# Bureaucratic Politics
### —— AND ——
# National Security

# BUREAUCRATIC POLITICS

—————— AND ——————

# NATIONAL SECURITY

Theory and Practice

edited by

# David C. Kozak
# James M. Keagle

Lynne Rienner Publishers • Boulder/London

*To Richard Rosser and Perry Smith*

*As teachers they taught the value of the bureaucratic politics paradigm; as practitioners they set a high example of honor, dignity, and the noblest standards of the profession. With them, bureaucratic politics was always a pleasant and positive process.*

The views and opinions expressed or implied in this book, edited and written in part by military officers, are those of the authors and do not necessarily reflect the views of the National War College, the United States Air Force, or the Department of Defense.

Published in the United States of America in 1988 by
Lynne Rienner Publishers, Inc.
948 North Street, Boulder, Colorado 80302

and in the United Kingdom by
Lynne Rienner Publishers, Inc.
3 Henrietta Street, Covent Garden, London WC2E 8LU

**Library of Congress Cataloging-in-Publication Data**

Bureaucratic politics and national security: theory and practice /
    edited by David C. Kozak and James M. Keagle
    Bibliography: p.
    ISBN 0-931477-91-3 (lib. bdg.) : ISBN 0-931477-92-1
    (pbk.) :
    1. United States--National security--Decision making. I. Kozak,
    David C. II. Keagle, James M.
    UA23.B787 1988                                    87-26837
    355'.033073--dc 19                                CIP

**British Library Cataloguing in Publication Data**
A Cataloguing in Publication record for this book
is available from the British Library.

Printed and bound in the United States of America

# Contents

# Foreword

Frequently, we like to remind ourselves of the blessings of liberty afforded to us by a constitutional system that intentionally divides and separates power. Pitting faction against faction, power against power, our forefathers thought, was the best way to avoid tyranny and the abuses associated with the wielding of absolute power. It was their belief that such a structure was necessary to preserve the freedoms for which so many had just given their lives.

This idea, most clearly expressed in *Federalist No. 10,* is the essence of what today we describe as "Madisonian pluralism." It has served us well during our two-hundred-year constitutional history as we have grown from a struggling new nation to our present position of leadership in the Free World.

Less often, however, do we reflect on the costs associated with our constitutional system designed to frustrate the exercise of power. Numerous agencies and institutions of government with independent power bases are important actors in the process of government. These "policy baronies" tug and pull at each other constantly, producing strategies and actions at times inconsistent with one another, at times almost incoherent, and producing at other times endless debate and stalemate.

During my years in government service, I have come to appreciate this process as democracy in action. Yet, a system that demands compromise and accommodation can be painfully slow, as I experienced while trying to put together a consensus position on strategic forces modernization that would satisfy the disparate actors in the national security arena.

Recent events of the Iran/*Contra* affair have served to highlight only too dramatically the degree to which the national security policy process is driven by such characteristics—and bureaucratic politics. Whether it is the secretary of state battling the secretary of defense, the White House staff fighting with the cabinet, or the president confronting Congress, the "invitation to struggle" does not produce a permanent winner for control.

This is how it should be. No matter how frustrated people in the process may get, no matter how much they may wish and attempt to circumvent the normal machinery of government in order to realize their particular policy visions, no matter how noble their motives, our process of government wisely does not tolerate such raw exercises of power over the long haul. It is a high price to pay, but not for securing and maintaining our freedom.

*   *   *

Dave Kozak and Jim Keagle are to be commended for this effort. Players in the national security policy process and lay people alike would be well served by a better understanding of how our government works in theory and in practice, which is exactly the aim of this book. As U.S. Air Force officers dedicated to the service of their country, these educators have for many years developed the ideas and issues raised in this text in their classrooms, first at the U.S. Air Force Academy and now at the National War College.

Our system will continue to function well only as long as our citizenry continues to commit itself to the process of learning, the world of ideas, and freedom of expression. It will require both constant work and vigilance. But again, such a high price is worth what it purchases—freedom and the preservation of our way of life.

*Brent Scowcroft*

# Preface

This collection had its inception in the early 1970s in the Political Science Department at the U.S. Air Force Academy, where both of us were struck by the conceptual value of the ground-breaking works of Morton Halperin, Arnold Kanter, Graham Allison, and Francis Rourke on bureaucratic politics and national security. At that time, Keagle was a cadet and Kozak a buck instructor. We agreed then that the bureaucratic politics approach provided many rich insights into how business was actually done in and between departments, agencies, and services. Our paths crossed again in the late 1970s as we together rejoined the Political Science Department at the Academy: Keagle fresh from a masters program at the University of Pittsburgh and now joining the faculty, and Kozak rejoining the faculty after doctoral studies at Pittsburgh. Our teaching only reinforced for us the great descriptive and explanatory power of bureaucratic politics. Consistently, we found it to be the most fruitful approach available for teaching the national security policy process and for imparting sophisticated notions of how and why business is done as it is.

Our next professional association was at the National War College in 1986 when we served as professors in the Department of Public Policy. Here, in conducting seminars in national security policy with mid-career professionals from the four armed services, Department of State, and other civilian agencies, we were doubly convinced of the merits of the bureaucratic politics model, especially after hearing the reflections of many of our speakers who were holding or had held top positions in the national security community.

Since we first conceived of this book, much new, quality material has appeared, covering some areas well but neglecting others. We have worked to bring together some of the classics with some of the new. Most importantly, we wanted to plug some gaps by commissioning original essays by practitioners to complement the many fine academic treatises available. We give our thanks and gratitude to those who labored to offer us the wisdom of their experiences, on time and in response to other editorial demands.

We also owe other major debts of gratitude. First and foremost, to Kay Keagle and Maryanne Kozak and to our children — Mark, Audra, and Gregory Keagle, Jeff, Tim, and Jackie Kozak—who supported us throughout, serving as our inspiration and enduring the demands on our time; to Roy Stafford, our dean of faculty at the National War College, who initially contributed in a major way to our chapter outlines, subdivisions, framework, and selections; to Myra Evans and Sue O'Keefe, who provided important clerical, typing, and editorial assistance; and to Maryanne Kozak, who edited all of the original pieces and significantly helped with manuscript preparation.

Finally, we dedicate this book to Richard Rosser and Perry Smith, both of whom led the Political Science Department at the Air Force Academy with a rare sense of intellectual inspiration and interpersonal skills. It is no small wonder that both went on to major positions of responsibility beyond the academy: Rosser became president of De Pauw University and is now the president of the National Association of Independent Colleges and Universities; Smith, a retired Air Force major general, served as Air Force planner and commandant of the National War College and is now a top authority on leadership. In our imperfect world, it is a shame that bureaucratic politics is not always practiced with the sophistication and public regardfulness of Rosser and Smith. Thanks, Dick and Perry, for your leadership and example!

*David C. Kozak*
*James M. Keagle*

# Contributors of Original Essays

*Terry Deibel* is professor of national security policy, the National War College.

*Richard Head,* brigadier general USAF (Ret.), has published *Case Studies of Crisis Decisionmaking* and is coeditor of *American Defense Policy.*

*Edward R. (Randy) Jayne II,* a former White House Fellow, was associate director of the Office of Management and Budget under President Carter. He is currently a senior vice president for General Dynamics.

*Chris Jefferies* is director of administration, Military Airlift Command. His experience includes assignments as staff assistant and policy analyst to the secretary of the Air Force; strategist and planner, headquarters, USAF; policy analyst and planner, U.S. Mission to NATO, Brussels, Belgium; and assistant professor of political science, U.S. Air Force Academy. In addition, he is a veteran of many hours flying strategic airlift missions in support of U.S. defense policy abroad, including 817 combat airlift sorties in the Republic of Vietnam.

*John Johns* is professor of organizational and personnel management, the Industrial College of the Armed Forces. A retired lieutenant general (Army) who served as deputy assistant secretary of defense from 1978 to 1979 and again from 1981 to 1984, he is the author of *Cohesion in the US Military* as well as articles on ethical conduct and leadership in the armed forces.

*James Jones* served for five years as the Marine Corps liaison officer in the U.S. Senate. He currently serves as a special assistant to the commandant of the Marine Corps.

*James M. Keagle* was formerly associate professor of political science, U.S. Air Force Academy and adjunct professor, Graduate School of Public Affairs, University of Colorado, 1977 to 1979 and 1982 to 1986. He is currently professor of national security policy and director of Latin American studies at the National War College and honorium professor of politics at The Catholic University of America. He is coeditor and contributor to

*Intelligence: Policy and Process* and has published articles in professional books and journals.

*John G. Kester* is a noted Washington, D.C., attorney who has written several well-cited essays on reform and reorganization of the joint chiefs of staff.

*David C. Kozak* was formerly associate professor, U.S. Air Force Academy; adjunct professor, Graduate School of Public Affairs, University of Colorado; and 1981-1982 American Political Science Association Congressional Fellow, serving on the staffs of Congressmen Jim Lloyd and Andy Jacobs and Senator J. James Exon. He is currently professor of national security policy at the National War College. He is author of *Contexts of Congressional Decision Behavior* and *Doing the Business of Congress* and coeditor and contributor to *The American Presidency* and *Congress and Public Policy.*

*John Macartney* is a former commandant of the Defense Intelligence College at the Defense Intelligence Analysis Center on Bolling AFB in Washington, D.C. An Air Force intelligence officer, former fighter pilot, and veteran of many bureaucratic engagements, he has taught at the U.S. Air Force Academy and the National Defense University. He currently is professor of national security policy at the National War College.

*Richard Thomas Mattingly, Jr.,* is assistant professor with the Department of Social Sciences, U.S. Military Academy.

*Allan A. Myer* is a former speech writer for President Reagan and a former staff member for the NSC. He is currently an executive vice president for Northrup.

*David M. Ogden, Jr.,* is director, Office of Power Marketing Coordination, U.S. Department of Energy.

*Albert C. Pierce* is currently professor of military strategy at the National War College. Previously, he was NBC pentagon correspondent and an assistant to the secretary of defense.

*Howard Shuman* is professor of national security policy at the National War College. Previously, he served as administrative assistant to Senators William Proxmire and Paul Douglas. He is author of *The Congressional Budget Process.*

*Perry Smith* is the author of several books on long-range planning and strategic vision. He is a former commandant of the National War College. Previously, he served in the Air Force as planner, command pilot, deputy commander for maintenance, and wing commander.

*Fred Thayer* is professor in the Graduate School of Public and International Affairs, University of Pittsburgh. Among his publications is *An End to Hierarchy and Competition*. A former Air Force officer retired at the rank of colonel, he served on both major command and Air Force headquarters staffs.

*George Edward Thibault* is a well-known author on naval strategy, and is a former chairman, Department ofMilitary Strategy, the National War College. He also was executive officer to Admiral Turner at the CIA.

*Earl Walker* is a tenured professor of social science at the U.S. Military Academy. Previously, he was a White House Fellow and a visiting professor at the National War College.

# ORGANIZATION FOR NATIONAL SECURITY

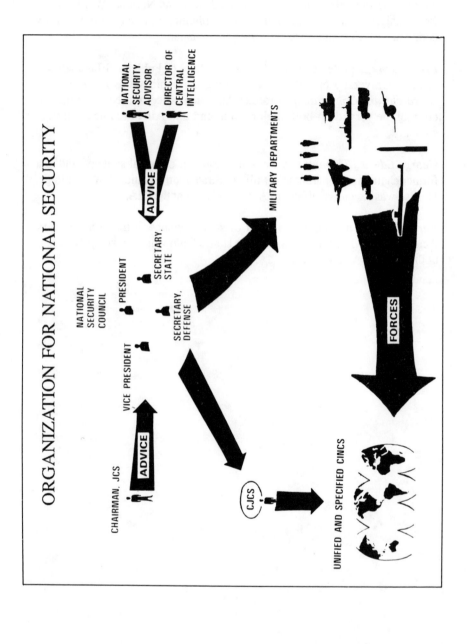

# Part I

# THE BUREAUCRATIC POLITICS PARADIGM

*The bureaucratic politics model is perhaps the best intellectual construct available for understanding national security policymaking. George Appleby and Norton Long pioneered the model in the 1940s and 1950s in reaction to the politics/administration dichotomy. In the 1960s Aaron Wildavsky and Francis Rourke made further developments, and in the 1970s and the 1980s Graham Allison, Morton Halperin, and Guy Peters refined this approach to depict the policy process as unfolding in a governmental structure more akin to a confederacy than a hierarchy. Decisionmakers are viewed as actors or players in a game of politics, promoting bureaucratic interests in competition for various stakes and prizes. Bureaucratic positions on policy issues are determined by bureaucratic interests (or, where one stands depends upon where one sits). Policy outcomes, more often than not, reflect a synthesis or compromise among different positions. The articles in Part I introduce and elaborate on these concepts, presenting frameworks and notions as derived from bureaucratic politics that are illuminating for the study of the national security policy process.*

# 1

## The Bureaucratic Politics Approach: The Evolution of the Paradigm

### DAVID C. KOZAK

*Public administration has contributed many rich insights for the study and practice of government. Among the most illuminating are the notions derived from the bureaucratic politics school. This article details the evolution of this approach and discusses its relevance to understanding defense policymaking.*

Public administration as a learned discipline and academic field of study has been described as both science and art, comprising an amalgam of various approaches and schools.[1] It is science in that it attempts to explain the reality of the public sector: how it is structured, how and why it does its business as it does, how processes actually work and actors actually behave. It is also art in that it aspires to prepare practitioners for service in the public bureaucracy by enhancing their understanding, increasing their sophistication, and prescribing for them a methodology for better statecraft.

The polymorphic nature[2] of public administration is readily apparent to those familiar with its literature. Those studying organizational structure and formalism, managerial ideology, bureaucracy as a social system, decision-making, policy process and policy analysis, and broader environmental contexts have made important contributions. But, perhaps the most illuminating insights are those emanating from what has come to be known as the bureaucratic politics school.

The bureaucratic politics approach provides some very sophisticated notions of public bureaucracy that are most relevant to studies of U.S. national security and defense policy. The purpose of this article is to trace the evolution of the bureaucratic politics paradigm, to specify its major concepts for understanding public bureaucracy, and to identify the relevance of these concepts to the study of U.S. national security.

3

## BUREAUCRATIC POLITICS: REACTIONS AGAINST THE POLITICS/ADMINISTRATION DICHOTOMY

Bureaucratic politics as an approach to learning has its origins in the adverse reaction of modern, post-World War II public administration to what has come to be known as the politics/administration dichotomy.[3] The politics/administration dichotomy was the dogma that dominated early twentieth-century administration. Essentially, it depicted politics (or policy-making) and administration as two separate realms. Politics was the domain of the elected office holder and policymaker. Administration—considered to be the mechanical execution of decreed policy—was the proper province of the professional public servant.

Classic statements of this older view are found in the writings of then political scientist Woodrow Wilson and German sociologist Max Weber. Although many others also subscribed to these arguments—most notably Frank Goodman (1900) and W. F. Willoughby (1927)—the works of Wilson and Weber have remained the most influential.[4] Writing in 1887, Wilson states that ". . . administration lies outside the proper sphere of politics."[5] To Wilson, "the field of administration is a field of business. It is removed from the hurry and strife of politics. . . . It is a part of political life only as the methods of the counting-house are a part of the life of society; only as machinery is part of the manufactured product."[6] Max Weber also depicts an apolitical bureaucracy. As he writes in his remarks first published in 1922,

> To take a stand, to be passionate . . . is the politician's element . . . indeed, exactly the opposite principle of responsibility from that of the civil servant. The honor of the civil servant is vested in his ability to execute conscientiously the order of the superior authorities. . . . Without this moral discipline and self-denial, in the highest sense, the whole apparatus would fall to pieces.[7]

The important thing to emphasize with regard to the writings of Wilson and Weber and the politics/administration dichotomy they fashion is that they each offer both descriptive and prescriptive propositions. To them not only are politics and administration in reality separate endeavors, but continued separation is a preferred arrangement. In other words, according to proponents of the dichotomy, not only never the twain meet, but never the twain should meet. The professional practice of public administration requires differentiation from politics and policymaking. The two functions are best handled by different institutions.

Notions of a politics/administration disjunction have not been confined to mere academic debate. For many years these ideas dominated thinking not just in academe but among practitioners as well, fostering what many have dubbed "the high noon of orthodoxy."[8] Nonpartisanship, hierarchical and mechanistic conceptions of public bureaucracy, emphases on unity of command and executive control and civil service, and preoccupation with efficiency and effectiveness—all of these flourished in an era of administration predicated on the independence of policymaking from policy execution. The Brownlow Committee (1937), the Hatch Act (1939), and the Hoover Commissions (1949, 1955) enacted into law the tenets of Wilson and Weber.

World War II produced the first significant stirring of skepticism concerning the validity of the politics/administration dichotomy. During that time of doubt, a generation of public administration scholars were educated by their experiences in government. Their service and the many insights it provided taught the inadequacies of an approach stressing a separation of politics and administration. For many, the dichotomy simply did not accurately grasp the reality of public administration as they had experienced and practiced it.[9] As Sayre stated in his 1958 review of the literature, ". . . to them, all administrative agencies and their staffs seemed to be involved in politics."[10] It was out of this adverse reaction to the politics/administration dichotomy—a reaction with a new emphasis on the involvement of administrators and administrative agencies in policy formation, the use of discretionary power, and the broader political process—that the bureaucratic politics paradigm was born.

## BUREAUCRATIC POLITICS: CLASSICAL STATEMENTS

If there is a consensus on any one item in modern, post-World War II public administration, it is the inadequacy of the politics/administration dichotomy as an accurate and valid description of the reality of the administrative process. From the seeds of post-war discontent, public administration scholars developed forty years of sophisticated debunking that has yielded many insights into the real world of government business. Pioneered by George Appleby and Norton Long in the 1940s and the 1950s, developed in the 1960s by Aaron Wildavsky and Francis Rourke, and refined in the 1970s and 1980s by Graham Allison, Morton Halperin, and Guy Peters, the bureaucratic politics approach emphasizes the political roles and relationships of bureaucracies, agencies and departments, and those who manage them. The scholars listed above and others make twelve major substantive points.

1. **Bureaucracy makes policy through the exercise of discretion.** To bureaucratic politics theorists, bureaucracy is anything but the mechanical and neutral implementation of policy. Although policy formulation and execution involve somewhat different roles and even dissimilar work cultures, responsibilities frequently blur. As many modern studies of public administration argue, bureaucrats make policy when exercising discretion

and giving advice. Paul Appleby stated in his 1949 treatise that the essence of bureaucratic power is delegated power. In his words, "with a great increase in numbers of affairs handled, and with the increased complexity of those affairs, both the Congress and the President have had to resort to delegation".[11] Legislation cannot anticipate every eventuality. For reasons of either necessity or expediency, many blanks and much fine print are left to bureaucracy. In filling in the details, government agencies exercise discretion, thus making policy and giving administration a definite political character.

2. **Administration is the eighth political process.** Appleby in the same 1949 piece states a theme that will be echoed numerous times: "The administrative or executive process, involving everything done by agencies other than legislative and judicial ones" is influenced by politics,[12] "by citizen sentiment, by agitation, by the prospect of elections and by the actuality of elections already held, by what takes place in or what can take place in nominating procedures."[13] No doubt some of the redefinition of administration as politics can be attributed to modern definitions of politics as more behavioral and analytical in nature, something more than electioneering. Harold Lasswell's definition of politic as "power,"[14] Easton's "authoritative allocation of values and resources,"[15] and Almond's "distribution of advantage and disadvantages," "conflict resolution," and "decision-making,"[16] greatly expanded an appreciation of administration's political nature. From such a perspective, Harlan Cleveland writes of the government executive as "a political animal" attempting to survive in "a political jungle,"[17] while V. O. Key writes of "administration as politics."[18] Harold Stein stated it most succinctly: ". . . it can be said that the concept of public administration as politics . . . is designed particularly to refer to the administrator's understanding and pursuit of his objectives and his relations with the social environment outside his agency that affects or is capable of affecting its operations."[19]

3. **Bureaucrats and bureaucracy are driven by agency interests.** In comparison to the other branches of government, administrative agencies are unique in that they lack a constitutional base or grant of power. As Norton Long has emphasized in his thoughtful treatises, as a result of both this lack of guaranteed existence and the inevitable efforts to insure survival of programs and professional values, "the lifeblood of administration is power. Its attainment, maintenance, increase, dissipation, and loss are subjects the practitioner . . . can ill afford to neglect.[20] In this pursuit of power, agencies, those who manage them, and those who do their business are driven by the highly particularized and parochial views, interests, and values of their organization. In Long's words, because of their insecurity, "agencies and bureaus more or less perforce are in the business of building, maintaining, and increasing their political support," "carrying" into the policy process a concept of agency "interests."[21]

**4. Agencies and bureaucracies are involved in an incessant competition, struggling for various stakes and prizes.** A major contribution of the bureaucratic politics approach is to depict bureaucratic and administrative processes as akin to a game of competition, within which participants vie, maneuver, and struggle for various stakes and prizes such as budget resources, personnel slots, morale, access, autonomy, missions, roles, and essence. In other words, agencies and those within them are constantly jockeying for power, position, and prestige, and this behavior has enormous consequences for public policy. This is certainly the conclusion of Graham Allison in *Essence of Decision: Explaining the Cuban Missile Crisis.* To Allison, bureaucratic politics is one of those nonrational factors at work that partially explain decisionmaking during the time of the Cuban missile crisis and the compromises made with the purely rational model that occurred.[22]

Morton Halperin applied the Allison approach to foreign and national security policymaking, arguing that foreign policy is usually the result of the interplay among interests, participants, rules, stakes, prizes, and actions.[23] The net result is a policy process whereby struggles for organizational survival,[24] expansion and growth,[25] and imperialism[26] are inevitable.

**5. Competition produces a common intra-agency bureaucratic culture and patterned role playing.** To students of bureaucratic politics, the struggle among contending bureaucracies fosters a distinctive internal mindset or perspective within each agency. As Halperin and Kanter note, "we believe that membership in the bureaucracy substantially determines the participants' perceptions and goals and directs their attention away from the international arena to intra-national, and especially intra-bureaucratic concerns."[27] Moreover, these mindsets involve patterned role playing, best captured by the dictum commonly referred to as "Miles's Law"[28] of "where you stand (on a policy issue) depends upon where you sit (in the bureaucracy)." In other words, policy positions are determined by or are a function of an actor's perspective as developed by his or her bureaucratic culture.

**6. Certain resources and strategies are associated with successful bureaucratic politics.** The very occurrence of bureaucratic politics, of course, gives rise to the employment of various strategies and ploys on the part of the contestants. A study of the behavior strategies people employ when adapting to or competing with one another is most productive in revealing how organizations function and how policy is processed.

Francis Rourke has written insightfully about how bureaucrats play the game of politics and which factors they correlate with success.[29] To Rourke, all bureaucracies are endowed with certain resources: policy expertise, longevity and continuity, and responsibility for program implementation. Some bureaucracies, however, are more successful than others in employing their assets. Rourke believes that agencies are more likely to succeed if they have the following four differentials: 1. a socially appreciated expertise, 2. the support of the bureaucracy's clientele and constituency groups, 3. good leadership, and 4. organizational vitality and energy.[30] To Rourke, the acquisition, maintenance, and expansion of these four characteristics becomes an objective of all organizations engaged in bureaucratic politics.

Aaron Wildavsky has written of the various tactics employed by agencies involved in the politics of the budgetary process. These tell much about the politics of bureaucracy in the U.S. system. According to Wildavsky, agencies playing the game of resource allocation engage in the following: acquiring a clientele, using "end round" plays to supportive congressional committees, cutting the popular programs and less-visible items, and expanding the base.[31]

7. **Policy made in an arena of bureaucratic politics is characterized by bargaining, accommodation, and compromise.** Bureaucratic politics depicts an organizational structure more akin to a confederation than a hierarchy. Decisions are made less through executive fiat and more in a bargaining arena. Allison writes about decisionmaking in systems so configured. Except in time of crisis or emergency, policy hammered out in a marketplace inevitably involves compromise, accommodation, and mutual adjustment—the mush that results from the clanging and banging and give and take of bureaucratic interests.[32] Charles Lindblom likewise detects a form of muddling-through incrementalism as a predictable consequence of the nonrational factors known as bureaucratic politics.[33]

8. **Bureaucratic politics involves strong political ties to clientele groups.** As Long, Rourke, Wildavsky, and other of the above-mentioned authors have emphasized, bureaucracies look to clientele groups for political security and support. All agencies have both internal and external constituencies: Internal constituencies comprise professional norms and associations; external constituencies are outside clientele groups who are affected by or otherwise have a strong interest in the business of the agency.

Clientele support is sought as part of a presumed symbiotic relationship between agency and clientele. The mutual benefit is that in exchange for the clientele's important political support for the agency, the clientele gets to have a major say in agency policymaking. There are two sides of this process. Phillip Selznick describes cooptation—agency use (if not commandeering) of outside groups ". . . as a means of averting threats to its stability or existence."[34] The other side is clientele capture, whereby through iron triangles of power consisting of agency personnel, relevant congressional committees and subcommittees, and affected outside interests, the clientele exercise inordinate, highly self-serving influence. I would like to emphasize that cooptation and clientele capture are two sides of the same coin. Both highlight the role of and problems with external groups in bureaucratic politics.

9. **Bureaucrats play politics as they interact with political institutions.** Many students of the policy process have argued that, in the main, policy is thrashed out in substantive subgovernments, subsystems, or

issue networks comprised of specialists representing different organizations: operating agencies, congressional panels, affected interests, the media, think tank consultants, and the Executive Office of the President (EOP).[35] These actors are the proximate policymakers within each of the programmatic areas of government. They constitute an indigenous power structure within which policy is hammered out in a give and take, push and pull, shove and haul process. It is here that bureaucrats interact with political institutions and it is here that political roles and relationships are most visible as bureaucrats attempt to defend their interests, influence events, and court favor.

Cronin writes of tugs-of-war between bureaucrats in the departments and agencies represented in the Cabinet on one hand and the White House on the other. This tension stems from conflicting role perspectives, as departments emphasize particularized programs and policies while presidential advisors are concerned with priorities and politics.[36] Wildavsky writes of conflict between advocates of spending (departments and agencies) and the Office of Management and Budget (OMB), which serves as a guardian on behalf of the presidency.[37] Ripley and Franklin illustrate the various and many interactions between bureaucracy and the Congress and the political character of the interactions.[38] In sum, all of these and many other works well-document the case that bureaucracies develop relationships with political institutions and that in the course of these relationships they give information, provide advice, make decisions, and administer programs in a political way. Chris Jeffries details some of the more obvious political ploys used by agencies: "tell the President only what is necessary to persuade him," "present your option with two obvious unworkable alternatives," "never agree to any position which might compromise yours," "always predict the consequences of not adopting your alternative in terms of worst cases," and "keep issues away from the president."[39] Each reveals the political nature of bureaucracy.

10. **Executive processes essentially involve efforts to coordinate, integrate, and synthesize bureaucratic politics.** In the world of bureaucratic politics, as Richard Neustadt has well argued, the position of president or chief executive is unique in that it is the one true centripetal force in the policy process, the one place where issues can be viewed in a comprehensive way and policy can be coordinated.[40] In fact, the distinctive charge and challenge of chief executives is to reconcile contending interests, transforming them into harmonious government.[41] Richard Fenno has stated it well: The presidency faces "the relative difficulty of promoting unity in the face of the basic pluralism of the American political system."[42] The challenge in the White House and its specialized policy shops in the EOP such as the OMB and National Security Council (NSC) is to reconcile the particulars of bureaucratic politics with general presidential programs.

11. **Proposals for organizational change and reform are politically motivated.** A major precept of bureaucratic politics is that proposals for

change and reform are essentially political phenomena. Organizational change is neither a technical nor a neutral exercise—it is the object of intense political pressure, conflict, and turmoil. Reorganizations have political purposes: They are not undertaken simply to conform to abstract principles; they are proposed and adopted not for therapeutic reasons but for political reasons and with political motives. As Harold Seidman states in his *Politics, Position and Power: The Dynamics of Federal Organization,* "Organizational arrangements are not neutral. They are a way of expressing rational commitment, influencing program direction, ordering priorities. Organizational arrangements give some interests, some perspectives more access."[43]

A corollary is that in proposals for reform, organizations are viewed as political objectives and objects—opportunity and boodle. Of course, agencies and departments have their own positions on reorganization issues as well as their own plans for what best serves organizational interests.

12. **By its very nature, bureaucratic politics raises profound questions concerning control, accountability, responsiveness, and responsibility in a democratic society.** Notions of semi-autonomous bureaucratic subsystems and narrow service empires pursuing organizational interests inevitably point to a series of fundamental issues and dilemmas concerning the role of bureaucracy in a democracy. May have invoked serious questions about how to make the diffused sovereignty and expertise of the bureaucracy respond to both executive direction and the popular will. Some have written of an unwieldy and unresponsive technocracy that needs to be brought under control. Others have discussed the representative nature of U.S. bureaucracy and the contributions it makes through its own intense advocacy to pluralistic democracy. No matter how one stands on these issues, they illustrate how a political approach to bureaucracy requires an interest in political questions previously ignored during the reign of the politics/administration dichotomy.

In sum, these twelve propositions explicate the major concepts and notions of bureaucratic politics as derived from the writings of its best known and classic proponents. They are premises that provide insights into the actual functioning and behavior of modern U.S. governmental bureaucracies. They are insights into how the government works.

## RELEVANCE OF BUREAUCRATIC POLITICS TO NATIONAL SECURITY STUDIES

Students of the U.S. national security policy process have long employed the bureaucratic politics approach in an effort to understand defense policymaking. For example, Hammond has discussed the synthesizing and integrating challenges to the NSC amidst rampant bureaucratic politics in the national security community.[44] Perry Smith highlights the political purposes of service doctrine and the use of doctrine in justifying and furthering bureaucratic interests.[45] Bauer and Yoshpe discuss the confederational nature of the Department of Defense (DoD),[46] while Katzenback discusses the difficulties of phasing out the U.S. horse cavalry in the early twentieth century due to the phenomena of bureaucratic politics.[47]

Many case studies also pinpoint the political role of bureaucracy. Ciboski points to competing technological interests and DoD politics in explaining the 1961 U.S. decision to cancel the skybolt missile program, an action with important ramifications for Britain.[48] Art examines the bureaucratic parochialism and rivalry that underlay the development of the TFX aircraft,[49] and Head explains the decisions in the development of the A-7 aircraft as a victory of some bureaucratic interests over others.[50]

In addition to the literature of academe, a bureaucratic politics approach is employed in governmental studies of the operations of the DoD and the national security policy process. For example, the 1986 report of the Packard Commission on Defense Management—*National Security Planning and Budgeting*—proposed expanding the responsibilities of Joint Chiefs of Staff (JCS) and Secretary of Defense in an effort to dilute service parochialism and enhance the generalist perspective in government.[51] Likewise, the staff report to the Senate Armed Services Committee *Defense Organization: The Need for Change* (commonly referred to as the Goldwater-Nunn Report) discusses operational failures and deficiencies, acquisition problems, lack of strategic direction, and poor interservice coordination as inevitable consequences of an imbalance "between service and joint interests."[52] The Tower Commission's report depicts a policy process involving a struggle between the national security advisor and NSC staff on the one hand and the cabinet secretaries and department officials on the other.[53] And, during his testimony before a special congressional inquiry into the Iran/Contra Affair, Lt. Col. Oliver North spoke of bureaucratic gridlock between the Central Intelligence Agency (CIA), the state, and the DoD as the rationale for his ad hoc approach to government policy.[54]

Combining and integrating these disparate insights yields a number of fruitful propositions that will underlie all subsequent pieces in this volume (see Figure 1.1). It should be emphasized that each proposition is a logical derivative from the tenets of bureaucratic politics.

## CONCLUSION

Bureaucratic politics as an academic approach has much to contribute to an understanding of the U.S. national security policy process. In reaction to the politics/administration dichotomy, the bureaucratic politics model has

## Characteristics of the National Security Policy Process as Seen from the Bureaucratic Politics Perspective

•The national security policy process is fragmented, nonhierarchical, and nonmonolithic.

•It is best conceived of as a confederation of functional and organizational constituencies and subsystems—a bargaining arena rather than a command structure.

•Decisionmaking requires inter- and intra-agency coordination and the integration of components.

•Bureaucratic professionalism, politics, particularism and parochialism, and outside affected groups color the process. Policy proposals bubbling out of the bureaucracy are influenced by these factors.

•Patterned role playing pervades. Adversarial advocacy is best explained with the dictum "where you stand depends upon where you sit!"

•Policy is hammered out in a political atmosphere with important inputs from the president and Congress. Hence, the name of the game is to influence those external institutions.

•Decisionmaking is constrained by fiscal, organizational, political, and cognitive limitations.

•Decisions are driven by SOPs, incrementalism, muddling through, satisfying, compromise, and accommodation.

•Crises and salience centralize organization to the NSC, Defense Review Board, budget process, and the White House.

•Declaratory policy can steer and guide but is not equivalent to policy programs and actions.

•Budget considerations drive strategy rather than vice versa, producing a strategy/resource mismatch.

•The policy process is personality dependent.

•Policy implementation is not automatic. It requires continuous negotiations and follow-through.

•Reorganization issues are intensely political, raising questions of authority, influence, and access.

Figure 1.1

developed with twelve major propositions, each of which sheds light on the reality of the policy process and decisionmaking in large, complex bureaucracies such as the NSC, DoD, and JCS. Too frequently, the application of the model to national security has been desultory and fragmented. Our purpose in this volume is to employ this model as thoroughly and comprehensively as possible in order to gain the full benefit of treating national security administration as public administration—a form of administration that is particularly amenable to a bureaucratic politics approach.[55]

Bureaucratic politics as a practice within the government, of course, will continue to be a matter of debate. No attempt will be made here to settle that debate. The reality of bureaucratic politics is both good and bad. The good is policy by compromise, consultation, and consensus; policy made in intense debate and deliberation with a sense of multiple advocacy; policymaking by specialists and experts; and dampers on policy extremism. The bad is problems of coordination, zero sum "dog eat dog" parochialism, and the lack of accountability. Regardless of either benefits or costs, recognizing bureaucratic politics leads to a realistic understanding of the U.S. policy process. Ignoring bureaucratic politics can only lead to ignorance and naiveté.

## NOTES

1. The classic statement concerning public administration as both science and art is found in the writings of Dwight Waldo, most notably *The Study of Public Administration* (Random House, 1955).
2. The term *polymorphic* is first applied to public administration in John C. Buechner, *Public Administration* (Dickenson Publishing, 1968), 18.
3. Politics/administration dichotomy as a descriptive concept seems to be first coined by Wallace S. Sayre, "Premises of Public Administration: Past and Emerging," *Public Administration Review* 18, no. 2 (1958): 102–105.
4. Frank Goodnow, *Politics and Administration* (Macmillan, 1900) and W. F. Willoughby, *Principles of Public Administration* (Johns Hopkins Press, 1927).
5. Woodrow Wilson, "The Study of Administration," *Political Science Quarterly* 2 (1887): 197–222. Reprinted in Jay M. Shafratz and Albert C. Hyde (eds.), *Classics of Public Administration* (Moore, 1978), 10.
6. Wilson, "Study of Administration."
7. Max Weber, "Politics as a Vocation," in *From Max Weber,* H. S. Garth and C. W. Mills, eds. (Oxford University Press, 1946), 95.
8. Donald Allensworth Sayre, *Public Administration: The Execution of Public Policy* (J. P. Lippincott Co., 1973), 147.
9. See, for example, Fritz Monstein Marx, ed., *The Elements of Public Administration* (Prentice-Hall, 1946).
10. Sayre, *Public Administration,* 104.
11. George H. Appleby, *Policy and Administration* (University of Alabama Press, 1949), 112.
12. Appleby, *Policy and Administration,* 29–30.
13. Appleby, *Policy and Administration,* 32.
14. Harold Lasswell, *Politics: Who Gets What, When, How* (Meridan Books,

1958).
15. David Easton, *The Political System* (Knopf, Inc., 1953), Chap. 5.
16. See Gabriel Almond and G. B. Powell, Jr., *Comparative Politics* (Little, Brown, 1966), Chap. 2; and Austin Rammey, *Governing* (Holt, Rinehart & Winston, 1971), Chap. 1.
17. Harlan Cleveland, "Executives in the Political Jungle," *Annals of the American Association of Political and Social Science* 307 (September 1956): 37–47.
18. V. O. Key, *Politics, Parties and Pressure Groups,* (Thomas Y. Crowell, 1958).
19. Harold Stein, *Public Administration and Policy Development* (Harcourt, Brace and World, Inc., 1952), i.
20. Norton E. Long, "Power and Administration," *Public Administration Review* 9 (Autumn 1949): 257. See also Norton E. Long, "Bureaucracy and Constitutionalism," *American Political Science Review* 46 (Sept. 1952): pp. 808–18 and "Public Policy and Administration: The Goals of Rationality and Responsibility," *Public Administration Review* 14 (1954): 22–31.
21. Long, "Power and Administration," 258.
22. Graham T. Allison, *Essence of Decision: Explaining the Cuban Missile Crisis* (Little, Brown, 1971), especially 256–257.
23. See Morton Halperin, *Bureaucratic Politics and Foreign Policy* (Brookings Institute, 1974); Morton Halperin and Arnold Kanter, eds., *Readings in American Foreign Policy: A Bureaucratic Perspective* (Little, Brown, 1973), 1–42; and Morton Halperin, "Why Bureaucrats Play Games," *Foreign Policy* 2 (1971), 70–90.
24. For an elaboration of the concept of survival see Herbert A. Simon, Donald W. Smithberg and Victor A. Thompson, *Public Administration* (Knopf, 1950), 381–401.
25. For an elaboration of the concept of growth see Anthony Downs, *Inside Bureaucracy* (Little, Brown, 1967), 5–23.
26. For an illustration of the concept of imperialism see Matthew Holden, Jr., "Imperialism in Bureaucracy," *American Political Science Review* 60 (December 1966): 943–951.
27. Halperin and Kanter, *American Foreign Policy,* 3.
28. For the origins of Miles's Law see: Richard E. Neustadt and Ernest May, *Thinking in Time* (Free Press, 1986), 157.
29. See Francis E. Rourke, *Bureaucracy, Politics, and Public Policy,* 3rd ed. (Little, Brown, 1984).
30. Rourke, *Bureaucracy, Politics, and Public Policy,* 91.
31. Aaron Wildavsky, *The Politics of The Budgetary Process,* 3rd ed. (Little, Brown, 1981).
32. Allison, *Essence of Decision,* 256.
33. Charles E. Lindblom, "The Science of Muddling Through," *Public Administration Review* 19 (Spring 1959): 79–88.
34. Philip Selznick, *TVA and the Grass Roots* (University of California Press, 1949), 13.
35. For the concept of subsystem issue networks see Hugh Heclo, "Issue Networks and the Executive Establishment" in *The New American Political System,* ed. Anthony King (American Enterprise Institute, 1979), 87–124.
36. Thomas Cronin, *The State of the Presidency,* 2nd ed. (Little, Brown, 1980), Chapters 5, 7, and 8.
37. Aaron Wildavsky, *Budgeting* (Little, Brown, 1975), 24–25.
38. Randall B. Ripley and Grace A. Franklin, *Congress, the Bureaucracy, and Public Policy,* 3rd ed. (Dorsey Press, 1984).
39. Chris L. Jeffries, "Defense Decisionmaking in the Organizational-

Bureaucratic Context," in *American Defense Policy*, 4th ed., ed. John E. Endicott and Roy W. Stafford, Jr. (The Johns Hopkins University Press, 1977), 236.

40. Richard E. Neustadt, *Presidential Power* (Wiley, 1980).

41. Colin Campbell, *Managing the Presidency: Carter, Reagan, and the Search for Executive Harmony* (University of Pittsburgh Press, 1986).

42. Richard F. Fenno, Jr., *The President's Cabinet* (Vintage Books, 1959), p. 271.

43. Harold Seidman, *Politics, Position and Power: The Dynamics of Federal Organization* 2nd ed. (Oxford University Press, 1976).

44. Paul Y. Hammond, *Organizing for Defense: The American Military Establishment in the Twentieth Century* (Princeton University Press, 1961); *Super Carriers and B-36 Bombers: Appropriations, Strategy and Politics*, Inter-University Case Program, No. 97. (Bobbs Merill Co., Inc., 1963); and "The National Security Council: An Interpretation and Appraisal," *American Political Science Review* 54 (December, 1960): 899–910.

45. Perry M. Smith, *The Air Force Plans for Peace: 1943–45* (The Johns Hopkins University Press, 1970).

46. Theodore W. Bauer and Harry B. Yoshpe, "Unity or Confederation: Defense Organization and Management," *American Defense Policy* 6th ed., eds. John Endicott and Roy Stafford (The Johns Hopkins University Press, 1977), 258–64.

47. Edward L. Katzenback, Jr., "The Horse Cavalry in the Twentieth Century: A Study in Policy Response," *Public Policy* 7 (1958): 120–49.

48. Kenneth A. Ciboski, "The Bureaucratic Connection: Explaining the Skybolt Decision," in *American Defense Policy* 4th ed., 374–88.

49. Robert J. Art, *The TFX Decision: McNamara and the Military* (Little, Brown, 1968).

50. Richard G. Head, "Doctrinal Innovation and the A-7 Attach Aircraft Decisions," *American Defense Policy*, 3rd ed., eds. Richard Head and Ervin Rokke (The Johns Hopkins University Press, 1973), 431–445.

51. "National Security Planning and Budgeting," *A Report to the President by the President's Blue Ribbon Commission on Defense Management* (June 1986).

52. "Defense Organization: The Need for Change," *Staff Report to the Committee on Armed Services, United States Senate* (October 16, 1985), 15, 636.

53. *The Tower Commission Report, a New York Times Report*, (Bantam Books, 1987), 95.

54. *Taking the Stand: The Testimony of Lieutenant Colonel Oliver L. North* (Pocket Books, 1987).

55. For an application of public administration to national security policy see: Chris Jeffries, "Public Administration and the Military," *Public Administration Review* (July/Aug. 1977): 321–333.

# 2

# Introduction and Framework
## JAMES M. KEAGLE

*Perhaps the greatest utility of bureaucratic politics is the systematic framework it offers for a sophisticated study of the defense policy process. Here, in an original essay, various facets of a bureaucratic politics approach are integrated for the study of national defense decisionmaking. This essay is an example of the type of organizing device emanating from a political view of the national security community and bureaucracy.*

*In the following essay, Dr. Keagle combines the systems model with the bureaucratic politics paradigm in a framework to enhance our understanding of the national security policy process. He utilizes the notions of structural functional lenses and centripetal/centrifugal forces to depict the play of politics. Each reader is left the difficult task of incorporating such a framework into an overall explanation and/or prediction of national security policymaking.*

Understanding national security policymaking is a difficult task for practitioners, lay people, and academics alike. Undoubtedly, national security policies are in part the output of large and complex organizations. Clearly, a variety of variables—the structure of the national security policymaking machinery, the multitude of players and personalities within the system, prevalent ideologies, private organizations, and the dynamics of institutional and personal interacting, among others—affect national security process and its outcomes. Moreover, the several intellectual constructs that are available direct attention and inquiry to different focuses.

Kenneth Waltz and Graham Allison have articulated such perspectives in their classic studies and demonstrated their frameworks' utility in acquiring some intellectual leverage on national security policy and process. Waltz directs our attention to three levels of analysis—humans, the state, and the structure of the international system—as mechanisms to examine the causes of war.[1] Alternatively, Allison offers three distinct conceptual models—rational actor, organizational process, and governmental (bureaucratic) politics—to explain nation-state behavior.[2]

While only a small sampling of the on-going debate, the number of different constructs does suggest the lack of consensus regarding the appropriate paradigm for an investigation of the national security policymaking that takes place today. Very few analysts, however, advance any particular viewpoint as producing all the right explanations and totally reliable predictions. Most analysts, as a close reading of Allison reveals, believe the varied perspectives are complementary and enhance our ability to comprehend the complex world in which we live.

## ANALYTICAL FRAMEWORK

It is our belief that the bureaucratic politics paradigm is perhaps the most useful construct available for understanding U.S. national security policymaking. Pioneered by George Appleby and Norton Long in the 1940s and 1950s, developed in the 1960s by Aaron Wildavsky and Francis Rourke, and refined in the 1970s and 1980s by Graham Allison, Morton Halperin, and Guy Peters, the bureaucratic approach depicts the policy process as unfolding in a governmental structure more akin to a confederacy than a unitary state. The game is politics: It is played by a multiplicity of actors with varying objectives, interests, and skills; the players operate within a certain organizational setting that is both fixed and malleable; persuasion and bargaining among the players drive the system, which produces no permanent answers; the game never ends.

Specifically, our framework combines the system approach as developed by David Easton with the notion of perceptual and structural/functional lenses to depict the structure of and dynamics inherent within national security policymaking. In this way we hope to illustrate the range and affect of the centrifugal and centripetal forces that play in the national security arena (see Figure 2.1).

## THE PERSONAL LENS—PLAYERS/INTERESTS

Real people operate the national security apparatus. While seemingly trite, this fact forms the basis for the first lens through which the policy processes flow. Each player sees the world uniquely, through his or her perceptual lens. Belief systems and ideologies are part of these lenses as players define situations, develop operational codes, and promote their interests as they compete for various stakes and prizes—for example, leadership, promotion, pay raises, prestige. No matter how hard we try, ultimately each of us views the world through only one pair of glasses—singularly our own.

Each player, too, is endowed with unique skills with which to participate

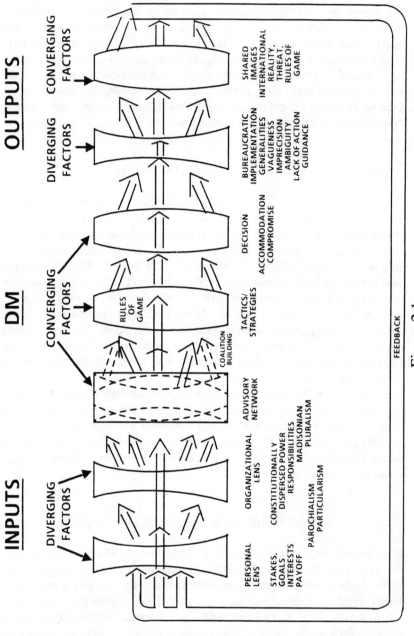

Figure 2.1

in national security policymaking. Such varying capabilities further complicate the process and suggest disharmony rather than unity, divergence rather than convergence in the policy process. Varying information processing and cognitive skills illustrate this point. Some individuals are adept working with large volumes of complex data and the intricacies of detail, as was President Carter. Others, like President Reagan, prefer broader visions that simplify reality. In any event, in a world in which we suffer not so much from a dearth of information as from its abundance to perhaps excess, one of a player's primary tasks is to discard irrelevant or erroneous data. What is superfluous "noise" to one is critical to another. Although the centrifugal effects of these differences can be abated via hiring decisions that emphasize loyalty and compatible ideological persuasions[3] the overall product from this lens is a set of markedly different personal perspectives and diverging inputs to the decisionmaking process.

## THE ORGANIZATIONAL LENS—MADISONIAN PLURALISM

One central feature of our system is that power was intentionally fragmented and that the government remains essentially nonhierarchical. Our constitutional framers consciously pitted ambition against ambition as they dispersed power among a multitude of actors. The list of players in national security is a familiar one and has grown over time to include, depending on the issue, the president, vice-president, cabinet officials and their respective departments, members of the White House staff, National Security Council (NSC), the director the Central Intelligence Agency (CIA), the intelligence community, ambassadors, Congress, and private organizations.

The distribution of organizational capabilities and responsibilities is not uniform. Each organizational setting offers a unique vantage point and set of resources to bring to bear on the process. Some analysts envision the executive departments as a collection of subgovernments, or fiefdoms, that add further to the plethora of perspectives emerging as inputs to the policy process, complete with the staff officers who are less contaminated with organizational baggage.[4] The suggestion is that organizations acquire lives of their own, seeking, as Morton Halperin and Arnold Kanter have noted, to influence the policy process so that any outcomes "maintain or improve their (1) essential role, (2) domain, (3) autonomy, (4) morale. . . , and (5) budgets."[5]

Thus, the United States has a Constitution that has ordained a pluralistic arena for debate. Arnold Miles so aptly described the essence of the debate within such a structural framework as, "Where you stand depends on where you sit." Moreover, a certain dynamic emerges in which the organizations adopt various tactics to sustain and/or enlarge themselves. The result is further divergence in the process, causing particularism and parochialism.

The situation at this point in the process is analogous to the problems facing a football coach. Given different individuals with different goals (salary, prestige, enjoyment) and different positions to play (quarterback, lineman, running back), a variety of demands follow as to how to best win the championship (if we are willing to accept for the moment for the sake of argument and simplicity that the team goal is commonly accepted). Defensive players would ask for a greater share of resources, arguing that defense, not offense, wins games. Running backs would be dissatisfied with a game plan that turned them into blocking backs so that the receivers and quarterback could accumulate impressive statistics (in the process of winning, of course). The list goes on. Yet successful football teams, by and large, do act as a cohesive unit, as political systems must do. What then, is the glue that brings these centrifugal forces in the political system under rein?

## CONVERGING LENSES

### Structure of the Decisionmaking Advisory Network Environment

Players do not compete and interact in an amorphous and unconstrained environment. For one, much as a coach positions his players, so, too, does the president enjoy a certain latitude to structure his organization and advisory network in ways compatible with operation style and preference. Richard T. Johnson has identified three distinct structures for the management of presidential advisors (formal, competitive, collegial), each with its own advantages and disadvantages, its own converging and diverging forces.[6]

Regardless of any formal structure created by the president, informal systems often may emerge that differ dramatically with any formal structures that may be in place. Hence, lines of communication, authority, and information flow are fluid, not rigid, and outcomes not easily predictable. Illustrative of this fluidity are the various roles performed by the secretary of state under different presidents. Some have been vicars of foreign policy while others have been faced with the reality that the authority and responsibility remained in the White House.

It appears, however, that the general centralizing effect of advisory networks, that the president particularly relies on in crises, works to strengthen national perspectives and override some of the centrifugal effects of parochialism and particularism stemming from the personal and organizational lenses. Moreover, in recent times, reorganization efforts have tended to focus on this need for improved management efficiency within the bureaucracy and have relied on centralization as a primary vehicle to achieve this end. The creation of the National Security Council and the DoD reorganization, 1947–1949, congressional reforms of the 1970s, the establishment of intelligence oversight committees, and Joint Chiefs of Staff changes, 1986–1987, represent such efforts to consolidate the number of fields upon which the actors involved in national security decisionmaking play and shape the structure of the advisory network so that it acts more as a converging lens rather than a diverging one.

## Rules of the Game

A second centripetal force that pulls divergent parochialistic perspectives together is the rules of the game. Assorted customs, statutes, and constitutional requirements establish certain rules of game for determining offices of primary responsibility, paper flows, and the direction of debate. Foremost among these is majority rule, which demands that the plural structures build coalitions in the hope of putting together a working majority. Parochial and particularistic perspectives begin to coalesce, and specific interests aggregate.

## Decisions

Decisionmaking in this environment requires significant degrees of both inter- and intra-agency coordination and integration of components in order to create the needed majority. Macro policies must mold together the inputs of the different players and subsystems. Regardless of a player's organizational resources and personal skills, no one can rule by decree. Bargaining drives the game, and no one can for long avoid its pervasiveness. Not even the president, no matter how preeminent he may be, can escape from this dictum.[7]

The bargaining process resolves disputes among players via compromises and mutual accommodations. Everyone gets a piece; no one receives the whole. Characteristically, outputs tend to satisfy the needs of the many, not to optimize the needs of the few. That is to say, in order to gain the support (or avoid the opposition) of a majority of the relevant players, extremes are tempered, made lukewarm rather than hot or cold. Bureaucratic players find it most comfortable to tinker at the margins of existing policies rather than to rethink and redo everything. Thus, creative leaps and bold innovations are rare. Rather, incrementalism and muddling through better describe the essence of national security policymaking.[8]

The heart of this process is the battle of the budget. Budgetary considerations are of paramount importance, influencing strategies and the development of fiscal requests. For instance, the defense budget request for (fiscal year) FY 1988 of $312 billion that President Reagan submitted to Congress in January 1987 was already trimmed to be more in line with the mood of Gramm-Rudman-Hollings and reduced defense expenditures. Beyond this, budget decisions often fund a particular system that is unwanted by the uniformed services. One needs only to point to the contemporary example of the T-46 trainer aircraft. Established as a priority by the foremost political document in the United States, the budget, the T-46 is an asset the U.S. Air Force (USAF) neither wanted nor requested. The USAF was faced with the task of identifying and justifying a role for the aircraft. Ultimately, the USAF waged a successful campaign to remove the T-46 funding from the budget.

The reverse is also true—the desired capability is not funded. Strategists must scurry intellectually to cover the void. The North Atlantic Treaty Organization's (NATO) longstanding reliance on nuclear weapons to deter a Warsaw Pact conventional attack illustrates this point. Because it has been budgetarily impossible to fund a conventional deterrent, NATO has cornered itself into reliance on a nuclear deterrent that encompasses the threat of first use of nuclear weapons, including U.S.-based strategic systems. The centrality of the budget process reminds us of a very poignant point—no decision is final, for next year's budget battle raises yet another opportunity for those previously denied to put together a winning coalition. "If at first you do not succeed, try, try again" is an age-old adage quite descriptive of the U.S. process that appears incapable of rendering a verdict with finality. Remembering the recent history of the Contras or development and deployment of the MX or B-1 brings comprehension of the unending nature of the process.

## Divergence Again—Implementation

The bureaucratic struggle does not end when the system produces a decision, no matter how watered down, accommodating, and consensual it may appear. For many the game has just begun. Policy executors enjoy a wide range for freedom of action for a number of reasons. For one, the language of decision is often vague and ambiguous. Imprecise or few, if any, guidelines for action accompany the decision, which leaves a broad opening for decisionmaking actions by those who may support or oppose the decision. Particularism and parochialism are reborn, with resultant organizational twists to implementation that can take the actors in numerous directions, each trying to apply the general prescription to the specific malady as viewed through different lenses.

## A LAST BIT OF GLUE

### Shared Images

As we complete the process circle and return to the personal and organizational lenses that so diverge policy inputs, it might appear as if the U.S. system were doomed to paralysis, if not eventual breakdown, due to the centrifugal forces at work. In fact, many feel this accurately depicts the current operation of the U.S. system. But I do not believe this to be the case for a very important reason. All the reasons I have outlined that might suggest victory for parochialism and particularism must be tempered with one remaining variable—shared images. The U.S. political system operates within a political environment of relatively broad consensus on the nature of international reality, the U.S. purpose in the world, and the threats confronting it. Debate is vigorous and parochialism is strong, but only within rather tight parameters as defined by U.S. political culture. Divergence beyond such rather strict limits, fortunately, has not emerged since the Civil War. The bond is strong.*

*Conclusion*

Despite the remarks above, I am not a bureaucratic determinist. The bureaucratic politics model is helpful in coming to grips with the many lenses through which national security policy is formulated and implemented. But it is only part of the puzzle. The personalities of the players involved are impossible to ignore. Lyndon Johnson was different from Dwight Eisenhower, and those dissimilarities mattered. They always will, whether the analysis includes presidents, cabinet officials, or lower-tier bureaucrats. Personalities (and skills) of the players involved do matter. Equally important is the field on which the players compete. As Johnson's study illuminates, the structure does matter. As much as chess would be an entirely different game if the board were another size and/or the pieces rearranged to begin the game, so, too, is the bureaucratic struggle affected by the field and the original positions of the players. Ultimately, I believe that the bureaucratic politics paradigm has a key role to play in shedding light on the functional activities, policy relationships, and issues of national security bureaucracy. It is a policy process that yields certain advantages and disadvantages for the players involved and blessings and banes for policymaking that affects all U.S. lives.

OUTLINE OF BOOK

Part I has addressed the bureaucratic politics paradigm and examined the political environment of national security administration. Drawing from the work of David Easton, Robert Dahl, and Karl Deutsch, David Kozak has reminded us of what is the essence of politics. From there he relied upon the classics of public administration literature in the hope of dispelling notions that a politics/administration dichotomy exists. Additionally, David Kozak summarized the historical evolution of the bureaucratic politics paradigm in

---

*Some may argue that the Vietnam War broke some of these bonds.

academia. Additionally, we drew on the work of Morton Halperin to suggest that bureaucratic politics is a game organizations must play—and must play well—in order to survive. Finally, we have examined a framework as a tool for improved understanding of the centripetal and centrifugal forces at work within the national security policymaking environment.

Part II focuses on the functional activities of administration—advice, choice, and implementation. The approach we have opted for in this section is a mixture of theoretical pieces, memoirs, and case studies, some old and some new.

Part III repeats this approach as we apply the bureaucratic politics paradigm to policy relationships (the presidency, Congress, and clientele groups). We conclude with several essays about the rules of the game and how to play and succeed in bureaucratic politics.

Finally, in Part IV, we will address some of the issues of bureaucratic politics—administrative change and reorganization; assessments of its strengths and weaknesses in producing "good" policy, relating to the paradigm's utility; and normative assessments of where the U.S. is and where it needs to go. Throughout this anthology we will offer a blend of academic and practitioner viewpoints through reprinted classic scholarly works and original essays by actual players.

In doing so we see two conclusions emerging. First, the explanatory and synthesizing nature of the bureaucratic politics model is valuable to those interested in comprehending and appreciating national security policy and process. Second, knowledge gained from such an understanding and awareness of the inner workings of the U.S. system can be applied by players involved to affect the outcome of the national security policy process. I hope this effort moves in that direction.

## NOTES

1. Kenneth N. Waltz, *Man, The State, and War* (New York: Columbia University Press), 1954.
2. Graham T. Allison, *Essence of Decision: Explaining the Cuban Missile Crisis* (Boston: Little, Brown), 1971.
3. See for example Richard P. Nathan, *The Administrative Presidency* (New York: John Wiley and Sons, 1983), 88. Nathan, in outlining the main ingredients of an administrative presidency strategy, emphasized loyalty and ideological compatibility over expertise.
4. A noted work here is Bert A. Rockman, "America's Departments of State: Irregular and Regular Syndromes of Policy Making," *American Political Science Review* 75, no. 4 (December 1981): 911-927.
5. Morton H. Halperin and Arnold Kanter, *Readings in American Foreign Policy: A Bureaucratic Perspective* (Boston: Little, Brown), 10.
6. See Richard T. Johnson, *Managing the White House* (New York: Harper and Row, 1974); also see Alexander L. George, *Presidential Decisionmaking in Foreign Policy* (Boulder, Colo., Westview Press, 1980).

7.  See Richard E. Neustadt, *Presidential Power* (New York: Wiley and Sons, 1980). A somewhat alternative perspective is offered by James MacGregor Burns, *Leadership* (New York: Harper and Row, 1978). Bert Rockman, *The Leadership Question* (New York: Praeger, 1984) compares and contrasts Neustadt's transactional president with Burns' transformative president as he explores the nature of presidential leadership in the U.S. system, which seeks a balance between governance, leadership, and efficiency on the one hand and legitimacy, consent, and accommodation on the other.

8.  See the sources listed in Note 7, particulary Rockman, who argues that the opportunities for presidential innovation, direction, and leadership are quite limited.

# Part II

# BUREAUCRATIC POLITICS AND THE FUNCTIONAL ACTIVITIES OF ADMINISTRATION

*Contrary to the tenets of the politics/administration dichotomy, adminis-*
*tration involves more than just the mechanical execution of policy.  As all*
*experienced practitioners know, administration also involves the giving of*
*advice, the exercise of choice, and the implementation of policy*
*declarations—all major activities.  This section will address these different*
*functional activities of administration, presenting essays that argue for a*
*broad view of the roles and scope of the activities of the national security*
*bureaucracy.*

# 3

## Bureaucratic Politics and the Giving of Advice: The Gathering, Processing, and Dissemination of Information

*Expertise is one of the most important political commodities of bureaucracy. Expertise stems not only from established substantive policy and program knowledge and from accumulated specialized information but also from the institutional memory accrued from the longevity of a career in bureaucracy. This expertise in policy, plans, and programs allows bureaucrats to have major input into policymaking deliberations through memos, studies, recommendations, and by playing the role of consultants and established governmental resources and assets. More often than not their advice and input is heeded in a major way. It might not be the final course of action, but the final outcome will usually not be too far from the recommended official position.*

*With regard to the national security community, questions of information, advice, and expertise inevitably raise issues concerning the U.S. intelligence network and its role in the policy process. Essays in this section discuss the components of this network from a bureaucratic politics perspective and the major issues raised by the politics of intelligence and information resources.*

# 3.1    Intelligence and Bureaucracy

## JOHN MACARTNEY

*Colonel John Macartney describes the National Foreign Intelligence Community as he elaborates on the business of intelligence—processing information. Throughout, he concerns himself with the bureaucratic realities that drive intelligence—fragmentation, subspecialization rank, essence. He specifically addresses the intelligence subculture in the military and the difficulties a knowledge-rich, intellectually stereotyped, and bureaucratically weak actor faces when the game is characterized as intel weenies versus jet jockeys.*

*Colonel Macartney reminds us that the intelligence community is not and should not be important in the policymaking arena. It has a crucial role to play if rational foreign policy is to be the outcome of the process. It must understand the realities of the bureaucratic policy struggle yet not slip over the line into policy advocacy, for its ultimate role is policy support, not policymaking, and that is a difficult mission indeed.*

Intelligence is information gathered for policymakers in government which illuminates the range of choices available to them and enables them to exercise judgment. Good intelligence will not necessarily lead to wise policy choices. But without sound intelligence, national policy decisions and actions cannot effectively respond to actual conditions and reflect the best national interest or adequately protect our national security.[1]

Bureaucratic politics can and often does drive intelligence, but the converse is rarely true. That is, the intelligence establishment exerts relatively little influence in the great bureaucratic policy wars that rage along the Potomac.

Despite a reputation for behind-the-scenes power manipulation, the reality is that intelligence is bureaucratically impotent. As Robert Gates, the deputy director of Central Intelligence, recently pointed out, "intelligence is a policy-support rather than a policy making endeavor."[2] Intelligence **information**, of course, is absolutely crucial to the policy process, but the

The suggestions and advice of Hans Heymann, Doug Hunter, Jim Lucas and J. T. Strong, faculty members at the Defense Intelligence College, are gratefully acknowledged.

**producers** of the information, intelligence organizations, are supporting players, not power brokers. Bureaucratic games are played within and between intelligence organizations, to be sure, but those games relate to **intelligence** policy, resources, and turf, not to the larger matters of U.S. foreign policy, the focus of this volume. In the national policy arena, intelligence players are everywhere in support but nowhere in the driver's seat. Furthermore, the policy struggle is especially dangerous for intelligence, a fragile actor among much more powerful bureaucratic contestants. The never-ending dilemma for intelligence is to try to maneuver just close enough to policy to be heard without becoming so involved that it is engulfed in bureaucratic crossfire. It's a delicate balance and the consequences are far from trivial. If intelligence withdraws or shies away from policy, or is excluded,[3] the stage is set for tragedy. At the same time, it fails when it gets too close and is captured.

Richard Betts tell us that intelligence failures are more often than not policy failures.[4] That is, policymakers may be predisposed to ignore intelligence information at odds with their preferred policy or with organizational interests. Or worse, intelligence players may succumb to pressures to get on the team, to produce and present intelligence that supports policy. Whoever is at fault, failures, when they occur, are likely to involve bureaucratic politics and occur at the policy-intelligence interface, where good intelligence is most important but also most vulnerable.

In his recently published and award winning book, *And I Was There,* Rear Admiral Edwin Layton writes that unpreparedness at Pearl Harbor resulted in part from bureaucratic feuding in Washington. Naval Intelligence, Layton reports, had been captured by Navy planners.

> The feud was rooted in the classic power struggle that has been endemic in military organizations since men first answered the call to arms: the struggle over who should control military intelligence. . . . Not only had it made a major contribution toward ensuring that the Japanese succeeded with their surprise attack, but had almost cost us the battle of Midway. In truth it had plagued our military commands throughout World War II—and it is still going on today.[5]

That intelligence is more policy-driven than policy-driving, the crux of Admiral Layton's book and the thesis of this article, stems from the very nature of the intelligence business, its place within the great bureaucracies, and the peculiarities rooted in the subculture of the profession.

## THE BUSINESS OF INTELLIGENCE

For the purposes of this paper, intelligence is defined as the collection, processing, analysis, and dissemination of foreign information.[6] Thus the

business of intelligence is really the processing of information—headlines,
spy novels, and Hollywood notwithstanding. To conjure up a realistic image
of intelligence, the layman would do better to picture a university research
faculty or a newsroom rather than a James Bond. The vast majority of
intelligence professionals go about their daily jobs within large bureaucratic
organizations on tasks closely resembling those of counterpart information
specialists in academia or the media.

The qualifier *foreign* is pertinent. It means the focus is on information
relating to the capabilities, intentions, and activities of foreign powers,
organizations, and persons. In this country, the intelligence establishment is
explicitly barred from the collection or analysis of domestic intelligence
information—by law.[7] Thus the loose conglomeration of organizations,
offices, and agencies commonly referred to as the intelligence community is
frequently, and pointedly, termed the National Foreign Intelligence
Community (NFIC).

## THE NATIONAL FOREIGN INTELLIGENCE COMMUNITY

The National Foreign Intelligence Community[8] is defined by Presidential
Executive Order 12333 as including these organizations and elements:

Central Intelligence Agency (CIA)
National Security Agency (NSA)
Defense Intelligence Agency (DIA)
Offices within the DoD for the specialized collection of intelligence through
    reconnaissance
Intelligence elements of the military services (Army, Navy, Air Force, and
    Marine Corps)
Bureau of Intelligence and Research of the State Department (INR),
    Intelligence elements of the Department of Treasury, Energy, and the
    Federal Bureau of Investigation (FBI)
Staff elements of the office of the director of Central Intelligence

The CIA has the largest analytical staff within the community and also
has primary national responsibility for the clandestine collection of human
intelligence (HUMINT). It is responsible for the production of finished
intelligence on political, military, economic, biographic, sociologic, and
scientific matters. Additionally, and uniquely, the CIA is charged with
conducting approved covert action missions. (Covert action is operations,
the carrying out of policy; it is not, in my view, intelligence strictly defined.)

The director of NSA reports to the secretary of defense and is
responsible for communications security (COMSEC) as well as collecting,
processing, and disseminating signals intelligence (SIGINT). Primarily an

information gatherer, NSA is less involved with all-source intelligence analysis and the production of finished intelligence products. Each of the military services also has a SIGINT element that operates under the coordination and management of NSA.

DIA is a joint organization that serves the foreign intelligence requirements of the secretary of defense, the Joint Chiefs of Staff (JCS) and the Unified and Specified Commands. The major producer of finished military intelligence for all national consumers, its director serves as the J2, or intelligence deputy, for the JCS and is responsible for coordinating the intelligence activities of the four military services as well as managing the worldwide Defense Attache System. DIA also provides a number of services of common concern for the larger intelligence community including, for example, photo processing and operation of the Defense Intelligence College. DIA focuses primarily on the analysis, production, and dissemination of finished intelligence. It also supplies current intelligence to the secretary of defense and JCS, staffs the intelligence watch at the National Military Command Center in the Pentagon, and provides intelligence support to top Pentagon policy makers and their staffs.

There is a good deal of personnel exchange between organizations of the NFIC and major elements of the community, especially DIA, NSA, and the community staff, are peopled by personnel on detail from other organizations. While many of the personnel in DIA and NSA are permanent civilian employees, almost half, including both agency directors, are military personnel on temporary loan (usually three years) from their services. That means there is high personnel turnover as well as multiple and quite different personnel systems and regulations to contend with. As any student of bureaucratic politics might expect, this organizational pluralism has bureaucratic implications.

For one thing, divided loyalties tug at the agencies' military members. Because the military come and go while the civilians stay, the two groups may develop different agendas and different informal networks. Also, because military assignments and promotions are primarily in the hands of service personnel shops, the services rather than the agencies themselves have the most to say about who will or will not work in DIA, NSA, and other joint intelligence organizations. Indeed, the very existence of large, joint, and civilianized intelligence organizations makes the military intelligence specialty quite different from other military career fields. Unlike pilots or artillerymen, for example, intelligence specialists can spend as much as half their military careers outside their service in joint (purple) assignments, usually working alongside civilian colleagues. That makes quite a difference in the armed services where service pride, esprit, and rivalry are fundamental to organizational culture.

The intelligence elements of the services are much more fragmented and scattered than the Washington-based agencies already discussed. Army intelligence includes the three-star assistant chief of staff for intelligence (ACSI) in the Pentagon as well as thousands of intelligence personnel assigned not to the ACSI but to various army field commanders worldwide, down through corps, divisions, brigades, battalions and companies. There are also separate army intelligence production centers such as the Missile and Space Intelligence Center at Huntsville, Alabama, as well as training centers at Fort Huachuca and Fort Devens. Whereas the Washington-based CIA, DIA, and NSA are primarily concerned with national-level or strategic intelligence, army intelligence interests are more tactical—focused on the weapon systems, battlefield terrain, and other threat or target information of immediate concern to army commanders in the field. Similarly, air force, navy, and marine intelligence each have a tactical focus and a Pentagon staff as well as dispersed elements scattered throughout the operating commands of their services.

Intelligence elements at the departments of state, treasury, and energy are small compared with the CIA and the DoD intelligence branches. Primarily in the business of analysis and production, along with some open source collection, they focus on the special interests of their respective departments but also contribute to the national intelligence analytical effort. The FBI has important counterintelligence responsibilities and its counterintelligence arm is part of the intelligence community, unlike its criminal divisions and other law enforcement elements, which are not.

The head of the CIA reports directly to the president and runs that agency but wears his most important hat as the director of Central Intelligence (DCI) with oversight, coordination, and guidance responsibilities for the entire intelligence community. Those responsibilities are exercised through a separate (from CIA) staff, called the intelligence community, or IC, staff. The DCI plays an important coordinating and leadership role for the community but, except for the CIA, does not really exercise direct control.

While not formally part of the community, several other actors deserve mention. Both houses of Congress have standing oversight committees, which have become consumers of intelligence as well as formulators of intelligence policy. Lobby groups also get involved. Some, particularly the American Civil Liberties Union (ACLU), have sought to restrict intelligence activities, especially covert action and counterintelligence. Others, such as the Association of Former Intelligence Officers (AFIO), urge more resources and wider latitude for intelligence. Additionally, there has developed a network of attentive and more or less professional intelligence watchers, especially in academia, the press, and think tanks. They too have influence.[9] Having defined our terms and described the intelligence community, we can turn to its bureaucratic environment.

## BUREAUCRATIC REALITIES

*Fragmentation*

To begin with, intelligence is not a unified organizational actor, nor really a community. Hans Heyman has called it a "hydra-headed agglomeration of competing institutions."[10] Not only is it divided into multiple national level organizations—CIA, NSA, DIA—but its elements, especially in the military, are further subdivided and widely parceled out to nonintelligence commanders. That means intelligence speaks with multiple voices while many nonintelligence actors, such as the secretary of state or the commander of U.S. Forces in Europe, also possess their own intelligence voices.

Fragmentation makes it hard for intelligence to develop, in Morton Halperin's terminology, an organizational essence.[11] What organization? Take, for example, the director of Naval Intelligence. A rear admiral, he has over twenty years of intelligence experience. But does he feel his essence is the navy or intelligence? If intelligence, does he identify with the defense intelligence community, or the larger National Foreign Intelligence Community? Most likely the answer is yes. He identifies with all of the above, and thus the notions of his organizational interest and essence are much diffused. They do not provide many cues to him or to the scholar who would use a bureaucratic politics paradigm to analyze behavior.

Actually, the fragmentation of intelligence goes still further. There are subcommunities generally clustered around the three major collection disciplines, HUMINT, SIGINT, and imagery intelligence (IMINT). Those subcommunities, particularly the *SIGINTers,* or *crippies* as they are called in the navy, have a self-identity that further blurs any picture of an organizational essence.

*Subspecialization*

A part of the national security bureaucracy, intelligence is also related to what is sometimes referred to as the knowledge industry, an economic subsector whose product is processed information. Both in and out of government, the business of processing information is a high-growth industry that includes public relations, education, the media, think tanks, consultants, research and planning organizations, advertising, the legal profession, and so on. Like its brethren, intelligence is labor intensive and employs a large proportion of highly educated professionals (Ph.D.s abound in intelligence organizations). Throughout the industry the common approach to knowledge processing is subspecialization, and intelligence is no exception. Its large analytical organizations are structured similarly to that of a university where the faculty is subdivided into academic disciplines, subdisciplines and narrow specialities.

Subspecialization gives both the university and the intelligence organization great breadth of knowledge. It is intended to provide the U.S. government with as wide a range of information as possible. But specialization has its flip side. First, detailed information does not always add up to knowledge. Second, the specialized intelligence analysts often cannot see the big picture while their generalist managers lack sensitivity to the fine nuances. Third, mosaic building takes a lot of specialists— intelligence is a very labor-intensive business employing tens of thousands. Finally, narrow specialization further fragments and dilutes organizational identity, or essence. An intelligence analyst who specializes in Soviet oil production, for example, may feel more professional kinship with counterparts in the Department of Energy or the oil industry than with the fellow down the hall whose intelligence speciality is Soviet artillery.

*Rank*

Within the bureaucracy, intelligence, especially on military staffs, suffers from the handicap of low rank. In working with operators and policymakers, intelligence is everywhere the junior partner. Even at the national level, the DCI traditionally lacks the status of the secretaries of defense, or state, or even the president's national security advisor. (Because of his unique status as a long time intimate of President Reagan, William Casey may have been a singular exception.) It gets worse at lower levels. The staff of the U.S. Southern Command in Panama, for example, is a key bureaucratic actor when it comes to formulating U.S. policy toward Central and South America. But the intelligence assistant, the J2, on that staff is only a colonel whereas the operations and plans deputies, the J3 and J5, are both flag officers. (At the U & S Commands as well as the JCS, the key staff deputies are numbered: J1, personnel; J2, intelligence; J3, operations; J4, logistics; J5, plans; J6, communications.) Furthermore, the J3 and J5 are not only senior, but like the commander in chief, are always bemedaled warriors—combat arms types—Steve Canyons rather than staff-support officers.

Other support deputies, like the J1, J4, and J6, are also outranked by the big two, J3 and J5. But these support elements work within their own specialties, while the J2 works intimately with the J3 and J5, the policy lions. "Here," in the words of Lt. Col. G. Murphy Donovan, an air force intelligence officer, "the intelligence ram is outgunned, outflanked and outranked."[12]

*Essence*

Despite fragmentation and subspecialization, we can make some general observations about organizational essence. There is, of course, more cohesion at the national level. Unlike military or departmental intelligence, the CIA is an organization unto itself and thus has a clearer bureaucratic identity. It is not subsumed as navy intelligence is, for example, within a much larger organization with a well-defined essence. CIA employees are inclined to see themselves as elite professionals. Conversely, they sometimes tend to view their colleagues elsewhere as indentured amateurs— soldiers or foreign service officers first, intelligence officers second, and perhaps captives of the larger bureaucracies they inhabit.

The SIGINT business is extremely technical. Thus NSA is staffed by many engineers and technical experts, which is a difference from most of the community where the intellectual center of gravity is in the humanities and social sciences. Also, primarily collection oriented, NSA has a greater interest in secrecy. Like other collection entities, it traditionally opposes the downgrading or public release of information to avoid providing clues to its ingenious but often vulnerable collection techniques.

DIA, on the other hand, more often favors downgrading or declassification. It is less collection oriented and more closely linked to the Unified and Specified Commanders who always feel a need to get intelligence downgraded and into the hands of troops and to share it with allies. Furthermore, DIA's annual publication *Soviet Military Power* has the express purpose of putting declassified intelligence information into the public domain. Only in the past few years has DIA overcome a bureaucratic inferiority complex, the legacy of its birth in the early 1960s, which occurred in the face of strong service opposition.

The organizational predispositions of the congressional oversight committees are still evolving. Born in the late 1970s in the aftermath of the Church Committee and Pike Commission investigations, both committees adopted watchdog attitudes towards intelligence. But by the mid-80s they were more with than against the Intelligence Community. In the aftermath of the Iran-*Contra* affair, the committees may be returning to an investigative mode.

## INTELLIGENCE SUBCULTURE

Despite its fragmentation, specialization, and military-civilian dichotomy, the intelligence profession is characterized by a discernable subculture.

### Egg Heads

First of all, intelligence is, as its name implies, an intellectual calling. Individuals who are attracted to and remain in the business are likely to be a different breed of cat than the movers and shakers who make policy.

In the military, for example, the route to command as well as to key policymaking positions is always up through the combat arms. The essence of the air force, as Halperin notes, is combat flying, and that service is dominated by fighter pilots. The senior combat officers who run the army, navy, and air force are all decisive, aggressive, action oriented, and sure of themselves. The intelligence officer, by contrast, usually lacks combat ribbons and the gung ho warrior flair; a man or woman of ideas, the intelligence officer is more cerebral, more comfortable with ambiguity, with both sides of an issue, with objectivity.

As a result of the difference in personality types, there may be and often is social and professional discrimination. In the machismo world of the young jet jockey, for example, the junior intelligence officer may not count for much. He's likely to be referred to behind his back as an "intel weenie." At senior levels in the Pentagon, the old discriminations of the flight line and stag bar are not as visible, but a subtle status differential may remain. To the warriors, intelligence has never been fully accepted as part of the profession of arms. The fact that senior intelligence officers are very likely to be serving or have served extended periods in joint agencies rather than within their own service can further undermine their social and professional acceptability.

This effect may be geographically reinforced. More than other military specialties, intelligence duty is not only joined with and alongside civilians, but also concentrated in Washington. One might expect that intelligence analysts, who are of an intellectual bent to begin with and who spend most of their lives inside the beltway, might be more subject to the influence of the eastern intellectual establishment than other military officers, the combat arms specialists who spend more of their careers assigned to bases abroad and in small towns across the United States.

## Objectivity

As George Thibault says in the next article in this volume, being right about the facts is what intelligence is all about. That, of course, implies not only analytical skill but above all objectivity, letting the chips fall where they may.

Objectivity, however, is the very last characteristic needed for bureaucratic engagements. In the adversarial give and take of the policy debate, determination, vigor, cunning, persuasion, aggressiveness, and single-minded loyalty are what count. Thus intelligence, which prides itself on being objective, is always at risk and under pressure. Facts and estimates that contradict established policy or organizational interests are resented and often rejected. Intelligence officers are always conscious of what may happen to the messenger who brings bad news.

If intelligence can be compromised by proximity to policy, it is irrelevant if it remains too distant.[13] There is a rich literature about this dilemma with the classic position, still dominant, being that intelligence should keep its distance and guard its objectivity. The newer view, much more evident in theory than in practice, is the notion, in Hans Heymann's words, that "intelligence, if it is to be at all relevant to policy, is very much a participant in the battle; that it must be attuned to the strategy and tactics being pursued, and that it is by no means invulnerable to being seesawed and whiplashed in the socio-political tug of war known as the policy making process."[14]

In practice the analyst, the narrowly focused expert deep down in the intelligence organization, is likely to be sheltered from the hurly-burly of the policy arena. His or her product will be edited, reedited, and carried to the fray by successive layers of intelligence managers. At each level, the managers will be more attuned to the big picture and the context of the policy issue but less objective and less familiar with the specifics. The bureaucratic politics axiom "where you stand depends on where you sit" is clearly visible within intelligence production organizations. Down in the trenches, the intelligence analyst has an objective, somewhat ivory tower outlook, relatively oblivious to the bureaucratic combat in the policy arena. The intelligence managers, on the other hand, especially those who operate at the ops-intel interface adopt a different stance where context, relevancy, and organizational interests come into play.

## Red But Not Blue

Several years ago, newly assigned to intelligence, I was being briefed on Soviet aircraft by a Soviet air analyst, a young USAF intelligence officer. The captain had encyclopedic knowledge of his subject: He seemed to know everything about the Soviets, especially their aircraft. But when I drew a parallel to a U.S. aircraft, I was stunned to realize the analyst knew little about the air force to which he belonged. He had never heard of an F-106 or an F-15. Intelligence specializes on foreign or red threat information and, to the consternation of operators and policymakers, is often ignorant of parallel U.S. information. This situation is an outgrowth of job specialization, as well as personnel recruitment and training paths. It is reinforced by legal prohibitions against domestic intelligence, and it is a problem.

First of all, it reduces the credibility of intelligence when the air analyst, for example, is recognized to be ignorant of his or her own air force. Second, consumers today are more and more demanding comparative data, red and blue. Estimates, background papers, and briefings that portray red only are sometimes criticized for being irrelevant, like a single bookend. Red versus blue comparisons (net assessments) not only double the workload for intelligence but open up a new and dangerous arena of bureaucratic vulnerability. The services resist such comparisons, and intelligence makes comparative evaluations at considerable peril. Any intelligence estimate that rates U.S. tactics, or equipment, or service personnel inferior to those of a potential adversary, for example, is sure to generate a firestorm of bureaucratic wrath.

## SUMMARY

This article began with the assertion that bureaucratic politics often drives intelligence but that intelligence players exert relatively little influence in bureaucratic policy struggles. After defining terms and describing the elements of the intelligence community, we turned to the bureaucratic environment.

Rather than being a single entity, intelligence was described as very fragmented—competing organizations with no one in overall charge, as well as being parceled out in bits and pieces to many other organizations. Intelligence was also shown to be labor intensive, employing a great many knowledge industry professionals, each with a narrow subspecialty. Furthermore, in the policy arena, especially on military staffs, the intelligence assistant is junior in rank and social status to the bemedaled operations and plans deputies who dominate the policy arena where intelligence is at risk and vulnerable.

Turning to the intelligence profession as a subculture, we found it is an intellectual calling that attracts a different sort than the movers and shakers who reign over the national policy process. Furthermore, we observed that by the very nature of their mission, intelligence professionals value objectivity—a concept that is dysfunctional in bureaucratic politics. Finally, we noted that intelligence focuses on red, or foreign, information. To an astonishing degree, intelligence specialists are likely to be ignorant of blue, or U.S., information.

## KNOWLEDGE IS NOT POWER?

One of the major axioms of bureaucratic politics is that knowledge is power. Why, it might be asked, does that not work for intelligence, which has knowledge yet lacks power? Part of the answer has already been given— knowledge is a source of power but it cannot overcome the handicaps of fragmentation, low rank, low status, and the impulse to be objective rather than persuasive. Moreover, intelligence is fundamentally in the knowledge dissemination business. Rather than guarding what it knows in order to be manipulative, intelligence gives away information as fast as it can. It must; that is its role, and, if it does not, it will be scooped by one of the many other sources within or without the intelligence community. (The press is a formidable competitor.)

Knowledge is indeed power, but it is the operators, the policymakers, who wield power and who can manipulate knowledge to enhance their power. While their intelligence staffs feed them *red* information, they, as planners and managers, already possess *blue*. Furthermore, they alone know the most critical information—their own future plans.

If intelligence lacks power as a bureaucratic actor, and if it does not have a monopoly on information, what about agenda setting? It is widely recognized that the media, the fourth estate, is a powerful actor in this country, often able to shape the national agenda. Is there a parallel for intelligence; can it shape the policy agenda? Yes, but only at the margins and only infrequently. There are times, of course, when a well-prepared intelligence briefing or estimate can rivet the policymaker's attention on a brand new issue, and, having done so, can be said to have shaped events. Those are intelligence successes, and intelligence continually seeks to make that happen. But in the big scheme of things, organizational interests, ideology, individual preconceptions, partisan politics, interest groups, and the national media usually have greater influence. More often than not, intelligence products are called up by policymakers whose real interest is promoting or defending their own agenda.

## CONCLUSION

If intelligence is a relatively weak and vulnerable bureaucratic actor that neither monopolizes information nor sets the policy agenda, does it have anything to do with policymaking? Absolutely! Policy cannot operate in a vacuum. Without intelligence, rational foreign policy is impossible. Policy cannot proceed without support from intelligence, while intelligence is irrelevant without policy. Nevertheless, there are strong impulses for policy and intelligence to go their separate ways. Policy hates to hear bad news, intelligence that might contradict or undermine established policy. Furthermore, policymakers are a different breed—they do not mix easily with their intelligence colleagues whose intellectualism makes them uncomfortable and whose objectivity is anathema. Intelligence, for its part, does not understand the policy process and tends to hang back, to stay clear of the fray, to avoid policy. Nevertheless, if it is to be effective, intelligence must get into the policy arena, close enough to know where the policymaker is trying to go, close enough to understand the context and, yes, the politics of the bureaucratic policy struggle. At the same time, intelligence can never itself become a policy advocate without compromising its credibility and, therefore, its utility.

Admiral Layton advises that the tenuous bureaucratic relationship between intelligence and policy has been present "since men first answered the call to arms."[15] This article has tried to point out why the very personality of the intelligence professional and the nature of the intelligence business are at odds with the policymaker and the policy business.

## NOTES

1. *Rockefeller Commission Report to the President by the Commission on CIA Activities Within the United States,* (Washington, D.C.: Government Printing Office, June 1975), 6.

2. Robert Gates, speech before an Intelligence Symposium sponsored by the Armed Forces Communications and Electronics Association (AFCEA), held at the Naval Surface Weapons Center, White Oaks, MD, October 7, 1986. A widely read 1964 expose of intelligence, *The Invisible Government* (New York: Random House, 1964), by David Wise and Thomas Ross argued, in effect, that the company (meaning the CIA) was part of an invisible cabal that secretly ran this country. Nothing could be further from the truth.

3. The exclusion of intelligence from policy, especially in early planning, is on the increase. Washington, unfortunately, has become a place where it seems virtually impossible to keep a secret. As a result, sensitive operations such as, for example, the 1983 Grenada invasion, must be very closely held to as small a group as possible—sometimes excluding intelligence. Even if top intelligence leadership is cut in, lower level analysts, the real experts, will probably still be cut out.

4. Richard K. Betts, "Analysis, War and Decision: Why Intelligence Failures are Inevitable," *World Politics* 31 (October 1975).

5. Edwin T. Layton with Roger Pineau and John Costello, *And I Was There,* (New York: William Morrow, 1985).

6. Conspicuously absent from my definition is covert action. While I believe covert action is one of the more important and useful of foreign policy tools, I am among those who do not consider it an intelligence function, although it is part of the CIA's mission. That doesn't make it intelligence. Covert action is operations, the carrying out of policy. Intelligence, on the other hand, is information—collecting, processing, analyzing, and disseminating it.

7. While maintaining internal security is considered part of the intelligence role in some foreign countries, that is emphatically not the case in this country. There may have been some ambiguity about that in the 1960s when some U.S. intelligence organizations, including military intelligence, were charged with collecting information on domestic dissidents and would-be revolutionaries. No more. Intelligence was severely chastized over that episode and an abundance of laws and regulations now restrict it to a foreign focus. Domestic security is a law enforcement, or police, function, not an intelligence activity. Counterintelligence, however, is part of the business of intelligence. It relates to information gathered and activities conducted to protect against espionage and other foreign intelligence activities, including sabotage and international terrorism. Counterintelligence is conducted both in the U.S. and abroad.

8. The descriptions and mission information that follow are extracted from Presidential Executive Order 12333, December 4, 1981; *Federal Register,* vol. 46, no. 235 (Tuesday, December 8, 1981), 59941–59954.

9. Roy Godson, "U.S. Intelligence Policy," in *American Defense Annual, 1986–87,* ed. Joseph Kruzel (Lexington, Mass.: Lexington Books, 1986), 194–195.

10. Hans Heymann, "Intelligence/Policy Relationships," in *Intelligence: Policy and Process,* eds. Mauer, Turnstaff, and Keagle (Boulder, Colo.: Westview Press, 1985), 58. There is a rich literature on the subject of the intelligence-policy interface and this article, by a former National Intelligence Officer who is now a professor at the Defense Intelligence College, is among the very best.

11. Morton Halperin, "Why Bureaucrats Play Games," *Foreign Policy* 2 (Spring 1971): 70–90.

12. G. Murphy Donovan, "Policy, Intelligence, and the Billion-Dollar

Petroglyph," *Air University Review* vol. 37, no. 2 (January-February 1986): 67. This article is an outgrowth of a paper done by Lt. Col. Donovan in Hans Heymann's (note 9, above) class at the DIC. Donovan does a superb job of portraying the junior partner status of intelligence as it provides support to the more powerful, and dangerous, policy lions.

13. Heymann, "Intelligence/Policy Relationships," makes this argument most elegantly.

14. Heymann, "Intelligence/Policy Relationships," 58.

15. Layton, *And I Was There.*

---

## 3.2 The Politics of Intelligence

### GEORGE EDWARD THIBAULT

*The following article highlights the pressures on the intelligence process, which Thomas Hughes described as "the fate of facts in a world of men." Specifically, although it is essential to be right about the facts, those who collect the facts, those who analyze the facts, and those who make national security policy based on information processed from a variety of sources see and interpret the facts differently. Some perspectives do not receive a proper hearing, for policymakers prefer believers, not critics. George Thibault develops these notions as he explores the difficulties in doing good intelligence work—an apt description of reality. Thibault rests his hope for improvement on the basic honesty and fairness of the intelligence officers in the field. Each of us must look for other ways to counterbalance those forces that play with the facts throughout the national security policy process.*

All too often analysts in our intelligence agencies are promoted not for being good interpreters of the real world but rather for being good soldiers in the intelligence community's intramural battles. If they stoutly uphold the office view, they are often preferred to those who prefer reality. It is often better to be wrong for bureaucratically acceptable reasons than to be right about the facts and galling to one's superiors.[1]

If there is a single most important attribute of intelligence, it is to be right about the facts. There must be enough information to help the decisionmakers—although it is said there is never enough to make their decisions sure, and too much to make them easy—and, it must reach them in time to be useful, which is usually too soon for the analyst who wants to wait for one more piece of the puzzle, and too late for the decisionmakers who want more time to decide. In the end, even when there is plenty of information on hand in time, it is of little use if it is not true to the facts as they are known. But is a fact a fact, or, is truth in the eye of the beholder?

As with most things, there are few absolutes in intelligence. Accuracy is a problem even for professional intelligence analysts because truth to one is distortion to another. Experiences, loyalties, and commitments to ideas and beliefs cause all of us to want to see different truths in the same set of facts, and often we do. For instance, two people see an automobile accident: One was the driver of one of the cars involved, and the other a passer-by. Not only do they see the accident from physically different vantage points, but also their responsibilities relating to the accident are different. The accident was the same, but their stories will not be. Even when we try consciously to suppress our biases, our perspectives and the ideological framework that gives order to our world remain, and they are different for every individual. "We could know truth if we could sublimate our minds to their original purity," said Plato. While the intelligence process tries to search for the truth, and works hard to understand it, it cannot succeed perfectly because in the end it is a human process. This article is about that process.

The value of any intelligence organization is measured by the quality of its product, and the quality of its product depends greatly on its courage to report only what hard evidence and solid analysis permit it to conclude. When the president's closest advisors reassure him that his dream of a perfect defense of the United States from nuclear weapons is just a question of money and time, his intelligence officers must tell him that many in the scientific community seriously doubt that his goal is technologically possible. They must inform him that some important U.S. allies will not support the effort because they do not see it in their best interests, that it could create a permanent barrier to arms control agreements, and that deterrence and stability will be affected in ways not entirely predictable throughout the development of this defense. His intelligence advisors may all support his dream—that is their choice as private citizens. However, if they support it officially with intelligence estimates and analytic efforts, those conclusions must come from an honest reading of the facts, not because more credence was given to some facts and less to others. Intelligence cannot take sides; it cannot advocate. The intelligence officer must strive to be the wise and thoughtful observer who understands more than most but places no bets at the gaming table.

Yet, a neutral bureaucrat, even an intelligence bureaucrat, is as hard to find as a neutral politician—the higher one goes in the administration the more that is true. Policymakers surround themselves with believers: There are seldom many critics, for example, around the president. Although the president may not see criticism as disloyal, (in fact, he may see it as extremely valuable), most of the others around him will. It is not accidental that the inner circle around the president is often referred to as his team. It is also not surprising that few in that inner circle will tolerate for very long anyone who does not seem to be on that team. Therefore, if the president's intelligence advisor does his job, if indeed he is the purveyor of the unbending truth as it is known to the intelligence professionals in the government, his role will be one of high risk. Career bureaucrats know from experience and political bureaucrats know from instinct that if they come to the White House with bad news too often their welcome will wear very thin very fast.

> There is a natural tension between intelligence and policy, and the task of the former is to present as a basis for the decisions of policymakers as realistic as possible a view of forces and conditions in the external environment. Political leaders often find the picture presented less than congenial. . . . Thus, a DCI[2] who does his job well will more often than not be the bearer of bad news, or at least will make things seem disagreeable, complicated, and uncertain. . . . When intelligence people are told, as happened in recent years, that they were expected to get on the team, then a sound intelligence policy relationship has in effect broken down. . . .[3]

> In the course of its investigation, the Committee concluded that the most critical problem confronting the DCI in carrying out his responsibility to produce national intelligence is making certain that his intelligence judgments are in fact objective and independent of departmental and agency biases. However, this is often quite difficult. A most delicate relationship exists between the DCI and senior policymakers.[4]

## THE DIRECTOR OF CENTRAL INTELLIGENCE

The director of Central Intelligence (DCI) is both the director of the intelligence community[5] and director of the Central Intelligence Agency (CIA). As director of the intelligence community he must try to cause many different government agencies to suppress to some extent their individual egos and join their efforts to produce the best combined intelligence picture for the president of which they are capable. To do this, he has little more than his personal power of persuasion.

The director might, by the usual measures of power, be considered to have the ultimate control lever over the community with his authority to prepare its single foreign intelligence budget. However, as approximately 80 percent of the foreign intelligence budget goes to the Department of Defense, and he does not have operational control of the Department of Defense, even his budget power has its limits. When there is disagreement over which programs will be funded and in what priority, the secretary of defense, who also has direct access to the president, is just as capable as the DCI of appealing his case directly to the president for decision. To prevail, the

DCI's argument must be valid and reasonable enough to persuade the secretary of defense to back down over his own initial judgment. Both are strongly motivated to do that privately, before firm positions are taken and reputations placed on the line. Sometimes, if subordinates feel strongly about an issue, or if an issue is highly political, they have been known to force their principal's hand by going public within the government, thereby making it extremely difficult for anyone to turn back without seeming to capitulate. Once positions are taken publicly they are not easily reversed at any level of government. The loser's credibility in his or her own department or elsewhere in the government will be damaged, and neither a DCI nor a secretary of defense can afford to let that happen very often.

During the Carter administration, the budget was managed by an independent intelligence community staff. Because the process was purposely transparent, no one felt threatened, and everyone cooperated to produce a sound budget. Disagreements were worked out below the cabinet level most of the time—less than a handful were ever taken to the president. All parties agreed that because the process was fully aboveboard, programs remained funded or were dropped on their merits and not on the patronage they could muster.

Largely in reaction to the Japanese attack on Pearl Harbor, where ample warnings existed but never came together to form a body of information decisionmakers could act on, the National Security Act of 1947 established the DCI and the CIA as the central control and gathering place for all intelligence collected in the U.S. government. Yet, presidents from Truman to Reagan have been reluctant to give the DCI full control over all intelligence. Perhaps they feared one person having too much power, or the potential loss of checks and balances on the quality of the work that some redundancy guarantees, or were concerned that a single funnel for all intelligence might in its own way be as bad as none. But because presidents have withheld the authority that the National Security Act originally envisioned, DCIs have seen the priority of their responsibilities differently.

Many DCIs have satisfied themselves with running the one agency they could control, the CIA, and letting the rest of the community operate more or less independently. Stansfield Turner tried to improve the director's control over the community when, before agreeing to be nominated for DCI, asked and received from President Carter a commitment to give the director control of the foreign intelligence budget. It was written into the president's executive order on intelligence and permitted Turner to establish a process for controlling community priorities, which was more than previous directors enjoyed.

But for day to day management of the community even that was not enough. The DCI has to walk a tightrope to have any influence over the community. The more he is perceived as being the active director of the CIA, the less the community is willing to trust him to look out for their interests first rather than the CIA's. The more he distances himself from the CIA to be seen as evenhanded in community affairs, the farther away he gets from the only soldiers over whom he had operational control and who can get things done for him. This balancing act leads to misunderstandings, distrust both in his own agency, the CIA, and everywhere else in the community, and an enormous drain on the DCI's time to develop and nourish trust in both camps.

Partially because the DCI has so many roles—the president's primary intelligence advisor, head of the intelligence community, and director of the Central Intelligence Agency—the DCI has more flexibility than probably any other incumbent in high office to interpret his role. He can be a collaborator with the president or the secretary of state to develop and implement policy as Allen Dulles did. He can look inward, eschewing an overtly political role, and be protective of the agency where he knows his real power lies as Richard Helms did. He can be aggressively involved in shaping foreign affairs through covert action as William Casey was. Many question whether the president's intelligence advisor, an appointed official not directly answerable to the public, should have such license to freewheel in the government. Certainly, Congress has raised this question on more than one occasion.

However, the DCI is a political appointee, ultimately answerable only to the president, and looked upon by most as a member of the president's team. He has no set term like the director of the Federal Bureau of Investigation (FBI), but serves at the pleasure of the president. No DCI of recent memory has been asked to step down because of incompetence; most have left with a change in administration. The president puts his own person in the job, someone in whom he has personal confidence and, it must be inferred, someone who he can rely upon not to undermine what he is trying to accomplish. While this is reasonable, it set up conditions that make it very difficult for the DCI to be apolitical.

Some DCI's have made no effort to justify their pro-administration activities. Others have been more sensitive to the danger that the intelligence community's credibility can be easily undermined if the DCI is seen as but another administration flag waver. Admiral Turner was faced with this dilemma early in his term as DCI. The CIA released a controversial oil study that supported the views of the administration at a time when the president was looking for support of his oil policy. The press believed the study a not very subtle maneuver to help the president. In his recent book,[6] Turner accurately describes how the completion of this study, started well before Carter came into office and over whose conclusions neither Turner nor Carter had had any influence, coincided with the mandate Carter had given Turner to declassify as much analysis as he could and get it out to the public. They discussed the alternative, to wait until a nonsupportive study came along, but that seemed just as much a manipulation, so they decided to go ahead and release the study and let the chips fall where they may. The White House might win on this one, but would certainly lose on others. The oil study became just one of many studies released when they were finished during the administration. As Turner and Carter expected, some studies supported and some undercut presidential initiatives.

Later, Admiral Turner's support of the president was expected in a different way. At the point when SALT II was to be sent to the Senate for ratification, senior members of the administration took to the lecture circuit to make the case for SALT II. Fellow administrators expected Turner to join in this effort and, it was assumed, he would be an especially convincing voice for the treaty because of his familiarity with its provisions and his detailed knowledge of nuclear strategy and systems as a professional naval officer. However, Turner knew he could not become an advocate for the treaty without losing credibility before the Congress where he would be required to testify on the treaty's provisions and especially on the U.S. ability to verify the Soviet Union's compliance with those provisions. So, he refused to comment on the treaty publicly. When asked in public what he thought about the treaty, he stated straightforwardly that his personal opinion was just that, and that officially, as the President's intelligence advisor, he was neither for it nor against it because to make a value judgment on the treaty would prevent him from doing what he was paid to do. He explained that his role was to tell the president and the Congress how confident the intelligence community was that they could detect Soviet cheating. Whether the extent of their ability to verify compliance was enough for them to conclude the treaty a good one was a political judgment which was the president's and the Congress' to make, not his. The president understood and accepted his DCI's logic. Others were less sensitive to the distinction.

Competing forces pull the DCI in many other directions. The president wants to hear that his policies are succeeding, the Congress (and its proliferating staffs) want to be fully informed of all clandestine and covert activities, and every intelligence agency wants to be a first-level player in presidential decisions without interference from the DCI.

## THE INTELLIGENCE COMMUNITY

"The truth is that the DCI, since his authority over the intelligence process is at least ambiguous, has an uphill struggle to make a sophisticated appreciation of a certain range of issues prevail in the national intelligence product over the parochial views and interests of departments, and especially the military departments."[7]

Competition between intelligence agencies is healthy. If more than one group looks at a problem, the chances are greater that important aspects will not be missed and that a range of views will result, giving the president a fuller set of options. In writing national intelligence estimates,[8] agencies with competence in the issue participate. Their disagreements over interpretations or conclusions are registered as majority and minority opinions, and all reach the decisionmaker. But to leave our discussion there would ignore the fact that each intelligence agency is a bureaucracy possessed of all the great and petty concerns of all bureaucracies: protection of turf; competition for dollars; sensitivity to pecking order; quest for prestige; fear of mission interlopers; and sundry other threats, internal and external.

Internally, some of the most senior and influential intelligence professionals have felt threatened by a profound change that has been taking place over the past twenty years. As sophisticated electronic equipment designed to collect and process intelligence has been introduced, the traditional spy[9] has seen what seemed to be a steady encroachment of technology on territory that formerly had been his or hers alone. The smart ones recognized that there would always be intelligence that only they could collect—the enemy's ideas, attitudes, concerns, intentions, and plans. As machines took over the more tedious and often exceedingly dangerous kinds of spying, the spies could become much more proficient at the jobs that only they could do. They could become more focused and even more valuable.

But some, especially among the older leadership, many of whom came into the CIA right after World War II, simply saw a threat to be fought. They made claims that DCI Turner was enamored of technology, did not understand human intelligence, and was downgrading it. He understood only too well that the most serious consequence of this inevitable transition would be to have the spies miss vital information no other collection means could get, while they continued, as if the world had stopped, expending energy and resources, and risking their lives, to collect information a technical system could get in a few minutes with no effort and at no risk whatever. However, the transition goes on and it has not been an easy one.

Internally as well, there has also always been an essentially destructive competition between the operations officers (the spy handlers) and the analysts. The operators have traditionally been first among equals. They were the ones who came from the Office of Strategic Services (OSS) after World War II to found the CIA. They were the quiet heroes as they are in any war, activists, individualists, colorful characters, and more often than not they wore an Ivy League tie. Other elements of the CIA and the intelligence community, except for state and military intelligence services, came afterwards. And, "afterwards" is like not coming over on the Mayflower. If you didn't, there is just no way you can be quite the equal of those who did. While this sense of self-importance is inevitably changing as the CIA moves into its second generation, operations has traditionally been the route to the top.

Consequently it is not surprising that the operations directorates in those agencies doing human intelligence collection believe they know best what intelligence needs to be collected. That is not to say that they are unresponsive when tasked by an analyst for certain information. But, in the end, it is the operations directorate managers who set the real collection priorities for their people in the field. Inevitably this affects the quality of analysis that can be done and the product that reaches the consumer.

Externally, there are many pressures that affect the quality of intelligence and ultimately policy outcomes. Some of the most influential are the pressures generated by the competition among the intelligence agencies, by policymaking departments to generate intelligence that supports their policies, by the desire of the Congress not just to oversee intelligence activities but to a degree manage them as well, by the tension that develops from trying to stay out of politics on the one hand and running politically driven covert action activities on the other, and by managing very sensitive relationships with allied intelligence agencies.

Looking first at interagency competition, we become quickly aware of each agency's struggle to pull out of the normal system for handling intelligence and be first to the president's ear with the latest news. This has two undesirable effects. First, it puts a priority in every agency on current intelligence rather than long range work. Current intelligence being where the action is, what everyone is most interested in, and unquestionably where the visibility and rewards are. Everyone would like to be the one with the scoop. This newspaper syndrome detracts from the United States' having a longer perspective that would permit it to foresee and perhaps avoid problems rather than simply reacting to them once they occur.

Second, informing the president in a piecemeal fashion precludes placing the latest news in a broader framework where it might be less startling or its meaning quite different. During the Carter administration some agencies regularly bypassed the DCI to take raw information or, at best, seat-of-the-pants analysis to the president. These agencies usually had no charter to do analysis nor analysts to actually interpret the information they collected. They seldom had the whole picture. Their job was to collect information and pass it on to analytic organizations who could integrate it with other information on the same subject. Although a scoop may boost the morale of an agency, when it causes the president to take a precipitous action that has international repercussions, as it did on at least one occasion, it is a disservice to the president and a danger to the nation.

Another pressure comes from the sponsors of some of the intelligence agencies. Every intelligence agency except the CIA works for a policymaking department, and although an agency may have good intentions and may try hard to do first rate analytic work, it is bucking some very strong internal pressures. Given those pressures, it is remarkable that each agency is as good as it is, and often the agencies are very good. Nonetheless, departments like defense and state have a great deal at stake both in terms of the status of the department and the security of the United States in the policies that they originate or are carrying out. Departments want their policies to succeed, and, just as important, to be seen as succeeding.

In foreign policy and military deterrence, perceptions become reality. What the agents believe is what is factored into their decisions. So, although the department may not consciously intend to skew its intelligence work, it is hard for that not to happen. By deciding what is or is not important, by analyzing some things and ignoring others, by being critical of some things and less so of others, by regarding some information as relevant and other information as less so, the agents give their work a policy cast, which, while unintentional, is inevitable.

For example, in the case of defense, your primary job is to be militarily prepared, if you are not absolutely sure of an aspect of enemy strength, it would be natural and, in fact, prudent, to err on the side of more than less. If you do not have that responsibility and there is no hard evidence that the enemy can do something, you have no reason to assume it can. Two different analyses of the same evidence, two different conclusions, or shadings of conclusions. Both are honest, but each was made as a result of different responsibilities.

The CIA, on the other hand, has no policymaking responsibility so does not feel the same pressures. A dispassionate observer might conclude that the CIA would be more likely to produce unbiased analysis, and in general that is true; however, former DCI James Schlesinger felt even the CIA was subject to bias:

> The intelligence directorate of the CIA has the most competent, qualified people in it, just in terms of their raw intellectual capabilities, but this does not mean that they are free from error. In fact, the intelligence directorate tends to make a particular type of error systematically in that the intelligence directorate tends to be in close harmony with the prevailing biases in the intellectual community, in the university community, and as the prevailing view changes in that community, it affects the output of the intelligence directorate.[10]

We can only conclude that no one is without some bias. Those biases become most evident within the intelligence community when it is expected to speak with a single voice on an issue. Unfortunately, no intelligence agency will concede that it might have an institutional bias that it needs to be careful does not find its way into its work, so the institution is often blind to where it stands, nonetheless standing firmly for the positions it takes.

Externally, the relationship between the intelligence community and Congress is a complicated one. It exists primarily through the Senate Select Committee on Intelligence and the House Permanent Select Committee on Intelligence, which oversee intelligence activities. For the first half-dozen years of its existence the intelligence community took pains to develop this relationship carefully. The White House recognized the authority of the Congress over foreign affairs, yet was wary that Congress not overstep the constitutional separation of powers. The Congress recognized that intelligence collection and analysis was an executive responsibility but was concerned that the White House not exceed its authorized powers secretly. By the early 1980s, a mutually respectful and trusting relationship grew up not unlike the description of porcupines making love—slowly and carefully. However, having been developed through careful, personal diplomacy, it was fragile, and since that time, the relationship has deteriorated considerably.

In the close relationship between Congress and the intelligence community, there exist benefits and liabilities on both sides. For a member of Congress there is little incentive to be a member of an intelligence committee: Most of the work is secret, entails little public credit for gains made, and cannot be talked about to constituents. Also, the risk of being tarred by association when an intelligence activity goes wrong is ever present. On the other hand, information is power: Members of Congress can use their deeper knowledge of world affairs to make more prudent judgments on other issues and influence their colleagues.

For the Congress in general, the benefits are substantial. In requiring the intelligence community to report all on-going sensitive activities, as well as covert actions that have been approved by the president, it exerts both an a priori control over what the community undertakes and a final control. If the congressional committees do not approve of an initiative, they can demand that it be modified or stopped. If the administration is unresponsive, it knows that as a last resort the congressional committee will go public to kill an activity. Usually, the intelligence community and the committees reach an accommodation that satisfies both, although this has not always been easy. As with covert action in Angola in the 1970s, Congress is sometimes pushed to legislating against an intelligence activity.

Although the intelligence community seldom sees it this way, the congressional oversight process ensures that it does not get out of step, as in the 1950s and early 1960s, with the kinds of activities the public would sanction if it knew about them. By keeping the Congress informed, intelligence enlists a powerful ally who, when things go wrong, must share the blame, and is therefore less inclined to blame in the first place. Finally, accountability is something the public rightfully demands of every agency of government but is unable to demand of the intelligence community because of the secrecy that surrounds what it does. Congressional oversight guarantees that accountability.

The intelligence community's aggressive pursuit of covert actions during the past few years is disquieting to many who feel the United States should not be a party to the inner struggles of other countries even if they are neighbors. Just as serious is the effect covert action has on the intelligence community's ability to collect and analyze information. Covert action is not intelligence; it is initiatives undertaken to influence the outcome of events without those who are doing the influencing becoming known. The problem here is that it is very hard for the CIA in general not to be influenced by what some in the same agency are doing, especially when they sometimes come from the same departments. If the CIA is working to make the administration's policy happen in Central America with one hand, it is extremely difficult for the other hand to not care how it all turns out. If the president's intelligence advisor is also the individual who is running the covert action and is responsible for its success, is it reasonable to expect the advisor to be neutral when reporting to the president?

Finally, traditional U.S. relationships with allied intelligence organizations materially affect the kind of analysis U.S. intelligence does. Normally, the United States does not spy on its friends, although Israeli activity against the United States uncovered recently might lead to other conclusions. The United States shares information with its allies and collects against third countries. For example, it may be easier to spy on Soviets in a third country than it is in the Soviet Union. However, working with allies is not always easy and, at times, it prevents the United States from knowing what is actually going on; that is, it degrades U.S. intelligence efforts.

In Iran under the Shah, the United States established virtually no independent knowledge of dissident groups in the country for fear of risking the Shah's friendship. All U.S. information on anti-Shah sentiment came from the Shah's own intelligence service, and U.S. intelligence contented itself with that. Consequently, the United States was as surprised as the Shah when forces got out of hand and he fell from power. It is easy to say that the United States should have ignored what the Shah wanted and really dug in to find out what was going on; however, each country must draw a fine line with its allies. To what extent should the United States risk its friendship with another country by secretly gathering information, even if it is ostensibly in their best interests. Most regimes are far too insecure to believe the United States, so often the United States satisfies itself with what it is permitted to know and what its friends will tell. In doing so, the United States compromises its national interests through inadequate information on which to base decisions—an often unavoidable situation.

## CONCLUSION

While this discussion is far from comprehensive, it is meant to point out some of the difficulties in doing good intelligence work. Many forces affect what is collected. Many agendas both inside and outside the intelligence community are at work between the collection and the production of a piece of finished analysis. It is surprising that the results are as good as they are, but then there are many fine people at every step of the process who are sincerely trying to be fair and honest. They are the ultimate counter-balance to the powerful forces pushing to make intelligence serve rather than inform the decisionmaker.

## NOTES

1. Angelo Codevilla, "The Substance and the Rules," *The Washington Quarterly*, (Summer 1983) p. 38.

2. Director of central intelligence. The DCI is the primary advisor to the president and the National Security Council on national foreign intelligence matters. He is the head of the CIA and of such other staff elements as are required for the discharge of his intelligence community responsibilities, and serves as chairman of the NSC's Senior Interagency Group when it meets to consider intelligence matters.

3. Final Report of the Select Committee To Study Governmental Operations With Respect To Intelligence Activities, United States Senate, 94th Congress, 2nd Session, Report No. 94–755, Book I, p. 75. Testimony of John Huizenga.

4. Final Report of the Select Committee to Study Governmental Operations With Respect to Intelligence Activities, Book I.

5. The intelligence community is comprised of the Central Intelligence Agency; the National Security Agency; the Defense Intelligence Agency; the offices within the Department of Defense responsible for collection of specialized national foreign intelligence through reconnaissance programs; the Bureau of Intelligence and Research of the Department of State; and the intelligence elements of the military services, the FBI, and the departments of Treasury and Energy.

6. Stansfield Turner, *Secrecy and Democracy*, (Boston: Houghton-Mifflin, 1985).

7. Final Report, Book I, p. 76.

8. An analysis of a national security issue or question which is a collaboration of the knowledge and experience of the intelligence community.

9. The term *spy* as used here is literally incorrect. A *spy* is usually a foreign national who agrees to obtain information for the United States overseas. Spies are managed or *handled* by operations officers who recruit them, tell them what information is needed, arrange to send that information back to the United States when it is obtained, and in every way protect the identity and well-being of the spy. In using *spy* here, I refer to the U. S. members of the Operations Directorate of the CIA and other agencies who manage human intelligence (HUMINT) collectors.

10. Final Report, Book I, p. 76. Testimony of James Schlesinger.

# 4

# Bureaucratic Politics and Decisionmaking: The Exercise of Choice

*The essence of decisionmaking is choice: choosing among options and alternatives, specifying ends and purposes, and selecting the means most appropriate to serve given ends. If any one overarching point emerges from the past forty years of sophisticated decision analyses, it is that most decisionmaking occurs under less than optimum conditions. Decisionmaking is constrained by many nonrational forces and factors that rule out certain options and militate toward the selection of others. Prominent among the list of such constraints—in addition to cognitive limitations, time, lack of information, dissension, and fragmented authority—is bureaucratic parochialism and particularism. Distinctive interest-promoting bureaucratic cultures, their internal professional norms, and external clientele frequently serve as decision constraints, strongly affecting the exercise of choice in the policy process. The articles in this section address bureaucratic politics and its impact on the choice of a course of public policy.*

# 4.1    Conceptual Models and the Cuban Missile Crisis

## GRAHAM T. ALLISON

*Graham Allison's 1969 article offered two alternative conceptual models to what he labeled the rational policy model, which were intended, as he wrote then, to "provide a base for improved explanation and prediction." One of these alternative models is the bureaucratic politics model. As we emphasize this model throughout this collection of readings, it is worth remembering that Allison's prescription for improving explanation and prediction of national security problems was to use the models together, not to each other's exclusion. Only in so doing can we hope to enhance our understanding, and improve the performance, of our national security policymaking machinery.*

The Cuban missile crisis is a seminal event. For thirteen days of October 1962, there was a higher probability that more human lives would end suddenly than ever before in history. Had the worst occurred, the death of 100 million Americans, over 100 million Russians, and millions of Europeans as well would make previous national calamities and inhumanities appear insignificant. Given the probability of disaster—which President Kennedy estimated as "between 1 out of 3 and even"—our escape seems awesome.[1] The event symbolizes a central, if only partially thinkable, fact about our existence. That such consequences could follow from the choices and actions of national governments obliges students of government as well as participants in governance to think hard about these problems.

Improved understanding of this crisis depends in part on more information and more probing analyses of available evidence. To contribute to these efforts is part of the purpose of this study. But here the missile crisis serves primarily as grist for a more general investigation. This study proceeds from the premise that marked improvement in our understanding of such events depends critically on more self-consciousness about what observers bring to the analysis. What each analyst sees and judges to be important is a function not only of the evidence about what happened but also of the "conceptual lenses" through which he looks at the evidence. The principal purpose of this essay is to explore some of the fundamental

Excerpted by the editors from the *American Political Science Review*, 63 (Sept. 1969), pp. 689–718 by permission of the author and the American Political Science Association.

## Summary Outline of Models and Concepts

| The Paradigm | Model I | Model II | Model III |
|---|---|---|---|
| | National government<br><br>Black box { Goals (objective function)<br>Options<br>Consequences<br>Choice | National government<br>Leaders<br>[A B C D E F G]<br>{ Organizations (A–G)<br>Goals<br>SOPs and programs | National government<br>[diagram of players in positions A–F]<br>{ Players in positions (A–F)<br>Goals, interests, stakes, and stands (r–z)<br>Power<br>Action-channels |
| **Basic unit of analysis** | Governmental action as choice | Governmental action as organizational output | Governmental action as political resultant |
| **Organizing concepts** | National actor<br>The problem<br>Static selection<br>Action as rational choice<br>Goals and objectives<br>Options<br>Consequences<br>Choice | Organizational actors (constellation of which is the government)<br>Factored problems and fractionated power<br>Parochial priorities and perceptions<br>Action as organizational output<br>Goals: constraints defining acceptable performance<br>Sequential attention to goals<br>Standard operating procedures<br>Programs and repertoires<br>Uncertainty avoidance (negotiated environment, standard scenario)<br>Problem-directed search<br>Organizational learning and change<br>Central coordination and control<br>Decisons of government leaders | Players in positions<br>Parochial priorities and perceptions<br>Goals and interests<br>Stakes and stands<br>Deadlines and faces of issues<br>Power<br>Action-channels<br>Rules of the game<br>Action as political resultant |
| **Dominant inference pattern** | Governmental action = choice with regard to objectives | Governmental action (in short run) = output largely determined by present SOPs and programs<br>Governmental action (in longer run) = output importantly affected by organizational goals, SOPs, etc. | Governmental action = resultant of bargaining |
| **General propositions** | Substitution effect | Organizational implementation<br>Organizational options<br>Limited flexibility and incremental change<br>Long-range planning<br>Goals and tradeoffs<br>Imperialism<br>Options and organization<br>Administrative feasibility<br>Directed change | Political resultants<br>Action and intention<br>Problems and solutions<br>Where you stand depends on where you sit<br>Chiefs and Indians<br>The 51–49 principle<br>Inter- and intra-national relations<br>Misperception, misexpectation, miscommunication, and reticence<br>Styles of play |

*Reprinted by permission from* Essence of Decision: Explaining the Cuban Missile Crisis, *p. 256. Copyright © 1971 by Little, Brown & Co., Inc.*

assumptions and categories employed by analysts in thinking about problems of governmental behavior, especially in foreign and military affairs.

The general argument can be summarized in three propositions:

1. Analysts think about problems of foreign and military policy in terms of largely implicit conceptual models that have significant consequences for the content of their thought.[2]

Though the present product of foreign policy analysis is neither systematic nor powerful if one carefully examines explanations produced by analysts, a number of fundamental similarities emerge. Explanations produced by particular analysts display quite regular, predictable features. This predictability suggests a substructure. These regularities reflect an analyst's assumptions about the character of puzzles, the categories in which problems should be considered, the types of evidence that are relevant, and the determinations of occurrences. The first proposition is that clusters of such related assumptions constitute basic frames of reference or conceptual models in terms of which analysts both ask and answer the questions: What happened? Why did the event happen? What will happen?[3] Such assumptions are central to the activities of explanation and prediction, for in attempting to explain a particular event, the analyst cannot simply describe the full state of the world leading up to that event. The logic of explanation requires that he single out the relevant, important determinants of the occurrence. Moreover, as the logic of prediction underscores, the analyst must summarize the various determinants as they bear on the event in question. Conceptual models both fix the mesh of the nets that the analyst drags through the material in order to explain a particular action or decision and direct him to cast his net in select ponds, at certain depths, in order to catch the fish he is after.

2. Most analysts explain (and predict) the behavior of national governments in terms of various forms of one basic conceptual model, here entitled the Rational Policy Model (Model I).[4]

In terms of this conceptual model, analysts attempt to understand happenings as the more or less purposive acts of unified national government. For these analysts, the point of an explanation is to show how the nation or government could have chosen the action in question, given the strategic problem that it faced. For example, in confronting the problem posed by the Soviet installation of missiles in Cuba, rational policy model analysts attempt to show how this was a reasonable act from the point of view of the Soviet Union, given Soviet strategic objectives.

3. Two "alternative" conceptual models, here labeled an Organizational Process Model (Model II) and a Bureaucratic Politics Model (Model III) provide a base for improved explanation and prediction.

Although the standard frame of reference has proved useful for many purposes, there is powerful evidence that it must be supplemented, if not supplanted, by frames of reference which focus upon the large organizations and political actors involved in the policy process. Model I's implication that important events have important causes, i.e., that monoliths perform large actions for big reasons, must be balanced by an appreciation of the facts (a) that monoliths are black boxes covering various gears and levers in a highly differentiated decisionmaking structure and (b) that large acts are the consequences of innumerable and often conflicting smaller actions by individuals at various levels of bureaucratic organizations in the service of a variety of only partially compatible conceptions of national goals, organizational goals, and political objectives. Recent developments in the field of organization theory provide the foundation for the second model. According to this organizational process model, what Model I categorizes as "acts" and "choices" are instead *outputs* of large organizations functioning according to certain regular patterns of behavior. Faced with the problem of Soviet missiles in Cuba, a Model II analyst identifies the relevant organizations and displays the patterns of organizational behavior from which this action emerged. The third model focuses on the internal politics of a government. Happenings in foreign affairs are understood, according to the bureaucratic politics model, neither as choices nor as outputs. Instead, what happens is categorized as *outcomes* of various overlapping bargaining games among players arranged hierarchically in the national government. In confronting the problem posed by Soviet missiles in Cuba, a Model III analyst displays the perceptions, motivations, positions, power, and maneuvers of principal players from which the outcome emerged. . . .

The space available does not permit full development and support of such a general argument. Rather, the sections that follow simply sketch each conceptual model, articulate it as an analytic paradigm, and apply it to produce an explanation. But each model is applied to the same event: the U.S. blockade of Cuba during the missile crisis. These "alternative explanations" of the same happening illustrate differences among the models—*at work*.[5] A crisis decision, by a small group of men in the context of ultimate threat, this is a case of the rational policy model *par excellence*. The dimensions and factors that Models II and III uncover in this case are therefore particularly suggestive. The concluding section of this paper suggests how the three models may be related and how they can be extended to generate predictions.

*   *   *

## MODEL III: BUREAUCRATIC POLITICS

The leaders who sit on top of organizations are not a monolithic group. Rather, each is, in his own right, a player in a central, competitive game. The name of the game is bureaucratic politics: bargaining along regularized channels among players positioned hierarchically within the government. Government behavior can thus be understood according to a third conceptual model not as organizational outputs, but as outcomes of bargaining games. In contrast with Model I, the bureaucratic politics model sees no unitary actor but rather many actors as players, who focus not on a single strategic issue but on many diverse intra-national problems as well, in terms of no consistent set of strategic objectives but rather according to various conceptions of national, organizational, and personal goals, making government decisions not by rational choice but by the pulling and hauling that is politics.

The apparatus of each national government constitutes a complex arena for the intra-national game. Political leaders at the top of this apparatus plus the men who occupy positions on top of the critical organizations form the circle of central players. Ascendancy to this circle assures some independent standing. The necessary decentralization of decisions required for action on the broad range of foreign policy problems guarantees that each player has considerable discretion. Thus power is shared.

The nature of problems of foreign policy permits fundamental disagreement among reasonable men concerning what ought to be done. Analyses yield conflicting recommendations. Separate responsibilities laid on the shoulders of individual personalities encourage differences in perceptions and priorities. But the issues are of first order importance. What the nation does really matters. A wrong choice could mean irreparable damage. Thus responsible men are obliged to fight for what they are convinced is right.

Men share power. Men differ concerning what must be done. The differences matter. This milieu necessitates that policy be resolved by politics. What the nation does is sometimes the result of the triumph of one group over others. More often, however, different groups pulling in different directions yield a resultant distinct from what anyone intended. What moves the chess pieces is not simply the reasons which support a course of action, nor the routines of organizations which enact an alternative, but the power and skill of proponents and opponents of the action in question.

This characterization captures the thrust of the bureaucratic politics orientation. If problems of foreign policy arose as discrete issues, and decisions were determined one game at a time, this account would suffice. But most "issues," e.g., Vietnam or the proliferation of nuclear weapons, emerge piecemeal, over time, one lump in one context, a second in another. Hundreds of issues compete for players' attention every day. Each player is forced to fix upon his issues for that day, fight them on their own terms, and rush on to the next. Thus the character of emerging issues and the pace at which the game is played converge to yield government "decisions" and "actions" as collages. Choices by one player, outcomes of minor games, outcomes of central games, and "foul-ups"—these pieces when stuck to the same canvas, constitute government behavior relevant to an issue. The concept of national security policy as political outcome contradicts both public imagery and academic orthodoxy. Issues vital to national security, it is said, are too important to be settled by political games. They must be "above" politics. To accuse someone of "playing politics with national security" is a most serious charge. What public conviction demands, the academic penchant for intellectual elegance reinforces. Internal politics is messy; moreover, according to prevailing doctrine, politicking lacks intellectual content. As such, it constitutes gossip for journalists rather than a subject for serious investigation. Occasional memoirs, anecdotes in historical accounts, and several detailed case studies to the contrary, most of the literature of foreign policy avoids bureaucratic politics. The gap between academic literature and the experience of participants in government is nowhere wider than at this point.

## Bureaucratic Politics Paradigm

*I. Basic unit of analysis: policy as political outcome.* The decisions and actions of governments are essentially intra-national political outcomes: outcomes in the sense that what happens is not chosen as a solution to a problem but rather results from compromise, coalition, competition, and confusion among government officials who see different faces of an issue; political in the sense that the activity from which the outcomes emerge is best characterized as bargaining. . . . National behavior in international affairs can be conceived as outcomes of intricate and subtle, simultaneous, overlapping games among players located in positions, the hierarchical arrangement of which constitutes that government. These games proceed neither at random nor at leisure. Regular channels structure the game. Deadlines force issues to the attention of busy players. The moves in the chess game are thus to be explained in terms of the bargaining among players with separate and unequal power over particular pieces and with separable objectives in distinguishable subgames.

*II. Organizing concepts.* A. Players in Positions. The actor is neither a unitary nation, nor a conglomerate of organizations, but rather a number of individual players. Groups of these players constitute the agent for particular government decisions and actions. Players are men in jobs.

Individuals become players in the national security policy game by occupying a critical position in an administration. For example, in the U.S. government the players include "Chiefs": the President, Secretaries of State, Defense, and Treasury, Director of the CIA, Joint Chiefs of Staff, and, since 1961, the Special Assistant for National Security Affairs;[6] "Staffers": the immediate staff of each Chief; "Indians": the political appointees and permanent government officials within each of the departments and agencies; and "*Ad Hoc* Players": actors in the wider government game (especially "Congressional Influentials"), members of the press, spokesmen for important interest groups (especially the "bipartisan foreign policy establishment" in and out of Congress), and surrogates for each of these groups. Other members of the Congress, press, interest groups, and public form concentric circles around the central arena—circles which demarcate the permissive limits within which the game is played.

Positions define what players both may and must do. The advantages and handicaps with which each player can enter and play in various games stems from his position. So does a cluster of obligations for the performance of certain tasks. The two sides of this coin are illustrated by the position of the modern Secretary of State. First, in form and usually in fact, he is the primary repository of political judgment on the political-military issues that are the stuff of contemporary foreign policy; consequently, he is a senior personal adviser to the President. Second, he is the colleague of the President's other senior advisers on the problems of foreign policy, the Secretaries of Defense and Treasury, and the Special Assistant for National Security Affairs. Third, he is the ranking U.S. diplomat for serious negotiation. Fourth, he serves as an administration voice to Congress, the country, and the world. Finally, he is "Mr. State Department" or "Mr. Foreign Office," "leader of officials, spokesman for their causes, guardian of their interests, judge of their disputes, superintendent of their work, master of their careers."[7] But he is not first one, and then the other. All of these obligations are his simultaneously. His performance in one affects his credit and power in the others. The perspective stemming from the daily work which he must oversee—the cable traffic by which his department maintains relations with other foreign offices—conflicts with the President's requirement that he serve as a generalist and coordinator of contrasting perspectives. The necessity that he be close to the President restricts the extent to which, and the force with which, he can front for his department. When he defers to the Secretary of Defense rather than fighting for his department's position—as he often must—he strains the loyalty of his officialdom. The Secretary's resolution of these conflicts depends not only upon the position but also upon the player who occupies the position.

For players are also people. Men's metabolisms differ. The core of the bureaucratic politics mix is personality. How each man manages to stand the heat in his kitchen, each player's basic operating style, and the complementarity or contradiction among personalities and styles in the inner circles are irreducible pieces of the policy blend. Moreover, each person comes to his position with baggage in tow, including sensitivities to certain issues, commitments to various programs, and personal standing and debts with groups in the society.

B. Parochial Priorities, Perceptions, and Issues. Answers to the questions: "What is the issue?" and "What must be done?" are colored by the position from which the questions are considered. For the factors which encourage organizational parochialism also influence the players who occupy positions on top of (or within) these organizations. To motivate members of his organization, a player must be sensitive to the organization's orientation. The games into which the player can enter and the advantages with which he plays enhance these pressures. Thus propensities of perception stemming from position permit reliable prediction about a player's stances in many cases. But these propensities are filtered through the baggage which players bring to positions. Sensitivity to both the pressures and the baggage is thus required for many predictions.

C. Interests, Stakes and Power. Games are played to determine outcomes. But outcomes advance and impede each player's conception of the national interest, specific programs to which he is committed, the welfare of his friends, and his personal interests. These overlapping interests constitute the stakes for which games are played. Each player's ability to play successfully depends upon his power. Power, i.e., effective influence on policy outcomes, is an elusive blend of at least three elements: bargaining advantages (drawn from formal authority and obligations, institutional backing, constituents, expertise, and status), skill and will in using bargaining advantages, and other players' perceptions of the first two ingredients. Power wisely invested yields an enhanced reputation for effectiveness. Unsuccessful investment depletes both the stock of capital and reputation. Thus each player must pick the issues on which he can play with a reasonable probability of success. But no player's power is sufficient to guarantee satisfactory outcomes. Each player's needs and fears run to many other players. What ensues is the most intricate and subtle of games known to man.

D. The Problem and the Problems. "Solutions" to strategic problems are not derived by detached analysts focusing coolly on *the* problem. Instead, deadlines and events raise issues in games and demand decisions of busy players in contexts that influence the face the issue wears. The problems for the players are both narrower and broader than *the* strategic problem. For each player focuses not on the total strategic problem but rather on the decision that must be made now. But each decision has critical consequences not only for the strategic problem but for each player's organizational, reputational, and personal stakes. Thus the gap between the problems the player was solving and the problem upon which the analyst focuses is often very wide.

E. Action Channels. Bargaining games do not proceed randomly. Action channels, i.e., regularized ways of producing action concerning types of issues, structure the game by pre-selecting the major players, determining their points of entrance into the game, and distributing particular advantages and disadvantages for each game. Most critically, channels determine "who's got the action," that is, which department's Indians actually do whatever is chosen. Weapon procurement decisions are made within the annual budgeting process; embassies' demands for action cables are answered according to routines of consultation and clearance from State to Defense and White House; requests for instructions from military groups (concerning assistance all the time, concerning operations during war) are composed by the military in consultation with Defense, State, and White House; crisis responses are debated among White House, State, Defense, CIA, and Ad Hoc players; major political speeches, especially by the President but also by other Chiefs, are cleared through established channels.

F. Action as Politics. Government decisions are made and government actions emerge neither as the calculated choice of a unified group nor as a formal summary of leaders' preferences. Rather the context of shared power but separate judgments concerning important choices determines that politics is the mechanism of choice. Note the *environment* in which the game is played: inordinate uncertainty about what must be done, the necessity that something be done, and crucial consequences of whatever is done. These features force responsible men to become active players. The *pace of the game*—hundreds of issues, numerous games, and multiple channels—compels players to fight to "get other's attention," to make them "see the facts," to assure that they "take the time to think seriously about the broader issue." The *structure of the game*—power shared by individuals with separate responsibilities—validates each player's feeling that "others don't see my problem" and "others must be persuaded to look at the issue from a less parochial perspective." The *rules of the game*—he who hesitates loses his chance to play at that point, and he who is uncertain about his recommendation is overpowered by others who are sure—pressure players to come down on one side of a 51-49 issue and play. The *rewards of the game*—effectiveness, i.e., impact on outcomes, as the immediate measure of performance—encourage hard play. Thus most players come to fight to "make the government do what is right." The strategies and tactics employed are quite similar to those formalized by theorists of international relations.

G. Streams of Outcomes. Important government decisions or actions emerge as collages composed of individual acts, outcomes of minor and major games, and foul-ups. Outcomes which could never have been chosen by an actor and would never have emerged from bargaining in a single game over the issue are fabricated piece by piece. Understanding of the outcome requires that it be disaggregated.

*III. Dominant interference pattern.* If a nation performed an action, that action was the *outcome* of bargaining among individuals and groups within the government. That outcome included *results* achieved by groups committed to a decision or action, *resultants* which emerged from bargaining among groups with quite different positions, and *foul-ups*. Model III's explanatory power is achieved by revealing the pulling and hauling of various players, with different perceptions and priorities, focusing on separate problems, which yielded the outcomes that constitute the action in question.

*IV. General propositions.* 1. Action and Intention. Action does not presuppose intention. The sum of behavior of representatives of a government relevant to an issue was rarely intended by any individual or group. Rather separate individuals with different intentions contributed pieces which compose an outcome distinct from what anyone would have chosen.

2. Where you stand depends on where you sit.[8] Horizontally, the diverse demands upon each player shape his priorities, perceptions, and issues. For large classes of issues, e.g., budgets and procurement decisions, the stance of a particular player can be predicted with a high reliability from information concerning his seat. In the notorius B-36 controversy, no one was surprised by Admiral Radford's testimony that "the B-36 under any theory of war, is a bad gamble with national security," as opposed to Air Force Secretary Symington's claim that "a B-36 with an A-bomb can destroy distant objects which might require ground armies years to take."[9]

3. Chiefs and Indians. The aphorism "where you stand depends on where you sit" has vertical as well as horizontal application. Vertically, the demands upon the President, Chiefs, Staffers, and Indians are quite distinct.

The foreign policy issues with which the President can deal are limited primarily by his crowded schedule: the necessity of dealing first with what comes next. His problem is to probe the special face worn by issues that come to his attention, to preserve his leeway until time has clarified the uncertainties, and to assess the relevant risks.

Foreign policy Chiefs deal most often with the hottest issue *de jour*, though they can get the attention of the President and other members of the government for other issues which they judge important. What they cannot guarantee is that "the President will pay the price" or that "the others will get on board." They must build a coalition of the relevant powers that be. They must "give the President confidence" in the right course of action.

Most problems are framed, alternatives specified, and proposals pushed, however, by Indians. Indians fight with Indians of other departments; for example, struggles between International Security Affairs of the Department of Defense and Political-Military of the State Department are a microcosm of the action at higher levels. But the Indian's major problem is how to get the *attention* of Chiefs, how to get an issue decided, how to get the government "to do what is right."

In policymaking then, the issue looking *down* is options: how to preserve my leeway until time clarifies uncertainties. The issue looking *sideways* is commitment: how to get others committed to my coalition. The issue looking *upwards* is confidence: how to give the boss confidence in doing what must be done. To paraphrase one of Neustadt's assertions which can be applied down the length of the ladder, the essence of a responsible official's task is to induce others to see that what needs to be done is what their own appraisal of their own responsibilities requires them to do in their own interests. . . .

## The U.S. Blockade of Cuba: A Third Cut

*The politics of discovery.* A series of overlapping bargaining games determined both the *date* of the discovery of the Soviet missiles and the *impact* of this discovery on the administration. An explanation of the politics of the discovery is consequently a considerable piece of the explanation of the U.S. blockade.

Cuba was the Kennedy administration's "political Achilles' heel."[10] The months preceding the crisis were also months before the Congressional elections, and the Republican Senatorial and Congressional Campaign Committee had announced that Cuba would be "the dominant issue of the 1962 campaign."[11] What the administration billed as a "more positive and indirect approach of isolating Castro from developing, democratic Latin America," Senators Keating, Goldwater, Capehart, Thurmond, and others attacked as a "do-nothing" policy.[12] In statements on the floor of the House and Senate, campaign speeches across the country and interviews and articles carried by national news media, Cuba—particularly the Soviet program of increased arms aid—served as a stick for stirring the domestic political scene.[13]

These attacks drew blood. Prudence demanded a vigorous reaction. The President decided to meet the issue head-on. The administration mounted a forceful campaign of denial designed to discredit critics' claims. The President himself manned the front line of this offensive, though almost all administration officials participated. In his news conference on August 19, President Kennedy attacked as "irresponsible" calls for an invasion of Cuba, stressing rather "the totality of our obligations" and promising to "watch what happens in Cuba with the closest attention."[14] On September 4, he issued a strong statement denying any provocative Soviet action in Cuba.[15] On September 13 he lashed out at "loose talk" calling for an invasion of Cuba.[16] The day before the flight of the U-2 which discovered the missiles, he campaigned in Capehart's Indiana against those "self-appointed generals and admirals who want to send someone else's sons to war."[17]

On Sunday, October 14, just as a U-2 was taking the first pictures of Soviet missiles, McGeorge Bundy was asserting:

I *know* that there is no present evidence, and I think there is no present likelihood that the Cuban government and the Soviet government would, in combination, attempt to install a major offensive capability.[18]

In this campaign to puncture the critics' charges, the administration discovered that the public needed positive slogans. Thus Kennedy fell into a tenuous semantic distinction between "offensive" and "defensive" weapons. This distinction originated in his September 4 statement that there was no evidence of "offensive ground-to-ground missiles" and warned "were it to be otherwise, the gravest issues would arise."[19] His September 13 statement turned on this distinction between "defensive" and "offensive" weapons and announced a firm commitment to action if the Soviet Union attempted to introduce the latter into Cuba.[20] Congressional committees elicited from administration officials testimony which read this distinction and the President's commitment into the *Congressional Record*.[21]

What the President least wanted to hear, the CIA was most hesitant to say plainly. On August 22 John McCone met privately with the President and voiced suspicions that the Soviets were preparing to introduce offensive missiles into Cuba.[22] Kennedy heard this as what it was: the suspicion of a hawk. McCone left Washington for a month's honeymoon on the Riviera. Fretting at Cap Ferrat, he bombarded his deputy, General Marshall Carter, with telegrams, but Carter, knowing that McCone had informed the President of his suspicions and received a cold reception, was reluctant to distribute these telegrams outside the CIA.[23] On September 9 a U-2 "on loan" to the Chinese Nationalists was downed over mainland China.[24] The Committee on Overhead Reconnaissance (COMOR) convened on September 10 with a sense of urgency.[25] Loss of another U-2 might incite world opinion to demand cancellation of U-2 flights. The President's campaign against those who asserted that the Soviets were acting provocatively in Cuba had begun. To risk downing a U-2 over Cuba was to risk chopping off the limb on which the President was sitting. That meeting decided to shy away from the western end of Cuba (where SAM's were becoming operational) and modify the flight pattern of the U-2s in order to reduce the probability that a U-2 would be lost.[26] USIB's unanimous approval of the September estimate reflects similar sensitivities. On September 13 the President had asserted that there were no Soviet offensive missiles in Cuba and committed his administration to act if offensive missiles were discovered. Before Congressional committees, administration officials were denying that there was any evidence whatever of offensive missiles in Cuba. The implications of a National Intelligence estimate which concluded that the Soviets were introducing offensive missiles into Cuba were not lost on the men who constituted America's highest intelligence assembly.

The October 4 COMOR decision to direct a flight over the western end of Cuba in effect "overturned" the September estimate, but without officially raising that issue. The decision represented McCone's victory for which he had lobbied with the President before the September 10 decision, in telegrams before the September 19 estimate, and in person after his return to Washington. Though the politics of the intelligence community is closely guarded, several pieces of the story can be told.[27] By September 27, Colonel Wright and others in DIA believed that the Soviet Union was placing missiles in the San Cristobal area.[28] This area was marked suspicious by the CIA on September 29 and certified top priority on October 3. By October 4 McCone had the evidence required to raise the issue officially. The members of COMOR heard McCone's argument but were reluctant to make the hard decision he demanded. The significant probability that a U-2 would be downed made overflight of western Cuba a matter of real concern.[29]

*The politics of issues.* The U-2 photographs presented incontrovertible evidence of Soviet offensive missiles in Cuba. This revelation fell upon politicized players in a complex context. As one high official recalled, Khrushchev had caught us "with our pants down." What each of the central participants saw, and what each did to cover both his own and the administration's nakedness, created the spectrum of issues and answers.

At approximately 9:00 A.M., Tuesday morning, October 16, McGeorge Bundy went to the President's living quarters with the message: "Mr. President, there is now hard photographic evidence that the Russians have offensive missiles in Cuba."[30] Much has been made of Kennedy's "expression of surprise,"[31] but "surprise" fails to capture the character of his initial reaction. Rather, it was one of startled anger, most adequately conveyed by the exclamation: "He can't do that to *me*!"[32] In terms of the President's attention and priorities at that moment, Khrushchev had chosen the most unhelpful act of all. Kennedy had staked his full Presidential authority on the assertion that the Soviets would not place offensive weapons in Cuba. Moreover, Khrushchev had assured the President through the most direct and personal channels that he was aware of the President's domestic political problem and that nothing would be done to exacerbate this problem. The Chairman had *lied* to the President. Kennedy's initial reaction entailed action. The missiles must be removed.[33] The alternatives of "doing nothing" or "taking a diplomatic approach" could not have less relevant to *his* problem.

These two tracks—doing nothing and taking a diplomatic approach— were the solutions advocated by two of his principal advisers. For Secretary of Defense McNamara, the missiles raised the spectre of nuclear war. He first framed the issue as a straightforward strategic problem. To understand the issue, one had to grasp two obvious but difficult points. First, the missiles represented an inevitable occurrence: narrowing of the missile gap. It simply happened sooner rather than later. Second, the United States could accept this occurrence since its consequences were minor: "seven-to-one missile 'superiority,' one-to-one missile 'equality,' one-to-seven missile 'inferiority'—the three postures are identical." McNamara's statement of this argument at the first meeting of the ExCom was summed up in the phrase, "a missile is a missile."[34]  "It makes no great difference," he maintained, "whether you are killed by a missile from the Soviet Union or Cuba."[35]  The implication was clear. The United States should not initiate a crisis with the Soviet Union, risking a significant probability of nuclear war over an occurrence which had such small strategic implications.

The perceptions of McGeorge Bundy, the President's Assistant for National Security Affairs, are the most difficult of all to reconstruct. There is no question that he initially argued for a diplomatic track.[36]  But was Bundy laboring under his acknowledged burden of responsibility in Cuba I? Or was he playing the role of devil's advocate in order to make the President probe his own initial reaction and consider other options?

The President's brother, Robert Kennedy, saw most clearly the political wall against which Khrushchev had backed the President. But he, like McNamara, saw the prospect of nuclear doom. Was Khrushchev going to force the President to an insane act? At the first meeting of the ExCom, he scribbled a note, "Now I know how Tojo felt when he was planning Pearl Harbor."[37]  From the outset he searched for an alternative that would prevent the air strike.

The initial reaction of Theodore Sorensen, the President's Special Counsel and "alter ego," fell somewhere between that of the President and his brother. Like the President, Sorensen felt the poignancy of betrayal. If the President had been the architect of the policy which the missiles punctured, Sorensen was the draftsman. Khrushchev's deceitful move demanded a strong counter-move. But like Robert Kennedy, Sorensen feared lest the shock and disgrace lead to disaster.

To the Joint Chiefs of Staff the issue was clear. *Now* was the time to do the job for which they had prepared contingency plans. Cuba I had been badly done; Cuba II would not be. The missiles provided the *occasion* to deal with the issue: cleansing the Western Hemisphere of Castro's Communism. As the President recalled on the day the crisis ended, "An invasion would have been a mistake—a wrong use of our power. But the military are mad. They wanted to do this. It's lucky for us that we have McNamara over there."[38]

McCone's perceptions flowed from his confirmed prediction. As the Cassandra of the incident, he argued forcefully that the Soviets had installed the missiles in a daring political probe which the United States must meet with force. The time for an air strike was now.[39]

*The politics of choice.* The process by which the blockade emerged is a story of the most subtle and intricate probing, pulling, and hauling; leading, guiding, and spurring. Reconstruction of this process can only be tentative. Initially the President and most of his advisers wanted the clean, surgical air strike. On the first day of the crisis, when informing Stevenson of the missiles, the President mentioned only two alternatives: "I suppose the alternatives are to go in by air and wipe them out, or to take other steps to render them inoperable."[40] At the end of the week a sizeable minority still favored an air strike. As Robert Kennedy recalled: "The fourteen people involved were very significant. . . . If six of them had been President of the U.S., I think that the world might have been blown up."[41] What prevented the air strike was a fortuitous coincidence of a number of factors—the absence of any one of which might have permitted that option to prevail.

First, McNamara's vision of holocaust set him firmly against the air strike. His initial attempt to frame the issue in strategic terms struck Kennedy as particularly inappropriate. Once McNamara realized that the name of the game was a strong response, however, he and his deputy Gilpatric chose the blockade as a fallback. When the Secretary of Defense—whose department had the action, whose reputation in the Cabinet was unequaled, in whom the President demonstrated full confidence—marshaled the arguments for the blockade and refused to be moved, the blockade became a formidable alternative.

Second, Robert Kennedy—the President's closest confidant—was unwilling to see his brother become a "Tojo." His arguments against the air strike on moral grounds struck a chord in the President. Moreover, once his brother had stated these arguments so forcefully, the President could not have chosen his initially preferred course without, in effect, agreeing to become what RFK had condemned.

The President learned of the missiles on Tuesday morning. On Wednesday morning, in order to mask our discovery from the Russians, the President flew to Connecticut to keep a campaign commitment, leaving RFK as the unofficial chairman of the group. By the time the President returned on Wednesday evening, a critical third piece had been added to the picture. McNamara had presented his argument for the blockade. Robert Kennedy and Sorensen had joined McNamara. A powerful coalition of the advisers in whom the President had the greatest confidence, and with whom his style was most compatible, had emerged.

Fourth, the coalition that had formed behind the President's initial preference gave him reason to pause. *Who* supported the air strike—the Chiefs, McCone, Rusk, Nitze, and Acheson—as much as *how* they supported it, counted. Fifth, a piece of inaccurate information, which no one probed, permitted the blockade advocates to fuel (potential) uncertainties in the President's mind. When the President returned to Washington Wednesday evening, RFK and Sorensen met him at the airport. Sorensen gave the President a four-page memorandum outlining the areas of agreement and disagreement. The strongest argument was that the air strike simply could not be surgical.[42] After a day of prodding and questioning, the Force had asserted that it could not guarantee the success of a surgical air strike limited to the missiles alone.

Thursday evening, the President convened the ExCom at the White House. He declared his tentative choice of the blockade and directed that preparations be made to put it into effect by Monday morning.[43] Though he raised a question about the possibility of a surgical air strike subsequently, he seems to have accepted the experts' opinion that this was no live option.[44] (Acceptance of this estimate suggests that he may have learned the lesson of the Bay of Pigs—"Never rely on experts"—less well than he supposed.)[45] But this information was incorrect. That no one probed this estimate during the first week of the crisis poses an interesting question for further investigation.

A coalition, including the President, thus emerged from the President's initial decision that something had to be done: McNamara, Robert Kennedy, and Sorensen's resistance to the air strike; incompatibility between the President and the air-strike advocates; and an inaccurate piece of information.[46]

## CONCLUSION

. . . The preliminary, partial paradigms presented here provide a basis for serious re-examination of many problems of foreign and military policy. Model II and Model III cuts at problems typically treated in Model I terms can permit significant improvements in explanation and prediction.[47] Full Model II and III analyses require large amounts of information. But even in cases where the information base is severely limited, improvements are possible. Consider the problem of predicting Soviet strategic forces. In the mid-1950's, Model I calculations led to predictions that the Soviets would rapidly deploy large numbers of long-range bombers. From a Model II perspective, both the frailty of the Air Force within the Soviet military establishment and the budgetary implications of such a buildup would have led analysts to hedge this prediction. Moreover, Model II would have pointed to a sure, visible indicator of such a buildup: noisy struggles among the Services over major budgetary shifts. In the late 1950's and early 1960's, Model I calculations led to the prediction of immediate, massive Soviet deployment of ICBM's. Again a Model II cut would have reduced this number because in the earlier period strategic rockets were controlled by the Soviet ground forces rather than an independent service, and in the later period, this would have necessitated massive shifts in budgetary splits. Today, Model I considerations lead many analysts both to recommend that an agreement not to deploy AMB's be a major American objective in upcoming strategic negotiations with the USSR, and to predict success. From a Model II vantage point, the existence of an ongoing Soviet ABM program, the strength of the organization (National Air Defense) that controls ABM's and the fact that an agreement to stop ABM deployment would force the virtual dismantling of this organization make a viable agreement of this sort much less likely. A Model III cut suggests that (a) there must be significant differences among perceptions and priorities of Soviet leaders over strategic negotiations, (b) any agreement will affect some players' power bases, and (c) agreements that do not require extensive cuts in the sources of some major players' power will prove easier to negotiate and more viable.

The present formulation of paradigms is simply an initial step. As such it leaves a long list of critical questions unanswered. Given any action, an imaginative analyst should always be able to construct some rationale for the government's choice. By imposing, and relaxing, constraints on the parameters of rational choice (as in variants of Model I) analysts can construct a large number of accounts of any act as a rational choice. But does a statement of reasons why a rational actor would choose an action constitute an explanation of the *occurrence* of that action? How can Model I analysis be forced to make more systematic contributions to the question of the determinants of occurrences? Model II's explanation of $t$ in terms of $t-1$ is explanation. The world is contiguous. But governments sometimes make sharp departures. Can an organizational process model be modified to suggest where change is likely? Attention to organizational change should afford greater understanding of why particular programs and SOP's are maintained by identifiable types of organizations and also how a manager can improve organizational performance. Model III tells a fascinating "story." But its complexity is enormous, the information requirements are often overwhelming, and many of the details of the bargaining may be superfluous. How can such a model be made parsimonious? The three models are obviously not exclusive alternatives. Indeed the paradigms highlight the partial emphasis of the framework—what each emphasizes and what it leaves out. Each concentrates on one class of variables, in effect, relegating other important factors to a *ceteris paribus* clause. Model I concentrates on "market factors": pressures and incentives created by the "international strategic market place." Models II and III focus on the internal mechanism of the government that chooses in this environment. But can these relations be more fully specified? Adequate synthesis would require a typology of decisions and actions, some of which are more amenable to treatment in terms of one model and some to another. Government behavior is but one cluster of factors relevant to occurrences in foreign affairs. Most students of foreign policy adopt this focus (at least when explaining and predicting). Nevertheless, the dimensions of the chess board, the character ᵒf the pieces, and the rules of the game—factors considered by international ᵐ theorists—constitute the context in which the pieces are moved. Can ᵒr variables in the full function of determinants of foreign policy ᵉ identified? . . .

# NOTES

1. Theodore Sorensen, *Kennedy* (1965), p. 705.

2. In attempting to understand problems of foreign affairs, analysts engage in a number of related, but logically separable enterprises: (a) description, (b) explanation, (c) prediction, (d) evaluation, and (e) recommendation. This essay focuses primarily on explanation (and, by implication, prediction).

3. In arguing that explanations proceed in terms of implicit conceptual models, this essay makes no claim that foreign policy analysts have developed any satisfactory, empirically tested theory. In this essay, the use of the term "model" without qualifiers should be read "conceptual scheme."

4. Earlier drafts of this argument have aroused heated arguments concerning proper names for these models. To choose names from ordinary language is to court confusion, as well as familiarity. Perhaps it is best to think of these models as I, II, and III.

5. Each of the three "case snapshots" displays the work of a conceptual model as it is applied to explain the U.S. blockade of Cuba. But these three cuts are primarily exercises in hypothesis generation rather than hypothesis testing. Especially when separated from the larger study, these accounts may be misleading. The sources for these accounts include the full public record plus a large number of interviews with participants in the crisis.

6. Inclusion of the President's Special Assistant for National Security Affairs in the tier of "Chiefs" rather than among the "Staffers" involves a debatable choice. In fact he is both super-staffer and near-chief. His position has no statutory authority. He is especially dependent upon good relations with the President and Secretaries of Defense and State. Nevertheless, he stands astride a genuine action-channel. The decision to include this position among the Chiefs reflects my judgment that the Bundy function is becoming institutionalized.

7. Richard E. Neustadt, Testimony, United States Senate, Committee on Government Operations, Subcommittee on National Security Staffing, *Administration of National Security*, March 26, 1963, pp. 82-83 (88th Cong., 1st sess.).

8. This aphorism was stated first, I think, by Don K. Price.

9. Paul Y. Hammond, "Super Carriers and B-36 Bombers," in Harold Stein (ed.), *American Civil-Military Decisions* (1963).

10. Sorensen, *Kennedy*, p. 670.

11. *Ibid.*

12. *Ibid.*, pp. 670 ff.

13. *New York Times*, August, September, 1962.

14. *New York Times*, August 20, 1962.

15. *New York Times*, September 5, 1962.

16. *New York Times*, September 14, 1962.

17. *New York Times*, October 14, 1962.

18. Cited by Abel, *Missile Crisis*, p. 13.

19. *New York Times*, September 5, 1962.

20. *New York Times*, September 14, 1962.

21. Senate Foreign Relations Committee; Senate Armed Services Committee; House Committee on Appropriation; House Select Committee on Export Control.

22. Abel, *Missile Crisis*, pp. 17–18. According to McCone, he told Kennedy, "The only construction I can put on the material going into Cuba is that the Russians are preparing to introduce offensive missiles." See also Weintal and Bartlett, *Facing the Brink*, pp. 60–61.

23. Abel, *Missile Crisis*, p. 23.

24. *New York Times*, September 10, 1962.

25. See Abel, *op. cit.*, pp. 25–26; and Hilsman, *To Move a Nation*, p. 174.

26. Department of Defense Appropriations, *Hearings*, p. 69.

27. A basic but somewhat contradictory account of parts of this story emerges, *Ibid.*, pp. 1–70.

28. Department of Defense Appropriations, *Hearings*, p. 71.

29. The details of the 10 days between the October 4 decision and the October 14 flight must be held in abeyance.

30. Abel, *Missile Crisis*, p. 44.

31. *Ibid.*, pp. 44 ff.

32. See Richard Neustadt, "Afterword," *Presidential Power* (1964).

33. Sorensen, *Kennedy*, p. 676; Schlesinger, *A Thousand Days*, p. 801.

34. Hilsman, *To Move a Nation*, p. 195.

35. *Ibid.*

36. Weintal and Bartlett, *Facing the Brink*, p. 67; Abel, *Missile Crisis*, p. 53.

37. Schlesinger, *A Thousand Days*, p. 803.

38. *Ibid.*, p. 831.

39. Abel, *op. cit.*, p. 186.

40. *Ibid.*, p. 49.

41. Interview, quoted by Ronald Steel, *New York Review of Books*, March 13, 1969, p. 22.

42. Sorensen, *Kennedy*, p. 686.

43. *Ibid.*, p. 691.

44. *Ibid.*, p. 691–692.

45. Schlesinger, *A Thousand Days*, p. 296.

46. Space will not permit an account of the path from this coalition to the formal government decision on Saturday and action on Monday.

47. A number of problems are now being examined in these terms both in the Bureaucracy Study Group on Bureaucracy and Policy of the Institute of Politics at Harvard University and at the Rand Corporation.

# 4.2    Crisis Decisionmaking: Bureaucratic Politics and the Use of Force

## RICHARD HEAD

*The following article by Brig. Gen. Richard Head (USAF, Ret.) should caution all of us who are advocates of the explanatory power of the bureaucratic policies paradigm. His detailed review of an actual U.S. crisis-management decision—the North Korean killing of two U.S. Army officers in the Joint Security Area of the Demilitarized Zone in 1976—exemplifies that in many instances bureaucratic politics plays a secondary role. General Head concludes by summarizing some procedural rules that permitted individuals, notably the field commander, to have a significant impact on the policy process. What remains to be addressed is how such useful procedures can become part of the routine of government's day-to-day operations.*

Since the publication of Graham Allison's seminal work, "Conceptual Models and the Cuban Missile Crisis," in 1969, there has been a rush to overstate the effects of bureaucratic politics in decisionmaking. Allison, for his part, was careful to posit his organizational and bureaucratic politics explanations as alternative models, but in the ensuing years many of the original caveats have been lost, neglected, or forgotten. One of the first critiques, Steven Krasner's "Are Bureaucracies Important?" was off the mark in many respects, but in one fundamental criticism, it was correct. A single focus on bureaucratics politics neglects other, more important variables and is dangerous when it obscures or dilutes the power of high officials to lead, manage, and direct the bureaucracy. The implication that lower-level officials seek to manipulate major decisions, and succeed, is wrong. That large organizations and the leaders who manage them affect government choice—Allison's major point—is certainly correct.

In a separate work Bud McFarlane, Frisco Short, and I argued that crisis decisions tend to be the product of the key policymakers' belief systems and the unique situation.[1] This article reiterates that finding and advances three other propositions for study.

1. Crisis decisionmaking tends to be centralized, elevated, and optimized, and it suffers from a lack of information. Bureaucratic politics plays an important, but a lesser role.

2. The primary political choice in a crisis is whether to use military force. The primary military recommendation is how it will be used. Additionally, military advice has been most persuasive when it has recommended against the use of inappropriate force.

3. Tactical successes tend to be likely when there is a clear military chain of command with combined arms resources. The role of the unified commander is central, and command arrangements are the most critical implementation factors.

Of these three propositions, the one that has stirred the most public discussion has been the issue of the role of force. When, under what circumstances, and by what means, does a political democracy resort to the use of force to resolve international disputes?[2] This issue has an extended history in U.S. politics, from George Washington's warning to stay clear of foreign entanglements in his second inaugural address to the mass cry of the 1970s—"No more Vietnams!" Throughout this long period, the traditional U.S. view of war has been conservative—a reluctance to get involved in foreign adventures, but when engaged, the nation tends to demand total victory, unconditional surrender in the terms of the Atlantic Charter of 1942. The U.S. view of war has been eloquently expressed by Gen. Douglas MacArthur in his speech to the Corps of Cadets at West Point in May 1962. "Yours is the profession of arms—the will to win, the sure knowledge that in war there is no substitute for victory; that if you lose, the nation will be destroyed."

The opposing view has its roots in the limited European wars of the seventeenth and eighteenth centuries. Its most famous spokesman was Karl von Clauswitz. Writing his classic work *On War* in the Napoleonic period, Clauswitz codified the dictum that war was only politics by other means—that the use of force was properly subject to political objectives. After the total mobilization of World War II, many thought that the overarching goal of statecraft would henceforth be the avoidance of a nuclear war, and thus all future wars would be limited. By *limited* most observers agreed that war "would be fought for ends far short of the complete subordination of one state's will to another's and by means involving far less than the total military resources of the belligerents, . . . leaving the civilian life and the armed forces . . . largely intact and leading to a bargained termination."[3]  To many, these limitations on force seemed morally and emotionally repugnant because they departed greatly from the desire for total victory. Yet they are consistent with the U.S. legal and ethical values of morality and expediency.

Over the four decades since the end of World War II, U.S. policy-makers, defense specialists, and the public have debated the merits of these two contrasting approaches to the use of military force. Diplomats have generally favored the more subtle, limited exploitation of military force to accomplish the goals of U.S. foreign policy, at the same time expressing concern about the dangers of escalation and superpower confrontation. It was the limitation of U.S. objectives and force that characterized the Korean and Vietnam wars and numerous crisis-management actions in between. In both wars U.S. civil-military relations witnessed tight political controls on the decisions of field commanders.

The public at large, on the other hand, has held wartime field commanders in high esteem. Charges of political interference produced huge support for General MacArthur after he was fired by President Truman in 1951. Many of the same limitations on military operations—bombing halts, target selection, sanctuaries, restrictions on ground offensives, pauses during negotiations—were present in Vietnam and contributed not only to a lowering of military morale, but confused the public and added to the already massive loss of public support.

Without any resolution of these two contrasting views, the Reagan administration had to face the same world of international relations as its predecessors, but one made more complex by the growing military power of the Soviet Union and greatly expanded terrorist operations. With the support of the U.S. people and the Congress, the country began a military build-up in 1981 that increased its readiness and sustainability while gradually expanding modernization and force structure. At the same time, the administration faced a series of crises and deployed Airborne Warning and

Control (AWACS) aircraft to the Sudan, a battalion of marines to Lebanon, and a Joint Task Force to Grenada. Anti-U.S. terrorist actions included the hijacking of a TWA airliner, the seizing of the *Achille Lauro*, car bombs on U.S./NATO bases in Europe, the bombing of the La Belle discotheque in Berlin, several kidnappings in Beirut, and the capture of Pan American flight 73 in Pakistan.

Since 1981 U.S. Secretary of State George P. Schultz has argued long and forcefully, within the government and in public presentations, that armed strength is essential in the conduct of diplomacy. He stresses that military forces need to be used as instruments of national policy in political-military crises as well as in combating terrorism. He not only advocated using military force to defend U.S. interests but also that U.S. responses "should go beyond passive defense to consider means of action prevention, preemption and retaliation."[4] Only in this way will the United States be able to prevent and deter future terrorist acts. Secretary Schultz stressed that there is a prerequisite for broad public consensus on the moral and strategic necessity for action, but that specific presidential decisions cannot be tied to the opinion polls. Broadly viewed, the policy articulated by the secretary and the Department of State advocated the use of military forces in a variety of political-military situations around the world to support and bolster U.S. foreign policy. Many considered these uses to be beyond the military missions of deterring war and preparing to defend the U.S. and its allies from attack. In many of these situations, the purpose of the military forces tended to be as broad as the role of the marines in Lebanon in 1982–1984.

The Lebanon crisis played a pivotal role in crystalizing policymakers' attitudes toward the use of force in the early 1980s. A brief review of the situation will be valuable for the purposes of this study. During the time of U.S. direct involvement in Lebanon, U.S. foreign policy was based on three objectives: "the withdrawal of all external forces"; "a sovereign, independent Lebanon dedicated to national unity and able to exercise control throughout its national territory"; and "security for Israel's northern border."[5] U.S. marines were deployed to Beirut in August 1982 as part of a multinational peacekeeping force to supervise the evacuation of 8,000 Palestine Liberation Organization (PLO) fighters who had congregated there in the wake of the Israeli invasion in June. By September 10, the PLO movement had been completed, and the marines were withdrawn. Four days later Lebanese President-elect Bashir Gemayel was assassinated, and the following day hundreds of remaining Palestinian refugees were massacred in their camps by phalangist militia. These two incidents jolted the administration into action, and, on September 29, it redeployed the marines to Beirut, this time increasing their numbers from 800 to 1200. Again the U.S. force was part of a multinational movement that also contained military units from France, Italy, and Great Britain, at the request of Amin Gemayel, the new president of Lebanon and Bashir's brother.

Six months later, on March 15, 1983, the marines suffered their first casualties in a direct attack on their forces. Their presence had stabilized the situation, but the first objective—the removal of all foreign troops—proved to be elusive when Israeli, Syrian, and PLO forces refused to be the first to leave. On April 18, a car bomb destroyed the U.S. embassy in Beirut and killed sixty-three people. The Syrian-backed Moslem factions more and more viewed the United States as being partisan in favor of the Israelis and the Phalange. As the credibility of the Gemayel government declined, so also did the support of the U.S. people for maintaining the marines there. In September the marines began firing their artillery for the first time, and the U.S. Sixth Fleet offshore began shelling. The Congress intervened at this point, and, despite a spirited debate, authorized the president to keep the marines in Lebanon for an additional eighteen months under the War Powers Resolution.

Secretary of Defense Caspar Weinberger and the Joint Chiefs of Staff had been skeptical about the marine mission to Lebanon from the start, not because it was not an important part of U.S. foreign policy to support Lebanon, but because they were concerned that others wanted to use military forces for political objectives that were vague and in some cases unattainable. The U.S. public shared these misgivings, with 44 percent favoring and 45 percent opposing U.S. participation in the multinational force in mid-October 1983.[6]

Then on October 23, a lone fanatic drove a truck loaded with explosives into the first floor of the marine barracks, detonated it, and killed 241 U.S. citizens. The outrage at the incident was widespread, touching virtually all those associated with the operation. Most people were dismayed at the vulnerability of the marine force and upset with its inability to bring peace to the area. Representative Sam Gibbons (D-Fla.), expressed some of the frustration, "If we are there to keep the peace, then we are far too few. . . . If we are there to die, then we are far too many."[7] The Department of Defense appointed Adm. Robert L. J. Long's commission to investigate the disaster, and they concluded the marine force "was not trained, organized, staffed, or supported to deal effectively with the terrorist threat in Lebanon."[8]

Public support plummeted. In January 1984 a public opinion poll taken by the *Washington Post* and ABC News reported that 58 percent of the people asked wanted the marines pulled out, and 59 percent thought the administration had "no clear goals" for their presence in Lebanon. On February 1–2, the Democratic caucuses of both the House and Senate called for "prompt and orderly" withdrawal of U.S. forces, and on February 7 the president announced their redeployment.[9]

Nine months later, Secretary Weinberger delivered one of the strongest and most-quoted speeches of the Reagan administration. He argued that military force was not appropriate in every crisis. If the U.S. military were to be used indiscriminately and as a "regular and customary part of our diplomatic efforts" it "would surely plunge us headlong into the sort of domestic turmoil we experienced during the Viet Nam War without accomplishing the goal for which we committed our forces."[10] Having stated the problem as he saw it, the secretary laid out six guidelines—major tests—to be applied when considering whether to use U.S. combat forces abroad:

- the commitment to combat should only be for engagements that are vital to our national interests or allies
- combat troops should be deployed with the intention of winning
- the forces deploying should be given clearly defined political and military objectives
- the relationship between objectives and forces—size, composition and disposition—must be continually reassessed
- before the decision to commit forces, there must be reasonable assurance that the American people and the Congress support such action
- finally, the commitment of U.S. forces to combat should be the last resort.[11]

Thus, the broad themes in U.S. crisis-management policy center on the proper conditions for the use of force, the overall purposes military forces can be expected to accomplish, and the importance of a popular consensus supporting the decision.[12] It is significant that neither the secretary of state nor the secretary of defense made an issue of who supports what policy or the bureaucratic politics of obtaining a presidential decision.[13] After this series of speeches in 1984, there was much discussion surrounding the secretary of state advocating the use of force more broadly than the secretary of defense. Both agreed on military combat as a last resort and the need for consensus, and they also agreed on specific employment decisions such as Grenada and the bombing of Libya on April 15, 1986. But the two views on military power are ones that have deep roots in U.S. policymaking, and understanding those views and their deep roots is a prerequisite for the study of crisis management.

With the description of these major issues forming the framework for analysis, it is useful to review an actual U.S. crisis-management decision and see the extent to which bureaucratic politics played a part. The North Korean killing of two U.S. Army officers in the Joint Security Area of the Demilitarized Zone in 1976 is a case that exemplifies most of the issues I have discussed. This example is particularly useful because it is one of the few that demonstrates the key role that the field commander can play.

## THE KOREAN DMZ CASE

*The Setting*

By August 1976 Gerald Ford had been president for almost two years and was running for reelection. He had traveled to Vladivostok to negotiate a framework for the SALT II agreement, ordered the evacuation of U.S. personnel as Saigon fell to the North Vietnamese, and acted resolutely in the *Mayaguez* seizure.

His secretary of state was Henry Kissinger, who was known to believe that crises present opportunities for executive action that are not available in routine times.[14] He argued that the United States was the leader of the free world and needed to counter Soviet expansion and client adventurism at all points. Kissinger also believed that force was an essential element of diplomacy but that its use brought moral risks that made it necessary to use sufficient force for both defense and deterrent purposes. Excess moderation in a crisis, he said, could bring about the very escalation one was trying to avoid. On the issue of popular support, Kissinger was adamant that "initiative creates its own consensus."[15]

The secretary of defense was Donald Rumsfeld, and the director of the Central Intelligence Agency was George Bush. The assistant to the president for National Security Affairs was Lt. General Brent Scowcroft, USAF, and his deputy was Lt. Col. Robert C. McFarlane, USMC.

In 1976 there were about 42,000 U.S. troops still in South Korea, under the command of Gen. Richard G. Stilwell, USA, who was also the commander-in-chief (CINC), United Nations (UN) Command. The purposes of these military forces were to provide tangible evidence of U.S. support for South Korea, deter an attack by North Korea, and dissuade the People's Republic of China (PRC) or the Soviet Union (USSR) from condoning such an attack.[16]

The cessation of armed hostilities in 1953 only transformed the nature and scale of the Korean conflict into less dramatic events. The formal political conference that was to provide for the peace never took place. Since the armistice, 49 U.S. citizens, 1,000 South Koreans, and over 600 North Koreans had been killed along the Demilitarized Zone (DMZ)—the 4-kilometer band that separates the two Koreas. In the period from 1967 to 1973 alone, the United States, the UN, and South Korea submitted nearly 2,000 formal complaints of incidents of harassment and violence along the DMZ. A large number of these were in the Joint Security Area (JSA)—the 800-meter diameter circle within the DMZ that houses the Military Armistice Commission (MAC) headquarters, intended as a neutral zone where both sides could travel freely and conduct meetings in an open environment.

On August 5, 1976, North Korea released a radio blast that was unusually strident in its attack, "The United States and the South Korean authorities, who have been stepping up preparations for war to invade the Northern half of the Democratic Peoples' Republic of Korea, *have now finished war preparations* (italics added) and are going over to the adventurous machination to directly ignite the fuse of war."[17]

On August 18 in the Joint Security Area, Capt. Arthur G. Bonifas and 1st Lt. Mark T. Barrett led a fifteen-man work detail of South Koreans and a security force of ten U.S. and Korean soldiers to trim a large poplar tree. The tree had long been a problem for UN guards because it grew so full that it obstructed the view between UN observation posts. In a period of thirty minutes, while the labor force was trimming the tree, twenty-eight to thirty North Korean guards appeared and surrounded the outnumbered UN force. Without provocation, the North Korean soldiers attacked the UN personnel with fists, clubs, and axes. In the ensuing fight, Captain Bonifas and Lieutenant Barrett were killed, another U.S. officer was wounded, and eight enlisted men were wounded.

## Notification and Initial Actions

Immediately after the incident, the U.S. Army/UN Command staff in the forward operations center at Yongson, in Seoul, formed a crisis action team, notified General Stilwell (who was in Japan), and sent out a message to the Joint Chiefs of Staff in Washington. Within an hour, the National Military Command Center (NMCC), the crisis communications hub of the Department of Defense, had received the message and activated its notification procedures.

The State Department Operations Center duty officer called the senior Korean desk officer shortly after receiving the call from the NMCC at 11:20 P.M. and relayed news of the incident. The Korean desk officer also received a call from a foreign service officer in the U.S. embassy in Seoul at about the same time. They discussed the fight, that *one* person had been killed, but that the details were still sketchy. The desk officer then called the deputy assistant secretary for East Asia who called the assistant secretary of state for East Asia and Pacific Affairs. It was decided the incident was not time-sensitive, did not require notification of any other officials, and could be handled the next day.

Secretary Kissinger was informed about 6:00 A.M. when his personal assistant, Lawrence S. Eagleburger, called him. Kissinger was outraged at the North Korean murders and furious that he had not been told earlier. He made two decisions: to inform General Scowcroft, who was in Kansas City with the president; and to call a meeting of the Washington Special Actions Group (WSAG) for 3:30 P.M.

General Scowcroft learned of the incident by cable traffic on the same morning, just before receiving the call from Secretary Kissinger. Scowcroft informed the president in his morning intelligence briefing at 9:00 a.m. The president was extremely upset by the brutal and apparently unprovoked killings, but he noted that the passage of time was not as critical to a successful response as it had been in the *Mayaguez* crisis. His instructions were that the WSAG be convened, options prepared, and that he be kept informed.[18]

## *The Decisionmaking Process: First WSAG*

The WSAG meeting began with an intelligence briefing from George Bush on the latest information on the situation. According to the *New York Times,* a participant commented afterward that there was no evidence of North Korean movement toward the DMZ. "Lacking such information, the session became more a discussion group, . . . without a sense of imminent conflict."[19] There was speculation on what the North Koreans hoped to achieve by such action.

In a review of military capabilities, the North's overall superiority on the ground did not appear significant, although the balance in the immediate area of the JSA substantially favored the North, particularly in artillery. The 60–70 U.S. fighters in South Korea were greatly outnumbered by the 588 of the North. No consensus emerged on a precise course of action. Secretary Kissinger argued that the U.S. needed to retaliate to redress this premeditated act of brutality, but the others were less inclined to support offensive action. They did agree on the need to deploy aircraft and ships to the area and to increase the readiness level of U.S. forces in Korea.

The WSAG members were all concerned about the impact of any U.S. action on the international community, the Soviet Union, and the People's Republic of China. The members agreed that Secretary Kissinger should contact representatives of the USSR and the PRC to indicate U.S. outrage and to make clear our intention to carry out strong measures in reply. They also agreed in their views of U.S. objectives, and their recommendations seemed less influenced by bureaucratic politics than by their personal appraisal of the situation.

Immediately after the meeting, Secretary Kissinger called General Scowcroft and the president in Kansas City and discussed the WSAG recommendations. President Ford approved each of the recommendations and authorized Kissinger to order the following list of diplomatic and military actions:[20]

- deployment of one F-4 fighter squadron from Okinawa to Korea
- an increase in the alert status of U.S. forces in Korea
- preparation for deployment of one F-111 squadron from the U.S. to Korea

- preparation for the use of B-52s on training missions from Guam to Korea
- preparation for deployment of the aircraft carrier *Midway* from its port in Japan to Korean waters
- notification of UN delegates and the Security Council

Meanwhile General Stilwell had arrived at his headquarters, immediately consulted with his staff, and taken several initial actions. In the next few hours he dictated the following:

1. A proposed text for the UN representative to the Armistice Commission
2. A proposed text of a letter to Kim Il-Sung, president and commander-in-chief of North Korea's armed forces
3. The initial concept of an operations plan to remove the tree: "I felt the minimum we had to do was to reassert our rights in the Joint Security Area and cut down the tree"[21]

General Stilwell's concept of an operations plan was sent to the JCS by message; it emphasized that the field commander had an inherent responsibility for the defense of his forces, and that the UN Command must maintain its legitimate rights in the DMZ. General Stilwell made the point very clear, "Thus, although it is only damn tree, it involves a major principle . . . to ensure the protection of our forces."[22]

There remained the issue of how much warning to give the North Koreans of the intended action. General Stilwell outlined the alternatives, no notice versus prior notice, and stated the arguments for each. In a concluding note, he summarized the dilemma of a military leader. "All my military instincts compel me to opt for the first course, but I appreciate that broader considerations may support the second course of action."[23]

The impact of General Stilwell's proposals in Washington was great. As an official noted later, "It was really General Stilwell's proposal that focused attention on going back into the JSA and reaffirming our rights there."

The next day Rear Admiral Frudden, the UN representative at the MAC, stated the full concern and outrage of the U.S./UN. He communicated the U.S. demands: 1. North Korean acknowledgement of its responsibility, 2. a promise that the security of UN forces in the JSA would not be challenged again, and 3. punishment of the men responsible. The North Korean general denied the charges and accused the UN forces of a "premeditated, well-organized provocation."[24]

Back in the United States, the country's attention was focused on the Republican National Convention, where President Ford had formally won the nomination.

## The Second WSAG Meeting

The White House situation room was the scene of the follow-up WSAG meeting, 8:00 A.M. August 19. It began with an intelligence briefing from CIA and led to a discussion of the available options, including General Stilwell's plan to cut down the tree. The tone of this meeting was more purposeful than the first WSAG, and the following moves were tentatively agreed upon:

- validation of the F-4 and F-111 squadron deployments
- agreement on the increased alert status, especially since North Korea had gone to a war-readiness posture
- recommendation to move the *Midway* task force to Korea
- continuation of the study of the War Powers Resolution and its applicability to executive actions
- recommendation to accept General Stilwell's basic concept of operations to enter the JSA with a show of military force and cut down the tree. (The Department of State had reservations about the large number of forces outlined in the plan, and General Stilwell was asked to reassess his requirements for minimum force, amplify his plan with details, and forward it for final approval. The no-notice version was accepted.)
- inclusion of a flight of three B-52s from Guam in the show of force over South Korea.

Secretary Kissinger then flew to Kansas City and met with General Scowcroft and the president to discuss the WSAG recommendations and possible North Korean reactions. He outlined the recommended course of action—a show of force—but noted that he believed a more forceful action was necessary. His reasoning was that retaliation was necessary to demonstrate the U.S. will to defend its interests, and he believed strongly that North Korea would not do anything in return. General Scowcroft agreed on the necessity of strong action up to the level of the original act—the death of the U.S. soldiers—but stressed the importance of assuring that the means chosen would not result in a North Korean reply in which we would be at a disadvantage. Specifically, he pointed out that the use of U.S artillery near the JSA (one 105mm Howitzer battery) could result in an artillery duel in which the U.S. would be at a serious disadvantage.

The president discussed the issue with Kissinger and Scowcroft for forty-five minutes and then tentatively decided on the tree-chopping and show-of-force option. He directed that the recommended deployments be implemented but decided to withhold final approval of the tree cutting until General Stilwell's detailed plan arrived from Korea that night.[25]

The plan was named Operation Paul Bunyan, and it had a series of tactical and strategic objectives. The tactical ones were to cut down the tree and to remove two illegal North Korean road barriers in the JSA. The strategic objective was to demonstrate U.S. and UNC resolve that erosion or denial of legitimate rights in the JSA and DMZ would not be tolerated. The plan proposed a primary task force to enter the JSA and a secondary task force to provide cover and reinforcement, if necessary. The primary task force was to enter the JSA precisely at 7:00 A.M. August 21, thirty minutes before the North Korean Army normally manned its guard posts. The detailed plan was completed on the evening of August 19 and sent to the JCS. It was approved by the JCS, the secretary of defense, the secretary of state, the NSC staff and forwarded to Kansas City for final decision.

General Scowcroft briefed the president on the morning of August 20 on General Stilwell's detailed operations plan. The president decided not to order any reprisal but approved the plan in its no-notice version. His personal belief was that it was essential to reassert U.S. prerogatives firmly but without overkill. He later stated that his reasons were related to the character of the adversary in North Korea. "In the case of Korea, to gamble with an overkill might broaden very quickly into a full military conflict, but responding with an appropriate amount of force would be effective in demonstrating U.S. resolve."[26] The president's decision was phoned to Washington, and the execute order was transmitted from the Joint Chiefs of Staff to General Stilwell by message and secure phone at 11:45 P.M., August 20 in Korea, seven hours before the operation was to begin.

*Operational Implementation*

The time for developing courses of action and making decisions had now passed. The forces were deployed and moving. B-52s from Guam arrived over their Korean training area, escorted by USAF Korean-based F-4s and Republic of Korea (ROK) F-5s. The aircraft were assigned flight paths to make their presence visible on radar but sufficiently far from the DMZ to remain nonprovocative. The task force inside the JSA had 110 personnel, including a U.S. engineer team with chain saws. Immediate backup was one JSA security platoon, an ROK force 300 meters away, and another U.S. force.

Maj. Gen. Morris J. Brady, the commander of the U.S. Second Infantry division and the joint U.S.-Korean I Corps group, commanded the secondary task force. It included a U.S. infantry unit airborne in twenty Huey helicopters, escorted by seven Cobra attack helicopters. These forces were placed so as to be easily monitored on North Korean radar and were intended as a deterrent or, if needed, for reinforcing and extracting the forces on the scene.

At 7:00 A.M. the engineers, the JSA security platoon, and the ROK force entered the JSA and headed for the tree. Five minutes later, North Korean officials of the Military Armistice Commission were informed that the UN force intended to complete peacefully the work begun on August 18, and that if the work party was not molested, there would be no further action. About 150 North Korean guards gathered across the bridge north of the tree, but no one challenged the operation.

The U.S. engineers took forty-five minutes to cut down the tree. Concurrently, another work party removed the two illegal North Korean road barriers inside the JSA. Both groups finished their work, and the task forces departed.

Within an hour, Maj. Gen. Han Ju-kyong, the senior North Korean representative to the armistice commission, requested a private meeting with Admiral Frudden and conveyed the following message from Kim Il-Sung: "It is a good thing that no big incident occurred at Pan Mun Jom for a long period. However, *it is regretful that an incident occurred* in the Joint Security Area, Pan Mun Jom this time. An effort must be made so that such incidents may not recur in the future."[27]

This was the first such use of a personal message from Kim Il-Sung to the UN commander in the twenty-three-year history of the Korean armistice. The message was immediately flashed to the UN Command, the U.S. embassy in Seoul, and Washington.

General Stilwell's opinion was that the message was totally unacceptable—that Kim was not only not accepting responsibility for the incident, he was blaming it on the UN Command for having inadequate security arrangements.[28] The State Department analyzed the message and noted two other aspects: a form of apology and a proposal for the separation of forces in the JSA. State working-group officials were surprised and commented that they were "amazed at the message," that it represented "uncharacteristic behavior of North Korea." They noted the statement partially met U.S. demands, but they also knew Secretary Kissinger wanted to be tough in this crisis. The Korean working group, without coordination with the secretary, released a statement that said, "The United States does not find acceptable a North Korean statement indirectly expressing regret for the killing of two American officers in the Demilitarized Zone between North and South Korea. . . . We do not find this message acceptable since it does not acknowledge responsibility for the deliberate and premeditated murder of the two U.N. Command officers."[29]

Murrey Marder of the *Washington Post* reported the State Department release in a Monday morning headline, "U.S. Says Message Fails to Admit Guilt in 'Brutal Murders.'"[30] When Secretary Kissinger read the negative interpretations in the Monday morning press accounts, he decided that the department should put a more balanced interpretation on the North Korean message, saying it was "a positive step," but that the U.S. still insisted on North Korean assurances respecting the safety of personnel in the DMZ.[31]

*Outcomes*

The aftermath of the crisis occurred in four areas: changes in the JSA; U.S. public reaction; congressional hearings; and international political results. The Joint Security Area changes came about as the North Koreans proposed establishing a military demarcation line through the JSA and that security personnel be restricted to their respective sides. The UN accepted the proposal and further negotiations resulted in the removal of all four North Korean guard posts in the south side of the JSA. U.S. officials never learned for certain whether any of the North Korean soldiers who participated in the murders were ever punished, but the senior lieutenant was reassigned shortly after the incident and has not been seen since.

U.S. public reaction was generally supportive. The *New York Times* treatment focused on the U.S. military actions and stated that the deployments of air and naval units into the area was a "necessary precaution." The deployments and the show of force were effective, it argued, in convincing the North Koreans of the firm commitment of the U.S. to deter any aggressive actions.[32] Newspaper editorials from the Midwest and West Coast tended to express general positions of disappointment that the U.S. response had not been stronger, while some were concerned that it had been excessive. The majority of U.S. newspaper editors agreed with the government decisions.

The House subcommittees on International Political and Military Affairs and International Organizations held combined hearings on the incident and invited executive branch witnesses from the departments of Defense and State. Congressman Fascell questioned the relationship of this and other past crises with U.S. security interests in the western Pacific. Those questions being answered satisfactorily, the committees then invited Representative Elizabeth Holtzman to make a statement questioning whether the president had complied with the provisions of the War Powers Resolution relating to notification of Congress.[33]

International political results were generally quite supportive of the U.S. actions, with the European and Japanese newspapers opining that Kim's message was a diplomatic defeat for North Korea.[34] The Soviet Union was very restrained in its reaction, maintaining silence for several days, then noting there had been "heightened tensions" and "provocative actions" by the U.S. forces in Korea. Peking was even more restrained in its public communications.[35]

In summary, the Korean tree crisis—like so many other modern military confrontations—had diverse and debatable outcomes. Its several results could not be called conclusive because the conflict between North and South Korea was not resolved. Yet, the local, tactical results were quite favorable for the United States and South Korea. There was a discontinuance of hostile acts in the JSA and along the DMZ generally for some time, and the realignment of boundaries within the JSA proved to be a permanent improvement. Although the long-term differences between the two Koreas were not resolved, the political influence of North Korea receded in the region, with the nonaligned nations, and in the United Nations forum. Internationally, the U.S. was seen to have defended successfully its legitimate rights in the JSA.

## CONCLUSIONS

When the U.S. actions in the Korean case are analyzed against Secretary Weinberger's criteria, the fit is very close. The commitment of additional forces deployed to Korea were supporting a U.S. ally and a national interest that had previously been designated as vital, extending as it did from the Korean War and the U.S. leadership of the United Nations forces there. While it is true that President Carter attempted to withdraw the Second Infantry Division from Korea, he reversed that policy decision when the full deterrent and symbolic effect of these forward-deployed forces became apparent. The combat forces that were deployed to Korea were integrated into on-scene forces that, in Operation Paul Bunyan, were fully prepared to defend themselves and win.

The deploying forces had clearly defined political and military objectives, including reassertion of UN rights in the Joint Security Area; self-defense and protection of U.S. forces; deterrence against future hostile acts; countering the North Korean actions and taking the initiative; extracting whatever apologies, reparations and assurances were possible, but avoiding provocation and incentives to escalate.

The relationship between the objectives and the size, composition, and disposition of the forces was assessed. When the Department of State objected to the size of the forces involved in the tree cutting, General Stilwell reduced the list in his final plan. Some believed the United States used more than the minimum force required to do the job. But the majority—including General Stilwell, the JCS, and the president—believed the forces chosen for the operation were the minimum necessary to complete the action successfully, which means using enough force to deter the North Koreans from taking any hostile action. Although the objective of self-defense was immediately accepted as the essential principle to be applied, there was far less support for a retaliatory strike. This was due primarily to the fear of escalation and the military advice against such action.

President Ford did not consult members of the Congress before taking his decision, as envisioned in the War Powers Resolution, partially because he believed the act was unconstitutional, an unwarranted restriction on the executive, and partially because it was impractical for reasons of communications and security. Nevertheless, with twenty-six years of U.S. defense policy supporting South Korea, he had more than reasonable assurance that the U.S. people and the Congress would support his actions.

Finally, the commitment of military forces was a last resort. There were no other viable alternatives in Korea. The Communist side had proved itself an intractable opponent in the Military Armistice Commission, and diplomatic avenues to influence directly North Korea were almost non-existent. The Soviet Union and the People's Republic of China were allies that might persuade North Korea from taking any drastic action over the long term, but in the routine hostility that characterized their behavior in the JSA, their influence was distinctly limited.

Beyond the guidelines for the use of force, the case tends to support the stated propositions. Bureaucratic politics, though it had an effect on the initial notifications and on the staff-to-staff relations between the departments of State and Defense, played a very minor role. The U.S. actions were much more the result of historical support for Korea and the unique situation in the JSA. What was new, and dramatically illustrated in this case, was the role of the overseas field commander, in touch with the political realities of his region, an expert on the use of force as an instrument of national policy, aware of both the strengths and limitations of his force, and under the command and control of the secretary of Defense as exercised through the Joint Chiefs of Staff. Further, the United States had in Korea a clear chain of command, with units that had worked together extensively.[36]

While the debilitating aspects of bureaucratic politics were notably absent, the process of crisis decisionmaking did follow established procedural rules. The process was useful and predictable. The advice and recommendations of the government department heads were presented and discussed in the Washington Special Actions Group at the call of the secretary of State. They were not random, and no one jumped the chain of command. The discussion was centralized and elevated to the White House rapidly, and the proposed courses of action were optimized to fit the situation at hand. No military operations plan was pulled from off the shelf for this crisis, but the general method of developing courses of action, identifying units that could contribute, and deploying fighter squadrons and ships into an overseas area had been practiced for years. The decisionmaking process did suffer from a lack of exact information on North Korea's intentions in the killings and on its possible responses to U.S. actions. Estimates of friendly, allied, and domestic reactions were fairly accurate, with support for the president approximating what had been anticipated.

The political decision to deploy military forces was taken almost immediately after the first WSAG meeting for three reasons: the moves demonstrated U.S. resolve and action in support of an important ally; they provided an added measure of military capability regardless of what subsequent courses of action either the U.S. or North Korea decided; and finally, they were essentially controlled, having been used repeatedly in previous crises. As mentioned, the novel aspect of this crisis was the military advocacy of a specific course of action to reenter the JSA, to cut down the tree, and to assert legitimate U.S. rights of self-defense. The fact that this action led in the following months to a realignment of the Joint Security Area, which provided even more security to UN forces, was a bonus.

## NOTES

1. Richard G. Head, Frisco W. Short, and Robert C. McFarlane, *Crisis Resolution: Presidential Decision Making in the Mayaguez and Korean Confrontations* (Boulder, CO: Westview Press, 1978). This article contains excerpts from Chapter 6.

2. For one of the most thoughtful treatments of the use of force, see Klaus Knorr, *On the Uses of Military Power in the Nuclear Age* (Princeton, NJ: Princeton University Press, 1966).

3. Robert E. Osgood, "The Reappraisal of Limited War," Problems of Modern Strategy, Pt 1, *Adelphi Papers*, no. 54 (London, 1969) and reprinted in *American Defense Policy*, 3d ed., ed. by Richard G. Head and Ervin J. Rokke (Baltimore: The Johns Hopkins University Press, 1973), p. 156 fn.

4. George P. Shultz, speeches at Yeshiva University, New York, December 9, 1984, and at the Trilateral Commission, Washington, D.C., April 3, 1984.

5. These objectives for U.S. involvement in Lebanon were expressed by Secretary of State George P. Shultz in testimony before the House Foreign Affairs Committee, September 21, 1983.

6. These public opinion figures are taken from an NBC News/Associated Press poll of October 18–19, 1983, as cited in Mary H. Copper, *American Involvement in Lebanon*, Editorial Research Report, March 2, 1984 (Washington, DC: The Congressional Quarterly), p. 172.

7. Ibid., p. 173.

8. Ibid., as quoted from the *Long Report*, released December 28, 1983, p. 173.

9. Ibid., p. 172.

10. Caspar W. Weinberger, speech to the National Press Club, November 28, 1984.

11. Ibid.

12. For a useful description of the factors affecting the use of force in the USSR, see Jonathan R. Adelman, "The Soviet Use of Force: Four Cases of Soviet Crisis Decision-Making," *Crossroads*, No. 16 (1985), pp. 47–81.

13. Other recent studies of the presidency are failing to take advantage of what has been published by Allison, Halperin, Kanter, and especially Neustadt on bureaucratic politics. For an example of cursory treatment, see Michael A. Genovese, "Presidential Leadership and Crisis Management," in *Presidential Studies Quarterly*, vol. 16, no. 2 (Spring 1986), pp. 300–309.

14. Interview with Dr. Kissinger. One of the best analytical descriptions of Kissinger's belief system was done by Stephen R. Graubard, *Kissinger: Portrait of a Mind* (New York: W. W. Norton, 1973). Of course read the policymaker's own words in Henry Kissinger, *White House Years* (Boston: Little, Brown and Co., 1979).

15. For a contrasting view, emphasizing the crisis-management philosophy of Dean Acheson, see Philip J. Romero, *Advising the President in a Crisis: Historical Lessons for Policy Planning* (Santa Monica: The Rand Corporation, 1984).

16. *Annual Defense Department Report, FY 1977*, p. 9.

17. North Korean News Agency broadcast, August 5, 1976, reprinted in U.S. Department of State message 182222Z August 1976, pp. 2–3.

18. Interview with former President Gerald R. Ford, April 29, 1977, Palm Springs, California, and material from General Scowcroft.

19. "U.S. Crisis Unit Takes up DMZ Killings," *New York Times*, August 20, 1976, p. 3.

20. These actions were described variously in the *New York Times* and *Washington Post* on August 20 and 21, 1976.

21. Interview with General Richard G. Stilwell, U.S. Army (Ret.), commander-in-chief, United Nations Command, March 9, 1977, Washington, DC.

22. Ibid.

23. Ibid.

24. *Washington Post*, August 20, 1976, p. 3.

25. Ford interview.

26. Ibid.

27. Unclassified message, "21 August 1976 Informal Meeting between the Military Armistice Commission (MAC) Senior Members, from CINCUNC to JCS, August 22, 1976." Also quoted in Korea Herald, *Axe-Murders at Panmunjom* (Seoul: Korea Herald, 1976), p. 28; *Washington Post*, August 23, 1976, p. 24; and Department of State answers to questions, Press Briefing, August 23, 1976.

28. Stilwell interview.

29. Associated Press, as quoted by the Korea Herald, *Axe-Murders at Panmunjom*, p. 27.

30. *Washington Post*, August 21, 1976, p. A2.

31. U.S. Department of State, transcript of Press, Radio, and Television News Briefing, August 23, 1976.

32. *New York Times*, August 24, 1976.

33. U.S. Congress, House, Committee on International Relations, *Deaths of American Military Personnel in the Korean Demilitarized Zone*, hearings before the Subcommittee on International Political and Military Affairs and the Subcommittee on International Organizations, 94th Cong., 2d sess., September 1, 1976.

34. Cited by U.S. Information Agency in *Worldwide Treatment of Current Issues*, 62 (August 26, 1976), p. 7.

35. Ibid.

36. For a review of the pitfalls of an ad hoc chain of command in a military operation, see U.S. Department of Defense, *Rescue Mission Report*, August 1980, known as the Holloway Report, pp. 15–18, 50–52. Also see the in-depth book by Paul B. Ryan, *The Iranian Rescue Mission: Why it Failed* (Annapolis: Naval Institute

Press, 1985), pp. 117ff. The Holloway Report was the result of the chairman, Joint Chiefs of Staff, appointing a Special Operations Review Group, headed by Admiral James L. Holloway, III, USN (Ret.). The report was released and discussed by Admiral Holloway at a DoD press conference, August 23, 1980, and is cited extensively by Ryan.

# 5

## Bureaucratic Politics and Policy Implementation: The Exercise of Discretion

*In addition to influencing policy through giving advice, disseminating information, and selecting choices, a bureaucracy strongly affects policy through the implementation process. Implementation is neither automatic nor mechanical: when officials enact a policy, they deliberately leave a great deal vague and unspecified. No law or policy can anticipate each and every eventuality. By necessity, those charged with policy execution must fill in the details and fine print. Thus, a major way in which a bureaucracy shapes policy is through the exercise of discretion when applying established policy. The implementation phase, however, also affords a bureaucracy another opportunity to weaken or obstruct enacted policies that have been institutionally opposed for being contrary to the interests, ideologies, or professional norms of the implementing bureaucracy. This is the infamous bureaucratic foot dragging, deliberate attempts to impede, dilute, or derail a policy now in the implementation stage that had been opposed during policy deliberation. Though such actions raise enormous concerns about accountability, control, and responsiveness, their occurrence is widespread, a challenge to executive authority, and an important illustration of how bureaucrats play politics and make policy.*

# 5.1    Excerpts from the Memoirs of Henry Kissinger and Richard Nixon

*The following excerpts from Richard Nixon's and Henry Kissinger's memoirs poignantly depict the dynamics of bureaucratic politics and interpersonal relationships that so directly affect the opportunities for success in national security affairs. Both were acutely aware of the range of variables to consider in shaping the National Security Council system. Their insights are extremely valuable to laypersons and practitioners alike as we seek to understand and improve the functioning of national security policymaking.*

There were conflicts of viewpoint and clashes of personality in the Nixon administration, but no human organization ever has been or ever will be free of them. The most important of these conflicts—because of its potential effect on policy—involved Bill Rogers, Henry Kissinger, and Mel Laird. When three such distinctive personalities and temperaments were added to the already volatile institutional mix of the State Department, the NSC, and the Pentagon, it was inevitable that there would be fireworks. To Rogers's credit, it must be said that in many cases his primary concern was simply to be kept informed of what was going on. He had to testify before several congressional committees, and the secrecy with which our decisions customarily—and usually necessarily—were surrounded often placed him in an embarrassing position. I once jokingly remarked that Laird did not have this problem because he would answer questions and state his views whether he was informed or not.

Rogers and Laird occasionally carried on sensitive dealings and negotiations without coordinating them with the White House. In some cases this was inadvertent, when they lacked information about our secret diplomacy; sometimes it was done to preclude Kissinger's or my own disapproval; and sometimes, I think, it was done just to show themselves, their departments, and the press that they were capable of independent action. In some cases the results were harmless or even positive, but in a few cases the outcome threatened to undercut our policy and credibility with foreign countries.

Reprinted by permission of Warner Books/New York. From *RN: The Memoirs of Richard Nixon* © 1978 by Richard Nixon.

Eventually the relationship between Kissinger and Rogers took on a fairly combative aspect. Kissinger bridled at my assignment in 1969 and 1970 of all Middle Eastern problems to Rogers. He felt that Rogers was overly influenced by the pro-Arab elements of the State Department, and that he did not have the necessary skill or subtlety or a sense of broad foreign policy strategy. Kissinger also worried when foreign policy power seemed to become dispersed, and he was concerned by Rogers's direct access to the Oval Office. Rogers felt that Kissinger was Machiavellian, deceitful, egotistical, arrogant, and insulting. Kissinger felt that Rogers was vain, uninformed, unable to keep a secret, and hopelessly dominated by the State Department bureaucracy. The problems became increasingly serious as the years passed. Kissinger suggested repeatedly that he might have to resign unless Rogers was restrained or replaced. . . .

*It was probably unfair to appoint to the senior Cabinet position someone whose entire training and experience had been in other fields. . . .

This is a particular problem for a Secretary of State. He is at the head of an organization staffed by probably the ablest and most professional group of men and women in public service. They are intelligent, competent, loyal, and hardworking. But the reverse side of their dedication is the conviction that a lifetime of service and study has given them insights that transcend the untrained and shallow-rooted views of political appointees. When there is strong leadership their professionalism makes the Foreign Service an invaluable and indispensable tool of policymaking. In such circumstances the Foreign Service becomes a disciplined and finely honed instrument; their occasional acts of self-will generate an important, sometimes an exciting dialogue. But when there is not a strong hand at the helm, clannishness tends to overcome discipline. Desk officers become advocates for the countries they deal with and not spokesmen of national policy; Assistant Secretaries push almost exclusively the concerns of their areas. Officers will fight for parochial interests with tenacity and a bureaucratic skill sharpened by decades of struggling for survival. They will carry out clear-cut instructions with great loyalty, but the typical Foreign Service officer is not easily persuaded that an instruction with which he disagrees is really clear-cut.

The procedures of the State Department are well designed to put a premium on bureaucratic self-will. Despite lip service to planning, there is a strong bias in favor of making policy in response to cables and in the form of cables. The novice Secretary of State thus finds on his desk not policy analyses or options but stacks of dispatches which he is asked to initial and to do so urgently, if you please. He can scarcely know enough about all the subjects to which they refer, or perhaps about any of them, to form an opinion. In any event, he will not learn from these draft cables what alternatives he has. Even if he asserts himself and rejects a particular draft, it

*The following are excerpts from Henry Kissinger, White House Years (Boston: Little, Brown and Co., 1979) pp. 27–29, 30. Reprinted by permission of Little, Brown and Co.

is likely to come back to him with a modification so minor that only a legal scholar could tell the difference. When I later became Secretary I discovered that it was a herculean effort even for someone who had made foreign policy his life's work to dominate the State Department cable machine. Woe to the uninitiated at the mercy of that extraordinary and dedicated band of experts.

The irony of Nixon's decision to choose as Secretary of State someone with little substantive preparation was that he thereby enhanced the influence of the two institutions he most distrusted—the Foreign Service and the press. For the new Secretary of State had in effect only two choices. He could take his direction from the White House and become the advocate of Presidential policy to the Department, the Congress, and the country, or he could make himself the spokesman of his subordinates. In a quieter time Secretary Rogers might well have been able to balance the demands upon him. But in the turmoil of the domestic discord caused by Vietnam, to do so required more self-confidence and knowledge than he could reasonably have been expected to possess. As a result, he seemed quite naturally concerned to avoid the assaults inflicted upon his predecessor, Dean Rusk. Since he tended to identify the public and Congressional mood with the editorial position of leading Eastern newspapers, and since these also powerfully influenced his subordinates, Rogers at critical junctures found himself unwilling to do battle for the President and often sponsored positions at variance with Nixon's.

Paradoxically, he may have been reinforced in that tendency by the memory of his friendship with Nixon in the 1950s. Then Rogers had been much the psychologically dominant partner. In consequence he could not really grasp that in the new relationship his was the clearly subordinate position. Even less could he face the proposition that he might have been appointed, at least in part, because his old friend wanted to reverse roles and establish a relationship in which both hierarchically and substantively he, Nixon, called the tune for once.

This curious antiphonal relationship between the two men had the consequence of enhancing my position, but my own role was clearly a result of that relationship and not the cause of it. From the beginning Nixon was determined to dominate the most important negotiations. He excluded his Secretary of State, for example, from his first meeting with Soviet Ambassador Anatoly Dobrynin on February 17, 1969, four weeks after Inauguration, at a time when it would have been inconceivable for me to suggest such a procedure. The practice, established before my own position was settled, continued. Throughout his term, when a State visitor was received in the Oval Office by Nixon for a lengthy discussion, I was the only other American present. . . .

The tug of war over responsibility for policy emerged early. For his part, Secretary Rogers took the position that he would carry out orders with which he disagreed only if they were transmitted personally by the President.

This was the one thing Nixon was psychologically incapable of doing. He would resort to any subterfuge to avoid a personal confrontation. He would send letters explaining what he meant; he would use emissaries. But since Rogers believed—quite correctly—that these letters were drafted by me or my staff, he did not give them full credence even though they were signed by the President. He frustrated the emissary, usually John Mitchell, by invoking his old friendship with the President and claiming that he understood Nixon better. This contest, which was partially obscured because both men blamed it on third parties, was unending. Nixon would repeatedly order that all outgoing policy cables were to be cleared in the White House. But this was frequently circumvented, and in any event, the means by which a Secretary of State can communicate with his subordinates are too manifold to be controlled by fiat.

As time went by, the President, or I on his behalf, in order to avoid these endless confrontations, came to deal increasingly with key foreign leaders through channels that directly linked the White House Situation Room to the field without going through the State Department—the so-called back-channels. This process started on the day after Inauguration. The new President wanted to change the negotiating instructions on Vietnam drafted at State that reflected the approach of the previous Administration. But he wished also to avoid a controversy. He therefore asked me to phone Ambassador Henry Cabot Lodge, our negotiator in Paris, to suggest that Lodge send in through regular channels, as his own recommendation, the course of action that the President preferred. Lodge readily agreed. Since such procedures were complicated and could not work in most cases, Nixon increasingly moved sensitive negotiations into the White House where he could supervise them directly, get the credit personally, and avoid the bureaucratic disputes or inertia that he found so distasteful. . . .

Once Nixon had appointed a strong personality, expert in foreign policy, as the national security adviser, competition with the Secretary of State became inevitable, although I did not realize this at first. The two positions are inherently competitive if both incumbents seek to play a major policy role. All the incentives make for controversy; indeed, were they to agree there would be no need for both of them. . . .

---

## 5.2  Of Presidents and Bureaucrats:
## A Look at Bureaucratic Politics
## Through the Eyes of
## National Security Decisionmakers

TERRY DEIBEL

*Dr. Deibel's essay contributes substantially to the bureaucratic politics paradigm by offering a representative sampling of the similarities and differences of perspectives of senior national security participants as they themselves admit to in their memoirs. Most striking of all are differences noted in Henry Kissinger's perspectives, first as assistant to the president for national security affairs and subsequently as secretary of state. Dr. Deibel concludes that the State-White House feud appears to be a continuing feature of U.S. national security policy in the post-Vietnam era. Although different management styles and organizational structures have been tried, no combination as yet has been able to overcome the bureaucratic struggle at the most senior levels of U.S. government.*

The memoirs of high officials constitute a rich and probably underutilized source for the study of statecraft. Reflecting on their experiences immediately after leaving office, presidents, national security advisors, and secretaries of state record in vivid, if often self-serving, terms their concepts and objectives, their trials and tribulations, their successes, and—occasionally—even their failures.

We can join the National Security Council's (NSC) deliberations on the SALT I treaty, sit next to Henry Kissinger as he works minute by minute through the first week of the October 1973 Middle East war, follow with Jimmy Carter the financial intricacies and political humiliations of the Iranian hostage crisis, look over Zbigniew Brzezinski's shoulder as he tells Soviet Ambassador Anatoly Dobrynin that the United States is about to recognize the People's Republic of China (PRC), or raise a glass with Richard Nixon and Leonid Brezhnev at the 1972 Moscow summit. These accounts more than make up in color and real-world feel what they lack in objectivity, and their authors' efforts at self-exculpation invariably draw on and thus more strikingly reveal the very characteristics that led to their original weaknesses. As a result, memoirs not only teach both substance and process simultaneously, they are also often far more revealing than their authors intended.

These observations apply with particular force to the utility of these accounts for the study of bureaucratic politics in national security decisionmaking. Remarkably, the memoirs of the Nixon and Carter administrations are equally rewarding in this regard, in spite of the fact that the two administrations were very different in party affiliation, political orientation, and internal cohesion. The memoirs of Richard Nixon and Henry Kissinger reveal that the top strategists of this relatively closed, Republican, and center-right administration were almost totally agreed on the broad lines and priorities of their foreign policy. They shared common assumptions about U.S. national interest and current world position, the use of power in international politics, the motivations and roles of other actors on the world stage—indeed, about virtually all the issues that influence decisions on national security policy.[1] In stark contrast, the books written by Jimmy Carter, Cyrus Vance, and Zbigniew Brzezinski show that those who directed this open, Democratic, and center-left administration had very different approaches to world politics, and that their chief had no fixed view on the basis of which to arbitrate his advisers' conflicting advice.[2]

Yet in spite of their fundamental differences, these two presidents and their national security advisers saw the bureaucracy as a major impediment to the accomplishment of their goals, while both secretaries of state viewed the bureaucracy as an ally in the struggle with the White House.

Richard Nixon, for example, repeatedly denigrates "the recalcitrant bureaucracy. . . ."[3] Kissinger, writing about Nixon, says:

> He had very little confidence in the State Department. Its personnel had no loyalty to him; the Foreign Service had disdained him as Vice President and ignored him the moment he was out of office. He was determined to run foreign policy from the White House. . . . He felt it imperative to exclude the CIA from the formulation of policy; it was staffed by Ivy League liberals who behind the facade of analytical objectivity were usually pushing their own preferences. They had always opposed him politically.[4]

Nixon's paranoid distrust of the bureaucracy was at least partially responsible for his deliberate appointment, in William Rogers, of a secretary of state largely ignorant of foreign policy, thereby magnifying the influence of the Foreign Service and further reinforcing his own "already powerful tendency to see himself surrounded by a conspiracy. . . ."[5] The result over time was the movement into the White House of many sensitive negotiations, utilizing backchannel communications that often left the State Department and even formal U.S. negotiators in the dark. This practice in turn encouraged Rogers and Secretary of Defense Melvin Laird to carry on secret negotiations of their own without clearing them with the White House—sometimes to avoid presidential disapproval but sometimes (Nixon thought) just to show they were still capable of independent action.[6]

As national security adviser, Kissinger admits, he shared and encouraged Nixon's negative view of State. Kissinger felt that any large bureaucracy tends to "stifle creativity" and confuse "wise policy with smooth administration." State could be expected to "exaggerate technical complexity" and favor the status quo while minimizing the "importance of political judgment," making policy tactical and reactive rather than strategic and forward looking.[7] These tendencies were amplified, Kissinger thought, by the procedures of the department, the tendency to make policy in response to and in the form of cables to overseas posts, so that decisionmakers receive "not policy analyses of options but stacks of dispatches" that covered up the real issues.[8] Kissinger was determined both that the president be given "the fullest range of choices and their likely consequences" and that policy make "a conscious effort to shape the international environment according to a conception of American purposes."[9] Neither seemed to him a likely consequence of reliance on the Department of State.

In time, of course, personal pique and prerogative were added to these institutional and intellectual differences. The relationship between Kissinger and Rogers, particularly, took on what Nixon called "a fairly combative aspect":

> Rogers felt that Kissinger was Machiavellian, deceitful, egotistical, arrogant, and insulting. Kissinger felt that Rogers was vain, uninformed, unable to keep a secret, and hopelessly dominated by the State Department bureaucracy. The problems became increasingly serious as the years passed. Kissinger suggested repeatedly that he might have to resign unless Rogers was restrained or replaced.[10]

Kissinger, for his part, admitted after the fact that "Rogers was in fact far abler than he was pictured"; but at the time Kissinger considered him an "insensitive neophyte" who might wreck foreign policy. "Rogers was too proud, I intellectually too arrogant, and we were both too insecure" to compose personal differences.[11] Meanwhile Nixon, who in Kissinger's view was "painfully shy," who "abhorred confronting colleagues with whom he disagreed," and who "could not bring himself to face a disapproving friend,"[12] "tried [as he himself put it] to keep out of the personal fireworks that usually accompanied anything in which they were both involved," leaving H. R. Haldeman "as a sort of DMZ between the two. . . ."[13] It was, to put it charitably, a rather complex triangular relationship.

Although not as harsh towards the bureaucracy as Nixon or Kissinger, Jimmy Carter was also determined that "the final decisions on basic foreign policy would be made by me in the Oval Office, and not in the State Department."[14] Carter characterized the department as "sprawling" and "compartmentalized," rarely able to produce "innovative ideas" and chiefly of value for the "inertia" provided by its "thoroughly researched information," "generally sound advice," and "mild and cautious" statements.[15] He told National Security Adviser Zbigniew Brzezinksi that he found Secretary of State Cyrus Vance's "restraining influence" useful since he and Brzezinski, being activists, "needed someone like Cy to rein us in."[16]

Brzezinski himself was more often opposed to the secretary of state than to the State Department; in fact, the national security adviser could develop close working relationships with Vance's principal lieutenants (like Deputy Secretary of State Warren Christopher), though he considered both Vance and Christopher "so much better playing supporting roles than when given predominant responsibility. . . ."[17] Moreover, he condemns the secretary's "contractual-litigational" approach to foreign policy for giving too little emphasis to the necessary role of force and argues that Vance failed "to provide a broad conceptual explanation for what our Administration was trying to do."[18]  He added, "Secretaries of State only too often . . . , and their State Department professionals almost always, tend to confuse diplomacy with foreign policy.  What they forget is that diplomacy is a technique for promoting national objectives abroad and not an end in itself."[19]  Still, it is interesting to note that Brzezinski felt pressured by his own staff into the conflict with Vance (and believed that Vance's staff also fueled the clash by feeding the press anti-Brzezinski material), while the secretary of state warned that "the tendency of the departments' staffers to dig in on their departments' positions has always had to be resisted."[20]

Not surprisingly, the view from the memoirs of secretaries of state is a polar opposite of these White House perceptions.  Vance, for example, had nothing but praise for the Foreign Service, "the most able and dedicated professional group in the federal government."[21]  The problem was how to make better use of this splendid resource, how to engage the service (and particularly overseas ambassadors) more directly in the development and implementation of major foreign policies after Kissinger's demoralizing tendency to rely on a small group of hand-picked aides.[22]  But with Brzezinski and the NSC machinery for policy coordination, Vance had real problems.  He found the sessions chaired by the national security adviser "tedious and often aimless," and regretted that he had not gone "to the mat" with the president over Brzezinski's exclusive right to draft the decision documents that came out of NSC meetings.[23]  Vance particularly objected to Brzezinski's increasingly taking on the role of policy spokesman, "in spite of repeated instructions from the president," until it "became a serious impediment to the conduct of our foreign policy."[24]  Unfortunately Carter, as in so many other cases, had different views: "Almost without exception, Zbig had been speaking with my approval and in consonance with my established and known policy.  The underlying State Department objection was that Brzezinski had spoken at all."[25]

Vance's and Brzezinski's memoirs are in agreement, though, as to the extent and import of their differences, which (like Rogers' and Kissinger's) were clearly more than a struggle for turf and had serious policy repercussions.  The national security adviser, for his part, contends that "on most issues, at most times we were in basic agreement," including on the Middle East, Africa, the Panama Canal treaties, human rights policy, and Third World relations generally.[26]  But as 1978 merged into 1979 and 1980, Brzezinski noted that they came increasingly to disagree strongly on such important matters as the conflict in the Horn of Africa, recognition of the PRC, and the Iranian crisis.[27]  Vance, too, maintains that while their substantive differences were "containable" during the administration's early years, after Afghanistan "it became increasingly difficult to hold the coalition together."[28]  When Carter decided to send a military mission to rescue the hostages in the face of Vance's protests, the secretary of state felt compelled to resign.

But perhaps the most telling vindication of the old saw that "where you stand depends on where you sit" lies in the way Henry Kissinger's attitudes shifted with his office. Like his new and spacious quarters overlooking Washington, D.C.'s monuments, the change from national security adviser to secretary of state "took some getting used to."[29] Seen from Foggy Bottom, the cramped White House quarters seemed to house an official with a "microscopic" staff and no more responsibility than to take the "big view," but the secretary was "responsible for a colossal enterprise" at State and a "vast catalogue of international relationships."[30] Not surprisingly, Secretary Kissinger soon discovered that the department was "staffed by knowledgeable, discreet, and energetic individuals," "dedicated men and women who supply the continuity and expertise of our foreign policy. I entered the State Department a skeptic, I left a convert. . . ."[31]

Although Kissinger continued to note the department's "mushiness and slow pace," its tendency toward "inertia rather than creativity," its elitism, clientism, and predilection for negotiation and problem solving rather than "conceiving a strategy and shaping events," he now felt that "in the hands of a determined Secretary, the Foreign Service can be a splendid instrument."[32] Moreover, he warned, "a President who succumbs to impatience with the ponderous State Department damages the country in the long run. A foreign policy achievement to be truly significant must at some point be institutionalized."[33] Kissinger noted, however, that making policy from State required a "confident partnership" between the president and the secretary, and he very nearly resigned in 1975 when it seemed that that relationship might be jeopardized by President Ford taking away his concurrent job as national security adviser.[34]

In two very different administrations, then, the memoirs of high officials reveal that perceptions of the White House by the State Department and vice versa have been strikingly similar. The one foreign policy memoir so far published from the Reagan administration hardly contradicts this picture, for Secretary Alexander M. Haig, Jr., brought the tradition of State vs. White House to a pitch of paranoia approached only by Nixon: Haig, like Vance, resigned after failing to manage or surmount the conflict.[35] The national security adviser's propinquity to the president and his freedom from the administrative, congressional, representational, and ceremonial responsibilities of the secretaryship all give him an enormous advantage in the struggle, if he wishes to use it and the president lets him do so. His freedom to be the conceptual thinker, to direct the interdepartmental machinery, to speak and even on occasion act for the president, all provide opportunities to nudge presidential decisions and shape events that the secretary of state lacks. As the history of the Shultz-Reagan relationship shows, even where the secretary uses the authority of his cabinet-level position and presidential confidence to the full, his control of the main lines of policy is hardly assured.

Throughout the memoirs, these general attitudes play themselves out in specific vignettes, often with no small impact on the formulation—and particularly the implementation—of various policies. Kissinger, for example, tears his hair out because the State Department will not implement Nixon's tilt toward Pakistan: "On no issue—except perhaps Cambodia—was the split between the White House and the departments so profound as on the India-Pakistan crisis in the summer of 1971. On no other problem was there such flagrant disregard of unambiguous Presidential directives."[36] The State Department, influenced by its "traditional Indian bias,"[37] used its control of the machinery of execution to restrict aid to Pakistan whenever Nixon ordered a cut in aid to India. "'It's hard to tilt towards Pakistan, as the President wishes,'" Kissinger told the Washington Special Action Group on December 3, 1971, "'if every time we take some action in relation to India we have to do the same thing for Pakistan.'"[38]

Eight years later we find Jimmy Carter, similarly "disturbed at the apparent reluctance in the State Department to carry out [his] directives fully and with enthusiasm," calling his Iran staff to the White House after the Shah's fall to tell them "that if they could not support what [he] decided, their only alternative was to resign." Earlier, he had ordered the recall of Ambassador to Iran William Sullivan (who "lost control of himself and . . . sent Vance a cable bordering on insolence"), but the secretary simply declined, defending his ambassador as an "outstanding career diplomat" who showed "courage and coolness" under fire.[39]

Similar conflicts of greater or lesser extent can be seen on Middle East policy, arms control, or indeed any matter in which either president maintained an active policy interest. To get the full flavor of these differences and their impact as participants viewed them, it may be particularly useful to follow one major policy initiative through both administrations. The opening to and eventual recognition of the People's Republic of China provides a particularly interesting example of how bureaucratic politics influenced what may be considered the most important single diplomatic initiative of the post-Vietnam era.

Characteristically, the Nixon White House made its first moves toward China during the summer of 1969 without consulting the State Department. Before the first NSC meeting on the subject, Kissinger sent Nixon a memorandum outlining the three different approaches to China policy within the government. The slavophiles, Kissinger argued, felt that Soviet fears of U.S.-Chinese collusion were so intense that any effort to improve relations would destroy the possibility of detente and should therefore not be attempted. The realpolitik approach took the opposite view: that U.S. contacts with China could be used as leverage against the Soviet Union to further U.S.-Soviet detente. Finally, the sinophiles argued that Soviet considerations should not be a major factor either way in decisions on the U.S. approach to China.[40]

Although Kissinger declared himself of the second school, it was the first that dominated the State Department reaction when the diplomatic channels were activated by a December 1969 Chinese invitation to resume bilateral talks in Warsaw. Llewelyn Thompson, the leading Soviet expert and slavophile in the Department, called on Nixon personally to argue that the United States should not try to use China against the USSR and to urge, so as not to alarm Moscow, that the Kremlin be informed of all U.S.-PRC contacts. Though Nixon and Kissinger flatly refused, the Department's machinery "more or less automatically" proceeded to inform U.S. embassies and allied governments worldwide about the invitation. Certain that "such dissemination of a fairly juicy piece of news was bound to radiate through the diplomatic world," Nixon sighed: "'We'll kill this child before it is born.' The difficulty of controlling the enormous bureaucratic communications machinery," Kissinger commented, "was a principal reason why control of China diplomacy was gradually moved into the White House."[41]

What Kissinger called "the bizarre rivalries within the Administration"[42] were also the major reason the national security adviser felt it necessary to move from talks between the two countries' ambassadors in Warsaw to direct contact at the highest level in Peking. He therefore wanted to suggest that the United States was ready to send an emissary to the Chinese capital, emphasizing that the administration wanted to make a fresh start on the basis of mutual interest rather than ideology and would not participate in a Soviet-U.S. condominium. "None of this," Kissinger relates, "was acceptable to those who had made China policy up to that time." Asian experts, cut off from the extensive secret contacts Kissinger had already had with the Chinese, were unaware of Peking's interest in a new beginning, and Soviet experts feared that Moscow would be upset by a high-level U.S.-Chinese meeting.[43]

When Kissinger went ahead with his proposal anyway, the department suggested that the United States not respond should China accept; when the Chinese did accept, the wrangle between the White House and State over arrangements for the mission was so prolonged that the next Warsaw meeting never took place. Fearing that the Chinese would use the United States for its own purposes, State now demanded that Peking allow trade and contacts, release U.S. prisoners, expand travel, and agree to peaceful settlement of the Taiwan issue "as an admission price to high level talks."[44] Kissinger, by contrast, thought that the mere fact of a meeting would provide the United States with enormous geopolitical gains: "the effect on Hanoi alone would be traumatic."[45] That last thing he wanted was prolonged negotiations in Warsaw over State's peripheral issues.

Nixon agreed and wanted to send a presidential envoy to the Chinese capital rather than an ambassador. Commented Kissinger, "This was, of course, exactly why State was so skittish about the enterprise."[46] When it came to selecting the envoy, Kissinger contends that Secretary Rogers's name "did not come up; nor could it have, given Nixon's determination that he, not the State Department, should be seen—justly—as the originator of China policy."[47] But Nixon writes that he did suggest Rogers, and that "Kissinger rolled his eyes upward," objecting not only on personal grounds but also because the secretary was too high-ranking and too public a figure for the initial, secret contact.[48] The choice eventually fell, of course, on the national security adviser, not only because he knew the background of the initiative best, but also because he was the emissary most subject to Nixon's control: "My success would be a Presidential success." "Only romantic outsiders," commented Kissinger wryly, "believe that men who have prevailed in a hard struggle for power make decisions exclusively on the basis of analytical ideas."[49]

Although Rogers did not know about these arrangements until the day before Kissinger secretly left Pakistan for China, the secretary objected anyway to the "information trip" Kissinger was to take through Asia as cover for the Peking mission.[50] Moreover, Rogers took unwitting revenge via a speech made right in the middle of the most sensitive negotiations over the secret trip that characterized Mao's invitation as "fairly casually made" and chastised China's policy as expansionist and "paranoiac," provoking the Chinese to publicly call Nixon's effort to improve relations "fraudulent."[51] These perturbations did not, however, persuade the White House to let the department in on the game; indeed, when Kissinger returned, Nixon insisted that Rogers receive only a sanitized version of the historic meeting.[52] Meanwhile, State set out to move U.S. policy on Chinese representation at the UN—"the one aspect of China policy unambiguously under its control"—toward a dual representation formula, which Kissinger was convinced would "raise havoc with our relations with Peking."[53] Nixon simply blocked the department by announcing at a press conference that he would not make a decision on the matter until July, well after the date set for Kissinger's visit.

However disruptive, these contretemps were nothing compared to the complications of Nixon's public and official trip to China in February 1972, a mission on which Rogers and the State Department had at least to be present, if not fully engaged. From the outset, in fact, Kissinger designed the summit to reflect the "bureaucratic intricacies" of the U.S. side, a complication that the wily Chinese accommodated with aplomb.[54] They were careful to place the president and his National Security Council staff in one building, the secretary of state and his entourage in another a few hundred yards away: "The Chinese . . . had re-created the physical gulf between the White House and Foggy Bottom in the heart of Peking."[55] More remarkably, all the summit meetings were divided into three levels, with Kissinger and his aides negotiating what became the Shanghai communiqué on one level while

Nixon and Kissinger met with Chou En-lai and Mao Tse-tung on another, leaving the two countries' foreign ministers on the third to discuss "the obsessions of our East Asian Bureau" so that "the State Department delegation [would be] occupied while Nixon was in meetings with Mao and Chou."[56] Extraordinary efforts were needed on both sides to keep the information for each level compartmentalized, but the Chinese "never dropped a stitch"—perhaps because, as Chou told Nixon, he thought that the Chinese foreign minister also had his "limitations."[57]

As in the earlier cases, though, a price had to be paid, and this time it involved the Chinese. Although Kissinger insists that State Department officials were only excluded from negotiating the Shanghai communiqué because Nixon blocked his request to let them in, the result was that Rogers did not see the communiqué until twenty-four hours before it was to be released and after both Nixon and the PRC politburo had approved it. Fortified with a list of changes proposed by his staff, the secretary of state told Nixon it was unsatisfactory, forcing on him the awful choice between the risk that leaks from a dissatisfied State Department might set off right-wing attacks on the communiqué and the possibility that a last-minute attempt to renegotiate the accord would wreck the visit itself. Storming around his bedroom in his underwear, Nixon was calmed only by Kissinger's willingness to endure yet another late night session with the Chinese. Though incredulous, the PRC delegation agreed to Kissinger's bizarre request and a *final* final draft was ready for the scheduled announcement.[58]

But neither the Shanghai Communiqué nor the end of the Nixon administration resolved the White House/State Department antagonism on China policy. The Carter administration, in its move from normalization to full diplomatic recognition, found the struggle reincarnated in the feud between Vance and Brzezinski. The new national security adviser, for his part, wanted to move quickly on recognition as a "strategic response" to Soviet geopolitical moves threatening Saudia Arabia, and for that reason he wanted to push the U.S. relationship with China into defense and strategic areas, with or without recognition.[59] Secretary Vance's primary goal, on the other hand, was a SALT II treaty with the Soviets, and he feared that "any U.S. security cooperation with Peking would have serious repercussions on U.S.-Soviet relations."[60] He also worried that "some of the president's advisors, particularly Zbig, were so anxious to move rapidly toward normalization that they seemed ready to compromise the well-being of the people of Taiwan."[61]

During the administration's first high-level trip to China in August 1977, Vance put forward the U.S. maximum conditions for recognition and concluded from the Chinese response that they were "not ready to negotiate seriously."[62] By early November, however, Brzezinski had "quietly encouraged" an invitation to visit China from the PRC's Washington Liaison Office, thus sparking "a prolonged struggle with State over whether [he] should make the trip."[63] The department's resistance, Brzezinski thought, was because State was "probably more 'turf-conscious' than any other agency in Washington," because Vance was concerned about the "political symbolism" of the national security adviser taking such a trip, and because of the growing differences between the two men over how to deal with the Soviet Union. Vance confirmed that he was mainly concerned that "a highly publicized trip would bring into sharp relief the question of who spoke for the administration on foreign policy," but that he also worried lest Brzezinski get into the recognition issue before State had finished studying it and consulting with Congress about Taiwan.[64]

As a result, it took the national security adviser a "sustained effort" of four months before he had "badgered" Carter into agreeing to the trip. Vance's insistence "that any negotiations be carried out through him," Carter presumed, was probably because "the State Department professionals were still smarting" over Rogers' having been bypassed by Kissinger seven years earlier.[65] All State could do was give the Soviet embassy advance word of the trip's announcement—making Brzezinski "very irritated"—and propose that Soviet Foreign Minister Andrei Gromyko be invited to the White House while he was gone![66]

As it turned out, Vance's forebodings proved right: The trip provoked a spate of magazine and newspaper articles about Brzezinski's foreign policy clout, highlighting the confrontation between the national security adviser and the secretary of state. Brzezinski added injury to insult by attacking the Soviets on television immediately after his return, earning himself a reprimand from the president and provoking a memo from Vance to Carter that decried the sharp, public differences within the administration and doubted that "playing the China card" was an effective way to deal with Moscow. Rather, wrote Vance, "we can help encourage a more cooperative attitude on the part of the Soviet leaders by conspicuous attention to the sense of equality to which they attach so much importance. And if they respond positively, we should refrain from crowing about any gestures they make."[67] "Obviously," observed Brzezinski, "Vance and I were in serious disagreement."[68]

Nevertheless, both State and the White House were in agreement on the basic desirability of recognition, and during the summer of 1978 they pulled together very effectively to negotiate the terms announced on December 15. Indeed, it would have been difficult to shut out the department, given its permanent representation in Peking in the person of Leonard Woodcock, head of the U.S. Liaison Office. The detailed negotiations on recognition were handled by Woodcock on the basis of instructions drawn up by Carter, Brzezinski, and Vance and transmitted for secrecy (at Vance's suggestion) over the White House communications system.[69] Meanwhile, Brzezinski was meeting with the head of the Chinese liaison mission in Washington, and Assistant Secretary of State Richard Holbrooke was handling technical matters with the Chinese UN delegation in New York. The only disputes recorded by the participants were over State's simultaneous effort to initiate diplomatic contacts with Vietnam (which Brzezinski thought "would be interpreted by the Chinese as a 'pro-Soviet, anti-Chinese move'")[70] and over the timing of the recognition announcement itself, which Vance wanted postponed until after a late-December meeting he had scheduled with Gromyko but was moved up when Brzezinski "blacked Christopher and Holbrooke out of the decision making for about six hours."[71] Again, in his memoirs as in the White House, Carter undercuts his secretary of state by relating that it was his decision to announce at once, lest secrecy break down and the matter be "leaked piecemeal to the press, perhaps in a distorted fashion."[72]

The case of the U.S. rapprochement with China, then, represents not only the persistence of the struggle between the White House and the State Department but also the benefits to diplomacy that can occur when agreement on fundamental objectives exists and personal and institutional egos can be controlled to permit a coordinated foreign policy. Zbigniew Brzezinski maintained right to the end of his term in office that he never wanted to be secretary of state,[73] and at the end of his book he argues that a "Secretarial system" of policy control is likely to be more and more difficult to operate efficiently.

> Few people outside the government realize the extent to which policy is hammered out through bureaucratic and personal rivalries, and how rarely it springs from the mind of a single dominant individual. This makes it all the more important that a single individual be the final arbiter, the source of national direction, lest security policy become simply the amalgam of bureaucratic compromise. Under the U.S. system, it has to be the President who is that final decision maker. That constitutional fact inherently drives decision making back into the White House.[74]

Brzezinski thus endorses a presidential system, with centralization of national security policy in the White House under a national security adviser who is confirmed by the Senate as a spokesman for—and even occasionally a negotiator of—U.S. foreign policy.[75]

Secretary Kissinger, on the other hand, comes down in favor of a strong secretary of state: "If the President does not trust his Secretary of State he should replace him, not attempt to work around him by means of the security adviser." Though he did "not understand" it when he was in the White House, Kissinger came to realize as secretary that Nixon's treatment of State was a self-defeating course: "The more the State Department was excluded from policymaking, the less incentive it had to safeguard any information it managed to acquire on its own."[76] The national security adviser should continue to run interdepartmental machinery as the only impartial arbiter of conflicting departmental views, Kissinger thought, but his contact with media and foreign diplomats should be reduced to a minimum so that the president and the secretary would alone articulate and conduct foreign policy—a way of doing business that would be very unlike Kissinger.[77]

Although as of this writing the Reagan administration has settled into a system closer to Kissinger's ideal than Brzezinski's, it has hardly been free of the State–White House struggle that seems to be a continuing feature of U.S. foreign policy in the post-Vietnam era. One can only await with interest the full story of those more recent battles as the participants lay down their policy papers and pick up their pens. It is hard to believe they will agree—or that we will not learn more about bureaucratic politics from the next phase of their personal and policy contests.

## NOTES

1. Richard Nixon, *RN: The Memoirs of Richard Nixon* (New York: Grosset and Dunlap, 1978); Henry Kissinger, *White House Years* and *Years of Upheaval* (Boston: Little, Brown, 1979 and 1982).

2. Jimmy Carter, *Keeping Faith: Memoirs of a President* (Toronto: Bantam Books, 1982); Cyrus Vance, *Hard Choices: Critical years in America's Foreign Policy* (New York: Simon and Schuster, 1983); Zbigniew Brzezinski, *Power and Principle: Memoirs of the National Security Advisor, 1977–1981* (New York: Farrar, Straus, Giroux, 1983). See, on this point, Walter LaFeber, "From Confusion to Cold War: The Memoirs of the Carter Administration," *Diplomatic History* 8 (Winter 1984): 1–12.

3. Nixon, p. 339.

4. Kissinger I, p. 11.

5. Kissinger I, p. 25.

6. Nixon, p. 433.

7. Kissinger I, p. 39.

8. Kissinger I, p. 27.

9. Kissinger I, pp. 39, 41.

10. Nixon, p. 433.

11. Kissinger I, p. 31.

12. Kissinger I, pp. 11, 45.

13. Nixon, p. 433.

14. Carter, p. 52.

15. Carter, p. 53. Brzezinski notes that Carter made the same comment to him about State's failure to come up with innovative ideas and the utility of Vance's "restraining influence." Brzezinski, p. 42.

16. Brzezinski, p. 42.

17. Brzezinski, p. 42.

18. Brzezinski, pp. 37, 42–43.

19. Brzezinski, p. 535.

20. Vance, p. 38.

21. Vance, p. 39.

22. Vance, pp. 40, 42.

23. Vance, pp. 37–38.

24. Vance, p. 35.

25. Carter, p. 53.

26. Brzezinski, p. 38.
27. Brzezinski, p. 38.
28. Vance, p. 394.
29. Kissinger II, pp. 432–433.
30. Kissinger II, pp. 432–433.
31. Kissinger II, pp. 442–443.
32. Kissinger II, pp. 439, 443–445.
33. Kissinger II, pp. 434.
34. Kissinger II, p. 437.
35. Alexander M. Haig, Jr., *Caveat: Realism, Reagan, and Foreign Policy* (New York: MacMillan, 1984). See, for example, Chapter 5.
36. Kissinger I, p. 864.
37. Kissinger I, p. 854.
38. Kissinger I, p. 897.
39. Carter, pp. 446, 449; Vance, pp. 317, 343.
40. Kissinger I, p. 181.
41. Kissinger I, pp. 189–190.
42. Kissinger I, p. 686.
43. Kissinger I, p. 686.
44. Kissinger I, pp. 688–690.
45. Kissinger I, p. 690.
46. Kissinger I, p. 691.
47. Kissinger I, pp. 715–716
48. Richard Nixon, *RN: The Memoirs of Richard Nixon*, Vol. II (New York: Warner Books, 1979), pp. 14–15.
49. Kissinger I, p. 717.
50. Kissinger I, pp. 728, 739.
51. Kissinger I, pp. 720–721.
52. Kissinger I, pp. 756–758.
53. Kissinger I, pp. 719, 726, 773.
54. Kissinger I, p. 775.
55. Kissinger I, p. 1055.
56. Kissinger I, pp. 1057, 1070.
57. Kissinger I, p. 1071.
58. Kissinger I, pp. 1082–1084.
59. Brzezinski, pp. 203–204.
60. Vance, p. 78.
61. Vance, p. 77.
62. Vance, p. 82.
63. Brzezinski, pp. 202–203.
64. Vance, pp. 114–115.
65. Carter, p. 193.
66. Brzezinski, pp. 206, 208.
67. Brzezinski, pp. 219–221.
68. Brzezinski, pp. 221–222.
69. Vance, p. 117.
70. Brzezinski, p. 228.
71. Vance, pp. 118–119.
72. Carter, p. 199.
73. "A Conversation with Zbigniew Brzezinski," *Bill Moyers' Journal* no. 702 (14 November 1980).
74. Brzezinski, p. 534.
75. Brzezinski, pp. 535–536.

76. Kissinger II, p. 434.
77. Kissinger II, p. 437.

---

## 5.3   Bureaucratic Politics in the Department of Defense: A Practitioner's Perspective

### CHRIS JEFFERIES

*Col. Chris Jefferies's experiences in the Department of Defense (DoD) serve as the backdrop for his essay on the relevance of the bureaucratic politics paradigm as a tool to explain the formulation of national security policy. Colonel Jefferies utilizes the analogy of bureaucratic politics as a game to describe the players and develop a series of axioms or rules of the game. His concluding assessment is a sobering one for those committed to defense reorganization as a panacea for DoD's problems. For Colonel Jefferies, such reforms are likely to have minimal impact, for all organizations, regardless of formal structure, are similarly driven by the realities of bureaucratic politics.*

The premise of our *Bureaucratic Politics and National Security* anthology is that to understand national security policy best, we must understand the bureaucratic-organizational processes by which national security is formulated: the participants, their positions on the questions at issue, and the means by which they exercise influence to incorporate their positions in a policy decision. My own experience with both the theory and practice of defense policy formulation convinces me evermore that this premise is valid. In any society, whether totalitarian, autocratic, or democratic, influence is wielded unevenly by people and groups or organizations. This phenomenon is particularly relevant in the U.S. polycentric democracy, which guarantees access and influence by many and varied interest groups and people. Thus, while other policymaking models may be relevant to a degree in explaining how policy decisions are made, it is finally the process by which these individuals and groups exercise their influence in competition with other individuals and groups that determines the extent of their influence and, thus, the policy itself. That process is bureaucratic politics. It is also described as a game, a definition that I find most nearly portrays the process if not interpreted too narrowly. The game has players, rules, standard plays or procedures, and goals or objectives. These we will explore below.


## THE CONTEXT

Because other authors in this anthology will have explained the theoretical basis of the bureaucratic politics paradigm, I'll not review it yet again except to emphasize that each of the writers goes a long way toward explaining the *why* of bureaucratic politics.[1]  However, lest the reader become too wrapped-up in a frequently prevailing view that bureaucratic politics—that is, the organizational self-interest part—works to the detriment of good defense policy, let me add two perspectives.

First, emphasizing the narrowness of bureaucratic self-interest obscures the broader fact that in a polycentric society, organizational self-interest is a legitimate and essential part of the interest aggregation. It assures access to and participation in our democratic processes. This is no less true within the government as well. To assure representation of relevant viewpoints within the structure of government, more, not less, bureaucratic politics should be the order, particularly when a bureaucracy represents a discrete function of government. I'm certain that a highly monolithic governmental organization with the discipline required to impose rational decisions from the top downward would not be to U.S. tastes. Without government organizations politicking for their functional needs, U.S. society would likely be highly skewed in directions it would not like. So, when the U.S. Air Force predictably lobbies and politicks hard for the B-1B bomber and the Peacekeeper missile, or the U.S. Navy politicks for fifteen carrier battle groups and the Trident SLBM system by advancing and defending their narrow self-interests through bureaucratic politics, our defense is better served than if neither service, nor competing elements within the services, were able to make the case for the defense capabilities each contributes to deterring attack on the United States. Bureaucratic politics assures that opportunity.

Second, good defense policy is in the eye of the beholder. To an individual or group whose views prevail in a policy decision, the policy is rational, far-sighted, and appropriate to U.S. needs. To an individual or group whose views are not reflected, the policy is ill-advised, short-sighted, and the result of bureaucratic infighting or a "war for turf."

From these more benign perspectives, let me provide my understanding of bureaucratic politics within the Department of Defense (DoD) as I experienced them. The Department of Defense is the largest executive department in the federal government, and manages the greatest single allocation of resources in the noncommunist world. About five million people work for the department as active-duty service members, civilian employees, and reserve forces—two million serving on active duty, almost two million in the reserve structure, and over one million civilians. It owns or operates over twelve hundred military installations in the United States and abroad. Its nearly $300 billion annual budget (6 percent of gross national product and about 30 percent of the entire federal budget) extends its influence throughout U.S. society and much of the world. It owns one of the largest office buildings in the world, a virtual city to which almost twenty-five thousand people go to work each day. It is in this context that bureaucratic politics occurs in the Department of Defense as policy decisions are debated and made, and, thus, a dynamic, fast-moving, unrelenting process challenging the skills and endurance of the most experienced participants is guaranteed.

## THE PLAYERS

The major organizational participants, or players, in the DoD are the secretary and his immediate staff, including the deputy secretary and his staff; about a dozen separate offices within the Office of the Secretary (OSD)—supporting staffs organized under under and assistant secretaries by geographical region or function; the Joint Chiefs of Staff (JCS) and their Office of the Joint Chiefs of Staff (OJCS); and the three military departments (army, navy, air force), each organized into civilian secretariats and a uniformed service (the Navy Department has two: the U.S. Navy and the U.S. Marine Corps).

Within each of these organizations are, likewise, suborganizations in a hierarchical structure representing regional or functional areas. For example, the Office of Assistant Secretary for International Security Policy is subdivided into East Asia and Pacific Affairs, African Affairs, Near East and South Asian Affairs, and Policy Analysis; the Office of Undersecretary for Research and Engineering is subdivided into the assistant secretary for research and technology, and deputy secretaries for International Programs and Technology, Research and Advanced Technology, Strategic and Nuclear Forces, and Tactical Warfare. The U.S. Air Force Air Staff has deputy chiefs of staff for Plans and Operations, Comptroller, Personnel, Programs and Resources, Logistics and Engineering, and Research, Development and Acquisition. All these offices are further subdivided into directorates, divisions, and branches, each one becoming a player with a position to argue and advance in the aggregration process of bureaucratic politics.

The object or ball used in the game, that is, the vehicle by which an organization can influence a policy decision, is a document—any piece of paper on which policy is recorded. It can be a policy statement issued by an organization; a speech delivered by or an article written for an organization's principal; a report; a memorandum between organizations; a letter signed by a principal to an individual or organization within or without the department; or an issue, background, or decision paper. If a decision is to be recorded on a piece of paper somewhere in the department, and an organization has the opportunity to participate in its drafting, then the organization is a player in bureaucratic politics.

Opportunities or requirements to generate a document, and thus participate in the policy process, come principally from two directions: from without and from within the department. From outside the Department of Defense come requests and requirements for information from Congress, the president or his executive office, other executive agencies such as the Department of State or Department of Commerce, the news media, and even prominent public figures or influential interest groups. These requests or requirements always result in a document of some nature being prepared to address the issue and thus provide an opportunity for organizations to play in the game.

From within the department are, first, recurring policy, planning, and programming documents. These are the Defense Guidance, the secretary's guide to defense agencies and military departments on policy, strategy, and programming priorities; the secretary's annual report to Congress; annual reports to Congress by the chairman, JCS, and each military department, called posture statements; and narrations accompanying an organization's program or budget submission. Beyond the recurring documents are, second, a wide range of reports, briefings, studies, analyses, speeches and public statements, memoranda, and position papers, all generated by a variety of an organization's requirements or perceived opportunities to advance a position, and all advocating an official position on the question at issue.

Two individuals in a DoD organization are most central to bureaucratic politics: the organization's principal, who will make the final decision and sign the document; and the action officer (AO), usually a major, lieutenant colonel or colonel, or equivalent rank civilian, who does the actual leg-work of drafting, coordinating, negotiating, defending and following-up to be sure his or her organization's position is not lost or cut out in the process of finalizing a paper.

The organization responsible for a document, or a portion thereof—that is, for an action—is the office of primary responsibility (OPR), and it is with this organization's AO that the AOs of other organizations (referred to as offices of collateral responsibility, or OCRs) must coordinate and negotiate.

Some documents, such as the Defense Guidance (DG), have many OPRs, each responsible for the portion reflecting their regional or functional interest. For example, although the overall responsibility for drafting the DG lies with the undersecretary for policy, successive sections, pages, paragraphs, even sentences and phrases, have separate OPRs under, among many, the assistant secretaries for International Security Affairs; International Security Policy; Command, Control, Communication and Intelligence; Force Management and Personnel; Acquisition and Logistics; and the director, Program Analysis and Evaluation. All these OPRs assign AOs to be responsible for their respective portions. Working with them are the OCR action officers from the military departments and services, the Joint Staff, and from any other defense or even nondefense agencies, such as the Office of Management and Budget, allowed to participate in the drafting process. It should not be difficult to understand the high intensity of activity involved in just this one example as each AO participates in reviewing, coordinating, negotiating, and drafting alternative wording that each must also coordinate within his or her own organization before putting the document into play on its behalf.

The most effective action officer is an individual comfortable in representing the views and positions of his or her organization and sincere in believing that the organization represents an important, perhaps crucial, part of the U.S. national security process. Indeed, if not, that individual would not likely be selected. However, a good AO does not confuse the organization's positions with personal feelings. One who does quickly becomes known among fellow AOs as a narrowly focused, single-issue zealot, a reputation limiting effectiveness; other AOs are inclined to avoid this type whenever possible. An effective AO, then, is willing to listen to the arguments of other positions, negotiate, compromise, and even lose gracefully from time to time, willing to take back to the principal the prevailing view and argue for a compromise.

An AO's effectiveness also depends upon credibility among the others; does he or she deliver, meet deadlines (suspenses), provide usable information and alternative draft language, return calls promptly, make good on quid pro quos, follow through on promises, and, above all, remain honest? That is, does he or she avoid "snowing" colleagues with misleading or incomplete data or other information? An individual for whom the answers are "yes" will be credible with peers, frequently sought-out for the organization's views and even his or her own opinions, and, most importantly, kept "in-the-loop" by fellow AOs with late-breaking, up-to-date information on the status of fast-moving actions.

An effective AO must also be credible with the principal. If not, the AO won't have the frequent access required for decisions and compromises. Credibility with the principal grows with credibility among the other AOs; he or she can provide the principal with information gleaned from the others about their organizations' positions and strategies. Likewise, an AO's credibility is enhanced among peers with quick and frequent access to the principal for short-suspense, quick-turnaround action. Credibility thus depends upon a cycle the AO nurtures with both peers and principal.

## THE GAME

The goal or objective of the bureaucratic politics game in the Department of Defense is to get the organization's view or position on an issue reflected in a document under consideration and, through it, in a policy decision. An almost always unrealistic expectation is that a single organization can get its position adopted totally as the final decision. Too many organizational players are involved in the process and are likely to have a view on the issue for this to occur. The best an organization can usually hope for is to see some element of its position in the final decision. The degree to which its position is incorporated becomes the challenge.

An organization has the best chance of getting its views reflected in a document if it can incorporate its position in the initial draft. This illustrates the first axiom of bureaucratic politics: *the first position on the street has the advantage.* Roughly analogous to the advantage an incumbent usually enjoys over a challenger, first on the street means that an organization's position on an issue is the first to find its way into print in a draft document circulating for coordination or comment. It carries with it the implicit assertion that it represents the official position until, or unless, other organizations are able to modify it.

The originating OPR for the document is best able to achieve this advantage because it owns the draft, or a portion thereof, and a useful measure of an issue's saliency is often the predraft efforts by other organizations to convince the OPR to modify the initial draft language to incorporate their views. For example, the AO for the assistant secretary, International Security Affairs, the OPR for the portion of the Defense Guidance, among others, addressing strategic nuclear defense policy, could each year count on visits by, respectively, the air force and army AOs about two weeks before the first draft of the DG was due out. Each would argue the service's view of the guidance language required to assist it in justifying increases in its respective contributions to strategic nuclear defense. During years in which expansion of force structure was at issue—that is, an increase in the number of weapon systems used by the services—the AO of DG could also count on a visit by the AO representing the director, Program Analysis and Evaluation (PA&E), who would argue for guidance language requiring the services, particularly the air force, to reassess the number of aircraft or missile systems needed for the air defense of North America. If the AO also got a visit on the same issue by the AO representing the assistant secretary for International Security Policy (ISP), arguing for language limiting the level of effort required, then that the issue will be hard fought throughout the cycle and the AO will therefore be little inclined to make any changes from the previous year's guidance. Instead, the AO will leave it to the interested OPRs, in this case the air force, army, PA&E, and ISP, to work out an agreeable compromise, but that would have to occur after the draft was on the street for comment and coordination.

An organization's success in influencing a document at the predraft stage depends upon the willingness of the owning OPR to be accessible. If the OPR is "hard-over" on an issue, then predraft influence will be minimal and the challenge must be made once the document is on the street and circulating, a much more difficult process. Accessibility, however, is a function of several factors, including the AO's personality, experience, and instructions from the principal; time available before the document *goes final*; and the nature of the document itself—short, single-OPR documents like speeches, memoranda, letters, and public statements are most difficult to influence before the draft is out, whereas large, multi-OPR papers, such as the recurring policy documents, are easier to influence because the volume of material involved lessens the chance that a particular paragraph, sentence, or phrase will stand out as changed. Indeed, every AO's dream is to slip unnoticed into a draft what appears to be an innocuous change supporting the organization's view but provides strong precedence later to make a major change elsewhere.

If an organization is unsuccessful in getting its views incorporated in the initial draft on the street then the challenge becomes greater as organizations follow the second axiom of bureaucratic politics: *if you can't get your best position in, then keep the worst position out.* Or, stated another way, half a loaf is better than none. During the Defense Guidance drafting process, the air force was anxious to include language requiring it to acquire a minimum level of intratheater, or tactical, airlift. Its major opponent, who also owned the draft section in question, was OSD/PA&E, who argued that a less costly alternative capability for intratheater movement of cargo was by truck. Logical justification existed for both sides: Surface transportation is much less costly to provide and operate, but in the theaters other than Europe it may not be practical or even possible. The air force, of course, wanted its best position reflected—that is, guidance requiring it to provide airlift to justify funding its intratheater airlift programs. Unacceptable was guidance requiring increases in intratheater movement by surface, its worst position. While the air force could not succeed in getting clear guidance in the draft requiring a minimum level of intratheater airlift, it did succeed in keeping out the specific requirement for additional surface transport. The requirement for intratheater movement of cargo remained sufficiently ambiguous to allow interpretation of either means and left open redressal of the issue in another context and part of the document. It also provided the opportunity for further analysis to determine if a mix of capability might be the answer.

Underlying the organization and functioning of the Department of Defense are two separate, yet intertwined, issues that probably more than any others affect the bureaucratic politics game within the department: Civilian versus military and centralization versus decentralization. These two issues lead to a third axiom: *whose position prevails in decisions can become more important than which position prevails.*

The civilian versus military issue, of course, has its roots in the constitutional principle of civilian military control and oversight, itself seldom at issue, and most explains the existence of separate civilian and military staff agencies within the department. Thus the Office of the Secretary of Defense, with its under and assistant secretaries and their respective staffs, finds itself in a natural and frequent tension with the uniformed military staffs. This tension exists to a lesser extent in the military departments between the civilian secretariats and the uniformed staffs, though it can develop there, too, as exemplified by the competition and conflict between Secretary of the Navy John Lehman and the uniformed navy staff. Although I do not wish to overstate the significance of tension (particularly as the uniformed staffs find themselves frequently allied with a civilian staff either advocating or opposing another organization's position, and as the civilian staffs also include a large number of military officers), in general the civilian OSD and military department staffs appear to see their role as counter-balancing the purely uniformed position.

Closely related is the issue of centralized versus decentralized control of the Department of Defense by the secretary. From the department's creation in 1947, which partially unified the separate armed forces under a secretary, the concept of a highly centralized defense establishment has been in one form or another the most constant and single overriding issue affecting bureaucratic politics. Although its saliency waxes and wanes with the secretary's personality and with national security crises occuring from time to time, and though it is related to the question of civilian control and oversight, centralization moves beyond by becoming a political issue of how power and influence is to be distributed within the department. Should it be mono-lithically unified under the secretary, or should it be decentralized as a confederation among the JCS, the military departments, and the OSD? Complicating and often resuscitating the question is Congress with its constitutional and political involvement in organizing and equipping the armed forces: a highly centralized and unified Department of Defense often means Congress has less influence on service activities affecting its constituents.

Significant legislation affecting centralization is the Defense Reorgani-zation Act of 1958, which appreciably strengthened the secretary at the expense of the separate military departments, and the Reorganization Act of 1986, which appears to strengthen the chairman, Joint Chiefs of Staff and the Joint Staff at the expense of the separate military services. However, incumbent secretaries have by personal philosophy exercised greater or lesser centralized control over the department. Interestingly, the issue of centralization appears to reflect political party philosophies as well: Democratic secretaries have attempted to impose greater centralization and control; Republican secretaries have tended to allow the military departments and uniformed services greater latitude through "participatory management" and "decentralized execution."[2]

This cycle of centralization-decentralization, together with the concept itself, has important consequences for bureaucratic politics. With the exception of the few political appointees at the second, third, and perhaps fourth echelons below the secretary, the civilian officers within OSD are career civil servants who have experienced the wax and wane of their authority, influence, and responsibility over many years in relation to the military departments and uniformed services. On more than one occasion I have heard many yearn wistfully for the "good old days" under McNamara or Brown when they had the authority to "make [their own] decisions stick."

During the FY86–90 Defense Guidance drafting process in 1983, one hotly fought issue concerned strategic mobility assets: how to provide rapid transportation for U.S. forces required in theater conflicts abroad, particularly to Europe. Should the services fund fast sealift or additional airlift? The navy justly feared that funding fast sealift ships might compete with funding already programmed for combat assets in its planned six hundred–ship navy. The air force likewise feared that funding sealift would compete with its programmed funding for the C-17 strategic airlift transport, already delayed by several years. The army supported the air force in its concern because the army needed the heavy airlift capability the C-17 would provide for its mobility. Opposing the services and the JCS (who of course supported the services) were principally the Office of Assistant Secretary for Manpower, Reserve Affairs and Logistics (MRA&L), supported by the directorate of Program Analysis and Evaluation (PA&E).

Although analyses and counter-analyses by the participants kept the airlift issue lively for almost the entire drafting cycle of six months, and clearly indicated the logic for a compromise providing both capabilities, the intensity of emotion, argument, and uncompromising positions grew well beyond the saliency of the issue itself. It became a litmus-test of Secretary Weinberger's policy of allowing the services equal voice with OSD in drafting his policy and programming guidance. This was the third fully developed Defense Guidance of the new administration, and the services were still smarting from what they perceived to be OSD's undue influence over their planning and programming in the past two editions, despite the secretary's stated policy. OSD (particularly MRA&L and PA&E, staffed by career civil servants who had exercised just such influence over the services under the previous administration, and themselves smarting from the breadth and intensity of the services' challenge), were adamant in their position. The intensity was finally diffused with an acceptable, reasoned compromise, but the principle of full service participation was reaffirmed. Though but one example of *whose* position becoming more important than *which* position, the same struggle was apparent over many other issues that year and continues to a greater or lesser extent as a major factor in bureaucratic politics today.

Bureaucratic infighting and turf wars, particularly interservice rivalry, appear often as a favorite theme of the news media. I briefly addressed the issue above in discussing the important role I believe organizational self-interest plays in formulating defense policy decisions, but the question of interservice or, more broadly, interorganizational rivalry suggests a fourth axiom of bureaucratic politics worthy of note: *All issues in dispute between organizations are more complex and multisided than appear on the surface.* There are few right-or-wrong, yes-or-no, best answers to policy questions.

This aspect of bureaucratic politics is well illustrated by the classic and continuing issue of the military services' roles and missions and reaches the core of the respective services' essence or raison d'être. The services jealously guard their traditionally assigned functions and tasks, arguing with sound justification that their training and equipping make each best qualified to perform them. So the air force resists army interest in developing a fixed-wing fleet of aircraft to provide combat ground support; the army resists navy interest in expanding its Marine Corps' capabilities for ground combat beyond that required to establish beachheads; and the navy resists air force interest in controlling all theater-assigned tactical combat air assets, regardless of service.

To the policy-maker in Congress or OSD, such turf wars seem to beg the more important question, What is the most effective way to get the job done? The answer that using whatever resources are available, regardless of service roles and assets, appears on the surface to be the right answer. But it may be neither the best nor the most simple. A myriad other factors must also be considered.

For example, one of the highest priority U.S. defense objectives in the future global war will be the same as it was in all past wars: sea-lane defense against enemy submarine, surface, and air forces to protect air- and sealifts carrying military cargo. But is the navy or the air force best trained and equipped to do the job? Or, the more likely question, Which of the two is more likely to be available? While the navy is clearly the candidate with its fleets of antisubmarine and antisurface warfare vessels and its aircraft carriers, the air force also has assets and capabilities that can be effective. Why not equip long-range air force heavy bombers with air-to-surface missiles, station shorter-range air force fighters on land locations near the sea-lanes, and assign air force airborne warning and control aircraft to coordinate these assets in support of sea-lane defense? Would not this blurring of the traditional navy and air force roles and missions be the best way to provide defense? In a relatively unconstrained resource environment, like that existing in World War II when land-based aircraft contributed to sea-lane defense, mixing the traditional service roles and missions would probably be the right answer. And so it seems today to many critics of U.S. military policy and strategy. But today's military is not resource unconstrained; simplistic arguments (such as interservice rivalry and turf protection prevent the optimum solution of mixing roles and missions) belie the complexity of the question and ignore many other crucial factors.

What other, more traditional and central, air force missions would have to be foregone to provide sea-lane defense? How many heavy bombers and crews assigned to one of the most critical U.S. strategic nuclear deterrent force components, a limited and carefully managed fleet of bombers, can the United States risk modifying, retraining and reassigning to sea-lane defense? How many fighter aircraft and crews can the United States risk modifying, retraining and transferring from their central missions of theater air superiority, interdiction, and close air support in Europe to globally scattered locations in small numbers near sea lanes? Does the United States risk depleting its continental-U.S. air defenses, which are increasingly critical as sea-launched cruise missiles proliferate among potential enemies, by shifting its limited numbers of airborne warning and control aircraft to sea-lane defense?

This is not to argue that the United States cannot or should not assign air force assets to the more traditional navy sea-lane defense role, or that in its military planning the United States should disregard the optimum mix and blur of traditional service missions, but only to illustrate that what might appear as a straight-forward, simple, and cost-effective best answer to such issues as resource-limited sea-lane defense is much more multisided than appears at first glance. And so it is with every issue in dispute in bureaucratic politics in the Department of Defense.

Related to the complexity of issues is a fifth axiom of bureaucratic politics: *No issue is decided once and for all in bureaucratic politics.* Though decisions are made and policies articulated and followed, they are nonetheless subject to constant pressure for change, a phenomenon reflecting the multiple-access and interest-aggregation nature of U.S. society and the policy process.

A wide range of examples of the phenomenon of change come quickly to mind: The B-1 strategic bomber, effectively shelved under the Carter administration in favor of B-52s armed with air-launched cruise missiles, yet now becoming operational; the MX or Peacekeeper strategic nuclear missile being resurrected in a mobile-basing configuration in an effort to acquire congressional approval to build and deploy a second group of fifty missiles; withdrawal of U.S. troops from Europe, either to reduce the defense budget, which it would not do, or to force the Europeans to contribute more to their own defense; a *two-and-one-half-war* to a *one-and-one-half-war* to a *one-large-and-two-small-wars* military strategy; continued questions over service roles and missions, such as army versus air force control of rotary-wing, ground-support aircraft in support of special operations; greater numbers of less sophisticated, less expensive weapons systems, rather than fewer high-cost, high-tech, more capable multirole weapons; the number and utility of aircraft carriers; the question of funding force readiness and sustainability or force modernization and expansion; and a myriad other perennial alternate views to current policy that continue to arise from year to year. Indeed, one of an AO's most discouraging experiences is seeing a position long-opposed, hard-fought, and effectively compromised in one document surface yet again in another document being circulated for coordination, or even rising again in the same document in subsequent years.

No issue is decided once and for all for several reasons. First is the fundamental fact that the defense process includes so many organizations, each continuing to advocate the position it inherently believes in and defends. Moreover, individuals within the organizations change. With the departure of a particularly skilled action officer or principal comes a shift in influence among organizations; it takes time for a new individual to master the issues and learn the game, usually at least one planning and programming cycle. In this process, it is usually the military officers who suffer from this disadvantage because they transfer much more frequently than their civil service counterparts. Even doubling the tenure of the average military officer would still leave the advantage with the civil servant who often spends an entire civil service career in the Department of Defense.

In addition, international crises occur and circumstances change. The concept of creating a rapid-deployment force able to move quickly anywhere in the world where U.S. interests might be threatened was advocated for years in the defense community. But it wasn't until the oil crises of the mid-1970s focused attention on the vulnerability of middle-eastern oil fields, and the change of government in Iran underscored the instability of the region, that the concept gained sufficient support to result in U.S. Central Command (USCENTCOM). Building special forces able to respond quickly to low-level conflict has likewise been advocated by defense organizations in several quarters over the years, but little support existed for the capability until terrorism and hostage-taking became wide spread. Providing funds for special forces meant that other important defense programs enjoying broader consensus would most likely suffer funding cuts.

To the axiom that no issues in the defense arena are settled once and for all is a corollary that must also be apparent, and I have found to be true: *there are few original ideas in the defense community.* An excellent example is a recent book about the Pentagon and its arts that argues for an extensive reorganization of the Department of Defense. While the book includes some valid critiques of the department and its processes and outlines a few potential changes that might result from the latest Reorganization Act, whatever influence the book exerts on reorganization will derive from its public relations and availability, not from its originality.

In concluding this essay on bureaucratic politics in the Department of Defense, let me address briefly the question of the current defense reorganization and its impact on bureaucratic politics. My assessment is that it will have little impact on the game. Reorganization will likely result in slight shifts of influence, for example from the uniformed military services to the Office of the Joint Chiefs of Staff, but it will not change the process of bureaucratic politics itself. A reformation would be required to achieve any impact of that nature, that is, an effort to change the rules or axioms such as I have addressed above. But even a reformation would probably change very little because bureaucratic politics is a phenomenon characteristic of organizations themselves; it is inherent in them.

## SUMMARY

I have attempted to illustrate bureaucratic politics in the Department of Defense with examples from my experience, and what I have found to be its axioms:

- The first position on the street has the advantage
- If you can't get your best position in, keep the worst position out
- Whose position prevails can become more important than which position prevails
- All issues in dispute are more complex and multisided than appear on the surface
- No issue is decided once-and-for-all in bureaucratic politics; Corollary: there are few original ideas in the defense community

While the essay is only a glimpse of the fascinating and dynamic processes within the department, I hope it will nonetheless provide the student of bureaucratic politics a better appreciation of its complexities and essential nature, an understanding that the processes are generic to bureaucratic politics in any context, and that they are a reflection of U.S. polycentric society. I can think of no better explanation of how national security policy is formulated in the Department of Defense.

## NOTES

1. Of the many theoretical constructs attempting to explain bureaucratic politics, there are two that I think have particular relevance. The first is by Philip Selznick (Philip Selznick, *The Organizational Weapon,* Santa Monica: Rand Corp., 1952, R-201), a sociologist who long studied organizational behavior in government and argues that organizational politics have their roots in sociological-organizational behavior. Organizations, he explains, are initially designed as technical instruments to mobilize human energies and direct them toward designated tasks—that is, as a means to an end. However, as people work within an organization, the relationships and processes that develop take on meaning and significance beyond the organization's purpose, with the result that maintenance of the organization and its processes become as important, if not more so, than the purpose for which it was organized. Thus, he argues, an organization becomes an institution, a responsive, adaptive organism fulfilling group and individual aspirations and social needs,

infused with value beyond the technical requirements of the task at hand. It becomes a valued source of personal satisfaction. Institutions are thereby marked by concern for self-maintenance, accommodating internal interests and adapting to outside influences in order to continue the organization as an entity. Within the political context of decisionmaking, these institutions then become actors themselves, with interests, goals, ambitions and viewpoints that may exist apart from those of individual members, or even the institution's leaders.

The second, closely related, is by Morton Halperin. In his article, "Why Bureaucrats Play Games," (Morton H. Halperin, *Foreign Policy*, 1971, No. 2, pp. 70–90) Halperin argues that an organization, even beyond a coincidence with its leaders, views the face of an issue in terms of its own interests, sensed dangers, and opportunities. It seeks influence to protect these interests, particularly those affecting its essential tasks and functions, or missions. In the defense arena, the organization's career officials equate these tasks and functions (roles and missions) to the security of the United States, arguing with sincerity and conviction that they are essential to U.S. security. Thus, the stand a bureaucrat may take on an issue is influenced by the issue's impact on the ability of the organization to carry on its essential programs and missions. An organization will oppose strongly any decision that will force it to share its missions with another organization. Both Selznick's and Halperin's perspectives go a long way to explain the *why* of bureaucratic politics.

2. Secretary Robert McNamara did more than any other secretary to institute the principle of centralization. Under him, OSD became synonymous with control, and he exercised strong restraint over the military departments in policy, planning, programming, budgeting, and acquiring weapons systems, particularly through his Office of Systems Analysis. Secretary Melvin Laird, to the relief of the military departments, particularly the uniformed military, loosened control by delegating significant responsibility to his deputy and assistant secretaries, and he allowed greater involvement of the military departments through what he termed *participative management.*

Although the change of administration that brought Secretary Harold Brown to the post of secretary of Defense also brought renewed emphasis on centralization and unity, control did not reach the intensity typical of the McNamara era. Nonetheless, defense policy and strategy planning, programming, and budgeting did once again become centralized within OSD, with the military departments frequently allowed little discretion. The trend was yet again reversed under Secretary Weinberger, who consciously, under his deputy, Frank Carlucci, allowed the military departments and uniformed services greater latitude and stronger voice in planning, programming, and budgeting. His approach to centralized decisionmaking, which allowed full participation by the military departments, uniformed services, the OJCS, and especially the regional and functional military commanders-in-chief, together with his emphasis on decentralized execution, has been very popular with the military departments.

---

# 5.4   Policy Preferences and Bureaucratic Position: The Case of the American Hostage Rescue Mission

## STEVE SMITH

*Using the U.S. hostage rescue mission of April 1980 as a case study to evaluate the usefulness of the bureaucratic politics paradigm; Steve Smith reminds us not only of its utility but also its limitations. As he outlines, bureaucratic position did significantly affect individual policy preferences in this particular example. We are left to examine that extraordinarily complex nexus between individual rational action and bureaucratic structure to make our analysis of national security policy more complete.*

Within two days of the seizure by student revolutionaries of the American embassy in Tehran on 4 November 1979, planning began on a possible rescue mission. Initial estimates of the probability of success were 'zero', given the severe logistic problems involved in getting to the embassy in Iran and back out of the country without losing a large number of the hostages as casualties. Nevertheless, as negotiations dragged on with very little promise of success, and as the 1980 American presidential election campaign approached, the decision was made to undertake a very bold rescue mission. Photographs of the charred remains of the burnt-out helicopters in the Dasht-e-Kavir desert provide the most vivid image of the failure of that mission.

The decisions about the mission were taken at three meetings on 22 March, 11 April and 15 April 1980 by a very small group of people (on average, there were nine participants). Since 1980, the hostage rescue mission has received considerable coverage in the press and in the memoirs of the participants in that decision-making process. As such, it is an excellent case-study for one of the most widely cited but rarely tested theories of foreign policy behaviour: the bureaucratic politics approach.

## THE THEORETICAL BACKGROUND

The dominant theories of why states act as they do derive from the basic assumption of rationality. Most theories of foreign policy are based on the premise that states act in a more or less monolithic way: foreign policy is, accordingly, behaviour that is goal-directed and intentional. Of course, many practitioners and academics quickly move away from the monolith assumption, but they can rarely command the kind of detailed information that would enable them to assess precisely what the factions are and how the balance of views lies in any decision-making group. It is, therefore, very common to talk of states as entities and to analyse 'their' foreign policies according to some notion of a linkage between the means 'they' choose and the ends these must be directed towards. Since practitioners and academics do not literally 'know' why state X undertook action Y, it becomes necessary to impute intentions to the behaviour of states. The rationality linkage makes this task much easier; hence the popularity of the idea of the national interest,

Reproduced by permission from *International Affairs*, vol. 61, no. 1, published by the Royal Institute of International Affairs, London, England.

which incorporates very clear and powerful views on what the ends of governments are in international society, and, therefore, on how the behaviour can be linked to intentions. The most important attack on this viewpoint has been the 'bureaucratic politics approach', most extensively outlined by Graham Allison in his *Essence of decision*.[1] According to this approach, foreign policy is the result of pulling and hauling between the various components of the decision-making process. Foreign policy may, therefore, be better explained as the outcome of bureaucratic bargaining than as a conscious choice by a decision-making group. As Allison puts it, the outcome of the decision-making process is not really a result but 'a resultant—a mixture of conflicting preferences and unequal power of various individuals—distinct from what any person or group intended'.[2] The critical point is that these conflicting preferences are determined, above all, by bureaucratic position. Foreign policy, according to this perspective, is therefore to be explained by analysing the bureaucratic battleground of policy-making, rather than imputing to something called the state a set of motives and interests. On the bureaucratic battleground, the preferences of the participants are governed by the aphorism first coined by Don Price, 'where you stand depends on where you sit'.[3]

Since the publication of *Essence of decision* in 1971, Allison's claims for the explanatory power of the bureaucratic politics approach have been challenged by several writers.[4] While the logical structure of his models and their applicability to countries other than the United States have come under attack, the most damaging criticism has concerned the extent to which Allison's theory of decision-making is able to explain the events of the crisis his book focuses on—the Cuban missile crisis. Allison's bureaucratic politics model has been criticized for not being able to explain the policy preferences of those who made US policy during the crisis: his aphorism 'where you stand depends on where you sit' does not fit the evidence. Although Allison goes into a detailed examination of who proposed what policy,[5] Desmond Ball has written, 'in the case of the Cuban Missile Crisis, Allison's bureaucratic politics approach would generally have been unable to have predicted from the basis of a person's position in the bureaucracy, what his position on the question of the missiles in Cuba would be'.[6] Robert Art, in turn, argues that the aphorism has to be qualified 'with so many amendments before it begins to work that when it does we may not be left with a bureaucratic paradigm, but may in reality be using another'.[7]

The decision of the United States government to attempt a rescue of the 53 American hostages held in Iran offers an excellent opportunity for a case-study to act as a further test of Allison's claims about bureaucratic position and policy preference. Whereas it has become broadly accepted that bureaucratic position is likely to have some impact on the more routine areas of foreign and defence policymaking, doubts about the applicability of the approach to crisis decision-making have constituted a serious weakness in its explanatory power.  The rescue mission offers a rare opportunity to examine the extent to which the approach can explain crisis decision-making: it was a decision taken over just three meetings; there were very few participants; there is ample evidence on the positions adopted by the participants; and, above all, it was a very controversial and bold decision, one which raised fundamental questions about the acceptability of the use of force.

The planning process for the rescue mission began on 6 November 1979, just two days after the hostages were seized in Tehran.[8]  During the winter and spring the planning continued, focusing on the composition and training of the rescue force, on the precise location of the hostages and the nature and location of their captors, and on the enormously complex logistic problems involved in mounting the mission.  These preparations continued in secret alongside an equally complex process of negotiation for the release of the hostages with the various elements of the Iranian government (including a secret contact in Paris).  Bargaining was also under way with the United States's allies, in an attempt to persuade them to impose sanctions on Iran. As noted above, there were three key meetings at which the rescue plan was discussed (on 22 March, 11 and 15 April 1980), although the actual decision to proceed, taken on 11 April and confirmed on 15 April, was in many ways only the formal ratification of what had by then become the dominant mode of thinking among President Carter's most senior advisers.  There were two schools of thought in the initial reaction to the seizure of the hostages: first, that the United States should impose economic sanctions on Iran; secondly, that it should make use of international public opinion and international law to force the Iranian government to release the hostages.  As these measures appeared less and less likely to succeed, the US government became involved in attempts to persuade its allies to join in economic sanctions—a move that succeeded just two days before the rescue mission.

President Carter's initial reaction to the seizure was to stress the importance of putting the lives of the hostages first.  He declared on 7 December 1979, 'I am not going to take any military action that would cause bloodshed or cause the unstable captors of our hostages to attack or punish them'.[9]  Yet leaks from the White House indicated that military plans were being considered.  By late March 1980, President Carter and his advisers were becoming convinced that negotiations were not going to be successful, a view confirmed by the secret source in the Iranian government.  At a meeting held on 22 March at Camp David, the President agreed to a reconnaissance flight into Iran to find an initial landing site for the rescue force (Desert One).  The plan called for eight RH-53 helicopters from the aircraft carrier *Nimitz* to fly nearly 600 miles, at a very low altitude, and with radio blackout, from the Arabian Sea to Desert One.  There, they would meet the rescue force of 97 men (codenamed 'Delta Force') who would have arrived from Egypt via Oman on four C-130 transport aircraft.  The helicopters would refuel from the C-130s and then take Delta Force to a second location (Desert Two) some 50 miles southeast of Tehran, where Central Intelligence Agency (CIA) agents would meet them and hide the rescue force at a 'mountain hideout'. Delta Force would remain hidden during the day before being picked up by CIA operatives early the next night and driven to a location known as 'the warehouse' just inside Tehran. From there they would attack the embassy and the Foreign Ministry where three of the hostages were held, rescue the hostages, and take them to a nearby soccer stadium, where the helicopters would meet them and transfer them to a further airstrip at Monzariyeh, to be taken to Egypt by the C-130s. The planning process had meant that very definite deadlines had emerged: by 1 May there would only be 16 minutes of darkness more than required for the mission; by 10 May, the temperature would be so high that it would seriously hamper helicopter performance. 1 May appeared to be the latest feasible date for the mission, and by late March the planners were recommending 24 April for the mission (primarily because a very low level of moonlight was expected that night). But the rescue mission failed. It never got beyond Desert One. Of the eight helicopters assigned to the mission, one got lost in a duststorm and returned to the *Nimitz*, and two suffered mechanical breakdowns. This left only five helicopters in working order at Desert One, whereas the plan had called for six to move on to Desert Two. The mission was subsequently aborted, and, in the process of manoeuvring to vacate Desert One, one of the helicopters hit a C-130, causing the death of eight men.[10]

It is critical, in any discussion of the applicability of the bureaucratic politics approach, to focus on the actual decisions that led to this mission, and to review the positions adopted by the participants. We have so much information available that this is not a very difficult task, although very important issues are raised by any attempt to ascribe policy preferences to bureaucratic actors (a point which will be taken up in my conclusion). Nevertheless, we know that the three meetings of 22 March, 11 and 15 April were the decisive ones, and we know who took part and what they said. The key meeting in terms of the actual decision was on 11 April, when the 'go-ahead' was given. The meeting on 22 March was important because at it President Carter gave permission for aircraft to verify the site for Desert One. The meeting of 15 April was important because Cyrus Vance, the Secretary of State, presented his reservations about the decision. As Zbigniew Brzezinski, President Carter's National Security Adviser, pointed out: 'In a way, the decision [on 11 April] had been foreshadowed by the discussion initiated at the March 22 briefing at Camp David. From that date on, the rescue mission became the obvious option if negotiations failed—and on that point there was almost unanimous consent within the top echelons of the Administration.'[11] A virtually identical set of people were present at those meetings. On 22 March, there attended President Carter, Walter Mondale (the Vice-President), Cyrus Vance (the Secretary of State), Harold

Brown (the Secretary of Defense), David Jones (the Chairman of the Joint Chiefs of Staff), Stansfield Turner (the Director of the CIA), Zbigniew Brzezinski (the National Security Adviser), Jody Powell (the Press Secretary), and David Aaron (the Deputy National Security Adviser). On 11 April, the same participants convened, except that Warren Christopher, the Deputy Secretary of State, replaced Cyrus Vance, and Carter's aide Hamilton Jordan replaced Aaron. The final meeting on 15 April was attended by the same people who attended on 11 April, except that Vance replaced Christopher.

In order to outline the positions adopted by the participants in this decision-making group, the participants can be divided into four sub-groups: President Carter, 'hawks', 'doves', and 'presidential supporters'. (These terms are only intended as analytical shorthand.) For reasons that will be discussed in more detail in the conclusion, the terms actually raise questions that are quite fundamental to the internal logic of the bureaucratic politics approach. Put simply, this concerns the issue, 'why are hawks hawks and not doves?' What this case-study shows is that this is indeed a critical theoretical concern which has been rather neglected in the study of bureaucratic politics. Before we discuss that issue in detail, it is sufficient to say that this case-study supports the contention that bureaucratic position explains policy preference. The evidence indicates that these four subgroups of people adopted consistent positions, positions which *a priori* seem predictable from their bureaucratic base. Although there is a risk of fitting evidence to a preconception, the conclusion to be drawn from the detailed press discussions and subsequent academic and personal accounts is that these groups acted in accordance with what the bureaucratic politics approach would suggest: namely, that the National Security Adviser, the Secretary of Defense, the Chairman of the Joint Chiefs of Staff and the Director of the CIA would support military action (the position of the National Security Adviser will be returned to in my conclusion); the Secretary of State, and in his absence his deputy, would oppose it; those individuals who were bureaucratically tied to the President (the Vice-President, the Press Secretary and the Political Adviser) would be fundamentally concerned with what was best for the Carter presidency; and President Carter, although clearly more than just another bureaucratic actor, would act in a way that reflected bureaucratically-derived as well as personal influences.

## PRESIDENT CARTER

The key to understanding President Carter's position lies in the interaction between his desire to avoid the blatant use of American military power and the great pressure on him to satisfy his public and 'do something'. From the earliest days of the crisis, he was attacked in the press and by the Republican

Party for failing to act decisively. 1980 was, of course, presidential election year, the President's public opinion rating was poor, and he was being challenged strongly for the Democratic Party's nomination. His promise not to campaign for the election so long as the hostages were in Iran made his situation worse. He was advised by his campaign staff that decisive action was needed (especially after the fiasco of the morning of the Wisconsin primary, on 1 April, when the President announced that the hostages were about to be released).[12] That inaccurate assessment was seen by many as a reflection of his lack of control over events; it was also portrayed as manipulating the issue for his own political ends.

Another factor which added to the President's frustration was the desire to make the allies go ahead with sanctions against Iran.[13] It later turned out that the allies' belief that the US administration was planning military action was their main incentive to join in the sanctions, in the hope of forestalling it. But the critical moment came when the President felt that the only alternative to military action was to wait until, possibly, the end of the year for the release of the hostages by negotiation. That was the impression he gained in the early days of April: information coming out of Tehran indicated that the release of the hostages would be delayed for months by the parliamentary elections due to be held in Iran on 16 May. Indeed, by the time the rescue mission was undertaken, the favourite estimate of how long the new government in Iran would take to negotiate was five or six months.[14] So, as a result of fear that the hostages might be held until the end of 1980, President Carter determined on a change in policy: 'We could no longer afford to depend on diplomacy. I decided to act.'[15] In fact, the President threatened military action on 12 and 17 April,[16] unless the allies undertook economic sanctions. This action (which, he said, had not been decided on yet) would involve the interruption of trade with Iran. (This was widely interpreted as meaning a naval blockade or the mining of Iranian harbours.)[17] Of course, this was a deliberate smokescreen: accordingly, when on 23 April the European countries agreed to the imposition of sanctions on Iran, the White House let it be known that this would delay any military action until the summer![18]

Yet the desire of the President for drastic action is only part of the story. It is evident that he was also extremely concerned to limit the size of the operation, in order to avoid unnecessary loss of life. At the briefing with the mission commander, Colonel Beckwith, on 16 April, Carter said: 'It will be easy and tempting for your men to become engaged in gunfire with others and to try and settle some scores for our nation. That will interfere with your objective of getting our people out safely. In the eyes of the world, it is important that the scope of this mission be seen as simply removing our people.'[19] W. Safire has argued that the reason why the mission was unsuccessful was precisely because Carter wanted the rescue to be a humanitarian rather than a combat mission, and stipulated only a small force with very limited back-up.[20] Hence, in explaining President Carter's position on the rescue mission, two factors seem dominant: a personal concern to ensure that the mission was not to be seen as a punitive military action, and a role-governed perception that American national honour was at stake. Although, in early March, the President had been unwilling to give the go-ahead even to a reconnaissance mission, when negotiations with the Iranian leadership suddenly broke down in the first few days of April (leading to his embarrassment over the Wisconsin primary statement) he decided to go ahead with the rescue mission. At the meeting of 22 March, the participants were informed that 1 May was the last deadline for a mission, and that the night of 24–5 April was the best time, owing to the low projected levels of moonlight. The need to get the rescue force into the area therefore meant that a decision was necessary by mid-April. At this juncture, the breakdown of talks, the fiasco of the Wisconsin primary announcement, the predictions of, at best, a five or six-month delay in the release of the hostages, and the feeling among his key advisers that he had to act resulted in Carter's decision to proceed.

Carter's actions were, of course, a response to a number of factors. The bureaucratic politics approach draws our attention to certain of these: specifically, his desire for re-election, and his perception of his responsibility as the individual charged with protecting American national honour. Clearly, Carter's personality was an important factor (and one can easily imagine other Presidents handling the situation in slightly different ways), but the bureaucratic politics approach seems much more useful in identifying the kinds of considerations that would be important to Carter than concentrating on notions of what would be most rational for the American nation. This is not to imply that bureaucratic factors are the only important ones in explaining what Carter did; but it is to claim that a bureaucratic perspective paints a far more accurate picture of what caused Carter to act as he did than any of the rival theories of foreign policy-making.

## THE HAWKS

The leading political proponents of military action throughout the crisis were Brzezinski and Brown. Drew Middleton wrote, 'for months, a hard-nosed Pentagon view had held that the seizure of the hostages itself was an act of war and that the United States was, therefore, justified in adopting a military response.'[21] Indeed, just two days after the hostages were taken, Brzezinski, Brown and Jones began discussing the possibilities of a rescue mission.[22] Their discussions led to the conclusion that an immediate mission was impossible, but Brzezinski felt that 'one needed such a contingency scheme in the event . . . that some of the hostages either were put on trial and then sentenced to death or were murdered. . . . Accordingly, in such circumstances, we would have to undertake a rescue mission out of a moral as well as a political obligation, both to keep faith with our people imprisoned in Iran and to safeguard American national honor.' In fact, Brzezinski felt a rescue mission was not enough: 'It would better if the United States were to engage in a generalized retaliatory strike, which could be publicly described as a punitive action and which would be accompanied by the rescue attempt. If the rescue succeeded, that would be all to the good; if it failed, the U.S. government could announce that it had executed a punitive mission against Iran.'[23] This punitive action, he thought, could take the form of a military blockade along with airstrikes. In the earliest days of the crisis, Brzezinski, Turner, Jones and Brown began to meet regularly in private and discuss military options; Brzezinski alone took (handwritten) notes. It was this group which directed the planning for the mission (which used military and CIA personnel) and gave the eventual plan its most detailed review.[24] Similarly, it was Brzezinski who pressed for the reconnaissance flight into Iran, agreed upon on 22 March, and the same group of four who proposed the rescue plan at the 11 April meeting, led by Brown and Jones. But it is clear from the available evidence that Brzezinski was the political force behind military action.

As early as February, Brzezinski felt increasing pressure from the public and from Congress for direct action to be taken against Iran. Brzezinski thought there were three choices: to continue negotiations, to undertake a large military operation, or to mount a small rescue mission. What swung him away from his earlier first choice, a punitive military operation, was the consideration that, after the Soviet intervention in Afghanistan in December 1979, any military action might give the Soviet Union additional opportunities for influence in the Persian Gulf and Indian Ocean: 'It now seemed to me more important to forge an anti-Soviet Islamic coalition. It was in this context that the rescue mission started to look more attractive to me.'[25] As negotiations failed, Brzezinski sent a memorandum to Carter on 10 April in which he argued that a choice must be made between a punitive military action or a rescue mission. Given his fears about the spread of Soviet influence, Brzezinski recommended the latter option, concluding, 'we have to think beyond the fate of the 50 Americans and consider the deleterious effects of a protracted stalemate, growing public frustration, and international humiliation of the US.'[26] At both the 11 April and 15 April meetings, Brzezinski spoke forcefully in favour of the mission.[27]

Brown and Jones were the main advocates of the actual rescue plan (Brzezinski still wanting more than the others in the way of a slightly wider retaliatory strike). These two men presented the plan to the 11 April meeting, and conducted the detailed private briefing with Carter on 16 April; it was Harold Brown who gave the detailed account, and defence, of the mission to the press after its failure. It was also Brown who spoke against the Christopher/Vance position at the 11 April and 15 April meetings.[28]

Finally, both Brown and Brzezinski spoke very strongly in justification of the mission after its failure, stating that it had been morally right and politically justified.[29]  Brzezinski was said to be 'downright cocky about it [the mission] in private and insisting that military action might be necessary in future.'[30]  He also warned America's opponents: 'Do not scoff at America's power.  Do not scoff at American reach.'[31]

Turner, the Director of the CIA, was also very much in favour of the mission, so much so that it appears that he did not voice the very serious doubts about the mission which had been expressed in a report by a special CIA review group, prepared for him on 16 March 1980.  According to this report, the rescue plan would probably result in the loss of 60 per cent of the hostages during the mission: 'The estimate of a loss rate of 60 per cent for the AmEmbassy hostages represents the best estimate.'[32]  The report also estimated that the mission was as likely to prove a complete failure as a complete success.  Yet it was exactly at this time that the review of the plan was undertaken by Brzezinski's small group.  To quote Brzezinski again: 'a very comprehensive review of the rescue plan undertaken by Brown, Jones, and me in mid-March led me to the conclusion that the rescue mission had a reasonably good chance of success though there probably would be some casualties. *There was no certain way of estimating how large they might be* [emphasis added].'[33]  Turner was involved in the detailed briefings of the President; at the meeting of 11 April he even said, 'The conditions inside and around the compound are good.'[34]  The evidence does not suggest that he made his agency's doubts public at any of these meetings, either in the small group or in the group of nine.

To sum up: the positions adopted by those classified here as 'hawks' could have been predicted in advance.  What is striking about the evidence is the consistency with which these four men—Brown, Brzezinski, Jones and Turner—proposed policies that reflected their position in the bureaucratic network.  (I must, however, point out one problem raised by this analysis concerning the issue of whether bureaucratic position *per se* causes these people to be hawks.  On the one hand, their position puts them in contact with certain ways of thinking, and they come to share ways of seeing the world; yet bureaucratic position alone might not necessarily determine whether a person is a hawk or a dove.  This problem, 'why are hawks hawks?', will be discussed again in my conclusion.)  Nevertheless, the evidence indicates strongly that bureaucratically-determined thinking on the part of Brown, Brzezinski, Jones and Turner was a major input to the decision-making process.  To the extent that the bureaucratic politics approach explains the policies adopted by these individuals, it illustrates the weaknesses of rationality-based theories of US foreign policy.

## PRESIDENTIAL SUPPORTERS

The next group to consider are those who do not fit into the traditional 'hawks-doves' characterization of US government. These are individuals whose primary loyalty is to the President, and who would therefore be expected to adopt positions that promised to bolster the President's domestic standing. Unlike those groups discussed so far, the first concern of this group is not the nature of US relations with other states, but, rather, the domestic position of the President. Mondale, Powell and Jordan seem to have been neither 'hawks' nor 'doves' in their views of the Iranian action; rather, their policy proposals show that their concern was first and foremost with the effect of the crisis on the Carter presidency. This can be seen very clearly in Jordan's memoirs,[35] which reveal both a loyalty to Carter and an evaluation of the rescue mission in terms of how it helped Carter out of a domestic political problem. 'I knew our hard-line approach would not bring the hostages home any sooner, but I hoped that maybe it would buy us a little more time and patience from the public.' The rescue mission was 'the best of a lousy set of options.'[36] Throughout his memoirs, at every juncture of the mission's planning, failure and consequences, Jordan's position is consistently one in which he advocates what he believed would benefit the President. This determined his reaction to Vance's objections (Vance was failing to support the President when he needed it, thereby putting Carter in an uncomfortable position), to the failure of the mission (Congress's reaction would be to concentrate on the lack of consultation and it might accuse Carter of violating the War Powers Resolution), and to Vance's resignation and his replacement by Ed Muskie[37] (the former created a problem for Carter, the latter was a vote of confidence in Carter's political future).

The evidence also unambiguously supports the contention that Mondale and Powell were motivated above all by an awareness of the President's domestic standing and their perceptions of how it might be improved. Brzezinski notes that Powell, Mondale and Jordan 'were feeling increasingly frustrated and concerned about rising public pressures for more direct action against Iran.'[38] All of them seemed to think that direct action was needed to stem this public pressure, *especially* after the Wisconsin primary announcement on 1 April. As Powell put it on 1 April: 'We are about to have an enormous credibility problem. The combination of not campaigning and that early-morning announcement has made skeptics out of even our friends in the press.'[39] Salinger argues that Carter's 'campaign for reelection registered the frustrations of the American public. While his political fortunes had risen after the taking of the hostages, he was beginning to slip in the polls and had lost a key primary in New York to Senator Kennedy. Jimmy Carter was now in the midst of a fight for his political life, and it looked as if he was losing. A military operation that freed the hostages would dramatically alter the odds.'[40] The position of the 'presidential supporters' was summed up in Mondale's contribution to the 11 April meeting, when he said, 'the rescue offered us the best way out of a situation which was becoming intolerably humiliating.'[41] (Interestingly, humiliation was also a concern of the hawks.) Before agreeing to the mission at that meeting, Carter informed those present that he had discussed the matter fully beforehand with Mondale, Powell and Jordan and that they all felt strong action was required.

The 'presidential supporters', then, proposed policies which reflected their own bureaucratic position. Mondale, Powell and Jordan had no vast bureaucratic interests to represent, nor was their chief concern the relationship between US foreign policy and other states. Each of them owed their influence to their position *vis à vis* President Carter (as, of course, did Brzezinski), and their concern was to act so as to aid his presidency, above all his domestic political fortunes. In contemporary press reports, it was these three men who voiced concern about the President's relations with Congress and his chances of re-election. This was in contrast to both the 'hawks' and the 'doves' who were far more concerned with Carter's relations with Iran, the Soviet Union and US allies. As in the case of the 'hawks', the policy preferences of the 'presidential supporters' seem to have been predominantly determined by their bureaucratic role.

## THE DOVES

The evidence that bureaucratic role determines policy stance is strongest of all in the case of the 'doves': Cyrus Vance, the Secretary of State, and Warren Christopher, the Deputy Secretary of State. Not only did the two men take virtually identical stands on the subject of the rescue mission, but, as will be discussed below, Christopher did not know what Vance's position was when he attended the 11 April meeting.

From the earliest days of the crisis Vance had advised against the use of military force.[42] At the meeting on 22 March, Vance agreed that a reconnaissance flight should go ahead in case a rescue mission should prove necessary (in the case of a threat to the hostages' lives), but argued against 'the use of any military force, including a blockade or mining, as long as the hostages were unharmed and in no imminent danger. In addition to risking the lives of the hostages, I believed military action could jeopardize our interests in the Persian Gulf . . . Our only realistic course was to keep up the pressure on Iran while we waited for Khomeini to determine that . . . the hostages were of no further value. As painful as it would be, our national interests and the need to protect the lives of our fellow Americans dictated that we continued to exercise restraint.'[43] After this meeting, Vance felt there was no indication that a decision on the use of military force was imminent, and on 10 April he left for a long weekend's rest in Florida.

But on the very next day the meeting was held that made the decision to go ahead with the rescue mission. Jody Powell explained to the press later that Cyrus Vance was on a well earned vacation and that 'Vance was not called back because it would have attracted too much attention when the operation had to remain a secret.'[44] There is no evidence as to why the meeting was called in his absence, but it is clear that Vance did not know that the mission was being so seriously considered, and that everyone else involved knew that Vance would disagree. Tom Wicker argues that Vance was deliberately shunted aside from the critical meeting in order to weaken his (and the State Department's) ability to prevent the mission from proceeding.[45] All the Carter, Brzezinski and Jordan memoirs say is that Vance was on 'a brief and much needed vacation' (Carter), 'on vacation' (Brzezinski), and 'in Florida on a long overdue vacation' (Jordan).[46] In many ways the exclusion of Vance can be interpreted as a symptom of what Irving Janis calls 'groupthink'; other symptoms can also be determined in this case-study of the phenomenon, which refers to the tendency for groups to maintain amiability and cohesiveness at the cost of critical thinking about decisions.[47]

The President opened the meeting of 11 April by saying that he was seriously considering undertaking a rescue mission, and he invited Brown and Jones to brief those present on the planned mission. At this point, Jordan turned to Christopher and said: '"What do you think?" "I'm not sure. Does Cy know about this?" "The contingency rescue plan? Of course." "No, no—does he realize how far along the President is in his thinking about this?" "I don't know . . . I assume they've talked about it."[48] When the briefing finished, Christopher was first to speak. He outlined a number of alternatives to a rescue mission: a return to the UN for more discussions, the blacklisting of Iranian ships and aircraft, the possibility of getting European support for sanctions against Iran. Brown immediately dismissed these as 'not impressive', and he was supported by Brzezinski, Jones, Turner, Powell and Jordan, all of whom wanted to go ahead. Christopher was alone in his opposition to the plan. He declined to take up a formal position on the rescue mission since he had not been told about it in advance by Vance; he therefore felt that Vance had either accepted the plan or had felt that the State Department could not really prevent its going ahead. According to one press report after the failure of the mission, Christopher 'was led to believe that the Secretary [Vance] already knew that the President had decided to undertake the mission.'[49] His impression was reinforced when Carter informed the meeting that Vance 'prior to leaving for his vacation in Florida, had told the President that he opposed any military action but if a choice had to be made between a rescue and a wider blockade, he preferred the rescue.'[50] Christopher knew that Vance had opposed the use of military force, but it is logical to assume that he felt all he could do was to offer non-belligerent alternatives (they were, after all, State Department people being held hostage) to any use of military force, but remain silent on the actual mission; particularly as it had been strongly suggested that Vance had *already* agreed to it. In support of this conclusion, it is interesting to note that Christopher did not contact Vance on holiday to tell him what had happened. When Vance returned on 14 April and was told what had happened at the meeting, Christopher explained that he had not telephoned him on holiday: 'Under the impression that Vance, who was taking his first time off in months, had given his tacit, if reluctant, approval to the plan, Christopher decided not to disturb him with word of the decision to go ahead.'[51]

Vance's reaction to the news was 'that he was dismayed and mortified.'[52] Vance writes: 'Stunned and angry that such a momentous decision had been made in my absence, I went to see the President.'[53] At this meeting Vance listed his objections to the mission, and Carter offered him the opportunity to present his views to the group which had made the original decision in the meeting to be held on 15 April. Vance's statement at that meeting focused on issues almost entirely dictated by his bureaucratic position.[54] He said, first, that to undertake the mission when the United States had been trying to get the Europeans to support sanctions on the explicit promise that this would rule out military action, would look like deliberate deception; secondly, the hostages, who were State Department employees, were in no immediate physical danger; thirdly, there were apparently moves in Iran to form a functioning government with which the United States could negotiate; fourthly, that even if it succeeded, the mission might simply lead to the taking of more American (or allied) hostages by the Iranians; fifthly, it might force the Iranians into the arms of the Soviet Union; and, finally, there would almost certainly be heavy casualties (he cited the figure of 15 out of the 53 hostages and 30 out of the rescue force as a likely death-toll).[55]

After Vance's comments, Brown turned to him and asked him when he expected the hostages to be released; Vance replied that he did not know.[56] No one supported Vance: his objections were met by 'a deafening silence.'[57] Although Vance said later that, after the meeting, a number of participants told him that he had indeed raised serious objections, no one mentioned them at the time[58]—an example of 'groupthink'? Carter noted that Vance 'was alone in his opposition to the rescue mission among all my advisers, and he knew it.'[59] In their memoirs, Carter and Brzezinski put Vance's subsequent resignation down to tiredness: 'He looked worn out, his temper would flare up, his eyes were puffy, and he projected unhappiness . . . Cy seemed to be burned out and determined to quit' (Brzezinski); 'Vance has been extremely despondent lately . . . for the third or fourth time, he indicated that he might resign . . . but after he goes through a phase of uncertainty and disapproval, then he joins in with adequate support for me' (Carter).[60] Even worries expressed by Vance about the details of the plan at the 16 April briefing were dismissed on the grounds that they reflected his opposition to the raid in principle.[61] On 21 April, Vance offered his resignation to Carter;

it was accepted, with the agreement that it would not be made public until after the rescue mission, whatever the outcome. Vance duly resigned on 28 April. The press reports about his resignation suggested that opposition to the mission was only the last incident in a long line, and that Vance's resignation stemmed from his battle with Brzezinski over the direction of US foreign policy. As a White House aide said, it had been 'clear for some time that Mr. Vance was no longer part of the foreign policy mainstream in the Carter Administration.'[62]

That Vance and Christopher opposed the rescue mission is not, in itself, proof of the applicability of the bureaucratic politics approach. What is critical is that their opposition was generated *not* simply from their personal views, but more as a result of their bureaucratic position (although there is a problem in weighting these). Three factors warrant this conclusion. First, Christopher, without knowing Vance's position on the rescue mission, and having been told (erroneously) that Vance supported it, still outlined alternatives. In fact, his opposition to the mission was on the same grounds as Vance's even though he was led to believe that his superior had given the go-ahead. Secondly, Vance's statement at the 15 April meeting very clearly reflected State Department concerns. The response of Brown and Brzezinski did not address the problems Vance had outlined (for example, the position of the allies), but stressed issues such as national honour and security. These are role-governed policy prescriptions. Thirdly, Vance was not opposed to a rescue mission as such, but only to one at a time when negotiation was still possible; his objection did not simply reflect a personal attitude towards violence.

## BUREAUCRATIC POLITICS AND IMPLEMENTATION

This article has tried to analyze the relationship between policy preference and bureaucratic position at three meetings. However, it is important to note that the bureaucratic politics approach subsequently developed by Allison and Halperin[63] is also significantly useful in explaining how the decision was actually implemented. Three features of their approach seem especially worth noting. First, their theory explains the composition of the actual rescue force. As Halperin and Halperin have argued, the 1948 Key West agreement on the division of responsibilities in the US armed forces resulted in the forces used for the rescue mission being made up of contingents from the navy, army and air force.[64] Because the navy had responsibility for any operations from ships, the helicopters used on the mission had to be navy ones—yet their pilots and equipment were simply not ideal for the job. None of the pilots concerned had had experience of such a mission; and the helicopter chosen was one normally used to sweep mines. Halperin and Halperin conclude: 'Because of the Key West boundaries, then, the presence on ships of the best-qualified fliers would tip off enemy intelligence that business was not as usual . . . Pentagon planners should not have had to chose a mine-sweeper helicopter and between pilots who knew the equipment and pilots who knew the mission.'[65] Secondly, bureaucratic politics operated in determining the nature of the command structure of the rescue force. The most surprising aspect of this was that there was no single overall commander. To quote Richard Gabriel: 'In typical "systems" fashion the operation was conceived and assembled in components, each with its own commander. Thus, at Desert One, there were no less than four commanders: the rescue force commander, the air group commander, the on-site commander, and the helicopter force commander. In addition, the Joint Task Force Commander was not even on the ground with his staff; instead he was located aboard ship in the Persian Gulf.'[66] The result was an inability to improvise when things went wrong. Each commander recommended aborting the mission, since the lack of a sixth helicopter at Desert One challenged each unit's planning assumptions. No commander could assume control outside his specific area. This problem of organization had recurred throughout the planning, with each service wanting a piece of the action. The eventual rescue force was arrived at not by logic but by bureaucratic bargaining. This was one of the conclusions of the Joint Chiefs of Staff's own review of the reasons for the failure of the mission.[67] Thirdly, there is strong evidence of a serious bureaucratically-determined clash between the President and leading Congressional figures. After he had decided to go ahead with the mission, President Carter, with conflicting advice from Brzezinski and Vance, decided not to inform Congress of the plans. He did call in Robert Byrd, the Senate Majority leader, and inform him that there were plans for a rescue mission, but he did not tell him that the mission was actually under way.[68] When the failure of the mission was announced, a large number of Congressional leaders attacked the administration for breaking the terms of the War Powers Resolution.[69] Indeed, Senators Frank Church and Jacob Javits had written to Cyrus Vance the day before the rescue mission took place, stressing that the President was required to consult Congress before sending US troops into a potentially hostile situation.[70] While executive-legislative struggles are built into the wider political setting in which decision-making occurs, these struggles were bureaucratically-determined to the extent that any President would have had to face these pressures simply by being President. The role of President, by being located in a network of bureaucratic relationships with, for example, the Congress, axiomatically involved these struggles. Bureaucratic battles thus detract from any conception of a US national interest.

## CONCLUSION

In the three key meetings that led to the decision to undertake the hostage rescue mission, the evidence presented here suggests that the participants adopted positions that reflected their location in the bureaucratic structure. The influence of bureaucratic structure makes it possible to explain the change in policy that occurred between the 22 March meeting and that of 11 April. In each case, the same group proposed a rescue mission, and the same group (Vance on 22 March, Christopher on 11 April) opposed it. The change came about because the 'presidential supporters' and President Carter himself felt that the situation had altered significantly. While this alteration was due in part to external events (the breakdown of negotiations), the evidence presented above suggests that an even stronger reason was the extent of domestic criticism of Carter's inaction (especially after the Wisconsin primary fiasco). The 'presidential supporters' felt it was 'time to act.' For similar reasons, Cyrus Vance's inability to change the rescue decision at the 15 April meeting is also explicable from a bureaucratic political standpoint. In the event, of course, his doubts were only too clearly vindicated. What this case-study shows, therefore, is the limitations of an attempt to explain foreign policy decision-making as if the state were monolithic and as if 'it' had interests. Such an approach makes policy-making appear rational, and this is a major reason for the popularity of such a perspective; but the case of the hostage rescue mission amply demonstrates the limitations of such conceptions of rationality, in that the key decisions are more powerfully explained by the bureaucratic politics perspective.[71]

However, this conclusion requires some qualification since it raises fundamental problems about the precise claims advanced by proponents of the bureaucratic politics approach. As was noted earlier, the question that must be addressed is whether bureaucratic position alone leads to the adoption of certain policy positions.[72] As it stands, the bureaucratic politics approach is rather mechanical and static; it commits one to the rather simplistic notion that individuals will propose policy alternatives because of their bureaucratic position. Two problems emerge when this is applied to a case-study such as this one. The first is that the bureaucratic politics approach lacks a causal mechanism; it cannot simply be true that occupying a role in a bureaucratic structure leads the occupant to hold certain views. The second relates to the wider issue of belief systems, in that certain individuals are 'hawkish' irrespective of their precise position in a bureaucracy. The latter problem is most clearly illustrated by the case of Brzezinski, since it is arguable that whatever position he had occupied in Carter's administration, he would have adopted roughly similar views. Together, these problems force us to focus on one issue, namely, the exact meaning of the notion of role in the context of the bureaucratic politics approach.

This issue has been dealt with in the literature in the work of Alexander George and of Glenn Snyder and Paul Diesing.[73] George is concerned with the ways in which US decision-makers use (and abuse) information and advice in the policy process. He examines in some depth the ways in which individuals and bureaucracies will select information to assist their rather parochial goals. In other words, through his study of the use of information, George arrives at precisely the same kind of concern that this study has led to, namely, the relationship between individuals and their policy advocacy. More saliently, in their comprehensive survey of crisis decision-making, Snyder and Diesing discuss the psychological make-up of those groups of individuals named in their study (as in this) 'hawks' and 'doves.' They believe that 'hard and soft attitudes are more a function of personality than of governmental roles',[74] and they offer a very useful summary of what the world-views of hard and soft-liners are. As such, the works of George and of Snyder and Diesing are the best available discussions of the impact of role on belief and of belief on information processing. Yet neither of these two pieces of work provides the kind of analysis that would be required in order to solve the problems this case-study has indicated in the bureaucratic politics approach.

While it is clear that it is simplistic to assume that bureaucratic position *per se* causes policy preference, it is equally clear that bureaucratic position has some impact. Role, in and of itself, cannot explain the positions adopted by individuals;[75] after all, the very notion of role implies a certain latitude over how to play the role. Further, a role does not involve a single goal, and there is therefore significant room for manoeuvre and judgement in trading off various goals against each other. Thus, for example, it is not a sufficient explanation of Vance's position just to say that he was Secretary of State. There was a complex interplay between his role, his personality, the decision under consideration, and other personal and bureaucratic goals. Yet role occupiers do become predisposed to think in certain, bureaucratic, ways, and for a variety of psychological reasons they tend to adopt mind-sets compatible with those of their closest colleagues. In addition, individuals are often chosen for a specific post *because* they have certain kinds of world-views. So for reasons of selection, training, and the need to get on with colleagues, it is not surprising that individuals in certain jobs have certain world-views. Neither George nor Snyder and Diesing unravel the problem this leads to—how to distinguish between personal beliefs and bureaucratically instilled beliefs—indeed, the evidence of this case-study indicates that this is too crude a way of thinking about the problem. To answer the question, 'why are hawks hawks?' it is not sufficient to say either, that is the individual's personal world-view (for no account is given of the origins of that personal world-view) or, it is because of their bureaucratic position (as this passes over the crucial issue of the individual's ability to interpret their role). Thus, while it is clearly the case that Brzezinski was a hawk, it is neither accurate to say that this was because he was National Security Adviser (since this would not in and of itself cause hawkishness), nor to say that his views were simply personal (since it is surely the case that, had he been Secretary of State, he would have had to argue for courses of action other than those he did argue for—given the State Department's concern with getting the allies to agree on sanctions).

This case-study therefore leaves us with some critical questions unanswered. On the one hand, the empirical findings are important in that they illustrate the weaknesses of the rational actor approach as an explanation of foreign policy behaviour. States are not monoliths, and we might impute very misleading intentions to them if we assume that decisions are rational in this anthropomorphic way. The evidence indicates that the bureaucratic politics approach is very useful in explaining the decision to make an attempt to rescue the hostages. The linkage between the policy preferences of those individuals who made the decision and their bureaucratic position is a more powerful explanation of that decision than any of the alternatives. But, as in the case of any theory, it is tempting to try to portray the outcome as something completely explicable by it. It is not: the bureaucratic politics approach overemphasizes certain factors and underemphasizes others. On the other hand, the theoretical implications of this case-study force us to consider the issue of the sources of the beliefs of decision-makers. The 'hawks-doves' dichotomy is brought out very strongly in this case-study; and yet the bureaucratic politics approach as it stands is not capable of supporting a convincing mechanism for linking position and world-view. Therefore, the empirical and theoretical implications impel us to consider precisely that mechanism. What is needed is to link the concept of individual rationality with the structural influence of bureaucratic position. Neither Allison's work nor the subsequent work of George and Snyder and Diesing does this. This article, therefore, points both to the utility of the bureaucratic politics approach and to its theoretical weaknesses. The very fact that bureaucratic position was so important in determining policy preference over the decision to attempt to rescue the hostages makes the clarification of the nature of bureaucratic role all the more important. The nexus between individual rational action and bureaucratic structure appears to be one of the most promising, but also one of the most complex, avenues for foreign policy analysis to explore.

## NOTES

1. Graham Allison, *Essence of decision* (Boston: Little, Brown, 1971). 0020-5850/85/1/0009-17$3.00 © 1985 International Affairs.

2. Allison, *Essence of decision*, p. 145.

3. See Allison, *Essence of decision*, p. 176.

4. These criticisms are summarized in Steve Smith, 'Allison and the Cuban

missile crisis: a review of the bureaucratic politics model of foreign policy decision-making', *Millennium: Journal of International Studies*, Spring 1980, Vol. 9, No. 1, pp. 21–40.

5. Allison, *Essence of decision*, pp. 193–210.

6. Desmond Ball, 'The blind men and the elephant', *Australian Outlook*, 1974, Vol. 28, p. 77.

7. Robert Art, 'Bureaucratic politics and American foreign policy', *Policy Sciences*, 1973, Vol. 4, p. 473.

8. For an account of the rescue mission see Steve Smith, 'The hostage rescue mission', in Steve Smith and Michael Clarke, eds., *Foreign policy implementation* (London: Allen & Unwin, forthcoming, 1984).

9. Robert D. McFadden, Joseph B. Treaster and Maurice Carroll, *No hiding place* (New York: New York Times Books, 1981), p. 197.

10. The details of the planning for and the subsequent failure of the mission are discussed in Smith, 'The hostage rescue mission.'

11. Zbigniew Brzezinski, *Power and principle* (London: Weidenfeld & Nicolson, 1983), p. 493.

12. See Hamilton Jordan, *Crisis: the last year of the Carter presidency* (New York: G. P. Putnam's Sons, 1982), pp. 248–9.

13. Brzezinski, *Power and principle*, p. 487.

14. Jimmy Carter, *Keeping faith* (London: Collins, 1982), p. 512.

15. Carter, *Keeping faith*, p. 506.

16. *New York Times*, 17 Apr. 1980, p. A.1; 18 Apr. 1980, p. A.1.

17. *Boston Globe*, 16 Apr. 1980, p. 1.

18. *New York Times*, 23 Apr. 1980, p. A.1.

19. Jordan, *Crisis*, p. 263.

20. W. Safire, *International Herald Tribune*, 29 Apr. 1980, p. 5.

21. Drew Middleton, 'Going the military route', *New York Times Magazine*, 17 May 1981, p. 103.

22. Jordan, *Crisis*, pp. 258–9.

23. Brzezinski, *Power and principle*, pp. 487–8.

24. Brzezinski, *Power and principle*, pp. 488–9.

25. Brzezinski, *Power and principle*, p. 489.

26. Brzezinski, *Power and principle*, pp. 492.

27. Jordan, *Crisis*, p. 251; Brzezinski, *Power and principle*, pp. 493–4.

28. Brzezinski, *Power and principle*, pp. 492–3, 494.

29. *Keesings Contemporary Archives* 1980, p. 30532.

30. *The Times*, 1 May 1980, p. 16.

31. *International Herald Tribune*, 28 Apr. 1980, p. 1.

32. Pierre Salinger, *America held hostage* (New York: Doubleday, 1981), p. 238.

33. Brzezinski, *Power and principle*, pp. 489–90.

34. Jordan, *Crisis*, p. 251.

35. Jordan, *Crisis*, pp. 248–89.

36. Jordan, *Crisis*, pp. 248–9.

37. Jordan, *Crisis*, pp. 264, 275, 283 & 285, respectively.

38. Brzezinski, *Power and principle*, p. 490.

39. Jordan, *Crisis*, p. 248.

40. Salinger, *America held hostage*, p. 235. See also *Newsweek*, 5 May 1980, pp. 24–6, for a discussion of the domestic context.

41. Brzezinski, *Power and principle*, p. 493.

42. Cyrus Vance, *Hard choices* (New York: Simon & Schuster, 1983), p. 377.

43. Vance, *Hard choices*, p. 408.

142     *Bureaucratic Politics and Administration*

44. *International Herald Tribune,* 29 Apr. 1980, p. 1.
45. Tom Wicker, 'A tale of two silences', *New York Times,* 4 May 1980, p. E.23.
46. Carter, *Keeping faith,* p. 506; Brzezinski, *Power and principle,* p. 492; Jordan, *Crisis,* p. 250.
47. See Irving Janis, *Groupthink,* 2nd edn. (Boston: Houghton Mifflin, 1982). For a discussion of to the extent to which groupthink was present, see Steve Smith, 'Groupthink and the hostage rescue mission', *British Journal of Political Science,* forthcoming, 1985.
48. Jordan, *Crisis,* p. 251.
49. Wicker, 'A tale of two silences', p. E.23.
50. Brzezinski, *Power and principle,* p. 493.
51. McFadden *et al., No hiding place,* p. 220.
52. Brzezinski, *Power and principle,* p. 493.
53. Vance, *Hard choices,* p. 409.
54. The following summary of Vance's views is based upon Vance, *Hard choices,* pp. 409–10; Jordan, *Crisis,* pp. 252–4; Brzezinski, *Power and principle,* pp. 494–5; Carter, *Keeping faith,* p. 507; *The Times,* 29 Apr. 1980; *International Herald Tribune,* 29 Apr. 1980; *New York Times,* 28 & 29 Apr. 1980; *Keesings Contemporary Archives* 1980, p. 30532; *Facts on File,* Vol. 40, No. 2060, 2 May 1980.
55. Doyle McManus, *Free at last!* (New York: New American Library/*Los Angeles Times,* 1981), p. 149.
56. Brzezinski, *Power and principle,* p. 494.
57. Wicker, 'A tale of two silences', p. E.23.
58. Wicker, 'A tale of two silences', p. E.23.
59. Carter, *Keeping faith,* p. 513.
60. Brzezinski, *Power and principle,* p. 496; Carter, *Keeping faith,* pp. 510–11.
61. Jordan, *Crisis,* pp. 263–4.
62. *International Herald Tribune,* 29 Apr. 1980, p. 1.
63. Graham Allison and Morton Halperin, 'Bureaucratic politics: a paradigm and some policy implications', in Raymond Tanter and Richard Ullman, eds.: *Theory and policy in international relations* (Princeton: Princeton University Press, 1972), pp. 40–79.
64. The 1948 Key West Agreement was a compromise between the three branches of the US armed services over which service would perform which missions and would be responsible for procuring certain kinds of equipment.
65. Morton H. Halperin and David Halperin, 'The Key West key', *Foreign Policy,* Winter 1983–84, No. 53, pp. 124–5.
66. Richard Gabriel, 'A commando operation that was wrong from the start', *Canadian Defence Quarterly,* Vol. 10, No. 3, 1980–1, p. 9.
67. Joint Chiefs of Staff, Special Operations Review Group, *Rescue mission report* (Washington, DC: Joint Chiefs of Staff, 1980), p. 50.
68. Congressional Research Service, *Iran: consequences of the abortive attempt to rescue the hostages* (Washington, DC: Congressional Research Service, 2 May 1980), p. 26.
69. *New York Times,* 28 Apr. 1980; *The Times,* 29 Apr. 1980.
70. *Keesings Contemporary Archives* 1980, p. 30534.
71. Allison's other approach, the 'organizational process model', clearly has implications for this case. See Smith, 'The hostage rescue mission.'
72. I am much indebted to Phil Williams for making me aware of the problems in my original formulation of this argument.
73. Alexander George, *Presidential decision-making in foreign policy: the effective use of information and advice* (Boulder, Colo.: Westview, 1980); and Glenn

Snyder and Paul Diesing, *Conflict among nations* (Princeton, NJ: Princeton University Press, 1977).

74. Snyder and Diesing, *Conflict among nations,* p. 297.

75. I am grateful to Martin Hollis for suggesting these problems of over-mechanistic role conceptions to me.

# Part III

# BUREAUCRATIC POLITICS AND POLICY RELATIONSHIPS

*Bureaucrats play politics if for no other reason than the fact that they have policy relationships with political actors. In a pluralistic democracy such as the U.S.—where policy is made in a politically charged, ceaseless struggle between the president and Congress—bureaucracy participates daily in the give and take, push and shove of politics. Political institutions such as the presidency, the Congress and its staff, and various outside groups (contractors, consultants, organized private interests) bring political imperatives to bear on the policy process. Bureaucracy as a partner in this process participates in the bargaining, negotiating, compromising, and accommodating that produce policy. This section examines the policy relationships of bureaucracy with political actors as examples of bureaucratic politics. We want to emphasize that each relationship should be viewed as a distinctive exchange process, with each actor, together with bureaucracy, bringing certain perspectives, roles, and resources to the relationship. This theme will be developed in each of the subsequent subsections.*

# 6

## Bureaucratic Politics and Liaison with the Presidency

*The U.S. presidency is best envisioned as a collective entity of offices, staff, and supporting institutions rather than just the activities of a single person, although the president's individual personality is important indeed. Presidents wear many hats, and presidencies perform many functions. For a study of national security, the most important are those functions pertaining to commander-in-chief and chief executive. If any one conclusion seems warranted from a contemporary study of the U.S. presidency, it is that except for nuclear command and control and crisis management where there is a centralization of authority in the White House, presidents do not have a strict, neat chain of command control over bureaucracy. The processes of the chief executive are more akin to a bargaining arena than a hierarchy. Presidents are just one of many competitors at the table in many policy domains, and, as the other participants, they must bargain to get what they want. Granted, they bring impressive resources to the game: chips in the form of central prominence, media access, budgetary tools, agenda setting and public mobilizing opportunities, and substantial leverage over Congress. But so does the bureaucracy: expertise, external support, longevity.*

*In considering the presidency and the national security bureaucracy, keep two thoughts in mind. First, the president's presence in the policy process is through the National Security Counsel (NSC) and the Office of Management and Budget (OMB). Second, there is an inevitable institutionalized adverserial relationship between presidential institutions and established line bureaucracy, with the presidency viewing bureaucracy as too slow, cumbersome, and ingrained in the status quo, and the bureaucracy perceiving the presidency as amateurish, short-term, and too political.*

# 6.1     The Power to Persuade

## RICHARD NEUSTADT

*Richard Neustadt's classic study of presidential power, originally published in 1960, characterizes presidents more as bargainers than commanders, working in an arena where persuasive skills serve the president better than authoritarian ones. As students study Neustadt, they need to be aware of the debate surrounding the ethics of his prescriptions. Some would have us believe that for Neustadt any president's primary end is to maintain and enhance his power and that anything done toward this end is justifiable. Others conclude that Neustadt at worst is amoral, offering a checklist to presidents whose power will constantly be tested and threatened.*

The limits on command suggest the structure of our government. The constitutional convention of 1787 is supposed to have created a government of "separated powers." It did nothing of the sort. Rather, it created a government of separated institutions *sharing* powers.[1]  "I am part of the legislative process," Eisenhower often said in 1959 as a reminder of his veto.[2] Congress, the dispenser of authority and funds, is no less part of the administrative process. Federalism adds another set of separated institutions. The Bill of Rights adds others. Many public purposes can only be achieved by voluntary acts of private institutions; the press, for one, in Douglass Cater's phrase, is a "fourth branch of government."[3] And with the coming of alliances abroad, the separate institutions of a London, or a Bonn, share in the making of American public policy.

What the Constitution separates our political parties do not combine. The parties are themselves composed of separated organizations sharing public authority. The authority consists of nominating powers. Our national parties are confederations of state and local party institutions, with a headquarters that represents the White House, more or less, if the party has a president in office. These confederacies manage presidential nominations. All other public offices depend upon electorates confined within the states.[4] All other nominations are controlled within the states. The president and congressmen who bear one party's label are divided by independence upon

Reprinted with permission of Macmillan Publishing Company from *Presidential Power* by Richard E. Neustadt. (New York: Macmillan 1980) pp. 26-35.

different sets of voters. The differences are sharpest at the stage of nomination. The White House has too small a share in nominating congressmen, and Congress has too little weight in nominating presidents for party to erase their constitutional separation. Party links are stronger than is frequently supposed, but nominating processes assure the separation.[5]

The separateness of institutions and the sharing of authority prescribe the terms on which a president persuades. When one man shares authority with another, but does not gain or lose his job upon the other's whim, his willingness to act upon the urging of the other turns on whether he conceives the action right for him. The essence of a president's persuasive task is to convince such men that what the White House wants of them is what they ought to do for their sake and on their authority.

Persuasive power, thus defined, amounts to more than charm or reasoned argument. These have their uses for a president, but these are not the whole of his resources. For the men he would induce to do what he wants done on their own responsibility will need or fear some acts by him on his responsibility. If they share his authority, he has some share in theirs. Presidential "powers" may be inconclusive when a president commands, but always remain relevant as he persuades. The status and authority inherent in his office reinforce his logic and his charm.

Status adds something to persuasiveness; authority adds still more. When Truman urged wage changes on his secretary of commerce while the latter was administering the steel mills, he and Secretary Sawyer were not just two men reasoning with one another. Had they been so, Sawyer probably would never have agreed to act. Truman's status gave him special claims to Sawyer's loyalty, or at least attention. In Walter Bagehot's charming phrase "no man can *argue* on his knees." Although there is no kneeling in this country, few men—and exceedingly few cabinet officers— are immune to the impulse to say "yes" to the president of the United States. It grows harder to say "no" when they are seated in his oval office at the White House, or in his study on the second floor, where almost tangibly he partakes of the aura of his physical surroundings. In Sawyer's case, moreover, the president possessed formal authority to intervene in many matters of concern to the secretary of commerce. These matters ranged from jurisdictional disputes among the defense agencies to legislation pending before Congress and, ultimately, to the tenure of the secretary himself. There is nothing in the record to suggest that Truman voiced specific threats when they negotiated over wage increases. But given his *formal* powers and their relevance to Sawyer's other interests, it is safe to assume that Truman's very advocacy of wage action conveyed an implicit threat.

A president's authority and status give him great advantages in dealing with the men he would persuade. Each "power" is a vantage point for him in the degree that other men have use for his authority. From the veto to appointments, from publicity to budgeting, and so down a long list, the

White House now controls the most encompassing array of vantage points in the American political system. With hardly an exception, the men who share in governing this country are aware that at some time, in some degree, the doing of *their* jobs, the furthering of *their* ambitions, may depend upon the president of the United States. Their need for presidential action, or their fear of it, is bound to be recurrent if not actually continuous. Their need or fear is his advantage.

A president's advantages are greater than mere listing of his "powers" might suggest. The men with whom he deals must deal with him until the last day of his term. Because they have continuing relationships with him, his future, while it lasts, supports his present influence. Even though there is no need or fear of him today, what he could do tomorrow may supply today's advantage. Continuing relationships may convert any "power," any aspect of his status, into vantage points in almost any case. When he induces other men to do what he wants done, a president can trade on their dependence now *and* later.

The president's advantages are checked by the advantages of others. Continuing relationships will pull in both directions. These are relationships of mutual dependence. A president depends upon the men he would persuade; he has to reckon with his need or fear of them. They too will possess status, or authority, or both, else they would be of little use to him. Their vantage points confront his own; their power tempers his.

Persuasion is a two-way street. Sawyer, it will be recalled, did not respond at once to Truman's plan for wage increases at the steel mills. On the contrary, the secretary hesitated and delayed and only acquiesced when he was satisfied that publicly he would not bear the onus of decision. Sawyer had some points of vantage all his own from which to resist presidential pressure. If he had to reckon with coercive implications in the president's "situations of strength," so had Truman to be mindful of the implications underlying Sawyer's place as a department head, as steel administrator, and as a cabinet spokesman for business. Loyalty is reciprocal. Having taken on a dirty job in the steel crisis, Sawyer had strong claims to loyal support. Besides, he had authority to do some things that the White House could ill afford. Emulating Wilson, he might have resigned in a huff (the removal power also works two ways). Or emulating Ellis Arnall, he might have declined to sign necessary orders. Or, he might have let it be known publicly that he deplored what he was told to do and protested its doing. By following any of these courses Sawyer almost surely would have strengthened the position of management, weakened the position of the White House, and embittered the union. But the whole purpose of a wage increase was to enhance White House persuasiveness in urging settlement upon union and companies alike. Although Sawyer's status and authority did not give him the power to prevent an increase outright, they gave him capability to undermine its purpose. If his authority over wage rates had been vested by a statute, not by revocable presidential order, his power of prevention might have been complete. So Harold Ickes demonstrated in the famous case of helium sales to Germany before the Second World War.[6]

The power to persuade is the power to bargain. Status and authority yield bargaining advantages. But in a government of "separated institutions sharing powers," they yield them to all sides. With the array of vantage points at his disposal, a president may be far more persuasive than his logic or his charm could make him. But outcomes are not guaranteed by his advantages. There remain the counter pressures those whom he would influence can bring to bear on him from vantage points at their disposal. Command has limited utility; persuasion becomes give-and-take. It is well that the White House holds the vantage points it does. In such a business any president may need them all—and more.

## II

This view of power as akin to bargaining is one we commonly accept in the sphere of congressional relations. Every textbook states and every legislative session demonstrates that save in times like the extraordinary Hundred Days of 1933—times virtually ruled out by definition at mid-century—a president will often be unable to obtain congressional action on his terms or even to halt action he opposes. The reverse is equally accepted: Congress often is frustrated by the president. Their formal powers are so intertwined that neither will accomplish very much, for very long, without the acquiescence of the other. By the same token, though, what one demands the other can resist. The stage is set for that great game, much like collective bargaining, in which each seeks to profit from the other's needs and fears. It is a game played catch-as-catch-can, case by case. And everybody knows the game, observers and participants alike.

The concept of real power as a give-and-take is equally familiar when applied to presidential influence outside the formal structure of the federal government. The Little Rock affair may be extreme, but Eisenhower's dealings with the governor—and with the citizens—become a case in point. Less extreme but no less pertinent is the steel seizure case with respect to union leaders, and to workers, and to company executives as well. When he deals with such people a president draws bargaining advantage from his status or authority. By virtue of their public places or their private rights they have some capability to reply in kind.

In spheres of party politics the same thing follows, necessarily, from the confederal nature of our party organizations. Even in the case of national nominations a president's advantages are checked by those of others. In 1944 it is by no means clear that Roosevelt got his first choice as his running mate. In 1948 Truman, then the president, faced serious revolts against his nomination. In 1952 his intervention from the White House helped assure the choice of Adlai Stevenson, but it is far from clear that Truman could have done as much for any other candidate acceptable to him.[7] In 1956 when Eisenhower was president, the record leaves obscure just who backed Harold Stassen's effort to block Richard Nixon's renomination as vice-president. But evidently everything did not go quite as Eisenhower wanted, whatever his intentions may have been.[8] The outcomes in these instances bear all the marks of limits on command and of power checked by power that characterize congressional relations. Both in and out of politics these checks and limits seem to be quite widely understood.

Influence becomes still more a matter of give-and-take when presidents attempt to deal with allied governments. A classic illustration is the long unhappy wrangle over Suez policy in 1956. In dealing with the British and the French before their military intervention, Eisenhower had his share of bargaining advantages but no effective power of command. His allies had their share of counter pressures, and they finally tried the most extreme of all: action despite him. His pressure then was instrumental in reversing them. But had the British government been on safe ground *at home*, Eisenhower's wishes might have made as little difference after intervention as before. Behind the decorum of diplomacy—which was not very decorous in the Suez affair—relationships among allies are not unlike relationships among state delegations at a national convention. Power is persuasion and persuasion becomes bargaining. The concept is familiar to everyone who watches foreign policy.

In only one sphere is the concept unfamiliar: the sphere of executive relations. Perhaps because of civics textbooks and teaching in our schools, Americans instinctively resist the view that power in this sphere resembles power in all others. Even Washington reporters, White House aides, and congressmen are not immune to the illusion that administrative agencies comprise a single structure, "the" executive branch, where presidential word is law, or ought to be. Yet . . . when a president seeks something from executive officials his persuasiveness is subject to the same sorts of limitations as in the case of congressmen, or governors, or national committeemen, or private citizens, or foreign governments. There are no generic differences, no differences in kind and only sometimes in degree. The incidents preceding the dismissal of MacArthur and the incidents surrounding seizure of the steel mills make it plain that here as elsewhere influence derives from bargaining advantages; power is a give-and-take.

Like our governmental structure as whole, the executive establishment consists of separated institutions sharing powers. The president heads one of these; cabinet officers, agency administrators, and military commanders head others. Below the departmental level, virtually independent bureau chiefs head many more. Under mid-century conditions, federal operations spill across dividing lines on organization charts, almost every policy entangles many agencies; almost every program calls for interagency collaboration. Everything somehow involves the president. But operating agencies owe their existence least of all to one another—and only in some part to him. Each has a separate statutory base; each has its statutes to administer; each deals with a different set of subcommittees at the Capitol. Each has its own peculiar set of clients, friends, and enemies outside the formal government. Each has a different set of specialized careerists inside its own bailiwick. Our Constitution gives the president the "take-care" clause and the appointive power. Our statutes give him central budgeting and a degree of personnel control. All agency administrators are responsible to him. But they *also* are responsible to Congress, to their clients, to their staffs, and to themselves. In short, they have five masters. Only after all of those do they owe any loyalty to each other.

"The members of the Cabinet," Charles G. Dawes used to remark, "are a president's natural enemies." Dawes had been Harding's budget director, Coolidge's vice-president, and Hoover's ambassador to London; he also had been General Pershing's chief assistant for supply in the First World War. The words are highly colored, but Dawes knew whereof he spoke. The men who have to serve so many masters cannot help but be somewhat the "enemy" of any one of them. By the same token, any master wanting service is in some degree the "enemy" of such a servant. A president is likely to want loyal support but not to relish trouble on his doorstep. Yet the more his cabinet members cleave to him, the more they may need help from him in fending off the wrath of rival masters. Help, though, is synonymous with trouble. Many a Cabinet officer, with loyalty ill-rewarded by his lights and help withheld, has come to view the White House as innately hostile to department heads. Dawe's dictum can be turned around.

A senior presidential aide remarked to me in Eisenhower's time: "If some of these Cabinet members would just take time out to stop and ask themselves, 'What would I want if I were President?', they wouldn't give him all the trouble he's been having." But even if they asked themselves the question, such officials often could not act upon the answer. Their personal attachment to the President is all too often overwhelmed by duty to their other masters.

Executive officials are not equally advantaged in their dealings with a President. Nor are the same officials equally advantaged all the time. Not every officeholder can resist like a MacArthur, or like Arnall, Sawyer, Wilson, in a rough descending order of effective counter pressure. The vantage points conferred upon officials by their own authority and status vary enormously. The variance is heightened by particulars of time and circumstance. In mid-October 1950, Truman, at a press conference, remarked of the man he had considered firing in August and would fire the next April for intolerable insubordination:

> Let me tell you something that will be good for your souls. It's a pity that you . . . can't understand the ideas of two intellectually honest men when they met. General MacArthur . . . is a member of the Government of the United States. He is loyal to that Government. He is loyal to the President. He is loyal to the President in his foreign policy. . . .There is no disagreement between General MacArthur and myself.[9]

MacArthur's status in and out of government was never higher than when Truman spoke those words. The words, once spoken, added to the General's credibility thereafter when he sought to use the press in his campaign against the President. And what had happened between August and October? Near-victory had happened together with that premature conference on *post*-war plans, the meeting at Wake Island.

If the bargaining advantages of a MacArthur fluctuate with changing circumstances, this is bound to be so with subordinates who have at their disposal fewer "powers," lesser status, to fall back on. And when officials have no "powers" in their own right, or depend upon the president for status, their counter pressure may be limited indeed. White House aides, who fit both categories, are among the most responsive men of all, and for good reason. As a director of the budget once remarked to me, "Thank God I'm here and not across the street. If the president doesn't call me, I've got plenty I can do right here and plenty coming up to me, by rights, to justify my calling him. But those poor fellows over there, if the boss doesn't call them, doesn't ask them to do something, what *can* they do but sit?" Authority and status so conditional are frail reliances in resisting a president's own wants. Within the White House precincts, lifted eyebrows may suffice to set an aide in motion; command, coercion, even charm aside. But even in the White House a president does not monopolize effective power. Even there persuasion is akin to bargaining. A former Roosevelt aide once wrote of cabinet officers:

> Half of a president's suggestions, which theoretically carry the weight of orders, can be safely forgotten by a cabinet member. And if the president asks about a suggestion a second time, he can be told that it is being investigated. If he asks a third time, a wise cabinet officer will give him at least part of what he suggests. But only occasionally, except about the most important matters, do presidents ever get around to asking three times.[10]

The rule applies to staff as well as to the cabinet, and certainly has been applied *by* staff in Truman's time and Eisenhower's.

Some aides will have more vantage points than a selective memory. Sherman Adams, for example, as *the* assistant to the president under Eisenhower, scarcely deserved the appelation "White House aide" in the meaning of the term before his time or as applied to other members of the

Eisenhower entourage. Although Adams was by no means "chief of staff" in any sense so sweeping—or so simple—as press commentaries often took for granted, he apparently became no more dependent on the president than Eisenhower on him. "I need him," said the president when Adams turned out to have been remarkably imprudent in the Goldfine case, and delegated to him even the decision on his own departure.[11] This instance is extreme, but the tendency it illustrates is common enough. Any aide who demonstrates to others that he has the president's consistent confidence and a consistent part in presidential business will acquire so much business on his own account that he becomes in some sense independent of his chief. Nothing in the Constitution keeps a well-placed aide from converting status into power of his own, usable in some degree even against the president—an outcome not unknown in Truman's regime or, by all accounts, in Eisenhower's.

The more an officeholder's status and his "powers" stem from sources independent of the president, the stronger will be his potential pressure *o n* the president. Department heads in general have more bargaining power than do most members of the White House staff; but bureau chiefs may have still more, and specialists at upper levels of established career services may have almost unlimited reserves of the enormous power which consists of sitting still. As Franklin Roosevelt once remarked:

> The Treasury is so large and far-flung and ingrained in its practices that I find it is almost impossible to get the action and results I want—even with Henry [Morgenthau] there. But the Treasury is not to be compared with the State Department. You should go through the experience of trying to get any changes in the thinking, policy, and action of the career diplomats and then you'd know what a real problem was. But the Treasury and the State Department put together are nothing compared with the Na-a-vy. The admirals are really something to cope with—and I should know. To change anything in the Na-a-vy is like punching a feather bed. You punch it with your right and you punch it with your left until you are finally exhausted, and then you find the damn bed just as it was before you started punching.[12]

In the right circumstances, of course, a president can have his way with any of these people. Chapter 2 includes three instances where circumstances were "right" and a presidential order was promptly carried out. But one need only note the favorable factors giving those three orders their self-executing quality to recognize that as between a president and his "subordinates," no less than others on whom he depends, real power is reciprocal and varies markedly with organization, subject matter, personality, and situation. The mere fact that persuasion is directed at executive officials signifies no necessary easing of his way. Any new congressman of the administration's party, especially if narrowly elected, may turn out more amenable (though less useful) to the president than any seasoned bureau chief "downtown."

*The probabilities of power do not derive from the literary theory of the Constitution.*

## III

There is a widely held belief in the United States that were it not for folly or for knavery, a reasonable president would need no power other than the logic of his argument. No less a personage than Eisenhower has subscribed to that belief in many a campaign speech and press-conference remark. But faulty reasoning and bad intentions do not cause all quarrels with presidents. The best of reasoning and of intent cannot compose them all. For in the first place, what the president wants will rarely seem a trifle to the men he wants it from. And in the second place, they will be bound to judge it by the standard of their own responsibilities, not his. However logical his argument according to his lights, their judgment may not bring them to his view.

The men who share in governing this country frequently appear to act as though they were in business for themselves. So, in a real though not entire sense, they are and have to be. When Truman and MacArthur fell to quarreling, for example, the stakes were no less than the substance of American foreign policy, the risks of greater war or military stalemate, the prerogatives of presidents and field commanders, the pride of a pro-consul, and his place in history. Intertwined, inevitably, were other stakes, as well: political stakes for men and factions of both parties; power stakes for interest groups with which they were or wished to be affiliated. And every stake was raised by the apparent discontent in the American public mood. There is no reason to suppose that in such circumstances men of large but differing responsibilities will see all things through the same glasses. On the contrary, it is to be expected that their views of what ought to be done and what they then should do will vary with the differing perspectives their particular responsibilities evoke. Since their duties are not vested in a "team" or a "collegium" but in themselves, as individuals, one must expect that they will see things *for* themselves. Moreover, when they are responsible to many masters and when an event or policy turns loyalty against loyalty—a day-by-day occurrence in the nature of the case—one must assume that those who have the duties to perform will choose the terms of reconciliation. This is the essence of their personal responsibility. When their own duties pull in opposite directions, who else but they can choose what they will do?

When Truman dismissed MacArthur, the latter lost three posts: the American command in the Far East, the Allied command for the occupation of Japan, and the United Nations command in Korea. He also lost his status as the senior officer on active duty in the United States armed forces. So long as he held those positions and that status, though, he had a duty to his troops, to his profession, to himself (the last is hard for any man to disentangle from the rest). As a public figure and a focus for men's hopes he had a duty to constituents at home, and in Korea and Japan. He owed a duty also to those other constituents, the UN governments contributing to his field forces. As a patriot he had a duty to his country. As an accountable official and an expert guide he stood at the call of Congress. As a military officer he had, besides, a duty to the president, his constitutional commander. Some of these duties may have manifested themselves in terms more tangible or more direct than others. But it would be nonsense to argue that the last *negated* all the rest, however much it might be claimed to override them. And it makes no more sense to think that anybody but MacArthur was effectively empowered to decide how he, himself, would reconcile the competing demands his duties made upon him.

Similar observations could be made about the rest of the executive officials encountered in Chapter 2. Price Director Arnall, it will be recalled, refused in advance to sign a major price increase for steel if Mobilization Director Wilson or the White House should concede one before management had settled with the union. When Arnall did this, he took his stand, in substance, on his oath of office. He would do what he had sworn to do in *his* best judgment, so long as he was there to do it. This posture may have been assumed for purposes of bargaining and might have been abandoned had his challenge been accepted by the president. But no one could be sure and no one, certainly, could question Arnall's right to make the judgment for himself. As head of an agency and as a politician, with a program to defend and a future to advance, *he* had to decide what he had to do on matters that, from his perspective, were exceedingly important. Neither in policy nor in personal terms, nor in terms of agency survival, were the issues of a sort to be considered secondary by an Arnall, however much they might have seemed so to a Wilson (or a Truman). Nor were the merits likely to appear the same to a price stabilizer and to men with broader duties. Reasonable men, it is so often said, *ought* to be able to agree on the requirements of given situations. But when the outlook varies with the placement of each man, and the response required in his place is for each to decide, their reasoning may lead to disagreement quite as well—and quite as reasonably. Vanity, or vice, may weaken reason, to be sure, but it is idle to assign these as the cause of Arnall's threat of MacArthur's defiance. Secretary Sawyer's hesitations, cited earlier, are in the same category. One need not denigrate such men to explain their conduct. For the responsibilities they felt, the "facts" they saw, simply were not the same as those of their superiors; yet they, not the superiors, had to decide what they would do.

Outside the executive branch the situation is the same, except that loyalty to the president may often matter *less*. There is no need to spell out the comparison with governors of Arkansas, steel company executives, trade union leaders, and the like. And when one comes to congressmen who can do nothing for themselves (or their constituents) save as they are elected, term by term, in districts and through party structures *differing* from those on which a president depends, the case is very clear. An able Eisenhower aide with long congressional experience remarked to me in 1958: "The people on the Hill don't do what they might *like* to do, they do what they think they *have* to do in their own interest as *they* see it. . . ." This states the case precisely.

The essence of a president's persuasive task with congressmen and everybody else *is to induce them to believe that what he wants of them is what their own appraisal of their own responsibilities requires them to do in their interest, not his.* Because men may differ in their views on public policy, because differences in outlook stem from differences in duty—duty to one's office, one's constituents, oneself—that task is bound to be more like collective bargaining than like a reasoned argument among philosopher kings. Overtly or implicitly, hard bargaining has characterized all illustrations offered up to now. This is the reason why: persuasion deals in the coin of self-interest with men who have some freedom to reject what they find counterfeit.

## NOTES

1. The reader will want to keep in mind the distinction between two senses in which the word *power* is employed. When I have used the word (or its plural) to refer to formal constitutional, statutory, or customary authority, it is either qualified by the adjective "formal" or placed in quotation marks as "power(s)." Where I have used it in the sense of effective influence upon the conduct of others, it appears without quotation marks (and always in the singular). Where clarity and convenience permit, *authority* is substituted for "power" in the first sense and *influence* for power in the second sense.

2. See, for example, his press conference of July 22, 1959, as reported in the *New York Times* for July 23, 1959.

3. See Douglas Cater, *The Fourth Branch of Government,* Boston: Houghton-Mifflin, 1959.

4. With the exception of the vice-presidency, of course.

5. See David B. Truman's illuminating study of party relationships in the 81st Congress, *The Congressional Party,* New York: Wiley, 1959, especially chaps. 4, 6, and 8.

6. As Secretary of the Interior in 1939, Harold Ickes refused to approve the sale of helium to Germany despite the insistence of the State Department and the urging of President Roosevelt. Without the Secretary's approval, such sales were forbidden by statute. See *The Secret Diaries of Harold L. Ickes,* New York: Simon and Schuster, 1954, Vol. 2, especially 391-393, 396-399. See also Michael J. Reagan, "The Helium Controversy" in the forthcoming case book on civil-military relations prepared for the Twentieth Century Fund under the editorial direction of Harold Stein.

In this instance the statutory authority ran to the secretary as a matter of *his* discretion. A president is unlikely to fire cabinet officers for conscientious exercise of such authority. If the president did so, their successors might well be embarrassed both publicly and at the Capitol were they to reverse decisions previously taken. As for a president's authority to set aside discretionary determination of this sort, it rests, if it exists at all, on shaky legal ground not likely to be trod save in the gravest situations.

7. Truman's *Memoirs* indicate that having tried and failed to make Stevenson an avowed candidate in the spring of 1952, the president decided to support the candidacy of vice-president Barkley. But Barkley withdrew early in the convention for lack of key northern support. Though Truman is silent on the matter, Barkley's active candidacy nearly was revived during the balloting, but the forces then aligning to revive it were led by opponents of Truman's Fair Deal, principally Southerners. As a practical matter, the president could not have lent his weight to *their* endeavors and could back no one but Stevenson to counter them. The latter's strength could not be shifted, then, to Harriman or Kefauver. Instead the other Northerners had to be withdrawn. Truman helped withdraw them. But he had no other option. See Memoirs by Harry S. Truman, Vol. 2, *Years of Trial and Hope,* Garden City: Doubleday, 1956, copr. 1956 Time Inc., 495-496.

8. The reference is to Stassen's public statement of July 23, 1956, calling for Nixon's replacement on the Republican ticket by Governor Herter of Massachusetts, the later secretary of state. Stassen's statement was issued after a conference with the president. Eisenhower's public statements on the vice-presidential nomination, both before and after Stassen's call, permit of alternative inferences: either that the president would have preferred another candidate, provided this could be arranged without a showing of White House dictation, or that he wanted Nixon on condition that the latter could show popular appeal. In the event, neither result was achieved. Eisenhower's own remarks lent strength to rapid party moves which smothered Stassen's effort. Nixon's nomination thus was guaranteed too quickly to appear the consequence of popular demand. For the public record on this matter see reported statements by Eisenhower, Nixon, Stassen, Herter, and Leonard Hall (the National Republican Chairman) in the *New York Times* for March 1, 8, 15, 16; April 27; July 15, 16, 25-31; August 3, 4, 17, 23, 1956. See also the account from private sources by Earl Mazo in *Richard Nixon: A Personal and Political Portrait,* New York: Harper, 1959, 158-187.

9. Stenographic transcript of presidential press conference, October 19, 1950, on file in the Truman Library at Independence, Missouri.

10. Jonathan Daniels, *Frontier on the Potomac,* New York: Macmillan, 1946, 31-32.

11. Transcript of presidential press conference, June 18, 1958, in *Public Papers of the Presidents: Dwight D. Eisenhower, 1958,* Washington: The National Archives, 1959, 479. In the summer of 1958, a congressional investigation into the affairs of a New England textile manufacturer, Bernard Goldfine, revealed that Sherman Adams had accepted various gifts and favors from him (the most notoriety attached to a vicuña coat). Adams also had made inquiries about the status of a Federal Communications Commission proceeding in which Goldfine was involved. In September 1958, Adams was allowed to resign. The episode was highly publicized and much discussed in that year's congressional campaigns.

12. As reported in Marriner S. Eccles, *Beckoning Frontiers,* New York: Knopf, 1951, 336.

# 6.2    Office of Management and Budget and National Security Policy in the Carter Administration

## EDWARD R. (RANDY) JAYNE II

*Often viewed as an outsider, the role of the Office of Management and Budget (OMB) in the national security policy process seldom receives the attention it deserves. In this article, Dr. Jayne explores OMB's performance during the four years of the Carter presidency. Dr. Jayne argues that OMB's functions are shaped significantly by presidential style and character. He draws the reader's attention to the broader issues of presidential leadership, White House staff function, and departmental interaction. He concludes by noting that OMB's involvement in national security policymaking was extensive and unique—and almost directly attributable to Carter's penchant for detail. Whether this degree of inclusion served the nation well or poorly is left to the reader to decide.*

Studies of presidential leadership are an important and enduring part of understanding U.S. politics. Our fascination with individual presidents often causes us to think of such works primarily as documentations of those personalities. However, accurate recountings of a president's style and management must include insight into more than just the men themselves and their political inner circles. The Rostows, Kissingers, Jordans, and Bakers play critical roles, but they do so in concert—or conflict, as the case may be—with the professional staffs within the Executive Office of the president.

The career organizations within the Executive Office are led by the president's men, but the institutions themselves maintain an identity all their own. The purpose of this chapter is to examine one such part of the Executive Office, the Office of Management and Budget (OMB). The focus is narrow, confined to a particular set of policies, that is, national security and the four years of Jimmy Carter's presidency. The story is about a president's influence on and use of OMB and correspondingly about the budget organization's impact on the president and his national security policy.

OMB's image among participants in and students of presidential leadership and management is rarely a neutral one; rather, it often appears to be one of two extremes. For some, OMB is the ultimate enduring institution, working its will of *less is more* throughout the federal program, independent of and in many ways indifferent to the particular political preferences of the person occupying the Oval Office. For holders of this view, the budget agency is a bureaucracy to be avoided, a barrier to work around and through as an administration endeavors to execute its political philosophy in spite of the many federal institutions in Washington. For other observers, this same OMB is instead a particularly potent resource of career civil service staff skills available to be applied, through an administration's own politically appointed leadership, to the president's agenda.

To preview to an extent the conclusions of this chapter, I find the real OMB somewhere between these two extremes, with the exact center of gravity of the institution varying significantly with the style and character of the president, his budget director, and the other senior advisers and cabinet members within each administration. In describing the role of OMB in national security policy in the Carter administration, a number of broader elements of presidential leadership, White House staff function, departmental interaction with the Executive Office, and other aspects of U.S. politics will by necessity be treated.

Before proceeding, two caveats are appropriate. First, no set of anecdotes such as this can provide full flavor or perspective on the subject at hand. I hope what follows will be sufficient to allow the reader to come to some independent judgments as to where on our theoretical spectrum of OMB roles Jimmy Carter's 1977–1980 system falls. Second, by way of a warning to the reader, it seems a somewhat universal characteristic of remembrances by those who serve and then write about those experiences that their roles are recalled as particularly deep and substantive.[1] With those warnings in mind, let us begin.

OMB's specific role in national security policy began to emerge even prior to the first days of the Carter presidency. Jimmy Carter's transition team had arrived in Washington in the last weeks of 1976 with a clear charter from the president-elect to overhaul a number of policies and institutions, and high on the list was the defense budget being structured by the outgoing Ford administration. The campaign promise to cut $8 billion dollars from that $123 billion program was a deep and personal commitment of the newly elected Democrat. The transition team had prepared detailed recommendations as to how the administration might act to fulfill the campaign commitment in FY78. Even before the inauguration, the OMB and National Security Council (NSC) staffs began analyzing the transition team material. In a series of meetings that started in the first week of the administration, the new president reviewed the defense program in depth.

In those early meetings, the campaign and transition staffs provided extensive plans as to specific cuts to be made in Department of Defense

(DoD) programs. It was OMB, however, that quickly emerged as the technical experts, the only source of data and perspective equal to the new president's voracious appetite for programmatic and financial detail. Out of that initial set of reviews, significant beginnings of both process and policy emerged. First, Carter created a budget review approach, not only for defense, but for most other functions, too, in which OMB Director Bert Lance and the senior OMB staff were first among equals in the Executive Office staff. Others participated, including the National Security Council staff, Domestic Policy staff, and others, but the center of discussion and debate involved the cabinet officer and his staff—in this case, Defense Secretary Harold Brown and his first deputy, Charles Duncan—and the OMB staff, including in many cases senior career civil servants as well as Carter's own recent political appointees.

The main participants in those sessions, accompanied by their staffs, were Vice President Walter Mondale, Secretary Brown, National Security Advisor Zbigniew Brzezinski, and Lance. As should be expected, the two principals able to engage in debate most actively were the two with large career staffs, Brown and Lance. Given the president's commitment to reduce military spending and his clear and oft-stated distrust of the bureaucracy, he quickly turned to his budget office as his primary source of independent data and analysis. Independence in this case of course really meant different from DoD. OMB's institutional role as budget slasher was in some cases partially suppressed but was never completely sacrificed in the name of independence. All presidents in the past two decades have used OMB's expertise in defense, but arguably no others did so to the extent that Carter did, and the trend and style of that relationship were set in those initial meetings.

The president's political advisors, including the OMB leadership, concluded early on that the $8 billion campaign reduction promise was not only politically impossible, but also not in the best interests of national security. The senior national security advisers—Brown, Brzezinski, Lance, Secretary of State Cyrus Vance, and the JCS Chairman Gen. George Brown—were unanimous in their view that $8 billion was too large a reduction, both for national security reasons and because of Congress' views. The president, having gone through the entire DoD budget in detail, agreed but only after hearing strong support for the original $8 billion commitment voiced by the vice president and several senior White House advisers. The budget that had been prepared by the Ford administration was cut, to a larger degree than DoD would have liked, but less than other key members of the president's staff wanted.[2]

The initial defense budget adjustments, while lower than the military services had feared, nonetheless challenged a variety of key service programs and set the stage for four years of continuous debate on certain of those items. By far the most controversial was the B-1 bomber. The president sought cancellation, and the air force fought to sustain the program. The resulting action was viewed by most of the public and media as a major cost-cutting cancellation. In fact, a compromise was made, terminating production plans, but continuing an extensive full-scale development (FSD) program for the B-1A. Further, a major commitment was made to both cruise missiles and the MX—selected by the president as preferable strategic force alternatives to the proposed new bomber. OMB joined Secretary Brown and the NSC staff in crafting this approach, and the then air force chief of staff, General David Jones, cemented his subsequent selection as JCS chairman by choosing to support rather than oppose this strategy.[3]

For military services accustomed to debating OMB primarily in the back rooms of the Pentagon early in the budget cycle, the new Carter environment was a radical and somewhat painful change. OMB had always sent its issue books to the Oval Office, recommending program cuts and policy changes. However, this president was accepting many of those recommendations, even over the objections of the defense secretary, national security adviser, and others. The service with the staunchest tradition of independence, the navy, reacted perhaps the most strongly to this pattern.

Beginning well before President Carter's term, the navy had worked to secure a major buildup of surface combatants. Of the three services, the navy had clearly suffered most in the Vietnam era, when what little major weapons procurement that occurred had concentrated on replacing older air and land forces. The navy simply and clearly stated its goal to achieve a 600-ship force. The shipbuilding program implied by that goal far exceeded the funding that the new president was willing to commit. In Jimmy Carter's mind, it was more than a question on money. The Naval Academy graduate and former nuclear submarine officer seemed to all those involved in the defense budget process to be particularly tough on his former service, especially when it came to arguments about surface force projection and ship vulnerability in combat.

The uniformed navy conducted an aggressive and effective three-pronged effort to increase their share of the new defense budget. Within the Pentagon, the service found active and expert support from its newly appointed civilian leadership, Secretary Graham Claytor and Undersecretary James Woolsey. Secretary of Defense Brown walked a thin line between implementing the letter of the president's position and representing the navy's views. Second, the navy used the media and public interchange to make its case. A major academic analysis led by faculty members of the Naval War College supported the 600-ship requirement.

Finally, as has been the case for many years, the navy found strong backing in the Congress. Both Armed Services Committees provided highly supportive and visible forums for the service to argue its views. It was a combination of these latter two aspects of the navy's effort—the War College study and Congressional support—that led to a significant and somewhat uncommon example of Carter OMB participation in national security policy.

In March 1978 the navy staged a major strategy conference at the Naval War College in Newport, Rhode Island, with a highly visible program of speakers who would talk on naval strategy, force requirements, and budgets. An invitation to speak was extended to me, who, as OMB associate director for national security and international affairs (NSIA), was asked to discuss resource requirements to support navy force structure. Sandwiched between senior navy spokespersons and advocates, it was an opportunity for the service to send its message even more clearly to the president and his advisors, and to a broader audience, as to why the 600-ship requirement was justified.

To many in the Executive Office, the conference had all the makings of a blockbuster media event in which a service would publicly debate the president. The OMB presentation could have taken any of a number of forms and tone. In the end, after significant exchange with the OMB director, national security adviser, Mondale, and others, and the approval of the president, I wrote the speech as a direct reflection of the chief executive's strong personal doubts as to the effectiveness and affordability of the navy's shipbuilding plan.

The result, unavoidably, was front page news.[4] The navy had delivered a volley, and Jimmy Carter had fired back. That much was not particularly unique. What was unusual, however, was that the messenger came not from the office of the secretary of defense or the NSC, but from OMB. Carter supporters, especially those concerned that military spending remained too high, voiced their approval at the public nature of the White House response. The navy's supporters, conversely, were extremely critical, challenging both the substance and the form of the OMB message. The budget office found itself, for better or worse, firmly in the middle of the defense policy process.

The final chapter of this navy story highlights some of the most negative reaction to this OMB role. Within the Congress, perhaps the strongest support for the 600-ship force came from the House Armed Services Seapower Subcommittee. Subcommittee Chairman Charles Bennett (D-Fla.), arguably the most informed naval expert in the House, was particularly upset by the OMB speech. Urged by his staff, Chairman Bennett invited the OMB associate director to appear before the subcommittee in the weeks immediately following the Newport speech. Historically, both Democratic and Republican administrations have followed a well established policy regarding such testimony. As a rule, Executive Office officials (OMB, Council of Economic Advisers, and others) do not appear before any authorizing committee or its subcommittees. Such appearances are the responsibility of the executive branch department or agency. OMB did appear before budget-related committees or those responsible for economic policy but historically avoided any and all authorization panels, leaving those to line management.

Congressman Bennett, however, was adamant and publicly threatened to issue a subpoena. After much White House debate, I was sent forth to meet the Seapower Subcommittee. Many of the president's advisers seemed anxious to continue the debate and urged a repeat of the Newport message. Others wanted to further stir the controversy by having the testimony remind the subcommittee that it was inappropriate for a Democratic panel to break years of tradition on Executive Office appearance rules, especially by threatening to subpoena a Democratic adviser delivering a message from their president.

The best advice, at least from the perspective of the testifier, came from three young Democrats on the subcommittee, congressmen Les Aspin, Tom Downey, and Bob Carr. All three held views on naval strategy more akin to the president's, and all three fully appreciated the need to avoid any needless alienation of conservative House Democrats already chafing at the Carter defense plan. With much help from these three legislators, the testimony took the form of a moderately worded outline of the president's overall defense program and budget priorities, and the role of the navy within that framework.[5] After being soundly chastised by certain members of the panel regarding OMB even thinking about policy matters (as opposed to budget matters, a distinction without a difference, of course), I was allowed to return to OMB, where the committee hoped I would, persuaded, confine myself in the future to more traditional *green eyeshade* types of work.

For reasons far broader than this minor confrontation, President Carter has been criticized extensively for a pattern of relatively weak and ineffective congressional liaison throughout his administration. We should not leave the subject of OMB, defense policy, and the legislative branch, then, without covering an example of cooperation and joint policymaking that worked quite well. Unlike the Reagan presidency, the Carter years found both President and Congress willing and able to work together on a plan of specific programs and funding levels to reduce the federal deficit. Granted, the absolute deficits were profoundly smaller then than in the 1980s, but they nonetheless represented comparably painful percentages of the federal program.

The administration joined forces with the House and Senate Budget Committees, led by Congressman Robert Giaimo and Senator Edmund Muskie, in an effort to make across-the-board reductions. OMB, represented by the new director, James McIntyre; deputy director, John P. White; executive associate director (EAD), W. Bowman Cutter; and the four program associate directors (or PADS, in the jargon), led the effort for the president.[6] Throughout most of the legislative session in 1979, joint meetings took place on Capital Hill, and they reached painful, yet effective agreements to lower spending in many nondefense areas.

These deliberations were directly influenced by another element of the Carter administration's national security policy, one that has had a profound and in many ways negative impact on the defense program and budget process for a decade. The issue was the policy, jointly adopted along with U.S. North Atlantic Treaty Organization (NATO) allies, of sustaining 3 percent real growth in defense spending each year. In the congressional-executive deliberations described here, the 3 percent growth policy was a continuous and contentious irritant, essential fencing off a level of defense budget dollars. That level, argued as sacrosanct by the president and certain of his key advisers, was set and defended purely by the mathematics of the 3 percent formula, independent of the programs and requirements involved.[7]

OMB's role in implementing the 3 percent policy was neither positive nor pleasant. It was difficult for the budget office or anyone else to oppose the original goal of the policy, for example, to help force U.S. allies into a sustained pattern of more significant and appropriate sharing of the joint defense burden. Further, most national security experts at the time shared the view that the decade of Vietnam had left a legacy of obsolete weapons and antique equipment. A long list of investment requirements called for sustained commitment of defense dollars at a higher rate than had been made in the 1972–1974 bottom of the Vietnam spending cycle.

From this understandable and reasonable beginning, the real growth policy grew under both Carter and Reagan into a shallow technical exercise involving inflation forecasts and outlay rate estimates. Although the Carter OMB labored to compare and trade off marginal funding requirements between programs across all the rest of the federal budget, it was not possible to do so with defense. The president demanded from his budget office, and exercised in his budget decisions, these trade-offs of education versus transportation, health versus agriculture, and so on, throughout the Executive Branch. If OMB chafed at its inability to include defense in the allocation process, so did Jimmy Carter. The 3 percent policy came to be both a ceiling and floor, and the president commented often, always privately, that this particular policy had removed from his hands some important elements of executive leadership.

## DEFENSE MANAGEMENT ISSUES

Although the image of OMB rightfully focuses on the agency's budget responsibilities, the *M* for management represents a significant part of the organization's role. The Carter administration OMB was chartered by the new president to conduct major reorganization efforts throughout the Executive Branch. In defense, this activity was not at all well received by the DoD and military services. As the management staff of OMB struggled to analyze and recommend changes to the Office of the Secretary of Defense, Joint Chiefs of Staff, and certain defense agencies, all of those institutions fought to resist any such effort. The program/budget side of the OMB organization found itself caught in the middle of this uncomfortable set of arguments. In the end, little of organizational substance occurred—of all the Carter reorganization initiatives, those in DoD appear to have been among the least effective and least enduring.[8]

In parallel to these reorganization efforts, a number of other politically charged management issues were key agenda items for the associate director for national security and the program side of the OMB staff. Two topics in particular found OMB directly and deeply involved in the president's personal drive for better efficiency in his defense program: military base closings and contracting out of in-house DoD functions. Across both these broad subjects, OMB's activism was driven by the continued demands of the president for data, analysis, and recommendations. The agency's responsiveness and activism were reinforced by the arrival in 1978 of a new OMB deputy director, former Assistant Secretary of Defense John P. White, who brought to the agency's front office strong expertise and interest in these topics.

By 1977 U.S. military staff had been reduced from the 1968 Vietnam peak of 3.5 million men and women back to a peacetime level of just over 2 million. Local political pressures, however, had prevented the Nixon and Ford administrations from cutting back significantly the large number of military installations required to house and support the wartime force. *Cutting the fat, not the bone* in the defense budget, then, focused immediately on the always difficult task of closing bases. The White House domestic policy staff, supported forcefully and vocally by Vice President Mondale, demanded action. The president told OMB, as keepers of the organizational and funding data needed to assist DoD in selecting closure candidates, to make it happen.

Reluctant at first, the Office of the Secretary of Defense (OSD) moved slowly in the process. OSD, and especially Deputy Secretary Charles Duncan, argued the politically painful risks of taking on so many senators and representatives. The center of gravity of military basing was in the South, with locations in many areas represented by conservative Democrats already vocally questioning Carter's defense policy. As the process gained momentum and potential candidate closures leaked out, even some political advisers in the White House asked that the president consider backing off somewhat in a process guaranteed to alienate target communities.

OMB's central staff role on a second management issue, contracting out government services and other functions, became a lightning rod of sorts for the agency. The goal was simple enough: identify a set of government functions that could be accomplished by private industry, conduct competitive bidding, and—where contracting out promised sufficient savings— award the business to a commercial concern, and reduce the government payroll accordingly. According to most analyses, such a plan would yield significant savings, due both to lower direct labor rates and to the avoidance of the relatively rich fringes (benefits, pensions, and so on) found in the blue collar civil service system.

Congress was of two minds on this issue. In pushing even broader procurement reform, Capital Hill had created, over the opposition of the White House at the time, the Office of Federal Procurement Policy (OFPP). OFPP, charged with administering the law and creating Executive Branch policy on procurement of goods and services, had been placed in OMB at its birth in 1975.[9] Together, OFPP and the OMB National Security Division set off to expand contracting out of DoD activities. From the start it was a lopsided struggle. The cost saving arguments, while quite real, attracted few supporters. The private services industry, poorly organized to lobby and fearful of angering its largest government customer, watched from the sidelines.

Faced with the prospect of layoffs in its huge civilian workforce, OSD argued the risks of depending upon contract labor should a military conflict occur. The civil service unions, always powerful voices in Congress and the Executive Branch, went to general quarters. The union arguments to OMB focused on concerns about degraded quality and reliability in functions contracted out. In parallel, the budget office was swamped by calls from irate legislators whose districts contained the major bases, depots, and shipyards targeted by contracting out studies. Legislators feared that OMB planned not just to swap private for government workers but to reduce or eliminate the jobs in their districts. For some congressional members, a 10 percent improvement in defense efficiency meant a 10 percent loss in district jobs. These legislators felt that the goal of a more efficient DoD should be pursued vigorously but only in other members' districts. In the end, contracting out moved forward, but with far less scope and rate of conversion than the president or OMB would have liked.

Throughout the push for base closings and contracting out, those in the White House most disappointed in the unimplemented campaign promise of an $8 billion defense cut continued to push OMB to make DoD deliver on these two issues. As noted above, the vice president and his staff were especially vocal on these points. Their obvious frustration at the spending implications of the 3 percent real growth policy seemed to heighten even further their insistence that OMB help the president execute individual reductions and savings.

Politics is full of ironies, in budgets as in all other areas. It was a memorable twist, then, when a major piece of the base-closing story came to an unexpected end. After months of agonizing effort inside the government and between Washington and the affected community, the administration came to the final steps required to close the venerable Philadelphia navy yard. OSD, the navy, OMB, and key congressional leaders had finally put together the arrangement, and the padlock was all but on the gates. The president had given his approval, and OMB was ready to turn to the next large base closure issue.

In a move that surprised many throughout the Executive Office and Pentagon, the vice president's staff announced publicly that the administration had, in its wisdom, decided not to close the yard. While the local constituency and many in the U.S. Navy celebrated, OMB wondered just what Mr. Mondale really wanted regarding defense budget efficiencies and reductions. The incident fostered a new budget office epithet, frequently uttered under the breath in response to new urgings from the vice president and his staff to be more efficient in defense spending: "Just like the Philadelphia Navy Yard."

## THE SPACE SHUTTLE

President Carter's appetite for detail, his strong and abiding interest in technology, and his reliance and apparent comfort with using the senior OMB staff as direct counterpoints to agency heads were manifested in each and every budget cycle in his administration. By far the most remarkable example of that style, at least in my view, came early in the term and involved the space shuttle. The OMB role and the nature of the policy debate were both unusual, and the ultimate impact of this event on U.S. space policy warrants its inclusion here.

The four OMB program associate directors (PADS), all political appointees, divide agency budget review responsibilities among themselves for the entire federal program. The associate director for National Security and International Affairs (NSIA) covers defense, foreign affairs, and intelligence, and was the position I held at the time. The associate director for Natural Resources, Energy, and Science (NRES) covers a variety of agencies, including the National Aeronautics and Space Administration (NASA). Given the president's charge to reduce federal spending wherever possible, Associate Director Eliot Cutler looked closely at NASA's shuttle program. As the shuttle moved from its development phase into full operational status, the funding requirements were staggering. After adding up its own science and exploration plans, commercial satellite launch projections, and planned military payload requirements, NASA programmed a five orbiter, dual (East and West coasts) launch pad system, with a pricetag of over $1.5 billion for FY78 alone.[10]

Cutler and his staff analyzed all aspects of this plan, including shuttle reliability, launch costs, turnaround rates, and projections of commercial satellite demand for launch services. After assessing this complex set of costs, risks, and requirements, the associate director for NRES recommended to OMB Director Jim McIntyre that the NASA plan be scaled back to a three orbiter, single (East) coast operation. This plan would save billions of dollars over the life of the program and provide a greater hedge against the many risks identified in shuttle performance and operation.

The recommendation was forwarded internally to the associate director for National Security for review. The defense budget included a variety of research and development, procurement, facilities, and operating costs associated with the NASA shuttle plan, and it was necessary that the ultimate budget reconcile those interactions. As expected, Director McIntyre asked Cutler and I to put together a joint position for use in the upcoming reviews with NASA Administrator Robert Frosch and Secretary Brown.

Because where one stands depends on where one sits, the OMB/NSIA view on the shuttle took a different approach from Cutler's. The two parts of OMB took similar views on issues of technical risk, potential for cost growth, nature of commercial launch demand, and likely real launch turnaround costs and schedules. As the NSIA associate director, however, I also racked up the costs of using the shuttle for a steady stream of military payloads, many of which were already being redesigned for orbiter as opposed to expendable rocket carriage. Alternatively, I had to consider the costs to shift missions back to expendable rockets because a three orbiter plan could not support many DOD requirements.

The two PADs, Cutler and I, shared an office suite and enjoyed a close working relationship, so we sat down to try to devise a mutually acceptable program. Cutler's good natured jibe to me that "it is always much easier to spend other people's money" was more than just a joke. The NASA funding profile was driven by significant requirements—West Coast polar orbits, large payloads, and rapid 1984 turnaround times—which came almost wholly from DoD. The Defense Department was contributing a significant amount of money to the shuttle effort, but we agreed that an even larger share was appropriate.

In the end, however, Cutler and I agreed to disagree on the fundamental issues of the numbers of orbiters and launch pads. If the program objectives were to be limited to NASA's civilian space science and some commercial satellite launch service, then Cutler's program was not only appropriate, but would allow DoD to perform a fair number of shuttle missions consistent with the Cape Canaveral limitations on orbit geometry. Under Cutler's proposed program, it was agreed that DoD would have to go back to the drawing boards for many planned launches, and both satellite and launch vehicle programs would require significant redirection and funding.

My NSIA recommendation, which would continue the five-orbiter, two-coast operation, attempted to weigh that program's costs and risks versus DoD's going it alone in a rejuvenated program to build Delta, Atlas, Titan, and perhaps a fourth, new, very heavy, lift booster. Both Cutler and I shared our cost and schedule assumptions with each other's staffs, and reached agreements as to the numbers that should be used. As directed, we presented both positions to the OMB director, and a series of spirited and intense discussions ensued.

The choice of either approach had far-reaching policy implications, above and beyond the obvious budgetary consequences. The NSIA argument was based on both national security and budgetary grounds. Essentially, it supported the NASA two coast, five orbiter plan as the lowest risk, lowest cost approach to meeting critical national security mission requirements. The NRES argument, citing the already large and alarming cost and schedule overruns in the program, took a more traditional OMB view as to the shuttle. Specifically, the three orbiter approach lowered cost and risk significantly for NASA, while scaling back the agency's long list of program goals and needs. At the same time, it urged DoD to adopt alternative ways to meet certain of its requirements that were generating unique shuttle costs and risks, most particularly the Vandenberg launch site and the maximum gross weight payload demands.

Budget Director James McIntyre heard the two positions argued by his respective associate directors. He heard, too, a variety of other inputs, from Defense, NSC, NASA, the president's science adviser, and others in the White House. Taken together, there was no clear answer so far as McIntyre was concerned, and two other senior OMB participants, Deputy Director White and EAD Cutter, shared the ambivalence. McIntyre's next move, while somewhat of a surprise to many of us at the time, was in hindsight quite understandable under the circumstances.

The president's approach to budget issues between an agency and OMB was to let his budget director decide and then hear only the more significant—measured in dollars or perceived political impact—appeals from his Cabinet. McIntyre would structure these meetings, held in the cabinet room and attended by the department or agency, OMB, and selected White House staff. OMB, controlling the agenda, would present the issues to the president in their terms, and then the agency head would provide counter arguments.

In the case of the space shuttle, Director McIntyre instructed his two associate directors to structure their arguments for presentation to the president. NASA, DoD, and the director of Central Intelligence, along with NSC and Domestic Policy Council staffs, would be invited and could themselves side with one or the other PAD, or suggest their own alternatives. The meeting occurred as scheduled, and the many participants were both shocked and bemused. For the first time in anyone's memory, the Office of Management and Budget was essentially arguing against itself.

The arrangement was an unmistakable sign of Jim McIntyre's confidence in his personal relationship with the president. The OMB director was clearly not worried about his not making the decision himself, knowing just how deeply Jimmy Carter was involved in the shuttle issue. McIntyre had every reason to believe that an appeals session would have ended with the same sort of discussion. Better to structure the questions on OMB terms and let the chief executive decide.

The meeting's outcome set the stage for the entire U.S. space program from that time through the *Challenger* accident. The president retained the dual launch pad, East and West coast plan, and this part of his decision was driven in great part by his commitment to arms control. Progress on the SALT II agreements then being debated depended in turn on U.S. ability to verify many Soviet actions. That verification in turn required a tight schedule of satellite launches, many from the Vandenberg Air Force Base West Coast facility.

The president accepted Cutler's projections of shuttle launch demand and turnaround time and cost between flights and scaled back to a four orbiter effort. These OMB projections, branded as cynical and *green eyeshade* by some shuttle advocates at the time, proved quite prophetic as the program began to fly. The agreement between OMB/NSIA and Secretary Brown to purchase a few more launch vehicles from the Atlas and Titan production lines essentially moved dollars from NASA to DOD.[11] Some in the air force understandably voiced strong objection to having to absorb these funds from within a fixed budget total. However, the use of these rockets in the early 1980s proved critical to the nation's military and intelligence programs as shuttle availability slipped more and more. Recent air force purchases of MLV (Delta) and CELV (Titan) boosters continue this thrust.

## TO COMPETE OR NOT TO COMPETE

In any administration, a key measure of how advisers and organizations influence the chief executive is the matter of who gets to *read the president's mail.* President Carter's staff secretary, Rick Hutchinson, managed the sensitive and sometimes controversial process of receiving policy memoranda and recommendations from the departments and forwarding them to selected Executive Office staff for comment or action.

The president found, like all his predecessors, that advocates have ingenious ways of circumventing the budget process in order to secure funding for their programs. Early in his term, Carter instructed Hutchinson to solicit OMB comments on all memos or recommendations that had any sort of budget implications. For agency requests for new programs the issue was straightforward, and OMB would receive the paperwork along with whichever White House staff offices had cognizance in the area. Other memos, especially in the national security realm, were sometimes not so clear. For example, a DoD request for congressional notification by the president on a foreign military sale (FMS) transaction generally reflected already approved budgets, so the real issues were approval of specific hardware and timing. The OMB approvals, or staffing, was often conducted through a brief phone conversation between the staff secretary and the OMB associate director.

As Executive Office advisers interacted regularly with the president, each individual developed a sense of what elements of policy were appropriate topics when it came to offering advice. Because of OMB's extensive interactions with President Carter, the associate directors were by and large quite comfortable when it came to offering advice that crossed that oft-cited but, of course, invisible line between policy and budget issues.

I can offer a personally memorable example of an OMB associate director advising on a budget/policy issue as a conclusion to this essay. The subject was fighter aircraft, and the specific question was foreign sales. President Carter continually strived, Camp David agreements notwithstanding, to limit the quantity and sophistication of U.S. weapons sold abroad. A focal point in that policy was the question of exporting current technology jet fighters. Having dictated that front line aircraft such as the F-15A, F-16A, and F-18A were not to be offered for third world (non-NATO) sale, the administration looked for ways to accommodate the fighter demands of countries like Taiwan, Pakistan, Venezuela, and the Middle East nations.

The Northrop Corporation, which had for years enjoyed strong U.S. government support for its F-5A and F-5E fighters in third world sales, had designed an upgraded version of that plane, designated the F-5G. In 1979, Northrop succeeded in securing formal DoD and State Department support for a policy recommendation designating the F-5G as a formal instrument of U.S. foreign policy. A presidential determination to that effect, staffed in DoD and State and endorsed in the White House by NSC head Brzezinski, arrived on Hutchinson's desk for Carter to sign.

The staff secretary, seeing the signatures of Vance, Brown, and Brzezinski, had the bulk of his staffing complete. However, he wondered whether there were any budget ramifications and placed a call to me as OMB associate director to ascertain that specific point. My late night response, on hearing the one-paragraph determination read, was a brief suggestion: "While there are no real budget issues involved, you may want to ask the president if he is comfortable making what is essentially an industrial source selection decision from the Oval Office. He should consider asking DoD to see whether other companies in addition to Northrop are willing to invest in such a market opportunity."

An early morning phone call from the president to me closed the loop. Carter's handwritten request to Secretary Brown, penned atop the rejected memo, asked DoD to solicit others in industry. Three additional firms responded, and in the succeeding months was born the administration's FX policy, which committed to the countries involved that the U.S. would offer one or more fighter aircraft approved for such export.[12] Northrop's F-5G, later to be renamed the F-20, therefore found itself competing head to head with other U.S. fighters and was unable to secure the obvious market advantage of having the company's updated version of the F-5A secure a sole source label as the designated instrument of U.S. foreign policy. The Reagan administration's subsequent approval of front line U.S. fighters for sale to countries like Pakistan and Venezuela effectively sidestepped—with many and far-reaching consequences—the earlier policies of designated export-only military hardware.

## CONCLUSION

The OMB associate director for the NSIA has additional responsibilities and roles in foreign affairs and intelligence matters that I will not discuss here. Defense programs and issues dominate the OMB interaction and conversations with previous and subsequent administrations' NSIA PAD's indicate consistency on this point. If the budget office's role was different in the Carter years, it was for the reasons already noted: The president's penchant for detail led to his regular interaction with both the political leadership and career staff of OMB, not only in defense but across the federal program.

Significant issues such as those mentioned here and others like the Camp David treaty negotiations, the verification aspects of SALT II, military draft registration, and the controversial carrier veto of the FY80 defense authorization bill found OMB deeply involved in the president's management and decisionmaking. For the political appointees serving OMB directors Lance and McIntyre, it was a challenging experience. For the career OMB staff, the challenge was even greater. The institution's tendency to operate as a quasi-academic critic of any and all government expenditures was put to the test. Carter demanded from OMB, and in many cases received, a more politically sensitive—some would also say more responsible—kind of advice.

If one can define a spectrum characterizing the extent to which OMB has been a substantive participant in national security decisionmaking, then the Carter years would seem to stand at one end of such a continuum. The Nixon/Schlesinger/Schultz and Ford/Rumsfeld/Lynn systems most likely fall somewhere in the center, and the recent Reagan/Weinberger/Stockman system must fall at the end opposite of Carter's because the OMB staff, and even the director, was relegated to the sidelines.

As I noted in introduction, this chapter is by necessity anecdotal, as I exercise selfish selectivity in choosing the policy examples presented. These pages could have treated the program issues in a particular year's defense budget review, or could have documented major debates on foreign service pay and benefits or on levels of P.L. 480 food aid as a foreign policy tool. These items, or any of the major national issues, however, would in my view have created the same perspective. The OMB director, the PADs, and the career staffs, were all brought fundamentally and for the most part totally into President Carter's decision processes whenever resources—dollars—

were involved.

Was this level of participation and involvement unique? For those of us who were political appointees, and therefore transient, the answer was of course "yes." We knew no other situation, at least not firsthand. A more useful judgement comes from the career OMB staff, the senior leadership of which has experienced twenty or more years in the Executive Office. For the careerists, a few of whose views of history are extensive enough to include a president from Missouri, the Carter style was indeed unique. Never before or since had OMB found so many of its staff, its issues, its analyses, and its arguments in direct exchange with the president as he set national security policy.

## NOTES

1. I served as OMB Program associate director for National Security and International affairs from April 1977 through July 1980. For the transition period and first months of the Carter administration, I served as a member of the National Security Council staff.

2. Approximately $6 billion was cut from the $123 billion budget prepared by President Ford. See *Budget of the United States Government,* (Washington, DC: U.S. Government Printing Office, 1977 and 1978).

3. General Jones argued forcefully for the B-1 program throughout the president's budget deliberations and did so in a universally hostile environment. Short of public protest and/or resignation, it is not clear to me what more the air force chief could have done on behalf of the bomber program. Nonetheless, many B-1 supporters accused Jones of caving on this emotional issue.

4. See "Navy Under Attack," *Time* III (8 May 1978):14–18; "U.S. Navy In Distress," *U.S. News & World Report* 84 (6 May 1978):24–27; and "Navy: All Engines Slow," *Newsweek* 91 (10 April 1978):34.

5. See "Statement of Edward R. Jayne II, Associate Director for National Security and International Affairs of the Office of Management and Budget before the Seapower Subcommittee of the House Armed Services Committee," April 13, 1978, OMB, Executive Office of the President.

6. See Gary Aderman, "Congress Reluctant on Legislative Savings," *National Journal,* 38 (22 September 1979):1571–1573.

7. See E. Kozicharow, *Aviation Week,* 108 (23 January 1978):14–15.

8. See Peter L. Szanton, *Federal Reorganization: What Have We Learned* (Chatham, NJ: Chatham House Publishers, 1981).

9. The Ford Administration had located OFPP inside OMB in part at least to curtail overzealous independence by the new procurement "czar."

10. See "Inflation Absorbs NASA Funding Growth," *Aviation Week* (30 January 1978) 28.

11. The FY79 and 80 budgets included additional Titan and Atlas boosters, representing final buys from production lines that otherwise would have shut down within months.

12. "Guides to Clear Way for Export Fighter," *Aviation Week* (14 January 1980) 17–18.

# 6.3    America's Departments of State: Irregular and Regular Syndromes of Policymaking

## BERT A. ROCKMAN

*This article (1) sketches a general explanation for the growth of coordinative machinery and of irregular personnel in modern governments; (2) identifies both general and specific reasons for this phenomenon in the United States with special reference to foreign policy making; (3) identifies within the American foreign policy-making context the modal charactericstics of irregular and regular syndromes of policy making, and the conjunction between personnel and institutional base; (4) traces the implications arising from these different policy syndromes; and (5) evaluates some proposals for improving the coherence and knowledge base of American foreign policy making. The problems of defining foreign policy authority, assuring an integrated perspective, and effectively using specialized expertise are best seen in terms of the larger problem of governance in Washington against which all proposals for reform must be abraded.*

The United States possesses two foreign ministers within the same government: the one who heads the Department of State, and the one who is the assistant to the president for national security affairs. The former heads a classically contoured bureaucracy. Proximate to him are appointed officials, often with substantial foreign policy experience. At greater distance is a corps of professional foreign service officers (FSOs). Beneath the national security assistant, on the other hand, is a smaller professional staff of somewhat variable size (ranging in recent times from about three dozen to slightly over 50) whose members typically are drawn from universities, other agencies, and research institutes.

This latter group—the National Security Council staff—is the institutional embodiment of White House aspirations for imposing foreign policy coordination. Its "director," the president's assistant for national security affairs, in recent years has come to be seen as the president's personal foreign policy spokesman as well as an influential molder, and sometime executor, of his policy choices. Though, at least publicly, the overt role of the president's national security assistant has been diminished in the Reagan

Excerpted by the editors from the *American Political Science Review*, 63 (Sept. 1969), pp. 689–718 by permission of the author and the American Political Science Association.

administration relative to the prominence it attained during the Nixon and Carter presidencies, a common perception is that, since the Kennedy administration, policy power has drifted steadily from the State Department to the president's team of foreign policy advisers (Campbell, 1971; George, 1972a; Destler, 1972a, 1972b, 1980; Allison and Szanton, 1976). If perceptions govern, this alone may constitute sufficient evidence of such a drift. Beyond perception, however, there is unmistakable evidence of growth in the role of the national security assistant (who postdates the founding of the National Security Council itself), and in the size and character of the NSC staff. Since McGeorge Bundy's incumbency, and especially because of the Kissinger and Brzezinski periods, the assistant to the president for national security affairs has become a visible public figure in his own right (Destler, 1980, pp. 84–85). In general, his role has evolved from one of coordinating clearance across departments to one of policy adviser. Similarly, the NSC staff itself has grown greatly, boosted especially during the Nixon administration. It is less and less composed of graying and grayish anonymous career foreign service officers, and more and more composed of foreign policy intellectuals and prospective high-fliers, many of whom are drawn from America's leading universities.

I do not mean to imply that the presidential foreign policy apparatus and the State Department always or even usually clash, nor that they have wholly overlapping functions. Nonetheless, it is clear that the NSC, at least in form, is today something far beyond what it was in Truman's time or in Eisenhower's. To some degree Truman, protecting what he believed to be his prerogatives, held the then-nascent National Security Council at arm's length as an advisory forum. Eisenhower, on the other hand, employed it frequently as a collegial body, one whose statutory members and staff were also, in some measure, representatiaves of their departments (Hammond, 1961; pp. 905-10; Falk, 1964, pp. 424-25). Since then, the role and character of the NSC staff, and especially that of the national security assistant, have mutated. This evolution into a role not originally envisioned for the NSC or the then special assistant (executive secretary in Truman's time) has notable consequences for policy making.

Even within the constricted sphere of executive forces on policy making, the foreign policy process involves a complex of actors and not merely a bilateral relationship between the NSC and the State Department. Although the State Department's position has been most eroded by the policy role of the NSC, neither it nor the NSC is a monolithic force. The national security assistant and the NSC staff are *not* the same actors, nor necessarily of common mind. Similar cautions are even more necessary to describe relationships between the secretary of state and the foreign service professionals of the State Department. A significant difference in intraorganizational relationships, however, is that the national security assistant to some extent selects his own staff, whereas the secretary of state has a department to manage and an established subculture that exists well below the level of those whom he selects. If the NSC staff is more nearly the creation of the national security assistant, the secretary of state, unless he divorces himself from the department, is more likely to be seen as its creation. This difference provides one of these actors with considerable strategic advantages in influencing the views and decisions of presidents.

As clearly as this somewhat ambiguous distinction permits, the NSC (and the national security assistant) and the State Department (though not necessarily the secretary) have come to embody, respectively, the differing commitments given to the roles of "irregulars" (those not bound to a career service) and of "regulars" (members of a career service) in the policy process. The correlation is quite far from unity, of course. There are mixes of personnel and outlooks within each organizational setting, but there are characteristically different career lines and perspectives as well. Above all, each setting provides for different roles. The operational responsibilities of the State Department give it the advantages of detailed knowledge and experience, and the political disadvantage of lacking an integrated world view. The NSC, on the other hand, is less constrained by the existence of operational responsibilities, by distance between it and the president, or by the communications complications typical of large hierarchically structured organizations. Its sterling political assets, however, are offset in some measure by the disadvantages of removal from day-to-day detail and highly specialized expertise. The differences between these organizational settings, to be sure, are quite significant. The NSC is a fast track. In contrast, the State Department can be a ponderously slow escalator. One setting is oriented to solving problems, the other to raising them. One is more oriented to attaining a bottom line, the other to journeying down a bottomless pit. In sum, the presidential foreign policy apparatus largely exhibits the advantages and disadvantages of an organ that is staffed to some degree by irregulars, and which is not charged with line functions. The State Department, in the main, illustrates the advantages and disadvantages of a hierarchically structured organization responsible for implementation, and which, therefore, tends to have a regular's orientation.

My objectives in this article then are (1) to sketch a general explanation for the growth of both coordinative institutions and of "irregular" personnel in government; (2) to identify both general and specific reasons for this phenomenon in the United States with respect to the official foreign policy community, in particular the tendencies toward Executive Office centrism; (3) to identify, within the foreign policy context, modal characteristics of the irregular and the regular syndromes of policy making, and in so doing, to discuss the conjunction between personnel and institutional base; (4) to trace the implications of these different policy syndromes; and (5) to evaluate some proposed solutions to the problem of both resolving foreign policy-making authority and of organizationally synergizing the "irregular" and "regular" syndromes in foreign policy making. Finally, I conclude by suggesting that the problem of defining foreign policy-making authority in American government is but an element of the larger problem of governance in Washington. Whatever specific palliatives emerge need to be fully grounded in these sobering facts.

## THE QUEST FOR POLICY INTEGRATION

The growth of coordinative institutions in modern governments and the growth in importance of irregular staffers in government are not the same thing, but they are traceable to the same sources, namely, the need to compensate for the inadequacies of traditional ministries in absorbing the policy agendas and perspectives of the central decision-making authority within the executive. The massive expansion of policy agendas themselves —"overload," as Klein and Lewis (1977, p. 2) call this phenomenon—is the signal cause of efforts to overcome the parochialness of the ministries and their civil servants. Problems of assimilation clearly have multiplied as governments pursue more and more complex, frequently conflicting objectives (Rose, 1976a; Neustadt, 1954). The forms taken by these coordinative mechanisms have varied across both political systems and policy arenas. The extent to which they have been composed of irregulars has similarly varied.

The more feeble the gravitational pull of directional authority in government, the more necessary it becomes to institutionalize coordinative functions. In Britain, the relatively strong pull of cabinet government, and the doctine of ministerial responsibility, means that the interface of politics and policy often takes place within the ministries themselves. There, irregulars are usually planted directly in the ministries. In the Federal Republic of Germany, the gravitational pull of cabinet government is substantially weaker, and the activism of the *Bundeskanzleramt* (the Chancellery) is greater than that of the British Cabinet Office (Dyson, 1974, pp. 361-62). In the case of the United States where the gravitational pull of political forces is exceedingly weak, mechanisms to achieve policy integration abound not only in the Executive Office of the Presidency, but even throughout Congress. The development of these mechanisms throughout the EOP is particularly intriguing in view of the fact that the American line departments are already well saturated with officials whose political pedigrees have been carefully checked out. American administration, as is well known, is laden with irregulars at some depth beneath the cabinet secretary, yet even this has often been considered insufficient to attain presidential control and integration over policy (Nathan, 1975; Heclo, 1975).

This, of course, brings us to the central issue, which is whether the quest for policy integration, defined as comprehensive control over vital policy objectives, can accommodate expertise defined in terms of specialized knowledge. The dilemma, as Paul Hammond once observed, is this (1960, p. 910):

> While the mind of one man may be the most effective instrument for devising diplomatic moves and strategic maneuvers and for infusing . . . creative purpose, its product is bound to be insufficient to meet the needs of the vast organizational structures . . . which are the instruments of foreign policy.

The growth of integrative machinery has brought to the fore officials who sometimes differ from their counterparts in the operating agencies.[1] At least as important, though, is that they are provided substantial policy-influencing opportunities without equivalent operational responsibility. To the extent that "central" staff agencies have challenged more traditional bureaucratic sources of policy, they have merely reflected the perplexing problems that nearly all modern democratic governments face in both integrating and controlling policy objectives, and in rendering them politically acceptable.

From these more general observations, I wish to take up the special case of the National Security Council and the assistant to the president for national security affairs as a remarkable example of how the facilitating function evolved into far more heady activities. This evolution also starkly illustrates the advantage of a staff agency at the expense of the traditional operating agencies. Put another way, it reflelcts the advantages that "irregulars" often have over "regulars."

## FROM MANAGER TO COMPETING SECRETARY OF STATE

From its inception in 1947, the National Security Council was designed to be a high-level policy review committee rather than a strictly staff operation (Sapin, 1967, p. 84). As a mechanism for arriving at major policy decisions, however, a support staff quickly emerged underneath the statutory membership of the NSC. Indeed, until the Eisenhower administration came into power in 1953, there was no overall coordinator who had immediate access to the president. In 1953, however, Eisenhower appointed a special assistant to the president for national security affairs whose responsibilities, among others, entailed playing an executive director's role with the NSC staff. An indication of how far the function of the president's national security assistant, and that of the NSC staff as well, has diverged from the original coordinating and facilitating function is the fact that it takes a monumental effort to recall who these presidential assistants were.[2]

Why has the national security assistant and the NSC staff moved from this relatively modest, if necessary, role to one which frequently has vied with the secretary of state and the State Department for foreign policy-making influence? At the outset of the Carter administration, for example, a sympathetic article referred to the NSC staff as the "other cabinet" (Berry and Kyle, 1977). There are numerous answers to this question, of course. At bottom, though, the "many" reasons are made particularly compelling by the peculiar political culture of Washington politics—an inheritance in part of extravagant institutional disaggregation.

It is true, of course, that whatever clout the national security assistant has exists only at the sufferance of the president (Art, 1973; Destler, 1977). Presidents can make or break the role of their national security assistants as policy advocates. They *can* minimize the visibility of their assistant; they *can* play down the substantive functions of the NSC staff relative to the State Department, for example. There are obvious manipulables in the relationship between America's "second State Department" and the White House, but the norms that have been established now seem firm in spite of the present and perhaps momentary diminution of the NSC role in the Reagan administration. The tendency to shift from central clearance to central direction has helped give the NSC apparatus and, above all, a policy-advocating national security assistant, an unusually important role. In the Reagan administration, Richard Allen has proclaimed his role model to be that of Eisenhower's anonymous special assistant, Gordon Gray. But Allen's own prior roles largely have been advocacy and advisory ones, rather than managerial or facilitative ones (Smith, 1981).

## Overload as an Explanation

Understandably, the National Security Act of 1947 which set up the National Security Council was enacted at the beginning of America's postwar eminence as the leading Western power. The role of global power with far-reaching responsibilities produces a busy agenda, and the busier that agenda the more the management of policy and of advice becomes important. According to a relatively recent report prepared for the president, there have been at least 65 studies of the U.S. foreign policy machinery since 1951 (*National Security Policy Integration*, 1979, p. 49). This abundance of studies bears witness to the great diversity of actors with some share of the foreign policy pie, to continuing problems of coordination between them, and to their reputed lack of responsiveness to the president. How, under these circumstances, is a president to make decisions without some final filter that reduces unmanageable complexity to at least endurable perplexity?

Undoubtedly, in an age of instant communication, some of the present NSC apparatus would have had to have been invented did it not already exist. Working out statements with counterparts in the Elysée, the Chancellery, or 10 Downing Street before the principals are themselves engaged is the kind of task that may need to be located close to the head of government. However, the enhanced role of the national security assistant over the past two decades (Destler, 1980) makes it unlikely that these tasks are sufficient to satisfy policy drives created by recent organizational practices.

## Institutional and Organizational Explanations

"Overload" explains the existence of coordinative mechanisms such as the NSC. It does not, however, explain the transformation of a once-anonymous role with a small staff to a prominent contender for policy-making power in foreign affairs.

Because government in Washington is as unplanned as the society it governs, criticisms of the foreign policy-making machinery overwhelmingly recommend organizational reforms (Campbell, 1971; Destler, 1972b; Allison and Szanton, 1976). As with virtually all governmental activity in the United States, fragmentation also characterizes the process of foreign policy decision making. Centrifugal tendencies begin at the top levels of American government, induced in part by the absence of effective mechanisms for cabinet decision making.[3] Lack of clarity at the top molds bureaucratic tendencies below. Thus, while the problems of bureaucratic politics exist everywhere, they are made more obvious by unclear boundaries of authority, by the fractionation of power centers, and by the ready availability of the press as a resource in policy struggles. Contemporary Washington epitomizes these conditions. It is not difficult, therefore, to find targets for reform.

Despite repeated calls for its resuscitation, the cabinet is to the functioning of American government what the appendix is to human physiology. It's there, but no one is quite sure why. Whatever initial presidential intentions may be, presidents soon learn that cabinet meetings are mainly for public relations benefits rather than for decision making. They also learn another lesson of particular importance in Washington, namely, that the probability of leaks to the press which may foreclose presidential options is geometrically expanded by the number of participants involved. Later I will discuss how an "information-leaky" environment, unique to Washington among world capitals, estranges presidents from their cabinet departments. For now it is useful merely to indicate that the extreme splintering of responsibilities means that presidents with innovative intentions will be desirous of centralizing in the White House that which is otherwise uncontrollable or unresponsive to them.

All leaders are apt to demand more responsiveness than they can or even ought to get. But American presidents crave responsiveness in part because so little is obviously available to them. Large organizations, and especially those that are highly professionalized, develop definable subcultures and resist intrusions from inexpert outsiders. Regardless of what it is that presidents order the first time, there is a strong tendency for them to be served fudge—or jelly, to employ the culinary metaphor used by President Kennedy. While this frustration is not peculiar to the foreign policy and national security agencies, foreign policy matters are often far more central to what it is a president, or a prime minister for that matter, must attend to (Rose, 1976b, pp. 255-56; 1980, pp. 35-38). Typically, too, there is less legislative direction of the foreign policy organs than of departments having primarily domestic responsibilities or impacts.

Among the agencies involved with foreign policy, moreover, the State Department largely deals with political analysis, impressionistic evidence, and judgment. Since politicians who become presidents are likely to defer to no one when it comes to making what are essentially political judgments, the vulnerability of the State Department becomes apparent. It is not only that the department moves slowly that frustrates presidents; it is often the message that it delivers that leads them to despair (Silberman, 1979).

In addition to its distance from the White House, a problem which to some extent affects all line departments, the culture and technology of the State Department are also factors in its organizational disadvantage. These factors interact with, indeed greatly exacerbate, its distance problem. The State Department is a regular organization *par excellence* with a highly developed professional subculture. The stock in trade of the regular foreign service officers, granted individual differences among them, is a large supply of cold water with which to dash ideas that emanate elsewhere or which challenge prevailing professional perspectives. In the words of one sympathetic observer:

> The most useful service that a senior State Department official can perform in a policy-making role is to douse the facile enthusiasms of administration "activists" in the cold water of reality. But most of them bring so little energy and skill to this task that they merely project an image of negativism (Maechling, 1976, pp. 11-12).

Put somewhat more generally, "Political appointees seem to want to accomplish goals quickly while careerists opt to accomplish things carefully" (Murphy et al., 1978, p. 181).

As a citadel of foreign service professionalism, the State Department is an inhospitable refuge for ideas and initiatives blown in from the cold. "It's all been tried before" is a refrain that may characterize the responses of professional bureaucrats whatever their substantive craft, but it is one that is at the heart of the department's perceived unresponsiveness.

Ironically, in this light, the professional subculture of the foreign service, as some have noted, ill prepares foreign service officers for the rough-and-tumble of bureaucratic politics (Destler, 1972b, pp. 164-66; Maechling, 1976, pp. 10-12; and even Silberman, 1979). Indeed, the recruitment of FSOs traditionally has made them America's closest facsimile of the British administrative class (Seidman, 1980, pp. 144-47). This is manifest also in operating style, a style characterized as one of "alert passivity" (Allison and Szanton, p. 126). While American bureaucrats in the domestic departments readily adopt the role of advocate to a far greater extent than their European peers (Aberbach, Putnam and Rockman, 1981, pp. 94-98), FSOs tend to be more like British bureaucrats, defusing programmatic advocacy so as to maintain the flexibility necessary to deal with the differing priorities imposed by new leaders. Unlike their colleagues in the domestic departments, officials in State lack domestic constituencies to help them weather episodic storms. In addition, the foreign service is oriented to serving abroad. The cost of this absorption is a lack of sophisticated political understanding of the policy-making machinery. In a system in which boundaries of authority are remarkably inexact, FSOs tend to lack both skills and bases for effective bureaucratic infighting—a considerable disadvantage.

As noted, the modal technology of the State Department is soft and impressionistic, and thus endlessly vulnerable. This helps to explain why the State Department is especially apt to be victimized. For as a former department official comments:

> New presidents and their staffs soon start to search for opportunities for leadership, areas in which to demonstrate that the President is on top of things and making policy. When this game is played, the loser is almost invariably the State Department and not, for example, the Pentagon. . . . To do more than scratch the surface of a few front page military issues would require a much larger White House staff than any President would want to contemplate. Foreign policy, on the other hand, is largely a matter of words, and the President and his staffers can step in at any time and put the words together themselves (Gelb, 1980, p. 35).

Once the staff has been constructed to oversee policy proposals, the next step toward advocacy seems nearly ineluctable unless the president is fully and unequivocally committed *in combination* to the secretary of state as the principal foreign policy maker *and* the State Department institutionally as the principal source of foreign policy advice—a combination that almost necessarily eliminates skilled policy entrepreneurs such as Henry Kissinger from the role. Why this combination of conditions is first unlikely to happen, but difficult to sustain if it does, is the question that needs to be addressed. To do so requires an exploration of the Washington political culture.

## The Political Culture of Washington as an Explanation

To explain the transformation of the NSC from a central clearance mechanism and a long-range policy planning one to an active center of policy making requires a focus on institutional and organizational features such as those we have just discussed. Yet the peculiar climate that pervades government in Washington helps to explain these institutional and organizational operations. For the distinguishing characteristic of government in Washington is its near-indistinguishability from politics in Washington. While politics in the capitals of all democratic states mixes together a variety of interests—partisan, pressure-group, bureaucratic, regional, and so forth—the absence of party as a solvent magnifies the importance of other interests. Above all, the overtness of the bureaucratic power struggle is likely to be in inverse proportion to the intensity and clarity of the partisan struggle.

Confronted with singular responsibility and inconstant support, presidents are often driven to managerial aspirations over "their" branch of the government. Sooner or later they sense that at best they are confronted with inertia, at worst, opposition. Rarely can they rely consistently upon their party for support, especially if they are Democrats; rarely too can they assume that their cabinets are composed of officials who are not essentially departmental emissaries. Cabinet ministers everywhere, of course, are departmental ambassadors to the cabinet. All ministers find it convenient, if not necessary, at some time to promote departmental agendas pushed from below. The late R. H. S. Crossman's assertion that "the Minister is there to present the departmental case" is universally true (1972, p. 61), yet he also observes that an American cabinet is only that—an aggregation of departmental heads (p. 67).

The basic themes of American governmental institutions are distrust and disaggregation. Together, they fuel suspicion. Presidents often come to divide the world into "us" and "them." "They" typically cannot be relied upon. "They" will be seen as torpid, bureaucratically self-interested, and often uncommitted or skeptical of presidential initiatives. Above all, "they" will be seen as an uncontrollable source of hemorrhaging to the press.

Unmediated by any tradition of, or basis for, a cabinet team, distance defines "us" and "them." There are always winners and losers in executive politics everywhere, but the more ambiguous the boundaries of authority, the less clear the adjusting mechanisms by which the winners and losers are determined, and the more pervasive the involvement of the media in policy struggles (a largely American phenomenon), the more ferocious the struggle. Under these conditions, the department heads will tend to lose ground to the White House because whatever advantages in autonomy distance permits, the more obvious are the disadvantages in accessibility.

Washington is a capital as obviously open as Moscow is obviously closed. The intimate involvement of the prestige press in internecine executive policy debates is legendary. Little remains confidential in Washington for very long, at least insofar as the exposure of confidentiality can assist any of the policy contestants. The lifelines connecting presidents to the cabinet departments are longer and perceived to be more porous than those that link presidents to the Executive Office. This perception undoubtedly is fortified by the belief that under most circumstances cabinet secretaries would as soon push their departmental perspectives or even their own special agendas than those of the White House. The secretary of state is not immune from this. Despite the "inner" role of the secretary of state (Cronin, 1975, pp. 190-92), *to the extent that he is perceived within the White House as someone who presses the interests and perspectives of the foreign service regulars, he is apt to be written off as one of "them."* The case of William Rogers is instructive in this regard, and even more so is that of Cyrus Vance who began in office with strong presidential support for his power stakes.

Although one must beware of self-serving tales that dribble *ex post facto* to the prestige American press from disgruntled ex-officials, the evidence, however partial it may be, is that leaks to the press are more likely to be blamed on the cabinet departments than on the executive office staff itself. A report in the *Washington Post,* for instance, indicates that after President Carter severely chastised noncareer and career State Department officials in early 1979 for suspected press leaks regarding policy toward Iran, Secretary Vance pressed upon him the view that the State Department was being unfairly singled out as a source of leaks that were regularly occurring everywhere, especially from within the NSC staff. The president's response, according to the report, was to meet with his national security assistant and several of his senior staff members and request them to smooth their relations with their counterparts at the State Department (Armstrong, 1980). To officials at State, the president threatened; to NSC officials, the president cajoled. "Us" versus "them," in other words, was not unique to the Nixon administration (Aberbach and Rockman, 1976).

The isolation of presidents from their cabinet departments, the absence of a common point of meaningful political aggregation—all of this within the information-leaky environment peculiar to Washington among world capitals—is a ready stimulant to the "us" versus "them" outlook that commonly develops in the White House, and in the departments as well. Distance and distrust are promoted on both ends of the tether line connecting departments to the White House. Departmental frustrations are often exacerbated by presidential distrust of bureaucratic institutions in an antibureaucratic culture. American politicians who enter through the gates of the White House have neither learned to endure the frustrations that arise through a slow and steady apprenticeship in party politics such as is found in Britain, nor to appreciate by virtue of living in their midst the skills and qualities that professional civil servants bring to government.

Because it contains memory traces from the past, bureaucracy is the enemy of novelty. Memory imposes constraint, while presidents typically want to make their mark as innovators.[4] Presidential frustrations derive, therefore, from the incapacity of large organizations to be immediately responsive to presidential wishes, and from the tendency of such organizations to protect their interests and core technologies from presidential intrusion. On the other hand, departmental frustrations arise when departments become the victims of imagined nonresponsiveness to presidents, as related in a recently revised version of the trade, proposed by the Soviets during the 1962 Cuban missile crisis, of American Jupiter missile bases in Turkey for those installed by the Soviets in Cuba.[5]

Thus far, I have outlined generally why presidents in America tend toward White House centrism—that is, why they seek to build a policy-making apparatus around them rather than relying exclusively upon the cabinet departments. I have not attempted to explain exhaustively this drive toward centrism, nor its ebbs and flows across particular administrations. My concern is with the trend line rather than the perturbations within it. Some aspects of the drive toward centrism are undoubtedly largely idiosyncratic, having to do with particular presidential styles and personalities within administrations. There are some reasons too that are probably universal, for example, the growth of technological capacity for central control, and some that are speculative, for example, hypothesized imperatives of leaders to try to exert control over policy without comprehending the mechanics—to reach, in other words, a bottom line without much concern for the algorithm. Of the reasons I explicitly cite, however, one—the increased agenda of governments—can be found in all modern democracies, and has resulted in efforts to devise coordinative machinery. The other reasons I have identified are more system-specific, and are rooted in institutional and cultural considerations. A dispersed policy universe generates needs for greater centrism. The weaker the pull of political gravity, the more the emphasis upon central staffing. Thus, according to one report, the load on central staff personnel in the EOP (at least during the Carter presidency) is immense when compared with staff counterparts in other nations (Campbell, 1980, p. 22). This apparently reflects White House obsessions for detailed policy control in an environment in which such control is as elusive as it is expected.

## FOREIGN POLICY BY IRREGULARS:
## WHITE HOUSE AND DEPARTMENTAL SETTINGS

The conditions that make American presidents turn to staff at the White House rather than bureaucrats, or even their appointees in the departments, undoubtedly characterize all policy sectors. Departmental appointees who have strong links to the career subcultures within their departments are often viewed with suspicion at the White House. They will be seen as advocates of parochial interests. Officials at the White House want presidential objectives to be "rationally" managed. Officials in the departments, on the other hand, want "rational" policies as they define them. This difference in perspective exists everywhere, and is by no means a peculiar characteristic of White House-State Department relations. What is peculiar about this particular relationship, however, is the extent to which the foreign service regulars are cut adrift from other sources of support in the political system and within their own department. Unlike their counterparts in the domestic agencies, they have no statutory-based standards to apply, only their judgments and knowledge to rely on. Unlike analysts in the domestic agencies, and in other national security agencies such as the Defense Department and CIA, their "data" are contained in imprints rather than print-outs.

Thus, at least since Dean Acheson's stewardship, most secretaries of state who wielded great influence (Dulles, Rusk under Johnson, and Kissinger) traveled light—in other words, without much departmental baggage. Strong secretaries often have been strong precisely because they ignored the department. When secretaries of state are perceived as representing departmental perspectives, they become especially vulnerable to competing sources of influence—most particularly from within the White House. Why?

One must begin with the fact that foreign policy is a *high-priority* item. By its importance, its capacity to push other items on the agenda to a lessr place, foreign policy, though not equally appetizing to all presidents, becomes the main course of the presidential meal. The extent to which foreign policy is a focal point of attention, of course, depends on the extent to which any nation is deeply involved and committed as an actor in world affairs. And that, understandably, is related to a nation's capacities for such involvement.

Crises especially lend themselves to central direction. Foreign policy is often nothing but crises—either reacting to them or creating them. Filled with crisis and presumed to be of first-order importance, foreign affairs are, in fact, glamorous. Much more than apparently intractable or technically complex domestic problems, foreign affairs often seem to be contests of will—games against other players rather than games against nature.

In such games, regular bureaucrats are unlikely to be key players. Their instincts are to think small, to think incrementally, and to see the world in not highly manipulable terms. The glitter that presidents often see in foreign policy is at odds with the cautious instincts of the professional service entrusted to deal with it. Unattached to specific operational responsibilities and accessible to the White House, the NSC can take on the qualities of a think-tank unencumbered by the more limited visions that flow from the State Department itself. Moreover, the NSC, like any staff organization, is far more readily adapted to the changing foreign policy themes of presidents than a line bureaucracy such as the State Department. State is, of course, highly adaptable to modulated swings in policy, but not to strong oscillations. Organizational memory and bureaucratic inertia preclude it from reinventing the world every four years.

This particular difference in settings—White House staff versus line bureaucracy—also implies a difference in styles of policy analysis. One setting is accessible to power, the other more remote. One is especially attractive to the ambitious and purposive, the other to the cautious and balanced. One setting is tailored for "in-and-outers" and "high-fliers" borrowed from other agencies, while the other is meant for "long-haulers." One effect of this difference in settings is that even though the NSC staff is not overwhelmingly composed of academic figures, more NSC staffers are apt to be academics than their counterparts at state. For example, a study of senior foreign service officers indicates that fewer than 8 percent are Ph.D.s (Mennis, p. 71), while 58 percent of the NSC staff with which Zbigniew Brzezinski began were holders of the Ph.D. degree,[6] as are 43 percent of the present staff. Such differences do not reflect merely ephemeral circumstance. The Reagan NSC also represents a mixture of scholars and government career officers with Washington experience (Smith, 1981). And as Destler describes the NSC staff under Presidents Kennedy and Nixon: "The typical staff members were not too different from the Kennedy period—relatively young, mobile, aggressive men, combining substantial background in the substance of foreign affairs with primary allegiance to the White House" (1972b, p. 123).

In other words, there is a correlation between background and organizational setting even though it is quite far from perfect. Backgrounds, of course, are only frail indicators of differences in syndromes of policy thought, and such differences need not imply substantive disagreement. Nonetheless, the correlation implies that the White House miniature of the State Department is more innovative than the real one at Foggy Bottom, more aggressive, and also more enthusiastic for White House policy directions.

The NSC staff and the national security assistant, of course, may conflict (as may the regulars in the State Department and their noncareer superiors). There have been notable clashes in the past, especially in the immediate aftermath of the American incursion into Cambodia in 1970 during the Vietnam engagement. The national security assistant and the NSC staff are not necessarily in agreement upon substance, but their *forma mentis* are likely to differ from those of their State Department counterparts. If presidents are served amorphous goo from the State Department bureaucracy (which they often see as representing other nations' interests to Washington), they may be provided with clear-headed principles from their in-house foreign policy advisers. Concerned with direction and results, presidents are usually predisposed to cut through the rigidities of complex bureaucratic systems and the cautions of the foreign policy regulars. In this, of course, lies the potential for isolating policy advice from implementation. Going through the bureaucracy often means spinning wheels, but ignoring the bureaucracy poses the prospect of personalizing policy rather than institutionalizing it. In this latter course, there is, to be sure, less wheel-spinning but there is, at least in the long run, also more spinning of castles in the air.

Finally, the soft technology of foreign relations means that it is just precisely the kind of thing that politicians think they are better qualified for than anyone else (Merton, 1968, p. 265). A former noncareer ambassador writes, for instance: "The average American has a sounder instinctive grasp of the basic dynamics of foreign policy than he does of domestic macro-economics. . . . Common sense—the sum of personal experience—will take one further in the realm of foreign policy than in macro-economics" (Silberman, 1979, pp. 879-80). Because little seems mystical or technical about foreign policy to presidents, reliance upon cumbersome bureaucratic machinery seems unnecessary. In most instances, presidents like to be directly engaged with foreign policy because it is more glamorous and central to their historical ambitions, less dependent upon congressional approval, and because it activates their "head of state" role (and in the event of possible military involvement, their "commander-in-chief" one also). In contrast to the trench warfare and haggling involved with domestic policy formulation, foreign policy making tends to promote self-esteem and presidential prestige. With all of these posssibilities, it is improbable, therefore, that presidents want the powers of foreign policy making to be distant from them. Usually, they want it close to them. Presidents need to legitimate White House centrism, then by investing it in a flexible staff operation headed by an unattached foreign policy "expert." These specific reasons, encapsulated within the more general determinants already discussed, have led the White House Department of State to loom as a contender for policy-making influence with the "cabinet" Department of State.

## IRREGULAR AND REGULAR SYNDROMES

In spite of the alluring differences implied by the personnel distinction between irregulars and regulars, neither end of this distinction is a monolith nor is it always generalizable in the same ways across policy sectors and political systems. One reason for this is that bureaucratic cultures reflect the character of the host political culture, as those who have contrasted British and American administrative styles have observed (Sayre, 1964). Both British senior civil servants and their American counterparts, for instance, are bureaucratic regulars, yet they differ substantially in the manner in which they confront their roles—a difference that results from the political ambi-ence surrounding them. Especiallly in administrative systems where there is little tradition of rotating officials across departments, there may be sharp differences in the characteristics of regulars across various departments. In the United States where these departmental subcultures are quite firmly implanted (McGregor, 1974, pp. 24-26; Seidman, 1980, pp. 133-73; Aberbach and Rockman, 1976, pp. 466-67), there is a stylistic gap between the entrepreneurial subcultures often found in social and regulatory agencies and the foreign service subculture of neutral competence.

Similar differences exist amongst irregular personnel as well, and as previously noted, American administration is permeated with irregulars. American elite civil servants' responsibilities began at a level of authority significantly below that of their British counterparts. Indeed, as defined earlier, the distinction between "irregular" and "regular" within departmental settings *must be* hierarchically related. Still, the appointed irregulars in the departments often have had prior experience in that department, 35 to 40 percent according to one estimate (Stanley et al., 1967, p. 41). The professional perspectives of their departments often have been assimilated by these officials, and at least in this respect it is possible to distinguish them from the corps of presidential policy advisers.

Precise comparisons of administrative structures such as those of Britain and the United States are always perilous, but it would not be stretching matters excessively to say that Executive Office irregulars are somewhat akin to the high-fliers of the British civil service without the latter's attachments to the civil service system. Typically, they have less experience in government than their senior line counterparts. With the growth of the institutional presidency, however, the American system has displayed a penchant for mismatching titles of formal authority and possibilities for influencing policy. The high-fliers, therefore, often are better positioned to exert more policy influence in the American system than are the senior officials in the line departments. In the American system, proximity breeds possibilities.

Two very broad distinctions need to be made. One is that between personnel and their relation to career service channels. The other is between organizational settings—central staff versus line department. Further differentiations, of course, can be made within each of these categories. Table 1 illustrates the possible intersection of personnel career channels and their organizational settings. Although I have no measure of the relative influence of setting and career channel on policy thinking and behavior, it is likely that departmental appointees (cell B of Table 1) will be subject, with varying degrees of susceptibility, to the magnetic pull of their departments. Similarly, central staff officials with career backgrounds (cell C of Table 1), also with varying susceptibility, may be inclined to retain their career perspectives and be sensitive to their promotion opportunities—in short, to maximize their departmental interests even while serving in integrative staff structures. This problem reportedly plagued the NSC to some extent under Eisenhower (Falk, pp. 424-25). The distinction between cells A and D is obviously the purest. I assume here the probability of interactive effects between structure and personnel.

Beginning with a broad distinction between irregular staff and regular bureaucratic settings, Table 2 sketches some of the important respects in which these settings differ. These differences point to modal variations in function, in vantage point, in personnel, and in orientations to policy. In the analysis that follows, however, I start with differences between personnel, work back to settings, and then to forms of policy thinking.

How do irregulars differ from regulars? First, irregulars are more likely to be charged with coordinating functions (policy planning, for instance) than are regulars even when they are each engaged in departmental responsibilities. These functions provide the irregular with greater breadth and the capacity to see a more integrated policy picture, but one limited in depth. On the other hand, the regular is located so as to see detail but is less able or likely to see beyond it. These structural features also lead to different interpretations of rationality. The irregular is apt to define rationality as coherence from the vantage point of policy management. The regular, however, is apt to see rationality in terms of informed policy making.

Free of operational responsibilities, irregulars are apt to be conceptualizing and deductive (more "theoretical" or "ideological") in policy thinking than are foreign policy regulars. Intimate detailed knowledge possessed by the regular tends to induce skepticism toward ideas that are abstract and aesthetically interesting. As the regular sees him, the irregular is a simplifier with tendencies toward an excess of imagination and a scarcity of discriminating judgment. Irregulars are rarely lacking in expertise; but the possibilities for thought are distanced from the immediacy of operational problems. Whether by role difference, by recruitment path, or by their interactive effects, the irregular is more desposed to theoretical thought than the regular. Theories are the precursors of activism for they simplify reality sufficiently to permit general, though not necessarily operational, plans of action. The inductivism that is more characteristic of the regulars leads them

Table 1. Career Channel and Organizational Setting Matrix

PURE

DIAGONAL

| Career Channel: Irregular<br>    Setting: Central Staff<br><br>A | Career Channel: Irregular<br>    Setting: Line Department<br><br>B |
|---|---|
| Career Channel: Regular<br>    Setting: Central Staff<br><br>C | Career Channel: Regular<br>    Setting: Line Department<br><br>D |

HYBRID

DIAGONAL

*Source:* Created by the author.

**Table 2. Differences between Irregular Central Staff Settings and Regular Bureaucratic Settings in Foreign Policy Making**

| | Irregular Staff Settings | Regular Bureaucratic Settings |
|---|---|---|
| Typical Responsibilities | Coordinating functions which provide breadth and integrative perspectives, and foster coherence | Implementing functions which provide detailed knowledge and particularistic perspectives, and foster local rationality |
| Location Relative to Decisional Authority | Proximate to political authority, therefore perceived as "Us" | Distant from political authority, therefore perceived as "Them" |
| Type of Personnel | Irregulars and regular "floaters" with few organizational commitments | A mix of irregulars and regulars toward the top, with regulars with long-term organizational commitments at the core |
| Typical Policy-Making Styles | Activists Theorists Conceptualizers Deductivists "Simplifiers" | Skeptics Specialists Inductivists "Complexifiers" |
| Dominant Policy Implications | Directive and thematic, initiatory and bold | Cautious and nonthematic, incrementalist and narrow-gauged |
| Resulting Policy Problems | Superficiality | Particularism |

*Source:* Created by the author.

often toward perceiving complication; it leads them frequently to be skeptical about generalized schemes of action; often it leads them into paralysis. It is both the virtue and the liability of the regular's "hands-on" involvement that he will be predisposed to illustrate the invalidity of proposals and the assumptions they are based on than to advance alternative solutions. After all, it is normally the regular who has to live with the consequences of "rashness."

Ideas and skepticism, while polar intellectual traits, are nonetheless each valuable ones. Large bureaucracies are the wellspring of skepticism and the depressant of ideas. This bureaucratic characteristic flows from the inertia associated with established routines as well as from the concreteness of the regular official's world. Met daily, concreteness and detail induce awareness of complexity. It is this awareness of complexity that ironically is at the heart of the State Department's self-perception as a protector of real long-term interests (Gelb, 1980, p. 34).

Given their natural proclivities, regular bureaucrats are apt to be oriented to the long term within their specialized realms, and likely to be skeptical of overarching themes. This characteristic is not especially attractive to presidents whose "common-sense" approaches to foreign policy often coincide with what is also politically supportable. Being policy generalists, presidents tend to be impatient with "can't-doers," failing to understand or appreciate the skepticism of the foreign policy regulars. From the presidential vantage point, sober thoughts are mere fudge, and skepticism rarely accords with presidents' political needs. Unattached foreign policy "experts," on the other hand, can articulate ideas and push proposals unencumbered by bureaucratic constraints or operational responsibilities. This gives them an obvious advantage over those representing the particularizers in the foreign policy bureaucracy. As for the secretary of state, his advisory and policy-making roles will likely be as large as his distance from the department is great.

There are dangers in the detachment of policy advice and policy influence from operational responsibilities. The triumph of theory over fact is obviously troubling. If regulars, by their skepticism (and probably also their convenience) tend toward incrementalist thinking, it is also true that, at least in the short run, no one ever died of incrementalism. Still, the failure to produce and institutionalize policy integration can be a long-term carcinogenic agent. For politics contoured only by those with operational attachments are likely to suffer from deficiencies of imagination.

## PROPOSED SOLUTIONS TO THE INTEGRATION PROBLEM

The problems of generating integrated and informed policy are obviously apt to receive attention in inverse proportion to the power of the political tools for achieving it. By this standard, America's foreign policy machinery is beset with continuing difficulties. Proposals, official and unofficial, to remedy the foreign policy machinery of the United States abound. They tend to fall into three broad classifications: (1) those emphasizing the role of a strong State Department with a powerful secretarial and presidential direction; (2) those emphasizing the importance of multiple streams of information with a national security assistant playing the more traditional role of traffic manager rather than the one of advocate acquired over the last two decades; and (3) those emphasizing strengthened cabinet-level coordination and the interchange of officials beneath this level. My intent here is to highlight their particular perspectives and their uncertainties.

## 1. Strengthening the Secretary of State

This is not only a common proposal, but also one that seems most obviously apt to connect political strength to institutional capabilities. As Destler put it:

> The issue is not whether the Secretary or the President has primacy. Rather it is who—the Secretary or the National Security Assistant—should be the central foreign affairs official short of the President and acting as his "agent of coordination." If the President is known to rely primarily on the Secretary of State for leadership in foreign policy-making across the board, he should prove far more formidable than a "mere cabinet officer" (1972b, p. 359).

A strengthened secretary of state, however, must have the confidence of the president, and this, in turn, requires a strengthened State Department which means, in Destler's view, a lessened diplomatic role for the secretary and a more forceful policy advocate and organizational management role. What Destler has in mind by the latter, however, is essentially a State Department so transformed that it would be a more coherent tool of presidential direction. In other words, an important element of Destler's proposed reforms is to do unto the State Department that which often has been tried in domestic departments: politicize it. Again, in his words:

> There will remain an inevitable tension between the interests and predispositions of Foreign Service officers and those of Presidents. So no Secretary of State who did not build a strong "political" component into the State Department could hope to satisfy a President bent on controlling the foreign affairs bureaucracy (1972b, p. 288).

Although it does not do full justice to Destler's arguments to say that coherence from the president's standpoint is the exclusive value with which he is concerned, his prescriptions move in the direction of making it the primary one. The potential trap, as Alexander George has noted, is that managerial rationality would come to displace substantive rationality, a likely probability if the State Department is to be politicized, if in essence it is to become a larger, deeper NSC (1972b, pp. 2811-83).

In this guise, a strengthened secretary of state necessitates a weaker national security assistant, indeed, a virtual elimination of the position. A strong secretary of state with a close relationship to the chief executive, Destler claims, has been the best check on the role of the national security assistant as a central policy advocate. But, as he also notes, the very existence of the assistant in the White House makes it difficult to generate that close relationship (1980, pp. 86-87).

The responsiveness of the State Department, of course, is also dependent upon a president knowing his own mind. Presidents differ in this regard, but it is not immediately clear how consistent they can be concerning policy directions to what, after all, are mostly reactive opportunities and necessities. Thematic agreement may be conducive to operational agreement, but it can be no more than that. Alternatively, overarching clarity in foreign policy may simply be dogmatism.

A more likely possibility, one that may be symbolized by personalities such as Alexander Haig and Henry Kissinger, is that of the entrepreneurial secretary of state who cuts a demanding figure in his own right. The entrepreneurship, however, may well come at the cost of organizational debilitation. While the relationship between Alexander Haig, the State Department, and the White House remains to be developed as of this writing, Kissinger, as secretary of state, was both a policy advocate and presidential spokesman, but in spirit he never left the White House in these roles. Nor, in fact, had he physically left it until late 1975. A secretary who draws nourishment from the Department's professional foreign service roots, however, is apt to find himself, sooner or later, designated as one of "them." This, at least since Dean Acheson, has largely been the case.

In any event, the problem lingers of generating political coherence (organizational rationality) in such manner as to effectively utilize substantive rationality (derived from specialized sub-units). A politicized State Department, one suspects, would be more coherent and responsive. But could it then effectively contribute to informed policy making?

## 2. Encouraging Multiple Advocacy

As proposed by Alexander George (1972a), the organizational strategy of multiple advocacy assumes the virtues of local rationality. In spirit, it is to foreign policy formulation an application of Chairman Mao's "Hundred Flowers Bloom" campaign. It makes a virtue of what is a necessary vice, the multiplicity of perspectives generated by the division of labor which bureaucratic sprawl leaves in its wake. George's interesting suggestion is to return to the basic concept of the old special assistant's role as a managerial custodian, a facilitator of varying perspectives so that the president may avail himself of the full play of diversity surrounding him. In its new form, the assistant would be constrained from playing the role of policy advocate, or from presenting foreign policy views to the public. His facilitating role would be greatly expanded, and in that presumably would lie his status. To some extent, this super-custodian presumably would be something akin to the director of the Office of Management and Budget, but without the capacity to pass judgment upon departmental requests—in other words, largely powerless. I am not the first to point out that in Washington those with status but without power quickly become worked around rather than through.

We may question, too, the assumption that presidents, or leaders of other large organizations, for that matter, are thirsting for information, diversity, and knowledge. Mao, after all, quickly came to disown the "Hundred Flowers Bloom" campaign. Facts, information, knowledge are great legitimizers of action. Not surprisingly, leaders often find it best to screen them selectively. A reasonable hypothesis is that the longer presidents (leaders in general) have been in power and thus the more prior commitments they have established and defenses they have constructed around them, the more likely it is that their tolerance for diversity declines. Even if at first presidents are predisposed to hunt facts, in the end facts are more likely to haunt presidents. Removed from electoral concerns, presidential interests in policy, per se, are often suspect (recall Nixon's response to Haldeman's request for policy direction on propping up the Italian lira), but whatever interests they do have also are apt to diminish as their term wears on and as more decisions become responses rather than initiatives. None of this perhaps would be so important were it not for the fact that George insists that presidents must assume a magistrate's role; otherwise, diversity becomes hyperpluralist babble. For without this particular role assumption, the rich flow of information and analysis likely would reinforce local rationality. Coherence and direction would famish.

The assumption that foreign policy contestants ought essentially to emulate lawyers in an American litigation proceeding by pressing their "interested" rendition of the "facts" before a disinterested presidential magistrate is curious. Being that presidents are neither disinterested themselves, nor unlimited in their attention spans, it is more likely that the chief magistrate will be the president's national security assistant. There is, in short, little incentive for the president to cope with detailed arguments, and none for the assistant to shy away from policy advocacy. As interesting as they are, proposals for functional changes that do not account for the costs to, and incentives of, the actors involved are more nearly prayers.

## 3. Strengthening the Cabinet and Rotating Officials

In *Presidential Power*, Richard Neustadt quotes a White House aide to President Eisenhower as saying, "If some of these Cabinet members would just take time out to stop and ask themselves, 'What would I want if I were President?', they wouldn't give him all the trouble he's been having" (1980, p. 31). The reasons for this estrangement are well known. And the underlying assumption about it, namely, that role alteration diminishes parochialness, is taken as the point of origin for its alleviation. To alleviate this condition, a two-pronged strategy has been advanced (Allison and Szanton, 1976, pp. 78-80; Allison, 1980). The strategy requires a dash of something a bit new and something old.

What is somewhat new is the recommendation that NSC staffers be continually rotated between the agencies and the White House so as to mold together agency and White House perspectives among individuals. The model for this suggestion is that of the British civil service generalist. As matters stand, of course, a substantial portion of the NSC staff previously served in another agency (State, Defense, and CIA, in that order) either indirectly or directly before arriving at the NSC. Estimates from the 1977 list show that nearly 40 percent had such experience (as compiled by Berry and Kyle, 1977), and to define things more narrowly, Destler (1972b, p. 249) indicates that as of April 1971 almost half of the NSC staff had some prior experience either in the State Department or the military services. Thus it is not that many of these officials are lacking experience in the agencies (though it should be kept in mind that over 60 percent of the 1977 staff had no prior agency experience), but rather that for most of them, present roles are likely to be especially compelling.[7] Recombinant socialization does not necessarily mean intellectual integration. In the face of a highly centrifugal structure of government, knowing how it looks from "there" may be merely a tactical advantage in the struggle to influence policy rather than a basis for policy integration. For such proposals to work, structures that provide for collectively responsible points of decision making are essential.

Thus, the other part of this recommended strategy is to create an Executive Committee of Cabinet Officials (ExCab) to provide ongoing high-level policy review. "A body like ExCab," Graham Allison claims, "would yield most of the advantages of the collegial participation of major department heads while avoiding the unwieldiness of the full cabinet" (1980, p. 46). ExCab, however, as even its promoter willingly admits, is not an altogether new idea. The Nixon administration after all, had proposed a set of "super cabinet" departments and, failing congressional approval, then created by executive fiat an informal set of "super-secretaries." Though Nixon's political demise brought this operation into formal disrepair, it is unfair to pass judgment upon it, since its creation only shortly preceded Nixon's calamitous, if protracted, fall from grace. To be sure, there are a number of operational problems that this approach does not automatically avoid. There is first the question of who is in and who is out. Only in a cabinet of nonentities of the sort Nixon tried to create for his second administration is it likely that department secretaries would accede to more powerful presences. Secondly, while the ExCab proposal potentially permits diversity to flow with decisional responsibility, many of the difficulties presidents have in dealing with the full cabinet also arise even with a reduced foreign policy-focused cabinet. It is not merely the presence of diversity within the executive that distresses presidents, for that evidently is a condition affecting top leaders everywhere to some degree. Rather, it is the ease with which opposition or losing forces within the executive can go to Capitol Hill or the press, usually reaching the former by means of the latter. It is difficult for collegial government, however reduced the number of relevant actors, to flourish under such conditions. Any proposal to reform the organizational apparatus of American foreign policy making needs to be sensitive to this problem. Though the possible, but as yet unknown, impact of organizational reforms should not be disconnected, these neither alter fundamentally the institutional framework of largely antagonistic forces in Washington nor the culture of openness that both sustains and reinforces this adversarial framework.

## CONCLUSION

Presidents ultimately determine foreign policy. Whatever system of advice and decision making exists can exist only with the president's approval. It is within the range of presidential discretion to permit the national security assistant to become a leading contestant for foreign policy influence. Similarly, it is within the scope of presidential judgment to permit the national security assistant to appear as the chief foreign policy representative for their administrations. Nixon and Carter did permit these things; indeed, they encouraged them, though for different reasons. Thus far, the Reagan model (if there is one) has resulted in decreased visibility for the national security assistant. The NSC professional staff, however, is no smaller than it was during the Carter administration, and at least one report indicates a more direct White House staff involvement monitoring operations through the NSC machinery (Evans and Novak, 1981). Additionally, somewhat reminiscent of Nixon's "administrative presidency" model, a loyal operative has been slipped into the deputy secretary's role at State. In the last 14 months of the Ford administration, the role of the national security assistant and, to a modest degree, that of the NSC veered closer to the Eisenhower model of a dominant secretary of state and a "neutral competent" national security assistant (Brent Scowcroft). The reason for this, however, now seems clear. Ford's secretary of state, Henry Kissinger, was his leading foreign policy spokesman and leading foreign policy maker, yet not really his foreign minister. To be both, foreign minister (representing departmental perspectives) and leading foreign policy maker has within it increasingly the seeds of an insoluble role conflict.

Presidents vary, of course, in their ideas as to how foreign policy making ought to be organized, what they want from it, and how much weight is given at least at the outset to the values of harmony and diversity. The difficulty lies in isolating which aspects of their variability will lead to a heightened emphasis upon staff irregulars, and how they will be used. Similar results, as the disparate cases of Nixon and Carter indicate, may flow from different organizational modes. While each held widely different models of the policy-shaping process in foreign affairs, each also further enlarged the role of the NSC as a policy mechanism. Early on, Nixon seemed to prefer policy to be shaped at the White House, and as much as possible to skirt around the bureaucracy. Carter's organization, on the other hand, seemed to exaggerate Alexander George's ideal of multiple advocacy except, quite importantly, that Zbigniew Brzezinski was meant to be an advocate and not just a mediator. Different intentions seem to have produced fairly similar results—a highly visible national security assistant and a "competing" State Department.

The variability of presidents notwithstanding, the overall thrust since Eisenhower seems fairly clear: more White House centrism in foreign policy making, and an enlarged NSC role. Presidential variability tells us a lot about form—the particular uses made of the NSC mechanism and of the national security assistant—but it does not tell us why the NSC today looks so different from the NSC of 25 years ago, nor does it tell us why the national security assistant has so often been a primary policy maker. While the water has both risen and receded, the watermark is a good bit higher now than it was then.

To explain this trend toward centrism, and thus the importance of policy irregulars, my analysis focuses upon a theory of government—a theme somewhat broader than its specific target. The proposals for reconstituting America's foreign policy mechanisms that have been examined here certainly represent a more precise approach. Yet, government and politics in Washington, and the open culture that surrounds it, represent the limits against which these various proposals bump. From the hyperpoliticized ambience of American government the role needs of foreign policy contestants are shaped. Institutional fragmentation and weak parties not only beget one another, they also promote a level of bureaucratic politics of unusual intensity—grist for the mill of a highly inquisitive press.

No wonder presidents find their political and policy needs better served from within the White House. From this vantage point, the departments sooner or later are perceived as representing or pursuing interests that are not those of the president. This is especially so for the State Department because it is frequently seen as representing interests of other countries. With virtuallly no domestic constituencies and reflecting a subculture that, much like the British civil service, emphasizes "neutral competence" and balance, the foreign service regulars in the State Department are singularly disadvantaged. The steamy adversarial climate of Washington's executive politics does not nourish such values. The White House (and often department heads) are anxious for "movement," and unreceptive to "let's wait a moment." In the long run, the danger in any such setting is that the tools of central clearance will metamorphose into mechanisms for central dominance.

In sum, the reasons why America has a competing State Department turn out to be both excruciatingly complex and yet remarkably simple. Its simplicity lies in the structure of antagonistic forces given form by the American Constitution. Its complexities lie in the conditions—the importance of foreign policy, the role of the media, the burgeoning of policy intellectuals—that have since ripened.

The problem of reconciling "the persistent dilemmas of unity and diversity" (Fenno, p. 339) remains to be solved as much in the foreign policy sphere as in the domestic one, especially as the distinction between these arenas erodes. In unity lies strategic direction and clarity, but also the dangers of a monocled vision. In diversity lies sensitivity to implementation and to nuance, but also the dangers of producing least common denominators. Ironically, during the Eisenhower presidency when the NSC performed most nearly like a cabinet committee producing consensus from diversity, it was criticized for the ambiguities remaining in its products (Destler, 1977, pp. 152-53). If not a fudge factory, it was at least a fudge shop.

Each president to some extent will develop mechanisms that suit him best. Among other things, the policy system established will reflect the idiosyncracies of interpersonal chemistry. Each, though, has inherited an in-house foreign policy apparatus defined in the last 20 years more by how it has been used than by its original statuatory rationale. How that apparatus will evolve cannot be foretold with preciseness. But how and why it has evolved from its inception to its present state is a saga that should be of as much interest to students of American government as to those of foreign policy.

## NOTES

1. Campbell and Szablowski (1979) note, for instance, that senior officials in the Canadian central coordinating agencies differ from the main-line civil servants in the traditional line ministries in that they are more likely to have entered laterally rather than to have moved upward through the civil service system.

2. From earliest to latest in the Eisenhower administration, they were Robert Cutler, Dillon Anderson, and Gordon Gray. During the Truman administration there were two executive secretaries of the NSC. Each, Sidney Souers and James Lay, reflected the "neutral competence" ideal.

3. This, of course, is a by-product of the presidential system. Ironically, the

Eberstadt Report which set forth the rationale for the National Security Act and, thus, the NSC, apparently was motivated by a desire to create a high level British type cabinet committee. As Hammond notes (1960, p. 899): "The Eberstadt Report assumed that the proposed National Security Council could be a kind of war cabinet in which the responsibilities of the President could be vested. . . . The premise arose . . . out of an inclination to modify the Presidency as an institution."

4. A recent study of organizational memory development among three EOP agencies, for example, finds that the NSC consistently has the least cross-administration continuity as measured by several indicators (Covington, 1981). The author of this report concludes that organizational continuity reflects presidential detachment, whereas lack of memory reflects intense presidential interest.

5. As Barton J. Bernstein (1980, p. 103 n.) observes from his study of recently declassified materials regarding this episode:

A chief executive may often express preferences (not orders) for policies, and that he may sincerely reinterpret them as *orders* when his own inaction leaves him woefully unprepared in a crisis. In this way, a president can place blame on a subordinate, and other aides who listen to his charges tend to believe that the president actually issued an order, and not simply stated a wish or a hope.

For a general review of this incident, see Bernstein (1980), and also Hafner (1977).

6. Compiled from data in Berry and Kyle (1977).

7. The Carter NSC figures are essentially reversed under Reagan. Among the present NSC staff, roughly 60 percent have had prior government experience, and 40 percent have not.

# REFERENCES

Aberbach, Joel D., Robert D. Putnam, and Bert A. Rockman (1981). *Bureaucrats and Politicians in Western Democracies.* Cambridge, Mass.: Harvard University Press.

Aberbach, Joel D. and Bert A. Rockman (1976). "Clashing Beliefs within the Executive Branch: The Nixon Administration Bureaucracy." *American Political Science Review* 70: 456-68.

Allison, Graham (1980). "An Executive Cabinet." *Society:* 17, July/August, 41-47.

_____, and Peter Szanton (1976). *Remaking Foreign Policy.* New York: Basic Books.

Armstrong, Scott (1980). "Carter Given Oaths on 'Leaks.'" *The Washington Post,* 16 July 1980, pp. A1, A4.

Art, Robert J. (1973). "Bureaucratic Politics and American Foreign Policy: A Critique. *Policy Sciences* 4: 467-90.

Bernstein, Barton J. (1980). "The Cuban Missile Crisis: Trading the Jupiters in Turkey?" *Political Science Quarterly* 95: 97-126.

Berry, F. Clifton, Jr., and Deborah Kyle (1977). "The 'Other Cabinet': The National Security Council Staff." *Armed Forces Journal* 114 (July): 12-20.

Campbell, Colin (1980). "The President's Advisory System under Carter: From Spokes in a Wheel to Wagons in a Circle." Presented at the annual meeting of the American Political Science Association, Washington, D.C.

_____, and George J. Szablowski (1979). *The Superbureaucrats: Structure and Behaviour in Central Agencies.* Toronto: Macmillan of Canada.

Campbell, John Franklin (1971). *The Foreign Affairs Fudge Factory*. New York: Basic Books.

Covington, Cary R. (1981). "Presidential Memory Development in Three Presidential Agencies." Presented at the annual meeting of the Midwest Political Science Association, Cincinnati.

Cronin, Thomas E. (1975). *The State of the Presidency*. Boston: Little, Brown.

Crossman, R. H. S. (1972). *The Myths of Cabinet Government*. Cambridge, Mass.: Harvard University Press.

Destler, I. M. (1980). "A Job That Doesn't Work." *Foreign Policy* 38: 80-88.

_____ (1977). "National Security Advice to U.S. Presidents: Some Lessons From Thirty Years." *World Politics* 29: 143-76.

_____ (1972a). "Making Foreign Policy: Comment." *American Political Science Review* 66: 786-90.

_____ (1972b). *Presidents, Bureaucrats, and Foreign Policy: The Politics of Organizational Reform*. Princeton, N.J.: Princeton University Press.

Dyson, K. H. F. (1974). "Planning and the Federal Chancellor's Office in the West German Federal Government." *Political Studies* 21: 348-62.

Evans, Rowland, and Robert Novak (1981). "The Education of Al Haig." *Washington Post*, 1 May 1981, p. A19.

Falk, Stanley L. (1964). "The National Security Council under Truman, Eisenhower, and Kennedy." *Political Science Quarterly* 79: 403-34.

Fenno, Richard F., Jr. (1975). "The President's Cabinet." In Aaron Wildavsky (ed.), *Perspectives on the Presidency*. Boston: Little, Brown.

Gelb, Leslie H. (1980). "Muskie and Brzezinski: The Struggle over Foreign Policy." *New York Times Magazine*, 20 July 1980, pp. 26-40.

George, Alexander L. (1972a). "The Case for Multiple Advocacy in Making Foreign Policy." *American Political Science Review* 66: 751-85.

_____ (1972b). "Making Foreign Policy: Rejoinder." *American Political Science Review* 66: 791-95.

Hafner, Donald L. (1977). "Bureaucratic Politics and 'Those Frigging Missiles': JFK, Cuba and U.S. Missiles in Turkey." *Orbis* 21: 307-32.

Hammond, Paul Y. (1960). "The National Security Council as a Device for Interdepartmental Coordination: An Interpretation and Appraisal." *American Political Science Review* 54: 899-910.

Heclo, Hugh (1975). "OMB and the Presidency: The Problem of 'Neutral Competence.'" *The Public Interest* 38 (Winter): 80-98.

Klein, Rudolf, and Janet Lewis (1977). "Advice and Dissent in British Government: The Case of the Special Advisers." *Policy and Politics* 6: 1-25.

Maechling, Charles, Jr. (1976). "Foreign Policy-Makers: The Weakest Link?" *Virginia Quarterly Review* 52: 1-23.

McGregor, Eugene B., Jr. (1974). "Politics and the Career Mobility of Bureaucrats." *American Political Science Review* 68: 18-26.

Mennis, Bernard (1971). *American Foreign Policy Officials: Who They Are and What They Believe Regarding International Politics*. Columbus: Ohio State University Press.

Merton, Robert K. (1968). "Role of the Intellectual in Public Bureaucracy." In R. K. Merton, *Social Theory and Social Structure*. New York: The Free Press.

Murphy, Thomas P., Donald E. Nuechterlein, and Ronald J. Stupak (1978). *Inside the Bureaucracy: The View from the Assistant Secretary's Desk*. Boulder, Colo.: Westview.

Nathan, Richard P. (1975). *The Plot that Failed: Nixon and the Administrative Presidency*. New York: John Wiley.

National Security Policy Integration (1979). Report of a Study Requested by the

President under the Auspices of the President's Reorganization Project. Washington, D.C.: Government Printing Office.

Neustadt, Richard E. (1954). "Presidency and Legislation: The Growth of Central Clearance." *American Political Science Review* 48: 641-71.

_____ (1980). *Presidential Power: The Politics of Leadership from FDR to Carter.* New York: John Wiley.

Rose, Richard (1976a). *Managing Presidential Objectives.* New York: Free Press.

_____ (1976b). "On the Priorities of Government: A Developmental Analysis of Public Policies." *European Journal of Political Research* 4: 247-89.

_____ (1980). "Government against Sub-governments: A European Perspective on Washington." In Richard Rose and Ezra Suleiman (eds.), *Presidents and Prime Ministers: Giving Direction to Government.* Washington, D.C.: American Enterprise Institute.

Sapin, Burton M. (1967). *The Making of United States Foreign Policy.* New York: Praeger.

Sayre, Wallace S. (1964). "Bureaucracies: Some Contrasts in Systems." *Indian Journal of Public Administration* 10: 219-29.

Seidman, Harold (1980). *Politics, Position, and Power: The Dynamics of Federal Organization.* New York: Oxford University Press.

Silberman, Laurence H. (1979). "Toward Presidential Control of the State Department." *Foreign Affairs* 57: 72-93.

Smith, Hedrick (1981). "A Scaled-down Version of Security Adviser's Task." *New York Times,* 4 March 1981, p. A2.

Stanley, David T., Dean E. Mann, and Jameson W. Doig (1967). *Men Who Govern: A Biographical Profile of American Federal Executives.* Washington, D.C.: Brookings Institution.

---

# 6.4   The National Security Council, the Conscience of the Presidency, and the Reagan Agenda

## ALLAN A. MYER

*Allan Myer, former member of President Reagan's National Security Council (NSC) staff, addresses the prominent role that the assistant for National Security Affairs and the staff of the NSC must play if the president's agenda is to survive the internecine bureaucratic battles. People and structural variables are crucial elements in this struggle. Myer's conclusion points to the dilemma with which the Iran-Contra investigation wrestled—namely, that White House control does not guarantee the protection and projection of the conscience of the presidency.*

On April 12, 1945, Vice President Harry S. Truman was summoned to the residence of the White House. There he was shown into Eleanor Roosevelt's sitting room, and she told him gently that President Roosevelt was dead. After a moment's stunned silence, Truman asked her, "Is there anything I can do for you?"

Mrs. Roosevelt shook her head and whispered, "Is there anything we can do for you? You're the one in trouble now."

How can the United States best protect its national interests and secure the objectives that would further those interests worldwide? To answer that basic national security strategy question, a typical discussion in graduate seminars and war college classrooms might go something like: First, understand the most important U.S. national security interests, interests that are global and, at times, at odds with those of the Soviet Union and other nations. Second, establish clear objectives that would secure those interests. Third, examine the threats to U.S. interests and national security objectives. Take into account all unfolding international trends. Fourth, thoroughly analyze available resources, capabilities, coalitions, alliances, and all other elements of national power. Finally, develop a rational, comprehensive, and objective national security strategy that can be achieved within the limits of existing U.S. national power.

This sequence might be the basis for a reasonable academic exercise—a straightforward, dispassionate, objective mechanism for developing national security policy. But from my vantage point as a former practitioner on the staff of the NSC, it is quite divorced from reality. Indeed, the use of any theory or model to explain actual circumstances is an abstraction and, typically, an unsuccessful attempt to reduce cluttered complexity to orderly relationships. Straightforward, dispassionate, objective mechanisms also fall short on one other account: The actual formulation of national security policy is rarely straightforward, almost always passionate, and, because the process is based on political perspectives and ideological influences, very subjective.

It does matter who sits in the Oval Office, and if the U.S. political process is intended to exercise the will of the people, it should matter. A president comes to office with a perspective—with very specific views on where the United States stands in the world, notions about where it should stand, and concepts on how to get there. There is an agenda, implied or otherwise. There is also the question of which issues should be addressed in what priority. There are questions of pace and timing. There are understandings about the intentions of adversaries. There are perceptions of allies and friends. Perspectives do matter. The presidential agenda always has some very tough obstacles to overcome. There is the Congress, of course, the media, think tanks, trade associations, political interest groups, and a host of other public policy centers. The agenda never has it easy, not even within the president's own Executive Branch. Political administrations come and go, but the bureaucracies within the Executive Branch stay forever. Career officers watch over the vested interests of the various departments. Officers of the Senior Executive Service, Senior Intelligence Service, and the Foreign Service have their own visions, perspectives, aspirations, and, yes, even agendas. In the end, vested interests in any particular department or agency may or may not coincide with those of a particular administration, and that's the rub.

From a viewpoint within the White House compound, the challenge is to keep the administration's perspective in force and the president's domestic agenda working. That is far easier said than done. There is no assurance that the president's perspective will lead the national security process. There is no guarantee that options being considered, much less chosen, for policy implementation will include the president's. There is no certainty that the priorities and pace of the national security agenda will be the result of direct presidential leadership. In fact, there is much evidence to the contrary. Without direct and continuing oversight by the Executive Office of the president (the White House staff), the departments and agencies of the Executive Branch tend to go their own way and do their own thing.

During the first year of the first term of the Reagan administration, the president chose to downgrade the role of his National Security Advisor and the staff of the National Security Council. The decision may have been a conscious attempt to avoid the internecine tensions that had developed between the White House and the State Department in at least three previous administrations. It was certainly an experiment in cabinet government, carried forward from the Governor's Mansion in Sacramento by the president, Ed Meese, Mike Deaver, and others who had been part of the California team. The problem was that California did not have to formulate and implement national security policy—California did not have a foreign policy. The experiment failed.

National security strategy in 1981 was, at best, a collection of departmental policies fought over in public. U.S. allies and adversaries alike tried without much success to interpret contradictory public statements made by various administration officials. No wonder. Cabinet secretaries and other officials would often take divergent positions, and the White House did not intervene.

The battle of the two Richards is a fitting illustration of that failed experiment. Richard Burt, an assistant secretary of state, and Richard Perle, an assistant secretary of defense, seemed to enjoy their widely reported skirmishes on everything from foreign and defense policy to arms control and the military balance. They fought over the basics of U.S. foreign policy, and over the particulars, and most everything in between. They argued at home and took their respective positions with them when they traveled overseas. These engaging and influential officials were near the center of the national security process; they were among the best and brightest in the Reagan administration, and they spent a year confusing everyone.

If the president's vision—whether it be in domestic or foreign affairs—is to be protected, the staffs within the Executive Office of the president are the ones to do it. The White House staff is the conscience of the presidency.

For domestic issues, the president has a counselor, a chief of staff, and offices of Policy Development, Political Affairs, Public Liaison, Legislative Affairs, and Cabinet Affairs. Each office is specifically charged with the responsibility to carry a piece of the president's domestic agenda forward, And each office sits astride a bureaucratic structure within the Executive Branch to do just that.

When it comes to national security affairs, the conscience of the presidency rests with the National Security Advisor and the staff of the National Security Council. The lines of authority in the national security decisionmaking process—what they are, and how they are used—determine whether or not the president's views, direction, and oversight are a key and continuing part of the game. To keep the president's wishes in the game, the starting point must be a a chain of command that points upward toward and through the National Security Council, its staff, and the president's National Security Advisor. At first glance, it might appear that because political appointments extend well down into the third and fourth tier of each department and agency, those officials should be able to keep the president's agenda on track. However, even disregarding the two Richards, that is hardly the way it really works.

The issue of technology transfer—exporting advanced technologies—is a case in point. The Department of Defense is concerned, as it should be, about the security implications of transferring military-relevant technologies that are likely to wind up in the hands of U.S. adversaries. The secretary of commerce is worried, as he should be, about the health of U.S. industry and its world market share. The United States trade representative wants to improve the U.S. trade balance, and he should do everything in his power to do so. The State Department, depending on the particular country involved and the technology transfer item in question, may not want to complicate or endanger other ongoing diplomatic efforts in that country, and it is correct in urging caution. The director of central intelligence is worried, as he should be, about the effect of previous technology transfers on the military balance and the security of the nation.

Where you stand on an issue depends, in large measure, on where you sit—fair enough. Departmental perspectives must be considered, and defended, during policy deliberations—as should the views of the person sitting in the Oval Office. In the end, competing perspectives must be reconciled, and, inevitably, reconciliation is principally a matter of organizational structure and administration. If the National Security Advisor and the staff of the NSC are not active and prominent players in policy analysis and formulation, and not fully engaged during policy deliberations at all levels of the process, the core national security beliefs of the president, and his foreign and defense policy agenda should not be expected to survive.

The crux of the matter is that during the first year in office, President

Reagan did not afford himself of the procedural and structural means to best exercise his will in national security matters, protect his core beliefs, and move his agenda forward. The situation began to change in January 1982, coincident with the appointment of Judge William P. Clark as national security advisor. The most immediate, and possibly the most substantive, change took place within the White House itself. Unlike Richard Allen, Judge Clark reported directly to the president, conducted the daily morning presidential briefing, and was granted rather unimpeded access to the Oval Office. With regard to the formal process, the role and authority of the national security advisor and the NSC staff were strengthened—albeit slowly at first.

The White House Press Office released a statement by the president titled *National Security Council Structure.* The guidelines in this seven-page document offered the Reagan administration's first detailed explanation of the responsibilities and lines of authority in foreign and defense policy within the Executive Branch. The national security advisor was to determine and publish the agenda of NSC meetings, ensure that the necessary papers were prepared and distributed in advance of NSC meetings to council members. Control of the agenda and the NSC meeting papers gave Judge Clark two potentially powerful roles. He was also given the responsibility for developing, coordinating, and implementing national security policy as approved by the president, but given the organizational structure detailed in the paper, this was an assertion without much substance.

Leadership for the organization of foreign, defense, and intelligence policy was assigned to the respective cabinet member. Under each of the three cabinet officers (state, defense, and central intelligence), the guidelines established Senior Interdepartmental Groups (SIGs), chaired by the deputy secretaries of state and defense, and the director of central intelligence. Each Senior Interdepartmental Group, as appropriate, established a number of functional or regional Interdepartmental Groups (IGs), chaired by assistant secretaries of the appropriate departments or agencies. The national security advisor chaired nothing; neither did any of the senior members of the NSC staff. Cabinet government was still very much alive in the national security process.

However, during the course of the next several years, the national security advisor assumed new tasks and responsibilities far beyond the guidelines established in January 1982. With the changes, the locus of analysis, coordination, and decisionmaking turned increasingly to a smaller group of people working in interagency groups outside the SIG-IG structure. In many cases, these interagency working groups were chaired by the national security advisor or his deputy. Although the SIGs and IGs remained operational and continued to produce important analyses, control of the coordination and decisionmaking processes steadily drew closer to the West

Wing of the White House.

As a result, by the end of the first Reagan term, the priorities and pace of the national security agenda were very much in the hands of the White House. Events of the second term would demonstrate the degree to which the conscience of the presidency was being protected and projected.

# 7

## Bureaucratic Politics and Liaison with the Congress

*The U.S. Congress is the most powerful independent legislative body in the world. Its authority over national security policy and operations is most impressive. Congress controls the purse strings, legislates, investigates, procures, structures, and micromanages. Everything that is done by the national security community eventually can be traced back to some congressional action in one form or another, and, of course, national security policy reflects, for better and for worse, the unique character of the national legislature with its penchant for incrementalism, delay, dispersed authority, watered-down compromises, and geographical parochialism.*

*Because of the important national security authority of Congress and its awesome policy tools with which to make its imprint felt, the bureaucracy expends enormous effort for the purposes of interfacing with the U.S. Congress. In every sense, this interface is political as agencies attempt to advance their interests by putting their best foot forward. Chapters in this section address the similarities and differences of bureaucratic and legislative cultures, their interface, and the enterprise of effective legislative liaison.*

# 7.1   Dateline Washington: The Rules of the Games

## STANLEY J. HEGINBOTHAM

*The Constitution creates an invitation to struggle. Differing rules of the game as perceived and played by executive and legislative officials, and executive officials who treat congressional partici- pants with "disdain and insensitivity," who "repeatedly sought to circumvent and deceive Congress rather than involve it in serious negotiations armed at compromise solutions" sounds much like a 1987 commentary on the state of executive-legislative relations in national security policy. Yet such is the essence of Heginbotham's 1983 analysis. As in 1983, success today and in the future calls for the national security players to transcend institutional games and work toward mutually accommodative policies and procedures—easier said than done.*

The debate over the appropriate relationship between Congress and the executive branch on matters of foreign policy has been revived in recent months. The Supreme Court's June 1983 decision in *Immigration and Naturalization Service* v. *Chadba,* which struck down legislative vetoes, has generated a debate about how Congress should exercise influence over arms sales to foreign countries, exports of nuclear materials, and other foreign- policy issues. And the dispatch of U.S. Marines to Lebanon and to Grenada has exposed, without fully resolving, competing perspectives on what role Congress should have in the deployment of U.S. armed forces into combat.

The *Chadba* decision in particular seems at first blush to strengthen the hand of the executive branch in this debate. But in fact it reaffirms the sepa- rate and countervailing powers and procedures of Congress and the executive as defined in the Constitution. Thus a careful reading of the *Chadba* decision should neither excessively buoy advocates of executive dominance in foreign affairs nor unduly dispirit supporters of a strong congressional role. Rather an analysis of the case should lead members of both camps, as well as those in the middle, to recognize that making the existing cumbersome system work more effectively is now even more important than ever.

Reprinted with permission from *Foreign Policy 2* (Spring 1971). Copyright 1971 by the Carnegie Endowment for International Peace.

Any effort to understand and improve the dynamics of congressional-executive interaction on foreign policy must begin by recognizing that the political cultures of the executive-branch foreign-policy arena and the congressional arena are fundamentally different. This gap creates both the tension that often hinders interbranch cooperation on foreign-policy matters and the stereotypes that players in each arena have developed, over time, concerning their counterparts.

Many executive-branch officials—including the staff of the National Security Council, State Department political appointees, and career Foreign Service officers—consider members of Congress and their staffs to be insensitive to the need for privacy and confidentiality in foreign relations. They view the legislators as predisposed to grandstanding, prone to disrupting important incremental day-to-day shifts in relations with other countries, dilatory and unpredictable in their legislative actions, ignorant of basic foreign-policy realities, and parochial in their approach to global issues.

Members of Congress and their staffs are often just as firmly convinced that foreign-policy officials are unquestioning in their advocacy of administration policies, obsessed with the minutiae of ritualized diplomatic exchanges, insensitive to broad patterns of American interests, more concerned with the interests and needs of their foreign counterparts than with the democratic processes of their own government, arrogant in their belief that their academic training and field experience give them a monopoly on foreign-policy wisdom, hypocritical in their claim exclusively to represent the national interest, and skilled primarily in stanching the flow of meaningful information to Capitol Hill.

To a great extent, these stereotypes accurately reflect behavior within one branch, at least as measured by the criteria for behavior in the other. But few participants in congressional-executive relations understand the demands and constraints of the culture of the other branch and generally underestimate the extent of their inherent differences between that game and the one they play.

Most participants know how to manipulate the dynamics of their own organizations. Accordingly, they follow the rules of behavior that are most likely to produce policy success and to advance their personal fortunes in their own arena. But because the rules of the congressional game and the foreign-policy game are often contradictory, when participants from the two arenas try to reach decisions jointly, conflict is almost always the result, no matter how completely they agree on substance.

This conflict occurs in large part because it is built into the system of government of the United States. Congressional electoral accountability and the separation of powers insure that members of the executive and legislative branches will apply different sets of rules to the management of U.S. foreign relations. The following eight pairs of rules shaping the behavior of members of Congress and their aides and of foreign-policy officials illustrate the potential for conflict created by these constitutional facts of life.

• On discretion and public pronouncements:

Foreign-policy Game: Career prospects depend largely on the ability to conduct sensitive diplomacy in private and to be discreet in interbureau conflict. Public-policy statements are inherently hazardous because they can constrain future flexibility and complicate private negotiations.

Congressional Game: Public-policy statements are keys to re-election prospects; be discreet in the procedural management of congressional conflicts but in general speak out on the substance of those conflicts.

• On unity and diversity in foreign-policy pronouncements:

Foreign-policy Game: Governments should speak to other governments with one voice. As representatives of the U.S. government, refrain from public statements that might conflict with or compromise U.S. policy.

Congressional Game: Cultivate a reputation for independence among voters; issuing public challenges to the executive branch's stated foreign policy is one effective means of doing so.

• On the significance of government-to-government relations:

Foreign-policy Game: Stable and friendly relations with foreign governments are goals worth pursuing for their own sake.

Congressional Game: Relations with foreign governments should be assessed in light of their importance to specific economic, strategic, political, and cultural interests of the United States and its constituent elements, whether those be regions, states, congressional districts, or interest groups.

• On continuous and sporadic attention to foreign policy:

Foreign-policy Game: Continuous monitoring and management of day-to-day relations with other countries are necessary to avoid needless misunderstandings and crises.

Congressional Game: Opportunities to influence foreign policy will arise sporadically, resulting from unanticipated events, public concerns, the legislative calendar, and occasional oversight activities. These opportunities must be exploited.

• On how to manage foreign relations:

Foreign-policy Game: Since governments are greatly concerned about maintaining stable and friendly relations with other governments, they are sensitive to relatively minor changes in the status of relations.  Send and receive important signals by carefully managing and interpreting those changes.

Congressional Game: Since only sporadic influence on relations with other governments is possible, the goal must be to correct misguided policies of the past.  In doing so, alienating those who are attached to the status quo and excessively reluctant to adjust to new realities will and should occur often.

• On timing and certainty:

Foreign-policy Game: Enhance the ability to maintain stable and positive relations with other countries by assuring foreign officials that any agreement reached in negotiations will promptly be ratified.

Congressional Game: The ability to use delay, procedural maneuver, and surprise to the disadvantage of congressional adversaries in the ratification of foreign-policy agreements will improve leverage over them in legislative bargaining.

• On critical skills:

Foreign-policy Game: Professional expertise—detailed knowledge, intercultural sensitivity, and diplomatic skills—is essential to the successful conduct of diplomacy.

Congressional Game: Abilities as a quick-study generalist are essential to political survival and to legislative success.

• On parochialism and the national interest:

Foreign-policy Game: Parochial, bureaucratic policy preferences should be expressed in terms that reflect concern for the national interest.

Congressional Game: Policy preferences in the national interest must often be expressed in terms that appeal to the parochial concerns of the electorate.

Many more examples of conflicting diplomatic and legislative imperatives can be cited.  The point is that these different sets of rules create problems when key actors do not recognize that they are playing in two arenas simultaneously or are unaware of the rules governing play in the other branch.  Much interaction between Congress and the foreign-policy bureaucracy is of this sort.  Congressional delegations traveling abroad, congressional inquiries concerning constituents' problems that are directed at State Department officials, and floor amendments on foreign-policy issues all provide settings in which the more parochial representatives of both branches come into conflict and negative stereotypes are reinforced.

Even with participants who are sensitive to the problem and skilled in both sets of rules, interbranch foreign-policy making efforts are likely to be strained and conflictive because the operating norms of the two systems are incompatible. The best that can be expected over any prolonged period and across a broad range of issues is that representatives of both branches be willing and able to compromise on both substance and process.

## THE COSTS OF CONSULTATION

The basic incompatibility of the rules of the congressional and foreign-policy games presents executive-branch officials who manage foreign-policy issues with a problem: To what extent should they consult with Congress? Influenced by experiences that have generated hardy stereotypes, many of these officials view as irresponsible and thoroughly misguided advice that they should routinely consult and compromise with Congress on foreign-policy issues. They argue that consultation should be avoided whenever possible and that this generally can be done without excessive cost.

They marshal numerous arguments in support of such a position. In this view congressional involvement in a foreign-policy issue complicates managing relations with foreign countries. Interbureau and interdepartmental negotiations that are necessary to achieve an executive-branch policy are complex and time consuming enough. Bringing Congress into that decision making further complicates the process and reduces chances of a timely resolution. Many policy decisions need to be made in secrecy, and even if congressional discretion could be counted on, it is bad practice to bring more participants than are absolutely necessary into such decision making.

In addition, the costs of consultation are very high. Power and jurisdictional claims are so diffuse within Congress, and professional staff on the Hill are so numerous that it is virtually impossible to limit consultation to a manageable number of members and their staffs. Besides, consultation by the executive branch runs the risk of mobilizing Congress into action on an issue it would otherwise ignore.

The temptation to avoid consultation with Congress that is motivated by these potential complications is reinforced by the fact that most foreign-policy decisions can be made and implemented without significant congressional intervention. The congressional calendar, crowded with other matters, leaves little time for foreign-policy oversight. This reality, combined with cumbersome congressional procedures, renders most foreign-policy issues too complex and fast moving for Congress to deal with. The executive can often complete confidential negotiations and make decisions before Congress becomes aware that there are decisions to be made. Efforts to consult, moreover, will often be fruitless because the responsibility and inflexibility in subsequent political posturing that result from informed participation in policy debates convince many members to remain uninvolved.

The chances of meaningful congressional intervention can be further reduced by tactics such as scheduling potentially contentious announcements when Congress is in recess, deluging Congress with many more decisions than it can seriously consider in an allotted time, conducting interagency and bilateral negotiations in secret, and persuading a few congressional leaders that congressional debate of an issue would seriously harm the national interest.

Faced with such numerous and persuasive arguments against consultation, many executive-branch officials will only rarely initiate consultations with Congress. They are most likely to do so when they believe that serious congressional involvement will strengthen their preferred outcome in an intrabureaucracy policy conflict, will help build public support for a policy, or will be inevitable because of legislative requirements or the contentiousness of an issue. Treaties and legislation dealing with aid and foreign trade, for example, present situations that promote interbranch consultation.

One can readily understand—and in many situations accept—the executive branch's consequent reluctance to consult. Nevertheless, this outlook has two serious flaws: First, it creates a tendency to gamble against high odds by trying to circumvent the need for consultation even when serious congressional intervention on an issue is likely. Second, when interaction with Congress becomes inevitable, it encourages foreign-policy officers to try to outmaneuver, underinform, and overpower congressional opposition rather than to engage it in serious discussions and negotiations. This approach cannot help but generate resentment, which risks reduced support in Congress for executive-branch foreign-policy initiatives.


## DEFENSIVE STRATEGIES

Several recent historical examples of executive-branch failures to anticipate the need for consultation with Congress and of subsequent executive-branch strategies for dealing with Congress that failed to produce effective foreign policy have been documented in a series of case studies by analysts of the Congressional Research Service (CRS).

In 1978 the Carter administration decided not to consult Congress as it moved to recognize the People's Republic of China (PRC). In his study of this episode, Robert Sutter argues persuasively that the decision reflected three primary calculations: that extreme secrecy was needed in the conduct of negotiations with the Chinese; that such negotiations could be sabotaged by the joint efforts of a China lobby within Congress and its allies in the executive branch; and that an announcement timed to coincide with a congressional recess for Christmas and the New Year would mute opposition from Capitol Hill.[1]

The costs of this strategy were much higher than many in the executive branch anticipated, but they should have been predictable. Congress had explicitly expressed its wishes to be consulted prior to any action that would adversely affect the status of Taiwan. The clear violation of those wishes not only severely complicated the administration's task of obtaining prompt passage of legislation to implement the recognition decision but also created a mood of distrust that troubles congressional-executive relations regarding the PRC to this day.

Following the Turkish military occupation of about 40 percent of Cyprus in August 1974, then Secretary of State Henry Kissinger aggressively rejected congressional involvement in formulating the U.S. response. It was a time of governmental instability in Turkey, Greece, and Cyprus, of the transfer of power from a discredited President Richard Nixon to an untried President Gerald Ford, and of continuing national debate over the Nixon administration's handling of the Vietnam war. Ellen Laipson argues that Kissinger's determination to exclude Congress from management of the Cyprus crisis stemmed not only from a determination to restrict the size of decision-making circles but also from judgments that diplomacy could resolve the crisis before effective congressional opposition could be mounted, that congressional policy interests were diffuse, and that the members who were most likely to cause trouble seemed to be poorly placed within the foreign-policy structure of Congress.[2]

The crisis dragged on, however, and powerful congressional interest—and opposition to administration policy—soon emerged. The intensity of the opposition was attributable in part to the Greek-American lobby, but Laipson argues convincingly that a far more important factor was Congress's sense that Kissinger was being unreasonably secretive, duplicitous, and uncompromising. The embargo on the transfer of arms to Turkey that resulted from the congressional-executive confrontation not only failed to achieve its goal of forcing Turkish withdrawal from Cyprus but also embarrassed American policy makers and continues to strain U.S. relations with Turkey.

Raymond Copson documents the failure of the Nixon administration to perceive the need for extensive consultation when the Byrd amendment on Rhodesian imports was under consideration in 1971.[3] That amendment forced Washington into a partial violation of the mandatory sanctions imposed by the United Nations on the regime of then Prime Minister Ian Smith by requiring that the United States permit the import of critical and strategic materials from Rhodesia. This case seems to be a clear example of inadequate executive-branch intelligence on Congress. The administration was simply surprised that then Senator Harry Byrd (I.-Virginia) and his colleagues were able to assemble a winning coalition to break the boycott. It failed both to anticipate and to observe the coalescence of supporters of the

Rhodesian regime, domestic chromium interests, advocates of strong national security, and opponents of the kind of Third World activism that had characterized the U.N.'s boycott movement. The resulting legislation was a significant source of embarrassment in U.S. relations with black Africa until 1977, when President Jimmy Carter successfully pressed for its repeal.

In mid-1981 the Reagan administration made clear its intent to sell Saudi Arabia airborne warning and command system (AWACS) aircraft, whose radar and communications systems could provide sophisticated radar surveillance and combat control over a large area, as well as equipment that would enhance the capabilities of its recently purchased F-15 fighters. Richard Grimmett details the administration's decision to delay formal submission to Congress of the letter of intent to make the sale and to impose on its own officials a moratorium on sale-related consultations with Congress in order to focus full attention on pushing the fiscal year 1982 budget through Congress.[4]  While this moratorium was in effect, opponents of the sale were successful in lining up 50 senators to cosponsor a Senate resolution to disapprove the sale as soon as it was formally proposed to Congress.

The administration was eventually able to reverse its losses but only after intensive lobbying that relied heavily on the argument—for which Congress has respect but limited tolerance—that the president should not be denied flexibility in foreign-policy making. Had the administration continued to involve key members of Congress in the months preceding formal proposal of the sale, it could well have come up with low-cost compromises on the precise terms of the sale that would have won congressional acquiescence with much less acrimonious public debate and at considerably lower political cost.

When executive-branch officials fail to anticipate and plan for the need to consult with Congress, they often respond to congressional demands for involvement in foreign-policy making with defensive strategies. The CRS case studies illustrate how such efforts can further aggravate interbranch relations and complicate foreign-policy making.

Executive-branch strategies that deny the legitimacy of a congressional role in a foreign-policy issue can destroy effective foreign-policy making. Kissinger's refusal to accept such a role during the boycott of Turkey became a major issue around which opposition to administration policy rallied. Less blatant, but still a cause of unnecessary tension, were Carter's insistence on prompt congressional action on the Taiwan Relations Bill and his threat to veto the bill if any of its provisions conflicted with his normalization agreement with the PRC. Both positions seemed to suggest Congress should simply act as a rubber stamp.

Refusals to bargain and compromise with Congress can have the same effects. After documenting Kissinger's repeated unwillingness to work out compromises with Congress, Laipson concludes: "[Kissinger's] diplomatic prospects in the eastern Mediterranean would have been greatly enhanced had he been prepared to bargain and negotiate on Capitol Hill with anything approaching the energy and skill he used internationally."

Faced with congressional opposition, administrations often seem to resort to deception. When congressional figures discover such subterfuges, their hostility and opposition are only intensified. Congressional leaders concluded very early in the Turkish embargo crisis that the administration was systematically lying to them. Hostility to the Carter administration's handling of the normalization of relations with the PRC was similarly perpetuated by a series of subsequent revelations that Congress had been misled on a number of key points in briefings and assurances it received on the normalization agreement. Sutter reports, for example, that senior administration officials assured members of Congress that, aside from the defense treaty, all other U.S. agreements with Taiwan would remain in effect. In fact, however, the administration had already assured the PRC that those accords would be replaced by unofficial arrangements. One administration official interviewed for that study spoke of a pattern of providing Congress with "disingenuous" answers to its questions.

Executive-branch officials plotting strategies and lobbying tactics for dealing with Congress on foreign policy tend to assume that base parochial considerations are the sole force motivating congressional opposition to their policies. Yet in both the PRC and the Turkey cases, several key congressional opponents of administration policy were more concerned about the coherence and effectiveness of U.S. foreign policy than about the parochial interests of the China lobby or the Greek lobby. Clear evidence that executive negotiators did not acknowledge legitimate bases for opposition stiffened their opposition significantly.

## DUAL-ROLE PLAYERS

What emerges most strikingly from a study of these cases is that much of the most vigorous and implacable congressional opposition to executive positions was generated by the disdain and insensitivity with which executive-branch officials treated congressional participants rather than by the specific political policies the officials espoused. They repeatedly sought to circumvent and deceive Congress rather than to involve it in serious negotiations aimed at compromise solutions. Unfortunately, such behavior has too often been directed at congressional participants who did understand both the congressional and the foreign-policy games and were making conscientious efforts to play responsibly in both.

There exists an inherent tension in congressional-executive relations that is likely to prevent extensive consultation with Congress and to perpetuate misunderstandings between the two branches when they do try to work out common approaches to foreign-policy problems. Nothing short of a major transformation of the U.S. constitutional system seems likely to change those patterns fundamentally.

For those seeking incremental improvements in congressional-executive relations on foreign policy, however, the far more important cleavage is the one that separates those who understand and are skilled in playing both the foreign-policy and the congressional games from those who focus single-mindedly on one game. Executive-branch officials who neither understand nor accept the legitimacy of the congressional game in foreign-policy matters are the ones most likely to avoid early and extensive consultation and then to circumvent and deceive Congress when it becomes involved. By the same token, those in Congress and staff aides who neither understand nor value the art of diplomacy are the ones most likely to embarrass executive-branch policy makers in their dealings with other governments or to pass restrictive legislation without good-faith efforts to achieve reasonable foreign-policy goals in less disruptive ways. But dual-role players who are skilled in both games can often anticipate and correctly interpret actions of the other branch and suggest ways to limit the damage from congressional-executive conflict on U.S. foreign relations.

The issue of restrictive legislation shows the value of individuals who understand the importance of and are skilled at playing both the congressional and the foreign-policy games. From the perspective of many foreign-policy officers, perhaps the most frustrating and frightening aspect of congressional-executive relations is the potential for disruption of policy built into restrictive legislation, such as the Turkish arms embargo and, until recently, legislative vetoes. In the officers' view, Congress is intent on achieving victories that inevitably produce serious defeats not only for U.S. foreign policy but also for the credibility of the U.S. policy-making process.

This interpretation, however, misreads the perspective of those congressional participants who understand that they must play both the foreign-policy and the congressional games. The point of such measure, in the view of many on Capitol Hill, is not to impose restrictions on the executive branch or veto its actions but to give Congress a measure of leverage in interbranch negotiations that the executive would otherwise dominate. From this perspective, congressional victory is achieved when restrictive legislation loses, but Congress extracts some policy compromises reflecting congressional concerns. Executive-branch officials who understand this congressional viewpoint see their goal—and their definition of victory—to be the defeat of such legislation by the negotiation of the least substantive compromise necessary to achieve a minimal winning coalition.

In this light, the defeat of a congressional motion to disapprove sale of uranium for India's Tarapur nuclear reactor can be seen as a congressional victory. The issue was pressed without irreversible damage to U.S.-Indian relations, but the difficulty of the administration's victory made very clear that further sales were likely to be disapproved. This action forced both the

U.S. and the Indian governments to recognize that a renegotiation of the fuel supply agreement was essential.

The Turkish arms embargo, in contrast, was widely seen in retrospect by its congressional advocates as a defeat rather than a victory. They recognized both the cost of such legislation for effective foreign-policy making and the limited effect on Turkey of such a blunt policy instrument. For many in Congress the goal had been not to impose restrictive legislation but to gain leverage by threatening to pass measures that would force the administration to modify its eastern Mediterranean policy. The passage of the legislation marked the failure—not the success—of that strategy. Similarly, the failure of SALT II to achieve Senate ratification is not a source of satisfaction to all of its opponents. For some at least, the primary motive seems not to have been defeating a treaty negotiated in good faith by their government but conditioning their support to higher levels of defense spending and some minor modifications in the treaty's terms. That a series of events intervened to make conclusive action on the treaty politically infeasible reflects the risky character of the way in which this political system tries to reconcile the foreign-policy and congressional games.

## MITIGATING THE STEREOTYPES

Such foreign-policy disasters resulting from congressional-executive impasses could be reduced in scale and frequency by expanding the roles of those who play both games. The influence of these key figures could be enhanced first by increasing their numbers. Exchange programs that bring Foreign Service officers to the Hill for intensive work experience have already created a core of midlevel State Department officials who understand congressional approaches to foreign-policy problems. Such programs should be strengthened and expanded. The regular raiding of experienced congressional staff members to fill policy positions in the bureaucracy and the hiring of experienced former executive-branch officials to fill staff jobs in Congress can increase mutual understanding in both branches. Such patterns of interbranch hiring are particularly important during presidential transitions and shifts in key committee and subcommittee leaderships.

Training programs, although probably much less effective than interbranch work experience, can also help mitigate the worst stereotypes held by those in Congress and in the foreign-policy bureaucracy. The Foreign Service Institute can clearly help by providing courses on congressional procedures. The CRS, through its programs for New Members of Congress and its Legislative Institutes and Public Policy Institutes for staff members, can play a comparable role on the Hill. Foreign-policy research organizations should be encouraged in their efforts to draw individuals from both branches into seminars and workshops on policy issues.

Second, those players who understand the workings of the other branch can help lay the groundwork for effective conflict resolution with outreach programs conducted during periods of little or no conflict. The involvement of members of Congress and their staffs in State Department activities such as preparing for visits by foreign heads of state or for bilateral or multilateral negotiations, for example, can sensitize those unfamiliar with diplomacy to some of its demands. Informal briefings on specific issues, although much more difficult to organize, can sometimes serve the same function. Such exposure is especially important for members and their staffs who serve on committees other than Foreign Affairs or Foreign Relations but have foreign-policy-related responsibilities or concerns. Conversely, those in Congress who are sensitive to the requirements of effective diplomacy can play a valuable role by stimulating discussions of foreign-policy issues with executive-branch officials in settings that encourage candor and serious policy assessment. The images of Congress held by too many such officials are almost exclusively the products of experiences with congressional inquiries relating to constituent problems, with congressional delegations abroad, and with public hearings.

Progress in congressional-executive consultation on foreign policy requires realism and perspective. No other country's political system demands a comparable effort to reconcile such divergent games as those played in the U.S. Congress and in the U.S. foreign-policy establishment. Both games are deeply rooted in the U.S. political system; both will necessarily be involved in the foreign-policy making process. Tensions between the branches on foreign policy are inevitable; they will be better managed, however, if both representatives and diplomats come increasingly to be judged on their abilities to transcend their institutional games and evolve mutually acceptable procedures and policies.

## NOTES

1. *Robert Sutter,* Executive-Legislative Consultation on China Policy, 1978–79, *U.S. House of Representatives, Committee on Foreign Affairs, 1980.*

2. *Ellen Laipson,* Congressional-Executive Relations and the Turkish Arms Embargo, *U.S. House of Representatives, Committee on Foreign Affairs, 1981.*

3. *Raymond Copson,* Executive-Legislative Consultation on Foreign Policy: Sanctions Against Rhodesia, *U.S. House of Representatives, Committee on Foreign Affairs, 1982.*

4. *Richard Grimmett,* Executive-Legislative Consultations on U.S. Arms Sales, *U.S. House of Representatives, Committee on Foreign Affairs, 1982.*

provision the United States could have a faceless, mindless, Kafkaesque society in which the bureaucracy was even less responsive to the individual problems of citizens than tenure, civil service regulations, and the Hatch Act have made it. Continued and expanding freedom of the people of the United States owes a considerable debt to the routine intervention, even interference, by the Congress with the bureaucracy in order to redress the everyday grievances of the people with their government. The ability of the bureaucracy to give the public the runaround—the failure to answer mail, the smothering of complaints, the harassment by the tax collector, the insolence of the immigration authorities, the arrogance of the diplomat, the power of the military, and the abuses of prosecutor and police—are regularly and extensively mitigated by this first amendment dictum. The Congress of the United States, through oversight by its individual members and the intervention of its committees, has tempered the power of bureaucracy and assuaged the discontents of the people in ways unknown and unprecedented not only in dictatorial states but in parliamentary democracies as well. In Britain, France, West Germany, and so on, no comparable intervention by the legislator in the affairs of the bureaucracy exists. The simple right to command the papers of a ministry is more often than not impossible.

Many in the executive branch of the U.S. government with considerably greater respect for the separation of powers and the system of checks and balances than Admiral Poindexter or Lieutenant Colonel North evidenced in the Iran Affair look upon Congress as the enemy. Although seldom taking the view of either the Nixon White House staff or the Reagan National Security Council that if one does not like a law it can either be circumscribed or need not be obeyed, the temper of the bureaucracy regularly and routinely is to disdain the Congress, to protect its turf, to act in secret, and to bury its mistakes. Public figures who should know better—cabinet officers, CIA directors, even presidents and vice presidents of the United States—often assert and sometimes act on the assumption that Congress should have no proper or substantive role in formulating foreign policy, determining the priorities of the purse, or deciding the issues of war and peace. Their view is that the executive decides and Congress should snap to attention and appropriate the funds. When asked if Congress should play any role in foreign policy, Lieutenant Colonel North replied to Senator Hatch, "There is a role, and that is the appropriation of monies to carry out that policy."[1]

This attitude is rampant among two schools of thought. The first is characterized by those who have either not read the Constitution or who do not understand it. They fail either to note or to understand in Article I of the Constitution that all legislative powers are vested in Congress and in Section 8 that Congress shall have the power to declare war, provide for the common defense, raise and support armies, provide and maintain a navy, and regulate commerce with foreign nations, as well as the right "to make all laws which shall be necessary and proper for carrying into execution the foregoing powers, and all other powers vested in this Constitution in the Government of the United States, or in any Department or Officer thereof." Even more they seem to be unaware that although the president has the power to make treaties and appoint officers of the government, he does so not only with the advice but the consent of the Senate.

The second school, a more knowing and sophisticated group, are those who understand the Constitution and its divided and shared powers but prefer either a different or a modified system.

The attitude of the first school is the result of their lack of institutional memory or the failure to study history. The United States was founded by a rebellion against the exercise of prerogative power by the British monarch or the prime minister acting in the monarch's name. On their own volition, they could, among other things, declare war, make treaties, appoint the cabinet, and nominate judges without so much as a by your leave from Parliament. They asserted the royal prerogative. Even in the 1980s, Prime Minister Margaret Thatcher went to war in the Falklands without a vote of the Parliament.

But the authors of the Constitution saw it differently. In a dozen or more ways, the powers exercised by the monarch or by the prime minister on the monarch's behalf in Great Britain are either divided or shared between the president and the Congress in the United States. Congress declares war by a simple majority vote of both houses without the approval of the president. The president, as commander in chief, carries out that declaration. The president also shares making treaties and appointing the cabinet and judges with the legislature: The consent to a treaty requires an extraordinary two-thirds vote of the Senate. As Edward S. Corwin has written, "The Constitution considered only for its affirmative grants of power capable of affecting the issue, is an invitation to struggle for the privilege of directing American foreign policy."[2] The system of checks and balances is cumbersome, slow, and inefficient but it has provided for two hundred years of growing and expanding political freedom.

The second school has studied history but sincerely and deliberately would like to delegate a considerably greater measure of prerogative power to the president. They want to increase presidential power at the expense of the Congress.

This battle, although not new (as was for example President Lincoln's use of prerogative power in the Civil War) is essentially a creature of the 20th century. In the 19th century, which was really the century of congressional domination, the relationship was largely settled. Since the days of the New Deal, not only the executive branch but its political science and academic supporters, have denigrated the Congress and glorified and even canonized the executive. Originally it was a battle between liberal activists who during depression and war urged the government to act and conservative stand-patters who opted for less government.

Ironically that has now changed as well. In the area of the president's war-making and foreign policy powers, in the use of government powers to put the social agenda in place (prayer in the schools, anti-abortion), to enforce the law (lie detector tests, compulsory drug testing, searches and seizures), and to enhance the president's power of the purse (item veto, budget reform), conservative politicians and judges have proposed massive increases in both the powers of the president and the authority of the federal government. These are not examples of limited government, but the essence of big government.

Another source of the conflict is that many members of Congress do not view the great departments of the government—State, Defense, Treasury, etc.—as the custodians of the public interest or the guardians of citizenship like the security forces who guard the gold at Fort Knox, as the departments would like to be viewed. Instead Congress sees the departments as the advocates, solicitors, and barristers of the interest groups; the patrons of the powerful; and the defenders, protectors, and champions of the clients of their departments. The State and Treasury departments fawn at the solicitations of their mighty clients, the national and international chambers of commerce, banks, and oil companies.[3] The Defense Department is too often incapable of disciplining either its contractors or suppliers or accepting the criticism of its internal whistle-blowers.

There are additional constitutional powers and legislative acts that provide for oversight and hence conflict between Congress and the bureaucracy. The most important among the constitutional powers is Article I, Section 9: "No money shall be drawn from the Treasury, but in Consequence of Appropriations made by Law." The power of the purse is the strongest of the oversight powers. It limits the president's actions in both domestic and foreign policy. In addition the constitutional authority by which Congress establishes departments, agencies, and bureaus is a potent source of conflict. Further, the power of impeachment, when taken with the confirmation power, is the method by which Congress can review both executive and judicial misbehavior. It is a more powerful weapon than ordinarily thought. Although it has only been used twice with respect to forty U.S. presidents, that is the equivalent of one in twenty, or 5 percent, of the holders of the office. It is of sufficient importance that it has become a powerful weapon to help keep the actions of the president and officers of the bureaucracy within both the letter and spirit of the Constitution. Finally, the power to legislate involves the authority to hold hearings, to compile information, and to investigate all areas of potential conflict with the bureaucracy.

With respect to legislation as a source of oversight and friction, there are hundreds of statutes. Of primary importance are the Legislative Reorganization Acts of 1946 and 1970, which strengthened the oversight functions of congressional committees; the 1921 Budget Act, which provided for the

General Accounting Office as the watchdog of Congress: the 1974 Budget Act, which established deferral and rescission as means to prevent the unauthorized impounding of appropriated funds; and the War Powers Resolution, which limits the president's prerogatives with respect to introducing troops into areas of imminent hostilities or into situations where imminent involvement in hostilities is clearly indicated by the circumstance.[4]

Finally, the rules of the House and Senate that require oversight by the standing committees and the creation of the House Government Operations Committee and the Senate Government Affairs Committee with powers to investigate virtually any agency or activity in the executive branch are clearly existing and potential sources of friction and conflict between Congress and the bureaucracy.

## BUREAUCRATIC CONFLICT WITH CONGRESS

If the foregoing is the perspective by which many in Congress view the executive and the bureaucracy, there is also a bureaucratic perspective that leads to conflict with Congress.

First and foremost are the constitutional commands. The executive power is vested in a president of the United States who has the authority both to appoint (with the advice and consent of the Senate for major posts) and to remove officers.[5] Where executive authority ends and legislation or legislative history begins is obviously a point of contention, especially in interpreting rather vague or general legislation often written obscurely to smooth over legislative disagreements.

The role of the president as commander in chief brings with it essentially unqualified acceptance of his orders by the uniformed military authorities. This is a major source of friction between the civilian and military officers of the executive branch and the Congress, for the first loyalty of the former (apart from the higher loyalty to the Constitution) lies not to the Congress but in the chain of command leading to the civilian president or the military commander in chief, the dual role the president plays. This fact, particularly since the *loss* of the Vietnam War, has led to a view among some officers among some officers and officials that, only after the Soviets and the press, Congress is the enemy. To the degree this view leads to action, such as lying to or misleading Congress, it is a source of friction. It is indeed a serious matter and stems from both the view that the war could have been won if only the services had not been fettered by the Congress and the press, on the one hand, and a limited view of both the letter and the spirit of the Constitution, on the other. But these views are by no means universally held and even less acted on, and they are more likely to be held by civilian than military officers. The historical record is that the U.S. military has, unlike the military in dozens of nations, been overwhelmingly loyal to the civil authorities of the country. In addition, unlike the British, who have had an elitist professional military, and the French, who have depended in part on a mercenary army, the U.S. military has been extraordinarily representative of the country. Selection and promotion represents meritocracy as opposed to aristocracy. It is an institution befitting a democratic society.

There is the further assertion of the primacy of the president in the field of foreign policy. The president may appoint and receive ambassadors, and he may make treaties, the general language of which largely expresses his foreign policy authority. Yet, the Congress shares foreign policy authority through the constitutional provisions of the power of the purse; the advice and consent procedures; the authority to regulate commerce with foreign nations by laying and collecting duties, defining and punishing piracies and felonies committed on the high seas and offenses against the law of nations; and the ability to declare war. Although the president's primacy in the field of foreign policy has been recognized by the Supreme Court, particularly in the *Curtis Wright* decision, its reality is a somewhat different thing. Woodrow Wilson and Jimmy Carter may have had primacy in making foreign policy, but Congress's failure to give assent to both the Versailles Treaty and SALT II should give one pause in asserting it as an absolute. In addition, the penultimate draft of the Constitution, changed only ten days before adjournment of the convention, provided that "The Senate shall have power to make treaties and appoint ambassadors." When the writers shifted that power to the president, they heavily circumscribed it with the limitations of Senatorial advice and the often impossible two-thirds majority requirement for consent. The assertion of presidential primacy, albeit highly questionable, is nonetheless an obvious source of conflict and struggle.

From the point of view of both the executive and the Congress, the War Powers Resolution is a source of friction. Presidents, White House counsels, and attorneys general have said they view its provisions as unconstitutional. Section 3 of the resolutions directs that the president "in every possible instance shall consult Congress before introducing United States Armed Forces into hostilities or into situations where imminent involvement in hostilities is clearly indicated by the circumstances." Section 5(b) says that the president shall remove the forces within sixty calendar days unless Congress has declared war, specifically authorized their use, extended the period, or is physically unable to meet because of an armed attack on the United States. The period can be extended for another thirty days if the safety of the troops requires it.[6]

During the first fourteen years of its existence, presidents often informed Congress that they were going to or had introduced troops in a potentially hostile situation, but in no instance have they consulted before the event with Congress. In addition, no president acting under the reporting procedures requiring him to state the constitutional and legislative authority under which the introduction of forces took place has acknowledged that he was doing so under the authority of the resolution. Instead, each has cited his authority as commander in chief and his oath of office to "preserve, protect, and defend" the Constitution.

The issue of removing the troops is a clash of authority that may never be resolved: It cannot be resolved by the Supreme Court as a theoretical issue, but it can be established by an actual event. However, the Court is quite reluctant in any event to take a case where it is required to decide a conflict between the other two independent branches of the government, especially during hostilities. Even the *Chadha* decision, which limited or outlawed the legislative veto, may not apply to the War Powers Resolution. Congress argued at the time the resolution passed that as Congress can declare war by a *concurrent resolution* between the House and the Senate, not requiring the signature of the president, it also can stop a war by a *concurrent resolution* requiring only a majority vote of the House and Senate, as provided in Section 5 of the resolution. Hence the strictures against the legislative veto would probably not apply. If Congress can declare war by a simple majority vote, it does not have to enact a statute requiring a two-thirds vote to override a presidential veto in order to stop a war the president has initiated without a congressional declaration. As a consequence, Congress will continue to assert its power to declare war and to make all laws that are necessary and proper under the elastic clause in order to carry out not only its own powers but the powers of other branches. The president will continue to assert his powers as commander in chief and his oath of office, and the issue will continue to cause friction and conflict from time to time.

In addition the executive branch and the bureaucracy feel that they have valid complaints against Congress in numerous other areas, one of which is that Congress holds too many hearings that waste time and duplicate the efforts of administration officials and their staff. The heads of the State and Defense departments appear not only before the foreign relations and foreign affairs committees and the armed services committees in both House and Senate, but the budget committees, the intelligence committees, the appropriations committees, the government affairs and government operations committees, and a variety of ad hoc and select committees from time to time. The time the officials take to prepare and give testimony makes it difficult if not impossible for them to carry out their administrative duties.

There are additional complaints against large congressional staffs, the massive amount of work the staffs generate for the administration, the requirements for myriads of reports and consultations as a result, the micromanagement of administration actions, the dangers of leaks, and the leisurely and protracted rate by which needed action on authorization or appropriation statutes is taken.

There is also a disdain for Congress generated by the bureaucracy's perception of the influence of particular interest groups on foreign policy, for example on Middle Eastern policies and relations between Greece and Turkey. Many assert that congressional decisions are corrupted by the influence of campaign funds and political action committees (PACs). The executive and the bureaucracy bristle at the double standard on ethical matters, outside income, and a variety of laws (civil rights, labor practices, the hiring of women and minorities), which applies to them or the public but not to Congress.[7] One could enlarge the list ad nauseum, but these issues and examples are sufficient.

## COOPERATION BETWEEN THE CONGRESS AND THE BUREAUCRACY

There are at least three noteworthy areas of cooperation between the Congress and the executive branch or bureaucracy. First is the extraordinary amount of collaboration between the Congress, on the one hand, and the military services and the entitlement agencies (social security, et al.) on the other, with respect to routine casework. The ability of citizens to petition the government for the redress of their grievances is one of the great successes of the U.S. system.

The second is the cooperation, or backscratching, among members of Congress and the congressional committees, the departments and the agencies, and the outside interest groups or clients that Congress and the agencies mutually serve. This is called the *Iron Triangle*.

Third is the cooperation that is the prelude to the vast amount of general consensus on public policy, which is noteworthy in multitudinous areas of government activity. Not all, nor even a majority, of the activities of the federal government represent areas of conflict between Congress and the executive branch.

### Casework

Apart from answering the legislative mail, the great bulk of the work of a member of the House or Senate is handling the routine problems that member's constituents have with the federal government. Most of these do not concern legislation or public policy but the application of existing laws to specific cases. Among the most numerous are the problems of service men and women, social security and medicare, veterans issues, passports and the problems U.S. citizens encounter when abroad, the indifference and indecisiveness of bureaucracies to the public, and a host of others, which include pardons, delivery of the mail, public lands, farm agencies, export licenses, regulatory agency rulings, housing, and students loans.

The military services have a coterie of specialists who occupy space in the House and Senate office buildings and who provide almost instant service to the caseworkers in members' offices. It is an ombudsman operation superior to the formal organization in Scandinavian countries. It is more efficient because it does not involve adding an additional bureaucratic layer between the citizen and the bureaucracy, as is the case when a formal ombudsman agency is established. Instead, the U.S. system involves the authority of elected legislative officials. This arrangement, backed by experienced and dedicated personnel on both the legislative and executive side, has brought speedy action in complicated cases because of the power of the intervener and the response of the agencies. It is one of the shining examples of legislative-bureaucratic cooperation but is largely unknown and unappreciated by the critics of both.

## *The Iron Triangles*

Cooperation in the second area, that of the Iron Triangles, is equally efficient but less meritorious than the cooperation in casework. The Iron Triangles comprise members of Congress, the agencies and departments, and economic or political interest groups. They involve virtually every activity the government undertakes, and they exist because of institutional arrangements.

First, the political heads of departments are almost always appointed from the groups served by the department. Almost every secretary of state comes from or is annointed by the foreign policy establishment. The treasury secretary routinely comes from the banking or financial community. The revolving door at the Defense Department—usually lawyers whose careers involve commuting between political appointments at the DoD and alternative work on behalf of the major contractors—needs no elaboration. A westerner regularly inhabits the post of secretary of the interior. The secretary of agriculture is drawn from the corn and soybean interest groups, when Republicans hold the White House, or the cotton, tobacco, and wheat interests when the Democrats control. The labor secretary, if not directly from the ranks of trade unions, is someone generally acceptable to them. The craft unions have more influence with a Republican administration and the industrial unions with Democratic administrations. Western water users, the mayors, governors, and local chambers of commerce influence dramatically the policies and water projects of both the Bureau of Reclamation and the Army Corps of Engineers.

Members of the House and Senate provide the third leg of the triangle. Members seek committee appointments serving the economic interest groups of their state or district. California senators routinely serve on the Armed Services Committee, the Agriculture Committee, the Banking Committee, and the Foreign Relation Committee because California is the home of the nation's largest defense industries, the biggest agricultural state in the Union, the center of the financial institution in the west, and the concentration of significant interests in trade and foreign policy in the Pacific. Mountain state Senators dominate the Interior Committee. Louisiana and lower Mississippi River states rush to the Public Works Committee, which is so essential to navigation and flood control on that great artery of transportation. Not only do they seek legislative committee spots but Appropriations Committee appointments, which fund the handiwork of their legislative committee efforts. Thus, in recent times, a senator from Idaho has not only chaired the Energy and Natural Resources Committee with jurisdiction over water projects and public lands (the bread and butter political and economic interests of his state) but has chaired the Interior Subcommittee of the Appropriations Committee, which funds such interests and projects as well. Similar relations exist among members on legislative committees serving banking, housing, health, public works, defense, and military construction, and the Appropriations Committee subcommittees funding the programs vital to those interests. Among congressional insiders this is called the *double whammy* and is reinforced by PAC funds to the Senator and lobbying from the interest groups that either initiate or carry out the programs.

The Iron Triangle relationship is perhaps the most formidable, although not the most noble, example of cooperation between Congress and the bureaucracy.

## Consensus

Because of provisions for both the division of power and the sharing of power built into the Constitution, the U.S. system of government is inefficient. It works best when the president and the bureaucracy, on the one hand, and the Congress, on the other, seek to reach agreement on major matters of public policy through constitutional means, the informing function, and the willingness to compromise. In recent times there has been a breakdown of the process. Witness the war in Vietnam, the budget deficit, and the foreign policy disagreement over Nicaragua and the contras. The backdowns were caused both by determined differences of opinion and the extraconstitutional means used to achieve conflicting ends.

There was a period roughly between December 7, 1941, and the end of 1965 when there was general cooperation and consensus in foreign policy. Although there was heated and protracted public debate, nonetheless general consensus in foreign policy was hammered out with respect to the Marshal Plan, Greek and Turkish aid, the Berlin blockade, the establishment of NATO, the Common Market, and Japanese-U.S. relations, among other issues. The fragile consensus fell apart following the Tonkin Gulf Resolution, the increased use of ground forces in Vietnam, the secret bombing and invasion of Cambodia, and the imperial presidency of Richard Nixon. Some areas of cooperation and consensus continued: for example, relations with Israel, the support of NATO, and the opening to China.

From the end of World War II until 1966 there was also a consensus in domestic economic policy. The Employment Act of 1946 worked very well indeed until inflation, induced by both additional domestic and foreign policy spending without a tax increase, took off after 1966.

The consensus in both foreign policy and domestic economic policy characterized by the war and post-war years originated and was carried out by a considerable degree of cooperation between Congress and the executive and was nourished by both political parties. The divergence of views, the breakdown in policy, and the disruptions associated with the Johnson and Nixon administrations over Vietnam, and the Reagan administration over Iran, were largely but not entirely the result of the unwillingness of the executive branch to seek consensus and the disdain for regular constitutional processes of compromise and cooperation.

## CONCLUSION

The purposes of divided and shared powers between Congress and the executive branch is not to avoid friction. On the contrary, one purpose of the checks and balances is to promote a healthy dialectic process in which the clash of thesis and antithesis results in synthesis or policy consensus. Such a dialectic is the basis of free institutions. It is found in the clash of parliamentary and congressional debate, the cut and thrust in the courtroom, and in academic and scientific procedures where new ideas and evidence are published in order that they may be criticized or validated.

Another purpose of divided and shared power is to keep people free. The democratic compact provides that in return for giving up rebellion and revolt, the minority is given the right to criticize and the opportunity to replace the existing government peacefully. Meanwhile, the majority is allowed to carry out lawful acts without fear that it will be replaced by force.

Consequently, both the friction and clash involved in free speech and debate, on the one hand, and the willingness to carry out decisions reached through the established institutions, on the other, are essential ingredients of the compact. This requires a respect for the Constitution and political institutions. When the respect is evident, consensus flows from conflict and friction and, when absent, provokes a breakdown in the fabric of government. On the whole very little is gained by reforming or changing the constitutional process. Very much is gained by respecting it.

## NOTES

1. *Washington Post*, 7/14/87, p. A7.
2. Edward S. Corwin, *The President: Office and Powers, 1787–1957*, 4th rev.

ed. (New York: New York University Press, 1957), 171.

3. Howard E. Shuman, *Politics and the Budget: The Struggle Between the President and the Congress* (Englewood Cliffs, N.J.: Prentice-Hall, 1984), 52–3.

4. Public Law 93-148, 93rd Congress, Sections 3, 4a, 4c, 5a.

5. The power to remove is not specifically granted by Article II, but inherent. If the president must "take care that the laws be faithfully executed," he must have the power to remove an officer who has failed to do so.

6. P.L. 93-148.

7. The basis for this is the immunity clause and the separation of powers, little understood by press, bureaucracy, and the public. If applicable to Congress, these laws would have to be enforced by the executive and the courts against an independent and separate branch of government, which both Congress and the courts would view as an intolerable situation.

---

# 7.3    Principles and Pitfalls of Legislative Liaison

## JAMES JONES

*This chapter focuses on legislative liaison from an institutional viewpoint. The opinions that follow have been derived from the author's five-year assignment as senate liaison officer for the U.S. Marine Corps from 1979 to 1984. It should be understood at the outset that there is no checklist for effective legislative liaison. No set formula exists that guarantees success by simple compliance. Rather, there exists a series of principles, admittedly loosely defined at times, which if correctly applied and shaped into cohesive philosophy and strategy can contribute to a mutually successful relationship with the U.S. Congress. Although the material that follows is oriented toward the military aspects of legislative liaison, the principles and pitfalls discussed apply to any institution whose welfare depends on a favorable relationship with the U.S. Congress.*

The first task any organization should assign itself in dealing with Congress is to establish institutional goals. What is it that needs to be achieved legislatively? Are the goals understood by the membership, and are the assigned priorities clearly established and articulated by leadership elements of the organization?

Frequently, and often incorrectly, institutional leadership assumes that there are understanding and consensus on goals and objectives within the organization. The reverse is frequently the case as conflicting policies and both corporate and private agendas struggle in what becomes a battle for the survival of the fittest program. No one who has served on a staff needs a lesson on friction in the pursuit of military objectives. Friction is not restricted to combat—it is alive and well on the legislative battlefield. Indeed, it is ever present. In large military organizations such as the army, navy, and air force, institutional goals are many and are usually evaluated for their success at the bottom line of the authorization or appropriations bill. For example, within the U.S. Navy it is clear . . . represented by the secretary of the navy and the chief of naval operations and expressed in terms of the surface navy, the sub surface navy, the aviation navy, the land-based navy and, the amphibious, or "gator" navy. Although these five "navies" compose the U.S. Navy (USN), each frequently has its own goals in terms of the U.S. Congress. The priorities for the goals of each are established and articulated by the secretary of the navy and the chief of naval operations. The implementor of the legislative priorities is the Office of Legislative Affairs of the Department of the Navy. Other services are organized in similar fashion. This system has survived the test of time and, with minor exceptions, is likely to remain as it is currently structured for a long time to come. Thus far, things are relatively simple: an institution decides what its goals are; the leadership establishes the priorities of the goals; and legislative specialists, who through liaison with the Congress must obtain authorization and funding, execute the task of achieving the goals.

Achieving institutional consensus on goals and objectives is a major accomplishment, and it is not easily done. Once achieved, however, those responsible for legislative strategy must understand these goals and must understand that goals will change. In the legislative arena, the institution with fixed, intractable goals propped up by a policy of inflexibility will experience frustration and failure unless the issues have the overwhelming popular support of the people of the United States and, therefore, the U.S. Congress.

I have been surprised by the number of legislative specialists who routinely interact with the Congress but have little understanding of how the Congress is supposed to function in academic terms, let alone how it works in reality. I was no exception to this observation. With little preparation I was reassigned from duties as a staff officer in the Headquarters of the U.S. Marine Corps (USMC) to being the marine senate liaison officer for the Department of the Navy. After a year of very hesitant performance and with the help of Brig. Gen. Al Brewster, USMC (Ret.), and Capt. (now U.S. Senator) John McCain, USN (Ret.), I was gradually able to function in the legislative arena. I am also particularly grateful to the helpful members of Senate staffs who aided me in that assignment. There are many short courses on the U.S. Congress offered in Washington, D.C. (As an example, see *Understanding Congress—A Seminar on the Legislative Process,* Washington, D.C., Washington Monitor, 1980). I strongly recommend that anyone being assigned to a legislative liaison billet be required to take one of the several courses available in order to become conversant on the subject of the U.S. Congress. As I mentioned previously, understanding how the Congress is supposed to work is one thing; understanding how it actually works is quite another.

The Congress is, very simply, the branch of government to which the military is accountable for its handling of personnel, money, material, and, yes, even success and failure on the battlefield. The rise of legislative micromanagement of the military that began in the 1960s continues unabated despite all forms of protestation. As frustrating as this is to accept, it remains a fact nonetheless. Having a very well-developed understanding of their constitutional responsibilities relative to the armed forces, modern day members of Congress are highly confident in their abilities to debate the issue on all aspects of military subjects. This is true despite the fact that there are increasingly fewer members with military active duty experience than at any point in U.S. history.

Accepting the reality of this situation for what it is will significantly assist anyone or any organization having the slightest hope of being successful legislatively. Senators and representatives are able to discuss articulately a multitude of complex issues, and military issues are but one of many. Because members of Congress usually have competent staffs experienced in the issues, they rarely seem to feel inadequate when speaking authoritatively on any military subject.

In my opinion, existing problems between institutions can usually be traced to flawed strategy and/or tender egos. As long as the Congress complies with requests from the armed forces, the atmosphere is cordial, full of deferences and well-articulated orations pledging support and mutual cooperation. With the advent of a controversial issue, however, both legislative and military hackles quickly rise. For the military, this can become a moment of perhaps long-lasting legislative frustration, depending on institutional response to the perceived obstacle. Displays of individual or institutional pique are usually fatal to an issue and should be avoided at all costs (this advice, however, is frequently difficult to embrace). Put another way, the legislative-military relationships are either win/win or win/lose situations; I need not point out which organization loses if, indeed, there needs to be a loser.

The history of the debacle of the ill-fated attempt to derail Department of Defense and Joint Chiefs of Staff reforms is a good example of how a strategy can turn sour regardless of the merits of its goals. Critics of this turn the other cheek philosophy frequently argue that at some point a position becomes a matter of principle, despite its unpopularity with legislators. I agree, but how a position is articulated is frequently as important as the issue itself in terms of long-term relations and results.

Another reason to avoid institutional (and personal) reactions is the ripple effect of such reaction. Although the target of legislative displeasure is frequently limited to a small group of individuals, when threatened by external forces, the Congress can and does unite to withstand criticism. It is understandably difficult to avoid the ripple effect because people very naturally tend to defend themselves when threatened, especially if the cause is just, but it is important to any service or institution to hold as closely as possible to a philosophy of acceptance and dignity, thus enhancing the long-range probability of institutional success, long after contemporary disagreement has been forgotten. I have seen many instances of personal relationships being so strained that effective liaison on any subject became virtually impossible. Faced with such a situation a service has two choices: It can remove the liaison officer(s) in question, as he or she will probably never be effective; or it can do nothing until the time for transfer normally occurs and a replacement attempts to repair months of damage. Neither alternative is pleasant, but situations such as these arise and can be difficult to recognize.

One of the realities of working in the Congress is that it can be brutally frank in evaluating liaison efforts. It is not difficult to obtain an assessment of how members of Congress perceive that certain liaison officers are performing their duties, nor is it difficult to obtain an evaluation of the entire legislative effort of a particular service. Capitol Hill is awash with generalizations that characterize navy liaison or army liaison as being effective or ineffective, cooperative or uncooperative, or any number of other such descriptions. As institutional behavior tends to reflect human behavior, it is easy to understand that legislative operations tend to avoid those in the Congress who are critical and uncooperative, dismissing their opinions as baseless, gravitating more willingly toward those whose opinions are more compatible with the easy achievement of institutional goals. Although I sympathize with the normality of this attitude, it is my opinion that this is a flawed strategy as it implies permanency of adversarial relationships and impedes the necessary growth and development of the legislative effort. In its infancy, a legislative organization's sphere of influence, or confidence zone, is very small. As time passes, if the organization and its philosophies are sound, and if the liaison officers are constantly developing their own potential, the areas of legislative operations expand. The organization becomes much more capable legislatively and is less restricted to limited options in the pursuit of its objectives.

Legislative liaison operations and the individuals within them begin to stagnate without a forward-looking strategy that seeks to constantly expand horizons throughout the Congress, to include staffs, senators, and representatives who may have no apparent ties to either the military or the Department of Defense. In excess of 10 percent of the Senate Authorization Bill is determined by efforts of the personal staff whose senator or representative has little or no connection with defense issues other than his or her vote. It therefore follows that any successful legislative liaison operation will be represented by people who can adapt to changing situations, different types of people, and frequently conflicting philosophies, all the while keeping the goals of the organization in sight despite many distractions.

If ever the need for personal discipline and restraint is required, dealing with the Congress may stand out as the consummate test of a career. In order to explain the problem, a word on the makeup of congressional staffs is in order. There are two types of staff: personal staff and committee staff. Committee staff occupy a position of first among equals in the Congress. Their many responsibilities require them to work with the committee chairs to fix agendas, arrange hearings, evaluate testimony, draft bills, write reports, marshall support among members for specific bills, and conduct investigations that lead to oversight hearings or the writing of new legislation. Personal staff refers to the employees of a member of Congress's personal office. Their focus is oriented toward the member's relationship with the constituency and with the assimilation of all issues before the Congress as they relate to that constituency and to the nation. In the Senate, for example, there are one hundred such personal staff, each different in size, organization, and emphasis. Each has a military legislative assistant (MLA) who represents the point of entry for any discussion on military-related matters. A relationship with each MLA is obviously desirable for a successful legislative program.

Rather than deplore the many complexities of staff relationships which, admittedly, require exhaustive attention, a productive strategy of developing and expanding staff relationships is far more rewarding than expected and offsets many problems. There are many ways to develop such programs. Briefings in Washington, congressional visits to military installations, and the development of personal friendships all go a long way to bridge whatever gaps may exist. This approach is not only necessary, it is a rewarding experience both personally and professionally: During this process a liaison officer may derive equal benefits in terms of expanding knowledge about his or her own service and other services, and, most importantly, increased education in understanding how the Congress functions. The dividend of a well-thoughtout and highly organized educational program assists both sides enormously. In developing such programs the liaison should attempt to include the widest political spectrum as possible. Services should always reflect a bipartisan approach in the pursuit of institutional objectives.

It is easy to understand why services should adopt a bipartisan philosophy. What could be more logical in terms of dealing with the Congress? Yet the reality is that few services actively pursue such a policy for reasons that relate primarily to near-term objectives being favored over long-term goals. Uniformed military personnel are, almost by definition, apolitical. Certainly most officers would (or should) not openly declare a preference for a particular political party while on active duty. Because of the nature of professional life within the military, changes in power positions are reflected by people being promoted to a new rank. Officers do not question the philosophies of those newly appointed to higher rank, rather they accept the new philosophies such people bring because of the higher rank. Fundamentally it comes down to institutional and personal loyalties, which are expected of members of the military establishment.

Capitol Hill, however, is different. Changes in the balance of power come about only as the result of elections. Certainly, changes in staff positions can affect the situation, but substantive changes only come about with the reelection or defeat of an incumbent member of Congress. The 1980 election in the U.S. Senate, which altered the balance of power in that forum for a period of six years, is an example of a dramatic shift in political philosophy with regard to the nation, and the balance of power with regard to the U.S. Senate. Every office in the Senate was affected. Democratic majorities on all committees, including all chairmanships and the attendant majority of seats were turned over to the victorious Republicans. Democratic staffs, holding nearly twice the number of members as their Republican counterparts, were forced to reverse the equation in favor of the new majority. This meant releasing key staff members from the Democratic side and hiring perhaps twice as many on the Republican side. In short, it was a dramatic event, the impact of which is complex and difficult to understand fully. Six years later, with the 1986 elections, the power balance in the U.S. Senate again reversed itself and a realignment of the Senate to reflect the will of the people again took place. Nothing compares to this process in the military, save perhaps the change of a service chief every four years, which brings a change in philosophy, perhaps, but never the type of institutional upheaval that can be generated by elections.

It is crucial that the military, then, adopt a bipartisan view in the pursuit of its objectives. Frequently, this view can be at odds not only with the legislature but also with the policy of civilian defense authorities who, after all, frequently hold political posts as a result of an election. The military establishment, therefore, can and frequently does find itself caught between conflicting political forces, each of whom is attempting to achieve success in the pursuit of separate agendas. Clearly, this can be an uncomfortable position to be in and great skill is required of service chiefs in navigating through such potentially difficult situations.

The battle lines are not always clearly drawn, even when they should be. For example, on both sides of Capitol Hill there has been an ongoing struggle between the Authorization and Appropriations committees. The former claims primacy in deciding what is going to be authorized for the military and considers its opinion to be paramount on military procurement issues. The latter considers that authorizers can only impose spending ceilings and that appropriators, who hold the purse strings, have great latitude in deciding to what extent authorized programs will be appropriated. Services frequently find themselves caught in the middle of legislative battles by politicians attempting to establish dominance of one committee over another.

Small wonder, then, that services generally choose the path of least resistance in pursing their objectives. Faced with such significant and constantly changing problems in the legislature, those involved in legislative affairs celebrate any welcome mat on Capitol Hill. Having to negotiate such a delicate minefield, they see no apparent reason why services should not be anything but bipartisan. Yet frequently they are not.

The reason that most services are not as bipartisan in their approach as they should be is twofold. First, as stated earlier, the complexities of the political struggles both in the Congress and in the Defense Department drive services to seek the paths of least resistance in the pursuit of their objectives. This requires legislative efforts to be directed principally and, unfortunately sometimes exclusively, toward those who are perceived to have the power to most affect institutional goals. Simply put, services play to the majority.

Second, the services are not always bipartisan because of something that cannot be easily controlled or even corrected. The military operates on a two- or three-year assignment policy. Officers who staff liaison billets serve for two or three years, rarely more and frequently less. This is true of most assignments in the military establishment. The corporate memory does not extend for a longer period of time. In working with the Congress, for the most part, members and their personal staffs, as well as committee staffs, have usually been in position longer. In terms of understanding issues, knowing program histories, having access to information, hearing well-articulated opposing view points, being subjected to sound lobbying pressures, let alone the desires of the military, congressional staffs are well-equipped to battle (if need be) with any service on any issue. Capitol Hill can and does take the long-term view in deciding issues, while the military, because of its assignment practices, finds itself trapped in a much shorter time frame. The key is in finding a mutually acceptable position between these two perspectives. Finding this common ground usually defines the success or failure of a legislative organization. I hasten to add that I do not consider all issues between Capitol Hill, the Department of Defense, and the military as being confrontational; the vast majority are not. I suggest however, that prior to entering the arena, military representatives should know the rules of legislative engagement before ever attempting to execute any strategy in the pursuit of legislative goals.

Having described the conditions that must be recognized, I shall turn the discussion toward some issues that impede services from achieving their goals. These problems were common to all services in varying degrees not long ago, and a few well-placed telephone calls have convinced me that these impediments remain in place during the current legislative period.

I have already discussed the problems associated with rapid personnel turnover common to all services. The air force, in my opinion, makes the best attempt of all services to develop corporate experience by returning officers with previously successful tours to the legislative arena at varying intervals during their careers. Successful liaison officers should be, if at all possible, left to execute a full three-year tour, or longer. Services could understand clearly that success in legislative affairs comes about slowly and incrementally. This means, in real time, that normally an officer reaches full potential in this field during the third year, rarely before. Services could also address the rotation problem by identifying reliefs early in order to acquire preassignment education, to familiarize newcomers with the congressional environment, and to permit as long a turnover period as possible with the incumbent officer. Short of civilianizing all legislative liaison billets, there is no way to solve the problem completely. Services can, however, enhance their positions with the application of forward-looking assignment policies. During the assignment process, care should be given in the selection of officers for legislative duties. The more responsible the billet the more important this becomes. Generally speaking, liaison officers whose personalities are gregarious and whose outlook is broad will tend to do well. Among the qualities I recommend as important to being content in the legislative field are patience, flexibility, adaptability, humility, self-confidence, and a secure ego. All of the preceding will be put to the ultimate test at some time during a normal tour of duty. Officers who are technically oriented and who prefer structure and clearly defined rules and objectives will have a predictably difficult time, as will officers who are not particularly people oriented. As I stated at the outset, there is no checklist for success, only adherence to a general set of principles that can lead to success and job satisfaction in working with the Congress.

Competing factions within each service is another institutional impediment to success in legislative affairs. All services share this characteristic in varying degrees despite the fact that the causative factors are understandable. Factional rivalries within each service are not new. They compete for their share of their service's budget. Ground versus air, missiles versus aircraft, submarines versus surface ships, pay raises versus more hardware, research and development funds versus operational and maintenance dollars—the list is extensive. Earlier I described the five navies as an example of the process through which priorities are developed, finally to be articulated by the military and civilian leadership of each service. If it ended there, things would be simpler. Concurrently with the official process, opposing factions with each service carry on, with widely varying degrees of activity, efforts to create support for their programs external to the system. Frequently it is not of their own doing. Supportive factions within the Congress ensure that conflicting issues receive visibility and actively encourage keeping options as alive as possible. It is impossible to ascertain the exact moment when a program is, legislatively speaking, dead. Battleships, B-1 bombers, the AV8-B, and many others have at one point or the other been pronounced terminated only to resurface again successfully. Services recognize that supporters of such causes ensure visibility of these issues in any appropriate discussions. Obviously, the more a service is capable of controlling the opposing factions, both internally and externally, the greater the ability that service, through such control, will be able to speak with one voice on Capitol Hill. The importance of achieving this capability should not be underestimated.

The one voice problem is common to all services' legislative operations. Externally, the goals and objectives must be clearly and positively articulated by each service, perhaps the most important precept for successful legislative operation. Yet, there is another, equally important principle that must be grasped and firmly controlled—the need for a legislative operation to express itself with one voice from within.

Each service has liaison officers on both sides of Capitol Hill. They are commanded by officers of colonel and navy captain rank. Their missions are to facilitate the flow of information from the Pentagon to the Congress and vice versa. They perform casework functions, request information from committees and staffs, are extensively involved in congressional travel, and serve as a very accurate barometer for the analysis of legislative trends in either the House of Representatives or the Senate.

Also very involved with the Congress is each service Committee Liaison Section, the legislative specialist in matters pertaining to programs. Without exception, each Committee Liaison Section is located in the Pentagon. They are also headed by a colonel or navy captain. Their main function is to work with the Armed Services Committees on either side of Capitol Hill. Each officer assigned to committee liaison work has responsibility for several programs and is tasked with legislatively achieving service goals for those programs. Although such an officer can usually achieve these goals through a close rapport with the appropriate staff on either the Senate (SASC) or House Armed Services Committee (HASC), he or she should be continuously searching for support, wherever it may be found, external to the committees. Industry also plays an important role in fashioning needed support for programs. Representatives and senators from districts and states potentially benefiting from programs that contribute to business growth, employment, and other potential voter support, are quick to offer help in obtaining legislative passage of a particular program.

The problem for the legislative liaison organization is that of success-fully coordinating the efforts of its sections in support of a well-thoughtout, cohesive legislative battle plan. Frequently this condition does not exist and the failure for not achieving this coordination can be significant. There are perceived to be conflicting missions between the Senate and House Liaison Sections and the Committee Liaison Sections. The former usually accept the generalist role and mission in support of the institutional goal. The latter, however, perceive themselves as the specialists, the ultimate spokespeople on matters of importance concerning programs. This is an accurate perception of their roles and mission.

The coordination problem arises when the two sections do not work in a coordinated manner toward the common goal of achieving service objectives. Small battles of territorial prerogatives, institutional rules inadvertently favoring one section over another, failures to analyze information obtained and reported by each section to the headquarters, and personal relationships all affect a service's ability to manage its own subordinate sections effectively in support of a one voice philosophy. As an example, there is a general policy among each of the services that Committee Liaison Sections have primacy in working with either the HASC or SASC. Frequently, House and Senate Liaison Sections are precluded from entering into a relationship with committee staffers on any program matters. This type of division of effort creates friction within the organization, lowers morale, reduces effectiveness, and can foster a we-they attitude among officers whose only objective is to support their service in the pursuit of legislative objectives.

Services that understand that an effective legislative operation rests with the development of an organization composed of people who understand service objectives and goals and create a climate in which all subordinate sections can act in support of the plan, each contributing in its own unique way in a coordinated, supportive manner, will enjoy far more success than services who allow petty jealousies and competing factionalism to dominate daily activities.

Some will respond to the above by claiming that as long as the goals are achieved all else is unimportant. Harmony, good working conditions, personal relationships, and the like are secondary according to such a philosophy, and there is much evidence to indicate that it has a strong following within the respective legislative liaison organizations. In my opinion, failure to identify and correct this condition certainly contributes to exposing service goals to unnecessary jeopardy. Services' ability to speak with one voice can be severely limited, staffers and members alike are quick to recognize conditions which reflect discord, misunderstanding, and lack of communication within a legislative organization, and the congressional perception of that particular service suffers unnecessarily. An appreciation of the very unique capabilities of each section and a blending of these capabilities in such a way as to foster harmony, teamwork, and a sense of purpose through coordinated effort is well worth the concerns of leadership in legislative organizations.

Finally, and perhaps the most important of principles in dealing with the Congress, communicating effectively with the Congress in a manner that establishes trust, integrity, honesty, and dependability over an extended period of time is the cornerstone of the relationship. This type of reputation is established by the service chiefs themselves at the outset of their respective terms.  Capitol Hill reads and hears but watches actions with great intensity.  Impressions of individuals and the organizations they lead or represent are quickly formed and difficult to change once established.  Thus, the relationship between a service chief's stated goals and philosophies and the manner in which they are carried out by his legislative experts is under constant scrutiny.  The more the actions of the implementors of legislative policy reflect the stated objectives of service leadership, the greater the credibility enjoyed by that service on Capitol Hill.

Effective legislative liaison is both complex and simple at the same time.  It is complex because the process of legislation is not easy to grasp, either theoretically or in actuality.  The understanding required must be acquired through study and time in the arena.  Yet it is simple in terms of human relations because being able to relate to people from all walks of life, respecting the existence of all views, and being honest in representing individual service objectives is enough to guarantee credibility and respect.  Failure to establish clear goals and to articulate and implement policies in support of stated goals that are understood by all will guarantee legislative frustration, contribute to bureaucratic infighting, and create unnecessary friction within any legislative organization.  The ability to maintain both an individual and collective perspective with regard to the role of the Congress in military issues is crucial to the establishment of a good legislative operation.  There is no place for either institutional or individual irritation toward the Congress because of either real or perceived congressional slight.  The only result from such flawed strategy is a loss of momentum in the pursuit of legislative goals.

A forward-looking, aggressive, responsive legislative organization will be staffed by personnel who have been carefully selected for their intellect and their ability to relate to people.  They will willingly subordinate individual egos for the good of the long-range goals of their respective service and will be balanced in their approach, favoring neither political party in their relationships with the Congress.  Within their respective organizations, these people will put aside rivalries and possible misunderstandings among colleagues in favor of a policy of mission accomplishment with little regard for personal reward or ego gratification.  In return, upon completing a normal tour length in the legislative arena, successful officers will remember the experience as one of the highlights of their careers and should look forward to further service in a related capacity.

# 7.4    The Reagan Doctrine: (As Yet) a Declaratory Policy

## ANGELO CODEVILLE

*A Reagan Doctrine has been associated with Presidential statements pledging the full U.S. assistance necessary for anti-communist liberation movements to regain their countries' freedom—notably in Nicaragua, Angola, and Afghanistan. Yet, purposeful policy to implement that Doctrine has yet to take shape: it has been mired on the bureaucratic battleground of the major foreign policy "baronies" in the U.S. Executive Branch and their allies in the Congress. The compromise of contending viewpoints has been the provision of a modicum of covert assistance to each liberation movement to keep it fighting, but not enough to enable it to win. The Doctrine, moreover, has been both weakened and distorted in each application by a "negotiations track" that both is unrealistic and contradicts the Doctrine's basic objectives.*

Over the past several years, the fact that most of the guerrilla wars in the world today are being waged against Soviet or Soviet proxy forces has provided a strong theme in the pronouncements of the Reagan Administration. In the Presidential campaign of 1984, the Administration's leading spokesmen invoked this fact as further proof that America's previously battered image had been refurbished by their competent stewardship, that the "correlation of forces" on the globe was shifting against the Soviet Union, and that American-style democracy was once again ascendant as the wave of the future. Throughout 1985 the Administration spoke increasingly about "anticommunist resistance movements," and "aid to freedom-fighters" rose into a major political issue in Washington.

President Reagan, for his part, went so far as to call Nicaragua's Contras "brothers." In his 1986 State of the Union message he announced what has come to be known as the Reagan Doctrine: that any people fighting to free itself from communist rule could count on the Administration's effective aid. Using the (original) words of the resolution on Afghanistan that the Congress had passed in September 1984, the President asserted that the aid would be

Copyright 1986, United States Strategic Institute. Published in *Strategic Review*, vol. xiv, No. 3, Summer 1986.

not just enough to help the freedom fighters fight and die, but enough to help them win.

Shortly thereafter, Jonas Savimbi, the charismatic leader of Angola's anticommunist forces, received a hero's reception in Washington. President Reagan introduced the three civilian leaders of Nicaragua's Contras by declaring that he was one of them. In May 1986 he received three leaders of the Afghan Resistance in the Oval Office. In June the President won hard-fought support from the House of Representatives to expend $100 million for the Contras. Earlier in the year, the *New York Times* reported that the Reagan Administration had agreed to send Stinger shoulder-fired anti-aircraft missiles to Angolan and Afghan (if not yet Nicaraguan) anti-communist forces.

## LIBERATION AND THE POLICYMAKING "BARONIES"

The very word "doctrine" over these Presidential statements has conveyed the image of a determined Administration policy aimed at the objective of driving the Soviets and their surrogates out of Afghanistan, Angola and Nicaragua. Yet, the test of policy in a democracy lies less in the declaratory statements of the head-of-state (irrespective of his sincerity) and more in the substantial decisions and actions taken by the government. Particularly in the current U.S. Administration, with its strong emphasis on the "cabinet approach," foreign policy is the "resultant," in the geometric sense, of the policy preferences of the major "baronies" involved in the policymaking process: the State Department, the Defense Department, the Central Intelligence Agency, and their respective allies in the National Security Council and the U.S. Congress.

Of course, it is risky—and perhaps less than fair to individual policy-makers who may diverge from the given "corporate" line—to generalize the policy preferences within the "baronies" and their interplay over the issue of U.S. assistance to anticommunist forces. Still, close observation of the interagency process in the Reagan Administration with respect to the issue has yielded consistent evidence of basic positions and themes.

There is first of all the Department of State. Given the central place of diplomacy in that agency's mandate and functions, there has evolved among its members—especially in the professional ranks of the Foreign Service—a disposition that assigns to negotiations the primary role in foreign policy. Short of being the instruments of "last resort," military power and armed force are seen as at best inputs into the negotiating process—as "strength-ening the bargaining hand." But the principal purpose of negotiations is to defuse conflict and tensions—from the vantagepoint of U.S. national interests, to ameliorate and constrain through negotiated agreement the threats posed to those U.S. interests.

It is in the very nature of negotiated agreements, moreover, that they are addressed to the status quo—to its stabilization rather than its revision. Applied to the situations in Afghanistan, Angola, and Nicaragua, it leads to what may be called a "minimalist" view in the State Department, which holds that the "insurrections" in those places may be harnessed to the search for regional arrangements which, while continuing the given Marxist-Leninist regime in power, might render it less threatening to its neighbors and to U.S. interests. There is also a "maximalist" view in the Department which suggests that the combined phenomenon of anticommunist movements may lead to a new global U.S.-Soviet *modus vivendi* based upon respect for the status quo. In neither the "minimalist" nor "maximalist" view, however, is there really room for victory by the anticommunist forces. In fact, it is fair to say that some would deem such victory "destabilizing" in the larger U.S.-Soviet context.

In contrast with such themes in the State Department, the civilians in charge of the U.S. Defense Department's policy generally favor the liberation of the three countries from communist control. They have pressed for formulation of national policy along those lines, but do not have a charter for dispensing aid. Moreover, they can count on resistance from the military services to giving liberation movements the weapons and other resources from their own hard-won shares of the military budget.

The Director of the Central Intelligence Agency, William Casey, is firmly aligned with the officials in the Defense Department, and personally seems to favor the victory of liberation movements. His Agency has the charter for dispensing the aid. But from among the CIA's senior personnel have come strong echoes of the State Department's view of the role of liberation movements in U.S.-Soviet relations. In their dealings with Congress and the NSC, CIA officials have often outdone even their colleagues in the State Department in reticence to provide aid to such movements quantitatively and qualitatively sufficient for victory, declaring that the Agency would rather be rid of the burden of supplying such aid at all. Nevertheless, the CIA has strenuously opposed proposals that the Defense Department be given primary responsibility for providing such assistance.

All of this is to say that, in the absence of more forceful Presidential leadership, the "resultant" of such contradictory forces within the Administration is a de facto policy neither of liberation nor of abandonment, but of what might be characterized as providing enough to anticommunist liberation movements to "keep the pot boiling," or to "raise the cost" to the Soviet Union and its surrogates of consolidating their holds over areas where such movements operate. Of course, few in the foreign policy establishment would be prepared explicitly to argue the case for such a "policy," given its cynical implications for those fighting the liberation cause, as well as the prospect of thereby conceding to the Soviet Union ultimate victories more meaningful—and more discrediting to the United States—than they would have been in the absence of any U.S. involvement. Yet, the various participants in the policy process seem reasonably content with governmental decisions that make such an outcome inevitable, because they represent "reasonable" compromises of intragovernmental differences.

Such compromises avoid the most vexing burden of policymaking: namely, casting the hard choices concerning the ends sought and the means likely to achieve them, and accepting the responsibility for success or failure. Instead, the Administration's foreign policymakers generally have dealt with their differences by adopting in foreign affairs in general, and with respect to the issue of anticommunist liberation movements in particular, the habits of domestic policymaking, which consist of giving a little to each side in a given controversy. This sort of policymaking permits the hard choices to be postponed—and ultimately to be foreclosed by the march of time and events. In foreign affairs, however, it has the effect of conceding to the opponent all the advantages of rationality that we deny to ourselves. But let us see how the phenomenon has applied in practice.

## NICARAGUA: GENESIS OF THE PROBLEM

All too soon after the Carter Administration had in effect helped the Sandinistas' victory in Nicaragua by isolating the Somoza regime from all possible sources of support, it was forced to confront the implications of a now-recognized fact that it had so recently dismissed: namely, that the Sandinista leaders were dedicated communists tightly allied with the Soviet Union. Clearly the Carter Administration decided that no U.S. government could agree to the establishment in Central America of a regime able to coerce its people into serving as the spearhead of a Soviet intrusion onto the hemispheric mainland and into the vulnerable "strategic backyard" of the United States itself.

Acting on that recognition, the Carter Administration in December 1978 notified Congress that it would engage in covert activities to forestall the "emerging totalitarian nature" of the Sandinista regime by giving assistance to democratic forces in Nicaragua. In 1979 most of the emergent democratic opposition to the Sandinistas was nonviolent. But already then the Sandinistas had begun labeling any and all who stood in the way of their consolidation of power and alignment with the Soviet Bloc as "*contra-revolucionarios*," or simply "*contras*." Over the following months, the opposition which the United States was helping gradually but inexorably became a paramilitary resistance.

By the time the Reagan Administration began to review its own program of assistance to the Contras, some thousand Nicaraguans per month, not to mention entire tribes of Miskito Indians, were asking for weapons with which to reclaim the freedoms they thought they had recently won. The Administration was generally favorable to meeting the demand, and its formulation of objectives did not differ from that of the Carter Administration: namely to change the Nicaraguan government. At the time, a spokesman for the Administration described its objective as follows: "do unto the Sandinistas what they are trying to do to El Salvador." Listeners were free to draw the conclusion: "change the government."

## EARLY DERAILING OF THE REAGAN NICARAGUA POLICY

Yet, a variety of people within the Administration, along with Democratic members of Congress who felt freer to oppose a Republican administration than their own, began to charge that it was illegitimate for the United States to seek to affect the nature of a foreign government by supporting armed actions against it. Although the opposition was to the *ends* of the Administration's policy, it was couched in objections to the paramilitary *means* to be employed. Thus, no sooner had the Reagan Administration announced that its intentions did not differ from its predecessor's than it felt pressure, both from within and without the Administration, to qualify or somehow blur those intentions.

The principal tactic of the opponents of actions against the Sandinista regime consisted of convincing the Administration that it could obtain appropriated assistance for the Contras only at the cost of pledging that this aid would not be used in an effort to change the Nicaraguan government. Throughout 1982 members of Congress led the Administration's witnesses into statements that the United States did not seek to involve itself in Nicaragua's internal affairs, but only intended to stop Nicaragua's intervention into El Salvador's internal affairs. Support for the Contras was a means of sending this message, and also of interdicting the flow of arms from Nicaragua to El Salvador.

In 1982, the annual appropriations for the Department of Defense were delayed until December's "lame duck" session of the Congress. At that time, Congressman (later Senator) Tom Harkin (D-Iowa) proposed an amendment prohibiting any and all expenditures for anyone seeking to overthrow Nicaragua's government. This was defeated easily, as was Senator Edward Kennedy's identical motion in the Senate. Thereupon the President was persuaded, reportedly by recommendations from the State Department and the CIA, to support an amendment offered by Congressman Robert Boland (D-Mass.) which barred the United States from expending any funds in order to overthrow the government of Nicaragua. The argument advanced to the President was that, inasmuch as the Administration's official line mentioned not "overthrowing," but "changing" and "democratizing"—which could theoretically be effected without overthrow—the Boland Amendment would strengthen rather than weaken the Administration's position by putting it beyond reproach. Predictably, however "the law," as the Boland Amendment was quickly dubbed by opponents of aid to the Contras, was elevated into a test for the Administration that it prove by deeds that it was *not* working to overthrow the Sandinista regime.

That burden of "proof" exacted a series of statements from the Reagan Administration in 1983–1984 to the effect that assistance to the Contras indeed was *not* intended at the overthrow of the Sandinistas—meaning in practical terms that the Contras would not win their struggle. The principal evidence for this was invoked in the Administration's refusal to supply the Contras with the heavy weapons, anti-aircraft and logistics essential to victory. Again and again the Administration contended that its policy was to seek a negotiated settlement, and that aid to the Contras was the primary prod toward such a settlement. Beyond that, in testimony before the Congress spokesmen for the Administration found themselves responding to questions—logically consequent to the Administration's stance—regarding the circumstances under which it would curtail aid to the Contras. It is noteworthy that the Sandinista radio in Managua repeatedly broadcast words by CIA Director William Casey to the effect of such a curtailment, making the point to friend and foe alike that the Contras were mere tools of the United States fighting for a hopeless cause.

That cause never seemed less hopeful than during the summer of 1984, when the Reagan Administration, having attached a request for arms for the Contras to an urgent supplemental appropriations bill in the Senate (in order to force the issue into a conference with the Democratic-controlled House of Representatives), thereupon agreed to have its request stripped from the bill. In October 1984, State Department officials were putting pressure on Honduras and Costa Rica to sign a treaty drafted by the representatives of Mexico, Colombia, Venezuela, and Panama, which would have cut off support for the Contras in exchange for a "commitment" by the Sandinistas to discuss reducing the role of its foreign supporters and better treatment of the opposition. Only when the Honduran Ambassador in Washington protested to the NSC staff and to members of Congress, who then protested to the President, did the State Department back off. The incident eventually led to the replacement of Langhorne A. Motley, the then Assistant Secretary of State for InterAmerican Affairs who became identified with the maneuver, with Elliot Abrams.

## THE 1985 ASSISTANCE DECISION

The October 1984 State Department initiative and its aftermath also led President Reagan to depict in clearer terms the struggle in Nicaragua as one between the Sandinistas and their legitimate internal opposition, and to insist that the United States would never deal with the Sandinistas behind the back of that opposition. More generally, the White House sometime in 1985 came face-to-face with the recognition that time was working for the Sandinistas and the Soviets and against U.S. interests in Central America—that while the United States had halted its help to the Contras, the Soviets were shipping ever mounting stockpiles of sophisticated weapons to Nicaragua to be used against the Contras. Once again the Administration had to confront squarely the dire implications of a consolidated, unchallenged Sandinista government and of the ensconcement of Soviet power in Nicaragua. The recognition prompted an increase in Administration pressure on the Congress, particularly on Democratic members seeking to avoid being placed on the wrong side of the line drawn by the President—namely that those refusing support to the Contras would bear ultimate responsibility for the establishment and expansion of communist totalitarianism close to America's southern border. Hence the Congress' agreement in the summer of 1986 to supply $100 million worth of food and weapons to the Contras.

Yet, in and of itself, this clearly did not—and could not—represent a decision either by Congress, or by the Administration, to seek the Sandinistas' ouster, nor even to declare to the world, to the Nicaraguan populace, or to the American people that the Sandinista regime is illegitimate. This was not a decision to give the Contras anything resembling the military odds that the Sandinistas had enjoyed in their rising against the Somoza regime. Had the United States made such a decision, it would be providing the surface-to-air missiles, the anti-aircraft weapons, the artillery, the transportation and the training necessary for fighting a modern army lavishly supplied by the Soviet Bloc.

One hundred million dollars worth of military aid over eighteen months—even assuming that it represents a significant fraction of what the Contras need to mount a serious military challenge—can be easily offset by increases in the tide of materiel (and men) from the Soviet Bloc to Nicaragua. A commitment to victory—or even the possibility of victory— would entail either a decision to supply the Contras with whatever they need to counter the Soviet Bloc flow, or a decision to limit that flow by a naval-air blockade or by even the threat thereof. In the absence of such decisions, the commitment of $100 million may be enough to "keep the pot boiling" in Nicaragua—at least for the time being.

## THE NEGOTIATIONS TRACK INTO THE WILDERNESS

According to at least one explanation of U.S. policy, there may be even less to the $100 million than meets the eye. In a speech to the World Affairs Council of Northern California on June 16, 1986, the President's Special Ambassador to Central America, Phillip Habib, argued for the assistance funds, and for the Contras themselves, as indispensable means to a negotiated arrangement in Central America. As did the Carter Administration, the Kissinger Commission and President Reagan, Habib explained that the United States—not to mention Nicaragua's immediate neighbors—cannot abide a Nicaraguan government both totalitarian and allied with Moscow. The Contras are worthy of support because they are legitimate Nicaraguan democrats and because, unless the Nicaraguan government turns to democracy, its neighbors can place no faith in its promises of coexistence.

The United States, Habib continued, fully supports the efforts of Mexico, Colombia, Venezuela, and Panama (the so-called Contadora countries) to fashion an agreement between Nicaragua and its neighbors that would end support for violence on all sides and rid the area of foreign, including U.S., military interference. The United States would abide by such an agreement while not being party to it. But, Habib emphasized, there is no getting away from the fact that the democratically elected presidents of Honduras and Costa Rica insist that any treaty involve not just agreements between nations, but also the democratization of Nicaraguan politics, without which neither of their countries could rest secure. They insist that any provision of Nicaraguan democratization come into force simultaneously with those requiring the neighboring countries to stop harboring the Contras, and they insist that any treaty provide for verifiable evidence that Nicaragua is living up to all of its provisions. Thus, the thrust of Habib's presentation of U.S. policy was that the price of a U.S. dismantling of the Contras is a Contadora treaty that is "comprehensive, simultaneous and verifiable."

Habib made no mention of who would *enforce* such a treaty. It has become standard in State Department formulations that the concept of verification crowds out the less comfortable one of enforcement of compliance. State Department officials tend to argue that if all provisions of a treaty, including arrangements for verification, go into force simultaneously, the treaty is self-enforcing: the U.S. side will not perform its obligations unless the other side performs its obligations. It is difficult to believe that those who wield this argument fail to foresee what would happen once the United States announced its intention to sponsor the dismantling of the Contras in exchange for Sandinista promises of democratization—promises whose fulfillment (or lack thereof) the United States might verify but would be in no effective position to enforce.

The Contras for the most part are not professional fighters whose campaign can be turned on and off, but ordinary people who have taken up arms in the hope of freer lives for themselves and a better life for their country. It is remarkable that they have fought for five years with so little tangible hope. An agreement that provided for their disbandment and the cut-off of American support would spell their end. Thus, by the time realization of the communist side's betrayal of the treaty's provision were to filter through the U.S. national security bureaucracy, the Contra option would no longer be available. The United States would have to choose in effect between doing nothing and going to war.

Of course, due to the objections from democratic Honduras and Costa Rica, a treaty is not around the corner. It hovers near enough, however, to help keep the U.S. foreign policy bureaucracy from focusing on reality and to justify giving the Contras enough to fight and die, day after day, as the Sandinistas and their Soviet Bloc allies tighten their hold on Nicaragua and prepare for the next step.

## A CLEARER ISSUE IN ANGOLA

In late 1985, even as President Reagan and Secretary of State George Shultz were echoing the widespread sentiment that Jonas Savimbi's Union for the Total Independence of Angola (UNITA) deserves the Free World's support in its fight against a Soviet-supported Cuban army of occupation—and as the Democratic-controlled House of Representatives was about to consider a proposal by Congressman Claude Pepper (D-Fla.) to provide some aid to Savimbi—Secretary Shultz wrote a secret letter to Congressman Robert Michel (R-Ill.), the leader of the House Republicans, asking him to quietly oppose aid to Savimbi. Congressman Michel, outraged, published the letter. This led a patently embarrassed Secretary of State to a series of meetings on Capitol Hill lasting into March of 1986, in which he sought both to remedy the impression of hypocrisy created by his letter to Michel, and to channel the Congressional pressure for aid to Savimbi into the policy framework he had sought to defend by drafting the letter to Michel in the first place. Let us see what that framework is, and how well Secretary Shultz has succeeded.

The issue in Angola is less complex than in Nicaragua. In 1975 the Soviet Union helped its client communist movement, the MPLA, to seize power by supplying an invasion force of some 20,000 Cuban troops. That number today is closer to 30,000, augmented by the usual contingents of East German internal security specialists, Bulgarians, Yemenis, etc. The Soviet Union devotes fully one third of its airlift capacity to supplying the expeditionary force in Angola. A Soviet hospital ship is permanently stationed off Luanda to care for the wounded.

On the other side of this war, Jonas Saimbi's UNITA controls one third of the country and actively contests another third. It has sanctuaries in Zambia and South Africa, and receives most of its aid from Europe, principally France. Although it once accepted aid from Communist China, UNITA is thoroughly pro-Western. The canard of the extreme left in the United States and Europe—that Savimbi is somehow the tool of South African racism—is clearly just that. In fact, UNITA is a thoroughly black movement, while its opponents, the leaders of the MPLA, are obviously dependent on white Cubans, Soviets, East Germans, etc.

The Soviet Union is determined to prevail in Angola. In 1985 Cuban forces under the direction of a Soviet general launched an attack across nearly a thousand miles of wilderness that inflicted heavy losses on UNITA and reached within 100 miles of its capital, Jamba. The Cubans used armor and aircraft to break through the defenses, and helicopters for enveloping movements. UNITA was saved by the remoteness of its capital, as well as by excellent fighting.

Yet, the 1985 attack foretold that UNITA is being outclassed. Between 1975 and 1985, UNITA had laboriously built a native organization with just enough foreign guns, trucks and radios to challenge the forces which had fashioned the communist victory in 1975. But by 1985 the Soviets had obviously upped the ante. In 1986 the Soviet-Cuban buildup, especially of aircraft, had further outclassed UNITA. Without a quantum leap in foreign assistance, UNITA seems ultimately doomed.


## THE NEGOTIATIONS TRACK IN SOUTHERN AFRICA

The question for U.S. policy is obviously whether or not to give Savimbi's UNITA enough to contend for victory at this higher level of violence, and to prepare to meet any ulterior Soviet escalation with even more massive assistance, or perhaps to prepare to prevent Cuban reinforcements from going to Angola. If the United States decided to do none of these things, it would have to prepare to live with the consequences of a Soviet victory in Angola.

U.S. policy, insofar as it exists, has been to obfuscate this choice. Since 1981 Assistant Secretary of State Chester Crocker has pursued what the State Department fancies as negotiations between Angola's ruling MPLA and South Africa. The objective of the negotiations ostensibly is a scenario in which South Africa grants independence to Southwest Africa/Namibia under conditions acceptable to the MPLA, and cuts off all support to Savimbi; in exchange for this the MPLA would expel the Cubans, Soviets and other Bloc nationals, and form a coalition government including UNITA. Of course, the United States, although not a formal party to the agreement, would respect it and cease its own support to Savimbi. Hence, Angolans would solve Angola's problem without interference.

In order to believe in the feasibility of this arrangement, one would first have to accept a string of propositions. The first is that the MPLA is free to order the Soviet coalition out. The second is that the MPLA's leaders would feel themselves secure enough to dispense with Cuban troops. The third is that South Africa could agree to hand Southwest Africa/Namibia over to Sam Nujoma's communist Southwest African People's Organization (SWAPO), as the MPLA demands, and help to destroy UNITA, thus leaving its northwestern border in thoroughly unfriendly hands.

So committed has the State Department been to this negotiation that in 1984–1985 it agreed to, and pressed upon South Africa, the MPLA's escalation of demands: namely that at the end of the process, after Savimbi was cut off and Namibia was in SWAPO's hands, some ten thousand Cuban troops would remain in Angola. After unfavorable publicity, however, the State Department returned to its original negotiating position that all the Cuban troops had to leave.

The Soviet-Cuban offensive of 1985 also convinced some officials in the State Department that U.S. aid to UNITA might not be a bad means of putting some pressure on the MPLA, and that without it the Savimbi bargaining chip might not last much longer. Moreover, by the winter of 1985–1986 Jonas Savimbi's prestige in the United States was high. In the wake of the furor over his letter to Congressman Michel, Secretary Shultz was not in a position to oppose aid to UNITA, which was supported by the Secretary of Defense as well as the Director of the CIA.

When President Reagan received Savimbi at the White House, the only question besides how much and what kind of aid he would receive was whether the aid would replace negotiations or be subordinate to them. Secretary Shultz seemed to ensure that aid would be subordinate to the negotiations by taking the initiative away from the Congress. He proposed that Savimbi receive $15 million of covert aid, administered by the CIA. The use of the covert mechanism tends to forestall the painful process of formulating U.S. policy in any given area.

## ABIDING QUESTIONS ABOUT U.S. ANGOLAN POLICY

By agreeing to give some aid to Savimbi, the U.S. Government had satisfied one set of pressures. The President's authority, after an intervention by several Senators, was enough to overcome resistance within the Administration—notably in the higher echelons of the CIA—to supplying some Stinger missiles to UNITA. But no one at the higher levels of the U.S. Government has (publicly) addressed the question: What will our $15 million a year do in Angola against a combined Soviet Bloc investment of over $1 billion?

The answer from the State Department would be, of course, that the U.S. aid is designed to keep pressure on the MPLA to accept the negotiated arrangement pushed by Assistant Secretary Crocker. But that answer cannot stand up to questions concerning its premises. Why should the MPLA and the Soviets-Cubans abandon one another so long as there is no serious prospect of disastrous defeat? Even if the communist side agreed to a deal, who would enforce it? Given what each of the sides in the affair is trying to do, and the means they are employing, what will the situation be in a few years hence? What are the likely consequences of a Soviet victory? Just how much should the United States be willing to commit in order to prevent it?

The decision to supply $15 million in covert aid to Savimbi was above all a decision not to confront those questions and to indulge a while longer the State Department's hope, at the same time satisfying pressures to do something in support of Savimbi. Meanwhile, the Soviets are pursuing a steadfast policy in Angola and Southern Africa.

## INDECISION OVER AFGHANISTAN

Because the issue in Afghanistan is clearer than even in Angola, its obfuscation in the Administration is all the more conspicuous. In December 1979, the Soviet Army invaded Afghanistan. The Soviets have changed the government in Kabul three times since the invasion. That government has absolutely no standing in the country other than as an agent of the Soviet Union. It is a foreign, atheistic abomination among devout, xenophobic Muslims. Perhaps one million Afghan civilians have been killed, and some three-and-one-half million have fled the country. The Mujahideen fighters are the only representatives of the Afghan people. Pakistan—especially its conservative Muslim ruling elite—has placed itself in great danger by acting as a conduit for foreign aid to the Mujahideen.

Yet, President Reagan, having invited the leaders of the Mujahideen to the Oval Office in May 1986, resisted their request that he withdraw recognition from the puppet government in Kabul. "Administration sources" explained that the President wants to maintain the U.S. embassy in Kabul in order to gather intelligence. This is in line with his decision to maintain recognition of the Sandinista regime in Managua, but it begs the question. Intelligence is information useful for implementing policy. In fact, the U.S. Government has not decided what it wants to do about Afghanistan.

What makes this indecision all the more poignant in the case of Afghanistan is that there is little, if any, opposition in the U.S. domestic arena to the proposition that the United States should help the Afghan freedom-fighters drive the Soviets out of their country. Indeed, each year since the Soviets invaded and the CIA began to funnel arms to the Mujahideen, the Congress has *increased* the Administration's requests for funds for this purpose.

In 1984 the Congress, led by the liberal Democratic Senator from Massachusetts, Paul Tsongas, passed a resolution requesting the Administration to supply aid to Afghanistan that would allow the Afghans to do more than fight and die. The resolution's original draft used the words that President Reagan later made the touchstone of the Reagan Doctrine: "enough to win." Ironically, because the Administration, in the persons of Secretary

George Shultz and CIA Deputy Director John MacMahon, lobbied so hard against these very words, Senator Tsongas reluctantly agreed to change them to "advance the cause of freedom."

## LACK OF ASSISTANCE POLICY TO THE MUJAHIDEEN

Even as Congress has sought to increase the flow of aid to the Afghans, it has asked the Administration to set a policy for using it. This the Administration has seemed unable and/or unwilling to do. The CIA, for example, has consistently demonstrated refusal to admit what every observer of the Afghan scene has noted about Soviet strategy there: namely, that the Soviet Union is waging a devastating war against the civilian population. By the same token, the CIA has refused to acknowledge the broad Afghan population's (not just the mainforce Mujahideen's) need for competent defenses against indiscriminate and pervasive strafing by Soviet aircraft. Indeed, even under pressure from Congress the CIA has resisted providing competent portable air defenses to the main-force Mujahideen.

Finally, the CIA has refused to address the Afghans' need to have the quantity and quality of weapons delivered to them tailored to the requirements of operations, and the need to have operations tailored to a winning strategy. For years CIA officials insisted that the Afghans were not to be trusted either with money or sophisticated weapons, and/or that Pakistan would not allow either more or more effective weapons or tactics. Finally, within the U.S. Government the CIA has argued against setting a policy toward Afghanistan more specific than one simply of delivering aid to the Resistance.

But as members of Congress came to see—and the Defense Department demonstrated within the NSC—that the CIA's contentions about Afghanistan were inaccurate, the NSC approved—and the President signed—a National Security Directive stating that henceforth the actions of the United States shall be tailored to help drive the Soviets out of Afghanistan. The first practical fruit of this NSDD was the decision finally to send a token number of Stinger missiles to the Afghans.

## STILL ANOTHER NEGOTIATIONS TRACK

Nevertheless, as the current year fades and another hungry winter faces the Afghans, the United States has made no plans to provide the general staff work, the weapons and training, the food and money, and the support to Pakistan without which the new NSDD will be a dead letter. On the contrary, as the Soviets further consolidate their position on the ground, while waging a scorched-earth offensive throughout the countryside, the State Department is encouraging negotiations among the Soviet Union, Pakistan and the Kabul puppet regime, the objective of which is to exchange the withdrawal of Soviet troops from Afghanistan for Pakistan's cessation of its role as sanctuary to the Mujahideen. Once again, the United States is not an official party to the negotiations, would sign nothing, but would stop all aid to the Afghan Resistance were the parties to reach an accord.

The State Department advertises the negotiations as a door kept open to encourage the Soviets' face-saving exit from Afghanistan. It is difficult to imagine that the Department's high officials do not realize that the negotiations are allowing an even more face-saving exit for Pakistan— indeed, that they allow Pakistan's internal opposition to offer itself as the fashioner of a deal that would rid their country of millions of aliens and of a dangerous enemy at its doorstep. In Pakistan as elsewhere, not only do the negotiations tend to destabilize the Resistance's sanctuary, but they offer yet one more excuse in the intragovernmental debate over U.S. foreign policy not to take the Reagan Doctrine seriously.


## THE MIRRORS OF DECLARATORY POLICY

The Reagan Doctrine is one more species of that present-day American phenomenon: the *declaratory* policy. In normal parlance, policy is the reasonable orchestration of action to achieve certain goals. The qualifier "declaratory" attached to so many U.S. policies, on matters ranging from nuclear targeting to liberation movements, reflects a widespread recognition that they are not policies at all, but rather rhetoric that satisfies some domestic political needs and may contribute to decisions regarding discrete actions in a particular field.

The Reagan Doctrine of helping anticommunist liberation movements to win sprouts from the political conscience of President Reagan—and from values deeply embedded in the American ethos. Perhaps the most salient effect of that conscience and those values is that those within the U.S. Government who do not share them find themselves compelled to pay lipservice to them even while they pursue their own policy preferences. This has given rise among other things, to a new type of diplomacy—one that might be dubbed "surrogate" diplomacy, in which representatives of the United States try to bring their country's influence to bear on third and fourth parties to strike covenants among themselves to which the United States is not a signatory—covenants which are never submitted to the scrutiny that the U.S. Constitution prescribes, but which bind the United States nonetheless. In other words, the political consciousness of which the Reagan Doctrine is an expression has led its opponents to seek through diplomatic legerdemain abroad the leverage they lack in the U.S. political process.

This and other declaratory policies may demonstrate that many of those responsible for the fate of the United States in the world, having ceased to be competent creators and executioners of policy, have become more clever at bureaucratic infighting.

# 8

## Bureaucratic Politics and Clientele Relations: The Pros and Cons

*As with any bureaucracy in a pluralistic system, the national security community is penetrated by outside groups and interests. These relationships are natural and inevitable and somewhat necessary and beneficial. In national security affairs, the major external actors are, of course, contractors, think tank and other beltway bandit consultants, and organized pressure groups with both a direct, supportive interest in the defense community (for example, the Navy League, Associations of retired or reserved officers), and those with only an indirect or nonsupportive relationship. Although the following essays detail some of the more pernicious aspects of relationships with outside actors, many of the relationships are positive and beneficial ones, providing bureaucracy with additional expertise and information, a second look, needed political support, and advice and counsel. From the perspective of the public interest, the cozy triangles of power that these relationships compose may in fact promote too narrow or specialized a focus in policymaking, yet signify a network of sustained power all but indispensable in pluralistic democracy.*

# 8.1   How National Policy Is Made

## DANIEL M. OGDEN, JR.

*Daniel Ogden, former director of Power Marketing Coordination, U.S. Department of Energy, believes national policy is made within a system of semiautonomous power clusters. Similar in many respects to the concepts of subgovernments, iron triangles, and issue networks, Ogden's power clusters come from a rich tradition. Beyond describing how such a system works, Ogden prescribes approaches for executive leadership and control of the said system. Today, as many charge the president with being excessively detached and disengaged, Ogden's advice seems most relevant.*

In the United States, public policy is made within a system of semi-autonomous power clusters. Each cluster deals with one broad, interrelated subject area, like agriculture, in which the government plays an active role. Each cluster operates quite independently of all other clusters to identify policy issues, shape policy alternatives, propose new legislation, and implement policy.

All clusters are bipartisan, or, in a sense, nonpartisan. They are organized to shape policy, not to win elections, and members of both political parties, as well as independents, participate freely and effectively in the decisionmaking process. The political parties participate very little in this process. Being organized to win elections, they do not focus on most specific policy issues that concern the power clusters. Issues of concern to the parties as parties usually are broad, intercluster matters such as taxes or budget levels, which seem likely to affect the outcome of the next election. Only 40 percent of the roll call votes in Congress are identifiably partisan, and of these, the parties average but 60 percent loyalty from their members.

The parties affect power cluster behavior, however, by winning elections. By electing the president, state governors, and organizing the Congress and the state legislatures, they decide which leaders within each

This article was originally published as part of a larger work entitled "Outdoor Recreation: Policy and Politics" in *The Political Economy of Environmental Control*, by Ogden et al., published by the Institute of Business and Economic Research of the University of California in 1972.

power cluster will hold key positions of power within the executive and legislative branches. Through presidential and legislative leadership selection of priorities among issues, they also affect the timing and chances of success of many specific policy decisions of concern to individual power clusters.

Many power clusters have subclusters that deal with specialized subjects within the broader policy area of the cluster. For example, the natural resources power cluster has identifiable subclusters in water, lands and forests, minerals, recreation, and energy policy. The subclusters operate with a considerable degree of autonomy within their parent power cluster but also interrelate actively with other subclusters on common cluster policy problems.

Individuals usually are active in one power cluster throughout their lifetimes. Only a few individuals are active in two or more clusters, and only a few individuals voluntarily move from one cluster to another.

The major power clusters include all of the major categories of foreign and domestic policy. Among them are agriculture, defense, natural resources, education, communications, transportation, justice and law enforcement, urban affairs, health, welfare, commerce, and banking and finance. Others could be identified.

Recognition of the power cluster system in recent U.S. political literature is usually dated from a 1964 book by Douglass Cater in which he described "sub-governments" that shape public policy,[1] and a 1965 book by J. Leiper Freeman.[2] They contended that public policy in the United States is shaped by interaction among the affected parties and identified the executive agencies, the congressional committees, and the organized interest groups—the iron triangle—as the most active participants. In 1971, as Royer Visiting Professor in Political Economy at the University of California, Berkeley, I introduced the term *power clusters* and suggested that a much broader range of participants was involved in most policy shaping.[3] Many writers during the 1970s, especially David R. Mayhew,[4] Richard P. Nathan,[5] John Kessel,[6] Kenneth A. Shepsle,[7] and especially Harold Seidman,[8] and James Thurber, described power cluster behavior in their books on Congress and the Executive Branch, although the narrower subgovernment and iron triangle concept retained currency. President Jimmy Carter, for example, speaking in Springfield, Illinois, on May 27, 1978, referred to the iron triangle as enemies of the president, saying, "an iron triangle of bureaucracy, congressional committees and well-organized special interests stands in the way of governmental reforms." The March 28, 1981, issue of the *National Journal* devoted much of its space to a series of articles dealing with particular iron triangles, and also treated them as enemies of the president.[9]

In 1980 Hugh Heclo published an article, "Issue Networks and the Executive Establishment," which pointed out that "the iron triangle concept

is not so much wrong as it is disastrously incomplete."[10] Noting proliferation and specialization at the subnational level of government in recent
years, and the increasing interdependence among federal, state, and local
governmental agencies in many subject fields, he pointed to the development
of "groups of policy specialists" which have come to constitute a
"professional-bureaucratic complex," many of whom make a living in
academic life, in private consulting firms, in law firms, or by freelance
activities. He offered the term *issue networks* to describe what he saw,
saying:

> The notion of iron triangles and subgovernments presumes small circles of
> participants who have succeeded in becoming largely autonomous. Issue
> networks, on the other hand, comprise a large number of participants with
> quite variable degrees of mutual commitment or of dependence on others in
> their environment. . . . Participants move in and out of the networks
> constantly. Rather than groups united in dominance over a program, no
> one, as far as one can tell, is in control of the policies and issues. Any
> direct material interest is often secondary to intellectual or emotional
> commitment. Network members reinforce each other's sense of issues as
> their interests, rather than . . . interests defining positions on issues.[11]

Power clusters are issue networks in Heclo's terms. They are informed
communications networks that are established by the participants in each
field of public policy.

Each power cluster is composed of the same basic elements: administrative agencies, legislative committees, interest groups, professionals,
volunteers, an attentive public, and a latent public.

The public administrative agencies include departments, bureaus,
services, and commissions at the federal, state, and local government levels
that deal in that subject area. For example, in transportation, they include not
only the Federal Highway Administration, but highway departments in each
state, county road departments, and city street departments. In education
they include all sorts of educational agencies from the U.S. Office of
Education through state superintendents of education and colleges of
education in state universities, county school superintendents and local
school district boards of education, right down to the principals and teachers
in a particular school. Among these officials are both elected and appointed
political leaders and career civil service employees who have status or tenure
in their jobs.

Legislative committees specialize in subject matter areas not only in the
U.S. Congress but also in state legislatures, county commissions or boards of
supervisors, and city councils. Especially in Congress, members seek
assignment to standing committees that deal with the subjects of most
interest to them and are most likely to help them politically back home.
Once on the committee of their choice, they become deeply involved

members of the power cluster to which the committee belongs.[12]

The appropriations process in Congress is similarly decentralized along power cluster lines. Each subcommittee on appropriations of both the House and Senate identifies with the power cluster in which it operates and relates to other elements in the power cluster more than to other subcommittees on appropriations. In congressional committees, three types of people belong to each power cluster: the members themselves, the professional staff to members who deal with the field of the power cluster, and the professional staff of the standing committees. In the Senate, members may belong to two major standing committees. Yet many senators have judiciously sought membership on only one standing committee that deals with a domestic power cluster and have used their other committee assignment either to serve on the appropriations subcommittee for their domestic power cluster or to serve on a nondomestic or noncluster centered second committee such as Finance, Government Operations, Post Office and Civil Service, Rules, Foreign Affairs, or Armed Services. Surprisingly rare is the senator who consciously seeks to be an influential leader in two unrelated domestic power clusters such as agriculture and urban affairs.

State Legislators tend to be less highly specialized and thus less involved in cluster policymaking than members of Congress. Many state legislative bodies retain large numbers of standing committees and permit members to sit on several committees simultaneously. This pattern, coupled with their part-time status, greatly dilutes the impact state legislators can have on decisionmaking in any power cluster. Moreover, state legislatures characteristically employ neither personal staff nor committee staff who could become involved in the clusters.

County commissioners, on the other hand, have sometimes become so heavily involved in one power cluster, usually agriculture or the highway subcluster of transportation, that they have been accused of neglecting the broader responsibilities of county government.

Each cluster has a large contingent of active special interest groups that deal with all other elements of the cluster, not just with the legislative committees. Interest groups include not only large membership service groups like the Grange, the Farm Bureau, and the Farmers' Union in the agriculture power cluster, but also private businesses that operate in that field, some as direct participants such as Swift and Company in the agriculture cluster, others as suppliers of major implements such as the John Deere Company, and still others in a wide variety of roles. Groups organized primarily to protect special interests through political action, and groups organized to promote particular goals also are active in each power cluster.

Certain professionals who make an independent living from serving each cluster also are active participants in the policymaking process. Some are lawyers who specialize, for example, in communications law, transportation law, or natural resources law. They may variously serve the legislative bodies, executive agencies, or interest groups as counsel or as advocates. Some are consultants dealing with highly professional subjects such as engineers, rate experts, accountants, or biologists who provide some specialized services or knowledge. They may testify at rate hearings before regulatory agencies, give expert advice to legislative committees, and similar services. Journalists are yet another type of professional in each power cluster. Many journalists specialize in one subject area of knowledge, such as outdoor writing, while others are employed by specialized journals who cater to a readership within a particular power cluster. Many college professors serve as professionals in one of the power clusters. For example, at the land grant universities, professors in the college of agriculture frequently contribute to decisionmaking in agricultural policy and professors in forestry contribute in natural resources policy.

Each cluster also attracts volunteers who make their living in other fields but who take a keen personal interest in the subject of that cluster and participate actively in it. A prime example is the role Laurence Rockefeller, brother of former Vice President Nelson Rockefeller, has played in the natural resources and environment power cluster. He not only chaired the Outdoor Recreation Resources Review Commission from 1958 to 1962, which led to the establishment of the Bureau of Outdoor Recreation and the creation of the Land and Water Conservation Fund, but later chaired the Citizen's Advisory Council on Recreation and Natural Beauty and its successor, the Citizen's Advisory Council on Environmental Quality. Three presidents of both parties appointed him to these posts. Some volunteers are very influential people, including excabinet officers, former governors, or members of Congress who have high status; wealthy persons who have time and the means to contribute to policy-making; or distinguished writers, lecturers, or commentators whose works had widespread influence.

An attentive public forms the backdrop for each power cluster. Many citizens pay special attention to one area of public policy—usually it is the area in which they make a living and hope to advance both economically and socially. Thus, farmers pay attention to agricultural policy and hikers, hunters, and fishermen pay attention to public land management policies. They selectively screen out news about other policy areas when reading a newspaper or magazine, watching television, or listening to the radio, but they pay attention to topics in their field of specialization. They read, listen, have opinions, and talk selectively about it. They can be aroused over a major controversy and may then get involved in an organized interest group or write to public officers. They help shape the policymaking process because they are currently and adequately informed about the subject field and have a continuing personal interest in it.

All power clusters also have a latent public to which they rarely give heed. These are people who have interests that are affected by the power cluster but who do not normally pay much attention to the cluster because they do not perceive that its policies will change to affect them adversely. They normally identify with another power cluster and focus their attention on its affairs. So long as the policy upon which they depend continues consistently, they are content not to interfere in the affairs of the other cluster and do not expect to be consulted about changes. However, a major switch in policy that affects this latent public may stimulate them to interfere in the cluster's internal decisionmaking to protect their own interests. A classic example of this sort occurred in 1974 when the Civil Aeronautics Board (CAB), to aid U.S. overseas-scheduled air carriers, proposed a rule to eliminate affinity charter flights. A policy decision that appeared to be an internal transportation cluster matter promptly turned into a major inter-cluster row. Higher education, fraternal organizations, churches, and even the gamblers in Nevada had been making extensive use of affinity charter flights to support their programs. They immediately descended upon the Civil Aeronautics Board and involved many interest groups and legislators from their own power clusters who normally take no part in transportation decisions. The CAB backed down.


## POWER CLUSTER BEHAVIOR PATTERNS

Each power cluster exhibits five important patterns of behavior which shape the policymaking process.


### Personal and Institutional Ties

First, close personal and institutional ties develop among the participants in each cluster. The key people get to know each other on a first-name basis, know the relative power and influence of all the principal participants, communicate frequently, and move from job to job within their cluster.

The flow of information is continuous and multidirectional. Legislators and executive agency people are in frequent touch. Both contact and are contacted by pressure group leaders and professionals. Some naive observers of the legislative process have sought to describe the policymaking process as though pressure groups were lobbying a relatively defenseless Congress who felt harried from all sides. The truth is that members of Congress are as likely to lobby the lobbyists or the executive agency people as the lobbyists, or executive agency people are likely to lobby the legislators or each other.[13]

To resolve any policy issue, a small group of intense communicators, the people directly charged with developing a solution to a problem in the executive and legislative branches and in the affected interest groups, talk to each other frequently. The contacts are both formal and informal, by letter, by phone, over lunch or coffee breaks, at hearings, in the corridors, and in direct meetings in their offices. Daily or even hourly exchanges may be made. Thus, many interest groups find a Washington office with a full-time professional staff essential if they are to participate in decisionmaking at this intensive level.

Beyond the intense communicators lies a circle of frequently consulted participants who are highly knowledgeable and who may be called upon for expert input, support, or approval. Some of these people are the key power holders in the cluster. They may be involved at the intense level early in the decisionmaking process to set out broad objectives, then expect only frequent consultation while their deputies conduct negotiations, and return to intensive participation in the final stages.

Outside these two inner circles are other participants. Some receive information on a regular basis, for they are active members of interest groups or field people in public agencies. Although not informed day-to-day on active negotiations, they keep in touch as often as necessary and can be called upon for help on short notice.

Still more remote from the center of decisions are the interested observers. They are the back-bench members of organizations, low-level field people, retired civil servants, and others with a continuing interest who receive their information from memoranda, newsletters, and the daily press. They can be mobilized, but only for a major effort.

Most participants in a power cluster move from job to job within the cluster, but never leave it. There is a great deal of this jobswapping, much of it by individuals who are moving upward in responsibility as they develop knowledge and skills, but some of it lateral as opportunities develop or change seems desirable for an individual. Many individuals serve for a time as staff in Congress either to a member or a committee, serve in the executive branch, and serve as a professional staff member for an organized interest group. The sequence of this service is as varied as the individuals involved.

Few persons move into key positions in a power cluster from outside the cluster. When a vacancy occurs in one of the key offices in the inner circle of power holders, members of the power cluster immediately cast about for someone already in the cluster who is capable of filling the post. Those who attempt to move in from outside the cluster are frequently deemed unqualified to fill the position they seek. An excellent example of this attitude was conveyed on February 13, 1975, by Senator William Proxmire of Wisconsin when President Gerald Ford nominated Mrs. Carla A. Hills to be secretary of Housing and Urban Development (HUD). Senator Proxmire unsuccessfully challenged her appointment, saying that "she has absolutely no known qualifications, experience, or background to become the Secretary of HUD."[14] If an outsider moves into a key post, he or she either learns to operate within the cluster very quickly or is by-passed by subordinates, one of whom usually takes over effective command of the unit because he or she is well established in the power cluster.

Some jobs within each cluster are partisan. These jobs are reserved for members of the cluster who are willing to identify themselves as Democrats or Republicans and to take the risks associated with gaining or losing office. Most professional staff positions in the Congress are partisan. In the federal executive a large number of jobs are partisan. They include all posts requiring Senate confirmation, such as secretary, under secretary, or assistant secretary of a cabinet department, and a host of lesser staff offices such as professional assistants to cabinet officers. The directors of many bureaus hold partisan appointments and sometimes lesser line officials fall in this category. Technically, all legal positions are subject to political appointment, but in fact, partisanship does not usually descend below the assistant solicitor level. Similar conditions exist in most states and even in many county governments.

When the Democrats come to power in the executive branch, they draw partisan professional leadership from the congressional committees, the liberal interest groups, Democratic state administrations, and the universities. Republicans use similar sources, but depend more heavily on private business and conservative interest groups than on the universities. When a shift in power occurs, the partisan staff people must find other employment, and a scramble ensues to find sufficient suitable positions to absorb them. Some return to their former jobs. Most find other jobs somewhere in their own power cluster where their added skills and experience continue to be used in the shaping of public policy.

Thus lines of communication do not break down with a change in control of the presidency or the Congress. The power clusters simply incorporate the role of the political parties in selecting people for office into their mode of operation. Some participants in each power cluster continue in their old positions. A few move to different positions, some with more power and influence, some with less. The new incumbents adjust to their new positions quickly and the old lines of communication are easily reestablished.[15]

Thus, it is foolhardy for presidents or governors to attempt to break up the lines of communication that have evolved through the years within each power cluster. A new president may well discover that the very men and women who were heading the cabinet and staff posts in the previous administration of the opposition party are now the key professional staff people on the standing committees of Congress and in the key interest groups that deal with their old agencies. But public programs must continue to be administered, unresolved policy issues must still be faced, and new policy questions are certain to arise. The continuing members of Congress of both parties, the career civil servants, the established interest group leaders, the professionals, and the attentive public expect to continue to participate in the decisionmaking process. They will continue to communicate with their established contacts and will expand to include the new appointees. They realistically face the probability that a change in administration four or eight years hence may well restore the former partisan officials to power and in the meantime they are in important positions requiring continuous participation anyway. So a change in jobs does not isolate an established participator from the policymaking process. He or she simply sits in a different chair and plays a different role.

A prudent new president or governor, then puts established leaders of each power cluster who are politically loyal in charge of each administrative department and expects them to provide a new direction of leadership from their new positions of power within their power clusters. President Jimmy Carter's selection of Representative Robert Berglund as secretary of agriculture and Professor Ray Marshall as secretary of labor and President Ronald Reagan's selection of Terrel H. Bell, a previous commissioner of education, as secretary of education and James G. Watt, a former deputy assistant secretary of the interior, as secretary of the interior are excellent illustrations of this principle.

*Participants Become Active in the Communication Network*

Second, the key participants in each power cluster are driven by their own need to be effective to become active participants in the power cluster communication network in which they are working.

Members of Congress, primarily concerned about reelection, actively seek membership on those committees that will do them the most good back home. Thus, Senators from the West vie for seats on such committees as Energy and Natural Resources and Environment and Public Works. Representatives of urban, manufacturing areas seek seats on Education and Labor, or Banking, Finance and Urban Affairs, while farm-state members prefer the Agricultural Committee. Membership on their preferred committees gives Senators and Representatives key roles in shaping public policy in the areas of their concern and places them in the center of their power cluster's communication network.[16]

Administrators are similarly drawn into the power cluster network. To succeed, the secretary of a major department must assume leadership within his power cluster. To exercise that leadership, and to shape the direction of policy, a secretary must have superior knowledge of the issues, events, and tides of opinion. Those who come from within the cluster to positions of leadership have an enormous advantage. Possessing background knowledge and contacts, they can lead their agencies and public policy in chosen directions. Two contrasting leaders in recent times have been Cecil Andrus, secretary of the interior for President Jimmy Carter, and James G. Watt, secretary of the interior for President Ronald Reagan. Both came from the natural resources power cluster, and both came from the West. Andrus emphasized environmental protection. Watt emphasizes development of natural resources, especially oil and gas.[17]

Whether new cabinet and subcabinet officials are drawn from the ranks of the power cluster or not, they quickly find they must join the communications network if they are to be effective. Moreover, they soon find themselves spokespersons for their agencies to other parts of the power cluster and for the power cluster. Richard P. Nathan provides keen insight into the pressures to join the cluster that all new officials encounter:

> Preidentification with a given program or viewpoint, as in the case of Romney and Hardin, however, is not the only explanation of why Cabinet members typically become spokesmen *to* rather than *for* the President. Forces that come into play after an appointment has been made also exert a strong influence in pulling new appointees into the orbit of the program interests of their agency. Both Nixon's Cabinet and sub-Cabinet appointees, particularly if they were new to the programs or agency they had been named to head, entered on their appointment into an almost ritualistic courting and mating process with the bureaucracy. They were closeted for long hours in orientation sessions with career officials, the purpose being for these career officials to explain to them program goals and accomplishments and to warn them about the need for support from powerful outside interests. . . . Thereafter, in many obvious and subtle ways, the praise and respect of the agency's permanent staff was increasingly made a function of the performance of these presidentially appointed officials as spokesmen and advocates for the agency's interests. As if in recognition of this point, John Erhlichman remarked at a Key Biscayne press briefing late in 1972 that after the Administration appointed key officials to high posts and they had their picture taken with the President, "We only see them at the annual White House Christmas party: they go off and marry the natives."[18]

Interest group leaders, similarly in need of a continuing flow of information, depend upon hired professionals who reside in Washington, D.C., and can be in constant contact with other parts of the power cluster. Elected group leaders commonly serve one-year terms and continue to live in their home cities. They may attempt to expand their contacts during their incumbency in national group office but are in the capital too infrequently to be an effective part of the inner circle of the issues network within their power cluster.

*Policy Decisions Made Within the Power Cluster*

Third, policy decisions normally are made within each power cluster. The several elements within each cluster try to work out acceptable policy agreements by intense negotiations among themselves before a bill is sent to

Congress for enactment. All clusters assume that the public interest will be served if most of the parties that are affected by a policy can agree on changes in it.

Outside elements—agencies, legislative committees, interest groups, and professionals from other power clusters—rarely contribute to such decisions and usually are not asked to make an input. Each cluster follows a live-and-let-live philosophy. Each expects to be left to resolve its own policy problems and expects to leave the other clusters to solve theirs. Thus, agriculturalists expect to make agricultural policy and do not expect to participate in deciding health policy nor do they expect the health people to try to shape agriculture policy.

Inviting in outsiders is akin to going outside the family to settle a family argument. Most participants in the power cluster look upon such an invitation as illegitimate. Moreover, asking for outside help creates debts that may have to be paid later by getting involved in someone else's fight. Those outside the power cluster respect this feeling and avoid involvement in an intracluster row in another cluster. They do not wish to take sides in a dispute that may have no political profit for them and may only make enemies of the opposition in the other power cluster. Moreover, they do not wish to create debts that can only be paid by involving others in their affairs.

Bills that have a serious chance for enactment, then, have been carefully worked out in advance by all of the key elements in the affected power cluster. Often, the executive agency that will administer the new law proposes it, with presidential approval. The leaders of the standing committees in the Congress sponsor the bill in both houses with as many cosigners as they can secure. The interest groups testify for the bill in hearings in both houses, generate letters of support from back home, and undertake other efforts to demonstrate widespread acceptance of the proposal. Specialists appear to testify to its virtue. Opposition, if any, is confined to a minority in the power cluster.

An excellent example of such prior consultation in the preparation of a serious bill was offered to the Senate on July 30, 1981, by Senator James Abdnor (R.-S.D.), in introducing S. 1553, a bill to authorize the secretary of the interior to develop irrigation projects in South Dakota:

> This measure has been drafted pursuant to long and arduous discussions with the administration, congressional officials, the Governor, and officials of the South Dakota Department of Water and Natural Resources, South Dakota's conservancy subdistricts, and local citizens. There have been extensive discussions among the members of the congressional delegation and among our staffs, and this measure reflects our best thinking as to how the needs and wishes of the South Dakotans may be served. Our legislative proposal today should be considered an extension of last year's agreement between the delegation and the Carter administration and the primary provisions appear to have the support of the Reagan administration.[19]

Congress does not look kindly upon bills that have not been carefully worked out to win approval of the affected power cluster. If a power cluster is having a continuing row over a major policy proposal, and part of the cluster comes in with a bill that actually gets to hearings, the committee members are very likely to tell the proposers to go back to the drawing board, get together with their antagonists in the cluster, and come up with an acceptable proposal with which all can live, even if no one is completely satisfied. The Redwood National Park proposal was an excellent example of this sort of hassle. Unable to work out a suitable compromise with the Sierra Club over the location of the proposed park, Secretary of the Interior Stewart L. Udall and his agencies chose to recommend a bill that had the approval of the Bureau of the Budget, the Save the Redwoods League, and Governor Brown's representatives. A two-year impasse was finally broken when the Senate Interior Committee, in a Solomonesque gesture, proposed a Redwood National Park that included acreage from both the administration's plan and the Sierra Club's plan. The committee's bill, with relatively minor modifications, became law.

Power clusters are therefore often tempted to try to solve problems by themselves that cannot really be solved in isolation. Some problems have significant intercluster impacts and many have fiscal implications that affect other clusters. Parochial power cluster decisionmaking, then, is one of the continuing problems of U.S. government and obliges chief executives to rise above power cluster lines in making decisions in the public interest.[20]

## Internal Conflicts Among Competing Interests

Fourth, each cluster has internal conflicts among competing interests. Some of these conflicts are so deep-seated and so well established that legislative bodies have become accustomed to taking sides over them. In the natural resources cluster, the public versus private power fight dates from the start of the twentieth century. In transportation, a perennial struggle goes on between highway users and the railroads and between the railroads and river navigators.

Most clusters have subclusters that may compete with each other but that also may have internal conflicts as well. The transportation cluster has clearly discernable subclusters in water, air, highways, and rail, all of which compete with each other in some degree.

Moreover, broad philosophical issues may run through the several subclusters, thus compounding the types of internal conflict. In natural resources, for example, three basic philosophical positions have greatly affected policy conflicts in all subclusters. One position is held by preservationists who wish to protect and preserve resources as they are, primarily for public use and enjoyment for outdoor recreation but also to protect the quality of living conditions for all. They urge such goals as the establishment of parks, protection of endangered species of wildlife, air pollution control, water treatment facilities, and the termination of drilling for oil off the coasts to prevent further oil spills. A second position is that of the multiple-use managers. They believe in the scientific management of natural resources to insure a continuous supply of water, forage, lumber, energy, minerals, and other natural products to maintain the nation's standard of living. They advocate constructing multiple-purpose dams, preventing forest fires, revegetating strip-mined areas, harvesting mature trees, and hunting managed species of wild game, among many policies. A third position is held by the regulationists. They see government ownership of one-third of the nation's land resources as a major device to regulate private industry in the public interest. They favor the yardstick principle—direct public ownership and development of resources such as water, electric power, and timber, in direct competition with private industry and have recently begun urging public development of federally owned coal, oil, and natural gas. They also support regulatory agency licensing and control of the service, rates, and accounting practices of utility industries such as electric power and natural gas.

## The Internal Power Structure of a Cluster

Fifth, each power cluster develops its own internal power structure. Even though the power cluster is itself an informal network for communication, it has within its composition certain figures who are recognized by all participants as holding key points of power—key cabinet or subcabinet posts in the executive branch, key committee chairs and ranking minority posts in the legislature, key policy-direction posts in the interest groups—or as possessing skills and prestige so that their points of view must be taken into consideration. A few congressional committee staff directors are so knowledgeable and so highly respected that their views carry more weight than those of some elected representatives.

The relative importance of any key figure within a power cluster varies with the issue and that figure's apparent interest in deciding the issue. But key figures can be by-passed if they display indifference to an issue or unwillingness to take a stand. Moreover, weak or ineffective bureau chiefs, assistant secretaries, committee members and staff, and interest group leaders may not be consulted before key decisions are made.

Stable political conditions contribute to the identification of such key leaders and to the building up of relationships and paths of communication among them. The twenty-six-year period of Democratic control of both houses of Congress from 1955 to 1981 contributed most significantly to this process. Executive agency people, interest group leaders, professionals, and volunteers became accustomed to dealing with certain key members of Congress and key staff members through the years. All parties had a basic interest in maintaining the flow of communications because all had benefitted from knowing what was going on. The election of 1980, by returning a Republican majority to the Senate, disrupted the communications network to the Senate for a time until committee assignments were made and key staff were chosen. There then followed a period of testing to determine which new leaders and which new staff would demonstrate skill, determination and ability—and thus become key figures in their respective power cluster communication networks.

When the party controlling the White House also has a majority in both houses of Congress, as has been the case with the last three Democratic presidents, but not with the last three Republican presidents, the flow of communications between the executive and legislative branches is viewed benignly by the White House. Richard Nixon, however, never enjoyed a majority in either house of the Congress, and apparently viewed the normal two-way and nonpartisan flow of information as subversive of his position. He made four attempts to curtail or destroy the power cluster system, all without success. First, he proposed consolidating eight domestic departments into four. Next, he proposed abolishing many categorical grants, by which federal agencies pass funds to their state and local counterparts, and substituting general revenue sharing. Meanwhile, he built a large central staff that could take decisionmaking away from the agencies, a process Richard P. Nathan called "the White House Counter-Bureaucracy Approach."[21] But a central staff can only impose red tape, review, and delay. It cannot deliver the mail. Being outside the power cluster system, it has no chance to participate in the real councils where policy continues to be made. Early in the second term, then, Nixon turned to "The Administrative Presidency." Three "super secretaries" were named with broad domestic policy responsibilities and many key White House staffers were assigned jobs in the agencies. Some even filled posts that had traditionally been occupied by nonpolitical career civil servants.[22] This, too, was doomed, for the new appointees either joined their power clusters to succeed, or failed, like Ron Walker, who was sent to head the National Park Service.

*The Chief Executive's Role.* What, then, must be the relationship of a chief executive—a president, a governor, or a mayor—to the power cluster system? Obviously, his or her responsibilities cut across power cluster lines, forcing the executive, in order to discharge the job, to make trade-offs among the interests of several clusters.

First, the executive must be aware of the power cluster system, understand it, know how it works, and accept it as a reality to be dealt with.

Second, the chief executive should select key appointees carefully, drawing them from among the most capable supporters within each power cluster, and choosing them because they are trustworthy in carrying their part of the government in the general direction the executive intends to go.

Knowing that each of them must be intimately involved in their power clusters if they are to lead successfully, the chief should anticipate that they will become spokespersons for their power clusters to the executive office and should also insist that they be spokespersons for the office to their power clusters.

Third, the executive should delegate to the key cabinet and subcabinet officials the resolving of intracluster issues and hold them accountable for achieving solutions.

Fourth, the executive should identify key intercluster issues, like national energy policy, which patently involves not only natural resources, but also agriculture, commerce, defense, transportation, housing, and other clusters, and insist that he and his immediate staff get involved in the resolution of such transcendent problems. Ronald Reagan early indicated a remarkable grasp of the power cluster system when he announced on February 16, 1981, the creation of six Cabinet Councils to deal with six broad intercluster areas: economic affairs; commerce and trade; human resources; natural resources and environment, including energy; food and agriculture; and national security. Other councils, or subgroups of these councils, may be needed to address specific intercluster issues as they arise.

Fifth, the chief executive should organize each department of government along viable subcluster lines to enhance communication and clearly and definitely fix responsibility. A classic example of how not to organize a department was demonstrated from 1977 to 1981 in the structure of the Department of Energy. Instead of assigning assistant secretaries to the obvious energy subclusters—oil, gas, coal, atomic energy, water power, and conservation and solar energy—the original organizers of energy divided program responsibility among a director of research, an assistant secretary for energy technology, and an assistant secretary for resource applications. Each of these officers expected to cover all six long-established and complex subclusters and at the same time determine where research left off and technological development began, and where that ended and commercial applications began. Reorganized twice by 1981, the department was finally restructured generally along subcluster lines.

Sixth, the executive should deliberately use the power cluster system to achieve stated goals. Propagandizing against them, or attempting to break them up betrays both ignorance and ineptitude.

The power cluster system is a natural product of the U.S. system of a federal government operating with a separation of powers. It may well be inherent in the government of any large, advanced industrial nation and may simply have evolved in a more open and pronounced way in the United States because of the independence of members of Congress and the resulting open participation of organized interest groups in the policymaking process. Because U.S. political parties are arenas of compromise— decentralized, multigroup, semipublic associations united to elect and appoint people to political office—public policy making in the United States always has been bipartisan. Partisanship focuses on office-seeking and office-holding, not on policymaking. Thus, Congress has specialized in its committee system and both majority and minority members share in shaping policy decisions.

The power cluster system has several strengths. It permits the president to delegate many policy issues to the cabinet. It contains conflict. Most issue-conflicts can be settled within the affected power cluster. It provides continuity and stability. A change in political power can take place without disrupting the orderly management of the public's business and without disrupting the communication networks within each cluster. It promotes professionalism and efficiency. Each power cluster has ties to professional training paths in the nation's universities and thus can recruit, train, and initiate new people to its functions in society.

Yet the power cluster system has weaknesses as well. Each cluster is parochial in its interests. The participants naturally attempt to find solutions to problems within their own consultation system, but some issues affect other clusters and cannot be wisely settled by the participants in one cluster alone.

Compounding this weakness is the lack of a communication network for settling intercluster issues. Indeed, there is not even an established process for one cluster to signal others when it encounters a problem that is recognized as intercluster. Its members who have contacts in other, affected power clusters, may attempt to involve these people without involving the real power structure of the other power cluster. President Reagan's Cabinet Council system offers a constructive method to identify such intercluster issues and a potential vehicle to open dialogue across cluster lines, at least within the executive branch. The success of such cross-cluster efforts is likely to turn on the success they have in enlisting the entire power structure of the affected power clusters so that the decisions that are reached will stick.

Still another weakness of the power cluster system is its tendency to resist change. The established leaders of the cluster have developed existing policy after delicate and sometimes elaborate political negotiations. Well aware of the fragility of the consensus that they have wrought on key policy matters, they argue, "When something works, don't try to fix it." Because legislative and interest group leaders continue in key spots, despite executive changes following elections, and because policymaking is decentralized, the group leaders can provide the support needed for career executive officials to advocate a continuation of accepted policy and to resist the imposition of new policy directions.

The power clusters can therefore resist presidential and gubernatorial direction. Indeed, they sometimes are powerful enough to place certain agencies and some policies beyond the reach of chief executives. The independent regulatory commissions are examples of such insulation.

President Reagan's effort in the spring of 1981 to slash the domestic budget ran headlong into power cluster resistance. Only by insisting on a package up-down vote were he and his followers able to prevail in the major thrust he wanted. Even then, many programs sought and obtained congressional restoration of funding.

The power clusters are not accountable to anyone. The power cluster system is not an institution with organized leaders and followers. It is, after all, an informal system of communication among people working in different parts of a single policy subject field. The cluster system therefore gives the impression that no one is in charge of making public policy. That may, in fact, be so. Many different people are continuously making inputs to public policy so that it is, in fact, the product of multiple interactions among many actors operating from various parts of the governmental and private scene. That may, in fact, be the only way any large democracy can work in our time.

A wise chief executive, thus, does not try to undo the power cluster system, for no one can hope either to destroy or to conquer it. Instead, the executive must strive to understand the system, make it work, and perceive that the power cluster system meets one of the crucial tests of politics: it offers a relatively efficient way to simplify an enormously complex and difficult task of reconciling policy goals and judgments. A great many policy issues are specialized and can safely be left to the appropriate power cluster for settlement. There is no need to consult everyone about such policies. However, some major policy issues require intercluster decision and in the process array one standing committee of the Congress against another or one cabinet officer against another, or both. Such broad issues require political leadership across power cluster lines and offer a chief executive ample opportunity to guide major public policy.

A president or a governor who chooses to let all policy be settled within the power clusters soon becomes a do-nothing chief executive. No president can hope to preside over the system in that fashion for many key decisions cannot be left to the parochial interests of the most affected power cluster.

A president or governor who wishes to alter public policy significantly must dare to override the interests of some clusters and to reshape the affected power clusters in the process. To succeed, the executive must enjoy both an overwhelming majority in Congress and public willingness to innovate.

Most presidents and governors are unwilling to be do-nothings and are unable to be innovators. To succeed they must understand the power cluster system and know how to deal with it effectively. All too often, with inadequate advice from inexperienced staff members who have themselves worked only within one power cluster, they attempt to confront the power cluster system instead of work with it.

## SUMMARY

Public policy in the United States is made through a system of power clusters that operate complex informal communications networks in each of the major fields of public policy. Each cluster includes at least executive agencies, legislative committees, interest groups, professionals, influential citizens, and an attentive public, which are concerned with that field of policy.

Each cluster displays similar behavior. Close personal and institutional ties develop among the participants in each power cluster. The key participants are driven by their own need to be effective to become active participants in their power cluster communication network. Policy decisions are normally made within each cluster. Each cluster has internal conflicts among competing interests and develops its own internal power structure.

Policy specialization in power clusters has developed as a practical way to make public decisions in a complex, advanced industrial democracy because the Constitution of the United States effectively requires two arena-of-compromise type political parties to select its public officials. The political parties provide the officers who guide policy in both the executive and legislative branches but rarely make public policy a partisan party matter.

Policy decisions, therefore, are a product of intense interaction among the basic component elements of one or more power clusters. Each element, including an open-ended, attentive public, makes significant inputs both in shaping and in executing the policies. Changes go on continuously.

Leadership falls to the elected chief executives, both federal and state, who must understand the power cluster system and know how to work with it. If a U.S. president or governor is to control the thrust of modern public policy effectively, one of the most important tasks is to specialize him- or herself by segregating the major policy issues within each power cluster that can safely be left to intracluster determination from the broad intercluster policy issues that require direct leadership and negotiation.

## NOTES

1. Douglass Cater, *Power in Washington* (New York: Vintage, 1964).
2. J. Leiper Preeman, *The Political Process* (New York: Random House, 1965).
3. Daniel M. Ogden, Jr., "Outdoor Recreation Policy and Politics" in Downs, Kneese, Ogden, and Perloff, *The Political Economy of Environmental Control* (Berkeley, Calif.: Institute of Business and Economic Research, University of California, 1972), pp. 98–103.
4. David R. Mayhew, *Congress, the Electoral Connection* (New Haven, Conn.: Yale University Press, 1974).
5. Richard P. Nathan, *The Plot That Failed: Nixon and the Administrative*

(Berkeley, Calif.: Institute of Business and Economic Research, University of California, 1972), pp. 98–103.

4. David R. Mayhew, *Congress, the Electoral Connection* (New Haven, Conn.: Yale University Press, 1974).

5. Richard P. Nathan, *The Plot That Failed: Nixon and the Administrative Presidency* (New York: John Wiley & Sons, 1975).

6. John Kessel, *The Domestic Presidency* (Scituate, Mass.: Duxbury Press, 1975).

7. Kenneth A. Shepsle, *The Giant Jigsaw Puzzle* (Chicago: University of Chicago Press, 1978).

8. Harold Seidman, *Politics, Position, and Power*, 2d. Ed. (New York: Oxford University Press, 1975).

9. See especially Timothy B. Clark, "The President Takes on the 'Iron Triangles' and so Far Holds His Own," *National Journal* (March 28, 1981), pp. 516–518.

10. Hugh Heclo, "Issue Networks and the Executive Establishment," in Anthony King, *The New American Political System* (Washington, D.C.: American Enterprise Institute, 1980), pp. 87–124.

11. Heclor, "Issue Networks," p. 102.

12. David R. Mayhew, *Congress, the Electoral Connection*, pp. 130–131.

13. Mayhew, *Congress, the Electoral Connection*, p. 131. "Congressmen protect clientele systems—alliances of agencies, Hill committees, and clienteles—against the incursions of presidents and cabinet secretaries." See also Harold Seidman, pp. 49–50.

14. *The Washington Post*, February 14, 1975, p. A-1.

15. Seidman, *Politics, Position, and Power*, pp. 80–84.

16. Mayhew, *Congress, the Electoral Connection*, p. 131.

17. See also *The Washington Post*, August 9, 1981, p. A10, for a perceptive description of the leadership exercised in the transportation power cluster by Secretary of Transportation Drew Lewis.

18. Nathan, *The Plot That Failed*, pp. 39–40.

19. U.S. Congress, *Congressional Record*, July 30, 1981, p. S 8868.

20. See Seidman, *Politics, Power, and Position*, p. 41, for a pointed comment.

21. Nathan, *The Plot That Failed*, pp. 45–54.

22. Nathan, *The Plot That Failed*, pp. 67–76.

# 8.2    The Military Industrial Complex: Yesterday and Today

*More than twenty-five years ago, President Eisenhower's farewell to the nation included a warning to guard against an immense military-industrial complex acquiring unwarranted influence. As Michael Weisskopf's 1986 analysis so aptly points out, the United States must continue to be wary of those who would serve their own interests rather than the nation's through a close and (to the taxpayers) expensive relationship with the Pentagon. Yet, two*

*other issues seem particularly noteworthy. First, the complex is
not a monolith. Second, the cost of underplaying the threat posed
to the United States by its adversaries may cost it dearly–not only
in dollars but also in lives.*

## President Eisenhower's Farewell to the Nation, January 17, 1961

My fellow Americans:  Three days from now, after half a century in the service of our country, I shall lay down the responsibilities of office as, in traditional and solemn ceremony, the authority of the Presidency is vested in my successor.

This evening I come to you with a message of leavetaking and farewell and to share a few final thoughts with you, my countrymen.

Like every other citizen, I wish the new President and all who will labor with him Godspeed. I pray that the coming years will be blessed with peace and prosperity for all.

Our people expect their President and the Congress to find essential agreement on issues of great moment, the wise resolution of which will better shape the future of the Nation.

My own relations with the Congress, which began on a remote and tenuous basis, when long ago a member of the Senate appointed me to West Point, have since ranged to the intimate during the war and immediate postwar period and, finally, to the mutually interdependent during these past 8 years.

In this final relationship the Congress and the administration have, on most vital issues, cooperated well to serve the national good rather than mere partisanship and so have assured that the business of the Nation should go forward.  So my official relationship with the Congress ends in a feeling on my part of gratitude that we have been able to do so much together.

### II

We now stand 10 years past the midpoint of a century that has witnessed four major wars among great nations.  Three of these involved our own country. Despite these holocausts, America is today the strongest, the most influential, and most productive nation in the world.  Understandably proud of this preeminence, we yet realize that America's leadership and prestige depend not merely upon our unmatched material progress, riches, and military strength but on how we use our power in the interests of world peace and human betterment.

# III

Throughout America's adventure in free government our basis purposes have been to keep the peace, to foster progress in human achievement, and to enhance liberty, dignity, and integrity among people and among nations. To strive for less would be unworthy of a free and religious people. Any failure traceable to arrogance or our lack of comprehension or readiness to sacrifice would inflict upon us grievous hurt both at home and abroad.

Progress toward these noble goals is persistently threatened by the conflict now engulfing the world. It commands our whole attention, absorbs our very beings. We face a hostile ideology—global in scope, atheistic in character, ruthless in purpose, and insidious in method. Unhappily the danger it poses promises to be of indefinite duration. To meet it successfully there is called for not so much the emotional and transitory sacrifices of crisis but rather those which enable us to carry forward steadily, surely, and without complaint the burdens of a prolonged and complex struggle—with liberty the stake. Only thus shall we remain, despite every provocation, on our charted course toward permanent peace and human betterment.

Crises there will continue to be. In meeting them, whether foreign or domestic, great or small, there is a recurring temptation to feel that some spectacular and costly action could become the miraculous solution to all current difficulties. A huge increase in newer elements of our defense, development of unrealistic programs to cure every ill in agriculture, a dramatic expansion in basic and applied research—these and many other possibilities, each possibly promising in itself, may be suggested as the only way to the road we wish to travel.

But each proposal must be weighed in the light of a broader consideration: the need to maintain balance in and among national programs—balance between the private and the public economy, balance between cost and hoped-for advantage, balance between the clearly necessary and the comfortably desirable, balance between our essential requirements as a nation and the duties imposed by the Nation upon the individual, balance between actions of the moment and the national welfare of the future. Good judgment seeks balance and progress; lack of it eventually finds imbalance and frustration.

The record of many decades stands as proof that our people and their Government have, in the main, understood these truths and have responded to them well in the face of stress and threat. But threats, new in kind or degree, constantly arise. I mention two only.

# IV

A vital element in keeping the peace is our Military Establishment. Our arms must be mighty, ready for instant action, so that no potential aggressor may be tempted to risk his own destruction.

Our military organization today bears little relation to that known by any of my predecessors in peace time, or indeed by the fighting men of World War II or Korea.

Until the latest of our world conflicts, the United States had no armaments industry. American makers of plowshares could, with time and as required, make swords as well. But now we can no longer risk emergency improvisation of national defense; we have been compelled to create a permanent armaments industry of vast proportions. Added to this, $3^1/2$ million men and women are directly engaged in the Defense Establishment. We annually spend on military security more than the net income of all United States corporations.

This conjunction of an immense Military Establishment and a large arms industry is new in the American experience. The total influence—economic, political, even spiritual—is felt in every city, every statehouse, every office of the Federal Government. We recognize the imperative need for this development. Yet we must not fail to comprehend its grave implications. Our toil, resources, and livelihood are all involved; so is the very structure of our society.

In the councils of government we must guard against the acquisition of unwarranted influence, whether sought or unsought, by the military-industrial complex. The potential for the disastrous rise of misplaced power exists and will persist.

We must never let the weight of this combination endanger our liberties or democratic processes. We should take nothing for granted. Only an alert and knowledgeable citizenry can compel the proper meshing of the huge industrial and military machinery of defense with our peaceful methods and goals so that security and liberty may prosper together.

Akin to and largely responsible for the sweeping changes in our industrial-military posture has been the technological revolution during recent decades. In this revolution research has become central; it also becomes more formalized, complex, and costly. A steadily increasing share is conducted for, by, or at the direction of the Federal Government.

Today the solitary inventor, tinkering in his shop, has been over-shadowed by task forces of scientists in laboratories and testing fields. In the same fashion the free university, historically the fountainhead of free ideas and scientific discovery, has experienced a revolution in the conduct of research. Partly because of the huge costs involved, a Government contract becomes virtually a substitute for intellectual curiosity. For every old blackboard there are now hundreds of new electronic computers.

The prospect of domination of the Nation's scholars by Federal employment, project allocations, and the power of money is ever present and is gravely to be regarded.

Yet, in holding scientific research and discovery in respect, as we should, we must also be alert to the equal and opposite danger that public policy could itself become the captive of a scientific-technological elite.

It is the task of statemanship to mold, to balance, and to integrate these and other forces, new and old, within the principles of our democratic system—ever aiming toward the supreme goals of our free society.

## V

Another factor in maintaining balance involves the element of time. As we peer into society's future, we—you and I, and our Government—must avoid the impulse to live only for today, plundering for our own ease and convenience the precious resources of tomorrow. We cannot mortgage the material assets of our grandchildren without risking the loss also of their political and spiritual heritage. We want democracy to survive for all generations to come, not to become the insolvent phantom of tomorrow.

## VI

Down the long lane of the history yet to be written, America knows that this world of ours, ever growing smaller, must avoid becoming a community of dreadful fear and hate and be, instead, a proud confederation of mutual trust and respect.

Such a confederation must be one of equals. The weakest must come to the conference table with the same confidence as do we, protected as we are by our moral, economic, and military strength. That table, though scarred by many past frustrations, cannot be abandoned for the certain agony of the battlefield.

Disarmament, with mutual honor and confidence, is a continuing imperative. Together we must learn how to compose differences, not with arms but with intellect and decent purpose. Because this need is so sharp and apparent I confess that I lay down my official responsibilities in this field with a definite sense of disappointment. As one who has witnessed the horror and the lingering sadness of war, as one who knows that another war could utterly destroy this civilization which has been so slowly and painfully built over thousands of years, I wish I could say tonight that a lasting peace is in sight.

Happily I can say that war has been avoided. Steady progress toward our ultimate goal has been made. But so much remains to be done. As a private citizen I shall never cease to do what little I can to help the world advance along that road.

## VII

So, in this my last good night to you as your President, I thank you for the many opportunities you have given me for public service in war and peace. I trust that in that service you find some things worthy; as for the rest of it, I know you will find ways to improve performance in the future.

You and I, my fellow citizens, need to be strong in our faith that all nations, under God, will reach the goal of peace with justice. May we be ever unswerving in devotion to principle, confident but humble with power, diligent in pursuit of the Nation's great goals.

To all the peoples of the world, I once more give expression to America's prayerful and continuing aspiration:

We pray that peoples of all faiths, all races, all nations, may have their great human needs satisfied; that those now denied opportunity shall come to enjoy it to the full; that all who yearn for freedom may experience its spiritual blessings; that those who have freedom will understand, also, its heavy responsibilities; that all who are insensitive to the needs of others will learn charity; that the scourges of poverty, disease, and ignorance will be made to disappear from the earth; and that, in the goodness of time, all peoples will come to live together in a peace guaranteed by the binding force of mutual respect and love.

---

## Profit, Patriotism Produce a Ubiquitous Alliance
### MICHAEL WEISSKOPF

Every 20 minutes of the business day a chartered bus shuttles men in uniform and pin-stripe suits to the high temples of the military-industrial complex.

From the Pentagon, the bus sweeps south one mile to the Crystal City office suites of scores of defense contractors and consultants, then returns to the Pentagon, delineating what President Dwight D. Eisenhower described 25 years ago today as the "conjunction of an immense military establishment and a large arms industry."

Eisenhower, in his farewell address as president Jan. 17, 1961, noted the emergence of a "permanent armaments industry of vast porportions" in the United States and acknowledged the "imperative need" of industry and government to manage it jointly.

Today, the military-industrial complex—in Eisenhower's enduring phrase—is larger and more pervasive than he could have imagined. Linked by profit and patriotism, the armed services, corporations, scientists, engineers, consultants and members of Congress form a loose confederation that reaches almost every corner of American society.

Reprinted from Michael Weisskopf, "Profit, Patriotism Produce a Ubiquitous Alliance," *The Washington Post*, Jan. 17, 1986.

A few measures cited by defense analysts illustrate the power of the complex. The Defense Department is the largest single purchaser of goods and services in the nation. One of every 20 jobs is directly or indirectly tied to defense spending. Defense employs as much as a quarter of America's scientists and engineers. In several states, defense employment is one of the largest sources of personal income.

The Pentagon plans to spend nearly $300 billion this year, including $34 billion for research and development—a sixfold increase over Eisenhower's last budget in constant dollars—spending that, critics charge, deepens the national debt and diverts resources from needy social programs.

Eisenhower also spoke of the "grave implications" of this union, and in a warning that has become a benchmark for defense analysts and social scientists alike, said:

"In the councils of government, we must guard against the acquisition of unwarranted influence, whether sought or unsought, by the military-industrial complex. The potential for the disastrous rise of misplaced power exists and will persist."

But despite its size, a statistical inventory of the military-industrial complex can be misleading in assessing its influence. For, despite its awesome dimension and extraordinary growth, the defense community today accounts for a smaller share of federal spending, national research and development and labor force than it did in 1961.

Whether this confederation has gained "unwarranted influence," as critics charge, by skewing national priorities, or whether it combines the forces needed to undergird national security, is an issue of intense debate a quarter-century after Eisenhower's admonition. That debate has been one of Eisenhower's most enduring legacies.

"It's defending our freedom," said Deputy Defense Secretary William H. Taft IV. "It's what brings us peace, it's what keeps the Soviets interested in arms reduction and protects our interests. What could be more valuable?"

Jerome B. Wiesner, former president of the Massachusetts Institute of Technology who served as science adviser to Eisenhower and President John F. Kennedy, contends that pressures from the military, industry and Congress often drive national decisions to build unneeded weapons systems that undermine arms control.

"It's no longer a question of controlling a military-industrial complex," Wiesner wrote recently, "but rather of keeping the United States from becoming a totally military culture."

The term "military-industrial complex" in popular usage has come to describe the merger of three main partners with a vested interest in the production of weapons: the armed services that use them; the defense industry that profits from building them, and members of Congress who gain constituent favor by landing military installations and defense factories for their districts.

Together they form what defense analyst Gordon Adams calls the "iron triangle," a powerful alliance that, he says, perpetuates itself and grows by advancing the common interest.

But the complex is hardly monolithic. The Joint Chiefs of Staff, shedding their hawkish reputation, have been a voice of restraint in the Reagan administration on matters ranging from continued observance of the SALT II arms control treaty to military reprisals against Third World terrorists.

"It has become more complicated since President Eisenhower issued his warning," said Paul C. Warnke, director of the Arms Control and Disarmament Agency in the Carter administration. "If you look at it today, the most rational people are in uniform. They recognize as military commanders that there's no sensible way to use nuclear weapons." In the procurement of those weapons, however, the military and its civilian managers readily join forces with industry and key lawmakers. It is in the growth and management of the nation's arsenal, critics said, where the "iron triangle" has gained undue influence.

Among defenders of the system, retired admiral Thomas H. Moorer, chairman of the Joint Chiefs in the early 1970s, said that armament decisions are driven by perceptions of the "threat," not by bureaucratic or corporate pressures.

"You don't work the problem backwards by building weapons and then formulating a policy to use those weapons," he said.

According to Wiesner, however, the Pentagon has exaggerated the Soviet threat to justify unnecessary weapons systems ranging from Eisenhower's B70 bomber to President Reagan's MX missiles. Prodded by self-interested military and industry leaders, he said, the "United States has been running an arms race with itself."

Other critics argued that the unhealthy collaboration of Pentagon and industry continues throughout the life of a weapons system, often resulting in bloated costs and substandard work.

Congress, while sharpening its scrutiny of defense spending in recent years, is generally eager to approve new weapons programs that mean jobs and income for constituents. The Navy assured support for its costly fleet expansion after dispersing new ports to the districts of lawmakers on key military committees.

"Some perfectly useless weapon systems continue to be funded because a member stands up in a closed meeting and says, 'Look, guys, I have to have this for my district,'" said Rep. Les AuCoin (D.-Ore.), a member of the House Appropriations defense subcommittee.

Karl G. Harr Jr., president of the Aerospace Industries Association who served as an Eisenhower aide, said a close partnership of government and industry is natural if the nation is to remain secure.

"I would recognize there would be a bias from those who feel defense is important," he said. "That's the way democracy works."

# 9

## How to Play and Succeed in Bureaucratic Politics: Being an Effective Participant in a Pluralistic Democracy

*Pluralistic democracy makes the game of bureaucratic politics inevitable. Yet some actors, either because of naïveté or incompatibility, feel frustrated with or uncomfortable in a fluid setting of adversarial advocacy, nonhierarchical organization, bargaining and compromise, and the mobilization of external support. To serve an agency or department well, one must be aware of the game of bureaucratic politics—how it is played and how to survive, serve, and succeed in such an environment. But national security managers need also to understand the limits of bureaucratic politics and the point at which the game becomes injurious to the public interest. Bureaucratic actors do grave disservice to themselves, their organizations, their programs, and the country when they cross the line with end-around plays, illegalities, freelancing, and other actions that evince contempt for representative democracy and an open society. The following chapters address appropriate personal strategies for effective participation in the maelstrom of bureaucratic politics.*

# 9.1　Political Executives and the Washington Bureaucracy

## HUGH HECLO

*In this essay Hugh Heclo discusses the limitations political appointees experience in managing the permanent bureaucracy. He devotes considerable attention to strategizing despite these constraints—that is, "to maneuver with limited resources so as to create relative advantage." More often than not, evoking conditional cooperation rather than invoking authority works best. The best leadership will acknowledge the tension inherent among government organizations and use it constructively. But as students and practitioners of the national security policy are well aware, striking the appropriate balance between creative tension and organizational havoc, unrest, and disunity is a difficult task.*

With every new administration, hundreds of new presidential appointees arrive in Washington to "take control of the bureaucracy." Only a few ever appear to succeed, if by success we mean changing government activity in some desired direction. Why do certain political executives do better than others in leading the bureaucracy?

Of course there are many reasons. During the past several years I have attempted to distill those reasons having to do with how public executives themselves choose to act—their statecraft. In a government peopled at the top by hundreds of short-term appointees, there is clearly wide scope for variation in how political executives will choose to act. The consequences of these choices are another matter. Forces inherent in our system of executive politics go far in determining, not how appointees will choose, but whether their choices prove prudent or foolish in coping with other people in government.

Here it is necessary to summarize only the five most important conditions that shape the content of political statecraft in the bureaucracy.

- The distinction in roles between political and higher bureaucratic executives is muddled in Washington, both formally and informally. For inexperienced participants in executive politics it is extraordinarily

Reprinted with permission of the author from *The Public Interest*, no. 38 (Winter, 1975), pp. 80–98. © 1975 by National Affairs, Inc.

difficult to know who's who.

- Would-be leaders among political executives are in a peculiarly weak political position in relation to each other and to career bureaucrats.
- The power of the bureaucracy is mainly passive, not active. It consists in the capacity to withhold needed services rather than in the capacity to oppose political superiors directly.
- Therefore political executives' first necessity is to help themselves. They do this by extending their networks and relationships throughout Washington so as to gain confidence about the nature of the surrounding political forces.
- But it also follows that self-help is not enough. The political leader's central problem in the bureaucracy is to gain the changes he wants without losing the bureaucratic services he needs.

Given these conditions, the essence of political statecraft in the bureaucracy is strategy—maneuvering with limited resources so as to create relative advantage. In talking with almost 200 appointees and bureaucrats representing all of the postwar administrations, one hears a number of recurring themes. There is no simple set of rules guaranteeing success but there are some regularities in the scars left by past mistakes.[1]

## THEORY Z: CONDITIONAL COOPERATION

Experts writing about private organizations have described two different orientations toward management control. Under so-called Theory X it is assumed that an average subordinate avoids work if he can, loathes responsibility, covets security, and must be directed and threatened with punishment in order to put forth sufficient effort to achieve managerial goals. Theory Y emphasizes a worker's need for identity and personal growth through work, rewards rather than punishment as a means of motivation, and the cooperation toward objectives that can be gained by commitments to mutually agreed upon goals rather than by strict supervision from above.[2]

What matters is not so much the academic models of "nice guy" or "tough guy" management but that public executives constantly come to Washington acting as if they subscribe to one or the other of these views. Consider one of the most extreme examples in recent years of hostility between political appointees and bureaucrats: the social service program of the Department of Health Education and Welfare during the Nixon administration.[3]

After several years on the job two of Nixon's leading appointees in these agencies pondered their different routes to ineffectiveness. Here is how one, a self-acknowledged muscleman, looked back on his approach to subordinates:

In the short run it probably helped me to be known as a monster. It established me as a force to be reckoned with. A lot of people were afraid to join battle with me. But in the long run it hurt a lot because it put people on the defensive. You'll get some reaction if people think you're mean enough or are going to be around a while or have enough powerful allies, but it can't last long enough to have much impact. You're not likely to know when you're getting real cooperation and when they're just acting out of fear. If I had to do it again, I'd spend more time getting to know the people under me and their programs. I'd keep asking why do we do it this way, Why that? It is not really effective trying to browbeat people and win every little battle.

The other political executive (in the same agency) avoided all the mistakes of his tough colleague, but reflected on the futility of his wholly compassionate approach:

I made the decisions but they [bureaucratic subordinates] just continued to argue. The delays went on until I left office. . . . The biggest problems were the procedures and paper work and special pleading by office heads under me. I was overburdened because I couldn't count on delegating it and have things turn out the way I wanted . . . I think they figured I would be an easy mark. . . . I made the same mistake the secretary did. He was too nice to knock heads and let people know he meant what he said. [A successor] came in and got things going. He let people know he expected orders to be followed in a timely fashion and when they weren't, heads got knocked, people transferred; there were early retirements.

Lessons can be drawn from these and similar experiences, but frequently only the bureaucrats are around long enough to do so and to learn from such failures. According to a high bureaucrat who watched both appointees:

They did all the wrong things. I don't think they ever understood that governing is about making a lot of different forces coalesce. The feudal bureaus, interest groups, congressional politics—these are all things to be used. There are pretty firm limits on your control and how far you can persuade people to change, but there is some room for progress by pulling these things together. . . . The smarter guys choose a manageable number of things they care about and promote key people already here who can help still the rebels. They try and bring around those opposing them. It can take three to four years and will never work if you start off by telling bureaucrats they're crap. . . .

You don't let people buck you and run behind your back. If you catch them at it, you can isolate them and get rid of them. . . . But you also don't get far by coming in and setting up separate people, programs, and ideas to the exclusion of existing ones. If it's going to stick, what you want has got to be associated with what's going to be here after you're gone. An appointee has got to make other people feel a part of the credit line.

Of course this bureaucrat is only one of the many people involved in executive politics who are constantly judging and ranking each other in numerous different ways. Though in Washington anecdotes of this kind are commonplace (and many of them naturally self-serving), there is a core of agreement about what has constituted the statecraft of effective political executives.

The basic point is that experience reveals the shortcomings of both Theory X and Theory Y and suggests the value of a third approach to working relations between political executives and ranking bureaucrats. It is what might be termed conditionally cooperative behavior. Any premise of compassionate cooperation and participatory management overlooks the bureaucracy's divided loyalties, its needs for self-protection, and its multiple sources of resistance. Unconditionally negative approaches fail to recognize the enduring character of bureaucratic power and a political leader's need to elicit the bureaucracy's help in governing.

"Conditional cooperation" emerges between these extremes. It implies a kind of cooperation that is conditional on the mutual performance of the political appointees and the civil servants. It emphasizes the need of executives and bureaucrats to work at relationships that depend on the contingencies of one another's actions, not on preconceived ideas of strict supervision or harmonious goodwill. Conditional cooperation rejects any final choice between suspicion and trust, between trying to force obedience and passively hoping for compliance. By making their reactions conditional on the performance of subordinates, political appointees create latitude for choice—possibilities for various types of exchanges with different bureaucrats. The basis for the executives' leadership becomes strategic rather than "take it or leave it."

As opposed to a set formula that assures success, conditional cooperation is a strategy that suggests a variety of resources and methods for trading services. It increases the likelihood that some political executives will do better than others in getting what they need from Washington's bureaucracies. Superficially, conditional cooperation might seem to be simply a matter of exchanging favors with the bureaucracy on a quid pro quo basis. The reality of executive leadership is more subtle. It involves bringing others to appreciate not so much what they have gotten as what they might get. Would-be executive leaders, remember, are like poor credit risks in a well-established credit market; they have had little chance to acquire a favorable standing or reputation in the eyes of other participants who are used to dealing with each other. The new political strangers have to work at building credit in the bureaucracy precisely because they have not had—and will only briefly enjoy—a chance to put anyone in their debt. Even so, memories are short and debts are often not repaid in Washington. The real basis of conditional cooperation lies in making bureaucrats creditors rather than debtors to the political executive; that is, giving them a stake in his future performance. Any past exchange of favors between appointees and careerists is far less influential than the general hope of grasping future returns. It is the grasping rather than the gratitude that drives executive politics.

## USING STRATEGIC RESOURCES

Strategic resources are important because they provide the possibility of exchanges with the bureaucracy that can create commitments to mutual performance. In theory, of course, it is conceivable that trust could be based on unconditional cooperation—a kind of gift relationship in which political and bureaucratic leaders expect little in return from each other. In practice, exchange is a way of life cultivated by those in the ambiguous executive roles of Washington. Political appointees cannot expect to stand—much less move—on the basis of their formal authority as appointed political leaders; neither can high careerists expect to be automatically accepted as carriers of the internal norms of civil service responsiveness. Even the institutionalist bureaucrat, the clearest example of a "model" civil servant, expects that his cooperation will be repaid with some degree of political respect for the integrity of government institutions. A distinguished academic "in-and-outer" colorfully described the public executives' strategic situation:

> I spent the first days up with [the secretary], and it was marvelous all the plans we were making—the executive suites, limousines, and all that. Then I went down into the catacombs and there were all these gray men, you know—GS 15s, 16s, and I understood what they were saying to me. "Here we are. You may try to run around us. You may even run over us and pick a few of our boys off, but we'll stay and you won't. Now, what's in it for us, sonny boy." And they were right there was nothing in it for them. The next time I got a presidential appointment, I made sure there was something I could do for them and they could do for me. We sat down together and did business.

Strategic resources in Washington are means by which executives and bureaucrats try to show "what's in it" for each other. These resources can be grouped into a few serviceable categories: goals and opportunities, procedures for building support, and ways of using people. But to many observers the most immediately obvious resource is an executive's political power. Paradoxically, a closer examination shows that political power may be one of the clearest but also one of the most limited assets for purposes of political leadership in the bureaucracy.

## POLITICAL CLOUT

Appointees with political clout—those who are willing and able to use many different means of self-help—not only extend their circles of confidence for dealing with outsiders but also create resources for dealing with civil servants inside. One such resource is a political executive's potential access to higher political levels. Career officials recognize that political contacts can mean the difference between the views of their agency being heard versus being merely tolerated or even ignored in the secretary's office or the White House. A careerist recalled longingly:

> Our last assistant secretary had terrific relations with [the secretary and two high appointees in the White House and the OMB]. He could call up, tell them our problems, and get them to listen and see if they could help. It improved our odds. Not everything, but an awful lot in Washington is done on the strength of these one-to-one relationships. Now we can't even get in the ball game.

Information carried back from higher political levels also aids top civil servants if their political executives convey it. It helps to know, for example, "whether it's just an ad hoc decision or something implying a policy," or "what's of interest and worrying the political people; maybe it's just some prior notice the President is giving a speech on a certain subject." Without such information higher civil servants know less in advance and worry more. "You spend your time on papers that no one really cares about . . . you have no idea of how the other political people are likely to react. . . . You don't know whether it really is a topside decision by the President or secretary or a call by some young political aid three times removed."

Thus the more adept a political appointee becomes in building his circles of confidence and in protecting his prerogatives, the more the value of his advocacy appreciates in the eyes of the bureaucrats below. In every department in every recent administration, one of the chief ways political executives gained support in the bureaucracy was by being, or at least appearing to be, their agency's vigorous spokesman. "Fighting your counterparts in other departments creates confidence and support beneath you," one acknowledged. In reference to a strong advocate in his department, a civil servant said: "He was well regarded on the Hill and dealt from strength with [the interest group]. A lot of White House people were afraid of him. You could get more of what was wanted approved and through Congress." Less politically effective executives may be personally admired by civil servants but have little to offer in return for bureaucratic support. As one such cabinet secretary was described by a bureau chief: "He had charisma, a really fine and open man who a lot of civil servants around here liked. But he never got a grip on the department. He didn't really fight for what was needed and if he made a decision it was because he got maneuvered into it by the staff." Experienced bureaucrats recognize that such appointees leave their agencies and programs vulnerable to more politically aggressive competitors elsewhere. In this sense, career officials will typically prefer a strong if unpleasant advocate to an amiable weakling.

A politically effective appointee is involved in speaking out, making claims, attacking other people. Openly exercising political muscle in this way involves a high degree of public risk-taking, which civil servants themselves are likely to shun. The very fact that a political executive not only is expendable but certain to be expended can paradoxically provide a strategic resource of sorts. Since any large bureaucracy is rarely of one piece, some civil servants consider a new face that is willing and able to expose itself politically to be an opportunity for support that had better be used while it is available. After serving under a string of cabinet secretaries, a bureaucrat observed:

> One thing I've eventually learned is that new people coming in can often get things done that others around a long time can't. People in the bureaucracy are telling them it's impossible, but they don't know that something can't be done and they do it. Like some Republicans have come in with no real obligations to the unions after an election, and that can be a big advantage. On the other hand, sometimes the unions will take things from a guy they regard as "one of them" that they'd never take from anybody else. It cuts both ways, and when you get a new guy who's tough and knowledgeable, you better make hay while the sun shines.

Thus a political appointee who shows himself able to take political risks can evoke responses that belie the stereotype of bureaucrats waiting to outlast political appointees.

Generally all these resources—political access, information, advocacy, and risk-taking—are by-products of any appointee's efforts to build credibility amid the maze of strangers in the government community. Political executives who can help themselves (like those already advantaged politically by the selection process) gain compound interest in dealing with the bureaucracy. For other executives, nothing fails like failure; political weakness in dealing with outsiders exacerbates all their problems of coping with bureaucratic insiders. To those who have, more is given, and those with scant political support are likely to have even that taken away by government infighting.

The resources derived from political clout, however, are also severely limited for would-be political leaders in government agencies. Risk-taking, advocacy, and so on, all point outward and are only very indirectly related to changing the behavior of officialdom itself. If political executives do not already agree with, or are unwilling to adopt, the bulk of the careerists' own agenda, then other resources for dealing with the bureaucracy are required. A politically powerful undersecretary explained: "We got along very well in the department because we wanted to and helped the bureaucrats do what they wanted to do." But the need for political leadership often goes further than bureaucratic advocacy. The same undersecretary's deputy recalled:

> We got a lot of loyalty and backup from the civil servants in return for his confidence in them. But the result too was that we got sucked in a number of times—I mean accepting and defending their advice that something couldn't be done. Then when the heat turned on in Congress or the press, you found out you could do these things after all. . . . What we didn't get was a lot of critical, innovative thought, because going along with the careerists in the accepted ways wasn't the way to get that. You also have to double-check, push bureaucrats, get mad sometimes.

The paradoxical fact is that the political clout of the appointees can help bureaucrats get more of what they want, but it offers little assurance that appointees can get what they want from the bureaucracy, especially if this implies changes in policy. If mere appeals to outside political power could compel changes among officials inside, the executives' lives would be easy; indeed their leadership would be unnecessary in the executive branch. But life is not so simple. As government leaders, the executives' problem is to gain the changes they want while acquiring the services they need from the bureaucracy. For that, they have to unite managerial brainwork and sensitivity to whatever political muscle they may have.

## GOALS AND OPPORTUNITIES

The pressure of time and circumstances forces political executives to confront many choices they would rather overlook. It also forces them to overlook many things they might like to consider.

In a general sense this need to focus attention is a constraint on leadership, yet in a strategic sense it can also be an asset. Experienced political executives have found that the process of goal-setting can be an important source of strength in dealing with the bureaucracy.

The underlying logic seems obvious, but it is often lost from view in the press of events and crises. A political executive who does not know what he wants to accomplish is in no position to asses the bureaucracy's performance in helping him do it. Likewise, an executive whose aims bear little relation to the chances for accomplishment is in an equally weak position to stimulate help from officials below. By trying to select goals in relation to available opportunities, political appointees create a strategic resource for leadership in the bureaucracy.

The operational word is selectivity. By the time they are leaving office, political appointees commonly regret the waste involved both in trying to do everything at once and in trying to do anything that is unrelated to the available chances for success. Here is how appointees from three different departments described what they had learned.

An assistant secretary:

> We didn't figure out what could and could not be moved in the department, with OMB, with the appropriations committee. . . . We bloodied our noses on things that couldn't really be changed.

An undersecretary:

> Deciding what you can win is important because then you don't use resources needlessly. For example, here are six decision memoranda on decentralization. I had no idea there'd be such a strong congressional backlash. Next time I wouldn't try and get some general authority through. I'd decentralize only a small bit of programs at first. It's a matter of what you can and cannot win and how you can or cannot win.

An assistant secretary, after eighteen months on the job; describing a standard situation:

> There's a budget cycle, a personnel cycle, a planning cycle—for what it's worth—and lots of other smaller recurrences in the department's business. It can take a year for these to unfold so you understand about them and see it is a matter of which cycles you leave for civil servants to keep running and which you try and make work for you. Doing it again, I'd spend less time trying to deal with 60 percent of everything and drop to 30 percent on some things and 90 percent on others I care about.

Obviously such comments have much in common with the bureaucratic dispositions mentioned earlier—gradualism, indirection, and so on. This does not necessarily mean that appointees have been captured by the bureaucracy, but it does suggest an accommodation to the need for fitting ends and means in the exercise of leadership. Such discrimination can be found alike in appointees who seek to expand or cut government programs and in those who see their aims as stemming from their own agenda or (as in the cases quoted above) from overall White House desires.

How do political appointees try to link choices on goals with available opportunities and thereby strengthen the incentives for bureaucratic cooperation? Specific circumstances obviously vary, but they have some common features.

### Preemptive Strikes

The early days in office—particularly with a new administration—constitute a particularly rich set of opportunities for any objectives aimed at major change. "After the first year the magic is gone, the weaknesses start to show, and you get bogged down with criticisms about what's gone wrong since you came in," one appointee remarked. A top appointee in another administration related how

> setting out major policy lines quickly means you're at an advantage because
> things are still loose and flexible in government. Later, people get more
> locked into positions; it's easier to get out-maneuvered. If people under you
> are confused in the first year about what's wanted and control is lost, then it
> is hard ever to get it back.

The advantages to be gained from scheduling major changes early, however, are extraordinarily difficult to realize in Washington. Most appointees cannot expect to enter office at the very beginning of a new administration. Even if they do, the incoming presidential party will rarely arrive with an operational plan for what it wants to accomplish in specific agencies. Moreover, the advantages of prompt action fit poorly with the needs of new political appointees to learn about their jobs and establish a network of relationships in the nation's capital. The exception to the normal situation was cited by one executive who had reorganized his agency, cut the work force by one-fifth, and won legislation to substantially redirect the major objectives of its programs:

> The only reason we could do it was because we knew what we wanted and
> moved between February and May, right after the inauguration and my
> confirmation. People in other agencies weren't quite sure what was happen-
> ing and anybody getting upset didn't know where to go. Later in the year,
> without the honeymoon feeling and confusion, I'd have been stymied.

## Areas of Relative Indifference

As political executives learn more about the particular views that seem to be locked into congressional committees, interest groups, and subordinate officials, they often seek advantages by choosing to act in areas of relative disinterest to other participants. They try, as one appointee said, "to charge down the corridors of indifference." Thus in many agencies the temporary executives generally find that they create less antagonism by concentrating on overall administration and organization rather than on detailed program delivery, on money grants rather than people services, on planning rather than implementation, and on squeezing rather than eliminating a program.

These strategic choices obviously reinforce inertia and marginal change in government. Such incentives can mean that many political appointees find it in their interest to deal with the easiest, not necessarily the most important, issues. But even (indeed especially) those appointees who recognize their leadership responsibility to cope with important controversial issues learn the value of selecting proximate goals that at least do not arouse a maximum of opposition initially. An executive trying to deal with programs in the

Department of Agriculture described the details of a common situation:

> This is not what you'd call a common sense environment. You can't just go
> after things. With the Agricultural Extension Service, state and local
> governments pay the majority of their salaries. The state directors of FHA
> [Farmers Home Administration] are appointed by state political groups.
> The county office heads of ASCS [Agricultural Soil and Conservation
> Service] are appointed by elected county committees, but it handles farm
> programs at the core of this department's operations. We can't end the pilot
> school milk program, even though we now have the school lunch program,
> because of the school lunch lobby, equipment manufacturers, milk lobby,
> and our own Nutrition Service. Each program also has a certain congress-
> man's stamp on it. Eliminate it and it's an affront to him, the clients, and the
> bureaucrats delivering it to them. There are just a lot of people around who
> can tell you to go to hell when you go after program delivery. We decided
> to leave this alone and not get into how they sit down with clients.

## Management Missions

Even if political executives are unable to take advantage of early opportunities or areas of indifference, they can acquire advantages in dealing with
the bureaucracy on the basis of objectives that are what some science
administrators call "project-like." Such goals identify a given point to be
reached with a particular set of resources and within a particular time.
Expectations between political appointees and civil servants become more
firmly based; the mutual performance that each expects of the other becomes
clearer. Everyone, as one official said, "knows the mission. You have a
schedule, costs, and a group of interlocking activities that have to be
performed in order to get from here to there."

Some potential executives fear the disadvantages of such engineering
analogies in government (among other problems, outsiders can more easily
assess the executives' own performance); others feel they make the job
easier. "You've got a better idea of where you stand, who's producing it, how
to motivate officials to pull together," one said. The space program of the
National Aeronautics and Space Administration (NASA) is the example
most frequently given, but other executives may point to a major building
program, a new accounting system, a given reduction rate in subsidies, and
similar "missions."

A number of efforts have been and are being made to systematize the
treatment of objectives in the executive branch, and no doubt further
improvements can be made. Indeed the ability to provide clear, measurable
objectives is often taken as the sine qua non of rational programs and
political leadership in government. There is no need to review the ample
literature on attempts to analyze (the planning, programming, and budgeting
system), monitor (management by objectives) and reevaluate (the current

program evaluation movement) agency objectives. Here it is enough to emphasize that as a practical matter the ability of most political executives to use project-type objectives in their working relationships with the bureaucracy are often severely limited. Businessmen experienced in government usually cite the lack of measurability compared with the situation in private enterprise. "In the private sector you know the name of the game—to get a percentage return, a certain productivity increase. Here there're no profit guidelines. Dollars aren't the measure of your performance." One explained that in government since "dollars aren't the bottom line, you get proxies for performance, input measure related to doing the work, providing a service, not producing an output." Knowing when a business has increased its market penetration from 40 percent to 42 percent is not like knowing when people have decent housing or proper health care.

Even beyond the problem of measurability, however, there are other powerful constraints on the political executives' use of mission-like objectives. One of these limitations is that what can be measured is often unrelated to the effectiveness that is judged and rewarded. "If I sweated fat out of my organization and increased productivity by 5 percent," said an executive, "I'd be a big man in my company. Here I could do that and be out of step with the secretary or a senator and get zinged every time. Or I may be a boob and with a politically favored program still get my funds increased in a way unrelated to how I'm doing as a manager."

Another inherent limitation is that since an executive's mission in Washington usually depends on contributing actions by a number of semi-independent outside participants, it can become extremely difficult to judge who is responsible for poor performance when objectives are missed. "At NASA we were lucky because there weren't six other agencies . . . involved in trying to put a man on the moon. If our people blew it, they couldn't pass the buck as easily as they can in most places." Political appointees will probably have to accept the legitimacy of much of the outside participation in their missions, even if this blurs accountability.

Still another constraint on mission-like political objectives lies in the temporary executives difficulty in learning enough about their organizations to asses the normal gamesmanship familiar in all organizational objective-setting. As one management analyst in government observed: "Objectives set unrealistically low just make people look good when they surpass the goals. Set very high they may just frustrate people into finding ways around them. The only way to get a sense of realism is to have good substantive knowledge and experience with the programs themselves." As noted, not many political appointees can be counted on for that kind of in-depth bureaucratic knowledge.

A final and most important constraint on the public executives' use of objectives is that political leadership commonly involves changing goals, not just hitting targets. An assistant secretary in one of the few agencies where measurable objectives were established by congressional statute acknowledged: "I was there just to get the program in place and running. There wasn't the time or opportunity to look back to ask if these are still the goals we should want to accomplish. It'll have to be someone else's job to worry about redirecting the agenda." Redirection may come from a new "man with a mission," but it is more likely to evolve slowly as new men cope with the circumstances. Goals are changed, not simply because political leaders renege on promises, but also because people who are affected complain about the old goals; or because some objectives (particularly in social programs that ore oversold) cannot be achieved or achievement does not have the desired effect; or because people and organizations interested in self-preservation realize that having only one finite aim can be a terminal occupation—in short because of the normal course of self-interested inter-action called politics.

## Climatic Pressures

Since discrete missions normally are difficult to use as a management tool, political executives improve their ability to deal with their organizations by treating goals, not as givens, but as part of an ongoing political process. "Climate" is a term frequently used to describe a variety of factors involved in adapting goals to prevailing circumstances. Sometimes a scandal may provide the impetus: "Billie Sol Estes was the best thing that ever happened to our plans for creating a post of inspector general [in the Agriculture Department]." Less drastic outside criticism can also help.

> Our secretary used to complain that the GAO [General Accounting Office] should get off his back. I was there when [the secretary of defense] told him he ought to get smart and do like he did: take advantage of every GAO report to get changes he wanted. With these reports he'd go to people in the interest groups and bureaucracy saying, "Look, these guys are breathing down our necks. Here's what we have to do." Sometimes he even did what GAO recommended.

Frequently less tangible "ideas in good currency" surround the bureaucracy and provide some of the best opportunities for realistic goal selection. Political executives who link their aims to ideas in good currency can gain a broader base to deal with even the most entrenched bureaucracy. One experienced official watched a succession of appointees gradually change a government agency that had once been considered to be an impregnable alliance with its powerful clientele:

> You can't really trace it to any one administration or appointee, but over time the bureau's budget was squeezed, some things taken away, nothing new added. A series of people coming in reflected the feeling in the air that there were broader policy issues that mattered more than the particular

prerogatives of this bureau.

The continuity to accomplish such long-haul change exists in points of view rather than in particular people. This gradualism, of course, may not provide very much gratification for political executives interested in big payoffs within their relatively short terms of office.

Hence, as a strategic resource, the selective intermixture of goals and opportunities is important. It helps a political executive specify how his exercise of political clout on the bureaucracy's behalf is conditional on the bureaucrats' performance. It sensitizes executives to the fact that working relations with the bureaucracy depend not only on winning fights but also on selecting, transferring, bypassing, and often running away from some fights in favor of others. Yet there are also considerable limitations. Political appointees in Washington may not be able to act early or to find areas of indifference. Neither can they count on acquiring clear missions against which to measure and climatic opportunities with which to spur bureaucratic performance. And as the next section shows, however well an appointee manages to point people in a particular direction, he will discover that his job in the bureaucracy is one of selling, not pointing.

## BUILDING SUPPORT

Since few political executives have the clear missions or massive public and political backing with which to generate spontaneous cooperation, they must usually work at procedures for building support in the bureaucracy. Changing words, plans, and pieces of paper is easy. Changing behavior, especially while not losing the constructive services of officials, is much more difficult.

Efforts to build support may embrace a specific policy objective or something as vague as improvising goals through the everyday interactions of government. Whatever an executive's aims, the inertia he faces in any agency is generally a compound of at least four elements. First are the Opponents, who see vital interests harmed by change and who are unalterably opposed to the efforts of political executives. Second are what might be called "Reluctants," people who may be opposed to change but who are not immune to persuasion that there are some hitherto unrecognized advantages: they will at least listen. Third, are the Critics—civil servants who feel they have views to contribute and are willing to be supportive as long as what they have to say is seriously considered. Finally, the Forgotten are those whose failure to support political executives stems from their failure to hear what is wanted or to hear correctly.

These four bureaucratic types can no doubt be found in any organization, but they are particularly important in the public agencies of the

U.S. executive branch, where a gulf of mistrust and many differences can separate the temporary leaders from those who spend their lives in government. Inexperienced appointees often visualize only the Opponents and respond with indiscriminate suspicions and withdrawal from the bureaucracy. Political executives more accustomed to the Washington environment make more efforts to cultivate the different sources of potential support, lest their reactions to Opponents prejudice possibilities of help from the others. Here I describe these efforts in terms of communications to deal with the Forgotten, fair hearings for the Critics, and consultation for the Reluctants. Outright Opponents fit more naturally into the discussion of bureaucratic sabotage and space limitations prevent dealing with this group here.

## Communication

Veteran bureaucrats usually cite failures of communication as the greatest weakness in the political appointees' relations with the bureaucracy. A typical comment: "Being so suspicious, political people are hard to talk to. They and bureaucrats aren't able to get their views through to each other. What you really need is better communications." Standing in isolation, this view is difficult to assess because the same official later noted that "when you do give out information it can leak all over the place, cutting off confidence and strengthening the opposition." Political information is a strategic resource that should not be dissipated. Like the warnings, orientations, and so on that bureaucrats can offer to new executives, information held by appointees is not a free good. Hence selectivity is obviously as important for communication—in the sense of passing strategically important information—as in goal-setting.

Communication in the sense of "getting the word out," however, is another matter. It seems difficult to have too much of this kind of communication. Executives cannot tap into potential bureaucratic support if large groups of people do not know what is wanted or, even worse, if they are only vaguely aware that an appointee exists. In the musical chairs at the top, political appointees typically begin communicating by at least trying to establish a personal "presence" in their agency, although how they do so varies with personal style. Some like to "press the flesh," to make the rounds of everybody in every office. Others are more comfortable with large meetings, and still others do better to avoid personal contact if it only betrays an insincere gesture.[4] Of course, a mere presence is unlikely to change anything, but it is a beginning.

In a larger sense, political executives often fail to recognize that they are always communicating—by example, by innuendo, even by a refusal to talk with people. The real need in building support is to communicate what is intended, for both intended and unintended signals are picked up in the bureaucracy.[5] For example:

- The agency was supposed to be preparing a tight budget, and here he was big-dealing it by flying all around the country with a huge staff contingent.
- We read [the appointee's] address to [an outside conference] pledging to meet the needs of these people. Then when we loosened up the program and it grew, word came down complaining that things were out of control. Everyone here was dumbstruck. It showed his ignorance about what he himself was doing.

As noted earlier, even an apparent refusal to communicate provides its own signals to civil servants. "Suddenly, you're not asked things or talked to, just told what must be done. You are supposed to be just a tool—not a professional."

Particularly in the Washington environment, communication cannot consist of simply saying something once in the bureaucracy. Persistence and follow-through lie at the heart of efforts to convey accurate messages. In part this is because the immense federal organizations find it difficult to transmit any messages through their many layers. Moreover, the executives' statements often produce little detailed guidance and leave much room for competing interpretations. There is another, less obvious reason why follow-through is probably the most important aspect of the political appointees' communication. The complex Washington environment makes it extremely difficult to separate the players' real moves from symbolic ones. Those on the receiving end of messages from political executives are accustomed to applying a heavy discount factor to mere proclamations. A supergrade explained that "over the years you see that a lot of the instructions aren't intended to be carried out. It takes extra effort to make it clear to people down the line that something is meant, not just another statement for the record or some speechwriter's inspiration."

Hence for political executives to say something once is a statement of intention; to show others what is meant and that it cannot be forgotten becomes a strategic resource. These extra efforts may take the form of reporting procedures, instructions committed to writing, informal reminders, complex management information systems, and a host of other techniques. But again, none of these techniques are substitutes for personalized networks and discussions. For purposes of communication follow-through, these networks need to include people at the operating levels of the bureaucracy. After describing the sophisticated reporting requirements he had helped create, an agency manager concluded by recognizing that "all these statistics and reports do is throw up some signals that things aren't happening at the point of impact. Our best techniques give only the signals, not the story. That's why you need personal contacts down there." There is therefore little point in advising political executives to concentrate on broad policy decisions rather than waste time on details. General decisions or guidelines may communicate little to subordinates without specific interventions and "casework" to demonstrate what is wanted in particular types of circumstances. But it is a waste of time and a source of confusion to impart details that are irrelevant to the executives' major purposes.

Follow-through often requires more persistence than appointees have time or inclination for, but there are few surrogates for the extra effort at communication required from political executives. Higher civil servants may help, but in Washington there are few generalist career officials with the responsibilities and stature that would permit them to oversee any broad-scale follow-through for a department of policy. "Try that," said one civil servant who did, "and you have political appointees jumping up against you all over the place saying that that isn't the way they understand administration policy."

### Due Process Again

Efforts to get the word out imply the reciprocal: listening to those who feel they have something to say. Political executives who are unwilling to provide a fair hearing to people in the bureaucracy generally find they have forced two otherwise distinct groups into the same camp. Working relations deteriorate not only with diehard bureaucratic Opponents but also with Critics who did not feel they had to win as long as they could gain access for their views.

For many civil servants, the complexity of many policy issues can reasonably justify a range of decisions by political appointees. For these bureaucrats a specific outcome may be less important than the kind of due process noted for relations among political appointees themselves. As one career supergrade said:

> The options aren't all that different regardless of which party is in power. Most of the [decisions] are in gray areas and could go either way. You're not facing a lot of moments of truth as long as you have a chance to have a serious input. What many career people do care about is that their sorting out of the alternatives comes into play, that however they [political executives] decide, there is evidence they've paid attention and at least had to wrestle with the issues worrying us.

Political appointees denied due process (at least those interested in self-help) can be counted on to raise a ruckus with each other; bureaucrats usually shop quietly among the many alternative listening posts in Washington and find other ways of getting their views heard. At any given time the consequences can be observed in a number of agencies. A GS 16 described a familiar set of choices and his own decision on what he regarded as an important issue:

> I think a lot of people feel they aren't being taken into account and are just
> expected to rationalize decisions from on high. It's when you are denied a
> voice that life becomes tough. You've got to decide if you can live with this
> and yourself or if you want to try and outlast it, or move. Or do what I'm
> doing now—find an ally elsewhere with more power than you to help make
> the case.

In another large agency a prominent bureaucrat described the slide into
demoralization:

> The feeling has grown in both the Johnson and Nixon administrations that
> the bosses didn't really want to hear what the career people had to say.
> You're not part of anything, just stuck out in an office somewhere, doing
> God knows what, that has an impact who knows where. I've seen the
> discontent filter through the whole structure. Productivity is falling, leaks
> are increasing, people are playing safer than ever before.

Obviously, listening to the bureaucrats' views on every issue may be
unduly costly and time-consuming for a political executive. The value of
working to establish a reputation as a leader who listens is cumulative, not
immediate. Such a reputation is a strategic resource because it contributes to
the trust that will undoubtedly be needed as specific pressures require
forbearance from those below. Moreover, whatever the substantive value of
the information communicated from lower-level officials (and it may be
considerable), fair hearings can create a competition among perspectives that
strengthens an executive's hand.

## Consultation

With the Reluctants in the bureaucracy, political executives face the choice
of seeking out or avoiding more active consultation. Such consultation may
involve anything from the initial selection of goals to discussions about
implementation. A great deal has been written about the pros and cons of so-
called participatory, or democratic, management. The argument in brief is
that "significant changes in human behavior can be brought about rapidly
only if the persons who are expected to change participate in deciding what
the change shall be and how it shall be made."[6] A number of case studies of
public agencies suggest that the degree of participatory management is
unrelated to effectiveness in accomplishing the intended goals of
reorganization but does improve the employees' support and reduce
resistance to change.[7]

These studies, however, also suggest a more important point: that the
arguments for or against active consultation with subordinates are highly

dependent on the particular situation and context. For purposes of political leadership in the bureaucracy, participatory management (trying to create a sense that "we are all in it together") seems largely irrelevant if it is followed simply as a maxim or proverb of good management. Only in an abstract sense are political appointees and civil servants in anything together, other than their agency. Consultation becomes relevant as a strategic resource when it is offered or withheld so as to serve the purpose of executive leadership. When and for what do experienced political executives feel a need to consult in detail with those bureaucrats who, far from being helpful, may actually resist the exercise of political leadership in "their" agency?

The answers from many different agencies and administrations seem clear. In-depth consultation (which is *not* the same thing as indiscriminate information-passing) makes sense when bureaucratic resistance may be susceptible to persuasion, either through intensified argument or by involving Reluctants in processes that lead toward largely unavoidable conclusions.[8] Consultation for what? To find what might be called the points of mutual self-interest. Since there is never enough agreement to go around, political executives generally do better by trying to search for these possible points of shared advantage rather than by assuming from the outset that initial resistance is immutable. Even if complete agreement between political and bureaucratic executives is impossible, consultation may reveal a partial overlap of interests that suffices for the purposes at hand. "You're looking for places where you can support him so he can support you," as one official put it. A former strong man in the Nixon administration learned to respect bureaucratic power in the agencies "because they could push as hard as I could push them." He concluded: "You can't mandate change there. It's a question of sitting down with people and showing how things can be of use to them."

Mutual advantage produces institutionalized change. As the desires of a political executive become connected with the interests of at least some of the officials who will remain behind, the chances of an enduring impact grow. Here, for instance, is how one fifteen-year veteran in the bureaucracy compared the results of the tenure of two assistant secretaries:

> The government is used to absorbing tigers. Thomas was bright and tough, but if you asked him what actually got done, what around here actually operates differently since he came and left, he couldn't point to anything. . . . It was all put in on top and like a big spring, things went back to normal when the topside pressure left. . . . Williams, I think, got people believing it was their own ideas. You still see some of the changes he got through because people [in various bureaus] were working out and adapting the system so it became their own way of doing business. To get rid of this after he left you'd have to change operating procedures and nobody likes to do that.

The particular bargaining tactics used to arrive at a sense of mutual advantage are far too numerous to discuss here. They range from the creation of formal task forces and joint decision documents, to quid pro quo side payments, to indirect leverage through third-party pressures. Again, some of the essential flavor can be conveyed by a compendium of experience, in this case from a political appointee who cited methods used to produce a variety of changes over the course of seven years.

> When we wanted a reporting system on things of interest to minorities, the statistics section said there weren't any data. I had them publish the table headings with empty columns. That got egg on their face, and they figured they'd better get some data on minority services before they were published again. . . .
>
> Quietly we started letting it be known about how the delays were hurting a lot of people in the agency. People started getting upset and asking how improvements could be made. "Well," we said, "here are some ideas that might work. . . ." The task forces helped show who was interested and where the pockets of resistance were. There's always somebody over in the weeds, and fifteen people sitting around a table can help bring that out and gang up on him a little bit. . . .
>
> We involved at least one person from each program division. The important thing was that with them working together, when it came out, you'd have some allies among the program people. . . . You could appeal to them by saying, "Look, why are you using all this manpower for things that aren't really connected to your bureau's objectives? With this plan you can use some of the cuts and reallocate them to things you really care about. . . ." Eventually they had to come up with suggestions themselves. The subsidies clearly were not working, and you could show that continuing in the same way meant at some point down the road we couldn't afford it; people would be hurt and there'd by a big hue and cry. Middle-level people fought like hell, but ultimately the division heads couldn't argue against the logic of the situation. . . .
>
> You know when you write the procedures you're the big gun in that field and anyone trying to change them is a threat to the foundation of your authority. The real back of the opposition was broken when we won over the dean of the budget officers, who'd built his power by letting the agencies go their own way on these things. Finally, through persuasion and a lot of argument, he was won over, and I remember as clear as day the meeting where he publicly capitulated. He said that if he'd known years ago what he now knew he'd have tried to put this through then.

As with other strategic resources, there are severe constraints on the political appointees' ability to consult and bargain toward mutual advantages with reluctant bureaucratic supporters. These processes require time, which temporary executives can often ill afford. Not everyone in large bureaucracies can be brought into discussions, and so a good deal of in-depth knowledge of the organization is likely to be required to identify at least proximate sources of resistance. Another obvious but often forgotten constraint is that any executive proposal needs to make substantive sense. There is little point in trying to persuade tenured officials with a case for change that does not have the merits to stand up against strenuous argument from those affected; often this requires more substantive knowledge than political appointees can muster. A related difficulty is that active consultation downward can strain a political executive's relations with his own political superiors, particularly if they are unwilling to tolerate compromises inherent in the give and take of any serious consultation. Without some leeway in what could constitute an acceptable outcome, consultation becomes perceived as a cynical attempt at cooptation and destroys rather than builds trust.

The various procedures described above for building support do not require that political executives avoid major fights with the bureaucracy, or accept whatever bureaucrats say, or cower behind the lowest common denominator of joint decisions. They do mean that some delicacy is required if appointees are to move among the natives in the bureaucratic villages without being captured. Experienced political executives do not necessarily make efforts to build support in the bureaucracy so that they can avoid the confrontations required by political leadership. They do it so that the fights, when they do come, are not one against all and to the death.

Many things—including personality, partisan politics, and intolerant political superiors—cause some political appointees to shun such delicacy in governing people. But the price of weak communications, restricted access for lower officials, and disregard for the self-interests of subordinates is the alienation of potential support in the bureaucracy. Many of the temporary executives in Washington choose to pay this price, and thus their initial suspicions about bureaucratic inertia and sabotage become self-fulfilling. What they cannot prudently do is to pretend that their actions exact no cost at all. The following comment by a Nixon appointee, who was surprised by the lack of bureaucratic cooperation he received, is an object lesson in the lack of statecraft:

> We began by going after the big issues and pretty much ignored the bureaucrats and opposition in Congress. The idea was to create some major points to rally Republican troops for the years ahead. . . . After a number of defeats in the first years it was decided to drop the legislative route and work through rules and regulations in the executive branch. The bureaucrats were very uncooperative toward this administrative strategy.

In this case the imprudence consisted, not of seeking partisan advantages, but of thinking that any "administrative strategy" could easily be built on bureaucratic relations that had already been cast aside in previous years.

## USING PEOPLE

So far strategic resources have been discussed in terms of political power, the selection of goals and opportunities, and methods of building internal bureaucratic support. People are also a resource that needs to be used for executive leadership. Political appointees often are unable to manage simply by motivating and bargaining with incumbent bureaucrats; in many cases changes in personnel are required in order to build a team that is in agreement about what needs to be done.

The idea of using people comes easily in Washington—too easily. Political executives naturally feel a need to have people around them who can be trusted from the outset and need not be won over. Given their own limited knowledge of people in government, inexperienced appointees are unlikely to believe they can count on this loyalty from below. More to the point, the civil service system—far from offering a basis for reassurance— often exacerbates doubts that good working relationships with career personnel can be expected. The labyrinthine civil service procedures and job-specific protections, the informal personnel practices and blurry intermixture of political and career jobs, the past attempts at politicizing the bureaucracy, the organizationally ingrown civil service careers, the standoffishness of civil servants who recognize the political vulnerability and career dangers that come in working closely with political appointees—all these offer public executives ample reason to doubt the people in government they inherit. Even if new executives harbor no ill will toward the Washington bureaucracy, they have to question whether this is a civil service system they can count on for help in exercising their legitimate leadership functions.

Thus the personnel system they walk into encourages the inclination of new appointees to think that their primary strategic resource and means of control lies in filling all key jobs with an outside retinue of personal loyalists. Unfortunately those who have watched the migrations of political appointees over the years generally seem to agree on one thing: importing a large number of outside lieutenants is usually an ineffective strategy for high political executives.

By now the reasons should be clear. The new subordinates can multiply all the difficulties of the executive's inexperience by bringing with them their own problems of self-help, short tenures, mistrust, needs for orientation, and so on. Not only do their personal loyalties fail to substitute for the institutional services the executive needs, but their intermediation can further separate the executive from bureaucratic services and vitiate opportunities for building support through communication, access, and consultation. Moreover, the proliferation and general bureaucratization of political appointees readily generates a false sense of security, a feeling that enduring changes in the behavior of government officials, and thus policies, are somehow being created just because more appointees are talking to each other.

One of the more aggressive assistant secretaries in recent years acknowledged his early admiration for "Machiavelli's advice: when you capture a town, bump off the top ten people, put in your own guys, and the rest of the population will settle down." Later he thought differently. "But you've got to realize this is a lousy communication system you're setting up. . . . There's nothing wrong with being tough, but doing it again I'd be more sensitive. I was having to work fourteen hours a day just to keep the place running myself until I got a good career deputy who knew how to get things done." The deputy described how this executive "had intimidated people so much that some were withholding bad news from him and others were beginning to play around with the statistics just to get results what would please him. . . . All the schedule C types had become a filter between him and the bureaucracy, calling their own shots and creating resentment. They were costing him more than he gained."

In the end a strategy of governing through outside placements also fails because it is normally an organizational impossibility. Without a massive reversion to spoils politics in government hiring, no top political executive can begin to place enough personal loyalists in all the important positions of his organization, i.e., in positions down to the level where discretionary guidance over the work of others shades into substantial routinization. "In this agency," said a top administrator, "we have six political slots; if you tripled that you'd still have less than two dozen of your guys in an organization of 62,000, and how long will it take for those 18 to figure out what's going on?"

Again, the more productive route lies in selectivity. Experienced political executives everywhere try to build strategy resources by selectively managing the various types of career personnel. In practice this means taking personnel actions to acquire officials already in the bureaucracy who show they can be of help, and if necessary bringing in outsiders to replace the unsuitable. Every cabinet secretary will want (though by no means will always get) his own lieutenants in top executive positions at the undersecretary and assistant secretary level. But below those levels the distinctions between civil servants and political appointees blur rapidly. It is here that political executives can gain a strategic advantage by using people in the bureaucracy.

The consensus of informed opinion on this point is impressive, among both bureaucrats and appointees and in Republican and Democratic administrations alike. Asked what advice they would give to new political appointees, most high civil servants would probably echo the one who said that "a smart guy should spend a while finding out who's productive, build on the ones who will help you do things, move them, use them to get other good people, and ride them as far as you can." Political executives with service in a variety of agencies report their experience in similar terms. For example, a Democratic assistant secretary with an expanding program said: "You can't motivate everybody. Some of these divisions are disaster areas with their leaks, but if you look, there are competent people around. I moved a regional director in to work in my office, replaced him with another good man I had watched. Then I took [a GS 15], consolidated some functions under him, and raised his status." In an agency where cutbacks were the executive's aim, a Republican undersecretary learned: "You didn't need to bring in a lot of new people because there was already an undercurrent of some who wanted changes; they could be found, encouraged, and promoted so you had a hard core of bureaucrats in key positions to ride herd on things."

The reason there is such consensus about using careerists goes back to all the bureaucratic services summarized best by the self-styled Machiavellian assistant secretary quoted earlier:

> I could have, and almost did, run around [an office director], and he could have beaten my brains out. But that isn't the point. The point is that no one understanding his function should want to run around him. I'm supposed to be smart enough to know what a guy like that is worth and realize that I should use him. [He] was a great civil servant, not because he did what you told him to, but because he would tell you how to solve the problems, what you could and couldn't do and why. With him I could get the changes through in one year instead of dragging on until I'm out of the picture.

To use bureaucratic personnel as a resource does not necessarily imply a political appointee's acceptance of the status quo. Sometimes political executives can create more flexible, innovative arrangements of officials and become less dependent on the established bureaucratic routines. The practical needs of decision-making, not management theory, lead experienced political executives to use bureaucrats in crosscutting and self-monitoring ways. These arrangements take many different forms. Career personnel may be used in policy analysis shops to foster competing analyses with program units; in an executive secretariat to make sure that views are canvassed, work processed, and decisions followed up; in mobile evaluation teams to report on activities further down the line. The reckless appointee may set everybody on edge by creating "my special strike force to go into the program divisions and report back only to me." The cooler agency head may get further with "a low-key special operations group that lives with the program people, gets in on things every step of the way, and plays it straight, letting those people know when and why they are reporting disagreements to me." By making these and other flexible uses of career people, government executives can provide a constructive service to both themselves and the bureaucracy. Such efforts show that if government officialdom is ingrown and cannot see new ways of doing things—as is often the case—there is an alternative to letting the career service go to seed and pushing political appointees ever lower in the bureaucracy.

If they are to use bureaucratic officials, even the toughest political executives need sufficient sensitivity to discriminate among the different capabilities of civil servants and match them to the appropriate jobs. Noticing that a civil servant is weak in one area, new appointees frequently overlook the needed help that could be given in other areas. "I almost made a mistake and dumped Williams because he couldn't negotiate with the other agencies," one said, "but he was superb in running the procedures. Starting a program, it's a two-fisted guy you want to bridge the torrent, but to keep things running smoothly you look for a diplomat who can still the tempest."

If political executives do not isolate themselves, they have ample opportunity to make these deeper assessments and go beyond the initial hearsay and apprehensions about Washington bureaucrats. These executives will watch meetings, responses to circulating papers, and special assignments. They will see that some "make serious efforts and are actively interested in finding ways of doing things" while others offer only "rote responses, reasons for not doing anything." An experienced political executive also looks for evidence of officials who avoid withholding information that puts him at a disadvantage. Some officials rarely create attention because they are anticipating and heading off problems; others may gain prominence by solving problems that are often of their own making, and still others may only look good because they leave the problems for someone else to solve. All of this requires more than superficial observation by political appointees interested in using civil service personnel actions as a strategic resource.

The real difficulty for executives in Washington does not lie in making these assessments but in finding the *constructive* flexibility in the civil service personnel system to do something about them. Contrary to popular beliefs, firing civil servants is not impossible, but it often requires experienced personnel experts to help work through the complicated procedures. There are such officials. As one said: "If you come up through the system you get to know procedures political appointees can't begin to cope with. I've fired civil servants who are incompetent or undercutting the leadership. The section in the book on firing is twice as long as the one on hiring, and it's dog-eared in my book." But what experienced officials will know and will usually encourage political executives to realize is that outright firings are extremely costly, not in dollars but strategic resources.

> Sometimes appointees seem to want to test you and ask "How do I fire a federal employee?" I tell him to give me the names and I'll have the employees out of the job in a month or two. But think of the implications, and you'll see there's a better, more indirect way of getting rid of a person you don't want on that job.

Given the nature of the civil service system, it is far easier and therefore much more common to use the indirect means available: quiet talks, early retirements, and exchanges (such as a favorable send-off in return for a graceful exit). Or as a former Civil Service commissioner said, "There are smart ways and dumb ways of getting rid of civil servants, ways that increase or decrease tension." Personnel advisers also recognize that the more hostile and unresponsive the civil servant, the more difficult removal becomes because of the likelihood of his using outside political connections. The general practice is to try to move unwanted officials to less troublesome positions. One career executive gave an accurate assessment of the options for anyone managing government personnel:

> What are you going to do with the guy who isn't doing you any good? You can make it known he isn't wanted, but some people don't get that signal. A confrontation can simply disrupt things and tie you up in procedures. You can try and make his job disappear [through a reorganization and reduction in force], but that's likely to backfire because he probably has got seniority and can bump young people below him who are better than he is. A transfer out of town is possible, but then he can use the grievance procedure that this is an adverse action. The normal thing is to move him to where he can do the least harm.

The difficulty for the public in these strategic moves is obvious: the other areas of the public's business used as dumping grounds are likely to suffer and the payroll costs and inefficiency of government employment are likely to grow.

But the problem of utilizing bureaucrats an executive does want, and of doing so without prostituting the concept of a career civil service, is a more important one than the oft-publicized inability to get rid of civil servants. The agency career ladders, the officials' vulnerability to political reprisals, the haphazard arrangements for broader executive development in the public service—these and more barriers obstruct efforts to utilize career personnel in a way that is both flexible for political managers and constructive for the civil service system. Good working relationships with political appointees are more apt to prejudice than to aid the bureaucrats' status and advancement as career public servants. Constructively using and moving permanent officials is a "hard sell" because bureaucrats recognize that, as one said, their "power base and career is a function of a particular job, or bosses, or relations and support from outside groups."

None of this means that experienced political executives fail to use career personnel as a strategic resource in support of their leadership. Quite the contrary. It is often precisely because institutional means are lacking that top government political executives can commonly go very far in using careerists. The point is that political appointees generally are not interested in the implications of their personal actions for the civil servants' careers, much less for the civil service as an enduring system. In fact there is every incentive for an appointee to "milk" civil servants for his own short-term advantages.

The selective efforts of political executives to use various bureaucrats readily shade into the development of personalized and politicized corteges. Rather than import a mass of outside loyalists or simply manage the capabilities of existing personnel, political appointees frequently nurture their own bureaucratic families of protégés. An assistant secretary described this common approach as follows:

> People you yourself hire are going to be more supportive than anyone else. They can be career guys, but they should be your guys and have primary loyalty to you. For example, Roberts is an excellent career man. I expected little but gave him some things to do and he performed wonderfully after plodding along in [the bureau] for eight years. I got him a promotion from a GS 14 to a 15 and took him with me to [a different agency] and made him a project director. Now he's an office head. That's the kind of person you have to attract and hold with you.

An undersecretary described how inexperienced people in the White House

> were stupidly checking into the party registration of career people. You can sense who in the agency is with you, working late, referring with approval to what you say. These are the guys who you move up rapidly, a GS 15 to a 16 and maybe an 18 in later years. These career guys tie their job prospects to the political appointee above them and so can succeed or fail spectacularly.

The costs of the tendency for career personnel management to merge into the development of personalized and politized bureaucratic protégés are not felt directly by political appointees, who typically move on to their own private careers. The price is paid by public officials who, although ambitious to move into challenging jobs, wish to retain some identity as career civil servants. Individual careerists can find they have indeed been used— "working your butt off for the guy and ending up as some executive assistant to a political appointee with no career development to show for it." A longtime participant in government described how those associated with a particular political executive can be "exposed, used up, and then become the holdovers and obstructionists for the next appointee to jump on." Of course, some careerists in this system will simply decide for very good reasons to cease being civil servants and to take political appointments. Others will have little choice. As one bright supergrade said: "Since he [the undersecretary] left government and [the assistant secretary] moved to HUD [Housing and Urban Development], I've got no clients for my work."

In a larger sense the real costs of the appointees' haphazard creation of bureaucratic families lie in the denigration of the concept of a career civil service. A well-known political executive went to the heart of the matter in describing the personal cortege that had moved with him between government agencies and the Executive Office of the President:

> In my experience these supergrade types in government compare favorably with almost any group I've seen in the private sector. A guy in his mid-thirties and a GS 15 has got to have a lot of political savvy and good moves. I've carried five of them with me in every job. They're my personal supporters and I look after them. . . . Civil servants identifying with people pose a real problem for the bureaucracy, but it doesn't bother me. It helps me as a political appointee because I can really deal with them. The whole civil service thing is so automated, promotions come automatically, grade-step increases, and pay changes. The only way for these guys to break through this automated system is through personal identification. What should happen if it were operating right is that the system should be throwing upwards and promoting the good, bright guys, not depending on personal identifications with patrons.

There is no need to idealize bureaucrats as "the" public service. Civil service systems are created to institutionalize a limited but important set of values in government. Among these are not simply nonpartisanship and obedience but also (and especially at higher levels) a continuous capacity to offer honest advice and uphold the integrity of government operations. Perhaps an obscure GS 15 said it best: "As the distinction blurs between an institutional career role and personalized loyalty, people start hedging. They hedge their best independent judgments, either so as not to be put into jeopardy of political identification or because once jeopardized they're trying to ingratiate themselves." Using career people as a strategic resource may help particular appointees, but it is no real help in establishing the civil service as an instrument of reliable government performance.

## IMPLICATIONS

My argument has been that political executives can usually do better by evoking conditional cooperation rather than by invoking their authority. Perceptive appointees from both the Theory X and Theory Y schools of management eventually see that the political executive's real job lies between the extremes of giving orders and of taking cooperation for granted.[9] They learn that political leadership in the Washington bureaucracy is not a task for martinets or presiding officers. For those both tough and sensitive enough, it is a job of managing a pluralistic, changing consensus with limited strategic resources.

In other words, there are no magical management systems or organizational changes for "getting control of the bureaucracy." Reorganization plans or techniques like management by objectives and zero-base budgeting are all executive proclamations that presume rather than create changes in subordinates' behavior. Instituting new management techniques and making them part of the bureaucracy's standard operating procedure lie at the end of statecraft not at the beginning.

In the preceding discussion I have also emphasized selectivity and calculation in dealing with the political resources, opportunities, people, and procedures for building support. This suggests that while would-be political leaders in the executive branch *can* be agents for changing what government is doing, convulsive root and branch changes fall outside the range of everyday statecraft. If political policy calls for revamping most of the major assumptions behind what an agency is doing, there is little point in a political executive appearing on that scene in the guise of a selective strategist who uses a variety of resources for encouraging bureaucrats to terminate their way of life. An entirely new organization will in all likelihood be required. Also needed will be a genuine, widely perceived sense of crisis—an economic disaster, an unambiguous foreign threat, an acknowledged need to "war" on some domestic problem—in order to galvanize the many disparate competitors for attention and agreement in Washington. Without that general sense of alarm, trying to shake up the bureaucracy by appealing to the American people for support simply misses the point.

A desire to capitalize on such opportunities for Big Change can therefore create one of the limits on mutual support between political leaders and bureaucrats. Fortunately for the stability of government institutions, such overwhelming crises seem relatively rare and are short-lived when they do occur. Moreover, once the bright new organization has been created, the familiar imperatives for statecraft reappear with time. These facts, along with the dispersed veto power and shortage of agreement that permeates most of everyday life in Washington, means that no political executive need apologize for working at relationships that are usually based on conditional cooperation with the bureaucracy.

Occasions for Big Change suggest a situation in which the political leaders' demand for performance is more than the bureaucracy can supply. Limits are also set on mutual support when bureaucrats demand more performance than political appointees can supply. Civil servants have their own expectations about what is due from political leaders in their agency. The tenure of officials who wish to remain civil servants but who also allow themselves to be used by political executives is conditional on the executives' own behavior. Appointees need to reduce the risk of added exposure and insecurity for such officials. When trouble develops— something upsets a political superior, the Office of Management and Budget attacks the agency's goals, a congressional committee takes offense—a political appointee who attempts to shift blame to subordinates quickly experiences an evanescence of bureaucrats, protégés or otherwise. As one observed, "The self-preservation instinct blossoms." Careerists involved in executive hearings and consultations expect to be serious participants dealing with issues of substantive importance, not "hacks rationalizing some piece of political propaganda." Officials helping a political executive will expect as their due some clear guidance in advance rather than to have to hope for support later. Since all strategic resources are limited, conditional cooperation breaks down when—for whatever reason—bureaucrats expect more in exchange for their cooperation than political executives are able or willing to provide.

Hence demands from either side can outrun the supply of mutual performance. But conditional cooperation involves more than bureaucrats and executives in their agencies. There are third, fourth, even nth parties implicated in the exchanges of executive politics and they too set limits on the degree of cooperation between the appointee and the bureaucrats. A political executive's primary constraint rests in his links to other appointees and political figures. An oft-quoted opinion of a former secretary of state is that "the real organization of government" at higher levels "is how confidence flows down from the President."[10] A similar but broader principle of confidence is at work throughout and across the levels of government. Depending on the political executives' specific allegiances and accidents of selection, their ability to deal with the civil servants below them is limited by their need for live political connections up to political superiors and out to the many sources of external power.

From this perspective it becomes clear why there is much more to the politics of executive branch leadership than simple-minded assertions about a natural animosity between presidents who long to control their administrations and parochial cabinet officers who love to be captured as departmental advocates. The fact is that requirements for statecraft in the agencies do not fit well with political prudence as seen from behind the White House gates. A president marshaling his power stakes expects to advance when there is credit to be had and withdraw as losses grow. When unpopular actions have to be taken in a government agency, his political appointees there should be hustling into the trenches of frontline support, not picking and choosing their advantages. After all, does not the President's generalship consist of using the strength of others and conserving his own? Bureaucratic politics contemplates quiet, behind-the-scenes workmanship, strategic reversals, caution, contentment with results for which everyone can share some of the credit. Presidential politics mobilizes its vital resources with the public by taking all the credit for dramatic, readily intelligible actions: big cuts, major new programs, flashy changes. Why, when the President has staked his reputation on getting something done in government, are his political executives reaching for the rapier instead of the bludgeon?

Executives in the agencies may argue that their achievements with the bureaucracy reflect favorably on the President, but to those in the White

House reflected glory may not be enough. Why not? Because a political executive's selection of goals and areas of indifference may not be what the President wants or would want if he could know what goes on throughout government; because to build support in the bureaucracy invites more delay and compromise; and because the people an executive uses may become his people but not necessarily presidential supporters. In these and many other ways an unconstrained use of his strategic resources may help a political executive with the bureaucracy but leave him vulnerable to the President's "true" supporters in the White House. Yet the more detached, broadly presidential view an executive takes of his agency, the more difficult it becomes to acquire support from its officials below and clients outside.

Hence the tensions of political leadership in its presidential and executive department guises are inherent. Being unavoidable, they suggest their own lesson for presidents: prudence for any president interested in the problem of controlling the bureaucracy consists in trying to use the inevitable tensions with his executives constructively, not in trying to eliminate or drive these tensions underground with simplistic notions of cabinet government and unified executive teamwork.

However, the implications of the preceding analysis go much further than the presidency. People in government can and do manage without conditional cooperation at the political-bureaucratic interface. When political appointees have little sense of direction or statecraft, the failure to establish a constructive working relationship with higher civil servants may be inconsequential, except that the bureaucracy is left freer to pursue its own agenda. Experienced bureaucrats become quite expert at helping themselves in the Washington scramble. Similarly, some political managers may feel no great loss if the careerists with whom they fail to build working relations have few analytic or administrative capabilities to offer or withhold; they become adept at creating their own personal teams in place of career civil servants. Appointees and bureaucrats can and do try to compensate for each other's inadequacies.

As each side maximizes its own convenience in this way, the overall quality of American democratic institutions is likely to decline. It is no consolation that appointees and top bureaucrats can compensate for having little that is worth exchanging with each other. If officialdom and professional specialists can get along very well despite an absence of political leadership above them, that should not reassure citizens who expect government bureaucracies to be guided by publicly accountable and removable political representatives. Likewise, political executives may manage without the institutionalized knowledge, continuity, and impartiality that government civil services are created to supply. That, too, is little consolation since the real strength of government machinery in a democracy is its ability to serve effectively, not just one particular set of political leaders, but any succession of leaders with a legitimate popular mandate. If democratic government did not require bureaucrats and political leaders to need each other, it might not matter so much when in practice they discover they do not.

## NOTES

1. For a fuller discussion see Hugh Heclo, *A Government of Strangers* (Washington, D.C.: The Brookings Institution, 1977). Research for this book was conducted from 1973 through 1976 and draws upon more than 200 interviews with political and career executives. All post-war administrations are represented in this sample.

2. The arguments are reviewed and set out in much greater detail in Douglas McGregor, *The Professional Manager* (New York: McGraw-Hill, 1967); Frederick Herzberg, *Work and the Nature of Man* (Cleveland: Cleveland World Publishers, 1966); and William K. Graham and Karlene H. Roberts, eds., *Comparative Studies in Organizational Behavior* (New York: Holt, Rinehart and Winston, 1972). One of the few relevant studies of civil servants is Fremont James Lyden, "Motivation and Civil Service Employees," *Public Administration Review*, 30 (May-June 1970). For a discussion of the generally lower level of commitment in government executives, see Bruce Buchanan, "Government Managers, Business Executives, and Disorganizational Commitment," *Public Administration Review*, 34 (July-August 1974), 339–47.

3. For detailed evidence on this particular disaster area during the Nixon years, see Joel D. Aberbach and Bert A. Rockman, "Clashing Beliefs within the Executive Branch," *American Political Science Review*, 70 (June 1976); and Martha Derthick, *Uncontrollable Spending for Social Services Grants* (Washington, D.C.: The Brookings Institution, 1975).

4. New department heads are especially prone to ritualistic mass handshaking sessions. As one bureaucrat said: "Everyone had to be lined up, one by one, to get the glad hand. It was like an internee camp. Besides, he was so dumb that he did it when everyone wanted to go to lunch."

5. Such indirect influence from the top is illustrated in Robert Sullivan, "The Role of the Presidency in Shaping Lower Level Policy-Making Processes," *Polity*, 3 (Winter 1970), 202–21. Similarly, the history of corruption investigations in Washington is replete with officials' claim that their actions were not intended to influence pending cases or decisions, even though others caught the significance of small signals, including a raised eyebrow. See Bernard Schwartz, *The Professor and the Commission* (New York: Knopf, 1959), p. 234.

6. Herbert A. Simon, "Recent Advances in Organization Theory," in Stephen K. Bailey and others, *Research Frontiers in Politics and Government* (Washington, D.C.: The Brookings Institution, 1955), pp. 28–29. For a more recent review of this subject, see Philip Sadler, "Leadership Style, Confidence in Management and Job Satisfaction," *Journal of Applied Behavioral Science*, 6 (January-March 1970), 3–19.

7. Frederick C. Mosher, *Government Reorganizations: Cases and Commentary* (New York: Bobbs-Merrill, 1967). See especially pp. 526 ff.

8. An official known for his wide-ranging use of interoffice consultations said: "This does not mean you bring the bureau chief into the secretary or undersecretary's office and lay out all the sensitive information that he can then use against you with [the interest groups] and Congress."

9. It is revealing that the opening quotations in this article, taken from office-holders in a domestic department, compare almost exactly with the lessons drawn by

a leading political executive in an organization as different as the State Department. See the extensive quotations and discussion in Donald P. Warwick, *A Theory of Public Bureaucracy* (Cambridge, Mass.: Harvard University Press, 1975), p. 209.
10. Dean Rusk, quoted in Morton H. Halperin, *Bureaucratic Politics and Foreign Policy* (Washington, D.C.: the Brookings Institution, 1974), p. 219.

---

# 9.2    Strategies for Professional Success: Making It in National Security Politics

## EARL WALKER and RICHARD THOMAS MATTINGLY, JR.

*U.S. Army officers Earl Walker and Richard Mattingly, Jr., review the bureaucratic politics framework and outline a series of strategies or courses of action for professional success in the national security environment. They conclude with a discussion of the necessity of maintaining ethical balance, which for them ultimately is based on each player's role as "the public's servant, not its master." In this year celebrating the bicentennial of the U.S. Constitution, all of us would be well served to remind ourselves that national security policymakers swear oaths to support and defend the Constitution, not a particular person or organization.*

For the professional in the world of national security policymaking, success is a matter of passionate concern. Success is perceived in many different ways.[1] For some professionals, it is defined in their own self-interest, that is as promotion, prestige, enhanced income, and prospects for later, outside employment. For others, it is the recognition that comes from advancing the interests and prowess of their organization. For still others, success is a sense of gratification that occurs with the promotion of the national interest, however that may be defined. Finally, many professionals are likely to perceive success as the happy coincidence of all these definitions simultaneously.

Success is pursued through various strategies or courses of action that professionals design to wind their way through the national security environment and the processes of decisionmaking and implementation that translate predispositions into recognized policies and programs. That environment is enormously complex, composed of numerous political institutions, public agencies, and individuals both inside and outside the government. The decisionmaking and implementation processes may be even more bewildering because unexpected twists and informal networks frequently overwhelm constitutionally mandated, formalized relationships.

What follows is in the nature of a brief, a condensation of conceptions, ideas, and recommendations about that environment, the national security policymaking process, and some of the successful strategies employed by professionals in this realm. As authors, we can make no claim that this brief will provide a complete description of the environment or the process of national security policymaking. The process and the environment are much too complex to summarize in a few pages. Nor can we claim that the strategies and concerns we outline here are always appropriate, complete, or sufficient to arm professionals for the task. These strategies are based on the experiences and observations of others, on our own (somewhat limited) personal experiences as players in the process, and on our own (more extensive) experiences in studying and teaching in this realm. Our aspirations for this article are to stimulate national security professionals to think creatively about success and about strategies that will enhance the prospects for achieving success. The sources we recommend for further, more careful review may be found in our endnotes.

Our framework for understanding national security policymaking relies upon the bureaucratic politics model and its emphasis that policy outcomes are the result of bargaining and negotiation among organizations and individuals, often described as actors or players. Such a model presumes that there is no best national security policy and recognizes that the actors or players in the process have different resources, varied stakes in the outcome, and conflicting positions or stands on the issue under consideration.[2]

National security issues focus on the creation of national and international political conditions that will protect and extend vital national values. These issues encompass economic, diplomatic, and military dimensions and involve those measures taken by a country to safeguard its interests and objectives against hostile interests, foreign or domestic. This definition identifies some of the key elements—values, government, and the dynamism of domestic and international environments—that must be examined in order to begin to understand national security policymaking.[3] Thus, given these diverse dimensions and elements, no cohesive, coherent, and integrated national security strategy can secure the nation's interests and guide the formulation of national security policies. Thus, because there is no single, discernible U.S. national security strategy, there exist many policies, sometimes in conflict one with another, that constitute the realm of national security affairs.

One must also be careful not to view any single policy as being tied to only one dimension of national security affairs.[4] Most policies operate in more than one dimension. Aid, such as the shipment of U.S. military equipment to Israel, is an example of the economic dimension of national security policy. Since these arms transfers can also affect the readiness of the U.S. armed forces, they have an impact on the military dimension of U.S.

national security as well. Furthermore, arms shipments to Israel have an impact on other nations in the Middle East and thereby affect U.S. diplomatic concerns abroad.

This perspective of national security affairs differs significantly from the view that this realm is dominated by a rational process that responds to international threats through a careful delineation of courses of action and the comparison of those courses of action against some predetermined criteria for choice.[5] This second perspective fails to discern the predominance of domestic and bureaucratic politics in national security affairs. Presidents and members of Congress care more about domestic constituencies than Third World debt; the sensitivities of neutral, emerging nations; or, for that matter, about allied reactions to U.S. initiatives. One need only to consider the lackadaisical U.S. response to the debilitating levels of debt piled up by Latin American nations or to the annual reductions in foreign economic aid to confirm this point. Some professionals in some organizations may care about promoting rational processes, but their agencies and organizational leadership value other things much more highly, such as institutional prowess and individual advancement. In such a contest over values, rationality rarely prevails.

The Reagan administration recognized early, even prior to the inauguration, that political factors contribute to bureaucratic intransigence and policy failure in the domestic policy arena. The strategies used by the Reagan team in domestic policymaking and implementation proved masterful in dealing with public agencies and Congress; they included a carefully planned and forward-looking transition organization for assuming the presidency, a cautious and thorough appointment process for political executives, and the use of a Cabinet Council process to coordinate the administration's initiatives. These strategies provided Reagan spectacular early successes. He was able to garner congressional acceptance and rally public support on many domestic issues, particularly those dealing with fiscal policy. Subsequent legislative and bureaucratic victories were later spun out from these early successes.[6] On national security matters, however, the Reagan record has been less impressive.

## THE NATIONAL SECURITY
## DECISIONMAKING ENVIRONMENT

The study of national security affairs in a noncrisis environment emphasizes the dynamics of the decisionmaking process and its central features of compromise, negotiation, and coalition building among the players. Participants are many and varied in the national security policy process, each influenced by his or her own definition of successful policy outcomes and colored by particularistic, organizational, professional, and political perspectives. Indeed, as Samuel Huntington has observed, "Policy is not the result of deductions from a clear statement of national objectives. It is the product of the competition of purposes within individuals and groups and among individuals and groups. It is the result of politics, not logic, more an area than a unity."[7] This competition, or game, as it has been referred to, determines who participates in policy decisions, what information is considered, which options are examined, and how decisions are implemented. Apparent discontinuities between the interested players in the game and a final policy often have their source in the structures and processes of the national security system. Thus outcomes are seldom what any single player, or any group of players would have expected. As President John Kennedy observed, "The essence of ultimate decision remains impenetrable to the observer—often, indeed, to the decider himself."[8]

A bureaucratic perspective emphasizes values such as checks and balances, opportunities for bargaining among diverse actors, and the demand for widespread participation by many interested parties. The emphasis here is on the representation of diverse interests by differing players, each of whom may see the stakes involved in a decisionmaking situation differently.[9] The final decision is evaluated on the basis of the opportunities that various actors have to influence the bargaining that produces some outcome, which may very well be maintenance of the status quo, because each of the various participants may check and balance each other too effectively for anyone to emerge as dominant. The origin of this model lies in the domestic policy process, a process not known for the most efficient, effective, or rational policy decisions.

There are very few substantial differences between domestic and national security policymaking. The most prominent is the degree that the latter is somewhat less affected by the conflict between domestic interest groups and by public opinion in general,[10] and somewhat more affected by the dominance of the president and his bureaucratic aides.[11] The similarities between the two areas are more numerous. National security affairs, like domestic affairs, are dominated by the interplay of different interests within the bureaucracy, with the president as arbiter, judge, or mediator, and Congress serving to sanctify or legitimate the outcome. Although the locale and actors differ, national security policies also share the same procedural style and substantive results as domestic policies.[12]

The great virtue of this system is that it produces policies that are tolerable to all the forces that have a stake in the outcome. The interests of bureaucracies, governmental officials and high-ranking advisors to the president, interest groups, Congress, the mass media and public opinion, and the prevailing ideological assumptions of the president and his national security advisors all play some role in the making of national security policy.[13] However, the emphasis on producing policies that reflect a consensus, irrespective of the substantive content of the outcome, has tended to result in particular kinds of policies. Typically, they are short-range, of limited scope, and very much like their predecessors. They are policies which are capable of only slow and marginal adaptation to new conditions. They are primarily effective in handling issues that are very much like earlier issues. Indeed, the policies that emerge often reflect the extraordinary complexities of a process that includes international issues and events, domestic concerns, and the nearly constant penetration of the American political system by global issues and forces. These external forces can range from the price of petroleum or the rate of inflation to questions of global survival.

## Organizational Clientele and Parochialism

A peculiarity unique to national security organizations is their clientele. Most organizations can be thought of as the institutionalization of the values of some group. In fact the highest achievement of any group is to see its interests permanently represented in the government. Thus, for example, farmers are represented by the Department of Agriculture and teachers by the Department of Education. However, for the Defense Department (DoD), the State Department, and the Central Intelligence Agency (CIA), the whole society benefits from their efforts to the national protect security, a function economists call a collective good. Such collective goods are seldom as vigorously defended as more particularized goods such as agricultural subsidy payments or student loans.

Lacking in intensely committed clientele, national security organizations find themselves more dependent on political leaders for support. Thus presidents and members of Congress have more capacity to influence national security policymaking than they do in many other policy arenas. Of elected officials, the president alone has a truly national clientele. Thus, his support and sponsorship are crucial factors in national security policymaking. He stands out as a dominant force with which all other players must contend.[14]

In spite of their clear constitutional mandate in national security affairs, members of Congress influence policymaking in varied ways. In time of crisis, they usually play little or no role. In matters of strategy, they serve more to oversee the process and check the president and function more as a source of appeal for disaffected professionals than as a sustained base of support. In structural matters involving weapons systems, personnel policies, foreign aid and organizational arrangements, their support is crucial—some would say seminal.[15]

The most prominent organizations in national security affairs are the National Security Council (NSC), Department of Defense, Joint Chiefs of Staff (JCS), Department of State, Central Intelligence Agency, Federal Bureau of Investigation (FBI), not to mention a two-house Congress that can challenge presidential initiatives with hundreds of legislative actions initiated by a multitude of committees and subcommittees. Also involved are such essentially domestic executive departments as Commerce, Labor, Agriculture, and Treasury, all of which have some interest in national security policy because they wish to enhance exports, protect U.S. labor, or seek a favorable balance of trade. No one political institution or agency has the authority or reach to coordinate and oversee all that is national security policy. The result is a series of U.S. policies characterized by discontinuity and, inevitably, inconsistency.

Although the Congress, the president, and national security agencies attempt to develop national policies that provide, from their perspective, the all-encompassing answer to national security problems, they invariably are able to consider only a few of the factors that constitute effective policy-making. The result is sometimes parochial national policies that fall far short of the nation's security needs. Such outcomes should not be surprising. After all, each organization in the national security policymaking process has different responsibilities, outlooks, and horizons.

Each agency in the national security structure shares three characteristics: it seeks to pursue its own goals, to enhance its own power, and to promote its own position in the government hierarchy. National security organizations are motivated by the desire to protect their own self-interests, and they define issues and take stands on them in a manner perceived to promote those interests.[16] This parochial tendency is natural, pervasive, and insures that the world and the issues of the day are seen from different perspectives.

Furthermore, the stakes for each organization and individual are different as well. Even within a given cabinet department, natural rivals submit claims on the budget. This rivalry is rooted in parochialism.[17] For example, within the Department of Defense each of the four armed services naturally feels that its contribution to the defense and security of the United States is the most important and, therefore, seeks the largest share of the budget in order to best equip itself for any missions it might be called on to carry out.[18] Within the State Department this same parochial rivalry can be seen in the competition among the regional and functional bureaus for budget, personnel resources, and influence. Between cabinet departments, for example the State and Defense departments, parochialism breeds competition.[19] Far from being neutral or impartial administrators, desiring only to carry out orders or maximize national interests, these national security organizations frequently take policy positions destined to maximize their own influence relative to that of other agencies.[20] What results then is an undeclared but understood competition between agencies for scarce resources, influence, and, ultimately, power.

Thus the parochial nature of organizations participating in national security policymaking is one of the core concepts of the bureaucratic politics approach. Each organization and subgroup within that organization sees its interests as being consistent with the national interest. Each defines the reason for its organization's existence in terms of "essence"—the core responsibilities and missions a particular organization has or should have. This "essence" reflects the organization's culture, which is the sum total of its experiences over time, the expectations of its clientele and overseers, the kinds of leaders it has attracted, and the cadres of professionals who have dominated the agency.[21]

## The Dominance of Professionals

The professional executives and administrators who participate in the game of bureaucratic politics, are late-career military, foreign service, and intelligence officers as well as policy analysts. It is the skills of these professionals that give national security organizations their problem-recognition and problem-solving capacities as well as their lore about prospects for policy success and future developments.[22]

The role of these senior professionals is extensive and decisive in the formulation and implementation of national security policy for four reasons. First, most routine decisions are delegated to senior professionals. Second, new issues within the organizational hierarchy take shape as they move up through succeeding levels of more senior professionals and are not drastically revised by the political executives who are disposed to give their imprimatur to what professionals have already worked out. Third, political executives need reliable and specific information that has been processed, verified, analyzed, and evaluated by senior professionals who can draw on long experience and accumulated knowledge.[23] Finally, decisions must be implemented by these same professionals. Senior professionals will see the policy or program through their own lenses, lenses developed through years of socialization, and will then enact it through repertoires they previously designed.

Thus professionals provide ideas on policy alternatives and make recommendations that the principal decisionmakers can discuss and act on. It is at the senior professional level of national security organizations that day-to-day decisions are made and programs carried out. Professionals also play a direct role in crisis decisionmaking—in most major policy decisions through analysis of information and alternatives for the principle decision-makers to act on.[24]

The ideal prize in the bureaucratic game of national security politics is that for his or her efforts, the individual receives personal and professional recognition at the same time that the essence of the organization is enhanced. There is not a necessary conflict between action that will advance the purposes of a bureaucratic organization in the national security apparatus and action that will advance the career of a single member of that organization.[25]

It is conceivable that an ambitious and intelligent person might never have to choose among (or for that matter recognize) the conflicting courses of action, one of which would promote the national interest, another the attainment of the objectives for which the organization is created, and still another that would advance one's own personal objectives.[26]

Therefore, in the end, professionals concerned with foreign affairs and defense policy have a profound impact on policy outcomes. They generally develop their positions on national security issues and policies largely by calculating the national interest in terms of the organizational interests of the career services to which they belong—be it the branches of military service, the State Department, or the CIA. This conclusion is not to discount the influence of individual self-interest and personal motivations for job performance such as power, promotion, prestige, and money income.[27] However, the world view of national security professionals is more strongly dominated by their particular organization, which has socialized and trained them to accept certain views and expectations about the world, the nation, and the role of politics. Thus their primary loyalty remains to their own career profession and to their organizations. Where several professions exist within one organization, the needs of the profession are more salient.

For example, in the Department of Defense, career army officers agree that the essence of their profession is ground combat capability, whereas navy officers generally see their principal mission as maintaining combat ships to control the seas against potential enemies. Although professionals at all levels of both these branches of the armed services have an unquestionable devotion to national security, there is an inherent conflict between the two when faced with limited budgetary and personnel resources that both must share.[28] Their definition of national security rests with skills and knowledge they have achieved through a lengthy process of training and socialization. One needs but a quick glance at the military profession to understand this point.

To pick one national security profession by way of illustration, army officers constitute the world's oldest public profession. Their traditions and ethics have accrued over centuries of war and condition how soldiers behave today. Active and retired army officers are among the principal architects of the modern state. They were responsible in the United States for building the first roads, bridges, canals, and railroads. Since the beginning of the republic, they also have been given a salient hand in governing as presidents, cabinet secretaries, and agency administrators.

The army officer's personnel system is archetypical. It carefully recruits, socializes, trains, promotes, and retires its officers with established milestones along the way for further education and training. The system is designed to inculcate a commitment to accepted viewpoints and ideals and to condition officers for service to the state. One author has summarized this world view as conservative realism, which celebrates order, obedience, and state security. The ideals of the officer corps are perhaps best summarized in the West Point motto of "Duty, Honor, Country." Those officers who cannot be conditioned for service to the state either select themselves out or are eliminated by the system.

Preparation for an army professional is extensive. A service's professional culture is very carefully inculcated. A senior army officer with twenty years of service will have attended at least four in-residence professional development courses varying from three to ten months duration, and each will have completed several courses on the conduct of staff actions and procedures. Similar requirements for initial training and ongoing professional development courses exist for foreign service officers and defense establishment policy analysts as well.[29]

## UNDERSTANDING THE GAME:
## THE NATIONAL SECURITY DECISIONMAKING PROCESS

Thus professional and organizational parochialism affect the national security policymaking process. Since professional participants are preoccupied with their career system and their organizations, they define the interest of the nation as a whole in these terms. For example, professionals provide information to political executives so that issues will be perceived in ways supportive of the career system. Similarly, options are presented in menu form, each of which will support and enhance the career system and the overarching organizational essence. Even when decisions are implemented, professionals will interpret orders based on the perspective of their career systems and may seek to delay, alter, or even disobey directives.[30]

Therefore, national security policymaking involves a struggle for power to control, and to influence those who control, national security decisions. It has also been called the art of the possible, or the process by which the conflicting demands of various individuals and subunits in the national security apparatus are satisfied through compromise. Indeed, the reason for the use of the word politics reflects the fact that national security policy emerges from a process of simultaneous conflict and accommodation among the multitude of participating professional groups, each with its own competing viewpoint. Policymaking means bargaining; negotiations are required and deals must be struck. Negotiations occur throughout the executive branch as political executives and professionals in one department seek support for their position in another. Since no one participant is powerful enough to force a decision when disagreement exists among the participants, the eventual decision is a result of compromises and consensus. Jerel Rosati points out in his discussion of the participants in the SALT I policymaking process that national security policies are "political resultants" in the following sense:

> What happens is not chosen as a solution to the problem but rather results from compromise, conflict, and confusion of officials with diverse interests and unequal influence; political in the sense that the activity from which decisions and actions emerge is best characterized as bargaining along regularized channels among individual members of the government.[31]

Thus decisions are the result of the pushing and pulling among the various participants as they attempt to advance their concepts of personal, group, organizational, and national interests.

It should not be surprising then that the type of national security policies that result from this give and take and mutual consent among the many participants are incremental in nature. Incrementalism is politically expedient because it is easier to reach agreement when the matter in dispute among the various competing groups are only modifications of existing programs rather than policy issues of great magnitude or an all-or-nothing character. The evidence is overwhelming that policymakers do not choose the option or set of options that has the maximum chance for realizing desired goals.[32] Instead, they settle for the first possibility that satisfies minimal requirements or expectations, one they believe will get them by and, at the same time, best promotes their interests. Herbert Simon has nicely labeled this *satisficing* behavior.[33]

Since national security decision makers operate under conditions of uncertainty with regard to future consequences of their actions, incremental decisions reduce the risks and costs of uncertainty. Incrementalism is also realistic because it recognizes that decisionmakers lack time and other resources needed to engage in comprehensive, or rational, analysis of alternative approaches to the issues at hand. Moreover, all participants in national security policymaking are essentially pragmatic, seeking not always the single best way to deal with an issue but, more accurately, something that will work. Incrementalism, in short, yields limited, practicable, acceptable decisions.

The consequences of such a national security policy process should not be alarming. The overwhelming complexity of the national security machinery limits what members of various organizations can do and inhibits the disposition of political appointees to act hastily in circumstances where action may not be appropriate. Expeditious, even impulsive initiatives by presidents and senior political executives in noncrisis situations are seldom acceptable to Congress; the dominant rule in U.S. politics is that consensus must be carefully built if initiatives are to be sustained.[34] The fact that policy is formulated and implemented by a large number of individuals in a complex institutional arrangement reduces the probability of taking decisive action. Political executives and professionals within different agencies usually disagree: they want different policies, and they define the situation differently because of their differing vantage points. The result is that policy formulation often boils down to a tug of war among competing agencies.[35] National security decisionmaking is a political game with high stakes, in which differences are usually settled with minimum costs to the participants.

## STRATEGIES FOR SUCCESS

Because of the variety of purposes among subordinate national security professionals, and especially among career military officers, the game of politics remains intense—with vested interests, interorganizational conflicts, intraorganizational rivalries, and the existence of best national security policies as varied and numerous as the individuals and organizations participating. Nevertheless, senior professionals have developed multiple strategies for playing the game of bureaucratic politics in national security policymaking. Participants report that these strategies will enhance prospects for individual success while at the same time advancing the purposes of their organizations.

### Accepting Environmental Constraints

It is a simple fact that there exist certain parameters within which individuals in the national security arena will have to operate during their careers and that will confront the national security policymaking environment over the rest of this century. Because these parameters will not change, successful national security professionals find it better not to waste time and energy objecting to them; rather, professionals take them as a given and go on from there.

For instance, it seems clear that national security decisions in the United States are shaped by the Constitution, which divides the making and implementation of national security policy among the different branches of government. One can not lightly dismiss the preeminent concern of the U.S. political culture for the potential of the abuse of power when in the hands of a centralized authority.[36] Consequently, successful professionals accept that the U.S. national security policymaking system encourages deliberation and incrementalism and prefer delay to impulsive action.[37]

The concept of rule of law is basic to the democratic form of government. Because this central tenet stipulates that laws and not individuals safeguard constitutional freedoms, national security professionals are constrained.[38] Thus, they may not initiate activities contrary to law. The investigation of the unauthorized sale of weapons to Iran and the use of the profits for assistance to *Contra* rebels in Nicaragua arranged for by Marine Lt. Col. Oliver North from 1982 to 1986 is an example of the fact that government officials are not above the law and that capricious behavior is not condoned by the U.S. public or by political elites.

Not only must professionals come to accept legal constraints, they must also accept resource and demographic constraints. Competing demands from other government programs ensure that there will never be enough money for the DoD to provide for all the forces that are thought to be needed. For example, when the Reagan administration assumed office in 1981, it added a little over $200 billion to the five-year defense program left by the Carter administration. However, because of economic constraints, mounting deficits, and competing demands from other areas of the budget, proposed defense expenditures were cut back by the president's Office of Management and Budget (OMB) and by the Congress.[39]

Demographic constraints must not be overlooked either. For example, in recruiting for the armed forces, the number of eighteen to twenty-one year olds is declining. By 1990 this age group will be almost 20 percent below the 1979 level, which was the peak year for that age cohort.[40] Concurrently, recruiting for the armed services will also be affected by economic growth in the private sector, which will increase competition for these personnel resources.

Successful professionals also recognize other more specific forces directly relevant to their own organization. For example, political executives within the agency and in superintending cabinet departments are worthy of careful study. Savvy professionals seek to understand the background and operating agendas of cabinet secretaries, under secretaries, and assistant secretaries who work in their area of responsibility. More specifically, professionals should seek answers to such questions as: What are the officials' educational backgrounds and professional training? Where have they been employed? What are their individual formative experiences? How do they think about problems? What historical experiences most likely have influenced their outlooks? From these questions a professional can infer likely reactions to proposed policies or programs and the best approaches for proposing new initiatives.[41] In essence, such knowledge is a boon to advocacy, a responsibility all professionals must undertake.

Professionals must also study and learn to accept the operating procedures of hierarchically senior staffs and executives. Thus, one might find dealings with budget examiners in the Office of Management and Budget and staffers on the House Appropriations Committee frustrating, but wise professionals accept these groups as givens in the environment and find ways to work with them to achieve organizational goals.

Another frustrating, but pervasive, reality is government reorganization. These reorganizations may change program emphasis, reflect the managerial style of a superior, and modify the power balance among individuals and organizations. The efforts to work out the bugs of the reorganization as well as the inordinant amount of time figuring out why a reorganization occurred and who are the resultant winners and losers are time consuming and frustrating.[42] For example, with the advent of the Reagan administration's Strategic Defense Initiative (SDI), it was necessary for agencies within the military service staffs of the Department of Defense to reorganize to meet the newly assigned (or perceived) responsibilities. Confusion was rampant within each service staff and between service staffs, as well as with the SDI staff agencies of the Joint Chiefs of Staff as to what agencies were responsible for various aspects of the SDI program and why. Each service staff agency had its own expert with recommendations and advice colored by his or her respective service and organizational perspectives. Yet, this should have been expected. In adapting to this change the military services were attempting to ingest or acquire control over the change. Reorganizations, like other environmental constraints, are best accepted as givens and exploited if possible.

Therefore, national security professionals confront a number of external and task-specific forces in their daily activities. These forces define the setting in which each national security organization must operate. At times these forces help enlarge the role of a particular national security organization and at other times they limit the organization's activities. Thus, professionals cannot view their organizations in isolation but rather must understand them as being immersed in a framework that imposes both constraints and opportunities.

## Respecting the Process

We have pointed out that the contrived nature of national security organizations means that they contain inherent sources of conflict. Externally, they have vigorous impulses to conflict with other agencies because their goals reflect differing priorities or interests. Internally, each organization functions by means of adjustment and compromises among competitive and even conflicting elements in their structure and membership.[43] Therefore, the national security process can be more readily understood if relationships between national security organizations are viewed as an outcome of a continuing tug of war. The success of one organization competing with another for increased resource allocation and influence with the principle national security decisionmakers rests on the strength it possesses in terms of effective and efficient use of its resources on hand, credibility, and expertise. Just as each side in a tug of war must carefully marshall its resources, national security organizations must position themselves to minimize weaknesses, recognize the importance of timing in employing organization strengths, and maintain a continual effort to enhance the essence of the organization. Not unlike the losing team engaged in a tug of war conflict, a national security organization can lose its enthusiasm for innovative ideas or may make a strategic error and employ its resources at the wrong time. The implications of this analogy are that national security organizations are always in the process of change and that the constancy sometimes attributed to the national security policymaking system is exaggerated by the fact that the label for describing the system remains the same even when the processes within each organization do not. Thus, because processes are in flux, careful attention must be paid to them.

Many participants feel that to succeed they must accept the political nature of the national security policymaking process. Such a recognition will help the mid-level and senior professionals better understand the diversity and seeming inconsistency of the goals that national security policy must pursue. Furthermore, such a recognition can save participants from excessive cynicism, which can cripple enthusiasm and fetter effectiveness. To be a successful player, professionals advise that one must jump into the game with both feet; hesitating means losing a chance to play at that point.[44] Finally, by accepting the political nature of national security policymaking, participants feel they can more realistically assess their probable impact on outcomes and the importance of policy and organizational advocacy.

Conflict should not be perceived as only dysfunctional to a national security organization.[45] It can improve morale, and it can lead to solutions that are creative both from an organizational and national standpoint. Thus the national security professional is best advised not to be concerned with the issue of how to eliminate disagreement or even all conflict, but rather how to guide the conflict so that wider organizational and national benefits may be attained.[46]

## Advancing the Organization

A national security professional who expects to succeed must recognize that organizational advancement must be a central priority. Organizational loyalty may be as necessary to a professional working in the national security hierarchy as is national loyalty to a person seeking election to the presidency. Because national security professionals have a relatively narrow outlook, they are preoccupied with the unique importance of their organization to the overall national security mission. In their view, national security can be improved primarily through the recommendations provided by their organization. Thus, professionals in the Department of the Army staff tend to feel that the questionable areas within today's national military strategy are derived from the influence of the sea mentality of the navy staff.

This loyalty to organizational goals is significant for national policy because it greatly affects organizational effectiveness. That is, in the absence of such a feeling of commitment by organizational professionals, their organizations are less likely to have a significant impact on policy outcomes. Thus, because each organization represents distinct values judged to be crucial to national security decisionmaking, the failure of professionals to take positions energetically may mean that all sides of an issue are not adequately represented, thereby unbalancing an initiative and creating later difficulties. For example, the failure of CIA professionals to energetically argue that the Shah of Iran was in considerable political difficulty in the late 1970s led to the nearly complete surprise of U.S. decisionmakers who did not forsee the Shah's precipitous downfall and the subsequent installation of the Khomeini regime. Had these professionals more energetically pursued organizational goals, a CIA failure might have been a CIA success.[47]

Demonstrated loyalty to the organization and its agenda also frees professionals from unwanted constraints by political executives. When political executives come to establish a relationship of trust with subordinate professionals, professional opportunities are considerably expanded. As Hugh Heclo has observed, political executives and professionals must exchange commitments (a relationship he describes as trust) in order for both to succeed in bureaucratic politics. The best way to build trust is through conditionally cooperative behavior in which both executives and professionals seek to sustain each other's goals as long as each side continues to perform in mutually supportive ways.[48] Through a relationship of trust, professionals can find their opportunities for success much enhanced.

*Developing Interpersonal Skills*

Two more essential skills that national security professionals must possess in order to succeed in the game of bureaucratic politics are interpersonal and negotiating skills.[49]

Interpersonal skills include the abilities to work effectively as a member of a group, build cooperative efforts within the group, and interact successfully with members of other organizations. Successful professionals recognize that national security organizations are staffed by people who bring many different attitudes, values, and personal characteristics with them and learn to work with diverse personalities to achieve results. Part and parcel of possessing these interpersonal skills is being aware of the existence and implications of informal groups. Organizational charts may specify the hierarchical chain of command as well as communications networks and formal rules; but human friendships, peer group support, or alliance networks alter these formal structural principles.[50] These informal groups and supportive ties can be beneficial to the national security organization and the individual because they can bypass ineffective people and augment a professional's influence to allow access to decisionmaking networks from which he or she might otherwise be excluded. Professionals learn to use these networks of former associates to promote organizational purpose.

To build such networks, or course, professionals have learned that the directive style of leadership, which served them so well in field, line organizations, is no longer successful. Because no individual is truly subordinate to another—rather all are carriers of certain organizational values in the seemingly never-ending rounds of negotiation that produce policy—relationships cannot be fostered if rank becomes the criterion for establishing and maintaining relationships. Furthermore, rank and hierarchy become almost meaningless when the essence of the exercise is not implementation of programs as is done in the field, but rather deciding what should be done by the organization and how that purpose is to be achieved.

In lieu of the directive style, a consensus-building, work-along-with style is preferred. That is, successful professionals recognize the value of their team, the need to sustain team or group morale and purpose, and to communicate openly not only with fellow team members, but also with members of other teams whose purposes are likely to be at cross purposes from one's own.[51] Such team play may at first strike professionals fresh from line duty in the field as horribly inefficient and ponderous, if not disloyal. Seemingly every detail must be coordinated and cleared and checked and consented to. Yet the end results are invariably superior because more human judgment is involved in the decision, and, with the agreement of all on the team and others on different teams, implementation is likely to be more successful.

Successful professionals find that they must act like politicians—a fate that many at first find abhorrent. That is, they must learn to persuade, coax, cajole, bargain, listen, and, yes, charm. In essence, successful professionals are required to learn another side of leadership, a side that most politicians have learned to use as a prerequisite for success. That side of leadership is more persuasive than directive, more receptive than responsive, more disposed to skills of conciliation and negotiation than to insistence upon obedience, and more inclined to warmth and humor.[52]

### Learning to Negotiate

Since all national security policy making involves varying perspectives, purposes, and principles, conflict among professionals within each group and across groups is endemic. Such conflict can become intensely bitter as human egos become attached to these purposes and principles and as perspectives are bounded by a human need to win the conflict rather than to satisfy the legitimate needs of the organization. Yet the reverse side of bitterness and winning may be to overemphasize relationships with others and thereby cede important organizational concerns in the hope of maintaining what professionals are fond of calling good working relationships.

Perhaps the best exit from this muddle is what Roger Fisher and William Ury call principled negotiation. Such a negotiation style refuses to be drawn into bargaining over the various positions that parties to the negotiation take. Arguing or debating over whether the other side's point of view is sensible makes no sense, because it is inefficient and likely to endanger ongoing relationships.[53] Rather, principled negotiation has four specific methods: separating professionals as people from the problem; focusing on interests and not positions; inventing options where all sides are likely to gain something (what Fisher and Ury call win-win strategies); and using objective criteria for negotiations.[54]

The first method of separating professionals as people from the problem recognizes the importance of maintaining close working relationships among professionals as they bargain. This entails frank recognition of the varying perceptions of the problem at hand; that is, each side seeks to understand the other side's point of view. Equally important are an open acceptance that emotions are likely to play a role in the negotiations and that active listening and purposeful, candid presentations are crucial to success.

The second method is to focus on interests that lie behind the positions professionals take on issues. By recognizing that such interests exist, that some interests of both or all parties may be shared as well as be at cross purposes, and that a candid exchange of their interests will promote understanding, the parties are will on their way to success.

Once professionals recognize that interests and not positions are at the root of the conflict, inventing options in which all may gain or win becomes more plausible. In essence, the ideal strategy for both sides is a win-win outcome in which both win, and not a win-lose or lose-win outcome, in which one side loses. If both sides win in the negotiation by advancing the organizational interests of all concerned parties, then negotiations have been a success and personal relationships can flourish.

Finally, professionals must recognize the importance of objective criteria in principled negotiations. Such criteria seek to produce wise agreements arrived at in an amicable fashion and involve fair standards and fair procedures for decision. Fair standards are legitimate ones that are viewed by each side as objective and reasonable. Fair procedures for negotiation and ratification of agreements must also be agreed upon. For example, during negotiations at the Law of the Sea Conference, India insisted upon a high initial fee for companies engaged in deep sea mining. The United States objected. Stalemate ensued until a researcher at the Massachusetts Institute of Technology developed a model that convinced both sides about the necessity for a small fee. In the end, the United States and India accepted the model's criteria.[55]

Thus, the art of negotiation is a crucial precursor to professional success in the national security community. All national security organizations and their members should realize that issues can divide and unify them over time. That is, one issue may divide two organizations today, but tomorrow another issue is likely to unify them against others.[56] Although conflict is endemic, achieving consensus is crucial because not only do all seek to win but also all must seek to promote harmonious relationships.

## Conceptualizing the Enterprise

Professionals also must possess the ability to conceptualize the enterprise that includes the organization itself, the people within it, and its purposes. Both intellectual skills and vision are crucial here. Intellectual skills are those stimulated by education, self-study, and reading. Specifically, successful professionals have developed abilities to write cogently and concisely without flowery language and without lapsing into jargon that can be understood only within the confines of their own organization. They also speak clearly and confidently; their presentations are well enunciated and rehearsed. Finally, these successful professionals have learned to reason in thoughtful and persuasive ways. They appeal to logic and to well-accepted criteria for reasoning through to a conclusion.

Vision is equally important in conceptualizing the enterprise. Vision is the ability to see the enterprise as a whole, its interconnections, the things that influence it, and the ways in which it influences others. In short, this is the coordinating, synthesizing function that is so much needed in national security policymaking. The high caliber, national security professional must be able to see things as a whole and in reciprocal, cause-and-effect relation. This ability to see things sensitively and simultaneously may be the most important skill of all.[57]

There are a variety of techniques to use in conceptualizing either an issue at hand, the organization with whom professionals are negotiating, or political executives with whom professionals must deal. Perhaps the most concise is offered by Richard Neustadt and Ernest May. They advocate a series of mini-methods to enhance prudent decisionmaking and discourage the ebullient candoism that new professionals often bring to national security affairs. They are suspicious that all things can be done in government, and they suggest more disciplined thought about what can realistically be achieved. Their plea is to harness history and experience, either past or very current, so that professionals might decide what to do today about the prospects unfolding tomorrow.[58]

To summarize their methods very briefly, they propose the following four steps: clear definition of the situation; careful testing of presumptions and analogies; thoughtful efforts to discern the history of the issue; and the placing of organizations and key political executives in context with other historical developments. First, to define the situation, they propose that professionals and political executives carefully identify the situation that seems to call for action. This definition is done by sorting details into lists of what is definitively known, what is unclear about the situation, and what is presumed to be true but has not been established as true. Once these lists are created, professionals can seek to attack what is unknown or unclear and what is presumed. To clarify the unknown, one always asks for the big picture; that is, one asks those who might know what is the story and thereby clarify more of the unknowns about the issue.

The second technique is to consider very carefully the presumptions or analogies others make about this situation and other situations that have occurred in the past. To Neustadt and May, analogies and presumptions constitute perhaps the largest danger in decisionmaking, for by comparing one event or issue with another, professionals and political executives substitute fallacious judgment for clear thinking. One way to test presumptions is to ask others two questions: How much of your own money would you wager on that analogy or presumption? What fresh facts would cause you to change this presumption?

Third, successful professionals study the history of an issue. Simply stated journalistic devices are useful here—ask the journalist's six questions: *When* did the issue arise? *What* did the matter concern then and now? *Where* did the issue arise and where does it now reside? *Who* has been and is now involved? *How* was it resolved in the past? *Why* has it been resolved that way?

Finally, to conceptualize the enterprise fully, professionals must seek to place key decisionmakers and organizations. Placing is comparing historical events and personal or organizational detail by creating a time chart in which events are portrayed simultaneously with details. Thus, placing decision-makers is to portray years on one column, large historical events on another (World War I, the Depression, Watergate), and then the personal details of the decisionmaker on still a third. Such a chart can be used to make inferences about where decisionmakers are likely to stand on an issue and can greatly enhance the professional's ability to persuade or advocate a position.

Placing organizations is a similar exercise, although instead of personal details, details of institutional history, hierarchical structures, professional cadres, personnel system incentives, and internal planning systems are arrayed in the third column. Organizational placement can help professionals better understand their own organization and its patterns, as well as other organizations and their patterns, thereby enhancing prospects for success.

Conceptualizing the enterprise is thus an important strategy in professional success. Not only must professionals develop intellectual skills to work effectively within the national security community, they must also seek a vision of the enterprise that attempts to see it as a whole.

## Maintaining Ethical Balance

Countless sermons have been preached and printed on the ethics of public service. These sermons formally recognize that definitive policy decisions made by national security professionals often have at their base conflicting ethical issues, such as whether to give precedence to the public interest or to the narrower demands of profession, department, agency or self. This ambivalent position has led some sensitive administrative theorists like Chester Barnard to say that the chief qualification of public service is the ability to resolve these competing ethical codes—legal, technical, personal, professional and organizational.  Dealing effectively with the moral complexities of national security organizations is a challenge all professionals and political executives must face.[59]

In a memorial essay to administrative theorist Paul Appleby, the late Stephen K. Bailey discussed what he believed were essential qualities of moral behavior in the public service.  At the core of Bailey's essay is his emphasis of three moral qualities that are applicable to professionals in national security policymaking: "optimism, courage, and fairness tempered by charity."[60]  Optimism is the ability of national security professionals to deal with morally ambiguous situations confidently and purposefully. Courage is the capacity to decide and act in the face of unclear circumstances when inaction, indecision, or agreement with the popular trend would provide the easy solution.  Fairness tempered by charity allows for the maintenance of standards of justice in decisions affecting the public interest. "The best solution," writes Bailey, "rarely is without its costs. . . . And one mark of moral maturity is an appreciation of the inevitability of untoward and often malignant effects of benign moral choices."[61]

We are not so naive as to provide a description of desired conduct in national security affairs.  Such descriptions are too often couched in such general terms that the professional can easily justify his behavior as proper. What we are emphasizing is an inner check—a professional's own sense of responsibility to the public.  We suggest that when national security decisionmakers are confronted with difficult choices, they talk to themselves in terms of various standards or principles.  They may have to compromise particular norms or values in a given situation (loyalty to superior or organization), but they can be reasonably comfortable if they recognize that certain other values, namely integrity and self-respect, are enhanced by so doing.  Granted, there are those who are frankly skeptical of this type of check; human nature being what it is, they are convinced that the main reliance must be placed on external controls over the national security professional.[62]  The disagreement is basically a question of emphasis, for we recognize that if national security professionals were to forget that their proper role is as the public's servant and not its master, a variety of institutions—including the Congress, the courts, and the press—would be quick to remind them of the subordinate nature of their role.[63]  However, the national security community will prosper in effectiveness and public esteem only when professionals and executives police themselves.

## CONCLUSION

In this article we have portrayed the national security environment and the process of decisionmaking in security affairs as a complex milieu dominated by bureaucratic politics. Our model of bureaucratic politics is one reliant upon the observations of others and cobbled together in a fashion that reflects our own experiences in this realm. Thus the world of national security affairs is not much different from domestic affairs. Politics predominates. It is not politics of the electoral, partisan sort, but rather politics as competition for power among elected public officials, appointed political executives, and highly trained professionals.

Given these realities, we have provided various strategies for public professionals, strategies that in fact are those most often adopted by successful politicians as well. These strategies are most likely to yield success in national security affairs. At the outset we defined success in a variety of ways: Success can reflect individual self-interest, organizational advancement, or the promotion if the national interest. We have not sought any one definition of success because each player in the game of bureaucratic politics has his or her own internalized measures. Our contention is that the strategies we advance will promote all or any one of these measures of success.

By accepting environmental constraints and respecting national and organizational policy processes, professionals can not only advance their interests, but avoid debilitating cynicism and frustration. Recognition that organizational purposes must be advanced if the national security decision process is to function effectively can provide professionals reassurance that their efforts need not be thought of as parochial. Interpersonal and negotiation skills as well as the ability to conceptualize the enterprise can enhance effectiveness. Finally, the maintenance of an ethical balance can sustain life-long careers.

These strategies for success are far from novel. Democratic politicians have used them for centuries. In the end, then, we are essentially calling for professionals to act more like politicians because, in fact, in the highly politicized atmosphere of Washington, D.C., everyone who is a success is part politician, part specialist. Politicians have a bad name. What we all forget too easily is that democratic politicians have sustained North American government for three centuries and the United States for two. In the process they have provided the United States more freedom than any other people at any time of history have ever enjoyed, economic prosperity that is the envy of the globe, and national security that has thwarted all enemies, be they foreign or domestic. National security professionals should set their sights by these achievements—not frown on politicians, but rather seek to be more political in their behavior.

# NOTES

1. J. Richard Hackman, "A New Strategy for Job Enrichment," in Fred Kramer, ed., *Perspectives on Public Bureaucracy* (Cambridge: Winthrop Publishing, 1981) discusses motivations for individual success. Also, a principal goal of most organizations is the maintenance and enhancement of the organization's health, defined in terms of growth in budget and personnel. Robert Trice, "The Policymaking Process: Actors and Their Impact," in John Reichart and Steven Sturm, eds., *American Defense Policy*, 5th ed. (Baltimore: Johns Hopkins Press, 1983) states the focus of most national security professionals is the nation as a whole and base their policy positions and actions on national interests. We are particularly grateful to David Kozak for his insistence that we write this paper. Thanks also to Daniel Kaufman and David Clark who provided us very useful comments, most of which we have included here.

2. The bureaucratic/government politics model is based on Graham T. Allison, *Essence of Decision* (Boston: Little, Brown, 1971); I.M. Destler, *Presidents, Bureaucrats and Foreign Policy* (Princeton, N.J.: Princeton University Press, 1972); Morton Halperin, *Bureaucratic Politics and Foreign Policy* (Washington, D.C.: Brookings Institution, 1974); Roger Hilsman, *To Move a Nation: The Politics of Foreign Policy in the Administration of John F. Kennedy* (New York: Doubleday, 1967); and Jerel A. Rosati, "Developing a Systematic Decision-Making Framework: Bureaucratic Politics in Perspective," in *World Politics*, 33 (January 1981). For an incisive critique of the bureaucratic model see Stephen Krasner, "Are Bureaucracies Important?" *Foreign Policy* (Summer 1972).

3. Frank Trager and Frank L. Simonie, "An Introduction to the Study of National Security" in Frank Trager and Philip Kronenberg, eds., *National Security and American Society* (Lawrence, Kans.: University Press of Kansas, 1973), 35–52. Lester R. Brown argues that in addition to the traditional military threat to national security, new threats that are ecological and economic in origin and are much less clearly defined pose serious national security problems. "An Untraditional View of National Security" in Reichart and Sturm, *American Defense Policy*.

4. Daniel J. Kaufman, Jeffrey S. McKitrick and Thomas J. Leney, eds., *U.S. National Security: A Framework for Analysis* (Lexington, Mass.: D.C. Heath, 1985), chap. 1.

5. Robert Dahl and Charles Lindblom, *Politics, Economics and Welfare* (New York: Harper and Row, 1953) see rational decisionmaking as an action that is correctly designed to maximize goal achievements, given the goal in question and the real world as it exists. Allison, *Essence of Decision*, defines rationality in the economists' sense of the term as "actions chosen by the nation . . . that will maximize strategic goals and objectives." Despite the diversity of meanings attached to the concept of rationality, and the attendant deficiencies associated with its use, it is a useful tool in describing the U.S. national security policy and the processes by which those policies are formulated. Theodore Sorensen, *Decision-Making in the White House: The Olive Branch or the Arrows* (New York: Columbia University Press, 1963) described policymaking in the Kennedy administration as aspiring to follow a multi-step procedure consistent with a rational policymaking model. Allison's study of the 1962 Cuban missile crisis reveals several points at which the deliberations of the key advisers resembled a rational policymaking model to include an agreement on facts, development of options, evaluation of costs and benefits, and making a decision because of presumed advantages.

6. See Wallace Earl Walker and Michael R. Reopel, "Strategies for Governance: Transition and Domestic Policymaking in the Reagan Administration" in *Presidential Studies Quarterly*, 16 (Fall 1986).

7. Samuel P. Huntington, *The Common Defense* (New York: Columbia University Press, 1961), 1.

8. As quoted in Allison, *Essence of Decision*, p. i.

9. In addition to the sources previously cited, see I.M. Destler, *Presidents, Bureaucrats, and Foreign Policy: The Politics of Organization Reform* (Princeton: Princeton University Press, 1974); William I. Bacchus, *Foreign Policy and the Bureaucratic Process: The State Department's Country Director System* (Princeton: Princeton University Press, 1974); Francis E. Rourke, ed., *Bureaucratic Power in National Politics* (Boston: Little, Brown, 1978); John Spanier and Eric M. Uslaner, *How American Foreign Policy Is Made* (New York: Holt, Rinehart & Winston, 1978); Stephen D. Cohen, *The Making of United States International Economic Policy* (New York: Praeger, 1977); Graham Allison and Peter Szanton, *Remaking Foreign Policy: The Organizational Connection* (New York: Basic Books, 1976); and Charles W. Kegley, Jr., and Eugene R. Wittkopf, *American Foreign Policy: Pattern and Process* (New York: St. Martin's Press, 1979). Although the latter two works never formally mention the bureaucratic politics model, they do utilize a bureaucratic politics approach. Charles E. Lindblom in his article "The Science of Muddling Through," in *Public Administration Review*, XIX (Spring 1959); 79–88, describes the governmental process as one of inherent bargaining.

10. Scholars in the past found interest groups to have much less influence in national security affairs. However, more recent articles suggest that the role of such outside groups is growing. For example, the thirteen contributors to George C. Edwards and Wallace Earl Walker, eds., *National Security and the US Constitution: A Bicentennial Reappraisal* (Baltimore: Johns Hopkins Press, forthcoming in 1988) found a considerable impact for these groups across all areas of security affairs. See particularly Edwards and Walker's concluding chapter on this point. For other older views see Lester W. Milgrath, "Interest Groups and Foreign Policy" in James Rosenau, ed., *Domestic Sources of Foreign Policy* (New York: Free Press, 1967) and Raymond A. Bauer *et al.*, *American Business and Public Policy*, 2d ed. (Chicago: Aldine-Atherton, 1982), 300–301.

11. Bureaucratic experts of various kinds exercise a pervasive influence over national security decisions. These professional groups include diplomats, military officers, scientists, policy analysts, and strategists. As Samuel Huntington describes the development of national defense strategy in *The Common Defense*, p. 147: "The relative absence of non-governmental groups concerned with strategy enhances the extent and importance of the bargaining roles of governmental officials and agencies." Public participation in actual national security policymaking tends to be indirect; the public participates as the officials making decisions take potential public reaction into account in reaching their own conclusions. William Quandt discusses in *Decade of Decisions: American Policy Toward the Arab-Israeli Conflict* (Berkeley, Calif.: University of California Press, 1977), 9–24, that some interest groups have succeeded in mobilizing the interest and support of nonexecutive, governmental allies and have been able to effectively override professionals in national security bureaucracies. For example, at least since 1968 the pro-Israel lobby has consistently been able to persuade the president and Congress to provide credits and grants to Israel for weapons systems. Also see Wallace Earl Walker and Andrew Krepinevich, "No First Use and Conventional Deterrence: The Politics of Defense Policymaking," in Gordon Hoxie, ed., *The Presidency and National Security Policy* (New York: Center for the Study of the Presidency, 1984).

12. Hilsman in *To Move a Nation* (New York: Doubleday, 1967) provides an insightful summary of the activities and the linkages that exist among the various participants involved in making U.S. national security policy by using a series of concentric circles representing levels of policy participants with the president at the center. See Francis E. Rourke, *Bureaucracy and Foreign Policy* (Baltimore: Johns

Hopkins University Press, 1986) and John Spanier and Eric Uslaner, *American Foreign Policymaking and the Democratic Dilemmas,* 4th ed., (New York: Holt, Rinehart, and Winston, 1985).

13. There are others who play a role. The academic world of research in universities has an influence and participates in the process. Most of the more effective political actors on Capitol Hill have academic experts whom they regularly consult. Other institutions do research of all kinds of contact with the government; they are staffed by national security policy experts and include the RAND Corporation, the Hudson Institute, Brookings Institution, and the American Enterprise Institute.

14. As Clinton Rossiter points out in *The American Presidency* (New York: Harcourt, Brace, and Co., 1960), 10, "a stubborn President is hard to budge, a crusading President is hard to thwart." Some references specific to presidential influence in national security policymaking include Alexander L. George, "Presidential Management Styles and Models," in George's *Presidential Decisionmaking in Foreign Policy: The Effective Use of Information and Advice* (Boulder, Colo.: Westview Press, 1980); Robert Hunter, *Presidential Control of Foreign Policy* (New York: Praeger, 1982); and Destler, *Presidents, Bureaucrats and Foreign Policy.* Standard references on the chief executive that provide primer chapters on his role in foreign policy include Edward S. Corwin, *The President: Office and Powers, 1787–1957,* 4th ed., (New York: New York University Press, 1957); Louis W. Koenig, *The Chief Executive* (New York: Harcourt, Brace, & World, Inc., 1964); Richard W. Neustadt, *Presidential Power, The Politics of Leadership* (New York: John Wiley & Sons, 1980); Richard Pious, *The American Presidency* (New York: Basic Books, 1979).

15. See Wallace Earl Walker "Domesticating Foreign Policy: Congress and the Vietnam War" in George Osborn, *et al., Democracy, Strategy and Vietnam* (Boston: Lexington Books, 1987). For a treatment of the role of Congress in foreign policy from the late 1930s to the early 1960s, see James Robinson, *Congress and Foreign Policy-Making* (Homewood, Ill.: Dorsey, 1962). Two very good studies of Congress's reassertion of its role in such policy are Cecil Crabb, Jr. and Pat M. Holt, *Invitation to Struggle: Congress, The President, and Foreign Policy* (Washington, D.C.: Congressional Quarterly Press, 1984) and Thomas Franck and Edward Weisband, *Foreign Policy by Congress* (New York: Oxford University Press, 1979). Philip Brenner, *The Limits and Possibilities of Congress* (New York: St. Martin's Press, 1983) contains case studies of congressional foreign and domestic policymaking. See also Richard Hass, Adelphi Paper 153, *Congressional Power: Implications for American Security Policy,* (London: International Institute for Strategic Studies, 1979). Edward J. Lawrence, "The Changing Role of Congress in Defense Policy-Making" in *Journal of Conflict Resolution,* (20 June 1976), attempts to explain the factors that have caused Congress to alter its role in defense policymaking. The factors he discusses include the Vietnam War, decreased public perception of external threat, rising non-DoD defense policy alternatives, increased control of military procurement, and continuing debate on national priorities.

16. Halperin, *Bureaucratic Politics and Foreign Policy.* Also, Vincent Davis, "The Politics of Innovation: Patterns in Navy Cases," Monograph #3, in *World Affairs* (Denver, Colo.: The University of Denver, 1967). A navy project officer's success in securing approval for a program to establish the navy's role in strategic nuclear bombing was due primarily to the organizational environment and astute, parochial bureaucratic maneuvering by some of the participants.

17. A leading work on budgetary politics, incremental policy, and parochialism is Aaron B. Wildavsky, *The Politics of the Budgetary Process* (Boston: Little, Brown, 1979).

18. The essence of the organizational perspectives captured by Alain Enthoven's

description of the "bomber general" in Amos Jordan and William Taylor, ed., *American National Security: Policy and Process* (Baltimore: Johns Hopkins Press, 1984), p. 209: "Picture if you will, a man who has spent his entire adult life in the Air Force, flying bombers and leading bomber forces. Bombers are his professional commitment and his expertise. His chances for promotion, public recognition, and success, and those of the officers serving under him are largely tied to the continued importance of bombers. He believes strongly in what he is doing, that is one of the main reasons he does it well." For discussion of interservice rivalry see Halperin, *Bureaucratic Politics and Foreign Policy* (Washington, D.C.: Brookings Institute, 1974), pp. 26–62; Samuel Huntington, "Interservice Competition and the Political Roles of the Armed Services" in *American Political Science Review*, 55 (March 1961); and John C. Ries, *The Management of Defense* (Baltimore: Johns Hopkins Press, 1964), 129–192.

19. Consider, for example, the potential for conflict between various DoD agencies whose response to their responsibility for national security might be a recommendation for an arms build-up, and the State Department's Arms Control and Disarmament Agency (ACDA) whose job it is to seek security through negotiated arms limitations. For a brief discussion of the history, tradition, and structure of both the Department of State and Department of Defense, which contributes to influence their organizational outlook, see Charles Kegley and Eugene R. Wittkopf, *American Foreign Policy: Pattern and Process* (New York: St. Martin's Press, 1982), chap. 10 and Jordan and Taylor, eds., *American National Security*, pp. 93–100.

20. For example, during a crisis over Laos in 1962, DoD wanted either massive intervention or complete withdrawal, while the Department of State proposed limited military steps coupled with an effort to make the nation neutral. Here the State Department prevailed. Hilsman, *To Move A Nation*, pp. 146–151. In Vietnam, especially after 1961, most Defense Department officials sought a military solution, while most State Department officials, especially Far East specialists, sought to subordinate military measures to political and social programs. Hilsman, pp. 28–34.

21. Halperin, *Bureaucratic Politics and Foreign Policy*, especially chaps. 2–4, 11, and 15; Wallace Earl-Walker, *Changing Organizational Culture* (Knoxville, Tenn.: University of Tennessee Press, 1986); and Edgar H. Schein, *Organizational Culture and Leadership* (San Francisco: Jossey-Bass, 1985), 1–22.

22. Samuel P. Huntington, *The Soldier and the State* (Cambridge, Mass.: Harvard University Press, 1957), 8–18 provides an excellent discussion of the distinguishing characteristics of a profession as a special type of vocation that is characterized by expertise, responsibility, and corporateness.

23. Frederick C. Mosher, *Democracy and the Public Service* (London: Oxford University Press, 1968). Professionalism produces multiple consequences. It provides skills and talents essential to fulfilling public goals. A professional mentality produces a commitment to do a job well and views a job as a career rather than a nine-to-five occupation. Professionalism may also enhance the desire to be of service and usually engenders honesty.

24. Harry Wriston, "The Secretary and the Management of the Department," and Don K. Price, "The Secretary and Our Unwritten Constitution" in Don K. Price, ed., *The Secretary of State* (New York: American Assembly, 1961), 76–112, 166–190, point out the importance of subordinate professionals in the analysis and implementation of a policy decision. Herbert Simon, *Administrative Behavior*, 2nd ed. (New York: MacMillan, 1957) has emphasized the importance of being able to shape the views and factual premises of senior decisionmakers as an important attribute of professionalism.

25. In a 1968 survey of Foreign Service Officers, 90 percent of those surveyed felt that a sense of service, dedication, and self-sacrifice was the preferred behavior in

their profession. See John Ensor Harr, *The Professional Diplomat* (Princeton, N.J.: Princeton University Press, 1969), chap. 6. Emmette S. Redford, *Democracy in the Administrative State* (New York: Oxford University Press, 1969), 46–49, found that professional military officers acquire a strong sense of duty, and they feel a personal responsibility to help defend their country.

26. Gordon Tullock, *The Politics of Bureaucracy* (Washington, D.C.: Public Affairs Press, 1965) is critical of this ideal view. Tullock in his general discussion of bureaucratic behavior in organizations believes in most cases the individual will have to make a choice between individual and organizational goals. In his view these goals seldom coincide. We disagree with this conclusion because most public organizations embody values that are synonymous with the values of their professionals.

27. Abraham H. Maslow, *Motivation and Personality* (New York: Harper and Row, 1954) discusses self fulfillment in organizations. Maslow concludes that every individual has a hierarchy of human needs. From highest to lowest they include self-actualization, self-esteem, social needs, safety needs, and psychological needs. Chris Argyris, "The Individual and Organization" in *Administrative Science Quarterly*, 2 (June 1957) and Victor Thompson, *Modern Organization* (New York: Knopf, 1961) provide excellent discussions of individual behavior, action, and techniques for coping with bureaucracies.

28. See note 16. Also Halperin, *Bureaucratic Politics and Foreign Policy*, pp. 26–62 and Huntington, *The Common Defense*, pp. 123–196.

29. Department of the Army, DA Pamphlet 600-3 *Commissioned Officer Professional Development and Utilization* (Washington, D.C.: Government Printing Office, 1986). For a similar discussion about the preparation of Foreign Service Officers see Harr, *The Professional Diplomat*.

30. Halperin, *Bureaucratic Politics and Foreign Policy*, pp. 26–62.

31. Rosati, "Developing a Systematic Framework," and Allison, *The Essence of Decision*, p. 162 discusses the concept of political resultants.

32. Hilsman, *To Move A Nation*, p. 5, sums up the incremental view of national security policymaking in the Kennedy administration: "Rather than through grand decisions or grand alternatives, policy changes seem to come through a series of slight modifications of existing policy, with new policy emerging slowly and haltingly by small and usually tentative steps, a process of trial and error in which policy zigs and zags, reverses itself and then moves forward." See also Charles Lindblom, *The Policy-making Process* (Englewood Cliffs, N.J.: Prentice-Hall, 1968) and Aaron B. Wildavsky, *The Politics of the Budgetary Process* (Boston: Little, Brown, 1984). For an excellent critique of incrementalism, see Robert Goodin and Ilmar Waldner, "Thinking Big, Thinking Small, and Not Thinking at All," *Public Policy* 28 (Winter 1979).

33. Herbert Simon, *Models of Man* (New York: John Wiley, 1957).

34. Bert Rockman, "Mobilize Public Support" in Edwards and Walker (forthcoming).

35. See Charles Kegley, Jr., and Eugene Wittkopf, *American Foreign Policy: Pattern and Process* (New York: St. Martin's Press, 1982), Chap. 13, for a discussion of consequences of organizational decisionmaking. Kegley and Wittkopf quote Henry Kissinger's critical commentary of the decisionmaking process: "This procedure neglects the long-range because the future has no administrative constituency and is, therefore, without representation in the adversary proceedings. Problems tend to be slighted until some agency or department is made responsible for them. . . . The outcome usually depends more on the pressures or the persuasiveness of the contending advocates than on a concept of over-all purpose." (p. 467)

36. U.S. national security policy is profoundly influenced by the set of values,

cognitions, ideas, and ideals that the majority of the people of the U.S. hold. For a broad overview, see Stanley Falk, *The Environment of National Security* (Washington, D.C.: Industrial College of Armed Forces, 1973); Kaufman, McKitrick and Leney, *U.S. National Security*, pp. 27–37; and James Oliver and James Nathan, "The American Environment for Security Planning," in Philip Kronenberg, ed., *Planning U.S. Security* (Washington, D.C.: National Defense University Press, 1981).

37. It is interesting to note that Alexis de Tocqueville concluded that in the conduct of foreign relations democracies appeared "decidedly inferior." According to de Tocqueville, "Foreign politics demand scarcely any of those qualities which are peculiar to a democracy; they require, on the contrary, the perfect use of almost all those in which it is deficient. . . . [A] democracy can only with great difficulty regulate the details of an important undertaking, persevere in a fixed design, and work out its execution in spite of serious obstacles. It cannot combine its measures with secrecy or await their consequences with patience." See *Democracy in America*, vol. 1. (New York: Vintage Books, 1945), 243. Yet Edwards and Walker in their concluding chapter find that this may in fact not be so.

38. An assessment of the problem of public servants operating above the rule of law can be found in a useful series of original essays on Watergate by Donald W. Harwood, ed., *Crisis in Confidence: The Impact of Watergate* (Boston: Little, Brown, 1974). Amitai Etzioni, *Modern Organizations* (Englewood Cliffs, N.J.: Prentice Hall, 1964), 110–111, points out that legal conditions are a component of the environment of a national security organization and that this reality is often overlooked.

39. By fiscal year 1984, projected multibillion-dollar deficits made Congress reluctant to continue funding large defense increases, and, as a result, the Reagan administration's request for a 10 percent real increase was cut in half.

40. Bureau of the Census, *The Projections of the Population of the United States, 1977–2050,* Table 8, Series II (Washington, D.C.: Government Printing Office, 1980). For critical analysis of the impact of this declining population see Martin Binkin, "Military Manpower in the 1980s: Issues and Choices," in *International Security,* 5 (Fall 1980).

41. President Roosevelt's inclination for a strong navy can be traced back beyond his tenure as secretary of the navy to his high school years during which he wrote and defended an essay about the importance of a navy. From a discussion with a historian in the Roosevelt museum, Hyde Park, New York.

42. Frederick Mosher, ed., *Governmental Reorganizations: Cases and Commentary* (Indianapolis, Ind.: Bobbs-Merrill, 1967) points out that reorganizations are actually efforts by officials to adapt their organizations to their surrounding environments. Reorganizations will occur at periodic intervals as part of organizational growth, change, or decline. Herbert Kaufman, "Reflections on Administrative Reorganization" in Joseph Peckman, ed., *Setting National Priorities: The 1978 Budget* (Washington, D.C.: The Brookings Institution, 1978), points out that the consequences of reorganizations are quite profound, not so much measured in terms of cost reduction or improved efficiency, but rather "the real payoffs are measured in terms of influence, policy, and communication."

43. Richard Hall, *Organizations: Structure and Process* (Englewood Cliffs, N.J.: Prentice Hall, 1972) and James D. Thompson, *Organizations in Action* (New York: McGraw Hill, 1967).

44. Ibid. See also James Anderson, *Public Policymaking* (New York: CBS College Publishing, 1984), chap. 2, for a concise discussion of the environment within which policymaking occurs, as well as some of the official and unofficial participants. Philip Taubman's "The Resident Rascal of the State Department," in *The New York Times,* September 4, 1984, discusses the individual style, strategies and techniques utilized by Langhorne Motley to make popular the Reagan

administration's Latin American policy.

45. Thomas Murphy, Donald Neuchterleig, and Ronald Stupak, *Inside the Bureaucracy: The View From the Assistant Secretary's Desk* (Boulder, Colo.: Westview Press, 1978), especially chaps. 2 and 4.

46. Richard G. Head, "The A-7 Decisions" in John Reichart and Steven Sturm, eds., *American Defense Policy*, 613–625. In his analysis of the USAF decision to buy A-7 aircraft, Head points out that interservice competition provides a powerful incentive to develop better, more efficient, and more capable forces. Bertram Gross, *The Managing of Organizations*, vol. 2 (New York: Free Press, 1964), is considered one of the most thorough expositions of the organization conflict/struggle theme. In fact, Gross suggests that the more competition in administration the better. See also Daniel Katz and Robert Kahn, *The Social Psychology of Organizations* (New York: John Wiley and Sons, 1966), 447–449. The constructive and positive role of conflict in heightened morale, in fostering creativity, and innovation should not be ignored. Some friction should exist between members in organizations as a condition for the generation of fresh ideas. A conflict-free national security organization will be static and operate at considerably less than capacity. See William Niskanen, *Bureaucracy and Representative Government* (Chicago: Aldine, 1971).

47. Gary Sick, *All Fall Down: America's Tragic Encounters with Iran* (New York: Random House, 1985), and William H. Sullivan, "Dateline Iran: The Road Not Taken" in *Foreign Policy* 40 (Fall 1980) for an insightful discussion of the intelligence failures and bureaucratic quarrelling that led to the tragic outcome in Iran.

48. Hugh Heclo, *A Government of Strangers* (Washington, D.C.: The Brookings Institution, 1977).

49. Jordan and Taylor, *American National Security*, pp. 209–214, provide a brief discussion of individual characteristics and position variables that increase a professional's chances of succeeding in influencing national security policymaking. Included in this discussion are the individual variables of education, the ability to write, speak and reason effectively, physical presence, and personal relationships with other key individuals.

50. Katz and Kahn, *The Social Psychology of Organizations*, p. 243.

51. Heclo calls this "due process" leadership, *A Government of Strangers*, pp. 164–166.

52. Peter Drucker's entertaining "The Deadly Sins in Public Administration" in *Public Administration Review*, 40 (March/April 1980) will assist the reader in understanding what individual strategies or actions *not* to pursue in national security policymaking. Drucker states that to commit any two of the six common sins of public administration will insure failure. The sins are as follows: having a too lofty objective, doing several unrelated things at once, throwing too many mass resources at a problem, being too dogmatic and failing to experiment, not learning from experience, and not abandoning pointless programs.

53. If this simple, but difficult, approach were adhered to, the intelligence and national security decisionmaking failures that surrounded the tragic outcome in Iran may have been averted. Sullivan, *Foreign Policy*.

54. Roger Fisher and William Ury, *Getting to Yes: Negotiating Agreement Without Giving In* (New York: Penguin Books, 1983).

55. Fischer and Ury, *Getting to Yes*, pp. 87–88.

56. On the point that conflict can both unify and divide, see E. E. Schattschneider, *The Semisovereign People* (New York: Holt, Rinehart and Winston, 1960).

57. Confidential interview with a senior OMB official who had many occasions to watch a variety of political executives and national security professionals in action.

58. Richard Neustadt and Ernest May, *Thinking in Time: The Uses of History for Decision Makers* (New York: Free Press, 1986); James Rosenau, "Pre-theories and Theories of Foreign Policy," in *The Scientific Study of Foreign Policy,* rev. ed. (New York: Nichols Publishing, 1980), stresses the importance of asking simple questions along the Neustadt/May theme to explain foreign policy decisions. To do so facilitates an appreciation of the numerous factors shaping foreign policy.

59. Chester I. Barnard, *The Functions of the Executive* (Cambridge, Mass.: Harvard University Press, 1938), 272.

60. Stephen K. Bailey, "Ethics and the Public Service" in Roscoe C. Martin, ed., *Public Administration* (Syracuse, N.Y.: Syracuse University Press, 1965), 283–298.

61. Bailey, "Ethics and the Public Service," p. 298.

62. Herman Finer, "Administrative Responsibility in Democratic Government," *Public Administration Review* 1 (Summer 1941). Finer states, "reliance on an official's conscience may be reliance on an official's accomplice."

63. Reaction by media and Congress to the Iran-*Contra* scandal to include scathing editorials by the media and the appointment of a Joint Congressional Committee to investigate the activities of members of the national security policymaking structure involved in the incident is evidence of this fact.

# 9.3    Operating in the Joint Arena

## PERRY SMITH

*Major General Smith's unique experiences give him a powerful vantage point from which to assess bureaucratic politics in the U.S. government. His rules of thumb for operating in the joint arena offer valuable tips for (potential) players of any experience level. Yet success in the joint arena or any bureaucracy is not guaranteed merely by reciting a certain checklist of the rules of the game. It is and will be the experienced and skilled who will know which rule is applicable at a particular moment and how best to apply their skills and resources to achieve their objectives.*

Of all the bureaucratic structures within the U.S. government, the Organization of the Joint Chiefs of Staff is clearly one of the most complex, most structured and most difficult to explain to outsiders. On the other hand, it is in the joint arena, both in Washington and in the Unified Commands in the field, that important planning and policy making take place. Anyone wishing to understand how national security policy is made must understand the rules of thumb for operating in the joint arena. The participants in the policy making and decision making processes within the joint arena tend to be hard-working, dedicated, and quite sophisticated individuals. The majority are military officers with anywhere from twelve to thirty-four years of service, mostly in the field and not in Washington. This lack of long-term Washington experience is quite unique since almost all other federal bureaucracies are staffed by long-term Washington hands.

Most military officers serving in Washington in the Office of the Joint Chiefs of Staff and in the military service staffs (army staff, navy staff, air staff, Marine Corps staff) serve for no more than four years and return to operational jobs in this country (or overseas) at the completion of two-, three-, or four-year tours in Washington. Although short in Washington experience, these officers are highly educated (a master's degree is common as is completion of one or more professional military colleges), and they have an excellent grasp of the operational aspects of their particular service. Those who serve in the Office of the Joint Chiefs of Staff are vastly outnumbered by those who serve on the military service staffs, and, as a result, the military service staffs are often able to overwhelm those serving in a joint position because they have ready access to more people, to more analytical resources, and so on.

Anyone examining the joint arena must understand that parochialism and provincialism are common phenomena at work at many levels and in complex patterns. For instance, an army lieutenant colonel from the infantry branch with a great deal of experience in airborne operations who works in the plans and policy area of the Joint Chiefs of Staff (JCS) has a number of loyalties. He must be loyal to the chairman of the JCS, who in most cases will be a four-star general or admiral from another service; he must be loyal to the director of the joint staff and the director of plans and policy, both three-star officers from different services; he must maintain his loyalty to the U.S. Army, the infantry branch, and the airborne infantry subbranch of the infantry, to which he will return in a few years; he must often represent and be loyal to a commander of a unified or specific command (such as the U.S. Commander of Europe or the Commander of the Strategic Air Command) since the paper he may be responsible for concerns one or more of these commands; and, of course, he must be loyal to both the secretary of defense and the president, to whom he has constitutional, legal, and traditional responsibilities.

An officer serving on the staff of a military service in Washington also has a hierarchy of loyalties, although this hierarchy is somewhat different in crucial areas. For instance, an officer from the staff of a military service often is expected to hold loyalty to his or her service higher than his or her loyalty to the chairman of the JCS or to a commander of a unified or specified command.

Hence, when the five key players (a joint staff officer and an officer from each of the service staffs) sit down to thrash out a study, action paper, message, and so on, these officers not only have different backgrounds but also different loyalties. If any of these five officers takes a parochial position favoring his or her individual service, the other officers normally feel obliged to take corresponding, but conflicting, parochial positions. Often the joint staff officer must work hard to draft a position that serves the overall interest of the nation and not just the narrower interest of one or two of the military services. Usually the result is a carefully crafted compromise that is not the best, or even nearly the best, solution to the problem, but is one that all can agree upon. Since the power of the joint staff officer is quite limited in the shaping and coordination of joint staff papers, the final papers are often disappointing to the chairman of the JCS, to the secretary of defense, and to the unified and specified commanders in the field.

## RULES OF THUMB AND RULES OF THE GAME

### Full Coordination

One of the worst mistakes an officer can make when operating within the joint arena is failing to gain full coordination on a joint paper. Lack of time, unavailability of key officials, and the desire to bypass a particularly recalcitrant official are some of the reasons that a joint or service action officer might fail to gain full coordination on a specific paper. Other less common reasons for skipping a particular office would be the sensitive or highly classified nature of the paper (some staff directorates do not have proper clearances to look at the paper) or when the officer responsible for the coordination process fails to realize that a particular officer has an interest in the paper.

A major responsibility of the senior officers in both the joint staff and the service staff is to look carefully at the coordination sheet normally attached to the staff paper to insure that the action officer has not skipped one or more key offices. In fact, one of the most common questions that I asked officers who were coordinating joint papers during my two years as director of plans for the air staff was, Why haven't you coordinated with X, Y, or Z?

### Identifying the Key Issues

Key issues are often missed in drafting action papers; consequently, senior officers must insure that all relevant issues are addressed. There are many reasons a paper may fail to deal with key issues: The joint staff officer who drafted the paper may be new, inexperienced, or not "tuned in" to the subject at hand; one or more service action officers may have convinced his or her colleagues to drop an issue in order to avoid damaging the interest of an individual service; or there may just be differences in judgment among the drafters of the paper about which issues are important. In any case, if the paper is to serve the purposes of the chairman of the JCS, key issues should be raised and addressed.

## Hidden Agendas

Actors in the joint arena should look for "hidden agendas," wherein one (or more) actors subtly interjects phrases that serve parochial interests. In recent years, individuals have rarely been blatantly parochial because the other four players will normally join hands to abort the effort. Subtle parochialism is the norm. In fact, hidden agendas are common in drafting or coordinating joint papers.

## The Importance of the Drafting Process

The first person "on the sheet" with a draft paper has the advantage over others in the process. Hence, clear advantages are gained from being both a good and a fast writer. Although the joint staff officer normally writes the first draft, he or she often asks an officer from an individual service staff to write a draft, particularly if he or she has strong expertise in the issue or issues at hand. One of the most important meetings in the process of developing a joint paper is when the five action officers first address the paper in draft form. The action officer who thinks and writes quickly and skillfully can often move the paper in the direction he or she desires. The joint staff officer must prevent the most skillful service staff officers from steering the paper in a parochial direction. From the joint perspective, it would be best if the joint action officer was the most experienced and skilled writer, but this is often not the case. In fact, a chronic problem has been that officers in the joint staff are somewhat less talented than officers on the staffs of the military services. The important legislation of 1986 was aimed, in part, at correcting this problem.

## Staying "Tuned In"

Although operational and staff experience, a grasp of technological issues, an understanding of international relations, and an understanding of public administration, bureaucracy, and decision making are all important attributes, the ability of an official to keep "tuned in" and to know where to get information quickly and accurately is the most important quality of all. These characteristics are gained by spending a great amount of time walking the halls of the Pentagon and learning who else in the building is able to keep up with disparate but important pieces of information. Information is power in this esoteric world. The most successful officers build up a network of contacts and nurture these relationships by sharing vital information and helping others. Trust and mutual respect in combination with a quick mind and much hard work can make and keep an officer "street smart" and "tuned in."

## Keeping in Touch with the Field

One of the worst mistakes an officer working in the joint arena can make is failing to stay in close contact with relevant agencies and individuals in the field. If, for instance, an officer is assigned to the Middle East Division of a service or the joint staff, he or she should travel often to the Middle East, should make contact with both foreign and U.S. officials visiting Washington from the Middle East, should get to know foreign officials who serve in Washington, and should spend much time on the telephone, sharing insights from the Washington scene and gaining information and insights from the Middle East. Officers may think they are creating superb policy on the Middle East in Washington, but, if they do not check their work often with people in the field who have the advantage of being totally immersed in the issues and the culture, they are making a grave mistake. The same is true of individuals who are working in more technical areas: Contact with laboratories, think tanks, and field agencies is an essential part of the job. The Washington-based staff officer must realize that with each passing day he or she becomes more and more removed from past experiences in the field and, hence, becomes more and more likely to err on the side of old experiences and outdated insights. After about four years, most military officers need to return to the field to reestablish currency, expertise, and contacts. However, a few officers in Washington have such a knack of staying in touch with the field that they can remain effective well beyond this four-year mark.

## "Kicking the Can"

One of the dysfunctional aspects of joint activities is a phenomenon known as "kicking the can." When one or more military services have a major objection to aspects of a joint paper, they try to change the paper to satisfy their concerns. If they succeed, as is often the case, they will try a number of delaying tactics so that the decision will not be made for months, years, or, preferably, ever. The postponement of a decision is common in the joint arena. In fact, it is probably the worst offense in the committee system known as the Joint Chiefs of Staff.

One way to postpone a decision is to initiate a study. Many studies are started, not because more complete data or analyses are needed by decision makers, but because one or more military services object to a decision being made. There are a number of unfortunate aspects of this tendency: First, a decision that should be made relatively quickly is not made for many months or even years; second, much time and money is spent, wastefully in many cases; third, the people involved often realize that they are participating in a sham, which leads to discouragement and cynicism. The JCS should work to overcome their propensity to postpone decisions.

Another way to postpone a decision is to "query the field." Often a service will push to have a message sent to the field, while at the same time working hard to insure that the field agency being queried will support the service's position. The skillful and manipulative action officer knows how to get field agencies to write messages to support his or her position. Some officers in Washington even go so far as to write messages for the field commands or agencies to send back to the joint staff. This kind of manipulation of the system needs to be watched carefully by the senior officials working on joint issues. Messages from the field to Washington should reflect the views of the field commanders and should not be written surreptitiously in Washington.

The worst example of this phenomenon that I am familiar with took place, not in the joint arena, but in a relationship with the U.S. Congress. An air staff action officer was enamored with a research and development program he had helped develop. When the air staff decided not to lend support to this program, the officer surreptitiously contacted his friends on Capitol Hill and got them to interject language in a defense appropriations bill allocating 50 million dollars to the program. In this case, his parochialism was not service parochialism but parochialism at a lower and more personal level. But this case demonstrates vividly that staff officers in Washington often hold strong views on issues and will at times take extraordinary steps to insure that their views prevail. It is the responsibility of the joint staff officers and the senior officers on the service staffs to make certain that national interest has highest priority in decisionmaking.

## The Implementation Process

Although most attention is paid to the decision-making process, the implementation process is equally important. Decisions that cannot or will not be carried out are of little value; too many decision papers lead nowhere. Actors in the joint arena have a responsibility to insure that they find solutions that can be implemented with a minimum of agony. Hence, decision papers must be written with clarity and precision and must contain the funding, manpower, logistics, and communications wherewithal to insure implementation. Once they realize they cannot prevent a decision by the Joint Chiefs of Staff, manipulative officers from various services will sometimes work to make the decision impossible to implement. In the vernacular of the joint arena, "Let's make this paper a real turkey so it will never fly." In other words, if an action officer cannot make the paper come out in favor of his or her service's position, he or she will often work to make the paper weak, confusing, and incapable of being implemented.

## The Reward of Parochialism

An unfortunate long-term phenomenon of the joint arena in Washington and in the field is that parochialism is often rewarded, whereas taking the broader, national view is not "career enhancing." Too many "street fighters" are rewarded, and too few statesmen are given accelerated promotion patterns. The common expression is "Colonel X on the joint staff has forgotten where his or her roots are," which means that Colonel X is so busy serving the national interest that he is "screwing over" his own service. Once the word is out that Colonel X is truly objective on all issues, his or her promotion opportunities often diminish appreciably. This is not because the leadership of the services dictates punishment for this objectivity, but because a significant number of senior officers hold loyalty to service as the most important value to be rewarded. So long as there are individual senior academies, career patterns in which individuals devote almost all of their professional time to a single service, and promotion systems that regard joint duty as "out of the mainstream," objectivity is more likely to lead to subtle punishment (or, at best, neglect) rather than reward.

## SUMMARY

The joint arena is much maligned and is considered by many to be an area in which there is much activity but little output. The trends that are evident in the mid-1980s are the strengthening of the power and influence of the chairman of the Joint Chiefs of Staff, the unified and specified commanders in the field, and the joint staff in Washington. Hence, it is more important than ever that students of public policy in Washington understand the rules governing the joint arena. The planning, policy-making, and decision-implementing aspects of joint activity will be fruitful areas for serious scholarly research in the years ahead.

---

# 9.4 The Department of Defense and Media Politics

## ALBERT C. PIERCE

*Albert C. Pierce in the following article, which is an adaptation of his remarks given at the George C. Marshall Leadership Conference, Lexington, Virginia, on 21 November 1986, argues that because the institutions and cultures of the military and press are different, they approach "their separate, legitimate, constitutionally sanctioned, necessary, and useful [national security] business" from distinct perspectives. The difficult task for both the media and the military, according to Dr. Pierce, is to manage such tensions productively and to avoid a destructive relationship that would be damaging to us all.*

The Pentagon and the press. The military and the media. The subject conjures up many images. One is of two scorpions in a bottle, ever wary and alert, each trying to strike the other first. Another, and one that probably applies more often, is of two apes on treadmills, each relentlessly, at times seemingly mindlessly, trying to do its separate job, working to keep moving forward, just trying to earn a day's worth of feed.

While both images apply some of the time, neither describes the normal state of relations, which is perhaps too complex to be captured in a single metaphor. To understand this complicated web of relationships, one should turn from the world of images to the field of anthropology, for, as Peter Braestrup has usefully pointed out, the military and the media constitute two quite distinctive cultures.[1]

At the outset, however, two other points should be made. The first is a clarification of terms. The subject here is not precisely the Pentagon and the press, or the military and the media. "Pentagon" narrows the focus to a five-sided headquarters building in Washington, D.C., and "the military" applies only to the uniformed members of the U.S. armed forces. For present purposes, it is more useful to think about those in uniform and those in mufti, those in Washington and those "in the field," indeed, the entire complex of those civilians and military officers who run the defense and national security establishment of the United States. Likewise, "the press" can be taken to apply only to print journalism, while "the media" generally means the electronic or broadcast news organizations. But here one should include both. "The Pentagon and the press" and "the military and the media," when not construed too strictly and thus too narrowly, become nicely alliterative and useful shorthand for larger concepts.

Second, both of these institutions are special. The U.S. Constitution is a short document; the Founding Fathers clearly wanted it that way. Yet they did find room in those few pages to make specific mention of the "common defense," "armies," and "a navy" as well as of "freedom . . . of the press." Not only are these two institutions constitutionally sanctioned, but they are vital, indeed essential elements of America and the American way of life. Without a strong military, we would be vulnerable to our adversaries, potentially dangerously so. Were we to be invaded or occupied, or politically intimidated short of invasion, the American constitutional system could change dramatically. On the other hand, we could be completely secure from invasion and intimidation, but were the free press to disappear, *that* would not be the United States of America as envisioned in Philadelphia in the sweltering summer of 1787.

But to return to an earlier point, it is more than a matter of two institutions or two professions or two ways of earning a living. Braestrup (from whom many of the following points are shamelessly borrowed) is right: These are two very different cultures, each with its own values, concepts, habits, skills, arts, institutions, language. Therefore, one begins with a bit of cultural anthropology.

## THE MILITARY CULTURE

The military is hierarchical and centrally organized. Every single American soldier, sailor, airman, and marine has the same commander-in-chief. Each one has a clear chain of command, to which he or she is ultimately responsible. Military people get promotions regularly, and the badge of each rank is displayed prominently on the uniform. The hierarchy—and where one stands in it—is always present and clear. People in uniform are accustomed to, and generally respectful of, authority. They are used to taking orders, and in the end will do so unquestioningly.

Career military personnel are comfortable in large organizations; they have chosen to spend their professional lives in one. They take pride in conforming to the norms and mores, standards and practices of their organization. They wear its uniform proudly.

The officer's code, not just for graduates of West Point, is simple: duty, honor, country. Though, to be sure, not all live up to it 100 percent of the time, it is the commonly accepted ideal one strives for and the standard one is held to. The Uniform Code of Military Justice is the same for all, regardless of rank or service.

Almost to a fault, the military respect—even revere—tradition. For example, every year on November 10, members of the United States Marine Corps, wherever they are in the world, perform a simple ceremony that commemorates the birthday of the corps. They read the same citation (from an early commandant of the Marine Corps), then they cut a cake. The first piece always goes to the oldest marine present, the second to the youngest. Every year, everywhere, it is the same ritual—tradition.

Military officers tend to be doers, to be active, to seek responsibility. The most valued and sought-after assignments are those that involve command—of a battalion, a ship, a squadron, whatever. This can be an enormous responsibility—anywhere from thousands to billions of dollars' worth of equipment and hardware—but it is even more than that. Civilian life has virtually no counterpart to what happens to hundreds of young army and Marine Corps lieutenants every year. They are given complete responsibility for the care, feeding, training, discipline, health, and well-being of a platoon of forty or so troops, very few of whom are older than the new lieutenant. The commander is also responsible for the lives of the troops' families as well, in ways most civilian supervisors would find hard to imagine. This at the age of twenty-three or twenty-four.

As commander, the officer is responsible not only for the troops' well-being in peacetime, but also ultimately for their lives in war. The peacetime mission of the U.S. military is to deter war, but if deterrence fails, commanders then become managers of organized violence. They try to kill people before those people kill them. For those who wear military uniforms, there is a bond of kinship that flows from this ultimate mission. It is a bond of secrecy also, for there are professional secrets that could spell the difference between who lives and who dies in war. Military officers do not like to share secrets, even with civilian members of the Department of Defense (DoD). Until recently, only two of the more than one million civilian employees of the DoD were authorized to read military war plans: the secretary and the deputy secretary of defense. In 1986, legislation widened the access to only a handful of others. So, it is not surprising that military officers do not like to reveal other secrets to outsiders, let alone to reporters and thus to the public at large and also to our adversaries and potential enemies.

## THE JOURNALIST'S CULTURE

To begin with an almost complete contrast, the world of American journalism is not hierarchical or centrally organized. Despite some recent trends toward conglomerate ownership of multiple newspapers, radio stations, and television stations, there is not now, and there never will be, one central organization to which all print and broadcast outlets report. The news business is part of the American capitalist, free-enterprise private sector, within which there is intense competition among independent news organizations.

Reporters themselves tend to be iconoclastic, nonhierarchical, and inquisitive. They are skeptical and at times even disrespectful of authority. They tend to be suspicious of large organizations and of the people who run and represent them. They generally do not even belong to any, and many of them spend their professional lives outside of, and trying to probe into, other people's large organizations. Professionally, many journalists are loners.

Within an individual news organization, what hierarchy there is is quite simple: There are reporters, and then there is management (editors, producers, executives). A thirty-year veteran reporter and a fresh-out-of-journalism-school rookie are both just reporters. While assignments, salary, and by-lines or air time vary, neither the old hand nor the newcomer wears any distinguishing badge of rank or seniority.

The business of reporters is finding out things and telling other people about them. That is what they do for a living. That often means finding out and telling things that certain people do not want others to know. Reporters are not doers; they are observers and story-tellers. Reporters say, "I've got a *story* on page one tomorrow," or "I'm working on a great *story* for next week." They do not write studies or publish research reports; they tell stories.

What journalists deal with in these stories are ideas, facts, words, images. They collect them, and then they make judgments about which ideas, facts, words, and images to put in their stories, to transmit to their readers or their audience. There is neither space nor time to communicate everything they know. Judgments about which stories to tell, with which facts, words, and pictures, are the essence of the news business.

Journalists take seriously their obligation—and their right—to discover and tell important, relevant, interesting stories to their readers or their audience. Despite more than occasional cynicism about the attentiveness and intellectual abilities of their readers, viewers, and listeners, people in the news business commonly describe what they do as informing the public. That, ultimately, is how they see their business, and they believe in it.

\* \* \*

One does not need a PhD in anthropology to realize that the military culture and the journalist's culture not only differ, but conflict. Inevitably there is tension between them. Much of that tension is necessary and productive; some of it is even desirable. The world of the military and the media, of government and journalism is not the peaceable kingdom in which the lion and the lamb lie down together. Rather, it is often a kingdom in which the lion tries to devour the lamb, and the real struggle is over which one gets to be the lion.

Over the last two decades, the tension between the two has not always been productive or desirable. In fact, there have been episodes, even extended periods, of bitter, harmful tension and bad blood. The examples come readily to mind—Vietnam, Grenada, the January 1985 classified Shuttle mission, various disclosures of sensitive intelligence information. These incidents pop up from time to time, feeding upon the inherent tension and turning it from something necessary and desirable into something harmful and counterproductive. Two apes on their treadmills suddenly become two scorpions in a bottle.

The central problem, then, becomes how both of these valued institutions can conduct their separate, legitimate, constitutionally sanctioned, necessary, and useful businesses without having the inherent tension deteriorate to the detriment of both institutions and ultimately of the American people. Perhaps a profitable way to proceed is to capture some of the past problems and to look toward the future by offering some prescriptive advice to both institutions from the perspective of someone who has worked both the DoD and the news media sides of the street.

## ADVICE FOR THE MEDIA

"Get it right, and get it first," is the standard order from the editor to the reporter. One problem is that in the intense competition in the news business, the desire to get it first sometimes overrides the obligation to get it right. For example, on June 9, 1983, "ABC World News Tonight" ran a story about Soviet troops in Cuba. Here is the transcript, as published by the DoD:

> U.S. Intelligence sources tell ABC News that the number of Soviet combat troops in Cuba has risen sharply in the last few months. The Russians already have a combat brigade in Cuba of 2600 to 3000 men. Sources say since early April, another 1500 combat troops have arrived.
>
> It was assumed that these forces were part of a normal seasonal rotational [*sic*] that would leave Cuba after completing a military exercise which is now under way. In the last few days, however, intelligence sources report that another 1700 troops have arrived from the Soviet Union by ship, troops which are not participating in the joint Cuban-Russian military exercises.
>
> Analysts are puzzled and concerned by these latest reports. The normal rotation of troops in the past has involved only half as many rotation forces. Sources fear what they are seeing now is a permanent buildup of Russian troop strength in Cuba which could plunge the U.S., Cuba, and the Soviet Union into a major confrontation.[2]

This story, with its ominous reference to a possible "major confrontation," was the first public airing of these particular alleged Soviet activities. Checking by other news organizations produced no confirmation of this ABC report of unusual Soviet activity in Cuba. Government sources described it as a normal rotation. The next night, ABC's anchorman announced: "The State Department said today it had no evidence at this time the Russians were increasing their presence in Cuba, but was watching it. More troops have arrived, but it is uncertain whether they have come to replace others who may be leaving."[3]

A little more checking before airing the first story would probably have yielded different, considerably less dramatic news, if any at all. They did get it first, but at the price of getting it wrong. Getting it first but not right, whether through inadvertence or carelessness, only feeds the cynicism many national security officials and military officers feel toward the media. Even worse, it misleads and misinforms the audience.

This leads directly to a second piece of advice. The news business simply does not do as good a job as it could and should of correcting its own mistakes. Leaving a sensitive story up in the air—such as the Soviet troops in Cuba—is unnecessary and wrong. If you stand by your story, say so. If you made a mistake, then admit it.

There is great concern in the news business about credibility, and rightly so, for credibility is essential to a successful newspaper or news broadcast. Too often, however, the in-house assumption seems to be that if you admit you made a mistake, your credibility will suffer. The unspoken corollary is that if you do not admit you made a mistake, maybe no one will notice and your credibility will remain intact. But there is another possibility: If you honestly and openly admit you made a mistake, perhaps your credibility will be enhanced, not diminished. And you would have—albeit belatedly—given your readers or viewers what Pogo used to call "the true facts."

Another piece of advice to national news organizations covering defense and the military is that there is more to the American military establishment than the military bureaucracy in Washington. As a veteran military correspondent recently observed, "There is a discouraging contrast between the forces in the field and the high command around the flagpole in Washington."⁴ Both are part of the story, and informing the public about defense requires careful, thoughtful stories about the field and the flagpole in Washington. Exclusive focus on either the field or the flagpole is telling only half of the story.

This one-sided reporting is related to one of the sources of tension between the military and the media: Most reporters do not know what the average soldier does every day to earn a living, and vice versa. The best defense correspondents always try to balance their routine in Washington with trips to the field to see real soldiers, sailors, airmen, and marines at work. The story is in Washington, but it is "out there," too.

News organizations should do a better job than most of them do in developing more specialists in complex areas like defense and national security. Critics, including not a few in the press, have called the military to task for rotating officers too frequently. Two- or three-year tours often mean that just when an officer has enough experience to do a job well, it is rotation time again. But the record of most major news organizations is not much better. For every Charles Corddry (of *The Baltimore Sun*) and Richard Halloran (of *The New York Times*), there are a dozen Pentagon reporters who are just passing through: Just when they really understand the issues, the forces, and the hardware, it is time for a new assignment. There are other exceptions, in terms of expertise if not longevity on the beat—retired Marine Lieutenant General Bernard Trainor covers military affairs for *The New York Times*, and former National Security Council (NSC) and Senate Foreign Relations Committee staffer Ric Inderfurth specializes in arms control issues for ABC News. Too many news organizations, however, seem to be afraid of that kind of expertise, or think that it is not necessary, or are reluctant to invest the time and effort it takes to convert a former government expert into a first-rate reporter.

One extremely sensitive area that always comes up when military people talk about the press is the way news organizations, especially television, cover grieving families at a time of tragedy—Beirut, Grenada, the Challenger disaster. There is something unseemly about the frenetic, voyeuristic invasion of the private grief of widows and parents. The bonds of kinship among military people are strongest in combat and in death, and they notice and remember how members of their "family" are treated at such times. Thus, managers of news organizations could take no better step to enhance their image with military people than to show a bit more human decency than they have in the past. Soldiers, sailors, airmen, and marines work for all of us, and when one or more are killed in the line of duty, we all suffer a loss. News coverage at its best—for example, the assassination of President John F. Kennedy—can create a national community of shared grief. The ghoulish death-watch stampedes seen recently serve no public good and cheapen a medium that has on other occasions shown us it can soar.

Last, news organizations should begin to open up a dialogue with government officials to work through some of the problems involved in revealing certain kinds of sensitive information. Unfortunately, this dialogue generally takes place only in the heat of intense deadline pressure when the secretary of defense or the director of the Central Intelligence Agency (CIA) calls news executives to request they not run a particular story. More often than not, such incidents are resolved in a way that allows the basic story to run with exceptionally sensitive details protected.

To be sure, much information is classified improperly and unnecessarily, but there are categories of genuinely important information, whose publication could seriously harm U.S. security. Often the information itself may seem somewhat innocuous, but the way the U.S. government obtained that information could be very sensitive. These are fine judgments, and the government usually has an advantage in technical expertise. No advance dialogue in noncrisis times could resolve future issues, but it could improve both sides' appreciation of each other's perspective and could make those crisis, deadline discussions better informed and more productive.

## ADVICE FOR THE MILITARY

The advice begins with the source of the military's most common complaint about the media: Vietnam. Regarding the media, the military should forget about Vietnam. Despite strong opinions on all sides of the issue, we will never resolve definitively whether or not the press turned the American people against the war and thus forced political leaders to cut back and withdraw prematurely. Most military officers seem to believe the press did, but they cannot prove it. (Neither can anyone else disprove it.) But that belief is the origin of much of the mistrust and ill-will between the military and the media, and many in the military seem determined to hang on to it.

An anecdote from a former marine public affairs officer illustrates the point. In the spring of 1984, a group of reporters, including several former war correspondents, was invited to meet with a class of junior marine officers in school at Quantico, Virginia. The young marines spent several hours intensely questioning, challenging, and criticizing the reporters; much of their bill of particulars revolved around Vietnam. After the bruised and bloodied journalists left, the public affairs officer asked several of the officers, virtually all of whom entered the Marine Corps after the United States left Vietnam, where they got the notion that the press had done such a poor job of covering the war. "Oh, the older guys told us," was the answer from one of them. Thus, not only is the military not putting Vietnam behind it, there is also an oral tradition being handed down which repeats and encourages this tale of bad blood between the military and the media.

A second important piece of advice is that defense officials should not "cry wolf" about national security. Every Pentagon correspondent has seen cases where the mantle of national security was wrapped around information whose release would do no real harm to the nation's security, but might to the image and reputation of certain officials, officers, or programs. Just as with the little boy, crying wolf when there is none runs the risk of not being listened to or believed when you need your credibility the most.

Credibility can be tarnished in other ways also, which leads to another bit of advice: Do your job, but do not overdo it. Reporters all understand that government officials try to put news, information, and events in the most favorable light. There is a fine line there, and crossing it can be counterproductive and even embarrassing. For example, in September of 1984, it was revealed in a public hearing that the coffeemaker on the C5A transport plane cost more than $7,000. An air force spokesman replied to the charge, "It's not really a coffee maker like your Mr. Coffee. It's really a hot beverage unit."[5] The air force went on to explain that the unit provides "coffee, tea, and soup"—as if that made it a real bargain! The reason the "hot beverage unit" cost so much is that it was designed to withstand many more times the force of gravity than would probably kill the plane's entire crew.

Here the advice to the military is the same as that given earlier to the media: If you make a mistake, admit it. Trying to put a good face on the news does not mean trying to put a good face on every bit of news. Do your job, but do not overdo it.

On a more serious level, national security officials should not threaten or try to intimidate the press. Two examples involve the January 1985 classified shuttle mission. A joint air force–NASA press conference was held in December 1984 to explain that this mission would be handled quite differently from previous NASA shuttle launches: Less information would be given out and there would be no live broadcasts of control-to-shuttle communications. Officials emphasized the classified nature of the mission.

At one point a reporter asked, "What reprisal, precautions, penalties, or whatever you want to call it, would you plan to take against any reporter who 'speculates' [about the mission beyond the officially released information]?" The senior air force spokesman, Brigadier General Richard F. Abel, replied, "I believe that would be something that would be investigated, and I would not speculate as to what would happen."[6] DoD officials later said they knew of no plans, or even any legal basis, for what Abel had threatened—that is, government investigations of reporters who speculated about the classified mission.

Defense officials tried to distance themselves from the position taken by Abel. But later when *The Washington Post* ran a story containing information about the mission beyond that officially released by the government, Secretary of Defense Caspar Weinberger said the *Post* story gave "aid and comfort to the enemy"[7]—words taken from the U.S. Constitution's definition of treason. Such threatening and intimidating language not only does not deter the press, it poisons relations further. On both counts, it is counterproductive and therefore unwise.

On a more day-to-day level, military officers should learn how to use the press to their own advantage. For example, during 1982 and 1983 when the Marines were in Beirut in that delicate, difficult, and ultimately doomed mission, there was great demand on the part of the press for interviews with the marines on the ground. Some of their commanders had an imaginative and practical idea: If a journalist wanted to spend time getting marines to tell their stories, then the reporter had to spend some time telling marine officers about what he had seen in other parts of Beirut or in the Shouf Mountains where the Druze positions were. Through this clever quid pro quo, the marines were able to collect significant tactical intelligence about hostile forces and hostile positions. The reporters were able to do their job, and the marines found a way to reap some tangible dividends for themselves.

George Marshall used to say, "Don't fight the problem." Many military officers tried to keep reporters out of tactical, operational situations, but since Grenada, this is a lost battle. The smart commanders will find ways to turn the (perhaps unwanted) presence of reporters to their own good ends.

Last, in dealing with the problem of military-media relations, the DoD should take advantage of its centralized hierarchy: It should establish a proper attitude and practice right from the top. Time and again—from racial integration to the antismoking campaign—the military has demonstrated that, while it is hard to change people's attitudes, it is feasible to alter their behavior patterns, which in the long run may lead to modified attitudes. To do so requires clear and direct policies from the top and vigorous enforcement of them.

Because the military and the media are different institutions and cultures, there will always be—and should always be—some tension between them. Ultimately both institutions serve and are responsible to the American people—as taxpayers and citizens and as readers and viewers. If this necessary and productive tension gets out of control and these two valuable institutions suffer at each other's hands, not only do they pay a price, but the rest of us do as well.

## NOTES

1. Peter Braestrup, *Battle Lines: Report of the Twentieth Century Fund Task Force on the Military and the Media* (New York: Priority Press Publications, 1985).
2. U.S. Department of Defense, *Radio-TV Defense Dialog,* June 10, 1983, p. 5.
3. Ibid., June 13, 1983, p. 5.
4. Richard Halloran, *To Arm a Nation* (New York: Macmillan Publishing Company, 1986), p. 142.
5. "No, It's not Mr. Coffee," *Des Moines* (Iowa) *Register,* editorial; reprinted in U.S. Department of Defense, *Current News,* main edition, October 1, 1984, p. 4-E.
6. National Aeronautics and Space Administration (NASA), "Public Affairs Policy for Department of Defense Space Transportation System Missions," transcript of December 17, 1984, press conference.
7. "Weinburger Hits Shuttle Report as Irresponsible," *The Washington Post,* December 20, 1984; reprinted in U.S. Department of Defense, *Current News,* main edition, December 20, 1984, p. 1.

# Part IV

---

# ISSUES OF
# BUREAUCRATIC
# POLITICS

---

*The value of a bureaucratic politics approach to national security studies lies not only in its describing and explaining of reality but also in its raising of important normative questions concerning executive control, decisionmaking, and reorganization—central and profound questions for both academicians and practicitioners. These issues go to the heart of the proper role of bureaucracy in a democracy.*

# 10

## The Politics of Administrative Change and Reorganization

*Nowhere can bureaucratic politics be observed better than in the conflicts surrounding proposed structural change and reform. Such proposals are not neutral. They cannot be considered apart from the substantive preferences of their proponents. Individuals who advocate and favor alterations in established institutions usually believe that such change will enhance the authority of those who think like they do and thus will enable them to produce the policies they prefer. Conversely, those who oppose change do so because they believe it will lead to their ox getting gored. Of course, for national security policymaking, the most salient reform proposals and movements are those pertaining to the Joint Chiefs of Staff (JCS). Many proposals have been made and enacted in the hope of enhancing the generalist's perspective in the Department of Defense and diluting the impact of the bureaucratic particularism of the individual services. Although time will tell how successful and beneficial these reforms will be in a policy sense, it is important to realize that the phenomenon of bureaucratic politics is at their roots.*

## 10.1    Politics, Position and Power: The Dynamics of Federal Organization

### HAROLD SEIDMAN

*Organizational structure has significant political implications because it can "imped[e] or facilitat[e] the achievement of basic political goals and the effective functioning of the democratic process," states Harold Seidman in the concluding chapter of his 1976 book,* Politics, Position, and Power. *Yet the tensions between general and particularistic interests, centralized and decentralized authority, and fancy slogans and unrealistic expectations point to some of the difficulties in managing effectively the federal system. Seidman proposes a series of questions to be asked to evaluate the effect of organizational structure and/or its reorganization. Our answers, he suggests, must be as sophisticated as the problems they address. That is a challenge we must be willing to face.*

By allowing political expediency to dictate the design of administrative systems, a President can create major obstacles to the accomplishment of his basic political goals and the effective functioning of the democratic process. If present trends are not reversed, we run the risk that the Federal structure will become not a reflection, but a caricature of our pluralistic society.

President Nixon spoke of the "precipitous decline in public confidence" in the Federal Government. As the major cause of this crisis of confidence he identified "the chronic gap that exists between the publicity and promise attendant to the launching of a new Federal program—and that program's eventual performance." Few would dispute President Nixon's conclusion: "If confidence in Government is to be restored, the gap must be closed."[1]

Regrettably the gap has not been closed and appears to be widening. As might be expected from an administration in which for the first time advertising and public relations men occupied positions as key advisers to the President, primary emphasis was given to "selling" the product. The influence of the advertising man was to be seen in President Nixon's addiction to hyperbole and the use of slick slogans and labels such as the "New American Revolution." Titles of Government agencies—ACTION, Conquest of Cancer—were selected by advertising criteria. The Conquest of

From *Politics, Position and Power: The Dynamics of Federal Organization* by Harold Seidman. Copyright © 1970, 1975, 1980 by Oxford University Press, Inc. Reprinted by permission.

Cancer agency not only makes questionable organizational sense, but also implies a result which the government cannot guarantee. It certainly raises false expectations, the very thing President Nixon decried. There is no sound reason to believe that a separate agency reporting directly to the President will be any more successful in finding a cure for cancer than the National Cancer Institute under the National Institutes of Health.

Confidence will not be restored by open guerrilla warfare between the White House and the career civil service. The stream of Presidential invective against the bureaucracy is self-defeating. It is not calculated either to make the bureaucracy more responsive, or to renew the people's faith in Government.

The gap will not be closed by an organization strategy ostensibly designed to counteract and contain the particularistic forces within the Congress, the bureaucracy, and the outside community, but whose true purpose is to aggrandize the President's personal power. One does not combat parochialism in the departments by bringing the interest-group brokers into the White House.[2] President Nixon's assumption that Cabinet members should be echoes of the President and that advocacy is somehow inherently evil have profound implications for the functioning of the American democratic system. The issue is not *whether* the departments should stand for something but *what* they should stand for. Distribution of power within the executive branch, just as the division of powers among the three branches of Government, is an essential restraint on the President and an integral element in the system of "checks and balances."

An organization structure that provides access for particular groups within the community is not necessarily flawed, unless it prejudices policy outcomes and permits private groups to exploit public institutions for their own benefit. The question is one of balance. In the design of any political structure, whether it be the Congress or the executive branch, it is important to build in arrangements that weight the scale in favor of those advocating the national interest.

President Nixon was correct in identifying as major problems: (1) multiplication and fragmentation of programs and increased compartmentalization; (2) narrowing of constituencies; (3) weakening of general purpose units of Government and general political executives at all levels within the Federal system; (4) diffusion of authority, particularly by making executive actions dependent on congressional committee agreement or subject to approval by advisory committees; (5) reduced administrative flexibility and discretion; and (6) over-centralization of decision making in Washington. President Nixon's proposals for broadening the program categories and permitting local governments greater discretion in using Federal grants (special revenue sharing); decentralizing decision-making authority to the field; reducing red tape; establishing uniform regional boundaries; strengthening State and local governments' decision-making and managerial capabilities; and authorizing joint funding of "program packages" were constructive. If accepted by the Congress and effectively implemented, these reforms would help to reduce, but would not eliminate citizen frustrations.

Follow through on the Nixon reforms was spotty. Organizational and administrative decisions continued to be influenced more by what served the President's immediate political interests than by what was deemed essential to assure effective program performance, equitable administration, and responsiveness to all elements within our society.

Structural arrangements and administrative systems can affect significantly the political balance and program results. But to prescribe repairs to the machinery as the cure-all for current frustrations reflects either a mistaken diagnosis or unwillingness to come to grips with the real problems. Waning of faith in government is the product of what Kermit Gordon, president of the Brookings Institution and Budget Director under Presidents Kennedy and Johnson, calls "the government's losing struggle to cope with the crisis of convulsive change in which we live."[3]

The Federal Government is well equipped to perform its traditional functions with reasonable effectiveness—to disburse money, to build dams, highways, and other public works, and to collect taxes. The Government has not yet developed the capability to deal with the highly complex social and economic problems confronting the nation which, if they are to be resolved, demand radically new approaches. Alice Rivlin's suggestions for test and experimentation in her provocative book *Systematic Thinking for Social Action* are persuasive, but they require a fundamental change in political values and in the traditional "pork-barrel" approach to problem solving.[4] General revenue sharing is a nonsolution and merely passes the problems on to the states and localities.

Atomization of political power is not the antidote. The notion that our central political institutions can be reformed by emasculating them persists, even though experience with special districts, independent public authorities, and, most recently, nongovernmental community action agencies, hardly supports this view. Significant changes will not be achieved if we start from the premise that it is impossible to build into established State and local government systems those institutions and procedures necessary to assure effective citizen participation, involvement, and responsiveness to the poor and politically powerless.

A persuasive case can be made that community action agencies played a constructive role in shaking up the old-line Government agencies and in acting as organizers and advocates of the poor.[5] But the 973 community action agencies still functioning in 1974 pose no threat to the political establishment and have become primarily service agencies for the poor. Previously hostile politicians, including Governor George Wallace of Alabama, have found that the CAA's provide a convenient buffer between them and their poor citizens.[6]

It is the Federal, State and City governments that control the allocation of resources. To accord any class, section, or neighborhood the trappings of political power without regard to its ability to obtain necessary resources is a cruel hoax. When political power is fractionalized, the capability to obtain positive action is seriously impaired. All that is left is the power to veto—a situation that favors those who want to hold down Government expenditures. Whatever satisfaction may be derived from firing unpopular school principals or teachers or blocking plans for new freeways is rapidly dissipated when it is discovered that these actions cannot produce urgently needed funds to modernize school facilities and to provide adequate mass transportation. Unless our political institutions and administrative systems create an environment in which power among the classes and sections is so balanced that they are compelled to make concessions to each other, no one can expect to benefit and ultimately everyone will lose. The creation of such an environment should be a primary objective of any organization strategy.

Confidence in our public institutions will not be restored by adopting uncritically Peter Drucker's policy of "reprivatization."[7] Drucker defines "reprivatization" as the systematic policy of using "the nongovernmental institutions of the society of organizations, for the actual 'doing,' i.e., for performance operations, execution." It is one thing for the Government to withdraw completely from an area of operations, as with the liquidation of the Reconstruction Finance Corporation or the sale of the Inland Waterways Corporation, or to contract with nongovernment institutions to provide services for or on behalf of the Government, but it is quite another to allow private institutions to exercise public power in their own right and to use public funds without effective safeguards to assure political accountability. In theory at least, elected directors of community action and city development agencies and farmer committees are responsible and accountable to the voters who chose them. The directors of such organizations as the National Home Ownership Foundation and the Corporation for Public Broadcasting, which are designated as private by congressional "fiat," appear to be responsible legally to no one but themselves and their corporations. The President may exercise some influence through his power to appoint directors, but even this restraint is absent in the Urban Institute and comparable "captive" corporations which have self-perpetuating boards of directors.

All citizens and groups will not be afforded an equal opportunity to share in the benefits of Federal programs by establishing institutional and procedural arrangements which tend to limit access to the chosen few, as in the Farm Credit Administration and the National Institutes of Health. One can defend consulting borrower organizations about agricultural credit policies or "peer groups" about research grants. But this does not justify conferring upon them the statutory right to determine how public funds are to be spent.

Administration of Federal services will not be brought closer to the consumers by so diffusing authority that effective delegation is impossible. Centralization of authority must precede decentralization. Whenever the exercise of executive authority is made contingent upon the agreement of others at the headquarters level, delegation outside of Washington presents difficult problems and is sometimes impossible. A department head can only delegate the powers vested in him.

Effective performance will not be achieved by clinging to an antiquated budgetary system which encourages waste and inefficiency. The annual budgetary cycle does not allow sufficient time for either the Federal agencies or State and local governments and private institutions which are increasingly dependent on Federal support to do the kind of advance planning which is essential to obtain program results. The cycle is compressed even further when the Congress does not enact appropriation bills until five or six months after the beginning of the fiscal year, and agencies must operate under continuing resolutions at the previous year's budgetary level. No agency can function efficiently when it is compelled either to disburse funds within a six-month period or to let them lapse. The period is even shorter when expenditures cannot be made until matching funds are provided or other actions taken by State and local governments. At a minimum, State and local governments and other institutions dependent on Federal financing require a firm commitment at least one year in advance as to the amount of Federal money that will be available so that they can develop their own budgets on a sound basis.

Proposals to break up the present constituencies by moving from a functional to a regional or geographic executive branch structure merely would substitute one form of particularism for another. National purposes will not be strengthened by reorganizing to give primary emphasis to sectional interests. These are even more difficult to deal with than conflicts among program areas. A congressman can defend politically measures which favor one program area over another, but he feels constrained to demand "equal treatment" for his State or district. The pressure on the Congress to "log-roll" and to spread the money around on a geographic basis without regard to peculiar local needs or national priorities would be increased rather than abated.

To revive the ancient debate about the relative merits of departmentalization according to major purpose, major process, clientele, materiel, or geography would be profitless and divert attention from the real issues. The doctrine of organization according major purposes advanced by the President's Committee on Administrative Management and the first Hoover Commission has brought about a more logical and consistent grouping of Government activities within the executive departments and eliminated such organizational anomalies as the assignment of health functions to Treasury and education functions to Interior—anomalies by no means uncommon in the period prior to 1939. Changes in our national values, goals, and priorities may well argue for additional reforms in executive branch structure. Persuasive arguments can and have been made for consolidation of land and water resources functions in a Department of Natural Resources, establishment of a Department of Education, and reconsideration of the present missions of the Commerce and Labor Departments. None of these reorganizations could be expected by themselves to curb appreciably the power of the centrifugal forces within our governmental system or to get at the roots of our current difficulties.

The benefits that are supposed to flow from departmentalization are by no means automatic. All too often the general purposes which ostensibly are to be served by a department may be obscured or lost altogether by the way a department is structured internally. A department composed of a collection of small semi-autonomous units, each speaking for its own limited constituency, will not act as a cohesive whole and will be highly resistant to change. The walls between bureaus within a department may be as impenetrable as those between departments, sometimes more so. A joint Bureau of the Budget, Civil Service Commission, Labor Department survey team found that the Labor Department had become so "compartmentalized" that it was almost impossible to fit new programs into the existing structure.[8] As a result, the Secretary was compelled to create a new bureau for each new program enacted by the Congress.

Reorganization commissions have concentrated primarily on the organization of the executive branch with only relatively brief reference to internal departmental organization. Yet, as a determinant of organizational behavior, the latter is the most important. As a result of the recommendations of the first Hoover Commission, the Congress has removed many of the legal impediments to the exercise of Secretarial authority. But it has shown no disposition to relax the extra-legal restraints against internal reorganizations which upset committee jurisdictions or threaten to alter the balance of power among constituencies or between the constituencies and the Secretary.

Cabinet Secretaries rarely bring to their jobs the unique combination of political insight, administrative skill, leadership, intelligence, and creativity required for the successful management of heterogeneous institutions with multiple and sometimes conflicting purposes. Most are content to be a "mediator-initiator" or a reactor to initiatives coming from the White House, the Congress, the bureaucracy, and the several constituencies represented by the Department. Anything other than a passive approach is likely to encounter opposition from the Congress, which believes that major bureaus should be allowed to run themselves without undue Secretarial interference. This is especially true of the so-called professional bureaus. We accept the principle of civilian control of the military profession, but not of the nonmilitary professions such as medicine, education, science, and engineering.

The Hoover Commission task force on departmental management recognized that "the external demands on a Secretary are such" that he cannot "give continuing attention to internal problems."[9] It assumed that the Under Secretary, or, in the case of the Department of Defense, the Deputy Secretary, would become the "top internal point of departmental direction." Deputy Secretaries of Defense have been used in this way, as have such Under Secretaries as Charles Murphy, who served under Secretary of Agriculture Orville Freeman, but these are the exceptions. An Under Secretary suffers from much the same disabilities as the Vice President and is subject to the same frustrations. Only under unusual circumstances is he able to establish the personal rapport and relationship of mutual trust with the Secretary which are essential if he is to act as an "alter ego." He can exercise authority in his own right only when the Secretary is absent or the Secretarial post is vacant. Since anything he says is construed to represent departmental policy, he must be highly circumspect if he is to avoid the appearance of usurping Secretarial prerogatives.

The failure of Under Secretaries generally to evolve into general managers or executive vice presidents has left a vacuum within the departmental management systems which has never been satisfactorily filled. This vacuum cannot be filled merely by multiplying the number of staff advisers to the Secretary. Attempts to use budget, planning, management, and analytical staffs to compensate for the deficiencies of line management are seldom successful and represent a misuse of staff talents. As one Secretary expressed it, what he needed were "people to do the job," not more people to tell him how someone else should do the job.[10] Former HEW Secretary Folsom was making the same point when he said that we had made considerable progress in strengthening the staff resources available to a Secretary and now his "chief concern was the need for more line officers."[11]

As departments are presently organized, a Secretary is confronted with a dilemma. If he utilizes his Assistant Secretaries as line officers, then he has no one at the top political level with department-wide perspective whom he can use for assignments which cut across program jurisdictions. If he uses his Assistant Secretaries as staff, then he has no one between him and the Bureau chiefs on whom he can rely to get jobs done. We find no consistent pattern within the executive departments, but the trend is toward using Assistant Secretaries in the line, with the notable exception of the Department of Transportation.

There is probably no pat solution to this dilemma. No two departments have identical managerial requirements. Each must have a system adapted to its own environment. It seems clear, however, that present restrictions on establishing executive positions at the Under Secretary and Assistant Secretary level, limiting the transfer or pooling of appropriations among organizational units to achieve common program objectives, and specifying the details of departmental organization and administrative procedures inhibit managerial innovation and experimentation. As James E. Webb points out, "if the organizational framework in which executives are fitted is rigid, the executive cannot be flexible."[12]

Departments are structured to administer national programs in accordance with uniform national standards. Solutions to many of our current problems require programs which are tailored to the special needs of a particular region or community. These types of programs by their very nature cut horizontally across established departmental jurisdictions at all levels of government. It is with respect to horizontal organization that the conventional wisdom of the orthodox doxology is least helpful. Hierarchical concepts of management cannot be applied to many of the new social programs which require the collaboration of a number of co-equal Government organizations on a single project, without any one having final authority over the other.

The rigidities in our departmental systems are major deterrents to lateral communications and cooperative efforts. Agencies find it difficult to work together when they have incompatible administrative systems. It is as if we had designed one system to operate on 25-cycle current, and another on 60-cycle. Converters are expensive and inefficient.

Up to now, insufficient attention has been given either within the executive branch or the Congress to the need for standardizing administrative provisions. Differences often reflect nothing more than historical accident or the predilections of a particular agency lawyer or congressional committee. Congress has no procedures for central review of proposed legislation to eliminate inconsistencies and conflicts in nonsubstantive administrative provisions. Administrative requirements in closely related programs may differ with respect to documentation to establish eligibility, control of property and funds, personnel standards, reporting procedures, geographic boundaries, auditing, planning, and definitions of common items such as "facilities."

The provisions of the Economic Opportunity Act and the Juvenile Deliquency Act which permit the waiver of certain incompatible legislative requirements for jointly funded projects are a step in the right direction, but do not go far enough. The Congress has been reluctant to authorize blanket waivers of conflicting technical and administrative rules for cooperative and jointly funded projects. The provision authorizing such waivers was one of the factors underlying congressional opposition to a general "Joint Funding Simplification Act" which would have permitted the pooling of grant funds from separate authorizations and appropriations to finance "program packages" developed by State and local governments.

Professional guilds have been able to exploit the differences in administrative requirements to protect their monopolies. Whatever may have been the original historical justification, the time has come to repeal those laws which confer exclusive privileges on single-State agencies and prevent their integration into a unified management system or stand in the way of cooperative programs. Federal regulations generally do not discriminate between the most competent and the least competent State and local governments. Rather than devise our regulations for the lowest common denominator of governors and mayors and States and cities, it would be preferable to provide for direct Federal administration in those instances where it could be demonstrated that State and local administration could not meet established standards of competence, honesty, and fairness.

For the horizontal programs, we need the "adaptive, rapidly changing temporary systems" advocated by Warren Bennis. Flexibility is essential so that the resources and people to solve specific problems can be drawn upon regardless of organizational boundaries. In designating project managers, there is a need for discretion to ignore traditional hierarchical distinctions among departments and agencies, Secretaries, Administrators, and Directors.

If the President and the Congress want to restore national unity and confidence in the Federal Government, they should first put their own houses in order. The President should restore the prestige of the Cabinet as the one visible symbol of the executive branch as a collective entity sharing common purposes. President Eisenhower was right in recognizing the institutional value of the Cabinet, but wrong in thinking that it could be converted into an effective decision-making mechanism. What is important is not so much what the Cabinet does as what it represents.

Recent Presidents have allowed the White House to develop into a separate institution more or less isolated from the other executive agencies. Richard Neustadt has observed that "In form all Presidents are leaders, nowadays. In fact this guarantees no more than that they will be clerks."[13] There is no more certain way to reduce a President to a chief clerk than to surround him with 100 or more personal helpers competing for his time and raising with him matters that would be better left to the institutional agencies in the Executive Office of the President or the operating departments. Creativity and energy within the executive establishment cannot be stimulated by limiting direct face-to-face communications with the President and by assuming that superior wisdom is necessarily possessed by members of the White House staff. Negativism is fostered when agencies either are placed in the position where they appear to be reacting defensively to White House staff initiatives, or are required to argue their case as adversaries in a tribunal where the President presides as a judge.

President Nixon acknowledged that a "leaner and less diffuse Presidential staff structure . . . would enhance the President's ability to do his job."[14] A National Academy of Public Administration panel has recommended that the White House staff be limited to not more than fifteen top aides to the President and not to exceed fifty supporting professional employees. The latter would be subject to the Hatch Act, which bars political activities.[15] The distinction between the personal, political staff of the President and the institutional staff in the Executive office of the President serving the Presidency needs to be restored. The Director of OMB and the Executive Director of the Domestic Council should not wear a second hat as Assistants to the President or be housed in the White House. Institutional staff should be recruited and evaluated on the basis of their professional competence, not loyalty to the incumbent President.

When the Congress disregarded the President's interests and abolished the National Resources Planning Board, it deprived the President of the professional staff support which is essential if he is to carry out his responsibilities for national planning and defining national goals in realistic and realizable terms. The National Planning Association, Rufus Miles, and William D. Carey have all stressed that the Executive Office of the President as now constituted does not have the capacity adequately to assist the President in setting national goals and priorities, analyzing policies, and evaluating program results.[16] *Ad hoc* task forces are useful, but they cannot do the in-depth staff work, or provide the continuity and follow-through which are essential. A planning or policy analysis staff within the Executive Office of the President will be effective, however, only if it is not expected to produce instant answers to highly complex and perhaps insolvable problems, or if it is judged by the President solely on its ability to produce politically attractive items for his current legislative program.

Hopes that the Domestic Council would fill the vacuum left by abolition of the National Resources Planning board have proved illusory. It has focused on "fire-fighting" and short-range tactical problems.

The President's task does not end with setting national goals and priorities and mobilizing public support for his programs. He must be as much concerned with means as ends. His decisions on program design, institutional type, organizational jurisdiction, and management system may well determine who will control and benefit from a program and, ultimately, whether national objectives are achieved. These decisions should not be governed solely by application of traditional organization doctrines. In evaluating the design and organization of new programs or proposed reorganizations of existing programs, the basic questions to be asked are:

1. What is the nature of the constituency that is being created, or acquired, and to what extent will it be able to influence policies and program administration?

2. Is the constituency broadly based or does it represent narrow interests antithetical to some of the public purposes to be accomplished by the program?

3. What committees of the Congress will exercise jurisdiction and to what extent do they reflect the interests of the constituencies to be served by

the program, or those of groups hostile to program objectives?

4. What is the culture and tradition of the administering department or agency? Will it provide an environment favorable to program growth, stunt development, or produce a hybrid?

5. What are the constituencies to whom the administering agency responds? Would there be any obvious conflicts of interest?

6. Where are the loci of power with respect to program administration: the President, the agency head, the bureaus, congressional committees, professional guilds, interest groups, etc.? Are provisions made to assure an appropriate balance of power and to prevent domination by any single group? Are the ultimate powers of the President protected and supported?

7. To what extent and in what way is access to those with decision-making power limited?

8. Does the program design foster dominance by a particular professional perspective and will this result in distortion of program goals?

9. Is provision made for an "open" system engineered in such a way that there are no built-in obstacles to joint administration with related government programs and cooperative efforts?

10. What safeguards are provided to assure that no group or class of people is excluded from participation in the program and an equitable share in program benefits?

11. Do the type of institution and proposed organization provide the status, visibility, public support, and administrative system appropriate to the function to be performed?

Whether or not meaningful improvements in executive branch organization and in the management of the Federal system can be obtained will depend in the final analysis on reorganization of the congressional committee structure. The particularistic elements in our society always will triumph over the general interest as long as they are nourished and supported by committees and subcommittees which share their limited concerns. At a minimum, committee and subcommittee jurisdictions should be compatible with current assignments of responsibilities within the executive branch and take into account interrelationships among programs so as to permit unified consideration of closely related and interdependent programs and evaluation of program objectives. Even modest reforms are unlikely, however, unless an informed and aroused electorate demands that the Congress modernize its organization and procedures. The assumption that only congressmen are affected by congressional organization is no longer tenable.

The Hoover Commission doctrines were somewhat dated when they were first published. They have served their purpose, and most of the basic recommendations have been implemented. Our Government has undergone revolutionary changes in the twenty-five years which have elapsed since the Hoover reports. The principles of organization advanced by the Hoover

Commission have not lost their validity, but read by themselves they do not contribute materially to our understanding of current problems of Government organization and management. It is fruitless to look to them for solutions.

We will compound the problems if we demand simple answers. The growing interdependence of the Federal Government, State and local governments, and many private institutions; increasing reliance on administration by grant and contract; and the greater utilization of multi-jurisdictional programs have added new dimensions to public administration. Whatever strategy is devised must be as sophisticated as the problems which it seeks to solve and retain sufficient flexibility to permit rapid adjustments to changing circumstances. It cannot deal with the executive branch as if it existed in isolation and must take into account the linkages between congressional and executive organization. If we persist in thinking of organization in terms of lines and boxes on an organization chart, our efforts to discover viable approaches to our current dilemma certainly will fail.

## NOTES

1. *Weekly Compilation of Presidential Documents,* October 13, 1969, p. 1399.

2. See Thomas E. Cronin, "The Swelling of the Presidency," *Saturday Review,* February 1973.

3. The Brookings Institution annual report 1970, p. 1.

4. Alice M. Rivlin, *Systematic Thinking for Social Action,* The Brookings Institution, 1971.

5. See James L. Sundquist and David W. Davis, *Making Federalism Work,* The Brookings Institution, 1969, Chapter 2.

6. *New York Times,* April 7, 1974.

7. Peter F. Drucker, *The Age of Discontinuity,* Harper and Row, 1969, pp. 233–42.

8. Joint Management Improvement and Manpower Review Team, "Review of Management Practices and Manpower Utilization in the Department of Labor," July 1963, pp. 2–2, 2–3.

9. Commission on Organization of the Executive Branch of the Government, task force report on "Departmental Management," January 1949, p. 11.

10. Based on notes of personal conversation.

11. Senate Committee on Government Operations, Subcommittee on Executive Reorganization, hearings on "Modernizing the Federal Government," January–May 1968, p. 221.

12. James E. Webb, *Space-Age Management,* McGraw-Hill Book Co., 1969, p. 141.

13. Richard E. Neustadt, *Presidential Power,* John Wiley & Sons, Inc., 1960, p. 6.

14. House Document No. 93-43.

15. Frederick C. Mosher and others, *Watergate: Its Implications for Responsible Government,* Basic Books, 1974, p. 37.

16. National Planning Association, "Program Planning for National Goals," November 1968; Senate Committee on Government Operations, *op. cit.,* p. 111;

William D. Carey, "Presidential Staffing in the Sixties and Seventies," *Public Administration Review*, Vol. XXIX, No. 5, 1969.

# 10.2   The 1986 Defense Reorganization: A Promising Start

## JOHN G. KESTER

*John G. Kester suggests in the following essay that the 1986 defense reorganization provides structural improvements for the realization of our national security objectives. He sees the enhanced power of the chairman of the Joint Chiefs of Staff (JCS) and the Commanders in Chief (CINC) as significant steps toward that end. However, he reminds us that regardless of formal organizational remedies, bureaucratic politics, or business as usual, will not be easily forsaken.*

On October 1, 1986, Congress went further in telling the Pentagon how to do its job than at any time since the fundamental defense organizational statutes of 1947, 1949, and 1958. The movement was bipartisan: The law carries the names of retiring Senator Barry Goldwater and House Armed Service Subcommittee Chairman Bill Nichols.[1] It could just as well have borne the names of Senator Sam Nunn and some diligent committee staffers on both sides of Capitol Hill who had pushed the effort for many years.

What strikingly distinguishes the new legislation from its predecessors is that it was unquestionably the child of Congress, not the Executive Branch. It was enacted not with Secretary of Defense Caspar Weinberger's blessing, but, figuratively, over his dead body. It became law in the face of protests by the sitting Joint Chiefs of Staff (who were disputed by some of their predecessors) that it was not needed—protests that finally became so strident and exaggerated that they were self-defeating.

Coming on the heels of flamboyant complaints about defense procurement—the allegedly overpriced hammers, coffee machines, and toilet seats—these long-needed organizational reforms secured passage partly on their merits and partly as a congressional vote of no confidence in the way the Pentagon had (or had not) been managed for the past six years. The Reagan administration understood the bill in the latter sense. The bill was quietly approved by the president without the usual signing ceremony that trumpets legislation drawing executive enthusiasm.

Congress, however, remains the Legislative Branch. It can pass laws, occasionally investigate, and intermittently micromanage. But it is up to the

Executive Branch, under the Constitution, to enforce the laws that Congress passes. The armed services committees have vowed to keep an eye on how well the reluctant targets of this legislation are saluting and moving out. The first promised checkup hearings were held in May 1987. "The devil, someone once observed, "is in the details." It will take a year or two of examining details of implementation before anyone will know for sure whether the 1986 Goldwater-Nichols Act is really, as House Armed Services Committee Chairman Les Aspin described it, "probably the greatest sea change in the history of the American military since the Continental Congress created the Continental Army in 1775."[2]

## ORIGINS OF THE NEW ACT

The new reorganization law is fundamental legislation. It addresses long-standing dissatisfaction with the way the U.S. military functions. The law has potential, if not sabotaged or ignored, to change permanently the way the armed forces are planned and the way they operate, and, in the process, it could reshape military careers.

In a tradition of complaints that goes back at least as far as General Maxwell Taylor's *The Uncertain Trumpet* in 1959 and the Symington Committee report to President-elect John F. Kennedy in 1960, the seeds for this reform were planted long ago. But they began to sprout during Harold Brown's time as secretary of defense, when he quietly started to streamline the sprawling and incoherent Office of the Secretary of Defense (OSD) by eliminating several assistant secretaries, pulling the giant defense agencies under OSD supervision, and securing congressional authorization to establish an under secretary of defense for policy, while at the same time dropping an unneeded second deputy secretary of defense. In addition to shaping up OSD, Brown had the larger goal of strengthening the joint (as opposed to service-dominated) elements of the bureaucracy, on the theory that, as Eisenhower had taught, war fighting was inevitably a joint proposition and the days of single-service combat were "gone forever."[3]

Brown's further plans for freeing the chairman of the Joint Chiefs of Staff (JCS) from the tyranny of the four service bureaucracies were soon stymied, however, by unexpected intervention from President Jimmy Carter's Office of Management and Budget (OMB), which wanted to meddle with Pentagon organization in order to play out its own grandiose (and fruitless) schemes to reorganize the entire U.S. government. Nothing came of the OMB activity, but it sufficed to hobble further progress at the Pentagon. The most visible step forward was a report by New York venture capitalist Richard Steadman in 1978 that pointed out flaws in the JCS system, but put forward only cautious suggestions for change.[4]

Over the next four years a series of articles appeared, further highlighting the ineffectiveness of the Department of Defense's (DoD) ponderous bureaucracy and suggesting far-reaching revisions.[5] The most controversial essay, given the author's position, came in 1982 from General David C. Jones, who was still in office as JCS chairman at the time.[6] (Until then, the practice had been for civilian and military critics of the JCS system to do nothing while in office and then later call for JCS reform when someone else would have to carry it out.) Jones relied not just on his own experience but also on a study filed by a group of retired four-star officers, including three former vice chiefs of staff, and chaired by former Assistant Secretary of Defense William K. Brehm. The study concluded (based in part on candid interviews with the chiefs themselves) that many criticisms of JCS parochialism and the ineffectiveness of the joint staff were well founded. Brehm also proposed a new joint-duty career field.[7]

Jones was more than backed up by outspoken Army Chief of Staff General E. C. "Shy" Meyer.[8] Both Jones and Meyer were attacked by uniformed colleagues for telling tales out of school. But both persisted, and cautious support was voiced by a handful of other distinguished senior officers who had completed their active careers. Later, several Washington think tanks also published studies urging action.[9]

The winds of change began to roil leaves on Capitol Hill in 1982 when Representative Richard C. White of Texas, in his final term, held subcommittee hearings on defense reorganization. After White's retirement, these hearings were continued by Representative Bill Nichols and led to enactment of minor legislative changes in 1984.[10] Such activity in the House was a break from tradition. The House Armed Services Committee for a generation had been ultraconservative, controlled by members and staffers tied to the navy. The navy's institutional views on interservice issues derived from a simple starting place: It had never wanted to be a part of the DoD.

## A NEW CAST OF CHARACTERS

However, and ironically, while Capitol Hill was opening its eyes to Pentagon reorganization issues, a totally opposite shift had taken place in the Pentagon. Caspar Weinberger, the new secretary of defense, soon revealed that he had no interest whatsoever in management. (Indeed, he quickly undid many of Brown's small reforms. The number of assistant secretaries of defense swelled from six to eleven, while Congress continued to add even more in a sort of interest-group approach to defense management.) Weinberger's answer to all organizational questions—and for a time his president's answer also—was to leave budget and policy decisions to the three military departments and to give the uniformed leadership whatever it wanted. The three military departments, not surprisingly, did not rise to the challenge; instead, they, predictably, pushed their pet programs (for example, fifteen carrier battle groups) without regard to overall capability.

The uniformed advocates of change were soon out of office. Jones retired in 1982 and Meyer in 1983. Jones was replaced by General John W. Vessey, Jr., not the least of whose attractions to the new administration was that he had been rejected for army chief of staff by Jimmy Carter. Vessey and the new chiefs spent the next four years assuring everyone that the JCS were one of nature's most nearly perfect creations since mother's milk. If the JCS were to be changed at all, they explained, it needed only minor adjustments of their own concoction—such as making the chairman a statutory member, coequal with his boss the secretary of defense, on the National Security Council (NSC).

Weinberger, egged on by the chiefs and following his hands-off management style, dug in his heels against meaningful change—to the point that his intransigence finally became an administration embarrassment. Meanwhile, public complaints about high-priced flukes of spare-parts pricing, and a growing desire to save money on defense, deepened loss of confidence in Weinberger's judgment.

## CONGRESS ACTS

In 1985 Barry Goldwater replaced John Tower as chairman of the Senate Armed Services Committee, and the Senate got busy. Goldwater, finishing up his career, teamed with ranking Democrat Sam Nunn, who as usual cared more for good results than for who took the credit. Three bold but thoughtful Senate staffers—James Locher, Jeffrey Smith, and Richard Finn—put together a comprehensive 645-page report that remains the best single compendium of the flaws in the old system and ideas for a new.[11] Their report was labeled as simply staff research, and they bore the brunt of emotional criticism from supporters of the *status quo,* thereby allowing the senators themselves a bit of distance and a freer hand in adjusting the final provisions.

By late 1985 it was clear that some change in how the Pentagon does business was coming. The only question was how much. To try to preempt the politically hot procurement issue, the White House circumvented Weinberger by appointing the Packard Commission, headed by Richard Nixon's Deputy Secretary of Defense. But in its 186 report on DoD acquisition, the Packard Commission concluded that many of the problems in Defense procurement resulted from gross flaws in DoD organization.[12] By that time, Congress was determined to act in a major way. Nevertheless, Navy Secretary John Lehman continued to lobby tirelessly against organizational change, both to protect naval interests and to seek elimination of some provisions in earlier leglislative pooposals that would have unduly weakened civilian authority. Lehman, while often overstating, at least raised some legitimate concerns about possible further decline of the position of service secretary, an office which he fearlessly filled to its full potential. However, Marine Corps Commandant General P. X. Kelley went completely overboard and blew his own credibility by announcing his apocalyptic vision that JCS reform "would create chaos . . . to the point where I would have deep concerns for the future security of the United States."[13]

In the end, basic change in U.S. military structure that for years had been dismissed as an impossible dream survived fourteen markup sessions, swept through the Senate in a single day, and passed on a unanimous vote. Many moderates had become convinced that legislation was the only way to force the administration to come to grips with fundamental organizational problems it had persistently denied even existed. The House, voting 406-4, passed a bill that had many provisions similar to the Senate's and even went further.[14] The conference to adjust the differences was tough but constructive. In a rare instance of the legislative process at its best, some ill-considered provisions in both bills were dropped along the way, and the final product probably is better than either the House or Senate versions would have been standing alone.

On October 1, 1986, the future began when the *Goldwater-Nichols DoD Reorganization Act of 1986,* as it was christened, became law. The new legislation is long and often too detailed, but its key provisions are not difficult to understand, and their purpose is so clear that no Pentagon administration will be able to ignore them. The main ones are as follows:

## The Secretary of Defense

The reorganization arrow almost hit the wrong target. The biggest problem in the DoD structure was that the four military services were too dominant, and the central military organization—the JCS and particularly its chairman—too institutionally weak. Yet some earlier House versions of the reorganization bill, as well as proposals pushed by the Weinberger administration at the behest of the JCS, would have cut back on the power of the secretary of defense, while leaving the service bureaucracies unscathed. The JCS chairman would have been made a military commander of all the forces, instead of simply head of the senior uniformed staff, and would have been added to the political leaders on the NSC (which he had always attended in a proper advisory role). All those bad ideas finally were eliminated.

The conference report starts out with a ringing reiteration that "the Secretary has sole and ultimate power within the Department of Defense on any matter on which the Secretary chooses to act." The law in several places prescribes qualifications for military appointees, and even suggests chain of command arrangements. But whenever it does so, it is careful to recognize the power of the commander in chief (CINC) and his secretary of defense to provide otherwise.

The new organization enhances CINC and JCS chairman power at the expense of service power, which is as it should be because that is where the problem was. And the law wisely leaves the chairman and the JCS in the purely staff role that the JCS has always occupied, the importance of which President Dwight D. Eisenhower, among others, emphasized. The conferees in fact directed the secretary of defense's office to take more charge, calling for greater "civilian oversight of the contingency planning process," a function for which the under secretary of defense for policy was created in 1978 but which no incumbent has ever fully performed.

## The JCS Chairman

Continuing a trend begun under the secretary's own authority by Secretary of Defense Harold Brown, the new law removes many functions from the service-dominated JCS—the corporate body—and reassigns them to the chairman alone. It is he, not they, who advises the president and secretary of defense, and it is to him that the joint staff now will answer.

## The Vice Chairman

The law also gives the chairman a four-star deputy. No longer will one of the service chiefs fill in as acting chairman on the frequent occasions when the chairman is out of town. Simple as it sounds, creation of this new second-ranking officer for the U.S. armed forces is a striking measure of the seriousness of the legislation, and of Congress' determination to change the present system.

The current service chiefs pulled out all the stops to lobby against this provision. Partly because no one likes to lose a chance to visit the White House, they urged that the new vice chairman should rank below them and never be acting chairman. They argued that the responsibility of acting as chairman gave each of them incentive to keep abreast of joint matters (which they are supposed to do anyway). They did not object to creation of a new office—but as they conceived it, the incumbent would have ranked behind them and never acted as chairman. In effect, Congress simply would have awarded the chairman's existing three-star assistant a fourth star.

The service chiefs' arguments failed. Congress recognized that substance as well as protocol was involved, and rejected the effort to keep the new office from exercising real authority. The new number two by law will have the clout to pull the programs together and really run the joint staff. The chairman is no longer alone; he and his vice chairman have the unequivocal mandate of Congress to be a potent team.

## The CINCs

Although there had been steps in Harold Brown's administration to pay more attention to the four-star commanders of the eleven unified or specified commands—the CINCs—in the new legislation they at last come into their own. This results in part from the tireless lobbying and graphic war stories of retired army General Paul F. Gorman, former assistant to General David Jones and former CINC for Latin America. Gorman impressed senators with true horror stories of his frustrations at trying to get the job done as a field commander whose resources were controlled by service bureaucracies back in Washington.

Some of the earlier versions of the legislation, in fact, read less like a law than an angry letter to the editor from a frustrated CINC. Some proposals would have gone too far, as in giving a CINC veto power over the secretary of defense's choices for his subordinates. The law as passed cures that by explicitly recognizing the secretary's authority and president's constitutional power to override CINC choices, while making clear that Congress now expects the heads of subordinate service elements to work for the CINC and not for their service headquarters back in Washington. The conferees also wisely eliminated many details, including a House proposal to set up a CINCs' council to rival the JCS. The last thing the DoD needs is another committee.

The law as passed finally gives the CINCs—who for too long have been generals without armies and admirals without fleets—great authority over the forces assigned to them. After objections and confusion in the House-Senate conference, the law stops short of calling their role "command," but the powers conferred are so broad that effectively it means nothing else, assuming that these positions are filled with officers not timid about using the invitation that has been handed them.

U.S. field commanders have not had such authority since Eisenhower and MacArthur, perhaps not even then. Exactly how it will mesh with the central uniformed authority in Washington remains to be seen. The new law probably goes about as far to rectify the balance as one might dare. CINCs, after all, by nature have limitations. It may well be the field commanders who in wartime become famous and later get aircraft carriers named for them. Yet no CINC will ever be in the best position to evaluate the country's overall military needs. General George C. Marshall, back at the Pentagon, was the key U.S. army officer of World War II, just as Admiral Ernest J. King surely outshone in important respects the principal naval field commander, Admiral Chester W. Nimitz. Central direction remains essential. The new law appears to provide a better balance without tilting the scales.

## The Service Staffs

Late in the House-Senate conference, several senior uniformed officers panicked over the House bill's requirement that civilian and military staffs be integrated in the military departments. If there were only one staff, they asked, reporting to the service secretary, then what would the chief of staff be? Just a chief of staff?

The House provision intended nothing sinister. Its idea, in fact, was to cut out the waste of having civilian staffs report to a service assistant secretary (for example, for manpower and reserve affairs) who duplicates and micromanages the work of other staffs that report to a three-star deputy chief of staff (for example, for personnel). The House bill would leave the service secretary with a palace guard of thirty or so close assistants in all, and force him to work with and use the uniformed staff if he wants to do something.

Uniformed officers, however, were aghast at such a plan. The truth is that the growth of civilian service secretariats reflects not so much secretarial aggrandizement as the desire of the career uniformed bureaucracy to give each transient secretary a staff of his own to order around, so that he can amuse himself and feel busy while not interfering too often in serious business—even though a chief of staff is, theoretically as well as etymologically, the chief of the staff of the service secretary, who by law heads the department. The idea that the Army General Staff, for example, is the staff of the secretary of the army had become well-high forgotten.

What also disturbed the senior military, though most were too polite to say so, is that many service secretaries have not been the sort of people to be trusted with serious business, being more in the tradition of Gilbert and Sullivan than of Henry L. Stimson. A few critics were willing also to acknowledge that when a service secretary does know exactly what he is doing, in the manner of Navy Secretary John Lehman, they often do not like that either. The remarkably unkind public attack on Lehman by the chief of naval operations, Admiral Carlisle Trost, as soon as Lehman was out the door, showed little charity or appreciation for the architect of the 600-ship navy.

Congress, somewhat puzzled, finally compromised, leaving the dual staff arrangement in place for most major functions. At Senator Sam Nunn's urging, a specific provision was added to the law to require the secretary of defense to specify the qualifications needed for appointment to each civilian office in DoD requiring presidential appointment and Senate confirmation. The conference members, going public with what many of them said privately, wrote that they "remain concerned about the lack of sufficient experience and expertise by persons appointed to political positions in the Department of Defense," and vowed that from now on the senators would "establish and exercise more rigorous confirmation standards."

## The Joint Career Field

Assignments and promotions are the currency of power in the U.S. military organization. Over the long run they shape the services far more than quibbles about who attends meetings at the White House.

Thanks to the stubborn insistence of the House conferees, the new law at last lays the foundation for a real U.S. general staff. Finally, by Congress' direction, there will be a career specialty for officers in joint-duty assignments. Their promotions are to be monitored to make sure able officers get into the field. (A House provision that went further and called for numerical quotas was wisely dropped.) Their big daddy will be the chairman of the JCS, and he will have what it takes to protect them. Unlike some of the passing enthusiasms that crop up every so often for one career field or another, this policy favoring joint duty is written into law and so will be difficult to ignore.

In a revolutionary new requirement, by statute every promotion board that considers officers who have served in joint-duty assignments now will have a joint-duty member—and that member will be appointed not by the service secretary, but by the chairman of the JCS. If the chairman is not satisfied with the board's results, he can return a promotion list with objectives to the service secretary, who must take action to satisfy him or else refer the disagreement to the secretary of defense. The chairman also is to establish career guidelines for joint officers and procedures to monitor them. By law, at least half the graduates of the National Defense University will be assigned immediately to joint duty (the House again would have gone further and would have required "significantly" more than half). Whether this requirement is feasible given the other constraints on shifting senior personnel remains to be seen. The law comes close to micromanagement; but the proclivity of the services in the past to cheat on even much milder directives from OSD amply explains the congressional insistence on detail.

Not only will real joint duty be a prerequisite for flag rank, but all the choice flag-rank positions, including chairman, vice chairman, service chief, and CINC, are to be reserved, unless there is a waiver, for officers whose careers show significant joint experience. Supposedly, the fast burners now will angle for billets on, of all things, CINC headquarters and the joint staff. For ambitious majors and lieutenant colonels—and, harder to believe, even for lieutenant commanders and commanders—joint duty is to be transformed from a stigma to the punchiest ticket around.

## Planning, Command, and Control

The new law also takes on the contingency planning process. It requires the secretary of defense to provide the chairman annual policy guidance for contingency plans, which the secretary is to review. This provides a statutory mandate for what should have been going on already and, if successful, will give civilian leaders more confidence in the military planning process, perhaps also eliminating the sort of command and control discontinuities that turned up in the Grenada invasion, as well as perennial logistics-mission mismatches. Plans prepared under resource constraints may end the frequent disconnections between the programming and budgeting process on the one hand, and military operational planning on the other.

## Roles and Missions

As a foot prying open the door toward future change, the new law retains the Senate bill's requirement for periodic reports by the chairman on whether roles and missions are sensibly distributed among the four services. The topic is the touchiest in the Pentagon; no one has prodded that hornets' nest since 1949. But, as a result, the country lacks adequate airlift and sealift because the army is prohibited from buying transport planes and ships, and the air force and navy think they have better things to do than drive buses. The new law at least points to a day when such issues may be faced.

## Testing the Law

The congressional authors of the new law tried as hard as they could to foresee, and to cut off, avenues for evading its central purpose of strengthening the joint military and freeing it from the grips of the service bureaucracies. Implementation will depend on what is done not just in the remaining time of the Reagan administration, but also by the next secretary of defense. After all, the last substantial changes to the National Security Act, which came in 1958, did not begin to reshape DoD until Robert S. McNamara began in 1961 to use them to their full potential.

Here are some tests to measure whether the new legislation is accepted in spirit as well as in law:

- Will naval components now be placed under direction of army and air force officers in the unified commands?
- Will there ever be a nonnaval CINCPAC?
- Is the new vice chairman committed to making the new organization work?
- Will headquarters staffs really be cut, as the new law mandates, or will Pentagon number-jugglers perform their usual magic act of sawing the lady in half, revealing later that all of her is still in place? The numbers already are flowing in, but it is difficult to know whether to believe them.
- Will the National Defense University, which has been getting somewhat better, become a real academy for the rigorous study of how

to plan and fight war, instead of a pleasant sabbatical of lectures and seminars on management theory and international relations?

Much of what happens next depends on the new chairman, Admiral William Crowe, Jr., and his first vice chairman, air force General Robert T. Herres. They both need to make sure that the right precedents are set and that the new vice chairman is not just an understudy, but an inside man who tears into long neglected problems, like military operations planning and execution and joint command and control systems. Crowe has already shown political skill on several occasions—not least by navigating through the JCS reorganization battle without making anybody angry at him and by leaving advocates of nearly every view with the feeling that deep in his heart the chairman is on their side. Now he will have to take some stands. Just as it took a conservative like Richard Nixon to sell the opening to China, so the sophisticated Crowe as an admiral has a particularly splendid opportunity to demand compliance with the spirit as well as the letter of the law and to bring U.S. military organization into the twentieth century before the twenty-first is upon us.

For organization does matter. The assignment of duties and authority in the defense hierarchy determines which problems are addressed and who makes the decisions. To shift the distribution of power in the organization, as the new law does, is a matter of substance. It is not to be dismissed lightly as fiddling with boxes on a writing diagram.

Not everything in the new law is right. For instance, it keeps Secretary Weinberger's bloated OSD organization and the service counterparts. It writes into law the office of administrative assistant in each service, for no apparent good reason. It does not touch the new under secretary of defense for acquisition, whose duties appear to duplicate those of many other officials, and whose inflated rank is the same as the deputy secretary of defense's only because David Packard (who fifteen years ago endorsed the bad idea of having two deputies) earlier this year urged his commission and Congress to make it that way. It repeals the secretary of defense's previous power to reorganize without legislation (because Congress does not trust Weinberger) and contains far more detail, particularly regarding personnel policies and CINC organization, than ought to be written permanently into a statute (again because Congress does not trust Weinberger). It falls short—but only by a hair—of setting up a central multiservice general staff, which is what should have been done and perhaps some day will be.

But those are small points. The legislative process has worked well, mainly because it was not rushed, because so many senators and representatives and their staffs took the trouble to learn the subject thoroughly, and because (a rarity these days) they could proceed without artisan politics at play. Now it is up to the civilian and military leadership of the Pentagon to forsake business as usual and deploy the potent organizational firepower that Congress has put in their hands.


## NOTES

1. *Goldwater-Nichols Department of Defense Reorganization Act of 1986,* P.L. 99-433, 100 Stat. 992 (1986).

2. "House and Senate Reach Accord on Military Command Structure," *The New York Times,* Sept. 12, 1986, p. A25, col. 1; "The Greatest Bill Since . . . ", *The Washington Post,* Sept. 24, 1986, p. A22, col. 1.

3. U.S., President, *Public Papers of the Presidents of the United States* (Washington, D.C.: Office of the *Federal Register,* National Archives and Records Service, 1953–  ), Dwight D. Eisenhower, 1958, p. 274.

4. Richard C. Steadman, *Report to the Secretary of Defense on the National Military Command Structure* (Washington, D.C.: Department of Defense, 1978).

5. For example, Colonel Trevor N. Dupuy, "Civilian Control and Military Professionalism," *Strategic Review* (Winter 1980): 36; John G. Kester, "The Future of the Joint Chiefs of Staff," *AEI Foreign Policy and Defense Review* 2, 1 (1980): 2; John G. Kester, "Designing a U.S. Defense General Staff," *Strategic Review* (Summer 1981): 39.

6. David C. Jones, "Why the Joint Chiefs of Staff Must Change," *Presidential Studies Quarterly* (Spring 1982). Vol. 12, No. 2, pp. 128–149. For a more accessible version of General Jones' views, see Jones, "What's Wrong with the Defense Establishment?" in Asa A. Clark et al., eds., *The Defense Reform Debate* (Washington, D.C.: Johns Hopkins Press, 1984) p. 272.

7. William K. Brehm et al., *The Organization and Functions of the JCS: Report for the Chairman, Joint Chiefs of Staff by the Chairman's Special Study Group* (Washington, D.C.: GPO, 1982).

8. General E. C. Meyer, "The JCS—How Much Reform Is Needed?" Armed Forces Journal International (April 1982): 82.

9. For example, Philip A. Odeen et al., *Toward a More Effective Defense: Final Report of the CSIS Defense Organization Project* (Washington, D.C.: University Press of America, 1985); Theodore J. Crackel, "Defense Assessment," in *Mandate for Leadership II* (Washington, D.C.: Heritage Foundation, 1984).

10. *Department of Defense Authorization Act, 1985,* secs. 1301–1303, P.L. 98-525, 98 Stat. 2492, 2611–2613 (1984).

11. U.S., Congress, Senate, *Defense Organization: The Need for Change, Staff Report to the Committee on Armed Services,* S. Print 99–86, 99th Cong., 1st sess. 1985.

12. U.S., President, Blue Ribbon Commission on Defense Management, *Final Report to the President by the President's Blue Ribbon Commission on Defense Management* (Washington, D.C.: GPO, 1986).

13. Frederick S. Hiatt, "Panel Backs Reorganizing of Military," *The Washington Post,* March 7, 1986, p. A1.

14. See generally U.S., Congress, House, *Hearings on Reorganization of the Department of Defense before the Investigations Subcommittee of the Committee on Armed Services,* 99th Cong., 2d sess., 1986.

# 11

## Differing Assessments
## of Bureaucratic Politics

*A major debate concerning the utility of bureaucratic politics has ensued among those seeking to optimize rational decisionmaking. Negative assessments of bureaucratic politics are made by those who feel it necessary to protect presidents and other high-level decisionmakers against bureaucratic particularism by strengthening executive staffs. This school counsels presidents to understand that bureaucracy advances its own interests and agenda and not necessarily the president's. Thus, presidents need to take particular care to ensure that their interests and priorities are those that are pursued. In other words, they must defend and buffer themselves against bureaucratic politics. A second school has a more positive view of bureaucratic politics. It believes executive decisionmaking can benefit from the rivalry, struggle, and competition among agencies and departments. It argues that out of this play come antidotes to mind-guards, hasty consensus, excessive concurrence, groupthink, and decisionmaking based on incomplete and biased information. In other words, bureaucratic politics—because it provides redundant channels—can be harnessed in a productive way to provide decisionmakers with a wide spectrum of advice, information, and input on which to devise a range of options and make decisions. This section presents examples of both perspectives.*

# 11.1   Domestic Structure and Foreign Policy

## HENRY KISSINGER

*More than twenty years ago, Henry Kissinger outlined the importance of domestic structure to foreign policy. Today more than ever, his discussion of the impact of administrative structure seems prescient. [One effect of this cumbersome structure is to rely on the status quo as a way to avoid the "whole anguishing process of arriving at decisions."] But note some of Kissinger's other remarks:*

Ideologies prevail by being taken for granted. Orthodoxy substitutes for conviction and produces its own rigidity. In such circumstances, a meaningful dialogue across ideological dividing lines becomes extraordinarily difficult.

Sophistication may thus encourage paralysis or a crude popularization which defeats its own purpose.

Faced with an administrative machine which is both elaborate and fragmented, the executive is forced into essentially lateral means of control.

*We are brought again to the issue of leadership. Decisionmaking in U.S. society tends toward compromise, the least common denominator, and accommodation, which work against bold innovation, aggressive policy initiatives, and radical change. We must ask whether the problems of today and the future can and should be solved by such a process.*

## I. THE ROLE OF DOMESTIC STRUCTURE

In the traditional conception, international relations are conducted by political units treated almost as personalities. The domestic structure is taken as given; foreign policy begins where domestic policy ends.

But this approach is appropriate only to stable periods because then the various components of the international system generally have similar

Reprinted by permission of *Daedalus*, Journal of the American Academy of Arts and Sciences, "Conditions of the World Order," vol. 95, spring 1966, Boston, MA.

conceptions of the "rules of the game." If the domestic structures are based on commensurable notions of what is just, a consensus about permissible aims and methods of foreign policy develops. If domestic structures are reasonably stable, temptations to use an adventurous foreign policy to achieve domestic cohesion are at a minimum. In these conditions, leaders will generally apply the same criteria and hold similar views about what constitutes a "reasonable" demand. This does not guarantee agreement, but it provides the condition for a meaningful dialogue, that is, it sets the stage for traditional diplomacy.

When the domestic structures are based on fundamentally different conceptions of what is just, the conduct of international affairs grows more complex. Then it becomes difficult even to define the nature of disagreement because what seems most obvious to one side appears most problematic to the other. A policy dilemma arises because the pros and cons of a given course seem evenly balanced. The definition of what constitutes a problem and what criteria are relevant in "solving" it reflects to a considerable extent the domestic notions of what is just, the pressures produced by the decisionmaking process, and the experience which forms the leaders in their rise to eminence. When domestic structures—and the concept of legitimacy on which they are based—differ widely, statesmen can still meet, but their ability to persuade has been reduced for they no longer speak the same language.

This can occur even when no universal claims are made. Incompatible domestic structures can passively generate a gulf, simply because of the difficulty of achieving a consensus about the nature of "reasonable" aims and methods. But when one or more states claim universal applicability for their particular structure, schisms grow deep indeed. In that event, the domestic structure becomes not only an obstacle to understanding but one of the principal issues in international affairs. Its requirements condition the conception of alternatives; survival seems involved in every dispute. The symbolic aspect of foreign policy begins to overshadow the substantive component. It becomes difficult to consider a dispute "on its merits" because the disagreement seems finally to turn not on a specific issue but on a set of values as expressed in domestic arrangements. The consequences of such a state of affairs were explained by Edmund Burke during the French Revolution:

> I never thought we could make peace with the system; because it was not for the sake of an object we pursued in rivalry with each other, but with the system itself that we were at war. As I understood the matter, we were at war not with its conduct but with its existence; convinced that its existence and its hostility were the same.[1]

Of course, the domestic structure is not irrelevant in any historical period. At a minimum, it determines the amount of the total social effort which can be devoted to foreign policy. The wars of the kings who governed by divine right were limited because feudal rulers, bound by customary law, could not levy income taxes or conscript their subjects. The French Revolution, which based its policy on a doctrine of popular will, mobilized resources on a truly national scale for the first time. This was one of the principal reasons for the startling successes of French arms against a hostile Europe which possessed greater over-all power. The ideological regimes of the twentieth century have utilized a still larger share of the national effort. This has enabled them to hold their own against an environment possessing far superior resources.

Aside from the allocation of resources, the domestic structure crucially affects the way the actions of other states are interpreted. To some extent, of course, every society finds itself in an environment not of its own making and has some of the main lines of its foreign policy imposed on it. Indeed, the pressure of the environment can grow so strong that it permits only one interpretation of its significance; Prussia in the eighteenth century and Israel in the contemporary period may have found themselves in this position.

But for the majority of states the margin of decision has been greater. The actual choice has been determined to a considerable degree by their interpretation of the environment and by their leaders' conception of alternatives. Napoleon rejected peace offers beyond the dreams of the kings who had ruled France by "divine right" because he was convinced that *any* settlement which demonstrated the limitations of his power was tantamount to his downfall. That Russia seeks to surround itself with a belt of friendly states in Eastern Europe is a product of geography and history. That it is attempting to do so by imposing a domestic structure based on a particular ideology is a result of conceptions supplied by its domestic structure.

The domestic structure is decisive finally in the elaboration of positive goals. The most difficult, indeed tragic, aspect of foreign policy is how to deal with the problem of conjecture. When the scope for action is greatest, knowledge on which to base such action is small or ambiguous. When knowledge becomes available, the ability to affect events is usually at a minimum. In 1936, no one could know whether Hitler was a misunderstood nationalist or a maniac. By the time certainty was achieved, it had to be paid for with millions of lives.

The conjectural element of foreign policy—the need to gear actions to an assessment that cannot be proved true when it is made—is never more crucial than in a revolutionary period. Then, the old order is obviously disintegrating while the shape of its replacement is highly uncertain. Everything depends, therefore, on some conception of the future. But varying domestic structures can easily produce different assessments of the significance of existing trends and, more importantly, clashing criteria for resolving these differences. This is the dilemma of our time.

Problems are novel; their scale is vast; their nature is often abstract and always psychological. In the past, international relations were confined to a limited geographic area. The various continents pursued their relations essentially in isolation from each other. Until the eighteenth century, other continents impinged on Europe only sporadically and for relatively brief periods. And when Europe extended its sway over much of the world, foreign policy became limited to the Western Powers with the single exception of Japan. The international system of the nineteenth century was to all practical purposes identical with the concert of Europe.

The period after World War II marks the first era of truly global foreign policy. Each major state is capable of producing consequences in every part of the globe by a direct application of its power or because ideas can be transmitted almost instantaneously or because ideological rivalry gives vast symbolic significance even to issues which are minor in geopolitical terms. The mere act of adjusting perspectives to so huge a scale would produce major dislocations. This problem is compounded by the emergence of so many new states. Since 1945, the number of participants in the international system has nearly doubled. In previous periods the addition of even one or two new states tended to lead to decades of instability until a new equilibrium was established and accepted. The emergence of scores of new states has magnified this difficulty many times over.

These upheavals would be challenge enough, but they are overshadowed by the risks posed by modern technology. Peace is maintained through the threat of mutual destruction based on weapons for which there has been no operational experience. Deterrence—the policy of preventing an action by confronting the opponent with risks he is unwilling to run—depends in the first instance on psychological criteria. What the potential aggressor believes is more crucial than what is objectively true. Deterrence occurs above all in the minds of men.

To achieve an international consensus on the significance of these developments would be a major task even if domestic structures were comparable. It becomes especially difficult when domestic structures differ widely and when universal claims are made on behalf of them. A systematic assessment of the impact of domestic structure on the conduct of international affairs would have to treat such factors as historical traditions, social values, and the economic system. But this would far transcend the scope of an article. For the purposes of this discussion we shall confine ourselves to sketching the impact of two factors only: administrative structure and the formative experience of leadership groups.


## II. THE IMPACT OF THE ADMINISTRATIVE STRUCTURE

In the contemporary period, the very nature of the governmental structure introduces an element of rigidity which operates more or less independently of the convictions of statesmen or the ideology which they represent. Issues are too complex and relevant facts too manifold to be dealt with on the basis of personal intuition. An institutionalization of decision-making is an inevitable by-product of the risks of international affairs in the nuclear age. Moreover, almost every modern state is dedicated to some theory of "planning"—the attempt to structure the future by understanding and, if necessary, manipulating the environment. Planning involves a quest for predictability and, above all, for "objectivity." There is a deliberate effort to reduce the relevant elements of a problem to a standard of average performance. The vast bureaucratic mechanisms that emerge develop a momentum and a vested interest of their own. As they grow more complex, their internal standards of operation are not necessarily commensurable with those of other countries or even with other bureaucratic structures in the same country. There is a trend toward autarky. A paradoxical consequence may be that increased control over the domestic environment is purchased at the price of loss of flexibility in international affairs.

The purpose of bureaucracy is to devise a standard operating procedure which can cope effectively with most problems. A bureaucracy is efficient if the matters which it handles routinely are, in fact, the most frequent and if its procedures are relevant to their solution. If those criteria are met, the energies of the top leadership are freed to deal creatively with the unexpected occurrence or with the need for innovation. Bureaucracy becomes an obstacle when what it defines as routine does not address the most significant range of issues or when its prescribed mode of action proves irrelevant to the problem.

When this occurs, the bureaucracy absorbs the energies of top executives in reconciling what is expected with what happens; the analysis of where one is overwhelms the consideration of where one should be going. Serving the machine becomes a more absorbing occupation than defining its purpose. Success consists in moving the administrative machine to the point of decision, leaving relatively little energy for analyzing the merit of this decision. The quest for "objectivity"—while desirable theoretically—involves the danger that means and ends are confused, that an average standard of performance is exalted as the only valid one. Attention tends to be diverted from the act of choice—which is the ultimate test of statesmanship—to the accumulation of facts. Decisions can be avoided until a crisis brooks no further delay, until the events themselves have removed the element of ambiguity. But at that point the scope for constructive action is at a minimum. Certainty is purchased at the cost of creativity.

Something like this seems to be characteristic of modern bureaucratic states whatever their ideology. In societies with a pragmatic tradition, such as the United States, there develops a greater concern with an analysis of where one is than where one is going. What passes for planning is frequently the projection of the familiar into the future. In societies based on ideology, doctrine is institutionalized and exegesis takes the place of innovation. Creativity must make so many concessions to orthodoxy that it may exhaust itself in doctrinal adaptations. In short, the accumulation of knowledge of the bureaucracy and the impersonality of its method of arriving at decisions can be achieved at high price. Decision-making can grow so complex that the process of producing a bureaucratic consensus may overshadow the purpose of the effort.

While all thoughtful administrators would grant in the abstract that these dangers exist, they find it difficult to act on their knowledge. Lip service is paid to planning; indeed planning staffs proliferate. However, they suffer from two debilities. The "operating" elements may not take the planning effort seriously. Plans become esoteric exercises which are accepted largely because they imply no practical consequence. They are a sop to administrative theory. At the same time, since planning staffs have a high incentive to try to be "useful," there is a bias against novel conceptions which are difficult to adapt to an administrative mold. It is one thing to assign an individual or a group the task of looking ahead; this is a far cry from providing an environment which encourages an understanding for deeper historical, sociological, and economic trends. The need to provide a memorandum may outweigh the imperatives of creative thought. The quest for objectivity creates a temptation to see in the future an updated version of the present. Yet true innovation is bound to run counter to prevailing standards. The dilemma of modern bureaucracy is that while every creative act is lonely, not every lonely act is creative. Formal criteria are little help in solving this problem because the unique cannot be expressed "objectively."

The rigidity in the policies of the technologically advanced societies is in no small part due to the complexity of decision-making. Crucial problems may—and frequently do—go unrecognized for a long time. But once the decision-making apparatus has disgorged a policy, it becomes very difficult to change it. The alternative to the *status quo* is the prospect of repeating the whole anguishing process of arriving at decisions. This explains to some extent the curious phenomenon that decisions taken with enormous doubt and perhaps with a close division become practically sacrosanct once adopted. The whole administrative machinery swings behind their implementation as if activity could still all doubts.

Moreover, the reputation, indeed the political survival, of most leaders depends on their ability to realize their goals, however these may have been arrived at. Whether these goals are desirable is relatively less crucial. The time span by which administrative success is measured is considerably shorter than that by which historical achievement is determined. In heavily bureaucratized societies all pressures emphasize the first of these accomplishments.

Then, too, the staffs on which modern executives come to depend develop a momentum of their own. What starts out as an aid to decision-makers often turns into a practically autonomous organization whose internal problems structure and sometimes compound the issues which it was originally designed to solve. The decision-maker will always be aware of the morale of his staff. Though he has the authority, he cannot overrule it too frequently without impairing its efficiency; and he may, in any event, lack the knowledge to do so. Placating the staff then becomes a major preoccupation of the executive. A form of administrative democracy results, in which a decision often reflects an attainable consensus rather than substantive conviction (or at least the two imperceptibly merge). The internal requirements of the bureaucracy may come to predominate over the purposes which it was intended to serve. This is probably even more true in highly institutionalized Communist states—such as the U.S.S.R.—than in the United States.

When the administrative machine grows very elaborate, the various levels of the decision-making process are separated by chasms which are obscured from the outside world by the complexity of the apparatus. Research often becomes a means to buy time and to assuage consciences. Studying a problem can turn into an escape from coming to grips with it. In the process, the gap between the technical competence of research staffs and what hard-pressed political leaders are capable of absorbing widens constantly. This heightens the insecurity of the executive and may thus compound either rigidity or arbitrariness or both. In many fields—strategy being a prime example—decision-makers may find it difficult to give as many hours to a problem as the expert has had years to study it. The ultimate decision often depends less on knowledge than on the ability to brief the top administrator—to present the facts in such a way that they can be absorbed rapidly. The effectiveness of briefing, however, puts a premium on theatrical qualities. Not everything that sounds plausible is correct, and many things which are correct may not sound plausible when they are first presented; and a second hearing is rare. The stage aspect of briefing may leave the decision-maker with a gnawing feeling of having been taken—even, and perhaps especially, when he does not know quite how.

Sophistication may thus encourage paralysis or a crude popularization which defeats its own purpose. The excessively theoretical approach of many research staffs overlooks the problem of the strain of decision-making in times of crisis. What is relevant for policy depends not only on academic truth but also on what can be implemented under stress. The technical staffs are frequently operating in a framework of theoretical standards while in fact their usefulness depends on essentially psychological criteria. To be politically meaningful, their proposals must involve answers to the following types of questions: Does the executive understand the proposal? Does he believe in it? Does he accept it as a guide to action or as an excuse for doing nothing? But if these kinds of concerns are given too much weight, the requirements of salesmanship will defeat substance.

The pragmatism of executives thus clashes with the theoretical bent of research or planning staffs. Executives as a rule take cognizance of a problem only when it emerges as an administrative issue. They thus unwittingly encourage bureaucratic contests as the only means of generating decisions. Or the various elements of the bureaucracy make a series of nonaggression pacts with each other and thus reduce the decision-maker to a benevolent constitutional monarch. As the special role of the executive increasingly becomes to choose between proposals generated administratively decision-makers turn into arbiters rather than leaders. Whether they wait until a problem emerges as an administrative issue or until a crisis has demonstrated the irrelevance of the standard operating procedure, the modern decision-makers often find themselves the prisoners of their advisers.

Faced with an administrative machine which is both elaborate and fragmented, the executive is forced into essentially lateral means of control. Many of his public pronouncements, though ostensibly directed to outsiders, perform a perhaps more important role in laying down guidelines for the bureaucracy. The chief significance of a foreign policy speech by the President may thus be that it settles an internal debate in Washington (a public statement is more useful for this purpose than an administrative memorandum because it is harder to reverse). At the same time, the bureaucracy's awareness of this method of control tempts it to shortcut its debates by using pronouncements by the decision-makers as charters for special purposes. The executive thus finds himself confronted by proposals for public declarations which may be innocuous in themselves—and whose bureaucratic significance may be anything but obvious—but which can be used by some agency or department to launch a study or program which will restrict his freedom of decision later on.

All of this drives the executive in the direction of extra-bureaucratic means of decision. The practice of relying on special emissaries or personal envoys is an example; their status outside the bureaucracy frees them from some of its restraints. International agreements are sometimes possible only by ignoring safeguards against capricious action. It is a paradoxical aspect of modern bureaucracies that their quest for objectivity and calculability often leads to impasses which can be overcome only by essentially arbitrary decisions.

Such a mode of operation would involve a great risk of stagnation even in "normal" times. It becomes especially dangerous in a revolutionary period. For then, the problems which are most obtrusive may be least relevant. The issues which are most significant may not be suitable for administrative formulation and even when formulated may not lend themselves to bureaucratic consensus. When the issue is how to transform the existing framework, routine can become an additional obstacle to both comprehension and action.

This problem, serious enough *within* each society, is magnified in the conduct of international affairs. While the formal machinery of decision-making in developed countries shows many similarities, the criteria which influence decisions vary enormously. With each administrative machine increasingly absorbed in its own internal problems, diplomacy loses its flexibility. Leaders are extremely aware of the problems of placating their own bureaucracy; they cannot depart too far from its prescriptions without raising serious morale problems. Decisions are reached so painfully that the very anguish of decision-making acts as a brake on the give-and-take of traditional diplomacy.

This is true even *within* alliances. Meaningful consultation with other nations becomes very difficult when the internal process of decision-making already has some of the characteristics of compacts between quasi-sovereign entities. There is an increasing reluctance to hazard a hard-won domestic consensus in an international forum.

What is true within alliances—that is, among nations which have at least some common objectives—becomes even more acute in relations between antagonistic states or blocs. The gap created when two large bureaucracies generate goals largely in isolation from each other and on the basis of not necessarily commensurable criteria is magnified considerably by an ideological schism. The degree of ideological fervor is not decisive; the problem would exist even if the original ideological commitment had declined on either or both sides. The criteria for bureaucratic decision-making may continue to be influenced by ideology even after its élan has dissipated. Bureaucratic structures generate their own momentum which may more than counterbalance the loss of earlier fanaticism. In the early stages of a revolutionary movement, ideology is crucial and the accident of personalities can be decisive. The Reign of Terror in France was ended by the elimination of a single man, Robespierre. The Bolshevik revolution could hardly have taken place had Lenin not been on the famous train which crossed Germany into Russia. But once a revolution becomes institutionalized, the administrative structures which it has spawned develop their own vested interests. Ideology may grow less significant in creating commitment; it becomes pervasive in supplying criteria of administrative choice. Ideologies prevail by being taken for granted. Orthodoxy substitutes for conviction and produces its own form of rigidity.

In such circumstances, a meaningful dialogue across ideological dividing lines becomes extraordinarily difficult. The more elaborate the administrative structure, the less relevant an individual's view becomes—indeed one of the purposes of bureaucracy is to liberate decision-making from the accident of personalities. Thus while personal convictions may be modified, it requires a really monumental effort to alter bureaucratic commitments. And if change occurs, the bureaucracy prefers to move at its own pace and not be excessively influenced by statements or pressures of foreigners. For all these reasons, diplomacy tends to become rigid or to turn into an abstract bargaining process based on largely formal criteria such as "splitting the difference." Either course is self-defeating: the former because it negates the very purpose of diplomacy; the latter because it subordinates purpose to technique and because it may encourage intransigence. Indeed, the incentive for intransigence increases if it is known that the difference will generally be split.

Ideological differences are compounded because major parts of the world are only in the first stages of administrative evolution. Where the technologically advanced countries suffer from the inertia of overadministration, the developing areas often lack even the rudiments of effective bureaucracy. Where the advanced countries may drown in "facts," the emerging nations are frequently without the most elementary knowledge needed for forming a meaningful judgment or for implementing it once it has been taken. Where large bureaucracies operate in alternating spurts of rigidity and catastrophic (in relation to the bureaucracy) upheaval, the new states tend to take decisions on the basis of almost random pressures. The excessive institutionalization of one and the inadequate structure of the other inhibit international stability.

### NOTES

1. Edmund Burke, *Works* (London, 1826), Vol. VIII, pp. 214–215.

---

# 11.2 Presidential Decisionmaking in Foreign Policy

## ALEXANDER GEORGE

*Alexander George, in the following article, makes a case for the selective use of multiple advocacy to be balanced with presidential-level initiatives from time to time. George reminds us of the limits of multiple advocacy—among others, that presidential style and temperament may not be well-suited for such an approach and that there is no guarantee that senior advisers can or will be effective advocates of the options presidents need to review. As a president's time is limited, George emphasizes the critical role of the National Security Council (NSC) special assistant as "custodian-manager" and reviews the potential role conflicts in both theory and practice. The ongoing Iran-Contra affair only reminds us of the crucial role the assistant to the president for national security affairs does play.*

From *Presidential Decisionmaking in Foreign Policy* by Alexander George. Reprinted by permission from Westview Press, Boulder, Colorado. Copyright 1980.

The present chapter outlines a policymaking system in which competition and disagreement among different participants is structured and managed in order to achieve the benefits of diverse points of view. The management model in question attempts to provide for a balanced, structured form of multiple advocacy. It should be made clear that achievement of the type of multiple advocacy outlined here is *not* left to the free play of internal organizational processes and bureaucratic politics; the top executive is *not* relegated to a passive role vis-à-vis the competitive struggle among his subordinates to define policy. Rather, the theory of multiple advocacy poses sharply defined requirements for executive management of the policymaking system. It requires considerable presidential-level involvement in that system. Strong, alert management must frequently be exercised in order to create and maintain the basis for structured, balanced debate among policy advocates drawn from different parts of the organization (or, as necessary, from outside the executive branch). As such, multiple advocacy encompasses but goes beyond what is usually meant by "adversary proceedings" or use of a "devil's advocate."[1]

Multiple advocacy is neither a highly decentralized policymaking system nor a highly centralized one. Rather it is a *mixed* system which requires executive initiative and centralized coordination of some of the activities of participants in policymaking. This management model accepts the fact that conflict over policy and advocacy in one form or another are inevitable in a complex organization. (Indeed, even the highly centralized system under President Nixon did not succeed in eliminating such disagreements, though it did not have a very effective way of utilizing such disagreements to supplement and improve the workings of the formal options system.) The solution it strives for is to ensure that there will be multiple advocates within the policymaking system who, among themselves, will cover a range of interesting viewpoints and policy options on any given issue. The premise of the model is that multiple advocacy will improve the quality of information search and appraisal and, thereby, illuminate better the problem the executive must decide and his options for doing so.

## REQUIREMENTS OF THE MODEL: THREE CONDITIONS

If a system of multiple advocacy is to function effectively, each participant must have minimal resources needed for advocacy, and certain rules of the game will be needed to ensure proper give-and-take.

A system of multiple advocacy works best and is likely to produce better decisions when three conditions are satisfied:

1. No major maldistribution among the various actors in the

policymaking system of the following intellectual and bureaucratic resources:

    a. Intellectual resources

        1) Competence relevant to the policy issues;

        2) Information relevant to the policy issues;

        3) Analytical support (e.g., staff, technical skills);

    b. Bureaucratic resources

        1) Status, power, standing with the president;[2]

        2) Persuasion and bargaining skills.

    2. Presidential-level participation in order to monitor and regulate the workings of multiple advocacy.

    3. Time for adequate debate and give-and-take.[3]

The first of these conditions is a forceful reminder that *the mere existence within the policymaking system of actors holding different points of view will not guarantee adequate multisided examination of a policy issue.* Competence, information, and analytical resources bearing on the policy issue in question may be quite unequally distributed among the advocates. As a result, one policy option may be argued much more persuasively than another. There is no assurance that the policy option which is *objectively* the best will be presented effectively, for this requires that the advocate of that policy possess adequate intellectual resources.

Maldistribution of resources needed for advocacy can take many other forms. A marked disparity in the bureaucratic resources available to the advocates may well influence the outcome of the policy disagreement to a far greater extent than the intellectual merits of the competing positions. For example, an option put forward by an advocate with superior competence, adequate information, and good analytical resources will not necessarily prevail over an option advanced by an advocate who is less resourceful in these respects but operates with the advantage of superior bureaucratic resources or unusual persuasive skills.[4]

## IMPLICATIONS FOR PRESIDENTIAL-LEVEL INVOLVEMENT

The potentially damaging effects on the policymaking process of maldistribution of the intellectual and bureaucratic resources relevant to effective advocacy pose some rather sharply defined requirements for managing the advisory system. There are three general tasks that the chief executive and designated staff aides will have to perform to ensure reasonably adequate forms of balanced multiple advocacy.

First, the executive may have to take steps if not to equalize resources among his chief advisors, then at least to avoid gross disparities in them.

Second, the chief executive and his immediate staff assistants in a given policy area must be alert to the danger that a sufficient range of policy alternatives may not be encompassed by those playing the role of advocates on a particular issue. In that event he may bring in outsiders or members of his own staff to serve as advocates for different interests or policy options.

Third, he may have to develop certain "rules of the game" to maintain due process for all advocates and fair competition among them, and to avoid "restraint of trade" among the advocates.

In brief, top-level authority in the organization—and at every lower level of decision making at which multiple advocacy is desired—has the task of maintaining and supervising the competitive nature of policymaking. Multiple advocacy does not just happen. The executive must want it and must take appropriate provision for securing it.

## THE NSC SPECIAL ASSISTANT'S ROLE AS CUSTODIAN-MANAGER OF THE POLICYMAKING PROCESS

The president cannot be expected to personally carry out the three tasks identified previously as necessary for maintaining a system of multiple advocacy. Historically the responsibility for doing so has evolved to the executive secretary of the NSC, which was established in 1947. At the onset of President Eisenhower's administration, the position of executive secretary was strengthened and retitled as special assistant for national security affairs. While the range of duties and influence exercised by the incumbent of this position has varied under different presidents, the executive secretary/special assistant always has had major responsibility for ensuring that the foreign-policymaking apparatus effectively serves the president's special needs for information and advice.

Thus, from the inception of the NSC, the central role assigned to the executive assistant/special assistant has been what might be called "custodian-manager" of the procedures by means of which presidential-level national security policy is made. The role of "custodian-manager" has embraced a number of subtasks and functions, which may be described as follows:

1. balancing actor resources within the policymaking system;
2. strengthening weaker advocates;
3. bringing in new advisers to argue for unpopular options;
4. setting up new channels of information so that the president and other advisers are not dependent upon a single channel;
5. arranging for independent evaluation of decisional premises and options, when necessary;
6. monitoring the workings of the policymaking process to identify possibly dangerous malfunctions and instituting appropriate corrective

action.

This "job description" of the special assistant's custodial functions is a composite of some of the most useful tasks performed on occasion by incumbents of the office. It seems useful to codify these tasks and institutionalize them as part of the duties of the special assistant, whoever he may be, in the future. In addition to his custodial functions, the special assistant's job has been broadened to include, from time to time, a number of additional major tasks.

## THE SPECIAL ASSISTANT'S ADDITIONAL ROLES
## AND POTENTIAL ROLE CONFLICTS

Over time, since the inception of the NSC, occupants of the executive secretary/special assistant's position have assumed important roles in addition to that of custodian-manager. Such a trend has been particularly prominent since 1961. A list of the other activities assigned to or assumed by the special assistants from time to time includes the following functions or roles: (1) policy adviser-advocate; (2) policy spokesman; (3) political watchdog for the president's power stakes; (4) enforcer of policy decision; and (5) administrative operator.

To many observers it has seemed natural and inevitable that the special assistant for national security affairs should add one or more of these roles to his basic responsibility as custodian-manager. Nor is this surprising, given the talents and personal qualities of some of those who have served as special assistant, their intimacy with the president, and the encouragement that he evidently has given them to participate more extensively in foreign-policymaking.

The acquisition of multiple roles, however, makes it likely that the special assistant will experience role conflict that will eventually undermine the effectiveness with which he performs his basic custodial functions. Once he becomes an adviser-advocate to the president as well as the custodian-manager, it will take a most exceptional person to continue to dispassionately oversee the flow of information and advice to the president; for to do so might well reduce his own influence as an adviser.

Similar conflicts with his custodial responsibilities arise when the special assistant assumes the additional roles of policy spokesman and enforcer of policy. As a result, the special assistant may lack the incentive to encourage timely and objective reevaluation of ongoing policy, which is one of the custodian's responsibilities. As Thomas Cronin has observed, aides who might be able to fashion a fairly objective role in policy formation often become unrelenting lieutenants for fixed views in the implementation stage.[5]

Another role conflict is likely if the special assistant assumes the role of watchdog for the president's power stakes. As such, his concern for maintaining and enhancing the president's political influence is likely to interfere with the performance of his custodial responsibility for serving as an "honest broker" of information and advice.

The custodial role also can be undermined if the special assistant takes on important operational duties, such as diplomatic negotiations, "fact finding," and mediation. Not only are such activities likely to be time consuming, they may distract the special assistant from his duties as custodian-manager. Besides, once he is plunged into the role of administrative operator, the special assistant risks becoming personally identified with the "line" activities that he is pursuing, and this can interfere with his custodial responsibility for encouraging timely evaluation and review of ongoing policies.

## THE EXECUTIVE'S ROLE AS "MAGISTRATE"

In addition to balancing actor resources and maintaining the rules for effective multiple advocacy, the executive must consider how to define his own role. When making use of multiple advocacy, the executive should adopt the stance of a magistrate—one who listens to the arguments make, evaluates them, poses issues and asks questions, and finally judges which action to take either from among those articulated by advocates or as formulated independently by himself after hearing them. There are also some things the executive must *not* do since they would undermine the workings and utility of multiple advocacy. Thus, he should not convey policy preferences of his own or offer a particular definition of the problem or of the situation as he sees it that may constrain the options the group of advisers will consider or tilt them in the direction he seems to favor. If necessary to avoid this, the executive should absent himself from early meetings of his advisory group.

The magistrate role is of central importance to effective multiple advocacy. It is only because a magistrate presides at the apex of the policymaking system that a constructive, disciplined form of multiple advocacy can be assured. The presence of a magistrate, together with the rules and norms he imposes on the policy debate, means that the controversy among the advocates is not one which they must resolve somehow by themselves (as would be the case in a fully decentralized bargaining system that lacked an authoritative leader). Rather, the advocates in this system are competing for the executive's attention and are seeking to influence his judgment, at his insistence, via analytic arguments.

## EMPHASIS ON DISCIPLINING ADVOCACY
## THROUGH HIGH-QUALITY ANALYSIS

Multiple advocacy does not attempt to eliminate partisanship, parochial viewpoints, and bargaining. Rather, it attempts to strengthen the analytical component of these familiar features of internal organizational politics. As systems analysts have suggested, analysis can usefully moderate bargaining processes and improve the quality of the debate.[6]  To this end, multiple advocacy not only encourages competitive analysis, but, at the executive's insistence, it also forces the "partisan" analysis offered by the advocates to meet high standards. To ensure this, the executive needs to maintain a competent analytical staff of his own and use it in such a way as to evaluate and discipline the analyses offered by advocates in support of their positions.

As this implies, in his role as magistrate the executive and his staff aides do not  passively accept the arguments of the advocates or simply decide in favor of the strongest coalition of advocates. Rather, the executive's central position, his own resources, and his ultimate responsibility give him the opportunity to force advocates to meet higher standards of analysis and debate. The executive's position also imposes on him the obligation to evaluate the relative merits of competing positions and, when necessary, to decide against the majority of his advisers.  In order to discharge these responsibilities, the executive who employs multiple advocacy will require a strong, independent, analytically-oriented staff such as that of the NSC.

## NOTES

1. The concept of "adversary proceedings," which is often recommended for incorporation into policymaking procedures, is borrowed from the judicial system. What the exponents of adversary proceedings in policymaking generally have in mind is that explicit provision be made that any policy recommended by staff or subordinates to the top decisionmaker be subjected to critical scrutiny by someone other than those who advocate that policy. Thus, Task Force VII, "Stimulation of Creativity," of the State Department's *Diplomacy for the 70s,* notes that "the lack of a system for subjecting policy to the challenge of an adversary view" has been "a major weakness in the department's organization" (p. 294). However valuable this suggestion, it clearly falls short of a system of multiple advocacy.

2. This includes a number of different things that determine the degree of influence and bargaining advantages that an advocate can muster vis-à-vis other advocates and the president himself: (1) the formal and traditional responsibilities accruing to the incumbent by virtue of the office (e.g., secretary of state, secretary of defense, etc.); (2) access to and standing with the president and other senior officials and the ability to use their confidence and trust as a bargaining asset; (3) responsibility for implementation of policies decided upon, which amplifies one's voice in policymaking; and (4) the ability to go outside the executive branch to secure powerful allies in Congress, among foreign-policy specialists, and in the media.

3. The time pressures of international crises are likely to strain the workings of multiple advocacy even while making such advocacy more important than ever for

obtaining a balanced, multisided examination of options. The range of effects that crisis-induced stress can have on information processing is discussed in Chapter 2.

4. This risk can be easily enhanced by personality factors. Individuals with hyperconfident, domineering personalities often rise to high levels in the advisory system. Once such individuals become convinced of the merits of a policy option, they can be exceedingly persuasive and forceful in selling it. The impact on the group's deliberations and on multisided analysis of options can be harmful if not countered by skillful balancing.

5. Quoted in A. L. George, "The Case for Multiple Advocacy in Making Foreign Policy," *American Political Science Review* (Sept. 1972):782–83.

6. See, for example, Henry S. Rowen, "Bargaining and Analysis in Government," and William Capron, "The Impact of Analysis on Bargaining in Government," both in Louis C. Gawthrop, ed., *The Administrative Process and Democratic Theory* (Boston: Houghton Mifflin Co., 1970), pp. 31–37; 354–71. See also Alain C. Enthoven and K. Wayne Smith, *How Much is Enough?* (New York: Harper & Row, 1971.

# 12

## Normative Perspectives: Control, Responsiveness, and Accountability

*Bureaucratic politics as a process of pluralistic government inevitably raises salient questions of both substance and control. The very incident of service parochialism, rivalry, and politics is seen by some as a major cause of deficiencies in strategy, operations, and ethics. Yet, before letting these indictments lead us to negative normative assessments, we should entertain the positive aspects of the system. Bureaucratic politics is perhaps best thought of as a marketplace where ideas and proposals for policy are subject to intense debate, deliberation, and scrutiny. Ideas bubble about in a huge policy caldron and only those surviving the process with some sense of consensus are likely to be enacted. At a minimum, this means that policy will be incremental, not radical; watered-down rather than impulsive and aggressive. Legitimacy comes not from executive command and mandate but from the give and take, push and shove, and banging and clanging of interests. It is policymaking as intended by the architects of the U.S. political system. Our tasks now are to identify its limitations and to devise ways that attenuate these without causing us to lose the benefits such a system provides.*

# 12.1    Defense Organization and Military Strategy

## SAMUEL P. HUNTINGTON

*This article pursues the argument that reorganization of the defense establishment can improve, albeit not make perfect, the performance of its mission—effective deterrence in peacetime and military success in wartime. To do so, Huntington recognizes the need to overcome parochial perspectives and inefficiencies, particularly in an era of budgetary austerity. As several of his key proposals have been adopted, we will let time judge their effectiveness.*

The U.S. Department of Defense is not as well organized as it should be to provide effective deterrence in peacetime or to achieve military success in wartime. That is the conclusion of almost all the participants—other than Navy admirals and Marine Corps generals—in the national debate on defense organization that occurred in 1982 and 1983. That debate was kicked off by critiques of the Joint Chiefs of Staff from two people who presumably could speak with authority: General David Jones, USAF, Chairman of the Joint Chiefs, and General Edward C. Meyer, USA, Chief of Staff of the Army. Their public criticism focused attention on defects in American defense organization about which officials, scholars, and study groups had expressed concern for years. The Jones-Meyer broadsides brought these concerns out in the open and stimulated the most widespread discussion of defense organization issues in over two decades. Hearings before House and Senate Armed Services committees led to the drafting in Congress of a bill mandating certain relatively modest changes in the structure of the Joint Chiefs. This bill met some of the criticisms, but its passage, if that occurs, clearly will end neither all the critical weaknesses in U.S. defense organization nor the debate over what should be done about them.

To some, this renewed attention to organizational issues seems like much ado about nothing. They argue that it is not the arrangement of boxes on a chart that counts, but rather the quality of the people in those boxes. Obviously capable people are important, but it is also a mistake to

Reprinted with permission of the author from: the Public Interest, No. 75 (Spring, 1984), pp. 20-46 ©1984 by National Affairs, Inc.

downgrade the significance of formal organizational structure. Organizational structure both reflects and shapes an entity's priorities: It can facilitate or inhibit innovation; it helps define the issues that come to top decision-makers; it is significant in determining who plays what roles in deciding what issues. It also shapes the nature of the decisions that are reached; decisions made by a committee, for instance, will differ from those made by an individual. Good organization cannot guarantee wise policy or effective implementation, but bad organization can make both of these impossible.

Criticism has been directed at many aspects of Defense department organization, including, for instance, procedures for weapons procurement. Varied as the criticisms have been, however, they have tended to focus on the strategic side of the defense establishment—i.e., how decisions are made on overall policy, on the development of military forces, programs, and weapons, and on the use of military force. Those criticisms tend to articulate in a variety of ways a single underlying theme: that there is a gap between defense organization and strategic purpose. This gap is the result of the failure to achieve the purpose of organizational reforms instituted 25 years ago.

## THE EISENHOWER AND McNAMARA REFORMS

The Department of Defense evolved through two major phases after World War II. The first phase, beginning with the end of the war and continuing until the early 1960s, saw the creation and gradual strengthening of the central defense organization. During this phase, the primary emphasis was on enhancing the authority and power of the Secretary of Defense. This was accomplished through a series of legislative enactments beginning with the National Security Act of 1947 and culminating in the Defense Reorganization Act of 1958. The latter bore the personal imprint of President Eisenhower and prescribed the basic legal structure of the department for the following quarter century. In the early 1960s, Secretary of Defense Robert McNamara exploited to the hilt the formal authority of his office and introduced the so-called Planning, Programming, and Budgeting System (PPBS).

The second phase in the evolution of the Defense department runs from the early 1960s to the early 1980s. During this phase, informed experts and official bodies often studied and frequently criticized defense organization, but virtually no significant change was made in the formal structure and processes by which the department conducted its business. The intense inter-service controversy which had characterized the 1940s and 1950s subsided; and a high degree of consensus both among the services and, after the departure of McNamara, between civilian and military leaders seemed to prevail.

The reforms initiated by President Eisenhower and Secretary McNamara concentrated on three areas, all related to ways in which the department went about constituting and planning to use military force: strategic planning, combat command, and resource allocation.

In transmitting his 1958 recommendations to Congress, Eisenhower stressed the "vital necessity of complete unity in our strategic planning and basic operational direction." The initiative for strategic planning should "rest not with the separate services but directly with the Secretary of Defense and his operational advisers, the Joint Chiefs of Staff. . . ." Eisenhower wanted to achieve unified strategic planning by making the Joint Chiefs of Staff and the Joint Staff serve as the military staff of the Secretary of Defense. Congress did not approve everything he wanted, but it did strengthen the overall authority of the Secretary over the military services, increase the size of the Joint Staff, and authorize the service chiefs to delegate more of their service responsibilities to their vice-chiefs, so that the chiefs themselves could give higher priority to their joint responsibilities as members of the JCS.

Eisenhower's second major goal, reflecting his experience as Supreme Allied Commander in Europe, was to ensure unity of command of the combat forces. "Separate ground, sea, and air warfare is gone forever," he said. "If ever again we should be involved in war, we will fight it in all elements, with all services, in one single concentrated effort." Hence combat forces must be "organized into combat commands." Congress implemented most of the changes Eisenhower wanted in this area. The President, acting through the Secretary of Defense, was authorized to "establish unified or specified combatant commands for the performance of military missions" and to determine what forces from the three military departments would be assigned to those commands. The chain of command for combat forces went from the President as Commander-in-Chief to the Secretary of Defense and then to the heads of these combat commands (known as commanders-in-chief, or CINCs). The CINCs had "full operational command" of the forces assigned to them from the services, but the services remained responsible for the "administration" of those forces. In due course, virtually all U.S. combat forces were assigned—at least in theory—to unified or specified commands.

The third major reform of this period was made legally possible by the increased authority given the Secretary of Defense in the 1958 reorganization act. It became a reality in 1961 and 1962 with McNamara's introduction of PPBS. Its purpose was to provide a more rational process for decisions on force structure, strategic programs, and weapons systems. It was to replace a system in which the Secretary of Defense set budget ceilings for the services, and the services then largely determined how they would spend that money. PPBS was an effort to tie together planning and budgeting, to look at programs "horizontally" across service lines, to determine in a comprehensive manner the true costs that might be associated with new programs, and to do all of this in terms of a rolling five-year planning cycle, instead of focusing simply upon next year's budget. McNamara moved quickly to introduce this system in 1961. Although congressional and bureaucratic resistance limited the extent of his success, he was, nonetheless, able to achieve a large part of what he wanted, and he created the framework within which resource allocation decisions were made within the department for 20 years thereafter.

The Eisenhower-McNamara reforms were thus designed to achieve the following: centralized and coherent strategic planning; the rational allocation of resources to forces, programs, and weapons; and unified command of combat forces. But during the following 20 years, none of these goals has been realized satisfactorily. The history of the Defense department has been a history of conflict between the intentions of Eisenhower and McNamara, on the one hand, and the interests of the services on the other. The outcome of that conflict was never in doubt. The services won, hands down. They successfully defeated the wishes of a five-star President and an awesomely vigorous Secretary of Defense and made the legislative language and administrative procedures of those officials work to serve service interests. Never have the American military services scored a more complete victory.


## THE SERVICES AND "SERVICISM"


Under the Eisenhower-McNamara system, the individual services *per se* were not supposed to fight wars, to make strategy, or to determine overall force structure. In fact, they continued to exercise a prevailing influence in each of these areas. Instead of developing a system for coherent central strategic planning, the Joint Chiefs continued to give priority to their role as spokesmen for their services, and Joint Staff officers bargain among themselves, each trying to get the most for his service. Instead of rational choices of programs and weapons most needed to serve national purposes, such choices are still largely determined by service needs and service interests, resulting in duplication of some programs, misallocation of resources to others, and, most important, neglect of still others. Instead of the unified command of combat forces, command is often fragmented and the unified commanders (CINCs) almost always find their authority over their forces second to that of the services that supplied those forces.

The root cause of these problems stems from the fact that, except for the Chairman of the Joint Chiefs, all military officers are *service* military officers. Their experiences, training, identifications, personal associations, and, most important, their futures—all are wrapped up in their services. As a result, the only source of non-service or trans-service advice, apart from the Chairman, to which a president or Secretary of Defense can turn, is civilians.

The growth of civilian influence in strategy is directly attributable to the failure of the military to approach strategy freed from its service blinders. Not "militarism" but "servicism" is the central malady of the American military establishment.

How can it be limited and its most pernicious effects be coped with?

Servicism could, in theory, be abolished by abolishing the separate services. Such drastic action is not, however, desirable, possible, or necessary. The services are invaluable in the specialized expertise they develop, the training they provide, the historical traditions they embody, the loyalties they breed. Tank warfare, submarine operations, and air combat do require very different skills. The organization of the armed forces on the basis of the element in which they operate may not be most rational for some purposes, but it makes a great deal of sense in terms of producing tactical combat units capable of defeating comparable enemy units. One country, Canada, tried to eliminate its three services and merge them into a single entity. This was a dismal failure, and has, in effect, been reversed in practice. Attempting to abolish the U.S. services would be inefficient, wasteful, and counterproductive.

Elimination of the services would be the most extreme approach. The most modest one would be to rely primarily on exhortation to persuade military officers to think and act in non-service terms. This has been tried—often. As has been mentioned, the 1958 reorganization act directed service chiefs to delegate more of their functions as service chiefs to their vice chiefs and to devote more time and energy to their joint responsibilities. Ideally this would have created a situation in which the vice chief would become the spokesman for the service point of view, while the chief of his service would think and act jointly with his colleagues on the Joint Chiefs. In fact, of course, the service chiefs could not act this way. They still wore their hats as service chiefs, their identifications were with, and their support came from, their services, and they continued to function primarily as service representatives. They also continued to give high priority to their duties as service chiefs, delegating to their deputies for operations a large portion of their joint responsibilities, thereby accomplishing just the reverse of what the reforms had attempted to promote.

Nor will exhortation through education suffice. Proposals have been advanced, for instance, for joint education for those selected for general or flag officer rank, or for one-year stints for all service academy cadets at the academy of another service. Such educational reforms may be desirable. They will not, however, deal with the problem of servicism. American military officers may learn the virtues of transcending service concerns at joint educational institutions, but when they leave those institutions they will respond to the incentives, rewards, and expectations of the environment in which they operate. Military officers want to serve their country ably and loyally, but the system is structured to make them want to serve their country by serving their service.

Neither elimination of the services nor exhortation to transcend service interests is an effective way of dealing with the evils of servicism. One is too much, the other too little. There are, however, three intermediate approaches that might offer some relief.

First, in some circumstances, incentives and rewards can be structured such that a service acting in its own self-interest will also be responding to national needs. Second, more military officers could be "divorced" from their services by offering them alternative careers in the central defense organization through a general staff corps or similar device, and by expanding the roles and strengthening the power of the JCS Chairman. Third, an enhanced role in the formulation and execution of strategy could be assigned to non-service-oriented civilians; though to some extent this has already occurred, civilians have not been adequately organized to make the most effective contribution to strategic planning and resource allocation. The application of one or more of these three approaches is essential in curbing the effects of servicism on the three most crucial functions of the military, as enumerated in the Eisenhower reform efforts—strategic planning, resource allocation, and combat command.


## STRATEGIC PLANNING


The Secretary of Defense is responsible for developing a national military strategy which, when approved by the President and acquiesced in by Congress, should provide the basic guidelines and framework for decisions on force levels, programs, and weapons systems, and for the development of operational plans for the use of military force. The national military strategy should serve the nation's foreign policy goals and, at the same time, be compatible with the fiscal constraints that inevitably exist. Strategic planning thus involves first the assessment of threats and of needs, and then the determination of priorities among regions (e.g., Europe versus the Persian Gulf), types of forces (e.g., nuclear versus conventional, regular versus reserves), force dispositions (e.g., forward deployments versus enhanced mobility), timing requirements (e.g., modernization versus readiness), and weapons (e.g., smaller numbers of highly sophisticated weapons versus larger numbers of less capable weapons). It also involves a whole series of closely related issues as to the circumstances under which and how American forces would be used in combat: for example, offensively or defensively, in long wars or short wars, unilaterally or in conjunction with allies, in gradual increments or in a massive initial commitment. These more general and conceptual issues lead into more specific questions of how much of what specific types of force (ground divisions, aircraft carriers, fighter bombers) may be necessary to implement the strategic plans.

   In many countries strategic planning is effectively dominated, if not totally monopolized, by the military acting through a central military staff. What is often lacking is an effective civilian counterweight to the strategic advice the military provides the government. In the United States, the situation is almost the reverse. Over the course of several decades, civilian agencies and groups have moved to shape strategy. The two principal offices in the Pentagon through which this has occurred are the Office of Program Analysis and Evaluation, created by McNamara to apply systems analysis to military issues, and the Office of the Undersecretary of Defense for Policy, which is an outgrowth of and has absorbed the earlier Office of International Security Affairs.

   Strategic planning, however, should not be dominated by civilian agencies. In the end, strategic plans have to be implemented by military officers commanding military units, and knowledgeable and responsible military officers ought to play a central role in the development of overall strategic plans. The agency through which the military engages in strategic planning is, of course, the Joint Chiefs of Staff. The most widely criticized deficiency in U.S. defense organization today is the failure of the JCS to play this role effectively.

   The litany of criticism of the JCS is long and has been repeated consistently over the years. While some changes and improvements have been made in how it functions, the fundamental problems are still those that existed 25 years ago. They basically stem from the composition of the JCS as a committee (except for the Chairman) of service representatives and of the Joint Staff as an organization of officers detailed from their services for brief periods of time and responsible to the JCS in its corporate capacity. Given this structure, the Joint Chiefs and its staff become the arena for the negotiation and resolution of an incredibly wide range of issues, trivial and important, that affect the services. This has several consequences for strategic planning.

   First, strategic planning tends to be neglected. Attention is necessarily focused on issues affecting service interests, including resource allocation, personnel assignments, roles and missions, administrative and logistical practices (which service's procedures will be used if they are standardized), and similar types of issues. As a result, the JCS rarely if ever has taken the initiative in developing new strategic concepts or approaches. Over the years these have come from civilians, from individual services, and, at times, even from theater commands (e.g., SHAPE's "deep interdiction" concept); they have not come out of the joint military structure. As one informed observer wrote in 1976: "The JCS has become so bogged down in the cumbersome process which is so concerned with protecting each chief's own service interests that it has become addicted to the status quo and has never been a source of innovation in the national security policy-making process."[1] The neglect of strategy is reinforced by the demands of the annual budgetary authorization and appropriations  process, which, to an extent unequalled in other countries, diverts the attention of top-ranking military officers from planning to fight next year's possible war to planning to fight next year's inevitable budget.  The military services are, understandably, more concerned with the latter than the former.

Second, to the extent that the JCS does develop strategic plans, these plans often are unrealistic because each service wants them to be based on assumptions that reflect its own estimate of the threat and the forces it will need to counter that threat. Ideally, military strategy should provide for the use of available resources to deal with perceived threats. If strategy is based on the assumption that unavailable resources can be put to use, it is not of much help.  But that tends to be the case.  This does, however, serve two purposes for the services.  First, it reduces conflict and facilities agreement among them.  Second, it enhances the ability of each service to develop the force capabilities it wants to develop.  (If a service is told to develop capabilities that would require $50 billion in expenditures, but only gets $35 billion, the service will have the primary responsibility for deciding which capabilities to emphasize and which to eliminate.)

That strategic plans will often be unintegrated follows as a natural result of this system.  The services may and often do plan to fight different wars. The interests of interservice harmony also dictate that almost all issues coming up within the JCS system be negotiated until a position is reached that all four services can accept.  The result is language that is often vague, ambiguous, and of little use to those who must make the tough decisions on strategic issues.

Third, as a result of the need to produce four-service agreement, the JCS process usually operates very slowly.  In times of crisis, of course, critical issues will be disposed of more expeditiously, but the snail's pace of JCS policy development has been a recurring theme for decades.  In the early 1960s, according to Paul H. Nitze, "it would sometimes take them [the Joint Chiefs] three days to blow their nose."  In 1970 the Blue Ribbon Defense Panel described JCS procedure as "ponderous and slow."  In 1982, said the Air Force Chief of Staff, the planning process was "cumbersome" and took "too long."[2]

Fourth, the quality of the people assigned to the Joint Staff has left something to be desired.  The services typically assign their best officers to their own staffs.  Officers who have been assigned to the Joint Staff have not been promoted at the same rate as comparable officers who have remained with their services.  Various directives requiring officers recommended for promotion to general or flag officer rank to have some joint service experience have not, so far, had much effect in countering this natural service tendency to keep their best for themselves.

Fifth, the functioning of the Joint Staff system creates obstacles to civil-military collaboration in strategic planning.  The Joint Staff is a purely military organization, staffed by the services. The Office of Program Analysis and Evaluation is, at present, almost entirely civilian. The Office of the Undersecretary for Policy is the only one of the three top offices in the Pentagon concerned with strategy that, as of 1982, had a reasonable balance of civilian and military talent among its top personnel (about a 60-40 ration, civilian to military). Effective military planning, as Army Chief of Staff Edward C. Meyer said, requires "much greater interplay between the joint military and civilian leadership" than exists at present.[3] A major purpose of the Joint Staff system, however, is to generate position papers upon which all four services agree. To achieve this, civilians are excluded and the services meet *in camera* (or, more accurately, in "the tank," as the JCS meeting room is called) to thrash out their differences so that they then can provide united military advice to civilian decision-makers.

## NON-SERVICE MILITARY INSTITUTIONS

How can those deficiencies in strategic planning be corrected? It is hard to conceive how service interests could be restructured so as to enable them to contribute positively to non-service-oriented strategic planning. Nor can failures in the military contribution to strategic planning be corrected by relying more on civilians. A responsible and powerful military role in strategic planning is essential. The conclusion is that curing the defects in U.S. strategic planning requires an increased role for *non-service* military institutions, and virtually all proposals to deal with the defects of strategic planning attempt to provide for this.

These proposals, roughly speaking, embody two different approaches. The more radical approach would be to create a general staff corps of officers divorced from their services. This would constitute a "purple suit" entity to whom civilian officials could turn for non-service-oriented military advice. A full general staff system has five key characteristics. First, officers are selected to enter the general staff corps relatively early in their careers. Second, their entire subsequent military career is within that corps; they thus pursue a different career line from those officers who remain in the services. Third, upon selection for the general staff corps, officers undergo rigorous and prolonged training (two or three years) in general staff academy. Fourth, their principal subsequent assignments are to the general staff, to other joint staffs, or to joint commands, with perhaps occasional rotation back to their services. Fifth, their assignments and promotions are made not by their services but by the head of the general staff. Not all general staff systems embody all these features to the same degree. Some minimum combination of them, however, is essential to constitute a general staff corps. Many countries, including the Federal Republic of Germany and the Soviet Union, have some variety of a general staff system.

The introduction of such a system in the United States would improve the effectiveness of military planning and the usefulness of military advice to civilian policy-makers. Given the inherent pluralism in the American defense structure, the creation of this additional unit would not threaten civilian control or the legitimate interests of the services. Creation of such an organization, however, would mark a major innovation in American military structure and would only be accomplished, if at all, after prolonged debate and controversy. It would probably require a major military disaster to bring such a system into being.

Given this situation, the more modest alternative for improving strategic planning is to enhance the power and roles of the Chairman of the Joint Chiefs of Staff. This could be done in a variety of ways. He could be given the authority to select officers for the Joint Staff and to have a decisive voice on their promotion while on that staff. He could be given authority in his own right, and not as now on behalf of the Joint Chiefs, to manage the Joint Staff. He could be designated, *vice* the Joint Chiefs, as the principal military advisor to Congress, the President, and the Secretary of Defense. This would not mean that the other chiefs would not also have direct access to these civilian officials, but it would place the initiative in making recommendations with the Chairman, the other chiefs being able to file dissents from his views if they so desired. The Chairman could also be given a deputy, who would preside over the chiefs in his absence and who could take the lead in resolving critical issues on behalf of the Chairman. Several of these measures were incorporated in the bills on defense organization that Congress considered in 1982, 1983, and 1984. Measures such as these would not replace the Joint Chiefs of Staff system with a general staff system. They would, however, enable the military to play a more useful, timely, and positive role in strategic planning. In part, they embody changes that the British have already made in their joint staff system, and without which top British military and civilian officials say they could never have conducted the Falklands War as effectively as they did.

Any major organizational change has a variety of consequences. The anticipated and planned consequence of the changes discussed above would be more effective strategic planning. One additional probable consequence of these changes may appear less benign: If power is centralized to a greater degree in the Chairman of the JCS, it is quite likely that the high level of consensus that has prevailed among the military chiefs will decline. At least some of the incentives to unanimity among the chiefs will be weakened. This does not necessarily mean a return to the age of contention that existed in the 1940s and 1950s. It does mean, however, that with the Chairman exercising an independent role of his own, more incentives will exist for individual service chiefs to appeal to the Secretary of Defense. This is, indeed, what is necessary to impart greater precision and clearer choices into the strategic planning process. If major contentious issues are not swept under the rug, they will be fought over. Less harmony among the chiefs is the price of clearer choices, more coherent strategy, and more meaningful civilian direction.

## RESOURCE ALLOCATION AND FORCE DEVELOPMENT

The second area where the Eisenhower-McNamara reforms did not achieve their objectives is the allocation of resources for force development. In various manifestations, PPBS has been followed in form, but it has not eliminated the irrationalities and imbalances in the assignment of resources to forces, programs, and weapons. Service priorities continue to prevail over strategic needs. The resulting deficiencies are many and important.

First, as with broader strategic issues, the tendency in the JCS process is for all services to approve the force goals and weapons programs of each. In the early 1980s, consequently, the Joint Chiefs approved requirements for 23 aircraft carriers (as against 14 then existing), 40 air wings (26 existing) and 33 Army divisions (24 existing). By endorsing each other's maximum goals, the chiefs created intra-military consensus at the expense of extra-military relevance. Even the Reagan administration did not endorse such ambitious force levels.

Second, over the years there has been an occasional tendency to return to the practice whereby the Secretary of Defense would set the budget figures for the services and then allow the services to decide, within broad guidelines, how they would allocate their funds. This tendency has been most noticeable under Laird and Weinberger. Its reappearance flew in the face of the whole theory of PPBS, but it was also a natural political development. The Secretary of Defense has to be concerned about expenditure levels, and if the services will acquiesce in ceilings that he and the President find acceptable, it is not unreasonable to let them have the dominant voice in deciding how the money will be spent. The service, on the other hand, will accept lower spending levels in return for greater freedom to allocate resources to those programs that it considers essential to its central missions and identity. The result, however, is that service interests rather than strategic needs play the dominant role in shaping program decisions.

Third, the role of service interests in shaping forces and programs leads to imbalances in military capabilities. Those "orphan" functions that are not central to a service's own definition of its mission tend to be neglected. For example, given limited resources, the Air Force and the Navy are not going to give high priority to air and sea lift for the Army, as against bombers and carriers for themselves. Somewhat similarly, the Air Force has been slow to emphasize close air support for the Army, and has done so at times only in response to Army attempts to develop its own capability for close air support. In other cases, no service may wish to give high priority to developing the capabilities to meet a perceived strategic need. This has traditionally been the case with counterinsurgency capabilities, and it was very much the case with the rapid deployment force for intervention in areas such as the Persian Gulf. President Carter ordered the creation of such a force in August 1977, but no service had a major interest in espousing this mission. Despite recurring prods from the White House, the concept languished in the Pentagon for over two years until the Iranian hostage seizure and the invasion of Afghanistan were able to produce a response that a presidential order had failed to generate. In general, extraordinarily active and sustained external prodding, as was the case with McNamara and airlift, is required to get services to develop capabilities that they do not see as central to their role.

Fourth, service dominance in determining programs tends to produce an overemphasis on procurement and investment, as against readiness. Lobbying for the latter has chiefly come only from the commanders-in-chief of the unified and specified commands. The CINCs' interest is to have forces that are well equipped, supplied, trained, and exercised to fight effectively in the near term. The services, on the other hand, are in large part procurement agencies, and they tend to look toward the longer-term needs of investment and modernization. Since the services have more influence than the combat commands in the resource allocation and budgeting process, investment needs tend to be emphasized over readiness needs. This tendency is reinforced by the interests of defense contractors, Congressmen, and their constituents in promoting major weapons systems. It is at times even reinforced by the interests of comptrollers and fiscal officers in holding down immediate expenditures—at the cost of allowing larger new authorizations, the expenditures for which will not peak for three or four years. Clearly a better balance is needed between investment and readiness.

In the competition for resources, the emphasis is thus on service programs to meet service goals. This was the case in 1948 when the Air Force undertook a major campaign to get 70 wings; it remained true in 1981, when the Secretary of the Navy waged a major campaign to get 600 ships. The problem, of course, is that 600 ships may or may not meet the strategic needs of the country, although they certainly meet the service needs of the Navy. A large navy is properly the *instrument,* not the *goal,* of strategy. The United States has no interest in a 600-ship navy as such. It does have an interest in having the right combination of ships to serve the strategic purposes of its foreign policy. Six hundred ships of one sort or another might or might not be necessary for those purposes, but that is something that is impossible for the Navy to determine rationally. As the process works, however, an instrumental, service goal supplants strategic goals.

The pre-eminence of service goals in the program development process stems from the failure of defense organization to reflect strategic purposes.

At the broadest level, most strategists would agree that the United States has three major strategic purposes: strategic deterrence, that is, to deter nuclear attacks on the United States and its allies, and to limit the damage from such attacks should they occur; NATO defense, that is, to deter and, if necessary, to defeat an attack on European allies; and regional defense, that is, to be capable of projecting the forces necessary to defend vital U.S. interests in East Asia, the Middle East and Persian Gulf, and the Western Hemisphere.

The most striking deficiency in U.S. defense organization today is the absence of any single official or office in the Pentagon with overall responsibility for any one of these strategic missions—and *only* for that mission. Individual officials and organizations are responsible for parts of each of these missions; other officials, such as the Chairman of the JCS and the Undersecretary for Policy, have a general responsibility for all these missions. The Secretary of Defense knows where to turn when he wants the individual officials responsible for the Air Force or the Marine Corps, for research and development of intelligence, for manpower or the budget. But where does he find an official with overall and exclusive responsibility for strategic deterrence? There is none. Nor is there any single official responsible for NATO defense or for force projection in the Third World. These are precisely the major strategic purposes of American defense policy, and they are virtually the only important interests in defense that are not represented in the defense organization.

How can this failure to represent strategic purpose in defense organization be remedied? There are three possible ways. One would be to restructure the services so as to make service interest coincide with strategic mission. In effect, this would involve a change in service roles and missions, as defined in the Key West Agreement of 1948, so as to define the competence of the services in terms of mission rather than in terms of element. Two proposals along these lines were advanced in 1983.[4] In general, they propose that the Air Force become the strategic deterrence force. It would lose its responsibilities for tactical air and airlift, but it would gain control of ballistic missile submarines and everything relating to ballistic missile defenses. The Army would be dedicated exclusively to land war and would gain control of everything necessary for the successful prosecution of land war, including tactical air, air lift, and sea lift. The Navy would lose its sea lift and ballistic missile submarines, but would keep everything else dedicated to the conduct of war at sea, including the Marine Corps, since amphibious operations cannot be separated from war at sea.

These changes, it is argued, would mean that the Air Force would no longer necessarily rule out basing MX missiles on small coastal submarines, since it would be assured that those submarines would be under its control rather than the Navy's. Similarly, the Army could greatly reduce its expensive and dubiously effective efforts to provide close air support by helicopters and instead purchase the cheaper and more effective fixed-wing planes which the Key West Agreement now bars it from procuring. Undoubtedly, such a realignment of service roles and missions would produce program and weapon choices better suited to serve U.S. strategic purposes. There are, however, several problems with this proposal. The division of service responsibilities among strategic deterrence, ground war, and air war does not entirely relate services to missions. Indeed, it mixes purposive (strategic deterrence) and elemental (ground, sea) definitions of service responsibility. Undoubtedly the Army would be primarily oriented to European defense and the Navy to sea control and force projection. One key element of European defense, however, is the ability of the United States to mobilize and transport personnel and materiel to Europe in the event of conflict. The Navy would have to protect them against Soviet submarines and aircraft. Yet the decision as to what resources would be devoted to this NATO mission would be made, not by someone with overall responsibility for European defense, but by someone who balanced this need against the need to project forces elsewhere. The Navy's decision on this issue might or might not be congruent with the Army's decision on its needs for reinforcement.

Another major difficulty of the service-restructuring solution is that the political problems involved in attempting to induce any of the services to surrender long-held responsibilities, even though secondary ones, are enormous. The agreement worked out at Key West is in many respects arbitrary. To reopen it, however, would be to shake up a hornet's nest of fears, animosities, and service lobbying that would effectively preclude serious consideration of other defense issues for some period of time.

A second way that has been proposed to relate strategic purpose to defense organization has been to enhance the role of the unified and specified commands and of the Chairman of the JCS as their spokesman. This proposal has received fairly widespread support. The CINCs, after all, are the officials who are responsible for using the military forces to achieve U.S. strategic purposes. Very modest steps to enhance their role in program determination and resource allocation have been taken under both Carter and Reagan, and the CINCs now appear semi-annually before the Defense Resources Board to present their needs.

Enhancement of the role of the CINCs undoubtedly would be useful. At the same time, however, it is not clear that such a move would satisfactorily close the gap between strategic purpose and defense organization. Many of the unified and specified commands are little more than service creatures and service fronts. Strengthening them will not create a strategic counterpoise to service interests. In addition, two or more commands contribute to each of the three major U.S. strategic purposes and hence no single CINC can represent the total needs of any such purpose. The physical location of the CINCs outside of—often at great distance from—Washington also makes it difficult for them to play a sustained role in the never-ending program-determination and resource-allocation process. Presumably the Chairman of the JCS might, as many suggest, attempt to articulate their needs in Washington. As we have noted, the CINCs do share an interest in readiness which often puts them at odds with the services on such issues as maintenance, spare parts, joint exercises, and other issues. On major resource allocation issues, however, the divisions among the CINCs will be as deep as those among the services. It is not clear how the Chairman can represent the views of the CINCs when those views can and must conflict with each other.

## UNDERSECRETARIES FOR STRATEGIC MISSIONS

Service restructuring is thus probably impossible. An enhancement of the role of the CINCs would be only partially effective. A third, more promising, approach would be *to create at the highest level in the Defense department offices concerned with each major strategic mission.* Such offices could be headed by undersecretaries of defense, who would replace and assume the functions now associated with the Undersecretary of Defense for Policy. Each such undersecretary would have the responsibility to ensure that the United States has military forces constituted, organized, trained, equipped, and deployed to carry out the mission for which he is responsible. Each undersecretary would thus supervise, direct, and coordinate all those activities in the Defense department primarily related to his strategic purpose. These would include both force development and operational planning. He would be the principal civilian advisor to the Secretary of Defense for everything connected with his mission, including budget allocations.

Each undersecretary should have general supervisory responsibility for the unified and specified commands relevant to his mission. He would also be their spokesman in the process of force development and resource allocation. It would be up to him to review the CINCs' statements of their requirements and make recommendations concerning their needs to the Secretary of Defense. Once he received guidance from the Secretary as to the resources that would be available to support his mission, it would then be up to the undersecretary to determine the most effective allocation of those resources among the various forces, programs, and weapons. Given limited resources, each undersecretary would have an interest in producing the combination of forces and programs that would most effectively and most efficiently meet the needs of his mission. The services and other Defense department agencies would, correspondingly, have interests in demonstrating that their programs would meet those needs more effectively and efficiently than those of the other services. Unproductive interservice rivalry over ownership of programs and functions would be replaced by a more productive rivalry to develop the best programs and weapons to meet the key strategic needs of the nation.

The responsibilities of individual undersecretaries might be defined in a variety of ways. The Undersecretary for Strategic Deterrence would presumably have authority over all strategic offensive and defensive forces and capabilities. He would also be responsible for offensive, defensive, and intelligence missions in space. He would have supervisory but not command authority over the Strategic Air Command (SAC), the Aerospace Defense Command, and Navy SLBM forces, and he would be the spokesman for their requirements in the process of force development and resource allocation. He would be the Defense department's person on strategic arms limitation negotiations.

The Undersecretary for North Atlantic and European Defense would be generally responsible for everything connected with NATO, including U.S. conventional forces allocated to that purpose, theater nuclear forces, and the naval forces designed to secure control of the North Atlantic. He would exercise supervisory authority over, and be the spokesman for the requirements of, the European and Atlantic commands. He would also be in charge of mobilization planning, since that process is driven by the requirements of a general war in Europe. He would also be responsible for developing the Defense department position for negotiations on nuclear weapons and conventional forces in Europe. He would share responsibility for antisubmarine warfare with the Undersecretary for Strategic Deterrence.

The Undersecretary for Regional Defense and Force Projection would be generally responsible for planning and preparations for military contingencies in East Asia, the Middle East and Persian Gulf, Latin America, and other Third World areas. He would have supervisory authority over and be the spokesman for the requirements of the Pacific, Central (Indian Ocean-Persian Gulf), Southern (Latin America), and Readiness Commands. He would coordinate military assistance programs for the countries in these areas. He would also have general responsibility for counterinsurgency and special operations. He would share responsibility for mobility capacities with the undersecretary for NATO affairs.

The undersecretaries clearly would compete with each other for resources to perform their missions. Unlike current interservice competition, however, where only service interests are at stake, this competition would involve critical issues of priority among central strategic missions. The differences among them would have to be resolved by the Secretary of Defense in meeting with them, the Deputy Secretary, and the Chairman of the Joint Chiefs of Staff. That six-man group would, in effect, be the top policy-making body in the Pentagon.

One of the most frequently voiced criticisms of the Office of the Secretary of Defense has been that its officials tend to get involved in administrative detail, which should properly be left to the services or other agencies, and attempt to "micromanage" the department. This tendency is in large part a result of the gap that exists in the department between strategic purpose and organizational structure. As one expert on governmental organization has observed, *"The failure to group related programs in major purpose agencies inevitably produces a shift of power to the policy and managerial offices grouped around the President."*[5] This is equally true within the Defense department, and the absence of "major purpose agencies" within the department has promoted the involvement of the Office of the Secretary of Defense in administration and management. Creation of major purpose agencies related to strategic missions would encourage the decentralization of authority and would tend to focus attention on the major strategic issues—which would be at stake among the undersecretaries—instead of on administrative details.

Movement in this direction would threaten neither the existence nor the roles and missions of the services. It would encourage the services to compete with each other in a more constructive fashion and would reward those services that came up with the most effective and least expensive programs to achieve strategic missions. The services would continue to do all that they do today, but their activities would be directed to a different mix of goals than they currently are.

In some measure, the creation of the three mission offices and undersecretaries recommended here would follow naturally from developments already under way in the department. During the early years of the Carter administration, the Secretary of Defense had an Advisor for NATO Affairs. In the Reagan administration, the Assistant Secretary for International Security Affairs has generally been responsible for matters concerning the Third World, while the Assistant Secretary for International Security Policy has handled NATO matters, strategic forces, and arms control negotiations. Neither of these officials, however, has had the statutory authority or the defined responsibilities to carry out the crucial duties in force development which the proposed undersecretaries would discharge. In the Defense department, assistant secretaries simply do not have the status and clout required for this task. Responsible as they should be for achieving the Defense department's major strategic purposes, these officials need to be undersecretaries and second only to the Secretary and his deputy in their authority and position within the department. In fact and in perception, they need to be mission "czars."

## COMBAT COMMAND

The need for unity of command was the dominant theme of the Defense Reorganization Act of 1958. Combat forces, President Eisenhower argued, must be "organized into unified commands . . . singly led and prepared to fight as one, regardless of service." The act attempted to accomplish this end through a radical break with the past. Before 1958, "unified" commands had existed, but, with the notable exception of Eisenhower's command in Europe, these commands were largely identified with individual services, even when forces from several services were assigned to them. After World War II, a service department served as the "executive agent" for each unified command, linking it to the Joint Chiefs of Staff and the Secretary of Defense. The 1958 act seemed to change this pattern drastically. Unified or specified commands would be directly under the command of the President and the Secretary of Defense; they would, at least in theory, have no direct ties with particular services; and the services would have no responsibility for the conduct of military operations.

The unification of command over land, air, and sea elements was achieved, however, only by accepting two other critical distinctions in military organization. The services were to be the *providers* of military forces: that is, they were to recruit, train, equip, and generally prepare military forces for combat. These forces would then be turned over to the unified and specified commands who would be the *users* of military force. They would plan for and actually direct the use of those forces in combat. There would be a balanced pattern of departmental organization, with a clear separation between an administrative hierarchy and a military command hierarchy. Under the 1958 act, the Army, Navy, Air Force, and Marine Corps thus would not fight wars; the unified and specified commands would fight wars. By removing the services in theory from military operations, the United States adopted an organizational pattern which, among major powers, it shares only with the Federal Republic of Germany (a very special case, because all its combat forces are under the operational command of NATO). The United States is thus almost alone in attempting to exclude its military services entirely from the conduct of military operations and relegate them entirely to supporting roles.

To the distinction between provider and user, the 1958 act also added another and more troublesome distinction, that between operational command and administrative command. Conceivably, once a military service had organized and equipped a military unit (ship, division, air wing) it could have turned full authority for that unit over to the unified command to which it was assigned—the unit only returning to service control when, for one reason or another, it was felt necessary fundamentally to reconstitute, retrain, or re-equip it. Short of this, however, it would be under the full command in all dimensions of the unified commander. The 1958 act, however, did not establish this system. Instead it provided that the CINC would have "full operational command" of the forces assigned to him, while the services would be "responsible for the administration" of those forces. The services have control over discipline, personnel, training, and logistics. The act thus provided for unified command of land, sea, and air forces at the expense of a divided command over the individual land, sea, and air components. Each subordinate component commander in a unified command is responsible to the CINC of his command on operational matters and to the chief of his service for everything else, which, in peacetime, is almost everything of importance.

The division decreed in the act between operational and administrative command in effect undermines the division of responsibilities between provider and user that was designed to ensure unity of command. The power of the CINCs over their service components remains highly constrained and limited. In 1970 the Blue Ribbon Defense Panel argued that the intent of the earlier reforms had been vitiated: "Despite the establishment of the unified command concept in the Defense Reorganization Act of 1958, as requested by President Eisenhower, the relationship and relative authority between the Unified Commander and the component commander, and between the component commander and his Military Department, remain substantially unchanged." Eight years later another official study made a similar comment. The CINCs "have limited power to influence the capability of the forces assigned to them. . . . The CINCs' forces are trained and equipped by their parent Services, who control the flow of men, money, and materiel to the CINC's components. The Services (and the components) thus have the major influence on both the structure and the readiness of the forces for which the CINC is responsible." As a result, the CINCs have to negotiate with their component commanders. Their only real power is the power of persuasion; they have only limited influence over what goes on in their service components.[6] The component commanders clearly exercise preponderant control over the combat forces assigned to unified commands. Unified commands, in short, are not truly unified.

The unified commands are also not truly unified in yet another sense. The 1958 act ended the system whereby a service department served as "executive agent" for each unified command. It could not and did not, however, end the identification of particular commands with particular services. The three specified commands—Strategic Air Command, Aerospace Defense Command, and Military Airlift Command—are composed entirely of Air Force units and are commanded by Air Force officers. The Pacific and Atlantic Commands are always commanded by naval officers. The European, Southern, and Readiness Commands have (with one brief exception) been under Army command. The Central Command, which developed out of the Rapid Deployment Joint Task Force (commanded by a Marine), is now commanded by an Army officer.

At least some of the designated unified commands are more unified in theory than in practice. The Atlantic Command has no Army or Air Force components regularly assigned to it. Except for three ships in the Persian Gulf, no Navy or Marine Corps units are regularly assigned to the Readiness Command or to the Central Command. Army units do exist in the Pacific

Command, most notably in Korea, but those are part of a subunified command headed by an Army general. The Southern Command includes modest Army and only minuscule Air Force and Navy forces. This leaves the European Command, with substantial forces from all service departments, as the only truly comprehensive unified command. Apart from the European Command, almost no naval forces are under the command of Army or Air Force officers, and only in the Pacific Command are significant Army and Air Force units under a naval CINC—and that is mitigated through the device of the subunified command. Despite Eisenhower's intentions and the 1958 act, in most cases the operational chain of command, as well as the administrative one, remains a service chain of command. To the extent a unified command is unified, it is not a command, because of the limited control of the CINC over components from other services. To the extent that a unified command is a command, it is not unified, because its forces come exclusively or overwhelmingly from a single service.

Such is the system in peacetime. The situation in war or crisis, when military forces have to be deployed and used, is not substantially different, except that, invariably, ad hoc arrangements have to be devised. In developing such command arrangements for military operations, the service members of the Joint Chiefs of Staff are driven by two urges. First, each chief wants his service to have a significant role in the operation. Second, each chief is under pressure to minimize the extent to which forces from his service are under the command of someone from another service. The efforts to harmonize these two principles can often lead to complex, uncertain, and fragmented command relationships. The Vietnam War, for instance, occurred within the geographical area assigned to the Navy-headed Pacific Command. Once significant Army forces were deployed to Vietnam, however, a subunified command, MACV, headed by an Army general, was created. In due course, Marine units were also assigned to Vietnam, and what was in effect a separate sub-subunified command was created for them in the northern provinces of South Vietnam. MACV, however, did not command the carrier task forces in the South China Sea or the B-52 bombers operating from Guam, both of which played significant roles in the air war. As a result, Vietnam was, as General Jones observes:

> perhaps our worst example of confused objectives and unclear responsibilities, both in Washington and in the field. Each service, instead of integrating efforts with others, considered Vietnam its own war and sought to carve out a large mission for itself. For example, each fought its own air war, agreeing only to limited measures for a coordinated effort. . . . Lack of integration persisted right through the 1975 evacuation of Saigon—when responsibility was split between two separate commands, one on land and one at sea; each of these set a different "H-hour," which caused confusion and delays.[7]

Comparable patterns have existed in smaller operations. Grenada is a relatively small island; but during the invasion, command over ground forces was divided between Marine and Army officers. In the Iran rescue mission, as the official Pentagon study concluded, command and control were "excellent at the upper echelons, but became more tenuous and fragile at intermediate levels." Within the Joint Task Force that had been created for this operation, command relationships "were not clearly emphasized in some cases and were susceptible to misunderstandings under pressure." Among other things, during preparation for the mission it was unclear as to whether a Marine or Air Force officer was in charge of training the helicopter units that were to undertake the rescue.[8]

The existing unified and specified commands are organized in terms of both mission and geographical areas. The mission commands, however, as is the case most notably with SAC, do not necessarily include all the major forces that are dedicated to that mission, while the geographical commands, on the other hand, do have full responsibility for their entire geographical area. It is difficult to see the logic that divides command of U.S. strategic retaliatory forces among four separate commands (Strategic Air, Atlantic, Pacific, European) and yet established a single command for all U.S. forces from the Golden Gate to the Persian Gulf. Geographically defined commands, oriented toward a particular area, service, or mission, may not be well suited to plan for and carry out operations that are at the margin of their responsibilities. Thirteen years before the invasion of Grenada, the Blue Ribbon Defense Panel argued that the Atlantic Command "tends to be oriented toward a general war maritime role as distinguished from a perhaps more probable contingency involving land operations in its geographical area of responsibility." Nor is it surprising that the Long Commission on the terrorist bombing of the Marines at Beirut airport should conclude that there was "a lack of systematic and aggressive chain of command attention" to the Marines' anti-terrorist security measures by European Command headquarters.[9] The current structure of unified and specified commands thus often tends to unify things that should not be unified and to divide things that should be under a single command.

The deficiencies in the command of combat forces will not be corrected by any single panacea. A wide variety of individual corrective actions is desirable. First, however, it is necessary to ask: What purposes is unity of command meant to serve? There are really two: cooperation and fungibility. Cooperation is served when all military forces assigned to a particular mission are under a single command. Fungibility is served when all military forces of a particular type are under a single command. The needs of cooperation and fungibility often conflict with each other, as well as with other important values in military operations. In a complex modern military establishment, as a result, absolute unity of command is virtually impossible to achieve. Unifying military forces along one dimension will create disunities along another. Some form of divided command will exist in almost all circumstances; the problem is to identify that form of division that is least injurious to the accomplishment of the mission at hand.

## MISSION COMMANDS, NOT AREA COMMANDS

The 1958 act was based on the absolute distinction between the provider-administrative role of the services and the user-operational role of the combat commands. This has, however, been a distinction impossible to maintain in practice. Much of the time, this effort at divorce is unnecessary and dysfunctional. Where there are operational missions that should be carried out with forces from a single service, no reason exists not to assign responsibility for that mission to the service. The assumption underlying the 1958 act—that all operational forces should be removed from the services—needs to be re-examined, particularly since in the specified commands and many "unified" commands they have never in fact been divorced. Conceivably, the United States might do well to follow a pattern comparable to that of the Soviets, in which in some cases the services are responsible for operational missions and in other cases they are not.

In keeping with this general approach, unified and specified commands should normally be organized in terms of mission, not area, and the scope of a command should be extended to all forces directly relevant to its mission. The Strategic Air Command, for instance, should be converted into a strategic retaliatory command incorporating the ballistic missile submarines that are now assigned to three other commands. In keeping with the recommendations of various groups, the Military Airlift Command might also be changed into a Logistics Command including sealift and related activities as well as airlift. Both of these commands would thus become unified rather than specified commands and should be commanded by Navy admirals as well as by Air Force generals. The Atlantic Command, on the other hand, should be converted into a purely naval Atlantic Sea Control Command, with that as its only mission. Responsibility for force projection and amphibious operations in countries bordering the Atlantic, on the other hand, should be transferred to the Readiness or Southern Commands. There is also little logic in the writ of the European Command extending over all of Africa and a good part of the Middle East. The European Command should be directed to the defense of Europe. Given the importance of the area, a separate Eastern Mediterranean-Levantine Command would clearly seem to be called for. In general, the scope of geographical commands should be limited to areas within which one mission is overwhelmingly dominant.

In some circumstances, services can serve strategic needs more directly. In other circumstances, however, the needs of cooperation will undoubtedly require the assignment of substantial forces from two or more services to a unified command which can and should be divorced from the services. In such commands, the position of CINC should, like the chairmanship of the Joint Chiefs of Staff, normally be rotated among the participating services. The circumstances that require the creation of a unified command also require that such a command not be the preserve of any particular service. In addition, the CINCs of those commands should have greatly enhanced authority over the forces assigned to them. It is difficult to see what is gained by the services' retaining jurisdiction over such matters as administration, discipline, unit training, and logistics. The unified commander has the responsibility to ensure that the forces under his command are ready to fight and to fight successfully. He should be given the authority commensurate with that responsibility, including the authority to assign officers as he sees fit and to relieve them from command when he deems that necessary.

In some cases, thus, the artificial distinction between operational command and administrative command can be broken down by giving operational as well as administrative command to the services. In other cases, as in Europe, for instance, it can and should be broken down by giving administrative as well as operational command to the CINCs. In all cases, the central need is to recognize that no particular form of unity of command is universally relevant and that the choice in particular circumstances should reflect the mission to be accomplished and the nature of the forces required for that mission.

## SUBORDINATING THE SERVICE VIEWPOINT

Militarism has been defined as that "doctrine or system" that, among other things, exalts "an institutional structure—the military establishment" and "accords primacy in state and society to the armed forces."[10]  In somewhat parallel fashion, servicism is the doctrine or system that exalts the individual military service and accords it primacy in the military establishment. The individual military services are and will remain indispensable elements in that establishment. Service interests, service needs, and service power, however, have dominated U.S. defense structure, warping and frustrating efforts to establish rational systems of strategic planning, force development, and combat command. The result is, inevitably, an undesirable weakening of the collective military contribution in these areas. In the United States, the military view, as Clausewitz recommended, is kept subordinate to the political view. The service view should, in a similar manner, be kept subordinate to the military view.

The evils of servicism cannot be remedied, however, by any single organizational reform. A variety of measures is needed. The principal organizational proposals suggested in this essay involve three different approaches: in strategic planning, strengthen the authority of the Chairman of the Joint Chiefs of Staff; in force development, create mission undersecretaries to represent the basic strategic purposes; and in combat command, orient commands to missions rather than geography, assigning responsibility for some to the services and enhancing the command authority of the CINCs of the others. Changes along these lines clearly will not solve all the organizational problems of the U.S. defense establishment.

Together, however, they will reinforce each other in elevating military needs over service interests, and in bringing defense organization more into line with strategic purpose. In its current incarnation, the U.S. defense establishment dates from World War II. It is middle-aged and it shows many of the characteristics of middle age. Like any large bureaucratic structure, it has tended to become top-heavy, overweight, sluggish, and loaded down with activities, offices, installations, and personnel, which may once have been vital to its functioning, but no longer are. So long as there is no shortage of resources for defense, such excrescences can be tolerated. Real constraints on defense will, however, almost inevitably be the dominant theme of the second half of the 1980s. To ensure that priority goes to what is needed for the wars the United States is most likely to fight, or most needs to deter, requires an effective and coherent military voice in the formulation of national strategy, the allocation of resources to forces, programs, and weapons so as rationally to serve strategic purposes, and unified command structures for combat forces relevant to the missions they are to perform. If service needs and service perspectives continue to prevail over national needs and national perspectives, the United States will face grave difficulties meeting future challenges to its vital interests.

## NOTES

1. Lawrence J. Korb, *The Joint Chiefs of Staff: The First Twenty-Five Years* (Bloomington: Indiana University Press, 1976), p. 24.
2. Paul H. Nitze, quoted in Geoffrey Piller, "DOD's Office of International Security Affairs: The Brief Ascendency of an Advisory System," *Political Science Quarterly* 98 (Spring 1983): 65; Blue Ribbon Defense Panel, *Report to the President and the Secretary of Defense on the Department of Defense 1 July 1970* (Washington, D.C.: Government Printing Office, 1970), pp. 126-128; General Lewis Allen, Jr., quoted in *Armed Forces Journal International* 119 (June 1982): 64.
3. Edward C. Meyer, "The JCS—How Much Reform Is Needed?" *Armed Forces Journal International* 119 (April 1982): 86.
4. John L. Byron, "Reorganization of the U.S. Armed Forces," *U.S. Naval Institute Proceedings* 109 (Jan. 1983): 68-75; Morton H. Halperin and David Halperin, "The Key West Key," *Foreign Policy* 53 (Winter 1983-84): 114-130.
5. Alan L. Dean, "General Propositions of Organizational Design," in Peter Szanton, ed., *Federal Reorganization: What Have We Learned?* (Chatham, NJ: Chatham House, 1981), p. 138.
6. Blue Ribbon Defense Panel, *Report*, p. 50; Richard C. Steadman, *Report to the Secretary of Defense on the National Military Command Structure* (Washington, D.C.: July 1978), p. 16; see also John H. Cushman, *Command and Control of*

*Theater Forces: Adequacy* (Cambridge: Harvard University, Center for Information Policy Research, Program on Information Resources Policy, 1983), pp. 3-58. Here and elsewhere I have drawn heavily on General Cushman's penetrating analysis of the history and problems of the unified commands.

7. David C. Jones, "What's Wrong with Our Defense Establishment," *New York Times Magazine* (November 7, 1982): 70.

8. Special Operations Review Group, "Report on the Iranian Rescue Mission," in *Aviation Week & Space Technology* 113 (September 15, 1980): 63-70.

9. Blue Ribbon Defense Panel, *Report*, p. 48; *Report of DOD Commission on Beirut International Airport Terrorist Act, October 23, 1983* (20 December 1983), p. 55.

10. Laurence I. Radway, "Militarism," in *International Encyclopedia of the Social Sciences* (New York: Macmillan and Free Press, 1968), vol. 10, p. 300.

---

# 12.2 "Bureaucratic Politics": The Ugly Attack on Professionalism

## FRED THAYER

*Dr. Thayer continues our examination of the bureaucratic politics model, postulating that such a theory has been used to attack the professional bureaucracy in general, and the military specifically, as being opposed, even disloyal, to the national interest. He argues that this conclusion need not inevitably flow from the theory of bureaucratic politics. Moreover, he concludes, only by putting an end to the ravaging of professionalism by elected officials unduly influenced by such bureaucratic-politics theorists can we hope to incorporate effectively the valued advice of professional public servants in national security decisions.*

This chapter outlines how a theory of politics and administration was transformed from a well-meaning attempt to define positive roles for career civilian administrators (bureaucrats) in many government agencies into a powerful weapon aimed not only at those administrators, but also at career military and foreign service officers, not to mention politically appointed department heads. Known as bureaucratic politics (BP), the currently dominant version of the theory (better labeled theology) has become an all-out attack upon professionalism, especially military professionalism. Under the leadership of alleged military reformers who have wholeheartedly adopted the theory, the attack has been increasingly successful. The drama is still unfolding, and there may yet be an opportunity to write a different final act than the champions of BP would prefer. Unfortunately, many of those who initiated BP dogma, especially academics in the field of public administration, do not yet see how others have completely reversed their original concepts.

As befits a drama, this chapter will proceed by looking at the "acts" that have been so important. These acts will take up the origins of the theory, its relation to other long-term attacks on military professionalism, the antigovernment alliance of President John F. Kennedy and Professor Richard Neustadt, the further expansion of the theory, and the body blows to military professionalism that have been delivered by the "reformers." The chapter will close with suggestions on how to reverse the trend by unmasking the gross fallacies of BP theology and mounting a spirited and forward-looking affirmation of professionalism.

## ACT I: THE FLOWERING OF A FLAWED THEORY

Almost any social science theory spawns variations of that theory in other academic "disciplines" or "fields." The origins of "bureaucratic politics" (BP) as a descriptive and prescriptive theory of activities *within* government are seen here as by-products of the political theory of pluralism. Whether particular variations of pluralist theory are valid or invalid, desirable or undesirable, need not be considered in detail. It is enough to note that while one school of thought argued that interest group competition was benign so long as group members have access to their leaders,[1] others complained that group leaders constituted an "elite" that did not really represent their memberships at all.[2] When pluralism was flying high, these disagreements were of little importance; the prosperity of the 1950s seemed to make it an unnecessary distraction to decide if rich private citizens had more power than elected officials at all levels of government. Political scientists, moreover, did not like the question: If the storied lobbyists and historic robber barons were in charge from the beginning, then what was the study of government all about?

The evolution of BP is more clearly discernible in the modern history of administrative thought and practice in the United States, especially by what has been important to the "field" of public administration and its self-conscious interfaces with the "discipline" of political science. A convenient point of departure, one that has long been recognized as such, is Norton Long's declaration that:

> There is no more forlorn spectacle in the administrative world than an agency and a program possessed of statutory life, armed with executive orders, sustained in the courts, yet stricken with paralysis and deprived of power, an object of contempt to its enemies and of despair to its friends. . . .
>
> The bureaucracy under the American political system has a large share of responsibility for the public promotion of policy and even more in organizing the political basis for its survival and growth. . . . The agencies have a special competence. . . . In the eyes of their supporters

and their enemies, they represent the institutionalized embodiment of policy, an enduring organization actually or potentially capable of mobilizing power behind policy. The survival interests and creative drives of administrative organizations combine with clientele pressures to compel such mobilization.[3]

Long's real preference, long popular among political scientists, was powerful parliamentary-type political parties that could develop coherent programs and mobilize public sentiment behind them, without the extensive involvement of career administrators. In his view, BP was the best the United States could do.

Long's influential but brief "think piece" (eight pages, no footnotes) appeared in the same year as Philip Selznick's landmark study of the Tennessee Valley Authority (TVA). Highlighting "co-optation" as "the process of absorbing new elements into the leadership of the policy-determining structure of an organization as a means of averting threats to its stability or existence," Selznick lauded TVA as a "relatively good example of democratic administration" and a "shining example of incorruptibility . . . in major matters," but also cautioned that political compromises might yet tarnish the agency's image.[4] He and Long concluded in effect that "good" policies and programs call for *political* commitment, activity and bargaining, day-in and day-out, by career civil servants. Inadvertently, however, these authors planted the seeds of a vicious counterattack, as did a third one who came along in 1963 to praise the bureaucracy for what had to be done:

> American bureaucracy is an independent force, and from its independence it draws much of its strength and prestige. It is a powerful and viable branch of government, not properly subject to complete control by Congress, the President, or the judiciary. . . .
>
> There has been much wringing of hands . . . about "the deadlock of democracy," the inability of the President and Congress to work together through a disciplined party system. . . . The bureaucracy, which is actually a more representative body than Congress, combines essential democratic ingredients at the same time that it formulates important policy. Administrative agencies, removed from the electoral process, can take action without consulting Congress, and such action is as responsive to the demands and needs of the community as any that Congress could take, even if there were no "deadlock." . . .
>
> American bureaucracy takes its place as an equal partner with the President, Congress, and the Judiciary.[5]

BP coincided nicely with the most widely accepted cliché among public administration academics. They have told their students for decades that no operational distinction can be made between making policy and carrying it out, between formulating it and implementing it; in short, there can be no separation of policy and administration. Career bureaucrats, so it is argued, perform precisely the same functions as elected and politically appointed officials, or, as Peter Woll argues, act on their own when elected officials are paralyzed. Having analyzed elsewhere why career administrators cannot be expected to agree publicly with this definition of their roles,[6] I use BP itself to show how this particular argument can be turned against those who make it.

The "survival interests" of academics include the luring of students into their programs so that universities will not abolish those programs. In marketing the distinctive study of public administration, U.S. academics could not borrow from European models because many of them were business-oriented[7] or military-oriented.[8] Business school students could look forward to a career ladder promising largely autonomous authority at the top, given the demise of family-run corporations and the ineffectual authority of boards of directors.[9] Public administrators, however, never have been able to think about becoming chief executive officers; they have been limited to aspiring at best to daily subservience to designated political superiors. With business schools training leaders, the "public administrationists" could not content themselves with turning out followers.

The deceptively attractive solution was to invent the pluralist-oriented doctrine of a unified public service elite. If administrators and elected officials could be labeled "partners," graduate degrees in public administration could become the equivalent of election to public office. This approach remains central to academics because it is more directly important to attract students than to establish fruitful dialogue with administrative practitioners who cannot act as though they are more important than their bosses. Yet academics still look upon bureaucrats as representatives of group interests.[10] Even the new public administration notion of the early 1970s, pledged to advancing social equity, wanted to find new administrators who would represent the unrepresented underprivileged.[11]

At the most general level, any claim that career administrators should be the equal partners of elected public officials is the intellectual equivalent of inciting a riot, but it also can convince others that the field of public administration is not worth attention. Whereas some administrative discretion in carrying out policy is inevitable and always has been,[12] this cannot be transformed into a doctrine of partnership without an accompanying theory of how to rewrite political constitutions, and not only the U.S. Constitution. Although such a fundamental change might make sense, the notion of informally adding BP to the Constitution is not a substitute, especially given the almost two-century-old fear that a technocratic elite may come to exercise permanent authority.[13]

At another level, BP has diverted the attention of public administrationists from the activities of the most important U.S. government agencies (the "inner cabinet" of state, defense, treasury, and justice) in favor of paying too much attention to the less significant "outer cabinet." This widely known schism has led to prolonged intellectual starvation,[14] leading to academic hallucinations because agencies with the longest administrative histories and the greatest dedication to accountable professionalism have been ignored, along with other dangerous aspects. Does Woll really prefer that the Central Intelligence Agency (CIA) and the Federal Bureau of Investigation (FBI) operate without any reference to Congress at all? Worse yet, BP invited counterattack by picturing career administrators as only lobbyists for special interest groups that, by definition, are opposed to the national interest.

The flawed doctrine was ripe for destruction at yet another level, especially given the tendency of public administration academics to focus on the federal government. Because the "outer cabinet" does in fact have some direct association with such clientele groups as agriculture, business, and labor, presidents often appoint to those cabinet posts individuals with long and direct experience in those areas. Who is surprised when a business executive becomes secretary of commerce? But these individuals, of course, can claim that their own expertise makes them self-sufficient in their relationships with career administrators. The members of the "inner cabinet," on the other hand, are unlikely to come from the ranks of professional diplomats, military officers, prosecutors, or even financiers. BP, therefore, was not only unsuited for its primary task of making careerists the partners of the "inner cabinet," but also turned out to be highly useful in ways its originators never imagined—tearing asunder national security decision-making and damaging the supremely important forms of professionalism nourished so carefully and so long in the foreign and military services.

BP's central logic had a gaping hole, one it shared with its pluralist parent. If careerists are only lobbyists competing against each other, how is the national interest to be determined? A true BP believer must agree that so long as the competition is "fair," then any outcome is acceptable. This readiness to accept any outcome made Charles Lindblom's "muddling through" a staple of public administration curricula.[15] Yet because pluralism cannot escape its "might makes right" logic, it also became necessary to hope that if muddling through seemed to be headed toward "bad" results, the ultimate guardian of the national interest would be the strong executive, a notion that for recent generations is still epitomized by the presidential tenure of Franklin D. Roosevelt. In a strange way, BP reinforced further centralization of authority.

As an integral part of the attack on military professionalism, BP really did not hit its stride until the unfortunate Kennedy-Neustadt alliance of 1960. In retrospect, however, it was inevitable that military professionalism would come under question in the 1950s, and that BP would become a handy baseball bat for those questioning the military. The Cold War produced an era unusual for the United States—that is, maintaining a large military establishment in constant readiness for war. A large budget request for equipment that may never be used is an immediate target, as are those who make such requests. BP, carelessly developed to begin with, was perfectly suited for such attacks. An agricultural bureaucrat, for example, is presumably for the interests of farmers and pays little attention to the interests of others (for example, urban consumers). The bureaucrat is at least credited with a proconstituency perspective. Because the official interest of the military leader is the defense of all citizens, a BP approach cannot credit that leader with being for any constituency except himself. The military, via BP, is thereby pictured as inalterably opposed to the national interest, even though that is the military constituency. As will be shown later, this sometimes comes close to an accusation that military chiefs are disloyal to the country. Attacks on professionalism began almost as soon as World War II ended.


## ACT II: THE TWILIGHT OF MILITARY PROFESSIONALISM

The downhill slide can be dated from the end of General George Marshall's service in the army and from some of Dwight Eisenhower's first actions as president. Attacks on military professionalism have taken different forms since that time, the latest one being that the senior officers of the military services really are not professionals at all, which is the essence of the contemporary military "reform" movement. This act of the drama, however, centers on the injuries to professionalism incurred in the 1950s and 1960s, except for the Kennedy-Neustadt wrecking crew that deserves its own act (to follow).

I have repeatedly discovered to my sorrow and even horror that today's reformers are not even aware that there was a Joint Chiefs of Staff (JCS) organization during World War II, and are wholly unfamiliar with its role and that of its chairman, Admiral William Leahy, who was recalled to active duty expressly for the purpose of coordinating (not directing or commanding) the work of the army, navy, and air force chiefs and their interactions with the president. All of this is outlined in appropriate histories, old and new,[16] but it is ignored by the reformers because it does not fit their cherished prescriptions for an ever stronger central authority (such as a powerful chairman of the JCS, or even a separate Defense Department "general staff") and weak heads of the army, navy, and air force. Marshall, the most famous of the World War II chiefs, along with his colleagues Admiral Ernest King of the navy and General Henry Arnold of the army air forces (technically subordinate to Marshall, but added to the JCS for air power expertise), led the way in demonstrating that professionalism combined responsibility, corporateness, service-based expertise, and a commitment to maintaining a separation of the political and the professional.

Marshall believed that "he had to hold the President at a calculated distance in order to keep his own freedom of action."[17]  He consistently declined to visit Roosevelt at either Warm Springs or Hyde Park, he attempted to avoid any informal meetings with the president, and he even made sure that he did not laugh at FDR's jokes.[18]  To do any or all of these, Marshall thought, would have compromised his ability to express professional disagreement, the highest duty of career professionals.  Few civil-military, policy-administration relationships have been as productive as this one, and it suffered not at all from Marshall's determination to keep his distance.  The movement toward the disruption of professionalism may have begun with a navy chief's public protest against the Truman administration's military budget in 1949 (and his subsequent firing by President Harry S. Truman), but antiprofessionalism took solid hold after the JCS members became explainers and defenders of Truman's Korean War policy in 1951, and also publicly supported his dismissal of General Douglas MacArthur.  Congressional Republicans publicly expressed a lack of confidence in the JCS, and Eisenhower concluded that he would have to replace them with appointees personally approved by his principal opponent for the 1952 Republican nomination, Senator Robert Taft.[19]

The new JCS chairman, Arthur Radford, had been a prominent participant in the protests by navy admirals against the Truman budget; in effect, he was rewarded for having fought Truman.  He became something of a republican chairman who was a vehicle for relaying the administration's views to the JCS rather than vice versa.  Because the chairman was by statute the only JCS member not involved with defense budgets (the responsibility of the individual services and their chiefs), he was encouraged to become unresponsible if not irresponsible.[20]  Eisenhower's reductions in army budgets and his apparent favoritism toward the navy and air force (an interesting development, given the insistence of today's reformers that administrators always favor the interests of the groups they have been associated with) later rankled the army's chief of staff, Maxwell Taylor, and another top general, James Gavin, to such an extent that after losing a number of budget battles, they left the army to write books of protest. Antiprofessionalism escalated.

Gavin wrote that the army, navy, and a part of the air force were "liberals" usually associated with the Democratic party, whereas the air force's bomber and missile components were "conservative" Republicans.[21] Taylor wrote along the same lines but without using party labels,[22] and even military sociologist Morris Janowitz distinguished between nonbomber "pragmatists" and bomb-oriented "absolutists."[23]  These swipes tended to portray Eisenhower as a lackey of the air force's bomber forces, and the identification of the army and navy as Democratic party in orientation was unusual in light of Eisenhower's two-term Republican presidency, MacArthur's earlier political ambitions, and Admiral Radford's role as the bearer of bad tidings for the army. Taylor's argument included even a proposal for a single chief of staff because the "cumbersome" JCS committee system did not work, and his published attack on Radford as a powerful JCS chairman who had overridden army views in the "best traditions of Tammany Hall" made it obvious that Taylor would not favor Radford as the single chief. Unprofessionalism, or antiprofessionalism, took on tidal wave proportions.[24]

Taylor and Gavin became official military advisers in John Kennedy's 1960 campaign. He often lauded them in speeches on security policy, and their roles were very important. They helped him make a (successful) case that a World War II hero-general had permitted the nation's defenses to crumble. (It is often forgotten that Kennedy's major promise in 1960 was a huge increase in defense spending.) After taking office, Kennedy appointed Gavin as his ambassador to France—a conventional political payoff. When the Bay of Pigs provided Kennedy a major disaster in his first months, he asked Taylor to study what had gone wrong. Later, he kept Taylor in the White House, dispatched him to Vietnam to make recommendations (that paved the way for large-scale escalation) and, in 1962, made Taylor the JCS chairman. And, while accepting responsibility for the Bay of Pigs fiasco, Kennedy removed all the service chiefs along the way even though their involvement had ranged from little to nothing.

Taylor's JCS colleague, air force General Thomas White, later labeled him a political appointee, adding that many professionals agreed.[25] The implications of Taylor's appointment were indeed far-reaching. His immediate credentials were wholly political, having used a campaign train as transportation to the chairman's office. Much of his anti-Eisenhower argument was the continuation of an old protest by paratroop generals during World War II that Eisenhower was using "their" transport planes to fly supplies to the front—a useful function, given the military uselessness of the airborne divisions. His major contribution to antiprofessionalism was to become the symbol of Kennedy's implicit announcement: He, as president, could not find a single officer on active duty worthy of becoming JCS chairman. A harsher and more sweeping indictment scarcely can be imagined. Kennedy obviously was looking for political and personal loyalty at whatever cost to professionalism. He should not have made the appointment, and Taylor, instead of leaping to accept it, should have declined it, just as General William Westmoreland later should not have followed Johnson administration "suggestions" to accept speaking engagements in the United States in order to defend the Vietnam war—in retrospect, an unforgivable absence from his combat post.

The attack on professionalism took another turn in connection with the McNamara Revolution of the 1960s, a revolution that can be distinguished in concept from the Kennedy-Neustadt alliance. The "whiz kids" who entered the Pentagon with Robert McNamara promised that their state-of-the-art

techniques of systems analysis would usher in a new era of sophisticated decision-making; it even would be possible to evaluate proposals without building prototype ships, tanks, or planes. Because these techniques provided the only valid way of evaluating budget proposals, military officers would have to acquire these skills. The intellectual skills of the analysts, that is to say, would become the bedrock of military professionalism. This promised to make civilian skills indistinguishable from military skills, in a sort of fusion of the two. Otherwise sane observers succumbed to the lure of promoting faddish techniques in the name of military professionalism.

One air force general, writing in *Foreign Affairs* (often a deliberate policy "signal"), seemed to attack the notion of fusion, arguing that while the old military approaches may have outlived their time, the military had to develop a new expertise that would transcend the "parochial boundaries of the services." The centerpiece of the Defense Department civilian staff should be a military director of operations with his own staff comprising military officers who had mastered the latest analytic techniques.[26] Edward Katzenback aimed his fire at the military war colleges that, he said, had become too "civilian" in their emphasis on international politics and technological trends. The war colleges would become more military if they added the McNamara techniques to their curricula. Better yet, all single-service colleges might be disbanded in favor of expanding the multiservice colleges.[27] Both of these arguments seemed to favor a clearly recognizable and distinct military professionalism, but at its core would be the new techniques brought to the Pentagon by McNamara's young civilian analysts. The arguments, somewhat sycophantic in nature, emerged when it was widely believed, and repeatedly stated by news media and other observers, that the McNamara Revolution had brought real and progressive change to the military. Disillusion with the Vietnam war had yet to be heard. Even today, the simple underlying premise of the early 1960s remains little understood.

If the content of military expertise is, by declaration, limited to the civilian forms of expertise available in the Defense Department, there is no need to consult those having military expertise because, by definition, they cannot add anything to what the civilians already know by virtue of having more such expertise than do the military people. Add to this mix just a dash of BP (all military proposals are "parochial," as noted by the air force general quoted above), and there is even less reason to consult the military people. While BP already had significantly crippled professionalism, the Kennedy-Neustadt alliance was busily attacking it from the top downward.

## ACT III: THE KENNEDY-NEUSTADT ALLIANCE

Neustadt's *Presidential Power*, appearing while he was a consultant with Senator Henry Jackson's famous Subcommittee on National Policy

Machinery, made him a natural as a postelection adviser to John Kennedy in 1960.[28] The latter later observed that Neustadt was the best publicity agent a political scientist ever had.[29] Such presidential anointing tends to exempt academics from even the pseudo-critical analysis of their intellectual output that is common in academe. Former colleagues may attack Henry Kissinger, for example, for his involvement with policies they dislike, but not because he is a low-quality thinker. Neustadt's bare-bones theory was and is a simple one; as he fleshed it out, it became half-baked and even deeply cynical. Worse yet, it remains powerfully influential.

Any president's power, goes the argument, is only the power to *"induce (all the relevant actors with whom he deals) to believe that what he wants of them is what their own appraisal of their own responsibilities requires them to do in their own interest, not his"* [emphasis in original].[30] This remains disarmingly attractive, as was Neustadt's prominent mention of Harry Truman, a president he admired: "I sit here all day trying to persuade people to do the things they ought to have sense enough to do without my persuading them. . . . That's all the powers of a president amount to."[31] Flaws quickly are discernible in this concept.

Neustadt's departure point clearly was "outer cabinet"—a president's cabinet officers "have departmental duties and constituents," and each operating agency "has a separate statutory base . . . statutes to administer . . . a different set of subcommittees at the Capitol . . . its own peculiar set of clients, friends and enemies outside the formal government."[32] Neustadt seemed not to notice that the "clients" of the "inner cabinet" (state, defense, treasury, and justice) are, in principle, the same as the president's. If an "inner cabinet" member makes a decision that is in the interests of that agency and its "clients" or "constituents" then, in principle, the decision is in the president's interest as well *unless* the president's interest is defined solely as reelection. If an "inner cabinet" concept had been included, it also should have been obvious to Neustadt that Harry Truman clearly had final, unilateral authority to use or withhold atomic bombs, and without having to persuade others to do his bidding. This kind of intellectual carelessness is harmless for the most part, but not when a particular theory is adopted by a president. How did Neustadt flesh out his skeleton?

Because the interests of presidents and cabinet officers are different, their relationships cannot be cooperative but must be adversarial. "The members of the Cabinet are a President's natural enemies," observed Charles G. Dawes, who had been Warren Harding's budget director, Calvin Coolidge's vice president, and Herbert Hoover's ambassador to England. To Neustadt, "Dawes knew whereof he spoke."[33] Neustadt even implied later that things were much better before presidents submitted integrated executive budgets to Congress. For example, Franklin Roosevelt was able to hoard his power by choosing to support only some of the appropriations sought by his department heads; "it's all your trouble, not mine," he once told

them. When a consolidated budget made presidents a "court of ultimate appeal," power shifted to department heads. Since they decided when and what a president should decide, the executive budget helped them in "getting service out of him."[34] This logic bears some resemblance to Ronald Reagan's quest for authorization to line-item veto appropriations by simply removing those that he dislikes even if his cabinet officers like them, but Neustadt has not rushed forward to support Reagan.

If cabinet officers are natural enemies, a president should keep them at a distance and maintain his own control over the issues to be addressed. When Kennedy applied this reasoning to the National Security Council (the statutory arrangement that brings presidents together with their chief security policy advisers to hammer out decisions), he also took account of criticisms that Eisenhower had relied too much upon military staff approaches and that committees generally were useless.[35] The National Security Council (NSC) quickly became a nonexistent forum that was brought together only to make trivial decisions or to be informed about decisions that already had been made.[36] Kennedy's major contribution in this regard, however, was to elevate the White House national security adviser to a position of public prominence as an advocate and explainer of policy, and to rely upon a coterie of other noncabinet advisers to criticize any proposals made by cabinet officers and to make their own proposals.[37] Since McGeorge Bundy and Walt Rostow operated the White House National Security Office in the early Kennedy years, each new adviser has operated the equivalent of a second State Department just outside the president's door. Hardly anyone can remember the names of those who served Truman and Eisenhower in that capacity, but this has changed. In various ways, the advisers have been engaged in constant battles with secretaries of state, have been more or less independent policy-makers, and, in recent years, may have kept secrets even from the president.

The prevailing view is that any president's rearranging of his administrative processes is a matter of personal style, but I suggest that the most important factor since 1960 has been the influence of BP and its Neustadt variant. Its logic is that department heads cannot be useful unless they are personally tied to the president and are themselves the enemies of members of their departments. In the Kennedy years, for example, only the attorney general (his brother), Robert McNamara (proposed by his brother-in-law), and Maxwell Taylor (from the campaign) clearly fit the requirements. Kennedy's sweeping adoption of Neustadt-style BP may not have been foreordained; the Bay of Pigs (1961), the Cuban Missile Crisis (1963), and the Vietnam war all made contributions.

Kennedy quickly adopted a Cuban invasion plan presented him by holdovers Allen Dulles and Richard Bissell of the CIA and JCS chairman Lyman Lemnitzer, who was the least enthusiastic.[38] Lemnitzer already was operating separately from the service chiefs because of a 1958 military reorganization act that increased the chairman's role. Only later did it become known that Marine commandant General David Shoup, a Medal of Honor winner from World War II invasions of Pacific islands, had pointed out that if the capture of tiny Tarawa had required an enormous effort, it was silly to assume that 800-mile-long Cuba would present no obstacles.[39] Roger Hilsman, then head of the State Department's Intelligence Bureau, concluded that because he was forbidden to evaluate the plans, the military intelligence offices also had been prohibited from analyzing them.[40] When the operation collapsed, Kennedy turned against "experts" in general, even though much of the expertise had been shunted aside to begin with. It is understandable that a political leader may superficially accept responsibility, but then let it be known that others really are to blame.

By the time of the Cuban Missile Crisis (CMC) in 1962, Kennedy had come to rely upon McNamara and Taylor, who repeatedly were giving him the "good news" that operations in Vietnam were a resounding success; their closeness to the president made dissenting views either unavailable or unwanted. McNamara, whose enthusiasm and prestige were at their highest, proclaimed in mid-1962 that "every quantitative measurement we have shows we're winning the war."[41] Taylor, the senior member of the Taylor-Rostow team that studied the war on the spot in 1961, was promising that success at little cost to the United States would be achieved by 1962 or, at worst, 1963.[42] From the BP perspective, NcNamara had tamed the military services, and Taylor's control of strategy made superfluous any advice from service chiefs.

The most definitive account of the CMC remains Graham Allison's *Essence of Decision* because much of the book was based upon the self-conscious application of Neustadt's BP doctrine and because Allison interviewed most of the participants in the CMC.[43]

On the day the crisis ended, Kennedy asserted that the military had "wanted" to invade Cuba, and "it's lucky for us that we have McNamara over there."[44] Yet it was the president who initially had favored an air strike on the Soviet missiles, and Robert Kennedy who first thought of a naval blockade. McNamara, who made no specific proposals to begin with, supported Robert Kennedy when he learned of the latter's preference. McNamara said later that he "came to know, admire and love Robert F. Kennedy by his behavior," and McNamara later wrote a glowing introduction to RFK's book on the crisis.[45] McNamara, of course, remained close to the family, shifting his position on the Vietnam war as RFK indicated that would be the theme of his bid for the presidential nomination in 1968, and joining the group that helped Senator Edward Kennedy prepare his public statements about his own personal crisis. RFK's book later praised Taylor as the only military chief who had given any consideration to the implications of military action against Cuba,[46] and their closeness became clear when RFK named a son after Taylor in 1965.

Following the pattern set before the 1960 elections, the air force, especially Chief of Staff Curtis LeMay, became the target of post-CMC analysis. LeMay repeatedly was pictured as an individual wholly committed to a military attack on Cuba, one whose continued "insensitivity" was "really not surprising." Allison asserted also that Air Force planners and General Walter Sweeney of the Tactical Air Command were wholly incorrect in telling the president that a "surgical air strike" might not be 100 percent effective. "Civilian experts," not identified by reference to a source, an agency, or a form of expertise, had studied the problem and had concluded that such a strike would indeed work, and that the surgical strike became a live option during discussions in the president's planning group (the Executive Committee, or ExCom, of the NSC). The navy's chief, Admiral George Anderson, became an object of scorn when he and McNamara argued, in the navy's operations center, about how U.S. warships would confront Soviet ships during the blockade; in due course, Anderson was made ambassador to Portugal. The military chiefs were blamed in general for "inflated plans," in connection with possible attacks on Cuba. Other whipping-boys of the postcrisis analyses were United Nations ambassador Adlai Stevenson, Secretary of State Dean Rusk, and CIA director John McCone; Allison seemingly concurred with these judgments by people close to the president.[47]

Had the CMC occurred a few years later, it might have been given more careful evaluation by outsiders not wedded to the image of a brilliant and courageous young president helped by the few "best and brightest." In Neustadt's BP, the job of these "insiders" is to pay close attention to the president's needs as defined solely in terms of presidential power. In praising Roosevelt's approach, Neustadt had laid it on the line: "He wanted power for its own sake; he also wanted what it could achieve. . . . His private satisfactions were enriched by public purposes and these grew more compelling as more power came his way."[48] If purpose is wholly secondary to "power for its own sake," then it is understandable that some cabinet officers and perhaps all career administrators will be labeled "adversaries" because they cannot be expected to put the president's personal political power at the top of their priority lists. Whether John Kennedy adopted this aspect of Neustadt's BP cannot be known, but the ultimate publicity on the CMC was managed so as to attribute success to the president and a few insiders. Neustadt later explained the difference between an outsider and an insider in terms that fit the Kennedy presidency.

Asked to comment on the roles of the secretary of state and the White House adviser on national security, Neustadt said to a congressional committee in 1963:

> All one really wants from State is this: on issues that the Special Assistant's office cannot handle because they aren't at the top of the President's own list, or because the President shifts off to something else after a decision has

been made while such issues must be tidied up and tended to—all one wants is that the staff in the Secretary's Office will, conscientiously and carefully, with a sense of serving the whole government, make sure that all the people with a right to know, a right to be involved and to express opinions, will get a crack at the right time and place.[49]

If the function of the secretary of state is to keep himself fully involved with issues that are not currently occupying the president's attention, then the secretary of state becomes the ultimate outsider. Had it not been for McNamara's position as the equivalent of a family retainer, he would have been as outside as Dean Rusk, and JCS chairman Taylor was a political, not a professional, insider. The other military chiefs were roundly criticized for their roles in the CMC, even though they never were brought into the inside planning process.

While the BP doctrine obviously can be used to explain what some department heads do some of the time, it was an act of debatable scholarship to expand unthinkingly the doctrine to the "outer cabinet" agencies. In retrospect, Kennedy's early death gave an extra boost to BP thinking because it became possible (and politically desirable in some cases) to blame Lyndon Johnson for the ultimate disasters that clearly were caused by decisions taken in the early 1960s. Thus, Kennedy still can be pictured as the leader of an intellectual renaissance in government, as represented by Allison's declarations that the "civilian experts" knew what the air force could accomplish in Cuba even if the air force did not. Although BP doctrine has taken different forms, it has been central to the presidency ever since.

## ACT IV: BP EVERYWHERE

BP has become more and more a description of what is wrong with government because its pluralist underpinnings have fallen into wide disrepute except for public administration textbooks. The military and foreign services have been dragged into this arena where all careerists become the targets. This survey shows only how pervasive the attacks have been by alleged intellectuals and practicing politicians. The approach will be generally chronological.

- Using pure economic assumptions of self-interest, Anthony Downs developed the concept of "territoriality." Bureaucrats, he said, "stake out and defend territories surrounding their nests or home bases." As in international politics, one can distinguish between a bureau's "heartland," where it has complete control; an "interior fringe," where it is not wholly in control; and a "no-man's land" of constant struggle with enemies. The objective is survival and, one hopes, invasion of neighboring territories.[50] Ironically, Downs produced his book while employed as a researcher at the Rand Corporation, financed by the U.S. Air Force. This situation may have led him to end his book with a chapter suggesting that bureaucracy in this country was not the major problem his theoretical argument might make it appear to be,[51] but only the other chapters are now remembered.

- Political theorist Theodore Lowi, perhaps inspired by his association with Robert Kennedy's presidential campaign, produced two all-out attacks on the supposed surrender of government's constitutional authority to a combination of special interests and career administrators.[52] He advocated that all legislation should be enacted in such detail that administrators would have absolutely no discretionary authority. This was the only way, he added, to recapture government from "interest group liberalism" and restore it to its rightful Madisonian position above the contending factions—a notion he labeled "juridical democracy."

- I. M. Destler, focusing on national security decision-making, used Neustadt's BP to propose changes in the State Department. The problem, he argued, was the "pet bureaucratic doctrines" of the permanent career group. The secretary of state should rely instead upon his assistant secretaries and, in turn, they should be given cabinet-level rank. The secretary also needed "in-and-outers" who would be "analytically oriented, more inclined toward aggressive involvement in issues and risk-taking" (always the description of those presumably ready to awaken slumbering agencies). The assistant secretaries and the "in-and-outers" would be known as the secretary's men, but also as the president's men, obviously engaging in combat with the Foreign Service. This was a significant change from Neustadt's BP, which holds that the president and secretary of state are natural enemies.[53]

- Frederick V. Malek served the Nixon administration for five years, getting the most recognition for selecting those to fill the presidentially appointed positions (about 650 in the federal government). Known as the resident "hatchet man," he later published his own views:

Government workers . . . want personal security. The idea of reform and innovation can be threatening to them because it may risk their security. Their instinctive reaction . . . is to perpetuate or enlarge their own areas of responsibility and to oppose any changes that might diminish their jobs or status. . . .
    They come to identify with the problem in which they have invested so many years of their lives. They tend to believe sincerely in the program's goals, and they spend enormous psychic energy in advocating it, running it and protecting it from change. . . .
    There is a great fear of risk-taking within the bureaucracy. . . . Unfortunately, dedication to the status quo is reinforced by the

government's personnel practices. Most individuals . . . enjoy almost total job security regardless of performance. . . .

There may be fifteen thousand employees in an agency, but the director may be entitled to fill no more than six positions with people of his own choice. The other employees cannot be easily fired, reassigned or given different pay. The sound business executive, of course, will not frequently use his power to fire people, but there is at least tacit understanding that the power exists. Employees who will not respond to normal, positive motivation will sometimes react more quickly if there is a "club in the closet." . . .

The most difficult problem . . . is the bureaucrats' propensity to avoid risks and shy away from innovation. Somehow we need to encourage people to be willing to accept an occasional failure—to stick their necks out . . . knowing . . . that a number of such measures will fail. . . . Top political appointees must be willing to accept the mistakes and take the public criticisms . . . recognizing this as a cost of more effective, more innovative government.[54]

To his credit, Malek admitted that the Nixon administration had made administrative mistakes. Despite its mistrust of careerists, it should not have withheld information from them because it feared they would oppose all changes. The Malek Manual that described "how to operate a political personnel system and . . . suggested subversion of the Civil Service merit system" should not have been prepared, even though Malek did not approve it and already had left office. Yet Malek praised the work of two political scientists who, after questioning 125 top career administrators, concluded that because only 17 percent of them were affiliated with the Republican party, "our findings document a . . . social service bureaucracy dominated by administrators ideologically hostile to many of the directions pursued by the Nixon Administration."[55]

- The wholly bipartisan Civil Service Reform Act of 1978 (CSRA) was ushered through Congress by the head of President Jimmy Carter's Civil Service Commission, Alan Campbell, the former dean of the prestigious Maxwell School of Public Affairs at Syracuse University. The primary motivation for CSRA was "a widespread public perception that public bureaucracies were bloated and inefficient,"[56] and Carter indicated as much. The bureaucracy, he said, suffered from "inadequate motivation . . . too few rewards for excellence and too few penalties for unsatisfactory performance." He was alarmed that only 226 of some 2 million federal employees had been fired for "inefficiency" in 1977, clearly not enough. The Civil Service, he asserted, was "ready and willing to respond to the risks and rewards of competitive life."[57] CSRA provided merit pay and bonus systems to reward those considered outstanding, and also made it easier to punish employees.

If these attacks upon careerists are reduced to their basics, they amount only to criticisms that bureaucrats do not always immediately agree with their bosses and sometimes question the latters' decisions, bureaucrats often believe that their agencies are performing useful service in the public interest, and bureaucrats enjoy their work and would prefer to keep their jobs. This type of thinking is not unique to bureaucrats; business executives and workers have been known to believe the same things. The elected officials of a community, state, or even nation may intervene in efforts to persuade employers not to close down factories and move elsewhere. From a slightly different perspective, the attacks convey the thought that "the boss is always right," an authoritarian point of view. Neustadt's ideal president, for example, would never need help from others in reaching decisions and never would make incorrect decisions.

At yet another level of analysis, some of the proposals seem hopelessly innocent. Does Destler really think it possible to elevate all assistant secretaries of state to cabinet rank? Malek endorses innovation and risk-taking, but his principal objective is to end bureaucratic resistance to changes directed from above; his real preference, that is to say, is obedience with no questions asked. And does he really expect presidents and cabinet officers to take the blame for failures initiated by bureaucrats when the latter have no legal authority to make policy innovations in the first place? Did Carter expect administrators with less job security to take more risks than before?

Nobody should be surprised at the continued expansion of BP doctrine. There have been intimations that the Reagan administration, or at least some of its members, devised and implemented national security policies without informing the secretaries of state and defense, the JCS, most of the CIA, and, in some instances, the president himself. Allegedly, some appointees to high posts at home and abroad were directed to bypass normal channels and report to individuals in the White House. Talk of "a government within the government," or even a "junta," has flowered. The more intense the belief that cabinet heads and administrators are not to be trusted, the fewer the people who will be consulted or informed. The unbroken trend since 1961 marches on, and the military reform movement gives us another example.


## ACT V: "REFORMING" THE MILITARY

BP doctrine has been used for years to attack the separate military services (army, navy, air force, and sometimes marines) for actively pursuing their "organizational imperatives" instead of the broader interests of the secretary of defense, the president, and the public at large. (Congress seldom gets much attention, despite its constitutional responsibilities for declaring war and equipping the armed forces.) The decibel count has risen steadily, and periodic changes in legislation have increased the authority of the secretary of defense and the JCS chairman, the only military officer who stands outside the dreaded services. The most recent "reform," the details of which need not concern us here, adds yet more authority to the chairman and secretary. It seems not to have occurred to the "reformers" that if previous increases in authority had not led to improved conditions but precisely the opposite, still more authority might not help.

Archie L. Barrett of the U.S. House of Representatives' Committee on Armed Services, and Edward L. Luttwak of Georgetown University were two of the more important intellectual contributors to the recent "reform." Barrett, a retired air force colonel, holds a doctorate from Harvard and is well located to influence legislation. General David C. Jones, a former air force general and JCS chairman, aggressively sought to expand the chairman's authority after he left the job (Admiral Thomas Moorer, another former chairman, disagreed with Jones). Jones asserted in a foreword to Barrett's book that "national security must be above politics—partisan, bureaucratic, sectional, or any other kind," a sort of "all politics is evil" declaration of war. Barrett's more genteel introduction is that "significant . . . decisions . . . derive from the interplay between the secretary of defense, whose control is tenuous at best, and each of the services, whose unflagging, skillful, and effective pursuit of their interests is deservedly legendary."[58] He adds:

> The Army, Navy, Air Force and Marine Corps exercise preponderant influence over the . . . Joint Chiefs of Staff (JCS) and the unified and specified commands. Consequently, no authentic, independent joint military presence exists to advise civilian leaders from a national point of view and employ the unified forces . . . in the field. . . .
> The members of the JCS, who are also the principal military officers of their . . . services, find it impossible to rise above service concerns and render advice on issues from a national perspective. Instead, their advice is the result of bargaining in which each member attempts to safeguard service interests. Because bargaining often fails to produce compromises acceptable to the services, the JCS avoids taking a position on a broad range of issues that shape the very core of the U.S. defense posture.[59]

In the standard BP view, any recommendation made by a service chief is, by definition, contrary to the national perspective. Because service chiefs are trapped by their loyalties, any bargains they reach also are contrary to that national perspective. Because service chiefs have too much influence over the JCS chairman and the unified commanders, neither the chairman nor those commanders can be an "independent military presence." The logic is far-reaching: A chairman close to the president (Taylor) cannot be an independent military presence, and Eisenhower, MacArthur, Nimitz, and LeMay were so trapped by their service loyalties that they could not be independent military presences in World War II. BP, as dogma, erases history. In fleshing out his argument, Barrett uses specific examples of how the system has not worked. The inner logic of those examples is worth attention.

## Case 1: Antiballistic Missiles (ABM)

In the mid-1960s, the army proposed an expensive ABM program, but the navy and air force initially agreed with McNamara that the available technology was not good enough. When it became clear that McNamara would refuse the army, however, the navy and air force chiefs suddenly agreed to support the army. Presumably, the services were so anxious to reassert their control over the assessment of weapons that two of them went against their own best judgment just to oppose McNamara. Worse yet, the navy and air force chiefs were endorsing an army program of $20 billion in an area in which they had no major interest.[60] The logic of this analysis includes several implicit premises.

One is that if the JCS do agree on an important question, the agreement is invalid unless it matches an earlier conclusion reached by the secretary of defense with no JCS assistance. A second premise is that, as suggested in the above quotation from Barrett, both JCS agreements and disagreements are contrary to the national perspective. Even an opinion (or opinions) on the conduct of the Vietnam War, or what to do in the Cuban Missile Crisis are, by definition, invalid. (Readers will recall that the air force was criticized for refusing to guarantee complete success for a surgical air strike against Soviet missiles in Cuba, yet it would have been in the "bureaucratic interest" of the air force to issue a guarantee.) A third premise is that no member of the JCS should say anything at all about the request of another service to develop a weapon, even if the service chief who wants the weapon cannot offer sound recommendations. Their opinions may be acceptable, however, if they echo the secretary's view. The fourth premise, also central to the military version of BP, is that the services are "log rollers"—each will approve any request made by the others. Following BP concepts, Barrett lists the size of the budget as of fundamental organizational interest to each service,[61] but elsewhere adduces evidence to the contrary without recognizing it as such.

Agreeing with the usual estimate of McNamara as an activist and dominant administrator, Barrett adds that the most recent secretaries have all been "inactive . . . administrators, passively accepting the existing . . . structure, processes and functional assignments." Yet he is forced to observe that McNamara failed to "secure military service cooperation during a period of ever-increasing defense budgets," while Melvin Laird, serving in the Nixon years and "emphasizing participative management," fostered "a cooperative attitude which prevailed throughout a time of relatively severe reductions in service programs and budgets."[62] Thus, the services disputed the secretary who was raising their budgets, but worked closely and well with the secretary who was slicing their budgets. Laird, a powerful congressional figure who accepted Nixon's request to serve, clearly is the most politically astute secretary ever to hold that position, and he had no significant problems at all with the JCS. Laird, of course, violated BP doctrine, simply by treating the service chiefs as important members of the decision process instead of dealing with them as natural enemies.

## Case 2: The Gaither Committee Report

The JCS opposed in 1957 the recommendations made by one of the "blue-ribbon" commissions that periodically analyze the military, even though committee's recommendations would have significantly increased military budgets. The opposition presumably was based on the fear of the JCS that service chiefs might lose some of their ability to control operations.[63] Leaving aside that Barrett says nothing about whether President Eisenhower fully supported the recommendations (he did not), Barrett's premise is that the committee was wholly correct. In retrospect, this is an amusing example.

Some readers may recall that in the late 1950s and early 1960s, some political leaders were convinced that the United States should undertake a massive civil defense program that would include both deep underground blast shelters and innumerable well-insulated fallout shelters to protect citizens from nuclear attack. At one time, President Kennedy even urged every home owner to convert a basement into a shelter or dig up the back yard and plant one there. The late strategic thinker, Herman Kahn, rode to fame on theories built around civil defense programs. The Gaither Committee was taken with the idea and, although its proposals were less extreme than most, it recommended a yearly outlay of $5–8 billion in total defense budgets of less than $50 billion. To the discomfiture of enthusiasts, most of the recommendations quietly were forgotten,[64] but the Kennedy administration did pursue fallout shelter programs to some extent. Typically, Barrett provides no reason why the JCS should have accepted Gaither Committee recommendations across the board.

## Case 3: The "Floating Warehouses"

There have been innumerable proposals on how the United States can prepare for "brushfire" wars in areas faraway from our overseas bases. The problem of the Gulf has been near the top of the list since at least 1979. The United States would have to land troops somewhere in order to fight in that region, but how long would it take to assemble the necessary vehicles and equipment for an army combat force? The Carter administration proposed that extra "sets" of equipment be stored on large ships that would remain near potential trouble spots. They could be moved to shore and unloaded if necessary, and troops flying from the United States could join the equipment and be ready to fight. The navy opposed the plan because it feared that cargo ships in the navy budget would reduce an already underfunded shipbuilding program, and because the cargo ships ultimately would have to be protected by warships.[65]

The logic, of course, is that the Carter administration was correct, and the navy's opposition was contrary to the national interest. The program was adopted, by the way, and is in operation, with at least some of the ships stationed in the Indian Ocean. The navy's questions, however, also may have been valid. If the ships were in the Gulf, closer to likely trouble spots, they might require protection. The navy's shipbuilding program, moreover, has been expanded considerably. As to the effectiveness of the "floating warehouse" concept, that has yet to be tested, but that is not to say that a test should be sought. There still is no reason to assume that the president is always correct and that a service-based question always is incorrect and out of order.

Edward Luttwak, the most passionate of military "reformers," seemingly writes with one hand while banging the table with the other; it is a joy to read him, even if one totally disagrees. Every secretary of defense, he literally shouts, learns quickly that it is "futile to expect any considered judgment from the Joint Chiefs and their Joint Staff" (a multiservice staff that serves the JCS), for the best they can produce is "the lowest common denominator on which all the services can agree." These agreements are "often unrealistic and . . . always violate the essential nature of strategy." The joint staff is especially "incapable of setting strategic priorities that cut across service preferences, and will unfailingly suggest the sharing out of raises and cuts among all the services." In the field, "rival service fiefdoms dominate the weak and sterile "joint" structures that are supposed to provide them with coherent guidance."[66]

Luttwak's preferred solution is to recruit an entirely new cadre of "national-minded officers" from the middle-high ranks (army and air force colonels and navy captains) and form them into a body of national-defense officers (NDOs) who never again will return to their services. They will become multiservice officers, but only if "they pass stiff entrance examinations and survive demanding interviews" (he does not say who the examiners will be, nor what will happen to those who fail the exams). The NDOs will then attend a national-defense training school before taking staff and command positions with multiservice forces and occasional "working tours with all services other than the one they came from." The result would be a "two-track (career) system" that would give some officers the "rewards of the kinship of men in the day-to-day life of the services" while the others were realizing the satisfactions of "working within the stream of national policy," occupying all top planning positions.[67]

Luttwak's basic assumption, of course, is that no careerist, civilian or military, can produce an idea compatible with the national interest unless that careerist has moved outside of government organizations. In his view, NDOs would be outsiders and completely identifiable, and they doubtless would compete for higher ranks within that cadre, but this would not cripple their devotion to the national interest. Luttwak is rather extreme; he contrasts the "deep-felt patriotism common in the officer corps" that would motivate the NDOs with the "narrower loyalty evoked by the services."[68] This could raise troublesome questions. If, for example, the commander of a warship (Luttwak admits this would be a job for a one-service officer, not an NDO) disputed the command of a superior NDO commander, would the disagreement turn on patriotism versus service loyalty? Because the NDO automatically would be correct, as Luttwak sees it, anything that went wrong would be attributed to sabotage or subversion. His second assumption does not stand up—as noted earlier, the JCS members do not always lobby for bigger budgets, as shown by their dealings with Laird. Even if this were correct, however, what would be wrong with it? A military planner who underestimates his requirements for achieving military success is far more dangerous than one who overestimates his needs, and nobody can know in advance what is needed.

If Barrett and Luttwak are correct, and they are typical of military "reformers," then no military advice ever given any U.S. president or any cabinet member supervising military forces has ever been correct. With other "reformers" Barrett and Luttwak avoid taking this position by focusing solely upon what has happened since military "unification" in 1947, and using only the BP theology (the only really correct label) as the framework for analysis. Although neither Barrett nor Luttwak expressly advocates total centralization of military authority in a proverbial "single chief of staff," they follow the typical BP line of constantly arguing that both the ability to recommend and the authority to decide must be completely removed from those who are members of the military services. The latter must obey without question whatever is handed down from an entity "above" them.

## CAN GOVERNMENT BE RESCUED FROM THEOLOGY?

The outlook is not immediately hopeful for saving either military or civilian professionals in government from further ravaging by the cultists who have orchestrated the BP scenario. The foregoing account, for example, does not even include the reinforcement of politically oriented BP by a version ("public choice") drawn from economic theory. Most readers probably are unaware that in an economic theory dedicated to private enterprise, all work performed by government employees is considered unproductive because it does not lead to the output of goods and services that can be sold in the market place. Technically speaking, government spending is wasteful; those in the military, for example, perform assigned duties in exchange for the equivalent of welfare payments. Essentially, they are in a "workfare" program. This view, in turn, leads to recommendations that government activities be kept to an irreducible minimum (the military is reluctantly accepted on grounds of societal survival) or, alternatively, that government functions be turned over to private enterprise so that the output of goods and services used by government will replicate conventional economic behavior (ideally, each citizen would purchase only those goods and services desired by that individual). Such approaches are nothing more than normal free-market economic theory, liberal and conservative alike. This economic version of BP theory cannot be further pursued here; the immediate task is to suggest how to recover some of the ground lost to BP theory in its political version.

BP theology appears vulnerable on two important counts. The first is that its weakness as political theory ("might makes right") leads believers to rely more and more upon authoritarianism to overcome that weakness. Some theologians dodge this issue, but it can and should be raised. The way to attack their prescriptions is to show that authoritarianism is invalid as organization theory—that is, nobody is competent to make any unilateral decision about anything. The second vulnerable aspect of BP theology is its resolute denial that anything in the nature of professional experience is useful in decision-making processes. These weaknesses will be taken up in order.

Neustadt presents the BP case as boldly as it can be stated, and it is surprising that such a gross falsehood is still unchallenged. Whatever the attractiveness of the phrase "power to persuade," it cannot hide the underlying premise that the president knows what each of his immediate subordinates can do and should do about every issue that might be of interest to him. "Power to persuade" implies that all he can do is hope they will do as he wishes, but his constitutional authority as commander in chief is something more, a truism quickly forgotten when careless thinkers confuse "outer" and "inner" cabinets. The premise is faulty because it is wholly at odds with the single most important contribution of modern Western philosophy and the scientific philosophy derived from it. That contribution, a sharp departure from previous philosophy, is that *all knowledge is uncertain,* a principle that is an outgrowth of the Protestant Reformation and the revolution against ecclesiastical authority based on the premise that knowledge is certain. When uncertain knowledge began to replace certain knowledge as the conceptual basis for legitimate authority, the very concept of unilateral authority was open to challenge, and that challenge has yet to be carried through.

This fundamental premise of modern Western philosophy comes to us most clearly in the context of what scientists are supposed to do. Almost any standard outline of scientific philosophy includes warnings of this sort:

> What is here involved is not only the freedom from personal or cultural bias
> or partiality, but . . . the requirement that the knowledge claims of science
> be in principle capable of test (confirmation or disconfirmation, at the least
> indirectly and to some degree) on the part of any person properly equipped
> with intelligence and the technical devices of observation and
> experimentation. The term *intersubjective* stresses the social nature of the
> scientific enterprise. If there be any "truths" that are accessible only to
> privileged individuals, such as mystics or visionaries—that is, knowledge-
> claims which by their very nature cannot independently be checked by
> anyone else—then such "truths" are not of the kind that we seek in science.
> The criterion of intersubjective testability thus delimits the scientific from
> the nonscientific activities of man.[69]

This prescription seems at first glance applicable only to those usually
designated as members of "scientific communities" who wear white coats in
laboratories, not to the everyday administrators of organizations and those
they supervise. There is no such distinction in real life, and this can be
shown in at least two ways. The first is that even the language of
administration often reflects a scientific perspective; how else account for
"scientific management," "management science," or even "policy science."
Political executives often seek to bring such bodies of thought to bear upon
the matters they face.

Second, any administrative decision can be nothing more and nothing
less than a decision to test the hypothetical statement that *if* the decision is
carried out as planned, *then* the desired outcome or objective will be
achieved. To recommend a course of action is to formulate a hypothesis; to
adopt that recommendation is to authorize the experimental test. Within
academic communities concerned with issues of public affairs, those of use
who research and publish do not "test" hypotheses; we suggest in print that
government test our hypotheses by implementing them. The lifeblood of
administrative activity is the testing of hypotheses.[70] This basic truth is
hidden by two conventions.

The first convention is that officials who decide to test hypotheses feel
uncomfortable about announcing that they are treating the citizenry as
"experimental subjects," so the language is prohibited except for minor-
league actions that are announced as pilot programs or experiments. The
second is that because organizations are structured as hierarchies that clearly
separate superiors from subordinates, those in charge are expected to pretend
they know what they are doing when they cannot possibly know. This gets
out of hand when presumably wise observers (Neustadt, for example)
undertake to advise a president that he does, in fact, know everything he
should know, indeed everything there is to know.

The scientific doctrine of intersubjectivity, therefore, really is a
prescription for how all social decisions should be made. It is sufficient to
point out here that unilateral decisions should be prohibited in important

matters, and, indeed, this was the philosophy behind the legislation that "unified" the armed forces in 1947 and established the NSC. The hope was that the president would meet and consult closely with appropriate subordinates before reaching decisions. The premise is simple and forthright: The president needs help and should not be encouraged to believe he does not. This does not guarantee "good" decisions, but, in scientific jargon, the probability of improving the quality of decisions is increased when an executive consults beforehand with those who have some knowledge (experience) that is relevant to the matters at hand.

BP theology dismisses all professional knowledge on grounds that even if there is such a phenomenon, it is erased by the evil motives of the professionals. Lest it not be obvious, the notion of knowledge-based authority is fundamental to organization theory and practice. Following Max Weber: "Bureaucratic administration means fundamentally the exercise of control on the basis of knowledge. This is the feature of it which makes it specifically rational."[71] "Knowledge" obviously connotes the experience of observing at close hand the testing of administrative hypotheses and, indeed, the conducting of such experiments. "Rationality" connotes the conscious effort to relate means (decisions and their implementation) to ends (objectives or values). This by no means implies that any professional knows enough to exercise unilateral authority, and even the military concept of "command" should include such humility—often learned late in the game, when survival is at stake. In a sense, the military is fortunate—the greater the risk, the greater the necessity to ask for as much information as possible. There is a recognizable tendency to use a literal definition of command in training environments.

If professionalism can be overdone by those who accept the encouragement to believe they know precisely what to do under all circumstances, and if it can be overrated for the same reason, this provides no license for BP theologians to dismiss it in favor of unabashed amateurism. Because the essence of professionalism is long-term association with those engaged in the same profession, the BP argument that only outsiders can compensate for the evils of professionalism is know-nothingism writ large. Expanded to include the notion that only family and close friends can be trusted, BP becomes a doctrine of "spoils." When military "reformers" add such ideas as a permanent general staff, multiservice NDOs, and long unified command experience, they choose theology over history. The United States never has had any significant military operations that even remotely correspond to the contemporary meaning of "unified" operations. The unified commands of this era are only the occupation forces put in place after World War II to manage the transition. To project today's proposals for military reorganization backward into history is to highlight the silliness.

In Luttwak's design, an army division commander would be a one-service officer presumably trained in land warfare. The high planners in

Washington, however, would be multiservice officers who had been outside their original services for perhaps two decades and who knew nothing at all about the inner workings of the services. Imagine if you can that General Marshall, a senior multiservice planner, was prohibited from exercising any influence upon the selection of division commanders for the land forces being deployed to Europe. Mind-boggling, wouldn't you say?

The attack upon professionalism descends into sleaze when directed against "outer cabinet" careerists in state, defense, treasury, and justice, none of whom have clear-cut interest group constituencies. In the case of the military, the ultimate cost of "bad" advice to presidents is casualties in battle; the "civilian experts" who promised a successful air strike in Cuba did not have to worry about such things. It is unforgivable for military "reformers," especially those previously associated with the profession, to imply that those on active duty are so obsessed with in-house politics that they do not give a damn about the lives of professional colleagues. Indeed, that concern is a primary motivation for substantial budget requests.

There is an outside hope that some BP theologians may yet have to recant, at least in part. These are the ones who have yet to notice that when the theology is applied at the top of government, all cabinet officers and careerists are enemies. In the Neustadt version, it makes little difference whether the top military officer: is a member of one of the services, a multiservice NDO, or an NDO freshly returned from a "unified" command. Either the president relies upon his own knowledge (a Neustadt president needs no advice) or he deals with a politicized professional whose personal loyalty is to the president—for example, Taylor.

Recanting will be slow because of BP's almost impenetrable defense. In using this occasion to further explore the logic of BP, I gradually came to understand why it is impossible to discuss the issues with "reformers" and other theologians. The doctrine assumes that the substance of any proposal or argument is wholly unimportant; only the underlying motivation is significant. Because cabinet officers and careerists have improper motives, their proposals and arguments must be rejected. It follows that anyone who disagrees with a theologian, or provides evidence to challenge the theology, must also have impure motives and, for that reason, has tainted the evidence. In the case of the "reformers," it becomes necessary to insist that Admiral Leahy was not the JCS chairman during World War II, that no such body existed at that time, and that the hard evidence of meetings and published output simply must be false.

If the country is fortunate, BP theology will become a casualty of careful analysis, except for the obvious truism that individuals do not relish being fired. The notion of the president as God (who else knows everything?) will fall, and even the notion of the entire government being the enemy may be opened to challenge. If it can be made clear that unilateral authority is impossible and that we have no reason to desert our basic philosophy and every reason to adopt it, the sharing of authority among policy-makers and professionals will be seen as the best possible solution available within the total system. If military professionals are fortunate, the wartime managerial structure put together by Franklin Roosevelt and his JCS may be rescued from the trash bin.

As for my academic colleagues in public administration, they have insisted for too long that the profession of careerists cannot be distinguished from the activities of elected and politically appointed officials. The two groups can actually function as informal partners in making important decisions, but neither can be expected to assert publicly that their tasks are identical. Norton Long, one of the early leaders of an optimistic BP doctrine, has more recently and correctly described the appropriate function of the Senior Executive Service, that cadre of high-level careerists established by the civil service reform of 1978: "A valued public service (could be) exemplified by a highly respected and widely recognized neutral competence of a senior executive service."[72] "Neutral" need not mean that administrators should be wholly passive about suggesting what should be done in areas familiar to them. What it does mean is that careerists need not be enemies of those elected and need not be required to demonstrate personal and political loyalty to them.

The careful reader may wonder by now why, given the U.S. system of government, Congress is so conspicuously absent from the foregoing analysis and argument. In BP theology, Congress generally is considered only another "enemy" of the president, especially because of its various associations with career administrators. Such phrases as "iron triangles" usually connote alliances among members of Congress and their staffs, bureaucrats and outside groups whose only collective objective is to thwart the (always correct) objectives of the president (provided the theologians like the president).

## NOTES

1. Robert A. Dahl, *Who Governs* (New Haven: Yale University Press, 1961).

2. F. Hunter, *Community Power Structure* (New York: Doubleday, 1953); and C. Wright Mills, *The Power Elite* (New York: Oxford University Press, 1956).

3. Norton E. Long, "Power and Administration," *Public Administration Review,* No. 9 (1949): 257–264.

4. Philip Selznick, *TVA and the Grass Roots* (Berkeley: University of California Press, 1949), pp. 262–266.

5. P. Woll, *American Bureaucracy* (New York: Norton, 1963), pp. 174–177.

6. Fred C. Thayer, "Woodrow Wilson and the 'Upstairs/Downstairs Problems: Is Change Possible?'" in *Politics and Administration,* eds. J. Rabin and J. S. Bowman (New York: Marcel Dekker, Inc., 1984), pp. 263–276.

7. C. S. George, *The History of Management Thought* (Englewood Cliffs, N.J.: Prentice-Hall, 1972), pp. 75–76.

8. Paul Y. Hammond, *Organizing for Defense* (Princeton: Princeton University

Press, 1961), p. 12.

9. John K. Galbraith, *The New Industrial State* (Boston: Houghton-Mifflin, 1971), Chapters 5–6.

10. R. Presthus, *Public Administration* (New York: Ronald, 1975), p. 64.

11. H. G. Frederickson, "The Lineage of New Public Administration," in *Organization Theory and the New Public Administration* ed. H. G. Frederickson (Boston: Allyn and Bacon, 1980), pp. 33–51.

12. C. A. Auerbach, "Pluralism and the Administrative Process," *Annals of the American Academy of Political and Social Science,* no. 400 (1972): 1–13.

13. M. Albrow, *Bureaucracy* (New York: Praeger, 1970), Chapter 1.

14. F. C. Mosher, *Watergate: Implications for Responsible Government* (New York: Basic Books, 1974), Chapter 3.

15. Charles E. Lindblom, "The Science of Muddling Through," *Public Administration Review,* no. 19 (1959): 79–88.

16. W. D. Leahy, *I Was There* (New York: McGraw-Hill, 1951), Chapter 8; and Eric Larrabee, *Commander-in-Chief* (New York: Harper & Row, 1987), pp. 20–21.

17. F. C. Pogue, *George C. Marshall: Education of a General* (New York: Viking, 1963), p. 324.

18. F. C. Pogue, *George C. Marshall: Ordeal and Hope* (New York: Viking, 1966), p. 23.

19. G. H. Snyder, "The 'New Look' of 1953," in *Strategy, Policy, and Defense Policy,* eds., W. R. Schilling, P. Y. Hammond, and G. H. Snyder (New York: Columbia University Press, 1962), pp. 410–415.

20. Hammond, *Organizing for Defense,* pp. 380–381.

21. J. M. Gavin, *War and Peace in the Space Age* (New York: Harper and Bros., 1958), pp. 248–253.

22. Maxwell D. Taylor, *The Uncertain Trumpet* (New York: Harper and Bros., 1960), pp. 202–203.

23. Mooris, Janowitz, *The Professional Soldier* (Glencoe, Ill.: Free Press, 1960), pp. 273–275.

24. Taylor, *Uncertain Trumpet,* pp. 108, 175–177.

25. Thomas D. White, "Strategy and the Defense Intellectual," *The Saturday Evening Post,* May 4, 1963, p. 10.

26. R. N. Ginsburgh, "The Challenge to Military Professionalism," *Foreign Affairs* 42 (1964): 225.

27. Edward L. Katzenbach, Jr., "The Demotion of Professionalism at the War Colleges," *U.S. Naval Institute Proceedings* (March 1965): 34–41.

28. Richard Neustadt, *Presidential Power* (New York: Wiley, 1960).

29. Graham T. Allison, *Essence of Decision* (Boston: Little, Brown and Co., 1971), p. 147.

30. Neustadt, *Presidential Power,* p. 46.

31. Ibid., pp. 10–11.

32. Ibid., pp. 8, 39.

33. Ibid., pp. 39–40.

34. Ibid., 856, 860.

35. Hans J. Morgenthau, "Can We Entrust Defense to a Committee," *The New York Times,* June 7, 1959.

36. Theodore C. Sorensen, *Kennedy* (New York: Harper & Row, 1965), p. 281.

37. S. Hyman, "Inside the Kennedy 'Kitchen Cabinet,'" *The New York Times Magazine,* March 5, 1961.

38. Roger Hilsman, *To Move a Nation* (New York: Doubleday, 1964, 1967), pp. 30–31.

39. David Halberstam, *The Best and the Brightest* (New York: Random House,

1969, 1970, 1972), pp. 66–67.
    40. Hilsman, *To Move a Nation*, pp. 30–31.
    41. Ibid., p. 411.
    42. Ibid., pp. 421–424; Halberstam, op. cit., p. 172.
    43. Allison, *Essence of Decision*, p. 147.
    44. Ibid., p. 198.
    45. Ibid., pp. 202–207.
    46. Ibid., p. 206.
    47. Ibid., pp. 123–126, 128–131, 197–199, 204–206. It has only now come to light, because of information released by then Secretary of State Rusk, that before the CMC was resolved, President Kennedy had decided that he would agree to a publicized trade—withdrawing U.S. missiles from Turkey in exchange for Soviet removal of the missiles in Cuba—because avoiding a nuclear exchange was the highest priority. Essentially, Kennedy was prepared to accept Adlai Stevenson's proposal to include the involvement of the United Nations. This secret decision was not acted upon because the Soviets agreed to an earlier proposal. After the crisis, however, the president himself orchestrated the "leaks" that pictured Stevenson as a weak appeaser so that the president's image would be that of a strong, "macho" head of state who had not backed down. Basically, the crisis was used to destroy Stevenson's political stature. Portraying him as an enemy whose defeat enhanced Kennedy's political power was in the best tradition of Neustadt's doctrine. On the released information, see *The New York Times,* Aug. 28, 1987; and *The Washington Post,* Aug. 29, 1987.
    48. Neustadt, *Presidential Power*, p. 162.
    49. Henry M. Jackson, ed., *The National Security Council* (New York: Praeger, 1965), p. 287.
    50. Anthony Downs, *Inside Bureaucracy* (Boston: Little, Brown and Co., 1967), pp. 212–216.
    51. Ibid., pp. 235–260.
    52. Theodore J. Lowi, *The Politics of Disorder* (New York: Basic Books, 1971), and Lowi, *The End of Liberalism* (New York: Norton, 1969).
    53. I. M. Destler, *Presidents, Bureaucrats, and Foreign Policy* (Princeton: Princeton University Press, 1972), Chapters 8, 9.
    54. Frederick V. Malek, *Washington's Hidden Tragedy* (New York: Free Press, 1978), pp. 100–102.
    55. Ibid., pp. 79–80, 96–97.
    56. P. W. Ingraham and C. Ban, *Legislating Bureaucratic Change* (Albany: State University of New York Press, 1984), p. 1.
    57. Jimmy Carter, text of address by the president to the National Press Club, White House memo, March 2, 1978.
    58. Archie L. Barrett, *Reappraising Defense Organization* (Washington, D.C.: National Defense University Press, 1983), pp. xxv, 1.
    59. Ibid., pp. 3–4. Note also that the senior military officer of each service doubles as a member of the JCS, whose chairman (as in the cases of Admiral Radford and General Taylor) is appointed to serve outside any of the services. The "unified" commands are those overseas commands (in Europe and the Pacific, for example) that often include units from all the services and presumably will conduct military combat operations, if necessary. The chain of operational command runs from the president to the secretary of defense to the unified commander (including one in the United States, whose command is kept prepared to deploy to trouble spots outside the areas of the other commands). "Specified" commands comprise members from a single military service. The Strategic Air Command, provided by the air force, has long-range bombers and intercontinental missiles. In the combat chain of command,

the JCS act as an advisory staff to the secretary of defense and the president. During World War II, the overseas commanders reported to the military head of the service primarily involved with their operations—that is, Eisenhower reported to Marshall, Nimitz to King, LeMay to Arnold, and so on.

60. Ibid., p. 36.

61. Ibid., pp. 37–38.

62. Ibid., pp. 209–285.

63. Ibid., p. 37.

64. Samuel P. Huntington, *The Common Defense* (New York: Columbia University Press, 1961), pp. 109–115.

65. Barrett, *Reappraising Defense*, p. 35.

66. Edward N. Luttwak, *The Pentagon and the Art of War* (New York: Simon and Schuster, 1984), pp. 269, 276, 284.

67. Ibid., pp. 272–279.

68. Ibid., p. 276.

69. H. Feigl, "The Scientific Outlook: Naturalism and Humanism," in *Readings in the Philosophy of Science,* H. Feigl and M. Brodbeck, eds. (New York: Appleton-Century-Crofts, 1953), p. 11, emphasis in original.

70. Martin Landau, "On the Concept of Self-Correcting Organizations," *Public Administration Review* 33, 6 (Nov./Dec. 1973): 591.

71. Max Weber, *The Theory of Social and Economic Organization* (Chicago: Aldine Press, 1947), p. 311.

72. Norton E. Long, "The SES and the Public Interest," *Public Administration Review* 41 (1981): 311.]

# 12.3    Why Our High-Priced Military Can't Win Battles

## JEFFREY RECORD

*Citing a long list of U.S. military failures, Jeffrey Record, an adjunct professor of modern military history at Georgetown University and noted author on military strategy, argues that "America's military record since Inchon has been one of persistent professional malpractice that in any other profession would constitute grounds for disbarment, denial of tenure, or legal action." He goes on to outline the intellectual and institutional deficiencies within the U.S. military. Record's attention to the differences between management and leadership has contributed significantly to the reform debate and will most certainly remain a centerpiece of discussions about the effectiveness of the U.S. military establishment in the years to come.*

The decimation last October of a U.S. Marine Corps battalion by terrorists in

Beirut was just the latest link in a chain of U.S. military failures stretching back to the Korean War. Indeed, the performance of American arms in combat since Gen. Douglas MacArthur's brilliant landing at Inchon in 1950 casts grave doubt on the effectiveness of the U.S. military establishment as an instrument of American foreign policy.

The issue is not the feasibility or morality of the political objectives that American governments have used armed force to pursue since World War II. Nor is it the willingness or reluctance of political leaders to use military power in specific circumstances, which is not within the province of the Pentagon. Nor is it the loyalty, tenacity and courage of the American fighting man. No, the issue is the competence of the U.S. military.

To bemoan or applaud the use of American force in one instance or another begs the critical question of whether the United States is any longer capable of applying force effectively on behalf of *any* political objective more difficult to achieve than the pacification of a tiny island like Grenada. The unsuccessful use of military power for the most compelling political ends can be just as detrimental to the nation as the successful use of force for unjustifiable reasons. A fundamentally flawed military instrument is itself a danger to national well-being.

Those who ascribe the Beirut disaster to inchoate or infeasible American political aims in Lebanon fail to recognize that the attack on the Marines succeeded—and would have succeeded irrespective of the political objectives underlying the Marine presence—because of professional military dereliction. A political decision did place the Marines in Beirut, but it did not leave open the gate to the Marine compound or prohibit the commander on the spot from undertaking proper security measures.

What is at stake in the wake of the Beirut disaster far transcends the future safety of the Marines in Lebanon. It is nothing less than America's military reputation, or ability to use force successfully to preserve and promote declared national interests.

Demonstrated military prowess is essential in a world where, sadly, force remains the final arbiter of international disputes. It is indispensable to the United States, whose myriad interests abroad are subject to potential violent threats and to whom others look for protection. A demonstrated capacity to use force effectively discourages adversaries and encourages allies. Such a capacity has not, unfortunately, been manifest in America's performance on the battlefield since Inchon. On the contrary, the United States seems to have lost touch with the art of war.

This is a painful litany, but it deserves careful consideration. It begins with the Yalu River rout. Following the Inchon landing and destruction of most of the North Korean army in September 1950, an imperious MacArthur, disregarding evidence of impending Chinese intervention, pressed northward to the Yalu with the aim of liberating all of Korea. The subsequent Chinese counterattack on United Nations forces, which were dangerously overextended and in some cases isolated, resulted in the longest retreat in American military history.

Then the Bay of Pigs. This abortive "covert" invasion of Cuba in 1961, mounted by the Central Intelligence Agency and Cuban exile forces, violated time-tested principles of successful amphibious assaults, such as the need for absolute air superiority over the landing area and dispersal of ammunition reserves for landing forces among more than one ship. The operation was compromised from the start by failure to keep it a secret.

Then Vietnam. Despite a pronounced superiority in all the measurable indices of military power, including troops, firepower and tactical mobility (in the form of helicopters), and possession of naval and air supremacy, U.S. and South Vietnamese forces were defeated by an army composed almost entirely of foot infantry. U.S. forces could always prevail in pitched battles, but could not win the war. The Pentagon's policy of rotating officers and men in and out of combat roles in Vietnam every six months was a classic example of what is wrong with our military establishment. That policy had a devastating effect on the cohesion of U.S. Army units, which nearly disintegrated in the early 1970s under the pressure of combat in Vietnam.

Then the loss of the Pueblo, an electronic intelligence-gathering ship, which was seized by North Korea in international waters in 1968 because of gross professional dereliction. Despite the nature of the vessel's mission and the manifestly reckless character of the North Korean regime, the Pueblo was provided neither armed escorts nor armaments of her own sufficient to fend off an attack. When the Pueblo began signaling for help, the U.S. military chain of command in the Far East proved unable to provide timely assistance. The commander of the Pueblo, when faced with the choice of surrendering or scuttling his ship, failed to do his duty.

Then there was the Son Tay raid in 1970, in which U.S. commandos conducted a brilliant operation to rescue 61 American prisoners of war from a prison outside Hanoi. Unfortunately, the intelligence information upon which the raid was predicated was faulty: there were no Americans at Son Tay.

And remember the Mayaguez? This attempt to recover the American cargo ship and her crew, seized by Cambodian forces in the Gulf of Siam in May 1975, quickly degenerated into a tragic comedy of errors. Hastily organized and plagued by inadequate intelligence, a rescue force composed of a mélange of U.S. naval vessels, Marines and Air Force helicopters assaulted a small island where the Mayaguez crew was thought to be held. The Americans met unexpectedly strong resistance, sustained heavy casualties (including 41 dead) and abandoned the operation upon discovery that the Mayaguez crew had already been released by the Cambodians.

Or consider the Iranian hostage rescue mission, an admittedly difficult and risky military venture, which collapsed before any contact with hostile forces. This was perhaps the most alarming display of American military inadequacy in the post-World War II era. Despite the benefit of five months' preparation, the rescue plan was doomed from the start because it disregarded fundamental rules for successful commando operations.

The plan was rigid and excessively complex. Resources committed to the operation, notably the number of helicopters and men assigned to the assault force, were inadequate to provide a reasonable chance of success. (Sending a man to do a boy's job is a cardinal principle of commando operations.) Nor was the plan ever fully rehearsed. Worst of all was a faulty command structure, the product in part of each service's irresistible desire to participate in the mission, which left no single person in a position of authority to improvise in the face of unexpected events. Accordingly, when the unexpected occurred—the breakdown of one too many helicopters and subsequent collision of a helicopter and cargo aircraft—the operation fell apart amidst such confusion that no one retrieved the bodies of the dead or the sensitive equipment aboard abandoned helicopters.

The conclusion that professional military negligence contributed substantially to the death of 241 marines in Beirut in 1983 is inescapable. Both the House Armed Services investigations subcommittee and the Defense Department's own commission (headed by retired Adm. Robert L. J. Long) charged with investigating the bombing concluded that the truck-bomb attack on the Marine compound in Beirut almost certainly would not have succeeded but for what, under the circumstances, were incredibly lax security precautions. They concluded that the responsibility for this lapse rested with the entire military chain of command, especially the senior officers on the spot.

The Long commission recommended that disciplinary action be taken against those officers bearing the main responsibility for the disaster.

To be sure, against this list of U.S. military failures must be counted some successes: Gen. Matthew Ridgway's masterful restoration of U.N. fortunes in Korea following MacArthur's dismissal; U.S. intervention in the Dominican Republic in 1965, and the downing of two marauding Libyan fighter planes in the Gulf of Sidra in 1982.

The U.S. invasion of Grenada in 1983 also must be deemed a success, although it is difficult to imagine how it could have failed—despite what proved to be inexcusably shoddy intelligence, tactical errors and a ponderous command and communications structure. Cuban forces on the island, denied reinforcement, were overwhelmed by sheer U.S. military might.

And, to be sure, the military alone cannot be blamed for the past $3^{1}/2$ decades of American defeats and miscarriages on the battlefield. The Pentagon was essentially excluded from the Bay of Pigs operation, and operational flexibility in both Korea and Vietnam was severely inhibited by overriding political considerations. Poor intelligence and what Frederick the Great called "His Sacred Majesty Chance" also exerted a deleterious influence, especially on the Son Tay and Mayaguez rescue missions. Yet all military operations must contend with external factors—weather, terrain, political objectives, luck, the mind and will of the opposing commander—that are not subject to control.

On balance, however, America's military record since Inchon has been one of persistent professional malpractice that in any other profession would constitute grounds for disbarment, denial of tenure or legal action. It is a record made all the more disturbing by the apparent absence in the Pentagon of a capacity for self-correction. The problem is rooted neither in the amount of resources made available to the Pentagon (which enjoyed a surfeit of resources in Vietnam) nor in debilitating political intrusion on the planning and execution of military operations (there was virtually none in the Son Tay, Mayaguez and Iranian hostage rescue operations). Only profound intellectual and institutional deficiencies within the U.S. military itself can explain so many failures on so many battlefields for so many years.

Unfortunately, it is far easier to recognize a manifest incapacity to use military force effectively than it is to determine its causes. Military establishments are peculiar organizations, and war remains among the most complex and least understood of human institutions. So there are no obvious explanations and remedies for the problem. But at least three points seem relevant here.

The first is that the American military is culturally, as well as by professional training and education, prone to disregard the fact that war remains first and foremost a human encounter—notwithstanding advances in weaponry. The outcome of combat is still determined less by the quantifiable ingredients of military power than it is, as the Israelis have repeatedly demonstrated, by such intangibles as generalship, strategy and tactics, training, morale, unit cohesion, combat experience and, of course, chance.

The American military harbors an unbridled—though historically unwarranted—faith in technology as the solution to most problems on the battlefield. That technology proved indecisive in Korea, ultimately irrelevant in Vietnam and unreliable in Iran seems not to have shaken that faith. Technological advance continues to be pursued for its own sake, even though its price is often paid in the form of unreliability in actual combat or in unit costs for weapons that prohibit their purchase in needed quantities.

To be sure, weapons are indispensable in war, and it is always better to have more and better weapons than one's opponent. Yet weapons are only tools. Even the best count for little in the hands of ill-trained or demoralized troops, or under the command of officers incapable of grasping battlefield opportunities. The Germans had fewer and less powerful tanks in 1940 than the French and British. The key to the Israeli slaughter of the Syrian air force in 1982 was not the superiority of the U.S. airplanes over Soviet MIGs, but the incomparable training, combat experience, innovativeness and esprit of Israeli pilots. Similarly, in the Falklands war, there was no contest on the ground between raw and wretchedly-led Argentine conscripts and experienced British regulars whose regimental system has for centuries produced a unit cohesion impervious to anything short of decimation.

A second observation: America's military malaise stems largely from the substitution of managerial and technocratic values for traditional warrior values that has taken place since World War II. The U.S. military has become another vast military bureaucracy whose *raison d'etre*—winning wars—has been supplanted by the overriding values of any bureaucracy: career advancement, maintenance of an orderly flow of people and paper *within* the system, and protection from outside disturbance. The result, obvious in Vietnam, has been a pernicious inability to distinguish between management and leadership, efficiency and effectiveness and technology and tactics—a confusion of bureaucratic (internal) imperatives and professional (external) goals. Too many military men forgot why they were in uniform. Promotion-hungry officers more interested in punching the "combat ticket" in Vietnam all too often failed to lead their men.

The men themselves, treated like interchangeable parts in some vast machine, were constantly shuffled from unit to unit and job to job by efficient, highly-centralized personnel management systems, despite the catastrophic effects of "personnel turbulence" on the social bonding critical to the cohesion of small units in the stress of combat. U.S. strategy in Vietnam boiled down to little more than the administration of massive doses of firepower.

Unfortunately for the Pentagon, men cannot be managed to their deaths; bunches of strangers can never be cohesive combat units, and firepower, though quantifiable and manageable, cannot be conclusive against an enemy, like the North Vietnamese, that refuses to provide decisive targets, or against one, like the Soviet Union today, that has superior firepower.

Finally, professional dereliction and incompetence have rarely been punished since World War II. This should not be surprising, since bureaucracies—and the Pentagon would seem no exception—compartmentalize professional responsibility to a point that is designed to exempt most bureaucrats from individual accountability for doing anything more than meeting the internal requirements of the bureaucracy itself.

While numerous officers have been cashiered for insubordination or court-martialed for criminal offenses since World War II, few have been sternly disciplined for professional malpractice. Failure to do so has bred an atmosphere of professional unaccountability that encourages, because it does not penalize, repetition of failure on the battlefield.

So the 1980 Defense Department report highly critical of the planning and execution of the Iranian mission cautioned that "no judgment of the able men who planned this mission or the brave professionals who executed it is intended nor should be inferred."

To its credit, the Long commission upheld the principle of professional accountability and recommended disciplinary action against those whose negligence contributed to the Beirut disaster. Yet it is highly unlikely that any will be court-martialed or cashiered, since the president, on the eve of the Long commission report's release, issued a statement that in effect pardoned everyone in advance. By taking the blame for an event for which he could not possibly be held personally responsible, President Reagan thwarted due punishment of those who are responsible.

It is encouraging that America's military record since 1950 has stimulated mounting pressure for reform in manpower policies, operational doctrine, weapons design and procurement. Some useful reforms are now being explored.

Several dozen concerned members of Congress have created a military reform caucus. Most are conservative, and are disturbed by the absence of any apparent correlation between the size of the defense budget and the effectiveness of U.S. forces.

The Army has begun testing a promising new manpower system designed to increase unit cohesion. The Army also has revised its operational doctrine, replacing an excessive emphasis on firepower with one encouraging greater reliance on maneuver. And last year, a group of defense intellectuals founded a Military Reform Institute here to encourage analyses of possible reforms.

Not surprisingly, the Pentagon, now awash in money but still convinced that money is all it needs to solve America's military problems, remains largely hostile to reform, although many younger officers are sympathetic to it.

Of course, not every proposal for reform has merit. Many reformers cannot be faulted for excessive intellectual or personal humility, and some of their proposed reforms would probably create more problems than they solve. Yet if the reformers do not have invariably correct answers, they are nonetheless asking the right questions. And the military reform movement is not responsible for the past 35 years of military malpractice.

---

# 12.4   The Ethical Dimensions of National Security

## JOHN JOHNS

*In this hard-hitting article, Dr. John Johns argues that many systemic factors work to compromise the integrity of the participant. "The pressures for conformity are so strong and the widespread deficiency in moral courage," he writes. A most serious consequence is the "precedent of military officers putting loyalty to ideological conviction and the executive chain of command above loyalty to the constitutional oath." By focusing attention on the U.S. moral crisis and the importance of senior national security officials in setting the appropriate example, Dr. Johns, himself a retired U.S. Army brigadier general, has taken a bold step toward a solution to U.S. ethical malaise.*

Our government cannot function cloaked in secrecy. It cannot function unless officials tell the truth. The constitution only works when the . . . branches of government trust one another and cooperate.

—Congressman Lee H. Hamilton, 1987

Trust is a social good to be protected just as much as the air we breathe or the water we drink. When it is damaged, the community as a whole suffers; and, when it is destroyed, societies falter and collapse.

Trust and integrity are precious resources, easily squandered, hard to regain.

—Sissela Bok[1]<br>*Lying*

The long-term security of any nation rests in large measure on the trust and confidence its people have in the institutions that serve the nation and in the leaders that populate those institutions. Perhaps the most critical institutions and leaders are those providing physical security for the nation.

The cover story in the May 25, 1987, edition of *Time*,[2] "What Ever Happened to Ethics," describes a nation in moral decay—a society plagued by hypocrisy, betrayal of public trust, and rampant greed. The moral malaise permeates every segment of our society—clergy, students, lawyers, doctors, bankers, business leaders, and, most unfortunately, public officials in the highest positions. Indeed, many of those entrusted with the duty of providing security and enforcing the constitutional laws have apparently violated that trust. The December 1986 *Gallup Report*[3] included the results of a survey that asked the public to rate a number of professional groups on honesty and ethical standards. Only clergymen (67%) and medical doctors (58%) were rated by more than half the respondents as either "high" or "very high" on those traits. U.S. senators and congressmen received less than 25% of the respondents' ratings in those categories. Since that poll was taken, the Irangate and televangelists scandals have been made public.

The growing concern about ethical conduct among public officials is not surprising. My Lai, Watergate, Wall Street scandals; record numbers of government officials charged with ethical misconduct; and, perhaps the most damaging of all, Irangate, have undermined the trust and confidence of the public. Undoubtedly, trust has been severely damaged; how close it is to being destroyed is open to debate. What is clear, however, is that a concerted effort is needed to stop the hemorrhage and rebuild the lost ground as much as possible. National security depends on the outcome.

National power, with which national security is achieved, requires a high degree of national cohesion/solidarity/will. Whichever term is used, the implication is that people of the nation will make personal sacrifices for the good of the nation—as defined by the national leaders. There are many factors that influence national will; a critical component and categorical imperative is trust and confidence in the leadership. This imposes an ethical duty on public officials to be competent in the service they offer and trustworthy in the exercise of the authority of their offices.

Perhaps no other institution depends more on public confidence for its effectiveness than does the federal government. The public can choose between competing private professionals; it cannot choose between national governments short of revolution. Individual members of the government can be replaced, but, when there is an overall crisis of confidence in the institution, there is a serious threat to the existence of a society. Of all segments of the federal government, none is so important for public trust as those elements which provide for national security.

The ethical obligations of public officials are reflected in the literature and in the oath of office of all federal officials—military and civilian—career, elected, and appointed. The Code of Ethics for federal government members became law on July 3, 1980, specifying certain behaviors—some rather concrete, some abstract principles. Among the prescriptions is to "put loyalty to the highest moral principles and to country above loyalty to persons, party or Government department." Government members are to uphold the Constitution and laws and never be a party to their evasion. Professional associations, such as the American Society for Public Administration (ASPA), have adopted codes of behavior for public officials; these codes carry variations of the theme that officials subordinate self-service to public service, that safeguarding the public trust is paramount, and that the constitutional process must be followed. These efforts to impose moral order through the use of laws, rules, and regulations—while noteworthy—are not sufficient.

Throughout the literature on military professionalism is the premise that the military profession rests on an ethical foundation. Trust and confidence is reflected in the oath of office and is at the heart of ethical codes, explicit or implicit. Recent polls indicate that the U.S. public gives high marks to the military (relative to other professions) for earning that trust and confidence. On the other hand, there are persistent criticisms from the mass media, Congress, the public, and even from within the ranks of the military itself, that standards of behavior leave something to be desired. A respected

Pentagon reporter, Fred Hiatt, has made serious accusations about the ethical conduct of the Pentagon Brass.[4] Members of Congress have expressed the view that senior DoD officials, civilian and uniformed, lack credibility on Capitol Hill. Although public polls show overall confidence in the military profession, they also show that the public questions many specific actions. In my classes at the National Defense University, many military officers express disappointment with the standards of conduct of officials in the Pentagon. One instructor teaching an ethics course in a military school stated that he had to call three general officers before one would agree to talk about ethical behavior in the Pentagon. The first two declined on the basis that they would have to be too negative if they described the real situation.

Where is the truth about this matter? One can easily pick out incidents in any large organization and make a case for either its being morally decadent or a citadel of integrity. Without a systematic analysis of behavior based on some given standard, I risk the danger of impressionistic generalizations that may reflect my own biases rather than the empirical world. Many of the senior military and civilian professionals in the Pentagon are colleagues of mine and most of these I consider to be men and women of strong personal integrity. Others seem to have lost their moral gyroscope. There are systemic factors at work in the Washington political milieu that influence all participants to compromise their integrity. Some handle those pressures better than others.

## INGREDIENTS OF INTEGRITY

### Honesty

One of the most difficult ingredients of integrity to keep intact in the Pentagon's bureaucratic struggle for resources is honesty. The challenges to this value do not come in the form of demands for face-to-face, bald-faced lies; rather, they are in the form of strategies and ploys used to gain decisions that favor a position in the bureaucratic struggle. In his analysis of how bureaucracies make decisions, Ralph Sanders[5] describes the various techniques of controlling information to support an advocate's position in the Department of Defense (DoD). Most of these techniques involve manipulation that can only be called deliberate deception. Reports that provide a biased assessment of an issue, suppression of dissidents' views, and hidden agenda are examples of deceptive practices that are widely used, within DoD and in the department's communication with Congress. Congress is forever suspicious of budget proposals that appear to be the "nose of the camel in the tent," but DoD claims to be the entire camel. However, the notion is that once Congress is committed to a program, it is easier to get follow-up funding to cover the rest of the camel. Caveat emptor has become the operative norm. Political hardball has replaced trust and

cooperation for the national good.

## Loyalty

Why do individuals who possess high personal integrity yield to the systemic forces that result in unethical behavior? There are several theories that suggest at least a partial explanation. During the discussions of ethics in my classes, it has become very clear that military officers have trouble with the concept of loyalty. On the battlefield, the concept is easily defined in terms of carrying out lawful orders, even if one does not fully understand the rationale for such orders. Any other response would be disastrous. In the realm of ideas at the national level, such obedience can easily translate into being a "yesman," barren of loyal dissent. Almost all military doctrine on leadership and ethics stresses the importance of having the courage of your own conviction, the willingness to take unpopular positions. I have never worked for anyone at any level who did not espouse that value; but some of those bosses displayed a very narrow range of tolerance for views that conflicted with their own. At least Samuel Goldwyn was honest when he allegedly said, "I don't want any yesmen around me. I want people who tell me the truth even though it costs them their jobs." In general, most officials want their subordinates to be ferocious competitors outside the organization, but docile followers inside.

Despite the above observations about the lack of courage to speak out, it is difficult to find a senior (or mid-level officer at senior service colleges) who will acknowledge that his or her freedom to speak up has ever been curtailed. I believe that most senior officials have had to make judicious decisions throughout their careers about when to speak up or stand mute. Such decisions take into account several variables such as the boss's attitude toward dissent and the importance of the issue, and some people are better at this kind of judgment. Courageous people who are inept judges of the situation are weeded out of the system. Others become windtesters and yesmen; most are never conscious of this behavior and are highly offended if accused of such behavior. Fortunately for them, only peers and subordinates perceive that behavior; therefore, they may rise to high positions.

The pressures for conformity are so strong and the penalties for dissent so severe, it is not surprising that we find widespread deficiency in moral courage. Again, this is not unique to bureaucratic behavior—it is endemic in U.S. society. Tocqueville observed "I know of no nation in which there is so little independence of mind and real freedom of discussion." And yet, the U.S. myth is that such freedom of thought is its great strength. One of my great frustrations at the National Defense University is the large number of students who resist critical thought when asked to question ideological sacred cows.

The various judgments of the behavior of the principal actors in the

Iran/*Contra* affair illustrates well how ideological beliefs dictate moral judgment. Ben Wattenberg describes the motives of the principals as a "patriot mentality" while Garry Wills describes the same behavior as a "junta mentality."[6] Wattenberg sees North, Poindexter, Secord, and McFarlane as patriots who were hamstrung by a Congress that does not recognize the true national interests. Wills views these same people as participants in a silent coup that violated their constitutional oath.

We need not question the motives of those four Service Academy graduates to condemn their behavior. Moral judgment can be based on principles of conduct, consequences of the behavior, or motives of the actors. Purity of motive is an important, but not determinate, factor. The principles of conduct involved in this issue are quite clear. All four took an oath of office to support the Constitution. The Constitution establishes a process that requires compromise and some semblance of consensus. The process is slow, frustrating, and sometimes seems to not serve national interests as perceived by patriotic military officers. The dilemma is most difficult for ideological zealots. At least some of the principal actors fit this categorization. Judging their behavior on the basis of principle, I must conclude that they violated their constitutional oath of office. I can think of no more serious breach of the military code of ethics. Deliberate violation of congressional legislation is not justified by an appeal to patriotism; sincerity of belief in, and commitment to, an ideological cause; purity of motive—the defense offered by the Nuremberg defendants.

Moral judgment can also be based on consequences of a given behavior. Many argue that the entire Iran/*Contra* affair would have been applauded if it had been successful. The criterion for success has never been clear to me, but let's assume it to include release of the hostages, better relations with Iran, and victory for the *Contras*. Would these consequences (assuming they represent U.S. national interests) outweigh the adverse consequences of bargaining with terrorists, strengthening Iran's position in the Gulf region, and the loss of moral stature caused by the hypocritical actions of the United States? This argument will go on indeterminately. Those consequences aside, a far more serious issue is the precedent of military officers putting loyalty to ideological conviction and the executive chain-of-command above loyalty to the constitutional oath. The very heart of the military code of ethics must be the inviolate nature of that oath.

Perhaps the most worrisome aspect of the distorted concept of loyalty is the danger of political polarization of the military. On the battlefield, there is little room for philosophical introspection about foreign policy and just or unjust wars. Most foreign policy issues are complex and defy simplistic, black-and-white characterization as right or wrong. An effective military must be imbued with the value of "my country, right or wrong." In practice, this usually results in a jingoistic attitude toward whomever, or whatever, is defined as an adversary. It should not be surprising, nor necessarily troubling if the officer corps tends to be, as regards national security, hawkish in its orientation.

There is a danger, however, when a natural tendency to be hawkish becomes identified with a particular political ideology to the extent that military officers are tempted to put ideological loyalty above loyalty to the constitutional process. That appears to have happened in the case of the Iran/*Contra* affair, where military officers, active and retired, demonstrated a hierarchy of values that places their personal concept of what is good for national security above that of what Congress has stated. It is absolutely essential that the U.S. military avoid becoming servants of a given political ideology other than that expressed in the Constitution.

The issue of conflicting loyalty is perhaps the most troublesome ethical dilemma facing public officials. Three cases illustrate the seriousness of this problem. The most notorious case is that previously mentioned, the Iran/*Contra* affair. Numerous military officers and civilian government officials apparently violated their constitutional oath by carrying out policies they believed (accurately so) to reflect their superiors' desires. At the time of this writing, the final story is yet to be told, but certain conclusions can be drawn with confidence. Prohibited by the constitutional process (congressional legislation) from doing what certain officials believed to be in the best interests of national security, officials at the highest level of government ignored those congressional restrictions and placed loyalty to their executive chain-of-command and ideological conviction before their oath to support the constitutional process. Defendants at the Nuremberg Trials also pleaded a just cause for their behavior, that is, "to stop Bolshevism." Military officers in the Pentagon and throughout the DoD structure assisted in implementing the illegal policies promulgated from the White House. When this issue was discussed in my ethics class at the National Defense University during the 1986–1987 academic year, almost all admitted that they would carry out policies directed by the White House, regardless of whether they thought Congress disapproved. Loyalty to the executive chain-of-command, so important on the battlefield, easily overrides abstract notions of congressional restrictions and constitutional oaths. This attitude is strengthened when illegal policies are consistent with one's ideology.

Several instances of the loyalty dilemma have arisen in the State Department concerning by the reinterpretation of the 1972 Antiballistic Missile (ABM) Treaty. Career officials were apparently systematically excluded from participation in the decisionmaking process and stood silent as the senior legal political appointee allegedly threatened firings if one of the career attorneys persisted in challenging the reinterpretation.[7] That individual later resigned in protest. Another State Department case involved the resignation of a senior career official, Francis J. McNeil, over what he considered an "exercise in McCarthyism." As one anonymous official commented, "What you had here was a classic juxtaposition between the true believer and the dispassionate professional analyst. . . ." In his letter of resignation, McNeil stated, "I thought you should hear directly from me as well as from elsewhere that I am leaving the Foreign Service in response to your exercise in McCarthyism. Confusing candor with disloyalty is a disservice to American interests and tradition. . . ." McNeil was highly regarded by his colleagues as a model professional diplomat noted for the candor of his advice and his nonpartisan loyalty to a succession of administrations of both parties.[8] The recipient of the letter, Assistant Secretary of State Elliott Abrams, lied to Congress and was later declared persona non grata by several senators.

The most glaring example of a distorted concept of loyalty in the Pentagon is probably that revealed by the chief of naval operations, Adm. Carlisle Trost, in comments regarding the former secretary of the navy, John Lehman. According to reporters, Trost made the following remarks: "The things that annoyed people about John Lehman were his disdain of senior military personnel, his tendency to override anyone who had a disagreement with him or contrary thought, and his habit of playing favorites: 'Play ball with me and you'll do well. Don't play ball with me and you're out.' There was a saying he had 'loyalty is agreeing with me.' Well, that's not the military definition of loyalty. Loyalty is not to the individual, but to the Service."[9]

While I disagree with Admiral Trost's notion that loyalty is to the service (First priority must be to the nation's interests as defined by the constitutional process. This does not preclude loyalty to one's boss, or service), he has exposed a serious ethical problem endemic to all bureaucracies. This problem appears to have been magnified under the Reagan administration, which has appointed more than its share of ideological true believers who confuse loyal dissent with disloyal behavior. It will take years for this legacy to be overcome. In the meantime, the environmental pressures for uncritical conformity will be strengthened and those who have the moral courage to offer loyal dissent will be sorely tested.

## NEGATIVE SYSTEMIC FACTORS

### Groupthink

A well-known phenomenon, *groupthink,* is a major contributor to ethical numbness in the Pentagon. Irving Janis[10] coined the term *groupthink* to refer to a condition where a functioning group becomes so cohesive and group loyalty so strong that members accept decisions by the leader or group without critical analysis. Centripetal social forces then operate to "circle the mental wagons" against alternative solutions. Intense pressure is applied to those members who break ranks, especially those who air differences outside the group, for example, in congressional testimony or by blowing the whistle.  Belief in the inherent moral superiority of their group leads to moral condemnation of those who are not team players.  Fawn Hall repeatedly emphasized that she was a member of the team.  There is a fine line between moral conviction and moral arrogance, but the implications are profound.

Groupthink leads to dysfunctional consequences in both decisionmaking and relating with other groups.  The adverse impact on group decisionmaking is perhaps the most serious consequence of groupthink.  The subtle suppression of critical thought puts a high premium on consensus and unity; group members not only fail to speak up against decisions, they accept the decisions as valid.  This lack of awareness that forces for overconformity are at work makes this phenomenon even more insidious.  Not only do many participants in the Pentagon decisionmaking system deny that groupthink exists, they become indignant at the suggestion that they themselves might be victims.

Groupthink is also an obstacle to effective intergroup cooperation.  The belief in the inherent moral superiority of the group's motives and beliefs, added to the tendency to stereotype adversaries, makes cooperation difficult. Pentagon officials view the mass media, Congress, and the Soviet Union as equally untrustworthy, characterized by faulty values and uncooperative behavior.  Given these perceptions, it becomes necessary to fight fire with fire—the normal rules of morality must be set aside for the group to be effective.  Hardball is not only legitimate, it is mandatory.  This attitude exists even within, and between, services.

## Ideologues

The pervasiveness of groupthink is exacerbated when key officials are ideologues or careerists dedicated to bureaucratic power for its own sake.  As recent administrations have strived to imprint their own ideology on the decisionmaking process, they have appointed more and more of the politically faithful to key positions.  As key group members become more homogeneous in their world view, loyal dissent is weakened.  Hard-line political loyalists weed out career individuals with different viewpoints whenever possible and ignore the views of those who remain.  The problem of political officials systematically excluding career officials from the decisionmaking process seems to have increased during the past few years, perhaps due to the increased number of political positions under the Civil Service Reform Act.  Not only are there more political appointees, the career members of the Senior Executive Service are vulnerable to transfer without due process—a tool that gives the political appointee considerable leverage in eliciting conformity.

Another reason for the apparent neglect of the career official in decisionmaking may be that many of the political officials take to heart the advice given by the Heritage Foundation in a special report published in late

1981.[11] The report paints a picture of a federal bureaucracy dominated by liberal careerists who cannot be trusted to carry out decisions made by the appointees. The report suggests a number of ways to neutralize careerists, for example, isolate, transfer, keep in the dark. I was told by authoritative sources that Secretary Caspar Weinberger condemned the report, and, based on my three years on the Office of the Secretary of Defense (OSD) staff during Weinberger's administration, the report was not taken seriously by most of the DoD political appointees. At least one senior OSD staff member, however, took it to heart and practiced it with Machiavellian glee.

Not all group cohesion, loyalty, and conformity is dysfunctional nor unethical. An organization cannot have constant dissension and members running to the press and/or Congress with every disagreement. This would destroy public confidence just as much as deception does. And, there are malcontents and bureaucrats who will drag their heels to block policies with which they disagree. It is a matter of degree, and a balance between conflict and cooperation must be maintained. My impression is that the kind of conformity produced by groupthink and ideological rigidity has taken the upper hand in the Pentagon. The reformers in Congress and elsewhere may be right in saying that the DoD is incapable of reforming itself.

## Loyal Dissent and Whistleblowing

Several legislative attempts have been made to protect loyal dissenters. Officials are encouraged to expose unethical behavior; indeed, this is a professional obligation. The U.S. Military Academy still retains that injunction as part of its Honor Code; that is, cadets will not tolerate violations of the code on the part of their colleagues. The other service academies have dropped that obligation—it simply is not workable because the norm against ratting on colleagues is too strong. In spite of the so-called whistle-blowing laws and offices set up to protect whistle-blowers, it is still better for your own self-interest to hear no evil, see no evil, speak no evil. The evidence that dissidents are weeded out of organizations without any semblance of justice is overwhelming.[12] You are better off to resign outright rather than try to expose unethical behavior. Why is this so? The fact is that one of the strongest values of social relations is that of loyalty. No one likes a snitch—a troublemaker.

Given these conditions, survival is based on rationalizing why not to stand up to unethical behavior. The most convenient rationalization is to blame it on the system (which is partially true); it's for a good cause; you can't be effective unless you play the game; or, the most effective, deny that anything is wrong. Groupthink greatly assists this process of denial. My impression is that many people unconsciously develop, over the years, a protective filter that desensitizes their moral gyroscope.

## THE NATIONAL PROBLEM

The moral malaise in which the United States finds itself has deep causes and will not be cured by simplistic slogans, scapegoating, nor moralizing about a return to traditional values. To solve this problem, we must understand its underlying causes and be willing to look at sacred cows of the value system. At the most fundamental level, U.S. citizens have to decide, as a people, what kind of society they want to have.

Members of the national security decisionmaking process do not operate in a closed system apart from that of the larger society. Indeed, the major actors in the governmental subsystem change frequently in the form of elected or political appointees. They bring with them the values of society-at-large, which, in general, emphasize individual rights and pursuit of self-interest. How, then, can we reasonably expect those values to be set aside and replaced by self-sacrifice and dedication to country? My conclusion is that such an expectation is unrealistic for many, especially those recruited from the business sector where a dog-eat-dog perspective dominates. Thus, the United States will need to continue to have explicit, detailed laws, rules, and regulations that prescribe behavior. These rules will have to be enforced by watchdogs such as inspectors general, auditors, oversight committees, and all the other bureaucratic mechanisms that are required to impose moral order. Must we use the same methods to elicit compliance of moral rules by career officials, or are they cut from the same bolt of moral cloth of the society at large?

A question that has occupied social philosophers throughout time has been, How is social order possible, given the myriad of individual interests represented in any large grouping of people? The question is not easily answered even when examining a social dyad, but becomes increasingly perplexing when one attempts to explain complex societies. Hobbes and Locke offered two classical answers to the question.[13] Both observed the turbulent times of the English Revolution and came to different conclusions. Hobbes believed humans were inherently selfish and aggressive and would pursue their own self interests—resulting in a "war of all against all." Social order can be obtained only if a political structure is established to regulate interpersonal behavior; that is, social order is imposed by political authority.

Locke disagreed with Hobbes. He believed that all people had common interests that could only be achieved through cooperative behavior. If people would communicate with each other and develop an understanding of how a cooperative endeavor would best serve the interest of all, social order would be more stable and enduring. According to Locke, agreed-upon values and norms of behavior would be internalized by individuals, and mutual trust and confidence would develop so that each would conform to those norms. Social order, according to this model, results from a sense of community—a moral obligation to behave toward others in a certain way.

Hobbes would have morality imposed, that is, moral order. Locke would have morality as a result of moral community. These different approaches to morality have profound implications for the nature of a society. No society is based on either model in its pure form; rather, societies vary in the mixture of the two means of control. Ideally, most people would prefer to rely more on the Lockean model than on the Hobbesian solution where such is feasible. But, the Lockean approach requires a socialization process that inculcates common values and norms of behavior in the members of a society.

Ethical norms define right and wrong behavior among a given community. In the final analysis, whether they be derived from divine revelation, philosopher kings, authorities, by common sense, or some combination thereof, these rules of behavior represent what the sources believe to be guidelines for a cooperative society. They involve compromises between individual freedom to do as one pleases and the rights of others. The effectiveness of the norms depends upon mutual trust and confidence that community members will voluntarily conform, and it is a matter of honor that individuals do not violate that trust. Watchdogs, in the form of police, inspectors, or other enforcers, are not needed.

Few, if any, groups rely solely on voluntary compliance with group norms of right or wrong. That form of control is usually supplemented by external controls, either hierarchical authority or peer pressure. For a society to function effectively over a period of time, however, voluntary compliance must account for the greatest part of the behavioral variance. Someone has hypothesized that 85 percent of the members of a society must voluntarily comply with rules 85 percent of the time if the society is to maintain social order. Without arguing over percentages, most would agree that the more a society can depend on voluntary compliance with ethical norms, the better the cohesion of the society.

Moral order (as opposed to moral community) can be imposed to a certain extent by political authority. Behavior can be regulated in this manner, but to the degree this is relied upon, voluntary compliance diminishes. Thus, the over reliance on laws, regulations, and other legalistic mechanisms to elicit compliance of society's norms of behavior weakens voluntary compliance and requires further reliance on legalistic control. This circular effect puts a society on a slippery slope. One index of the degree to which a society has moved toward legalism as a means of social control is the number of lawyers it has. In this regard, it is interesting to note that the per capita number of lawyers in the United States is over 40 times that of Japan.

The United States is a highly individualistic society with a strong emphasis on individual rights as opposed to community welfare. The authors of the Constitution reflected this bias and, coupled with the fear of centralized control in the hands of an elite, wrote a constitution that tilted in favor of the individual rights. The dominant political philosophy stresses that pursuit of individual self-interest is the best way to attain the good of the nation. U.S. economic philosophy of laissez-faire private enterprise is equally biased toward pursuit of self-interest. Again, this pursuit of self-interest theoretically will produce the greater good for all. Some argue that such pursuit of self-interest also dominates U.S. social and psychological values in the form of social Darwinism and psychological egoism.[14]

If indeed U.S. dominant societal values emphasize the individual rights and pursuit of self-interest then it is not too surprising that it is a litigious society relying on external regulations to curb its pursuit of self-interest. There is reason to believe that it has always been a legalistic society rather than a community. Moral order, rather than moral community, has maintained social order. The United States has adopted the Hobbesian solution rather than the Lockean approach. "Let the buyer beware" in business relations imposes no limits based on moral sentiment of fairness, honesty, and full disclosure. As a result, laws have proliferated to protect the buyer, although the true believers of laissez-faire economics might argue that in the long run the marketplace would eliminate the unethical vendor. Apparently in the long run is too long; the United States has attempted to legislate moral order.

As the federal government's involvement in distributing economic goods has increased, we should not be surprised by, nor critical of, the practice of political representatives looking out for the self-interest of their constituents (and their own political fortunes). After all, U.S. political philosophy supports such behavior. Advocates of specific federal spending, however, do not see their particular hobby horse as inimical to national welfare. Military proponents lobby congressmen strongly for defense spending and tend to label as less than honest those congressmen who do not share their views. Ideological orientation sometimes determines moral judgment; for example, anything is justified if it serves one's ideological cause.

Amitai Etzioni has well described the moral malaise resulting from these dominant economic, social, psychological and political philosophies.[15] He concludes that duty to the common good has been subordinated to the pursuit of self-interest in all walks of life. Patriotism is in vogue if it requires nothing more than rhetoric. People want government services but do not want to pay for them; they want a strong defense but want to borrow the money and pay others to serve. The argument to reduce the role of government is often no more than a fig leaf to conceal a philosophy of social Darwinism; the United States is wedded to laissez-faire mixed with libertarianism and the pop psychology notion of me-ism. As Etzioni explains, U.S. citizens have been brought up on a highly simplified notion of the invisible hand: Everybody goes out and tries to maximize her- or himself—and the economy thrives for all. There is no need to curb self-interest, even greed; it is the propellant that fires up economies. Special interest groups and lobbies dominate the political process, each putting self-interest above the general welfare.

Etzioni's observations are supported by attitudes of college students expressed over the past two decades. In a recent survey of students identified as the *best and brightest* of a fine university, a reporter found cynicism to be the order of the day.[16] He found their dominant value to be that of making money, and if it required playing the game to make that money, they were prepared to play the game. Their reaction to the recent scandals on Wall Street was that it was just part of the game. The end justifies the means, and this is a dog-eat-dog world. They all do it; survival of the fittest. The reporter found these students to be largely unconcerned about moral and ethical questions. These impressions are supported by data collected in 1984 by the American Association of Higher Education, which showed that 70 percent of freshmen listed as their top concern "being well off financially." Fifteen years ago, a similar survey indicated the highest value was "developing a meaningful philosophy of life."[17]

## THE FUTURE

The moral malaise that affects U.S. society cannot be cured with political rhetoric and scapegoating. We must reexamine fundamental values as well as the socialization process for inculcating those values. It will not be an easy task because it will require the examination of sacred cows that form the bedrock of U.S. economic, political, and social philosophy. My experience in teaching ethics tells me that few U.S. citizens are willing to question these fundamental values.

Moreover, the United States has allowed its moral socialization process to become fragmented and largely ineffective. The public school system, a critical component of the socialization process where the diverse elements of society can have common values taught, is paralyzed by an acrimonious struggle of competing ideological camps, each insisting that their respective version of morality is the only acceptable one. As a result, little is taught. Due to sociological reasons that are beyond the scope of this discussion, the family role in the socialization process has been significantly reduced. Even such a simple example as national holidays illustrates how the socialization process has deteriorated. Holidays are designed to be a symbol of certain values a nation wants to foster. The ritual and ceremony associated with a holiday can be very useful in strengthening those values. Instead, they are currently little more than days off for recreation and shopping bonanzas.

The degradation of the family and schools as socialization institutions has been accompanied by the increased role of the arts and mass media. Music, movies, magazines, books, and television have filled the void.

There is a moral crisis in the United States that represents a serious threat to national security. A systematic effort will be required to reverse the trend. A significant element of such an effort must be a better example by senior officials in the national security community.

## NOTES

1. Sissela Bok, *Lying: Moral Choice in Public and Private Life* (New York: Vintage, 1979).

2. "Whatever Happened to Ethics?" *Time*, May 25, 1987.

3. *Gallup Report,* October 1986, p. 3.

4. Fred Hiatt, "A Parting Slot," *The Washington Post,* 17 August 1986, p. C1.

5. Ralph Sanders, "Bureaucratic Ploys and Strategems: The Case of the U.S. Department of Defense," *The Jerusalem Journal of International Relations,* vol. 4, no. 2 (1979).

6. Ben Wattenberg, "Patriot Mentality," and Garry Wills, "Junta Mentality," *Baltimore Sun,* May 15, 1987, p. 23A.

7. Michael R. Gordon, "Ex-Aide Says Reagan Got Flawed Advice on ABM's," *The New York Times,* April 30, 1987, p. A3.

8. John M. Goshko, "Top Aide Retires, Assails Abrams," *The Washington Post,* February 11, 1987, p. A19.

9. Jim Stewart, "Navy Brass Erasing Lehman Legacy," *Atlanta Constitution,* April 28, 1987, p. 2.

10. Irving Janis, "Groupthink," *Psychology Today,* vol. 5, no. 6 (November 1971).

11. Charles L. Heatherly, *Mandate for Leadership II: Continuing the Conservative Revolution* (Washington, D.C.: The Heritage Foundation, 1981).

12. N. R. Kleinfield, "The Whistle Blowers' Morning After," *The New York Times,* November 9, 1986, pp. F1, F10, F11.

13. J. Bronowski and B. Mazlish, *The Western Intellectual Tradition* (New York: Harper and Row, 1975), pp. 193–215.

14. Richard Gabriel, *To Serve With Honor* (Westport, Conn.: Greenwood Press, 1982), pp. 15–17.

15. Amitai Etzioni, "Duty: The Forgotten Virtue," *The Washington Post,* March 9, 1986, p. C5.

16. Haynes Johnson, "Goals of the Best and Brightest," *The Washington Post,* April 22, 1987, p. A2.

17. Sarah Tippit, "University of Maryland Takes Steps to Combat Cheating on Exams," *The Washington Post,* May 7, 1987, Md 1.

# 12.5   The Need for Change

*The following excerpts from the Packard Commission Report, the Tower Commission reports, and the Goldwater-Nunn Defense Organization Staff Study point to the need to improve the functioning of U.S. national security policymaking machinery. All recommend structural changes that have largely been implemented by the 1986 Goldwater-Nichols Reorganization Legislation and presidential actions, respectively. Although such attempts to enhance the efficiency of U.S. government apparatus appear laudatory initially, serious students of political culture will recognize that such adjustments only invoke the central dilemma of Madisonian pluralism—namely, to a great degree, democratic government and efficient government do not go hand-in-hand. Managing the balance between the two is a central question facing the United States today and in the years to come.*

---

## The Packard Commission Report[1]

### THE ROLE OF THE PRESIDENT IN NATIONAL SECURITY PLANNING

In our *Interim Report*, the Commission found that there is a need for more and better long-range planning to bring together the nation's security objectives, the forces needed to achieve them, and the resources available to support those forces. It is critically important that this relationship be clearly established through a national military strategy. At the same time, military strategy cannot be carried out in isolation from the larger questions of the nation's overall foreign policy and its domestic economic and fiscal objectives. Within the Executive Branch, only the President can make the decisions necessary to balance these elements of national policy. For this reason, the Commission sees a need to streamline the present extensive process for defense planning and budgeting within the Executive Branch by establishing a mechanism for early, firm Presidential guidance. . . .

*Recommendations*

To institutionalize, expand, and link a series of critical Presidential determinations, we recommend a process (Appendix E) that would operate in substance as follows:

The National Security Council would develop and direct a national security planning process for the President that revises current national security decision directives as appropriate and that provides to the Secretary of Defense Presidential guidance that includes:

- A statement of national security objectives;
- A statement of priorities among national security objectives;
- A statement of major defense policies;
- Provisional five-year defense budget levels, with the advice and assistance of the Office of Management and Budget, to give focus to the development of a fiscally constrained national military strategy. Such budget levels would reflect competing demands on the federal budget as well as projections of gross national product and revenues; and
- Direction to construct a proposed national military strategy and strategy options for Presidential decision in time to guide development of the first biennial defense budget for fiscal years 1988 and 1989. . . .

## A NEW PROCESS FOR PLANNING NATIONAL MILITARY STRATEGY

To provide the President and Secretary of Defense with military advice that better integrates the views of the nation's combatant commands and Military Services, the Commission in our *Interim Report* recommended legislation creating new duties for the Chairman of the Joint Chiefs of Staff (JCS). In the Commission's view, the Chairman should become the principal military adviser to the President, the National Security Council, and the Secretary of Defense, representing his own views as well as the corporate views of the JCS. The Chairman should be given exclusive direction of the Joint Staff, and other elements of the Organization of the Joint Chiefs of Staff, to perform such duties as he prescribes to support the JCS and to respond to the Secretary of Defense. To further assist the Chairman in performing his new duties, a new position of Vice Chairman of the JCS should be created. We note that in a message to Congress on April 24, 1986, the President endorsed these recommendations and that the Senate and House have separately passed legislation along these lines.

In making these recommendations, the Commission envisioned that the new duties of the Chairman would include a major role in national security planning. The Commission recommended that the Chairman, with the advice of the other members of the JCS and the Commanders-in-Chief (CINCs) of the combatant commands, be given responsibility for preparing and submitting to the Secretary of Defense a fiscally constrained national military strategy, with strategy options, based on the President's initial guidance on national security objectives and priorities, and his provisional five-year budget levels. The Chairman would also, with the assistance of the other members of the JCS, and in consultation with the Director of Central Intelligence, prepare a military net assessment of the capabilities of United States and Allied Forces as compared to those of potential adversaries. The net assessment would be used to evaluate the risks of the strategy and the strategy options. . . .

## Recommendations

The Secretary of Defense, following receipt of the Presidential guidance described previously, should direct the Chairman of the Joint Chiefs of Staff (JCS), with the advice of the other members of the Joint Chiefs of Staff and the Commanders-in-Chief (CINCs) of the Unified and Specified Commands, to:

- Appraise the complete range of military threats to U.S. interests and objectives worldwide;
- Derive national military objectives and priorities from the national security objectives, major defense policies, and priorities received from the President; and
- Provide the Secretary of Defense a recommended national military strategy that:
  Best attains those national security objectives provided by the President, in accordance with his policies and priorities;
  Identifies the forces and capabilities necessary to execute the strategy during the five-year planning period; and
  Meets fiscal and other resource constraints directed by the President during the five-year planning period.

At the direction of the Secretary of Defense, the Chairman also should develop strategy options to achieve the national security objectives. Such strategy options would:

- Frame explicit trade-offs among the Armed Forces;
- Reflect major defense policies and different operational concepts, in terms of different mixes of forces or different degrees of emphasis on modernization, readiness, or sustainability;
- Respond to each provisional budget level provided by the President;
- Explore variations within a particular provisional budget level; and
- Highlight differences in capability between the recommended national military strategy, on the one hand, and feasible alternatives, on the other.

At the direction of the Secretary of Defense, the Chairman of the Joint Chiefs of Staff, with the assistance of the other members of the JCS and the CINCs, and in consultation with the Director of Central Intelligence, should also prepare a military net assessment that would:

- Provide comparisons of the capabilities and effectiveness of U.S. military forces with those of forces of potential adversaries for the Chairman's recommended national military strategy and other strategy options;
- Reflect the military contributions of Allied Forces where appropriate;
- Evaluate the risks of the Chairman's recommended national military strategy and any strategy options that he develops for the Secretary of Defense and the President; and
- Cover the entire five-year planning period.

The Secretary of Defense, following his review and analysis of the Chairman's recommendations, should provide to the President:

- The Secretary's recommended national military strategy and its corresponding five-year defense budget level, consistent with the President's policy and fiscal guidance;
- Appropriate strategy options and corresponding five-year defense budget levels sufficient to provide the President a wide range of alternatives in choosing a national defense program; and
- A military net assessment of the recommended national military strategy and strategy options. . . .

## Recommendations

*Congress.* A joint effort among the Appropriations Committees, the Armed Services Committees, the Office of Management and Budget (OMB), and the Department of Defense (DoD) should be undertaken as soon as possible to work out the necessary agreements, concepts, categories, and procedures to implement a new biennial budget process for defense. Biennial budgeting for defense should be instituted in 1987 for the fiscal year 1988–89 defense budget. Congress should authorize and appropriate defense funding for those two years. The second year of this new biennial budgeting process should be used by both Congress and the DoD to review program execution where appropriate.

Congress should reduce the overlap, duplication, and redundancy among the many congressional committees and subcommittees now reviewing the defense budget.

The leadership of both parties in the House and the Senate should review the congressional process leading up to annual budget resolutions with the intent of increasing stability in forecasts for defense budgets for future years. We cannot stress strongly enough that a responsible partnership in providing for the national defense means agreement between Congress and the President on an overall level of a five-year defense program early in a new President's term in office and adherence to this agreement during his Administration.

The chairmen and ranking minority members of the Armed Services Committees and the Defense Appropriations Subcommittees should agree on a cooperative review of the defense budget that has the following features:

- Review by the Armed Services Committees of the defense budget in terms of operational concepts and categories (e.g., force structure, modernization, readiness, and sustainability, etc.);
- Review and authorization of individual programs by the Armed Services Committees that concentrate on new defense efforts at key milestones—specifically the beginning of full-scale development and the start of high-rate production—in terms of their contributions to major defense missions; and
- Review by the Appropriations Committees, using the new budget structured in terms of operational concepts and categories, to adjust the President's defense budget to congressional budget resolution levels through refinements based on information not available when the President's budget was formulated months earlier.

Congress should adhere to its own deadlines by accelerating the budget review process, so that final authorizations and appropriations are provided to DoD on time, and less use is made of continuing resolutions.

Congress should review and make major reductions in the number of reports it asks DoD to prepare and should closely control requirements for new reports in the future.

*Executive Branch.* The President should direct the Secretary of Defense and OMB to institute biennial budgeting for defense in 1987 for the fiscal year 1988–89 defense budget and budgets thereafter.

The Secretary of Defense should develop and submit to Congress defense budgets and five-year plans within an operationally oriented structure. He should work with the appropriate committees of Congress and with OMB to establish the necessary mechanisms and procedures to ensure that a new budget format is established.

The Secretary of Defense should institute a biennial programming process within DoD to complement the proposed biennial planning and budgeting processes.

The Secretary of Defense should work with the Armed Services Committees to define procedures for milestone authorization of major defense programs.

Baselining and multi-year procurement should be used as much as possible to reinforce milestone authorization. . . .

To accomplish meaningful, long-range defense planning, certain modifications are needed in our defense establishment.

The President and the Secretary of Defense require military advice that better integrates the individual views of the nation's combatant commanders and the Chiefs of the Services. Today, there is no one uniformed officer clearly responsible for providing such an integrated view, who can draw upon the best thinking of, and act as an effective spokesman for, our senior military leadership. The current authority of the Chairman of the Joint Chiefs of Staff is insufficient to enable him to perform effectively in this capacity. The Chairman's advisory relation to the President and the Secretary of Defense, the Chairman's mandate over the Joint Staff and the Organization of the Joint Chiefs of Staff, and the Chairman's place in the channel of communications between the Secretary of Defense and the Commanders-in-Chief of the Unified and Specified Commands (CINCs), all must be strengthened to this end.

So, too, must the views of the CINCs be more strongly and purposefully represented than they are at present within the councils of the Joint Chiefs and in weapons requirements decision-making. Because it is the responsibility of the Chairman to integrate the sometimes conflicting advice of the Service Chiefs and the CINCs into a national strategy, the necessity for impartiality and objectivity in doing so argues for another voice in the Joint Chiefs of Staff to represent the views of the CINCs. For these purposes, and to assist the Chairman in his existing and additional responsibilities, we conclude that the position of Vice Chairman of the Joint Chiefs of Staff should be established.

There is an important need to provide for continuity of advice to the Secretary of Defense and the President in the absence of the Chairman of the Joint Chiefs of Staff. The current system, in which the members of the Joint Chiefs of Staff (JCS) rotate quarterly as Acting Chairman, has provided continuity better than earlier systems. It also has served to enhance a needed joint perspective among the Service Chiefs and increase their effectiveness in both their JCS and Service roles. The establishment of a Vice Chairman as a member of the Joint Chiefs of Staff having special responsibilities for representing the interests of the CINCs and reviewing weapons requirements would be an important innovation. While underscoring the importance of continuity, the Commission believes the procedures under which an Acting Chairman is designated should remain flexible. Under the President's direction, the Secretary of Defense should be permitted to adopt those procedures which are best suited to the particular circumstances and to revise them in accordance with changing needs. . . .

## Recommendations

The Commission recommends the following reforms in federal law and DoD practices.

Current law should be changed to designate the Chairman of the Joint Chiefs of Staff (JCS) as the principal uniformed military advisor to the President, the National Security Council, and the Secretary of Defense, representing his own views as well as the corporate views of the JCS.

Current law should be changed to place the Joint Staff and the Organization of the Joint Chiefs of Staff under the exclusive direction of the Chairman, to perform such duties as he prescribes to support the JCS and to respond to the Secretary of Defense. The statutory limit on the number of officers on the Joint Staff should be removed to permit the Chairman a staff sufficient to discharge his responsibilities.

The Secretary of Defense should direct that the commands to and reports by the Commanders-in-Chief of the Unified and Specified Commands (CINCs) should be channeled through the Chairman so that the Chairman may better incorporate the views of senior combatant commanders in his advice to the Secretary.

The Service Chiefs should serve as members of the JCS. The position of a four-star Vice Chairman should be established by law as a sixth member of the JCS. The Vice Chairman should assist the Chairman by representing the interests of the CINCs, co-chairing the Joint Requirements and Management Board, and performing such other duties as the Chairman may prescribe.

The Secretary of Defense, subject to the direction of the President, should determine the procedures under which an Acting Chairman is designated to serve in the absence of the Chairman of the JCS. Such procedures should remain flexible and responsive to changing circumstances.

Subject to the review and approval of the Secretary of Defense, Unified Commanders should be given broader authority to structure subordinate commands, joint task forces, and support activities in a way that best supports their missions and results in a significant reduction in the size and numbers of military headquarters.

The Unified Command Plan should be revised to assure increased flexibility to deal with situations that overlap the geographic boundaries of the current combatant commands and with changing world conditions.

For contingencies short of general war, the Secretary of Defense, with the advice of the Chairman and the JCS, should have the flexibility to establish the shortest possible chains of command for each force deployed, consistent with proper supervision and support. This would help the CINCs and the JCS perform better in situations ranging from peace to crisis to general war.

The Secretary of Defense should establish a single unified command to integrate global air, land, and sea transportation, and should have flexibility to structure this organization as he sees fit. Legislation prohibiting such a command should be repealed.

# The Goldwater-Nunn Defense Organization Staff Study[2]

## EXECUTIVE SUMMARY

### A. Introduction

This study, as its title—*Defense Organization: The Need for Change*—indicates, is critical of the current organization and decision-making procedures of the Department of Defense (DoD) and of the Congress. The underlying problems within DoD have been evident for much of this Century. The inability to solve these problems is not due to a lack of attention or a failure to have the issues examined by the most experienced and learned experts. At regular intervals during the last 85 years, these issues have been vigorously addressed by highly capable and well-intentioned individuals, both from the public and private sectors as well as from civilian and military life. It is the complexity of the Department of Defense—the largest organization in the Free World—that has served to frustrate previous efforts. Adding to the difficulty of these issues are the quickening pace of the technological revolution, the increasing and changing demands of protecting U.S. security interests in a dynamic international environment, and the resistance to needed changes by a substantial portion of the defense bureaucracy. While the problems in congressional review and oversight of the defense program have emerged more recently, their resolution has not been possible despite serious study and concern by Members of Congress. . . .

### B. Principal Organizational Goal of DoD

The principal organizational goal of DoD, both in 1949 and now, is the integration of the distinct military capabilities of the four Services to prepare for and conduct effective unified operations in fulfilling major U.S. military missions. In this study, this goal is termed "mission integration". Mission integration is necessary at both of the distinct organizational levels of DoD the policymaking level, comprised basically of Washington Headquarters organizations, and the operational level, consisting of the unified and specified commands. Effective mission integration is critical to U.S. national security because none of the major missions of DoD can be executed alone by forces of any single Service. Without effective mission integration, unification of the four Services—as provided in the National Security Act of 1947—means little. . . .

### C. Problems and Broad Recommendations

1. Limited Mission Integration at DoD's Policymaking Level

The three principal organizations of the Washington Headquarters of DoD—the Office of the Secretary of Defense (OSD), the Organization of the

Joint Chiefs of Staff (OJCS), and the Military Departments—are focused excessively on functional areas, such as manpower, research and development, and installations and logistics. This functional structure serves to inhibit integration of Service capabilities along mission lines, and, thereby, hinders achieving DoD's principal organizational goal of mission integration. The focus of organizational activity is on functional efficiency (or, in other terms, management control of functional activities) and not on major missions and their objectives and strategy. Without extensive mission integration efforts, numerous deficiencies occur:

In colloquial terms, material inputs, not mission outputs, are emphasized.

A sharp focus on missions, where DoD must compete with potential adversaries, is lost in the functional diffusion.

Strategic planning is inhibited by the absence of an organizational focus on major missions and strategic goals.

Service interests rather than strategic needs play the dominant role in shaping program decisions.

Functions (e.g., airlift, sealift, close air support) which are not central to a Service's own definition of its missions tend to be neglected.

Tradeoffs between programs of different Services that can both contribute to a particular mission are seldom made.

Opportunities for non-traditional contributions to missions (e.g., Air Force contributions to sea control) are neither easily identified nor pursued.

Headquarters organizations are not fully attuned to the operational, especially readiness, requirements of the unified commanders.

Interoperability and coordination requirements of forces from the separate Services are not readily identified.

Beyond these major shortcomings, the functional structure encourages OSD micro-management of Service programs. . . .

2. Imbalance Between Service and Joint Interests

Under current arrangements, the Military Departments and Services exercise power and influence which are completely out of proportion to their statutorily assigned duties. The predominance of Service perspectives in DoD decision-making results from three basic problems: (1) OSD is not organized to effectively integrate Service capabilities and programs into the forces needed to fulfill the major missions of DoD; (2) the Joint Chiefs of Staff (JCS) system is dominated by the Services which retain an effective veto over nearly every JCS action; and (3) the unified commands are also dominated by the Services primarily through the strength and independence of the Service component commanders and constraints placed upon the power and influence of the unified commanders. In sum, the problem of undue Service influence arises principally from the weaknesses of organizations that are responsible for joint military preparation and planning. . . .

### 3. Imbalance Between Modernization and Readiness

The imbalance between Service and joint interests is a major cause of the imbalance between modernization and readiness in the defense program. Overemphasis on future needs deprives operating forces of capabilities needed to respond to today's or tomorrow's crisis. Current warfighting capabilities are robbed to pay for hardware in the distant future. For the most part, the Washington Headquarters of the Services are focused on future requirements and the modernization of their equipment. The constituency for readiness is the operational commands which are among the joint organizations whose interests are under-represented in senior decision-making councils. Correcting this modernization-readiness imbalance will require a strengthening of the representation of the operational commanders, especially the unified commanders, in the resource allocation process.

### 4. Inter-Service Logrolling

While strong criticism of destructive and disruptive inter-Service rivalry is frequently voiced, DoD suffers more from inter-Service logrolling. The intensity of the postwar rivalry among the Services was so great that its continued existence has been assumed. It is true that inter-Service secretiveness, duplication, lack of understanding, and inconsistencies continue to exist. These are found at lower levels of organizational activity where they continue to undermine coordination and cooperation. However, over the last 20 years, the Services have logrolled on the central issues of concern to them in order to provide a united front to the Secretary of Defense and other senior civilian authorities. The natural consequence of this logrolling has been a heightening of civil-military disagreement, an isolation of OSD, a loss of information critical to effective decision-making, and, most importantly, a political weakening of the Secretary of Defense. The overall result of inter-Service logrolling has been a highly undesirable lessening of civilian control of the military. Actions to correct this problem will need to ensure that senior civilian authorities are informed of all legitimate alternatives.

The current system in many regards represents the worst of many possibilities. On critical issues, the Services logroll and deny the opportunity for effective decision-making. On lesser issues, the Services remain determined rivals and preclude the degree of cooperation and coordination necessary to provide efficient and integrated fighting teams.

### 5. Inadequate Joint Advice

The JCS system has not been capable of adequately fulfilling its responsibility to provide useful and timely unified military advice. The institutional views of the JCS often take too long to prepare; are not in the concise form required by extremely busy senior officials; and, most importantly, do not offer clear, meaningful recommendations on issues affecting more than one Service. As General David C. Jones, USAF (Retired), a former JCS Chairman, has stated:

. . . the corporate advice provided by the Joint Chiefs of Staff is not crisp, timely, very useful or very influential.

Former Secretary of Defense James R. Schlesinger concurs in his evaluation of formal JCS advice:

. . . The proffered advice is generally irrelevant, normally unread, and almost always disregarded.

Symptoms of inadequate joint advice are found in many activities within DoD, including strategic planning, programming, operational planning, force employment, roles and missions of the Services, revision of the Unified Command Plan, organization of the unified commands, and development of joint doctrine.  The JCS are viewed as the key military advisors on a substantial range of important strategy, resource, operational, and organizational issues.  Shortcomings in their ability to meaningfully address these issues have had a serious impact on the ability of DoD to prepare for and to conduct military operations in times of crisis.  Moreover, the JCS have failed to provide adequate staff support to the Secretary of Defense in his mission integrator and chain of command roles.  As a result, the Secretary has been forced to rely on civilians, whether they are qualified or not, for advice on issues for which independent military recommendations would have been preferred.

The dual responsibilities of the Service Chiefs—often referred to as "dual-hatting"—to their individual Services and to the Joint Chiefs of Staff is the primary cause of the deficiencies of the JCS system.  "Dual-hatting" poses an inherent conflict of interest for the Service Chiefs.  They have one job that requires them to be effective advocates for their own Service.  Their second job as JCS members requires them to subordinate Service interests to broader considerations.

6.  Failure to Adequately Implement the Concept of Unified Command

The concept of unified command, as formulated in the immediate postwar period and articulated by President Eisenhower in 1958, has not been adequately implemented.  At that time, President Eisenhower stated:

Because I have often seen the evils of diluted command, I emphasize that each unified commander must have unquestioned authority over all units of his command. . . .  Today a unified command is made up of component commands from each military department, each under a commander of that department. The commander's authority over these component commands is short of the full command required for maximum efficiency.

Despite President Eisenhower's efforts, the authority of the unified commanders remains extremely limited.  They have weak authority over their Service component commands, limited influence over resources, and little ability to promote greater unification within their commands.  As a result, the unified commands remain loose confederations of single-Service forces which are unable to provide effective unified action across the spectrum of military missions. In essence, there is limited mission integration at the operational level of DoD. As the 1970 *Blue Ribbon Defense Panel Report* noted: "The net result is an organizational structure in which 'unification' of either command or of the forces is more cosmetic than substantive."

The operational deficiencies evident during the Vietnam War, the seizure of the *Pueblo*, the Iranian hostage rescue mission, and the incursion into Grenada were the result of the failure to adequately implement the concept of unified command.

7. Unnecessary Staff Layers and Duplication of Effort in the Top Management Headquarters of the Military Departments

Each Military Department has two separate headquarters staffs (three in the Navy) the Secretariat and the military headquarters staff. This arrangement results in an unnecessary layer of supervision and duplication of effort. Moreover, the existence of two separate staffs leads to delays and micro-management and is counterproductive and inefficient.

8. Predominance of Programming and Budgeting

9. Lack of Clarity of Strategic Goals

10. Insufficient Mechanisms for Change

11. Inadequate Feedback

12. Inadequate Quality of Political Appointees and Joint Duty Military Personnel

13. Failure to Clarify the Desired Division of Work

14. Excessive Spans of Control

15. Insufficient Power and Influence of the Secretary of Defense

16. Inconsistent and Contradictory Pattern of Congressional Oversight

## D. Specific Recommendations

Many of the broad recommendations of the staff study are presented in preceding text of the Executive Summary. The study also makes a total of 91 specific recommendations to solve the problems identified in Chapters 3 through 9. The twelve most important specific recommendations are:

1. Establish three mission-oriented under secretary positions in the Office of the Secretary of Defense for (1) nuclear deterrence, (2) NATO defense, and (3) regional defense and force projection.

2. Disestablish the Joint Chiefs of Staff and, thereby, permit the Service Chiefs to dedicate all their time to Service duties.

3. Establish a Joint Military Advisory Council consisting of a Chairman and a 4-star military officer from each Service on his last tour of duty to serve as the principal military advisors to the President, the National Security Council, and the Secretary of Defense.

4. Authorize the Chairman of the Joint Military Advisory Council to

provide military advice in his own right.

5. Designate one of the members of the Joint Military Advisory Council, from a different Service pair (Army/Air Force and Navy/Marine Corps) than the Chairman, as Deputy Chairman.

6. Specify that one of the responsibilities of the Joint Military Advisory Council is to inform higher authority of all legitimate alternatives.

7. Authorize the Chairman of the Joint Military Advisory Council to develop and administer a personnel management system for all military officers assigned to joint duty.

8. Establish in each Service a joint duty career specialty.

9. Make the Chairman of the Joint Military Advisory Council (JMAC) the principal military advisor to the Secretary of Defense on operational matters and the sole command voice of higher authority within the JMAC system while ensuring absolute clarity that the JMAC Chairman is not part of the chain of command.

10. Remove the Service component commanders within the unified commands from the operational chain of command.

11. Fully integrate the Secretariats and military headquarters staffs in the Departments of the Army and Air Force and partially integrate the Secretariat and military headquarters staffs in the Department of the Navy. (The Department of the Navy is treated differently because of its dual-Service structure.)

12. Create the position of Assistant Secretary of Defense (Strategic Planning) who would be responsible for establishing and maintaining a well-designed and highly interactive strategic planning process.

---

# The Tower Commission Report[3]

## ORGANIZING FOR NATIONAL SECURITY

Ours is a government of checks and balances, of shared power and responsibility. The Constitution places the President and the Congress in dynamic tension. They both cooperate and compete in the making of national policy.

National security is no exception. The Constitution gives both the President and the Congress an important role. The Congress is critical in formulating national policies and in marshalling the resources to carry them out. But those resources—the nation's military personnel, its diplomats, its intelligence capability—are lodged in the Executive Branch. As Chief Executive and Commander-in-Chief, and with broad authority in the area of foreign affairs, it is the President who is empowered to act for the nation and protect its interests. . . .

What emerges from this history is NSC staff used by each President in a way that reflected his individual preferences and working style. Over time, it has developed an important role within the Executive Branch of coordinating policy review, preparing issues for Presidential decision, and monitoring implementation. But it has remained the President's creature, molded as he sees fit, to serve as his personal staff for national security affairs. For this reason, it has generally operated out of the public view and has not been subject to direct oversight by the Congress.

## THE REAGAN MODEL

President Reagan entered office with a strong commitment to cabinet government. His principal advisors on national security affairs were to be the Secretaries of State and Defense, and to a lesser extent the Director of Central Intelligence. The position of the National Security Advisor was initially downgraded in both status and access to the President. Over the next six years, five different people held that position.

The Administration's first National Security Advisor, Richard Allen, reported to the President through the senior White House staff. Consequently, the NCS staff assumed a reduced role. Mr. Allen believed that the Secretary of State had primacy in the field of foreign policy. He viewed the job of the National Security Advisor as that of a policy coordinator.

President Reagan initially declared that the National Security Council would be the principal forum for consideration of national security issues. To support the work of the Council, President Reagan established an interagency committee system headed by three Senior Interagency Groups (or "SIGs"), one each for foreign policy, defense policy, and intelligence. They were chaired by the Secretary of State, the Secretary of Defense, and the Director of Central Intelligence, respectively.

Over time, the Administration's original conception of the role of the National Security Advisor changed. William Clark, who succeeded Richard Allen in 1982, was a longtime associate of the President and dealt directly with him. Robert McFarlane, who replaced Judge Clark in 1983, although personally less close to the President, continued to have direct access to him. The same was true for VADM John Poindexter, who was appointed to the position in December, 1985.

President Reagan appointed several additional members to his National Security Council and allowed staff attendance at meetings. The resultant size of the meetings led the President to turn increasingly to a smaller group (called the National Security Planning Group or "NSPG"). Attendance at its meetings was more restricted but included the statutory principals of the NSC. The NSPG was supported by the SIGs, and new SIGs were occasionally created to deal with particular issues. These were frequently chaired by the National Security Advisor. But generally the SIGs and many of their subsidiary groups (called Interagency Groups or "IGs") fell into disuse.

As a supplement to the normal NSC process, the Reagan Administration adopted comprehensive procedures for covert actions. These are contained in classified document, NSDD-159, establishing the process for deciding, implementing, monitoring, and reviewing covert activities. . . .

## RECOMMENDATIONS

"Not only *** is the Federal power over external affairs in origin and essential character different from that over internal affairs, but participation in the exercise of the power is significantly limited. In this vast external realm, with its important, complicated, delicate and manifold problems, the President alone has the power to speak or listen as a representative of the nation." *United States* v. *Curtis-Wright Export Corp.,* 299 U.S. 304, 319 (1936).

Whereas the ultimate power to formulate domestic policy resides in the Congress, the primary responsibility for the formulation and implementation of national security policy falls on the President.

It is the President who is the usual source of innovation and responsiveness in this field. The departments and agencies—the Defense Department, State Department, and CIA bureaucracies—tend to resist policy change. Each has its own perspective based on long experience. The challenge for the President is to bring his perspective to bear on these bureaucracies for they are his instruments for executing national security policy, and he must work through them. His task is to provide them leadership and direction.

The National Security Act of 1947 and the system that has grown up under it affords the President special tools for carrying out this important role. These tools are the National Security Council, the National Security Advisor, and the NSC Staff. These are the means through which the creative impulses of the President are brought to bear on the permanent government. The National Security Act, and custom and practice, rightly give the President wide latitude in fashioning exactly how these means are used.

There is no magic formula which can be applied to the NSC structure and process to produce an optimal system. Because the system is the vehicle through which the President formulates and implements his national security policy, it must adapt to each individual President's style and management philosophy. This means that NSC structures and processes must be flexible, not rigid. Overprescription would, as discussed in Part II, either destroy the system or render it ineffective.

Nevertheless, this does not mean there can be no guidelines or recommendations that might improve the operation of the system, whatever the particular style of the incumbent President. We have reviewed the operation of the system over the past 40 years, through good times and bad. We have listened carefully to the views of all the living former Presidents as well as those of most of the participants in their own national security systems. With the strong caveat that flexibility and adaptability must be at the core, it is our judgment that the national security system seems to have worked best when it has in general operated along the lines set forth below.

## Organizing for National Security

Because of the wide latitude in the National Security Act, the President bears a special responsibility for the effective performance of the NSC system. A President must at the outset provide guidelines to the members of the National Security Council, his National Security Advisor, and the National Security Council staff. These guidelines, to be effective, must include how they will relate to one another, what procedures will be followed, what the President expects of them. If his advisors are not performing as he likes, only the President can intervene.

The National Security Council principals other than the President participate on the Council in a unique capacity.[1] Although holding a seat by virtue of their official positions in the Administration, when they sit as members of the Council they sit not as cabinet secretaries or department heads but as advisors to the President. They are there not simply to advance or defend the particular positions of the departments or agencies they head but to give their best advice to the President. Their job—and their challenge—is to see the issue from this perspective, not from the narrower interests of their respective bureaucracies.

The National Security Council is only advisory. It is the President alone who decides. When the NSC principals receive those decisions, they do so as heads of the appropriate departments or agencies. They are then responsible to see that the President's decisions are carried out by those organizations accurately and effectively.

This is an important point. The policy innovation and creativity of the President encounters a natural resistance from the executing departments. While this resistance is a source of frustration to every President, it is inherent in the design of the government. It is up to the politically appointed agency heads to ensure that the President's goals, designs, and policies are brought to bear on this permanent structure. Circumventing the departments, perhaps by using the National Security Advisor or the NSC Staff to execute policy, robs the President of the experience and capacity resident in the departments. The President must act largely through them, but the agency heads must ensure that they execute the President's policies in an expeditious and effective manner. It is not just the obligation of the National Security Advisor to see that the national security process is used. All of the NSC principals—and particularly the President—have that obligation.

The tension between the President and the Executive Departments is worked out through the national security process described in the opening sections of this report. It is through this process that the nation obtains both the best of the creativity of the President and the learning and expertise of the national security departments and agencies.

This process is extremely important to the President. His decisions will benefit from the advice and perspective of all the concerned departments and agencies. History offers numerous examples of this truth. President Kennedy, for example, did not have adequate consultation before entering upon the Bay of Pigs invasion, one of his greatest failures. He remedied this in time for the Cuban missile crisis, one of his greatest successes. Process will not always produce brilliant ideas, but history suggests it can at least help prevent bad ideas from becoming Presidential policy.

## The National Security Advisor

It is the National Security Advisor who is primarily responsible for managing this process on a daily basis. The job requires skill, sensitivity and integrity. It is his responsibility to ensure that matters submitted for consideration by the Council cover the full range of issues on which review is required; that those issues are fully analyzed; that a full range of options is considered; that the prospects and risks of each are examined; that all relevant intelligence and other information is available to the principals; that legal considerations are addressed; that difficulties in implementation are confronted. Usually, this can best be accomplished through interagency participation in the analysis of the issue and a preparatory policy review at the Deputy or Under Secretary level.

The National Security Advisor assumes these responsibilities not only with respect to the President but with respect to all the NSC principals. He must keep them informed of the President's thinking and decisions. They should have adequate notice and an agenda for all meetings. Decision papers should, if at all possible, be provided in advance.

The National Security Advisor must also ensure that adequate records are kept of NSC consultations and Presidential decisions. This is essential to avoid confusion among Presidential advisors and departmental staffs about what was actually decided and what is wanted. Those records are also essential for conducting a periodic review of a policy or initiative, and to learn from the past.

It is the responsibility of the National Security Advisor to monitor policy implementation and to ensure that policies are executed in conformity with the intent of the President's decision. Monitoring includes initiating periodic reassessments of a policy or operation, especially when changed circumstances suggest that the policy or operation no longer serves U.S.

interests.

But the National Security Advisor does not simply manage the national security process. He is himself an important source of advice on national security matters to the President. He is not the President's only source of advice, but he is perhaps the one most able to see things from the President's perspective. He is unburdened by departmental responsibilities. The President is his only master. His advice is confidential. He is not subject to Senate confirmation and traditionally does not formally appear before Congressional committees.

To serve the President well, the National Security Advisor should present his own views, but he must at the same time represent the views of others fully and faithfully to the President. The system will not work well if the National Security Advisor does not have the trust of the NSC principals. He, therefore, must not use his proximity to the President to manipulate the process so as to produce his own position. He should not interpose himself between the President and the NSC principals. He should not seek to exclude the NSC principals from the decision process. Performing both these roles well is an essential, if not easy, task.

In order for the National Security Advisor to serve the President adequately, he must have direct access to the President. Unless he knows first hand the views of the President and is known to reflect them in his management of the NSC system, he will be ineffective. He should not report to the President through some other official. While the Chief of Staff or others can usefully interject domestic political considerations into national security deliberations, they should do so as additional advisors to the President.

Ideally, the National Security Advisor should not have a high public profile. He should not try to compete with the Secretary of State or the Secretary of Defense as the articulator of public policy. They, along with the President, should be the spokesmen for the policies of the Administration. While a "passion for anonymity" is perhaps too strong a term, the National Security Advisor should generally operate offstage.

The NSC principals of course must have direct access to the President, with whatever frequency the President feels is appropriate. But these individual meetings should not be used by the principal to seek decisions or otherwise circumvent the system in the absence of the other principals. In the same way, the National Security Advisor should not use his scheduled intelligence or other daily briefings of the President as an opportunity to seek Presidential decision on significant issues.

If the system is to operate well, the National Security Advisor must promote cooperation rather than competition among himself and the other NSC principals. But the President is ultimately responsible for the operation of this system. If rancorous infighting develops among his principal national security functionaries, only he can deal with them. Public dispute over external policy by senior officials undermines the process of decision-making and narrows his options. It is the President's responsibility to ensure that it does not take place.

Finally, the National Security Advisor should focus on advice and management, not implementation and execution. Implementation is the responsibility and the strength of the departments and agencies. The National Security Advisor and the NSC Staff generally do not have the depth of resources for the conduct of operations. In addition, when they take on implementation responsibilities, they risk compromising their objectivity. They can no longer act as impartial overseers of the implementation, ensuring that Presidential guidance is followed, that policies are kept kept under review, and that the results are serving the President's policy and the national interest.

## The NSC Staff

The NSC Staff should be small, highly competent, and experienced in the making of public policy. Staff members should be drawn both from within and from outside government. Those from within government should come from the several departments and agencies concerned with national security matters. No particular department or agency should have a predominate role. A proper balance must be maintained between people from within and outside the government. Staff members should generally rotate with a stay of more than four years viewed as the exception.

A large number of staff action officers organized along essentially horizontal lines enhances the possibilities for poorly supervised and monitored activities by individual staff members. Such a system is made to order for energetic self-starters to take unauthorized initiatives. Clear vertical lines of control and authority, responsibility and accountability, are essential to good management.

One problem affecting the NSC staff is lack of institutional memory. This results from the understandable desire of a President to replace the staff in order to be sure it is responsive to him. Departments provide continuity that can help the Council, but the Council as an institution also needs some means to assure adequate records and memory. This was identified to the Board as a problem by many witnesses.

We recognize the problem and have identified a range of possibilities that a President might consider on this subject. One would be to create a small permanent executive secretariat. Another would be to have one person, the Executive Secretary, as a permanent position. Finally, a pattern of limited tenure and overlapping rotation could be used. Any of these would help reduce the problem of loss of institutional memory; none would be practical unless each succeeding President subscribed to it.

The guidelines for the role of the National Security Advisor also apply generally to the NSC staff. They should protect the process and thereby the

President.  Departments and agencies should not be excluded from participation in that process.  The staff should not be implementors or operators and staff should keep a low profile with the press.

## PRINCIPAL RECOMMENDATION

The model we have outlined above for the National Security Council system constitutes our first and most important recommendation.  It includes guidelines that address virtually all of the deficiencies in procedure and practice that the Board encountered in the Iran/Contra affair as well as in other case studies of this and previous administrations.

We believe this model can enhance the performance of a President and his administration in the area of national security.  It responds directly to President Reagan's mandate to describe the NSC system as it ought to be.

The Board recommends that the proposed model be used by Presidents in their management of the national security system.

## SPECIFIC RECOMMENDATIONS

In addition to its principal recommendation regarding the organization and functioning of the NSC system and roles to be played by the participants, the Board has a number of specific recommendations.

1. *The National Security Act of 1947.*

We recommend that no substantive change be made in the provisions of the National Security Act dealing with the structure and operation of the NSC system.

2. *Senate Confirmation of the National Security Advisor.*

We urge the Congress not to require Senate confirmation of the National Security Advisor.

3. *The Interagency Process.*

It is the National Security Advisor who has the greatest interest in making the national security process work, for it is this process by which the President obtains the information, background, and analysis he requires to make decisions and build support for his program.  Most Presidents have set up interagency committees at both a staff and policy level to surface issues, develop options, and clarify choices.  There has typically been a struggle for the chairmanships of these groups between the National Security Advisor and the NSC staff on the one hand, and the cabinet secretaries and department officials on the other.

Our review of the operation of the present system and that of other administrations where committee chairmen came from the departments has led us to the conclusion that the system generally operates better when the committees are chaired by the individual with the greatest stake in making the NSC system work.

We recommend that the National Security Advisor chair the senior-level committees of the NSC system. . . .

### 4. *Covert Actions.*

We recommend that each administration formulate precise procedures for restricted consideration of covert action and that, once formulated, those procedures be strictly adhered to.

### 5. *The Role of the CIA.* . . .

We emphasize to both the intelligence community and policymakers the importance of maintaining the integrity and objectivity of the intelligence process.

### 6. *Legal Council.*

The Board recommends that the position of Legal Adviser to the NSC be enhanced in stature and in its role within the NSC staff.

### 7. *Secrecy and Congress.* There is a natural tension between the desire for secrecy and the need to consult Congress on covert operations.

We recommend that Congress consider replacing the existing Intelligence Committees of the respective Houses with a new joint committee with a restricted staff to oversee the intelligence community, patterned after the Joint Committee on Atomic Energy that existed until the mid-1970s.

### 8. *Privatizing National Security Policy.*

We recommend against having implementation and policy oversight dominated by intermediaries. We do not recommend barring limited use of private individuals to assist in United States diplomatic initiatives or in covert activities. We caution against use of such people except in very limited ways and under close observation and supervision.

## NOTES

1. The Packard Commission's Report on Defense Management, *A Quest For Excellence* (Washington, D.C.: U.S. Government Printing Office, 1986), pp. 10, 13, 15, 19–20, 28–30, 35–36, 37–38.

2. Barry Goldwater and Sam Nunn, *Defense Organization: The Need for Change* (Washington: U.S. Government Printing Office, 1985), pp. 1–12.

3. John Tower, Edmund Muskie, and Brent Scowcroft, *The Final Report of the President's Special Review Board* on the future role of *The National Security Council Staff* (Washington, D.C.: U.S. Government Printing Office, 1987), pp. 6, 13–15, 87–93, 94, 95, 96, 97, 98, 99.

# 13

## Conclusion
### JAMES M. KEAGLE

As the United States begins its third century of constitutional government, the world in which it operates poses serious questions and challenges to the national security policymakers. Some would even suggest that the demands on and responsibilities of a great power in today's world are incompatible with a structure of government that disperses and distributes decisionmaking power and authority and favors inefficiently produced outcomes as preferable to tyranny.

We do not believe that such a tension inevitably will force the United States to choose between its Madisonian system and effective use of power in the formulation and execution of national security policy. It is our thesis that within the limitations imposed by the real play of bureaucratic politics and dictated by the U.S. system of checks and balances—separated, divided, overlapped, and shared powers—it is possible to construct and implement national security policies that can preserve for the foreseeable future the values for which so many U.S. citizens have dedicated their lives.

Although necessarily a frustration on bold, energetic, executive initiatives (Hamiltonianism), a pluralistic structure (Madisonianism) creates sufficient opportunities for leadership and innovation that we see reason to be optimistic that the U.S. system can continue to work toward the achievement and preservation of its most cherished values—freedom and democracy (Jeffersonianism).

It is our hope that this book, by further exploring the nature and importance of bureaucratic politics as a characteristic of the U.S. system of government, will serve as a useful tool for those who participate in the national security policy process—as voters, soldiers, professional bureaucrats, elected officials, and informed citizens. U.S. national security will continue to depend on players and organizations knowledgeable of the rules of the game of this system of government intentionally designed to frustrate the exercise of personal and institutional powers; so, too, will our freedom.